CONTENTS
*

PART ONE
Gardening Foundations

PART TWO
Choice of a Garden

5

Contents

PART THREE

The Garden Beautiful—Flowers and Foliage

6

Contents

PART FOUR

The Garden Beautiful—Flowering Shrubs and Trees

PART FIVE

Food Production—Fruit

PART SIX

Food Production—Vegetables

Contents

COLOUR PLATES

MONOCHROME PLATES

9

Monochrome Plates

Monochrome Plates

ACKNOWLEDGMENTS

The Author gratefully acknowledges the courtesy and help of the following :

Mr. Michael Haworth-Booth for the colour plates and for monochrome illustrations Nos. 29 and 58-61;

The Horticultural Photo Supply Service for Nos. 1-9, 11, 21, 23, 26-7, 40-1, 47-8, 62-3, 70, 74-5, 77-8, 80-2, 86-8, 90-2, 98, 100, 102-7, 109-10, and 119-25;

The Editor of the Smallholder for Nos. 10, 22, 28, 32-6, 38-9, 46, 56-7, 65, 67-9, 71-3, 76, 79, 83-5, 89 and 93-7;

The Cement and Concrete Association for Nos. 12-18 and 30-1;

The Editor of My Garden for Nos. 19-20 and 24-5;

Messrs. Sutton & Sons, Ltd., for No. 37;

Mr. J. Allan Cash for Nos. 42-3;

The National Rose Society for Nos. 44-5;

Reginald A. Malby & Co. for Nos. 49-55, 64, 66 and 101;

The Mushroom Growers Association for No. 99;

The General Electric Co., Ltd., for No. 108;

The Shell Photographic Unit for Nos. 111-18;

Mrs. Dorothy Edwards, Messrs. Evans Bros., and the National Federation of Young Farmers' Clubs for the figures in the text Nos. 20-8 ;

Mr. Charles Green for figures 1-19 and 29-40.

PREFACE

AT LAST I have had time to write the book that large
numbers of readers of my other books—rightly or wrongly
—have been asking for. It has not been easy to choose what to
put in and what to leave out. Have I said too much, I ask myself,
or have I said too little, about any one subject?

You must be the judge, and do please let me know what you
think about it. I have tried to keep you in mind all the time.

Many people have been kind enough to help me. Miss
Maria Dehn, B.Sc. (Hort.), N.D.H., Dip. Hort. (Swanley), one
of my staff, did trojan work on the Flower Section. I miss
her now that she is on the staff of Ambler College in the U.S.A.
Other members of our staff have also gladly lent a hand, viz.
Miss K. Bekh, Dip. Hort. (Swanley), Miss Russell, Gold Medallist
R.H.S., and Miss Margaret Call, Dip. Hort. (Studley).

I want to thank them all for their great interest and hard work.
Michael Haworth-Booth was asked by the publishers to advise
and write on the Shrub section and I am most grateful to him
for his help.

Since writing the original preface—a good deal of horticultural
water has flown under the bridge. I wrote the book just as I was
leaving the Swanley Horticultural College for the Thaxted
Horticultural College and now I am at Arkley Manor in Hertford-
shire continuing my researches with no digging—no hoeing—
on use of chemical fertilisers and in fact comfort growing in its
entirety. When I wrote the book The Good Gardeners' Association wasn't born and now as the book reaches its tenth edition
and over 100,000 copies have sold, the Association is well on to
its 5,000th member.

I do hope you will like this new revised edition.

W. E. SHEWELL-COOPER

PART ONE

GARDENING FOUNDATIONS

CHAPTER I

The Beginning of Things

THE SOIL AND ITS PROPERTIES

*

ALL gardeners have to begin somewhere and all gardens have a beginning too. Some people start their gardening long before their 'teens, as I did ; others take to it when they are married and so have a plot of their own. Some men and women have to make gardens from a bare field ; others take over a garden that has been planned and prepared by somebody else, and maybe they dislike the lay-out and hate the trees and shrubs that have been planted. How then is it possible in a book like this to start at " the beginning of things " ?

Most people intend to garden in soil. There are super-enthusiasts, it is true, who go in for growing crops in tanks of water, regularly fed with mysterious concoctions. There is no proof, however, that the crops they produce are as valuable to health as those grown in nature's way. However, let others speak of hydroponics, as this special system of culture has been called. This manual deals only with the basic principles connected with soil cultivation.

SOILS

How THEY ARE FORMED

Soil does not only contain disintegrated rock or minerals, it also consists of certain quantities of organic matter which have developed as the result of vegetation. It contains living organisms, moisture, and certain gases. Where there is any depth of soil on cultivated land the top 8 ins. or so are usually darker in colour, owing to the organic matter in the process of oxidisation.

(a) *Worms*

Good soil contains earthworms whose function is to draw leaves and other organic matter into the ground and, in addition, to pass vegetable matter and soil through their bodies and eject this on to the surface of the ground. Land containing a good earthworm population may easily have a desposit of " worm cast material " exceeding 10 tons to the acre. The part, therefore, that the worms play is extremely important.

(b) Soil Bacteria

In addition to the worms there are the soil bacteria, or micro-organisms, which, like Peter Pan, never grow up. They have a big part to play and they deal mainly with decomposition and, as decomposition leads to recomposition, their work must be encouraged. They provide the fresh material on which the live plants may live. Some bacteria may be said to be scavengers ; some attack the cellulose in decayed plants ; some use the carbonic acid in the soil for their energy. There are bacteria and fungi that work on the nitrogenous types of matter, breaking them down to substances of an ammonia type from which the roots of plants can easily feed. One microbe will do one job and work on it till it is finished. Then another microbe will come along with all his friends and deal with the new problem in the conditions produced by the first. Thus the work is automatically passed on from one to another. The bacteria, as a group, set about preparing food for the generations of plants that are to come. Without their voluntary help, life would cease.

The soil, therefore, is not only a place where the roots of plants can anchor ; it is not only a storehouse of plant food. It is a large manufacturing centre where millions of living organisms will work all day and night to help the gardener, providing they are given the right conditions. Cultivate the ground properly ; dig in the manure or organic matter and the countless organisms will get to work to prepare the food for the plants that are to come. I sometimes call the soil bacteria the " cooks," or " chefs," of the soil.

(c) Azotobacter

There is another group of bacteria known as the Azotobacter which must be mentioned briefly. These bacteria do not break down organic matter ; they build up. They get to work on gases and other compounds which might be lost in the soil and they build them up into such a condition that they can be held in the ground and be used by the plants later. Some live on the roots of plants in symbiosis, that is, they do no harm to the plants, but they help to supply nitrogenous foods to them and the plants, in return, give them a supply of sugar. It is the pea and bean family, the *Leguminosæ*, as it is called, that does this, and actually, in addition to peas and beans, it contains lupins, clovers and other plants that have hooded flowers, like vetches. Little white nodules are found on the roots of these plants and it is advisable to leave the roots in the ground when the crop is over, and just to cut away the top. Thus the nitrogen, " manufactured " by these bacteria on the roots, is left in the soil for other plants to use later.

HUMUS

The gardener must see to it that sufficient organic matter is added to the soil each year, so that plenty of humus is assured. Humus may be considered the by-product of bacterial activity, and microbes work at their best when they've plenty of material to deal with. Nature's plan is to build up the humus year after year, and this can only be done with organic matter. The gardener must replace and return that which has been taken out of the soil year by year for, when replacement is not carried out, soil erosion and soil sickness may occur. This passing back into the soil of humus has been called the Wheel of Life. Death is Nature's way of providing for new life. There can be no permanently perfect soil. There must be change and the gardener should aim at having a vigorous, living, breathing soil ; a soil in which the capital is never removed, and the capital is the humus content. Every bit of work done in the garden helps to break down the humus, and every crop grown reduces the organic content of the soil. Thus, to keep the soil as it should be, organic matter must be dug in each year.

Some reading this may already say, " What is humus ? " It is the complex residue of partly oxidised animal and vegetable matter, together with substances, synthesised by fungi and bacteria, used to break down these wastes. It is the key material of the Wheel of Life. During its formation, all sorts of chemical changes have taken place. The soil organisms have worked on the proteins and the carbo-hydrates and have broken them down into simpler substances. Humus may be called the organic colloid of the soil and may be simply described as a brownish-black jam or jelly. It makes all the difference to successful gardening ;

it can store water; it can store plant food; it can prevent valuable minerals from being washed away. It helps to keep the soil open; it ensures the right aeration; it gives the ideal insulation against heat and cold.

TYPES OF SOIL

There are five main types of soil. These are : sand, clay, loam, calcareous soils and peat. Even these soils differ, and you can have combinations of one or more of them.

SAND
Sandy soils contain less than 10% of clay, and consist of very small particles of silica and quartz. The amount of humus present will alter the colour and the texture. Sand may be said to be light and dry; it is one of the warmest soils. One of the advantages of a sandy soil is that it can be worked at any time of the year and is comparatively easy to cultivate. But it is poor in plant foods, coarse-grained and does not retain moisture easily.

CLAY
Clay is very fine-grained, smooth and silky to the touch. It is much richer in plant food than sand and this, in addition to its water-retaining properties, makes it valuable in a dry season. A regular application of lime prevents clay soil from becoming " sticky " and " opens " it up.

LOAM
Loam is an ideal blend of sand and clay. There are various types of loams, depending on the proportion of clay or sand present. It is the best soil for large numbers of plants. The ideal loam has all the advantages of sandy and clay soils and none of their disadvantages.

CALCAREOUS SOILS
Calcareous or chalky soils are often very deficient in plant food and rather shallow ; they are often lacking in humus. When wet they are sticky and unpleasant, and during droughts they suffer badly from lack of water. Owing to what is known as lime-induced chlorosis, the leaves of plants often become bright yellow in colour. The club root disease does not flourish on chalky soils.

Marls are really chalky clay soils and are therefore treated in the same way as clays, except that heavy dressings of lime are not usually necessary.

Peat

Peaty soils are absolutely void of lime ; their sourness is produced by the decaying vegetable matter present. Celery loves peaty soil and so does celeriac. Once peaty soils are well worked and limed, they prove valuable.

THE IDEAL SOIL

The ideal garden soil may be considered to consist of $\frac{1}{2}$ sand, $\frac{1}{4}$ clay, $\frac{1}{6}$ humus, and $\frac{1}{12}$ lime. There are few of these soils about, and the only reason the ideal constituents are given is to encourage gardeners to carry out judicious improvements to the soils they have to contend with.

SUB-SOIL

Most soils are about 12 ins. deep, though there are some in Kent that have a depth of only 3 or 4 ins. Below this you have the sub-soil. If the sub-soil consists of gravel you know that all excessive moisture will be quickly carried away. If, on the other hand, the sub-soil is sticky clay there may be a danger of water-logging. If it consists of ironstone then it may be impervious, and so have to be broken up with a crowbar. Sub-soils should never be brought to the surface when digging.

SECTION TWO

THE CULTIVATION OF SOIL

*

DRAINING THE SOIL

In small gardens drainage is often difficult to arrange. Soils, however, that are well drained are much warmer and you must have a warm soil to ensure fervent bacterial activity. When arranging to drain a garden three types of drains are used, the mains, the sub-mains and the small drains which lead into these. The main drain should be laid in the direction of the greatest slope and the sub-mains enter into this. At the junction where the sub-mains enter the main a hole is made in the larger drain-pipe so that the smaller one fits loosely into it. It is important to see that the drains enter in at an angle in the direction of the flow of water. Agricultural drain-pipes are laid down end to end and are not joined by cement. The water from the soil then passes into the system at the open joints.

The fall, as it is called, should be at least 1 in 100 for the mains and 1 in 75 for the sub-mains. Always start laying the drains from the lower end, as it is only in this way that you can ensure an even fall. At this lower end, there must be a ditch or some similar gulley to take the water away and, if this is impossible, a square well should be dug and be lined with brick. This, in addition to taking away the excess water, may be useful as a reservoir.

Those who cannot afford to use agricultural tile drains may dig out trenches to the depth of 2 ft. 6 ins., and of a spade and a half's width, and fill the bottoms of the trenches up to 9 ins. with stone, rubble, clinkers, tins and other insoluble rubbish. Such drainage material helps to get the excess soil moisture away. Those who live in the country may find it easier to bury bundled brushwood or heather and, over this, turves may be placed upside down to prevent fine soil from working through.

Fig. 1 shows, perhaps more clearly than the text above, how the drainage work should be carried out.

FUMIGATING THE SOIL

One of the problems when digging up grassland is that it is often infested with wireworms and leatherjackets. This makes it

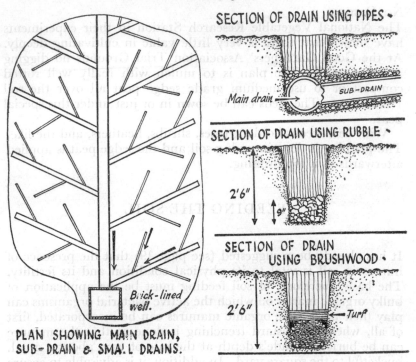

SECTION OF DRAIN USING PIPES

Main drain   SUB-DRAIN

SECTION OF DRAIN USING RUBBLE

2'6"   9"

SECTION OF DRAIN
USING BRUSHWOOD

2'6"   Turf

PLAN SHOWING MAIN DRAIN,
SUB-DRAIN & SMALL DRAINS.

*Brick-lined
well.*

FIG. 1

necessary to fumigate the soil in some way. As a matter of fact, it is possible to get quite a serious wireworm infection in land that has not been cultivated for a number of years.

There is only one safe way of treating the soil: with Carbon Bi-Sulphide.

CARBON BI-SULPHIDE
Carbon Bi-Sulphide is a highly inflammable liquid with a stench resembling rotten eggs. It must be applied, or at any rate is best applied, by the use of a Soil Injector. The mechanism of this machine ensures a perfectly regular distribution of the Bi-Sulphide in measured doses. The propelling force is very powerful, so that, however compact the soil may be, the chemical is at once diffused around the hole of injection and a gas is generated which kills all insect life. The depth of the holes, which may be up to 15 ins., can be regulated by the use of a movable pedal.

No Digging

The National Vegetable Research Station in their experiments have shown that there is very little value in cultivating deeply. At the Good Gardeners' Association Trial Grounds no digging is done at all. The plan is to mulch with really well rotted compost or to use medium grade sedge peat all over the soil 1 inch deep. The seeds can be sown in or just under this special peat.

With herbaceous borders, roses, shrubs, heathers, and the like. The planting is done in undug soil and the sedge peat is applied afterwards as a top dressing.

FEEDING THE SOIL

It has already been suggested (see page 19) that the presence of humus in soil is vital to its physical condition and its fertility. The basis, therefore, of soil feeding must be the application of bulky organic matter on which the active bacterial organisms can play their part. The organic manures can be incorporated, first of all, when the bastard trenching is done so that the manure can be buried a spade's depth at the rate of, say, about a 2 gal. bucketful to the square yard. In addition, it is advisable to ensure that there is sufficient fine organic matter worked into the top 2 or 3 ins. This can be incorporated when the forking and raking is done in the spring, summer or autumn in order to get land ready for seed sowing or planting out. Horticultural peat is often used for this purpose, or very fine, fully rotted, composted vegetable refuse. It is during this incorporation that any organic fertilisers needed can be applied.

ORGANIC MANURES COMMONLY USED

Farmyard Manure

Animal manures are undoubtedly valuable not only for their organic contents but for the way in which they assist in liberating plant foods already present in soils. They differ, of course, firstly, as to the amount of straw and other litter used; secondly, as to the animal concerned, be it horse, cow or pig; thirdly, as to the method in which the animals are kept; and lastly, as to the way in which the manure has been stacked and stored. Manure heaps that are not kept under cover lose a lot of their value through leaching. Fresh manure, when dug in, has what is called a denitrifying effect, that is to say, it takes the bacteria away from their normal work of " producing " nitrogen to working on the straw to break it down. It is always advisable, therefore, to use well-rotted manure. A good dressing of well-rotted manure in the garden would be at the rate of one really good barrow-load to 10 sq. yds.

POULTRY MANURE

This is quite a good manure, being rich in nitrogen, phosphates and potash. Fresh poultry manure contains approximately 18-25 lbs. nitrogen, 12-24 lbs. phosphate and 6-12 lbs. potash per ton. It should be stored in a lidded bin and when " powdered " should be applied with care. It is used at 2-3 ozs. to the square yard. Poultry manure is useful when applied as an accelerator at 4 ozs. to the square yard for every 6 ins. thickness of vegetable matter put on to the compost heap.

RABBIT MANURE

This is not produced in sufficient quantity as a rule to make it of value to use alone, but it is excellent for adding to the compost heaps as advised for Poultry Manure.

It can be used with the straw from hutches as ordinary dung dug into the ground at 1 bucketful to the square yard.

VEGETABLE COMPOST

A very good substitute for dung may be made from all the vegetable refuse from the house and garden. It is possible to use the tops of peas and beans ; the tops of potatoes ; old cabbage stumps, when bashed up with the back of an axe ; tea leaves ; orange peel ; bought-in baled straw and, in fact, any rottable material of this kind. Such material should be put into heaps and should be treated with a suitable activator (see below). There are various schools of thought with regard to this, but all agree on certain basic principles, and they are : (1) that the layers of plant refuse used should be from 6-12 ins. in depth ; (2) that the heap should have some shelter from wind and sun to obviate drying out and loss of heat ; (3) that woody material, such as apple prunings, should be excluded ; (4) that the heap should not be too large or high (maximum height 8 ft.) and (5) that it may be necessary to use a certain amount of hydrated lime every, say, 2 ft.

For the normal garden the bins used might be 6 ft. high, 6 ft. wide and 6 ft. deep, or 8 ft. by 8 ft. by 8 ft. The surrounding walls should be preferably of wood. Old railway sleepers are excellent for the purpose, although, when this is impossible, corrugated iron will do, or even wire netting. The vegetable waste should be put into the bins evenly. There is no need to shake any soil off the roots of weeds, neither is there any need to be frightened of putting on diseased potato crops, for the heat engendered in the heap during the rotting-down process should kill weed seeds and disease spores—and in fact does. For every 6-8 in. thickness of vegetable waste collected, a sprinkling should be

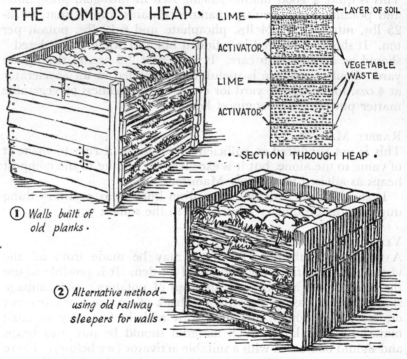

THE COMPOST HEAP

① Walls built of old planks.

② Alternative method— using old railway sleepers for walls.

FIG. 2

given with the activator. This may consist of rabbit or poultry manure at 3-4 ozs. to the square yard, or of sulphate of ammonia at 2 ozs. to the square yard. After 3 layers have been sprinkled with one of these materials, it will be necessary to apply lime to the fourth layer in the form of hydrated lime at 4-5 ozs. to the square yard. Another 3 layers will, of course, be put on above this, each one treated with the droppings or the chemical and the eighth layer receiving the lime. The heap will gradually be built up in this way. Of course, as the material rots, it starts to compact and, therefore, it may be a long time before the 5-ft. height is reached. (See Fig. 2.)

If any of the material is dry, it should be thoroughly soaked before the sulphate of ammonia is applied. It is surprising the amount of water that straw needs. If it is convenient, it helps matters to sprinkle the more bulky material, like cabbage stumps, with the finer products, like lawn mowings, as this helps the rotting down to be more even. If labour is available it is a good plan " at half-time " to turn the heap so that the outside becomes the inside, and vice versa. It may be necessary to build the heap gradually day by day, week by week. On the other hand, there may be a large amount of vegetable refuse available at one time and then a number of layers will, of course, be built in one day. In this case, it will probably be necessary to tread the material down well. If the heap should suddenly grow to the height of 4 ft. or so in one day, it might be advisable to cover the top with a layer of soil 3 or 4 ins. thick, in order to help retain the heat and moisture.

When the compost is ready, which it should be in about six months' time, it should have a pleasant earthy smell and should feel rather like a slightly moist sponge. If it is wet and sour-smelling then something is wrong and it would be advisable to turn the heap and add a little more lime and soil. If, on the other hand, it has a musty smell and there seems to be a whitish-grey growth present, you can be sure that the heap is too dry and the answer is to soak the heap well. It is convenient to start one heap in the early summer ready for use in the autumn, and another one in the summer for use in the spring. Many gardeners keep four bins going so as to have compost available at any time.

A number of " prophets " have arisen with regard to the composting of vegetable refuse. The Indore method insists on the use of animal manure, plus the turning of the heaps. The Bio-Dynamic School, and Miss Maye Bruce with her Quick Return method, both insist on the use of certain herbs. The great thing, however, is to compost and not to waste any vegetable refuse at all. When made and ready the compost can be dug in at a similar rate to farmyard manure.

Wool Shoddy
This is more valuable than cotton shoddy (which for this reason is not mentioned separately) and may be used when obtainable. It

is a waste product of the woollen trade and to be really valuable should be free from oil. Shoddies take a long time to rot down and should always be dug in during the autumn. It is slow in action and may take years to rot down properly. It is usually applied at the rate of one bucketful to the square yard.

HOP MANURE

This is the residue left behind during the manufacture of beer. It normally contains no phosphate or potash and only a little nitrogen. Sometimes, however, those who sell this product add some plant foods. Hops may be dug in in the autumn or spring, or used as a top dressing during the summer. Dig them in at the rate of half a bucketful to the square yard.

SEAWEED

Seaweed is a useful manure. It is low in phosphates but apart from that is valuable, especially when rotted down. It should be applied at the same rate as dung and may be dug in in the autumn and also used as a top dressing in the spring.

NIGHT SOIL AND SEWAGE SLUDGE

Human excrement is similar in value to that of animals but is very seldom used except in the country. Town sewers often terminate in sumps and from these cesspools the liquid naturally drains away. The solid material left is of little value as a manure, but it is quite useful in pushing up the organic content of soil. Some Town Councils compost sewerage wastes and they are then in a position to sell an excellent substitute for dung to the gardeners and allotment holders in the district.

GREEN MANURE

One of the ways of adding humus to the soil is by means of green manure. This consists of growing plants of any kind which should be dug in well before they mature. Unfortunately, it cannot be relied on to produce as good results as farmyard manure, as it does not add phosphates or potash. It is also very slow acting, and it may take about eight months before it is rotted down into a suitable condition for plants to grow in.

Most green manures, like Rye and Mustard, merely give back to the soil the food taken up during growth. But when legumes are used, such as clovers, peas, vetches and lupins, a good deal of nitrogen is taken from the air and given to the soil. It is quite a good plan for a gardener to sow all the seeds he has over at the end of the season on a patch of land to act as green manure.

Another method of enriching the land with organic material, and also cleaning it at the same time, has been devised by Mr. Y. L. Scarlett, C.D.A. The land should be dug during the winter and early spring and tares broadcast at the rate of $\frac{1}{2}$ oz. to the square yard. These should be " mushed up " with a spade and nitro-chalk applied at the rate of 1 oz. to the square yard, when the flowers appear in late June. The material should be left for eight days and then dug in. The surface of the ground is then cultivated and sown with rye, say the third week in July, and this rye is dug in any time between October and December.

PEAT
Horticultural Sedge peat which has been deacified is a very valuable moisture-holding material to apply to soil. It is usually worked into the top 2 or 3 ins. of soil before seed sowing or planting, at the rate of half a bucketful to the square yard. If the ground is dry the peat should be thoroughly damped before use. It is also much used as a mulch, applied to a depth of 1-2 ins., round soft fruit bushes and flowering shrubs, as well as along the rows of runner beans, and similar crops which like plenty of moisture.

Peat is excellent for use along the rows of strawberries at flowering time in order to keep the berries clean as they ripen. It can then be forked into the ground after harvesting. It is important, however, to use Sedge peat and not sphagnum peat.

ORGANIC FERTILISERS

There are a number of organic fertilisers which not only add the necessary plant foods but, in addition, because they are organic in origin, they do help to build up the humus content of any soil. Those who fear to use the normal chemical artificial fertilisers, because they believe them to have a depressing effect on the soil's humus content, can use any of the following without fear of this happening.

FISH MANURE
Fish manure is made from fish waste and now offered free from objectionable odour. It is rich in nitrogen and phosphates but contains no potash. Some manufacturers add potash during the drying process. Fish manure rapidly rots down and feeds the soil and, because of the organic matter it contains, stimulates bacterial action. It is usually applied at 3-4 ozs. to the square yard, being raked in to the top 2 ins. of soil.

GUANO

Guanos are rather expensive, but on the whole they decay rapidly and yield a continuous supply of nitrogen throughout the season. The best guano is probably the Peruvian, but there are meat and bone guanos to-day made from slaughter-house refuse. They are usually applied at 3-4 ozs. to the square yard a fortnight before sowing seed or planting out.

MEAT AND BONE MEAL

See GUANO *above*

HOOF AND HORN MEAL

This is a slow-acting fertiliser which contains nitrogen and phosphates but no potash. Use at the rate of 3-4 ozs. to the square yard.

SOOT

Soot is a nitrogenous manure which darkens soils and so enables them to absorb and retain heat better. More generally used as a top dressing in the spring. Suitable chiefly for all members of the cabbage family. Usually applied at 5 ozs. to the square yard.

STEAMED BONE FLOUR

This is a slow-acting manure supplying phosphates only. It is used for plants like peas and beans and is generally used at 2 ozs. to the square yard.

BONE MEAL

Bone meals are slower in action than steamed bone flour and do not give as good results. When sold they contain the gelatine which the steamed bone flour does not.

WOOD ASHES

These contain a small percentage of potash being about one-twelfth as valuable as sulphate of potash. They are usually applied at the rate of about ½ lb. to the square yard. They are best stored in a dustbin with a lid in order to keep them dry.

FLUE DUST

A potassic fertiliser only, generally about a sixth as valuable as sulphate of potash, and applied at about 5 ozs. to the square yard. Much used by those who dislike using a chemical fertiliser. There are a number of proprietary flue dusts on the market.

DRIED BLOOD

A very valuable organic nitrogenous manure containing approximately 12% nitrogen It is applied in the spring and summer at the rate of 2-3 ozs. per square yard to growing crops, or to pot plants, giving a teaspoonful per plant. It is particularly useful for cucumbers.

INORGANIC FERTILISERS AND THEIR FUNCTION

Fellows of the Good Gardeners' Association do not use purely chemical fertilisers. The author for 15 years now has given no chemical fertilisers at all to the soil in his garden. Providing, however, fertilisers are looked upon only as "tonics," and not as the main food, there seems little harm in adding very small doses when absolutely necessary. Cabbages require more nitrogen than most crops. Peas and beans need more potash; root crops, more phosphates. These three plant foods, with others, should be present in the right proportions if perfect growth is to be obtained, and if it were possible to give sufficient well-rotted dung or compost over a period of years, there is no doubt that these three foods would always be present.

THE THREE MAIN PLANT FOODS

What then are the functions of the 3 main plant foods—Nitrogen, Phosphates and Potash?

NITROGEN

This has to do with the building up of the stems and green leaves of a plant. Nitrogen-starved plants are light green in colour and generally smaller in size. When two much nitrogen is given all the energies of the plant seem to be directed towards the production of leaves and rank shoots. If a plant is soft owing to an overdose of nitrogen, then the insects will feed ravenously on the lush growth, and the plant will be more liable to fungus diseases. Too much nitrogen defers ripening.

The main nitrogenous chemical fertilisers are:

Sulphate of Ammonia, which is not readily washed away in the soil, does not encourage the worm population. Use at 1 oz. per square yard.

Nitrate of Soda, which is very quick acting and may be used, if necessary, at any time of the year to hurry plants along. Use it at 1 oz. per yard run if plants seem to need a stimulant. Do not let any drop on the leaves.

Nitro-chalk, which contains about the same amount of nitrogen as Nitrate of Soda, plus lime, has the advantage of being in a granular form, and so can be more easily applied to growing crops. It is quick acting and is a fertiliser used on acid soil. It is used for members of the cabbage family as a tonic at 1 oz. per square yard.

PHOSPHATES

The application of phosphates has an effect on root growth. Phosphatic fertilisers therefore are used in the vegetable garden and for pot plants. Phosphates help to ensure a steady, firm, continuous growth.

The main phosphatic fertilisers are:

Superphosphate, which does not wash out easily from the soil and so may be applied before sowing the seed or putting out plants. It is a greyish, dry powder and can be mixed with sulphate of ammonia and may be applied at $1\frac{1}{2}$ ozs. per square yard.

Rock Phosphates, which are much used by growers as they are " natural."

Basic Slag, which is applied at the rate of 2 ozs. to the square yard sometime early in the winter to be of use the following spring. Its best use is for soils rich in humus, like the peats, and for very heavy clays. It contains a certain amount of lime.

POTASH

Potash is needed by all crops, particularly by peas and beans. It plays an important part in the production of firm, well-flavoured vegetables and fruits and high quality flowers. Plants grown with sufficient potash have firm leaves which are more resistant to disease, and a healthier, better plant with strong fibre results from potassic applications. The lighter soils are normally deficient in this plant food.

The main potassic chemical fertilisers are:

Sulphate of Potash is probably the safest artificial to use where produce of good quality is required. It can be mixed with Sulphate of Ammonia and Superphosphate. Application is generally made in the spring, and a good dressing would be 1 oz. to the square yard. It is not easily washed away.

Muriate of Potash, which has a similar taste to ordinary common salt. This has an " irritating " action on the roots of growing plants and may do damage, and so is never recommended for the garden.

1. *Mulching fruit trees*

2. *Mulching strawberries*

3. *Mulching beans*

4. *Crocking and filling seed boxes.* (*Note presser*)

5. *Stages in seed sowing in boxes.* (*Note the template with holes to ensure even spacing of seeds*)

6. *Rubbing seeds in lime to whiten them*

Kainit, which is the cheapest form of potash to be had. It is more impure than Muriate of Potash and contains a variety of chemicals like Epsom Salts and Chloride of Magnesia. It should not be used on any soils, especially on clays, which are apt to set down hard like cement.

Dangers in Mixing Fertilisers
It is dangerous to mix one fertiliser with another unless you know that there will be no adverse chemical reaction. Further, of course, fertilisers as a whole should NOT be mixed with Lime.

Organics Best
It is always better to use an organic fertiliser such as a fish manure which has been " prepared " by the manufacturer and so " balanced " as to contain Nitrogen, Phosphates and Potash. Different types of balanced fish manure are available to suit the requirements of various crops. Many of them contain trace elements.

Trace Elements
In addition to the three main plant foods mentioned above, and also calcium, magnesium and sulphur which are also required by the plant, there are other elements necessary for the plant but in quite minute quantities. These are called " trace elements " and comprise manganese, boron, zinc, copper and molybdenum. Of these boron is the most important as lack of this element can cause deficiency diseases in some crops, particularly cauliflower, turnips and celery. If sufficient organic matter is given regularly the need for trace elements is supplied.

THE ROLE OF LIME

Lime, as well as being important in sweetening soil and preventing it from becoming acid, plays its part as a plant food. It is the calcium content that is valuable as a plant food. It also helps to release other plant foods and aids in decomposing humus and organic compounds in the soil so that they, too, can be used.

Lime should always be used for the cabbage and pea and bean family, but it is not so important for potatoes and roots, with the exception of turnips and kohl rabi which are crucifers and so liable to be attacked by Club Root (see page 681). Some plants of course hate lime. I refer to some heaths—rhododendrons, azaleas and the like. Regular applications of lime make it possible to keep down the club root disease. It should be possible to keep ordinary soil in good condition if lime is applied at 5-7 ozs. to the square yard.

Lime should never be dug in for it washes down into the soil very quickly. It should be sprinkled on the surface of the ground and will of course be forked or hoed in during the cultural operations.

The three main types of lime are :

Hydrated lime, which is the most important type for the gardener. It is convenient to handle, but is not so valuable as quicklime.

Quicklime, which is difficult to obtain. It has to be slaked down on the soil, and is more unpleasant to handle than hydrated lime, and will not store.

Chalk, or Limestone, which is often sold as ground limestone, and is half as valuable as quicklime and must, therefore, be used at a heavier rate. It is usually applied at the rate of 7 ozs. to the square yard of hydrated lime, and for ground lime 5 ozs. to the square yard will be sufficient.

LIME MEASUREMENT IN SOIL

Scientists have agreed to express the degree of acidity of soil by what to the outsider seems a queer notation, i.e. pH 7. pH 7 represents the neutral point ; figures less than 7 indicate the degree of acidity and figures more than 7 show the degree of alkalinity. It will be seen, therefore, that pH 4 is much more acid than pH 6.

In this country the extremes of soil acidity and alkalinity usually run between pH 4.5 and pH 8.5, and it can be said that most crops do best in soils which range from pH 6 to pH 7.5. Different crops will, of course, grow under varying acid or alkaline conditions. Peas and beans seem to like a soil between pH 6 and 7. Potatoes quite like a soil from pH 4.7 to 5.7.

To raise land that you have found to be pH 4 to pH 7, might take 4 tons of lime per acre in the case of sands, and as much as 12 tons per acre in the case of clays, whereas to raise pH 6 to pH 7 takes about $1\frac{1}{2}$ tons of lime per acre in the case of sands, and 3 tons per acre in the case of clays.

Excess of lime can cause trouble in soils as well as acidity, and there is what is known as lime-induced chlorosis. This is common in the case of fruit trees in Kent grown on chalky land.

The home gardener can test his soil accurately for acidity by using what is called an indicating fluid. This fluid is green, and when it comes into contact with the soil it turns red if the land is very acid, orange if it is less acid, and yellow if it is less acid still. The British Drug House offers for sale a soil—indicating fluid which enables the gardener to make tests of his garden or allotment in a few minutes.

TABLE OF LIME APPLICATIONS FOR DIFFERENT SOILS

Dressings of quicklime (burnt lime or lump lime, builders' lime or Buxton lime) required on different soils and for different degrees of acidity :

pH	Clay	Peat	Heavy loam	Light loam	Sand
4·0	18	18	16	12	10
4·5	16	16	14	10	8
5·0	14	14	12	8	7
5·5	12	12	10	7	6
6·0	10	9	8	6	5
6·5	9	8	7	5	4

All figures are for ounces per square yard.

TABLE SHOWING EQUIVALENT VALUES OF DIFFERENT TYPES OF LIME

Quantities of different forms of lime required to produce the same effect :

Lump chalk ..	4	12	16	20	24	28	32	36	40
Finely ground limestone	2	6	8	10	12	14	16	18	20
Hydrated lime ..	$1\frac{1}{3}$	4	$5\frac{1}{3}$	$6\frac{2}{3}$	8	$9\frac{1}{3}$	$10\frac{2}{3}$	12	$13\frac{1}{3}$
Quick lime	1	3	4	5	6	7	8	9	10

All figures are for ounces per square yard.

MULCHING

Mulching may be described as the application of some type of organic matter on the surface of the ground around a tree or shrub or along rows of vegetables or fruits. (See illustration facing page 32.) Keeping the top 1 in. of soil well hoed is described as a dust mulch. The Americans use strips of paper and stones for mulching (see also page 60).

LIQUID MANURING

There is a lot to be said for liquid feeding. Plant foods are always taken up in solution and, of course, when minerals of any kind are applied to the soil they can only be used when they pass into solution. When liquid manures are applied to the ground the root hairs are able to take the food in immediately. The great advantage of liquid feeding is the universal distribution of the plant food throughout the area of soil in which the plants are growing. It is as if the liquid food fills up the " pores " in the soil with the solution. It may be said that each particle of soil will be coated with a thin film of the liquid manure, and so all the fine root hairs are able to get on with their work of " drawing in " moisture and food from the soil.

People's ideas differ as to the amount of diluted liquid manure that ought to be used and a good general guide is to suggest 2 pts. of diluted liquid manure per foot run of normal crops, which means about 8 gals. per 30 ft. row. If the soil were very dry it would be necessary to give a normal watering first. If the plants were smaller and were sown broadcast a good general guide would be 1 gal. of liquid manure per square yard. For individual plants like cucumbers, tomatoes or melons, 1 qt. per plant will do when they are young, and 1 gal. per plant when they are bearing a large number of fruits. Beans and peas can be given as much as 1 gal. of diluted manure per foot run, especially runner beans which grow so tall. These applications are necessary once a month, though in the driest and hottest months of the year, once a fortnight would probably be necessary.

Trees, shrubs and bushes may be fed with liquid manures if desired. The aim here will be to give 1 or 2 gals. of liquid manure per square yard for an area covered by the branches and 2 ft. beyond. Roses will normally be given 1½ gals. per bush once a month, say, between the middle of April and the beginning of September. In the olden days liquid manure was made by hanging a sack of animal droppings in a barrel of water. It was a slow, somewhat unpleasant, job and of course no one could tell exactly the value of the manure nor what plant foods it contained. There was no chance, therefore, of doing any balanced feeding. It was just a hit-and-miss affair. To-day, however, there are liquid manures sold in bottles which contain what may be called dissolved humus, all the necessary plant foods and small proportions of the " trace elements " required to provide for possible deficiencies in the soil. Such liquid manures are made up to different formulæ so as to satisfy the needs of various types of plants. For instance, you can buy a bottle of liquid manure with a high percentage of potash for tomatoes or gooseberries, while another balanced liquid feed will contain a higher percentage of " nitrogen " and so be more suited to the brassica crops. Furthermore, these manures are free from any disease spores which is more than you could say for the old-fashioned sack and tub method.

For those who are going to carry out liquid manuring on a large scale, it is possible to purchase an automatic diluter which enables the liquid manures to be applied with a hose. By means of a special attachment, the water in the hose can be made to suck in the necessary liquid manure in exactly the right dilution, and, therefore, by the time the water issues through the jet at the end, the liquid manure is correctly diluted. It is possible, by these means, to deliver anything between 50 and 200 gals. per hour and to make certain that exactly the right amount of food is being given to the soil during this period.

SOIL STERILISATION

Though the words " soil sterilisation " are used, the correct term is " partial soil sterilisation," the object being to kill insect pests, to destroy injurious fungi and protozoa, to kill weed seeds, to eliminate all non-spore-producing bacteria, but *not* to kill the ammonia-producing bacteria. These latter can produce hard-walled " spores " and are able, during the time of sterilisation, to remain dormant and immediately afterward to multiply at a tremendous rate and carry out unrestricted operations. It is only when the soil is heated that all these things take place.

There are three ways of partially sterilising soil by heat : (1) by electricity ; (2) by steaming ; (3) by baking.

(1) ELECTRICITY
It is possible to buy electric soil sterilisers which can treat soil at the right temperature automatically with the minimum of trouble.

(2) STEAMING

(*a*) *Commercial*

Glasshouse growers with large areas pass steam into the soil *in situ* by means of grids, and thus bring the temperature up to 212° Fahr. for about 15 minutes. It is essential to steam the soil efficiently, for if a small pocket of soil is missed, the diseases will spread from this and multiply more rapidly than in non-sterilised soil.

(*b*) *Steaming at Home*

It is also possible to sterilise soil in a domestic copper. 2 gals. of water are poured into the bottom and 2 ins. above the water a perforated bucket is hung, or supported, on an open framework, and in this the soil to be sterilised is placed. The water is then boiled, the lid is put into position over the copper and thus it is possible to heat the water to a temperature of 200° Fahr. for about half an hour. There are a number of proprietary low-pressure sterilisers advertised which can sterilises oil by steam in about an hour. These may contain anything from 4 to 18 bushels of soil, depending on the size and price. A thermometer should always be used for measuring the temperature of the soil, especially the top inch or two and the corners of the container which seem to heat up last.

(3) BAKING

Years ago, the author carried out experiments on soil sterilisation and, with the help of Mr. W. Priestner, evolved what came to be known as the Reaseheath Steriliser. This was a long, brick trough in which 3 tons of soil could be placed, and having been covered with sacks, a fire was lit in the stoke-hole and the flames encouraged along the trough. Though the structure was simple, it worked, and in case there are those who wish to build a similar steriliser the dimensions now follow : trough of quick brickwork, 3 ft. 1½ ins. wide, 23 ft. long, and 1 ft. 2 ins. deep (all inside measurements) ; flues, 4½ ins. wide and 15 ins. high ; firebox, 2 ft. 9 ins. by 18 ins. Except where otherwise specified, common brick is used throughout. There is a rise of 9 ins. in the whole length.

In the construction of the steriliser, a hole 4 ft. 6 ins. wide by 25 ft. long is dug. It is 4 ft. 6 ins. deep at the chimney end, and 5 ft. 3 ins. at the fire-box end, with a well at the latter end excavated 2 ft. deep for the stoke-hole. A concrete bed 6 ins. thick was then laid over the platform, and the fire-box built in with quick fire-brick walls. The outside walls of the trough were carried up 15 ins., and three mid-feathers, each a single brick in thickness were put in at $4\frac{1}{2}$-in. intervals. *Of course, it is possible to build a far smaller steriliser of appropriate dimensions suitable for a small garden.*

To facilitate draught, the ends of the outside feathers were " cut away," or chamfered, and the central feather set back 9 ins. Fire-brick was used for the first 4 ft. 6 ins. of the bottom of the trough, fire-clay flags 24×12 ins. were used for the remainder of the length. The flues were covered in with common brick. The outside walls of the trough were then carried up to the ground level. The flues were carried through into the base of the chimney, and small iron doors were introduced into the wall to allow for cleaning.

Owing to the position of the steriliser, it was necessary at Reaseheath to carry the chimney sideways before commencing the rise (under ordinary circumstances a straight chimney should serve equally well). At the commencement of the rise, the chimney was tapered gradually to an inside measurement of 9×9 ins. at 2 ft. from the ground. It was carried up in 9 in. brick to a height of 8 ft., and capped with 6 ins. of concrete and a pot. A curved baffle or damper was introduced into the chimney at 3 ft. from the ground to allow for regulation of draught, and for fuel economy. To prevent the earth falling in, the stoke-hole was bricked round, and steps were introduced for convenience of access.

Earth to be sterilised is wheeled in until the trough is full ; the " charge " amounting to about 3 tons. A coke fire in the fire-box brings the whole to an average temperature of 205-210° Fahr. in 8 hours. Various materials have been tried for covering over the earth to conserve heat. Iron plates are effective, but as they cause the moisture to condense the surface layer becomes very sodden. Thick sacking has proved the most suitable material so far tried for this purpose—old sacks serve quite well. After baking for 4 hours, the earth is completely double dug, and the heating is continued for 4 more hours. By this means the whole of the soil receives similar treatment. At the end of the second period of baking, the soil can be removed and allowed to cool. It should not be used immediately after removal, and an addition of about $\frac{1}{2}$ cwt. slaked lime to the 3 tons of soil is advisable.

CHEMICAL STERILISERS

Chemical sterilisers are by no means as effective as heat. They do not control weed seeds and there are no chemicals yet used which are both fungicides and insecticides. Three are commonly used: Formaldehyde, Cresylic Acid and Tar Oil Derivatives.

FORMALDEHYDE

Formaldehyde is a fungicide but does not kill insects. It should be diluted by adding 1 part to 49 parts of water and 1 gal. of the diluted produce is sufficient for a bushel of soil. The earth needs to be thoroughly soaked and then to be covered with sacking for 48 hours. At the end of this period, the sacking should be removed and the earth forked over thoroughly so as to allow the volatile gas to escape. As Formaldehyde is highly toxic to plant life soil cannot be used until all traces of the smell have disappeared, which usually takes 14 days. It should never be used in a greenhouse where plants are growing.

CRESYLIC ACID

Cresylic Acid is diluted by adding 1 pt. to 39 pts. of water. This should be applied at the rate of 1 gal. to 1 bushel of soil. You should then cover the soil as for Formaldehyde for 48 hours and then fork it over from time to time over a period of 3 weeks, so as to allow the fumes to escape. Cresylic Acid will kill soil pests but is useless as a fungicide.

TAR OIL DERIVATIVES

The Tar Oil Derivatives are usually sold under proprietary names and should be used according to the directions given by the makers. Unfortunately, extravagant claims are sometimes made for them.

N.B.—The author prefers not to have to sterilise soil and has shown that if the soil is properly fed with organic matter, and so is really rich in humus, then it is alive and healthy and remains so. In the whole ten years at the Horticultural College, Thaxted, the greenhouse soils were never sterilised and in the last 10 years at Arkley Manor, Arkley, the soil in the College greenhouses has never been sterilised either.

CHAPTER II

Give Us the Tools and We Will Finish the Job

NO gardener can function properly without the use of the appropriate tools. These must be well made and of good quality and, of course, strong enough to do what they are expected to. In the case of hand tools it is never advisable to buy sizes and weights too large or heavy for the user. Buy tools made by reliable makers and never attempt to economise by purchasing inferior implements.

Having purchased them it is most important to keep them clean and thus, every time they are used, they should be wiped over with old pieces of sacking and then rubbed with an oily rag so as to keep off the rust. Tools that are bright and clean cut through the soil more easily and thus save effort. They also last longer. Each tool should have its place on the shed wall and should be hung up on a nail or hook when not in use. If this is done it is a matter of a few seconds to see if any tool is missing, and far more tools can be stored in a small space if they are properly hung in place. The shed itself must be rainproof and sufficiently strongly constructed to carry the weight of the implements when in position. It is always better to hang the sharper tools like the scythes or sickles high up so that they cannot easily be got at by young people.

TOOLS REQUIRED

The Spade

Be sure to buy a spade and not a shovel. A spade has a straight blade and is used upright. It should have a sharp cutting edge and the blade should be bright. The handle should be smooth and made of good ash. Most people like a flange or ridge on the top of the upper side of the spade so that the instep is not cut into when the gardener thrusts the spade into the ground with his foot (see Fig. 3).

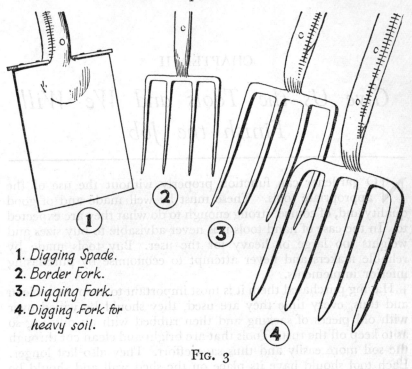

1. Digging Spade.
2. Border Fork.
3. Digging Fork.
4. Digging Fork for heavy soil.

FIG. 3

THE FORK

A fork will normally have four rounded tines or prongs, though when it is used, as it sometimes is, as a digging tool in heavy clay soil it may have flat tines. Like the spade, it should have a nice strong ash handle with a " D " or " T " grip at the end. The tines should be pointed and should be kept bright and clean. It is used principally in the spring and summer for forking over land so as to get it down to a finer condition. It is also used for lifting potatoes, for spreading manure and for putting rubbish on to a barrow. It is usual for the upper part of the fork to be of iron and the lower part of each prong to be of steel. The prongs should be 9-10 ins. long, almost straight. (See Fig. 3.)

THE HOE

There are two main types of hoe—the draw hoe and the Dutch hoe, sometimes called the thrust hoe. The handle of these hoes should be from 4-6 ft. in length, depending on the height of the user. On the whole, the handles of the draw hoes can be shorter than those of the Dutch hoes. The draw hoe is used walking forwards and the Dutch hoe walking backwards.

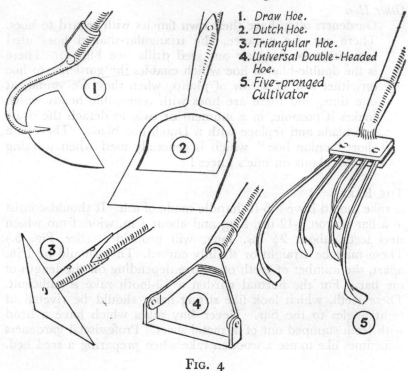

1. Draw Hoe.
2. Dutch Hoe.
3. Triangular Hoe.
4. Universal Double-Headed Hoe.
5. Five-pronged Cultivator

FIG. 4

Draw Hoes

This has an upright blade which should be approximately at right angles to the handle. It may be used for drawing soil up to plants, as in the case of earthing potatoes, or drawing out drills in which to sow seeds, or for chopping down weeds when they are somewhat thick. Most gardeners prefer a draw hoe with a swan neck (see Fig. 4), and like the tool to have a 6-in. blade. Some double pronged draw hoes with swan necks have slots at the end into which blades of different widths can easily be fixed).

Dutch Hoes

The blade of these hoes should be attached to a strong 6-ft. ash handle. When the gardener is standing upright and is holding the far end of the handle at full arm's length at his side the blade should be parallel to the surface of the soil. It should be used between the rows of plants all through the summer before the weeds appear, and then no weeds will appear. (See Fig. 4.)

Other Hoes

Gardeners often have their own fancies with regard to hoes. There are, for instance, the triangular-shaped hoes used sometimes for drawing out seed drills (see Fig. 4). There is the double-bladed hoe which enables the gardener to hoe on either side of a row of plants, when they are young, at one time, and there are hoes with removable heads which makes it possible, in a moment or two, to detach the draw hoe blade and replace with a Dutch hoe blade. There is a short " onion hoe " which is generally used when working among plants on one's knees !

The Rake

A rake should have a 6-ft. handle made of ash. It should consist of a bar of iron 6-12 ins. long and about $\frac{1}{2}$ in. wide, from which steel teeth, about $2\frac{1}{2}$ ins. long, will protrude. (See Fig. 5.) These may be straight or slightly curved. They should be 1 in. apart, the number of teeth of course depending on the length of the bar. For the normal garden a 12-tooth rake is sufficient. These teeth, which look like strong nails, should be riveted at right angles to the bar. Never buy rakes which have a head with teeth stamped out of a metal sheet. Professional gardeners sometimes like to use a wooden rake when preparing a seed bed.

The Cultivator

A cultivator is very similar to a hoe : it usually has 3 or 5 steel prongs instead of the blade. The handles are 5 ft. long and the prongs 9 ins. long. Some cultivators have removable prongs, so that they may be used on both sides of a row at a time : others have adjustable prongs. Cultivators are used for breaking down soil among crops. (See Fig. 4.)

There are wheeled cultivators, known as Planet Juniors, and wheeled hoes which are simple to push along in a rather jerky motion between the rows of plants. These are very popular with market gardeners. There are, of course, motor cultivators of various sizes which can do admirable work in the garden. The National Institute of Agricultural Engineering may always be consulted on the best types of motor cultivator to use for a particular garden.

The Dibber

The dibber (see Fig. 10) is still much used, though the more modern gardeners prefer to use a trowel. It is liked because it is quicker in operation than a trowel, especially in loose ground. It

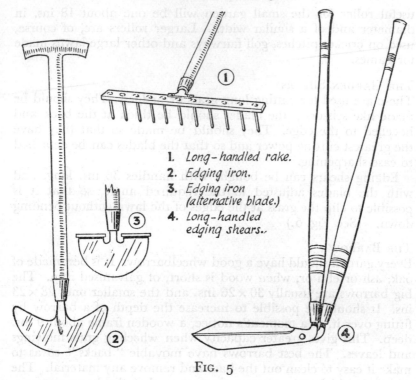

1. *Long-handled rake.*
2. *Edging iron.*
3. *Edging iron (alternative blade.)*
4. *Long-handled edging shears.*

FIG. 5

consists of a piece of rounded wood with one blunt end and a handle at the other, in fact it is often made from old spade handles which have got broken.

It is most important not to have a dibber with a sharply pointed end or else the roots of a seedling may easily find that there's an air pocket below them when they are planted. Sometimes dibbers are shod with steel so as to make them easier to push into the ground.

THE TROWEL

A trowel should be slightly scoop-shaped and the blade may be 5, 6, 7 or 8 ins. long. Strong riveted trowels should always be purchased with smooth, short, easy-to-grip handles.

THE ROLLER

Rollers are useful for consolidating soil, but should never weigh over a hundredweight. It is always better to buy what is known as the double cylinder type, especially if this has self-oiling bearings. The handle should be balanced so that it always comes up naturally into position and doesn't drop on to the ground. A useful roller for the small garden will be one about 18 ins. in diameter and of a similar width. Larger rollers are, of course, used on cricket pitches, golf fairways and other large lawns made for games.

THE GARDEN SHEARS

These are used for cutting long grass or hedges. They should be made like scissors ; the blades should be thick at the back and bevelled to the edge. They should be made so that they have the greatest cutting power and so that the blades can be detached to ease sharpening.

Edging shears can be bought with handles 36 ins. long, and with the blades adjusted to the required angle, so that it is possible to clip the grass at the edges of the lawn without bending down. (See Fig. 5.)

THE BARROW

Every garden should have a good wheelbarrow. It is best made of oak, ash or elm or, when wood is short, of galvanised iron. The big barrows are usually 30 × 26 ins. and the smaller ones 28 × 23 ins. It should be possible to increase the depth of a barrow by fitting over it, at a moment's notice, a wooden frame about 9 ins. deep. This gives greater capacity when wheeling grass mowings and leaves. The best barrows have movable " backs " so as to make it easy to clean out the base and remove any material. The wheel should have a pneumatic tyre so that the barrow is easy to move about and so that it leaves the least possible mark on the soil or path.

Long, narrow double-wheeled barrows are very useful indeed for they make it unnecessary for the gardener to take the whole weight of the barrow on his shoulders. Such barrows are often 5 ft. long and 3 ft. wide, and are fitted with pneumatic tyres of motor bicycle size, plus the usual ball bearings.

All barrows should be kept painted regularly to preserve the wood or metal (if it is not galvanised) and should always be stored under cover. The bearings should be oiled once a fortnight.

THE INCINERATOR

It is useful to have somewhere to burn diseased and woody material. Some people build small brick incinerators with special fire bars and a grate below so as to be able to start the heap burning at any time. Others just buy corrugated iron incinerators which are portable ; these have a kind of cast-iron stove funnel in the centre to carry the smoke away and ensure a good draught. They are usually about 20 ins. in diameter and 30 ins. in height.

The Tools and the Job

THE WATERING CAN

Watering cans should always be made of strong galvanised metal and should always be stood upside down when not in use. The Haw's patent type of can is best for the greenhouse. It has a long spout and may be gripped by the handle or by the cross-bar that goes from the opening to the spout. It's a perfectly balanced can and is easy to dip into a tank. The length of the spout allows plants at the back of the staging to be watered easily. The pressure from the weight of the water in the can forces the water out evenly through the finest rose. It is useful to have roses with various sized holes punched in them.

THE SPRINKLER

One of the best ways of watering the garden in the summer is by the use of the overhead sprinkler. There are various types of sprinklers on the market and they all aim at making the water reach the soil as much like rain as possible. They are attached to the hose and, when the tap is turned on, the pressure of the water keeps them either whirling round or makes the nozzles work backwards and forwards and thus applying the water finely over a given surface.

THE SPRAYING MACHINE

There are various kinds of spraying machines, varying from a syringe to a motor-driven machine. A very simple one is the Solo which looks like a syringe and has a double-acting pump, and thus it can give an almost continuous spray. It is provided with about 10 ft. of tubing, fitted with a strainer at the end, this being placed in the bucket of spray fluid. The nozzle has a mystifier fitted to it, so as to ensure a fine spray, but when this is removed it is possible to throw a straight jet of liquid a distance of some 25 ft. It weighs just over 3 lbs. and the actual syringe itself is 2 ft. in length.

Other spraying machines suitable for the small garden are: the bucket-pumps, which are similar to those used in the 1939-45 war; the knapsack sprayers, which are carried on the back and hold about 3 gals., and the movable tank sprayers which have a pump fitted to a tank on two wheels so that the machine can easily be moved about.

These machines are used for applying insecticides and fungicides as and when necessary.

THE DUSTING MACHINE

The advantages of using dusts are: (1) that no water has to be used or carried; (2) that less labour is required; (3) that the powder cannot be used too strongly, and (4) that dusting can be carried out in a quarter of the time needed for spraying.

The disadvantages are : (1) that a dust never penetrates as well as a liquid ; (2) that you, therefore, never get as good control of an insect or a fungus, and (3) that dusting can never take the place of winter spraying in the case of fruit trees and bushes.

There are various hand-dusting machines on the market fitted with a non-return valve in a special chamber to prevent the return stroke of the plunger drawing the powder into the barrel of the air pump. They may cost anything from a few shillings to a pound or so ; the bigger ones will have the same non-choking arrangements as the smaller ones but, in addition, they will have a bigger container which will probably be protected inside by a sulphur-resisting lacquer. There are knapsack types for carrying on the back, with double-acting bellows which give a continuous distribution of powder, and there are rotary fan dust guns which ensure a powerful blast of air plus a dust distribution over a large area. The dust gun is fitted to the front of the worker's body and is operated by turning a handle. These machines sell for a few pounds.

THE SYRINGE

For very small gardens, and for little greenhouses, ordinary garden syringes are often used. These may be fitted with two or three interchangeable nozzles. They should always be rinsed out with clean water after they have been used for a chemical.

PRUNING TOOLS

A number of tools are needed in connection with the pruning of fruit trees and bushes.

(a) *Knife*

Preferably, this should have a fixed handle so that the blade cannot close up when you are working among the trees. The blade should be about 4-5 ins. long and should be slightly curved towards the end. It should always be kept very sharp and it is useful if the pruner can keep a small whetstone in his pocket for this purpose.

(b) *Budding Knife*

This may close up like an ordinary pocket knife, but the handle should be tapered so that it can be used for opening up cuts made in the bark. It should also be kept sharp.

(c) *Secateurs*
These should be of a
type with a removable
blade, like the Rolcut,
and should be kept
sharp and oiled.

(d) *Long-handled Pruner*
A special tool with a
long handle and a curved
head which can be
hooked over branches.
The blade is operated by
means of a handle at
the base of the tool
which is able to close up
the knife-cutting edge
and so sever the branch.
(See Fig. 6.)

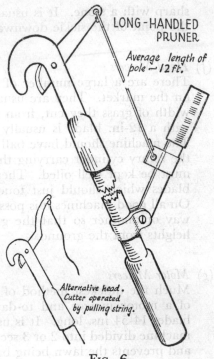

LONG-HANDLED
PRUNER.

*Average length of
pole — 12 ft.*

*Alternative head.
Cutter operated
by pulling string.*

FIG. 6

TOOLS FOR CUTTING GRASS

(a) *Shears*
(See page 46.)

(b) *Edging Shears*
(See page 46.)

(c) *Scythe*
Very little used in the garden to-day. It is much more an
agricultural tool.

(d) *Edger*
This is a half-moon-shaped tool used for cutting turf and
edging the lawn. The blade should be kept sharp and
bright, the handle should be similar to that of a spade or fork.

(e) *Sickle*
A tool that is sometimes called a Brushing Hook and sometimes a Britching Hook. Semi-circular in shape, it is used
with a quick side movement for cutting long grass. Is often
" set " so that the handle is 3 or 4 ins. above the blade, as
that makes for easy labour. The blade should be kept

sharp with a stone. It is usual to start this sharpening from the point of the sickle downwards.

(f) Hand Mowers

There are a large number of good hand mowing machines on the market. They are usually classified according to the width of grass they cut, from 8 ins. up to 24 ins. A mower with a 12-in. blade is usually sufficient for a small garden. The machine should have ball bearings in the drive and in the rotary cylinder carrying the cutting blades. These parts must be kept well oiled. There should be 5 to 8 revolving blades which should just touch the stationary lower knife. On all good machines it is possible to adjust the blade in one way or another so that the grass may be cut at different heights from the ground.

(g) Motor Mowers

Much the quickest method of cutting the lawn is by means of a motor mower and to-day these may be bought with blades 14-54 ins. long. It is useful to have the rollers of the machine divided into 2 or 3 sections, as this facilitates turning and prevents the lawn being badly marked when the ground is rather soft.

(h) Motor Rotary Scythes

These are quite useful for cutting either a lawn or longer grass, and are thus a very useful dual purpose machine. But they have two disadvantages: (1) that they do not roll as they cut, as do the normal motor mowers, and (2) that they do not leave the lawn looking as neat and trim as an ordinary mower does, because you do not get that "roller vista" effect.

(i) Hover Mowers

The hover, or air cushion, mowers recently introduced have several marked advantages. Because the machine is "floating" on a cushion of air it makes for light work. It will also cut wet grass, can be used on slopes and banks, and makes it possible to cut over paving stones embedded in a lawn as well as cutting right up to and over the edge of the lawn. Its low hood also makes it easy to use under bushes and shrubs.

CHAPTER III

Doing the Job

THERE are a large number of operations that have to be carried out in the garden and this is where the craftsman comes in. Gardening is not only a science—it is very definitely a craft, and the man who can grow good vegetables, produce beautiful flowers and ensure an abundance of fruit, is a man who can use his hands as well as his head. Furthermore, the practical work in the garden should be done so that you get the maximum amount of effect with the minimum amount of physical effort, and for this reason details are given in many cases as to how the work should be done from the point of view of using the right muscles and holding the body in the right way.

DOUBLE DIGGING

This used to be thought an important garden operation. It is usually carried out in the autumn, or early winter, and allows the organic matter to be incorporated. It makes it possible to leave the land rough and so let the cold winds and frost act on the lumps and break them down ready for the spring. It makes it possible, too, to get down to the bottom of the trench and fork over the " spit " that lies below so as to aerate it and help with the drainage. It is important in double digging or bastard trenching to see that the bottom spit remains at the bottom and the top spit at the top, and when the gardener talks about spit, he really means spadeful.

Mark out the piece of ground to be double dug by putting down a line at one end of the plot so as to make a strip 2 ft. wide, remove the top spit and wheel this to the other end of the plot where the double digging will finish. Get down into the bottom of the trench just made (it will be a spade's depth, 2 ft. wide) and fork it over, leaving the forked soil where it is. On top of this forked soil, place the manure or properly composted vegetable refuse, together with any annual weeds that may be at hand.

Now move the line back another 2 ft. and, spadeful by spadeful, fill in the first trench with the top soil from this area, and you will thus produce another trench similar in size to the first one,

DOUBLE DIGGING

1ˢᵗ STAGE ·

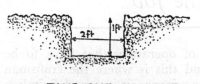

2 ft

1 ft

TAKE OUT TOP SPIT

2ⁿᵈ STAGE ·

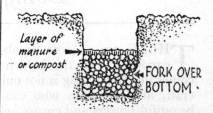

Layer of
manure
or compost

← FORK OVER
BOTTOM ·

3ʳᵈ STAGE ·

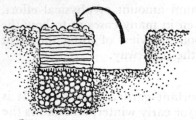

FILL FIRST TRENCH WITH
SOIL FROM SECOND · ·

4ᵀᴴ STAGE ·

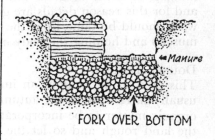

← Manure

FORK OVER BOTTOM

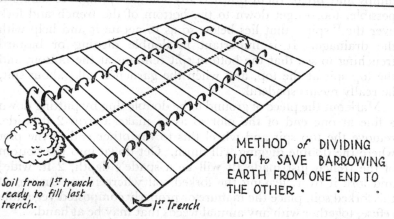

Soil from 1ˢᵗ trench
ready to fill last
trench.

1ˢᵗ Trench

METHOD of DIVIDING
PLOT to SAVE BARROWING
EARTH FROM ONE END TO
THE OTHER · · ·

Fig. 7

which should be treated in the same way. You will then continue this work 2 ft. by 2 ft. until you reach the end of the plot, where you will find a heap of soil to fill in the last trench made.

Another method, which saves barrowing in the case of large plots, is to divide the piece of ground to be dug lengthways into two portions, and then to dig down the whole of one strip, filling in the last trench with the soil of the first trench from the other strip, and thus you will eventually come to the pile of soil from the first strip marked " A " which you have put at the head of strip 2. This is very difficult to explain in writing, but the diagram below should make it quite easy to understand.

When digging, the bulk of the work should be done with the leg and the dorsal muscles. The blade of the spade will be thrust into the soil with the foot, one arm will be used for levering up the soil on to the spade, while the other arm will grip the handle of the spade low down and then, with the bent knee and the bent elbow, almost the whole weight of the spade can be taken on the knee. Now it is only necessary to bend forward slightly and give a slight twist with the hand on the handle and the soil will slide off the blade upside down well ahead into the trench. (See Fig. 7.)

RIDGING

In the case of very heavy clays, it may be worth while ridging in the autumn or early winter. Land in ridges exposes as much surface as possible to the weather and also enables excess moisture to be carried away. The soil in the spring is, therefore, much warmer. When marking out the ground, a strip 2 ft. wide should be chosen, running the whole length of the plot, north and south. The trench is then opened out as for

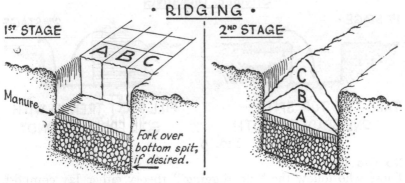

Fig. 8

bastard trenching (see page 51) and the soil taken to the end of the plot. The strip is now divided into three; spadeful A is placed in the centre of the trench thus made, spadeful B on top of it, and spadeful C on top of that. (See Fig. 8.) The operation should be continued right the way down the strip, and thus it will be found that a ridge has been made the whole length of the ground. Further strips are then marked out with a line and the ridges run parallel one to the other. It is possible to bury the manure while ridging, in exactly the same way as for bastard trenching.

SINGLE DIGGING (regarded as the deepest cultivation necessary) Single digging consists of turning the ground to one spade's depth and is often done in the summer when the gardener is in a hurry to prepare the ground for another crop. A trench should be got out first of all, at least a spade's width and about a spade's depth at one end of the plot. As the ground is dug over, the top inch or so of soil should be skimmed off and put into the bottom of the trench ahead before the next strip of land is dug over. (See Fig. 9.) In this way the weed seeds will be buried. The actual operation of digging is, of course, similar to that of bastard trenching, except that there is no question of getting down into the trench and forking it over, nor is there any need, as a rule, for the spit of soil dug over to be deeper than 6 or 7 ins. Care should be taken, when digging, to remove all perennial weed roots, and, as the ground will be used shortly afterwards, there is no need to leave the surface soil rough. The gardener can chop up the spadefuls of soil with the side of the spade as he digs them over, in order to help fine them down.

SINGLE DIGGING

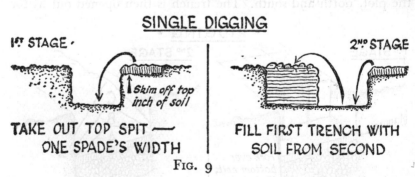

1ST STAGE

Skim off top inch of soil

TAKE OUT TOP SPIT — ONE SPADE'S WIDTH

2ND STAGE

FILL FIRST TRENCH WITH SOIL FROM SECOND

FIG. 9

No DIGGING
Those who follow the " no digging " theory either lay compost all over the ground 1 in. deep in the autumn of one year and then

in the spring of the next scratch out drills in the residue of the
compost and sow the seeds ; or they sow the seeds on the surface of
the ground and cover the actual strips where the seeds are with
well-rotted compost 2 ins. deep. There are of course a number
of modifications of these schemes.

Non-diggers have to make a tremendous amount of good
compost each year, and I find it works out at about 200 tons
to the acre.

There is no doubt that non-diggers can get good results, and
do in various parts of England. The thing that worries me is
that all those I know who are doing this work have gardens
that were dug for years past and maybe the plants are " cashing
in " on work done in the past.

Forking

The forking over of ground is done in a similar manner to
digging, except that the fork may be driven in at an angle of
45° or even less, so as to cover as big an area as possible. There
is no need to have a trench ahead. The object is merely to turn
the ground over and get it down to a fine condition. The gardener,
therefore, works regularly, methodically driving his fork in, lifting
it very slightly and turning the soil upside down and then, if
necessary, knocking it about a bit more with the prongs in order
to produce what he calls a fine tilth.

Hoeing

As has already been seen on page 43, there are two main types
of hoes, the draw hoe and the Dutch hoe. The draw hoe is used
walking forwards with a kind of chopping motion. One hand
should grip the hoe handle about three-quarters of the way up
and the other about half-way up (see illustration facing page
489). As the gardener walks forward the hoe will, of course,
move with him. He takes, therefore, one pace forward, the hoe
blade touches the ground. He draws it towards him cutting
through the soil to a depth of, say, $\frac{1}{2}$ in. He thus cuts off any weeds
there may be and disturbs the soil to this depth. He then walks
forward one more pace. Again he allows the hoe to touch the
ground and draws it towards him once more, again cutting
through the soil. He can do this work with a regular rhythm
and thus work up the rows of plants, doing all the hoeing that is
necessary with the minimum amount of labour.

A draw hoe is normally used when the weeds have got
rather bad, for if the blade is kept sharp it can cut through
them.

In the case of the Dutch hoe the operator works backwards. He holds the end of the hoe handle in one hand and uses the other hand merely to guide it. He shouldn't have to grip the hoe with both hands. He then uses the blade, which should lie parallel to the ground, to cut through the top ½ in. of soil, and he walks back gradually while so doing. Thus, with short jerky movements, he covers the strip of land on which he is working, leaving the top ½ in. of soil loose and providing what is called a " dust mulch." At the same time he is killing off young weeds.

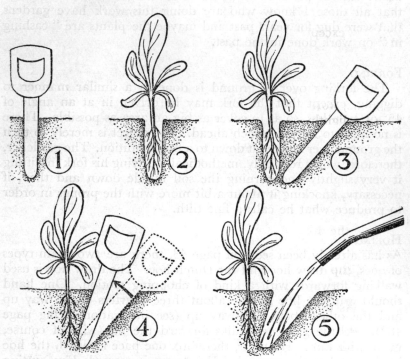

FIG. 10   PLANTING SEEDLING WITH DIBBER

USING THE DIBBER

The dibber is pushed into the ground perpendicularly so as to make the necessary hole. The gardener should use the weight of his body to do the work, so he should be well over it. It is a mistake to try and push the dibber in at arm's length. Once the hole is made the plant roots are put into position, and another hole is made at an angle of 45° at the side. The dibber is then levered up towards the plant and thus firms it in position. The hole is left at the side so that it can be filled up with water if necessary, from time to time.   (See Fig. 10.)

USING THE TROWEL

The trowel is used in a similar way to the dibber but the weight of the body is over the trowel. The back of the trowel should be towards the line which is stretched tightly over the ground to make sure that the row is straight. A half-moon cut is thus made. Take out the trowel, make another cut with the concave surface of the trowel towards the line, so that the edges of the cut meet the edges of the cut previously made. It should then be possible to lift out an almost circular piece of soil and put it on the side near the hole. The plant is then put into position, the roots are spread out, and the semi-circular pieces of soil then goes back into the hole in approximately the same order ; thus the lower damp soil is kept in the lower part of the hole. It is always better to use a trowel than a dibber if possible.

When setting plants out in rows, a line should be put down and the trowel should then be thrust into the ground with its back to the line, and in this way it can be ensured that all the plants are in a straight line. Sometimes, in the case of small seedlings, it is only necessary to push the trowel into the ground with its concave surface towards the gardener and convex surface against the line and then to pull the handle of the trowel forwards, thus forming a hole. The roots of the plant can then be inserted in the hole and the earth pushed back into position again. This can only be done when the root system is small.

In the case of plants with larger roots it is necessary to make certain that the hole is deep enough to accommodate them all. Roots should never be allowed to be bunched up, for if they are they never uncurl themselves again. The blade of the trowel should be kept bright and clean and the edge sharp.

WATERING

Most amateur gardeners give far too little water and, therefore, it is always better in the open to use an overhead sprinkler on the end of a garden hose and allow it to be in position for at least half an hour. If watering is done with a machine that throws the water well up into the air, there is no reason why it should not be applied at any time. It is when watering is done with a can, and the drops not aerated, that there is a danger of scorching foliage, and in this case it is best to do the watering when the sun has gone down.

It is always better to water soil when it is firm than when it is loose and puffy. Therefore, if land is going to be dug, it is better to do the overhead irrigation before the digging rather than afterwards. The great thing is not to adopt the " little and often " plan. Give a good soaking once a week, rather than dribs and drabs every day, and aim at applying, say, at least 6 gals. of water per square yard.

Watering differs from soil to soil. The gardener on the heavy clay may have to water seldom. The gardener who has a light sandy soil or a gravelly soil over chalk may have to flood twice a week in dry weather. It is possible to feed plants with Liquinure automatically while the overhead irrigation is being done (see page 37).

Details of watering with regard to plants grown in pots, will be found in Part Seven, " Growing Under Glass."

PLANT PROTECTION

Plants sometimes need protection from hot sun, frost or wind.

Sun

In the case of sunshine such protection is only necessary in the greenhouse, in the frame, or under continuous cloches, and the method usually employed for giving this protection is to fleck the outside of the glass with lime wash, so as to break the sun's rays. Certain firms sell a proprietary product known as " Summer Cloud," something similar to a green distemper, which is sprayed over the outside of the glass and thus leaves a thin deposit. It is only necessary to give protection, however, to some plants and details will be found in the text dealing with these subjects. Under cloches it is usual to give slight shade for tomatoes, cucumbers and melons in mid-summer. Occasionally, exhibitors protect individual blooms from hot sunshine by putting over them a paper cone shaped like a dunce's cap.

Frost

Plants need protection from frost in the spring and in the autumn. For vegetables and any dwarf growing plants, continuous cloches are ideal for the purpose. (See pages 581-85). The cloches may be put into position to warm up the ground in the spring a fortnight before seed sowing, and they may be used equally well late in September to protect crops that are growing and to cause them to continue " fruiting." Cloches give the ideal protection because they admit a certain amount of air automatically.

It is possible to use pea sticks, bracken and straw to protect other plants during the winter. It is important to keep plants dry during cold weather, for when they get wet and frozen they are invariably killed. In the north, and in exposed localities, it is often advisable to protect dwarf roses by covering them with straw or bracken and by drawing soil up to the stems. Tender shrubs may be protected by having sacking or garden matting tied round them. Frames may be protected in a similar manner and in this case the mats or sacks are just laid over the top.

Sometimes it is necessary to protect the blossom of early flowering fruit trees in the spring. This is usually done by hanging fish netting over the trees, though if the trees are trained against walls or fences, it is possible to purchase wall cloches to cover them.

Wind

It is surprising what damage wind can do, in fact I would say wind often does more damage than frost. It can harm plants in the summer as well as in the spring and winter. Continuous cloches are ideal for giving protection against wind, but it is always worth while pushing pea sticks into the ground on the windward side of plants whenever they are being grown in a windy situation. It is particularly necessary to protect from wind early in the spring and, very often at this time, temporary " fences " may be put up of wattle hurdles or of sacking hung from wires. Curiously enough, wire netting will break the force of wind, even though it is not generally believed that this is possible. In small gardens plants often suffer from draughts, which whistle round the side of the house, especially down paths to the back door.

PLANT SUPPORTING
There are some plants that need supporting, staking or tying, and details with regard to the use of these will be found under many of the headings dealing with the individual plants. The great thing with staking and supporting is to see that the pea sticks, poles, bamboos or whatever is going to be used, are in position in plenty of time. A good general rule is that all plants that grow over 2½ ft. high need supporting.

Flowers. (See pages 95 and 96.)
Vegetables. (See pages 493 and 518.)
Fruit trees. (See page 394.)

The tying material used will differ in accordance with the plant to be supported. However, the modern cotton twist or twill, coloured green, is rightly very popular because it cannot easily be seen. For fruit trees, however, tarred string is better. It may be that special elastic tying materials will become available shortly which can be used with advantage on plants like tomatoes and cucumbers, whose stems swell as they grow, because then the tie will give and the plants will be properly supported all the time.

BLANCHING

Blanching means that some method is employed to keep certain parts of a plant in the dark so as to cause etiolation and thus prevent the green colouring matter in the stems or leaves from developing. Certain vegetables have to be blanched to prevent their being bitter and to ensure that they are tender and crisp, e.g. endive, celery, leeks, cardoons, chicory and seakale. The latter two are usually forced with heat during the blanching process. Cos lettuces like a little blanching and this is usually done by tying them up. Details of the various methods of blanching advised will be found under the heading of vegetables in Part Six, Food Production.

MULCHING

Mulching is done during the summer months and is particularly important in May, June and July. It aims at preventing moisture evaporation from the soil and, incidentally, at the same time provides organic matter (with two exceptions—dust mulching and paper mulching) which the worms pull into the ground. It is a good method, therefore, of increasing the humus content of soil without disturbing the roots of plants.

Materials often used for mulching include lawn mowings, properly composted vegetable refuse, well-rotted dung, damped horticultural sedge peat, hop manure, malt culms, seaweed, etc. The mulching material is put down along rows of plants to a depth of not more than 1 in. or so and for a width of, say, 6-9 ins. on either side. It is often used for peas and beans, for strawberries or raspberries. Mulches may also be placed right round individual plants, such as Brussels sprouts or cauliflowers or around black-currant bushes or blackberry plants. When a material like sedge peat is used, the mulch may be as thick as 1 in., but it is when rotting material is applied that it must not be deeper than an inch, or during its rotting heat may be evolved which can easily damage the plants. Furthermore, the mulching material may form a hard crust which would, for instance, prevent fresh young canes from growing up in the raspberry row.

The best mulching material is undoubtedly medium grade sedge peat. It never forms a crust. Mulching helps to keep the moisture in the ground. (See illustration facing page 32.) Mulches can be used anywhere in the garden in the summer. (See also page 35.)

TOP DRESSING

Top dressings are sometimes confused with mulches and there is no doubt that sometimes a mulch does act as a top dressing as well, especially when well-rotted dung or properly composted vegetable refuse is used. Top dressings, however, are concerned with feeding the plants and therefore they are often hoed lightly in. Organic fertilisers are very useful in this connection, particularly a fish manure to which some potash has been added to balance it up. Rock plants sometimes need a top dressing with limestone chippings or peat or fine leaf mould (for details see page 149).

THE USE OF HORMONES

Several hormones have been discovered in recent years which have proved to be of great value to the gardener. There are four main uses for hormones in the garden :

(1) The treatment of cuttings to encourage better and more rapid rooting.

(2) The prevention of pre-harvest fruit-drop on apples and pears.

(3) Encouraging development of fruits without fertilisation —particularly in the case of tomatoes.

(4) Weed control—there are several " selective " weed killers now on the market which destroy the weeds without damaging the crops. These are particularly useful on lawns.

Hormones for these various uses are sold under proprietary names and may be obtained from any good horticultural sundriesman.

MOVING PLANTS

It is necessary to move plants at various stages of their career. I have known it advisable to transplant apple trees when they were over 20 years of age because the orchard was far too thick, and the operation was carried out with great success. The main thing with all transplanting is to keep the roots out of the ground for as little time as possible, and with big subjects, like fruit trees and shrubs, it is vitally necessary to stake them properly so that they cannot possibly move about, however slightly, when they are in their new position. It is necessary for them to make baby fibrous roots and if they can rock about at all these continually get broken so that the tree has little chance of establishing itself again.

With smaller subjects, it is advisable to dig the plants up with as big a ball of soil to their roots as possible. This can be done, for instance, with herbaceous plants, with small fruit bushes, and so on. With vegetables, and with many flowers and alpines, it is advisable to get the transplanting done when the plants are very young. They thus get over the moving far more quickly. Taken by and large, few people move a plant at a small enough stage. Lettuce seedlings, for instance, should be moved when you can just see the two first leaves.

Trees, fruit and most shrubs like being moved late in the autumn or early in the winter so that they can get established before the spring. The evergreen shrubs on the whole prefer to be transplanted in the spring. They like protection from wind after planting and they also like to have their leaves syringed over once or twice a day during dry weather until they get thoroughly established.

Vegetable and flower seedlings can be transplanted in the spring, summer and autumn and if the weather is dry they like to be watered until they establish themselves ; and when it is possible they are glad to have protection from sunshine. Some people use flower-pots and put these upside down over the individual plants of lettuces, cauliflowers and the like during the day-time and remove them at night-time. This shading operation may only be necessary for four or five days. It is surprising what a difference shading makes in the hot, sunny weather. It may be possible to shade plants just by putting a few dock leaves over them, a rhubarb leaf, or in fact anything that will act as an umbrella.

Transplant carefully, transplant quickly, transplant very firmly. Don't pull up more plants per day than you can handle for transplanting.

SHOWING FLOWERS

Flower Shows are always popular, and a few hints on preparing flowers for exhibition might not be out of place.

Great care must be taken with the cutting, and this is more important than many people imagine. If possible the blooms should be cut in the early morning—the earlier the better—

especially if the weather is warm. If midday cutting cannot be avoided, the flowers should be got out of the sun as soon as possible, and be placed in a cool shady place in a bucketful of water for a few hours before packing.

For packing, long flat boxes are best. These should be lined with tissue paper, the blooms laid in very carefully and held in position by one or two sticks across the stems. These should be cut the exact width of the box so that they fit tightly. Of course always take more flowers than you actually need.

Upon arrival at the show the flowers should be unpacked without delay, the vases filled and the blooms arranged. It should have been planned out beforehand exactly how the exhibit is going to be arranged, so as to avoid waste of time.

The flowers should not be sprayed or syringed over with the idea of keeping them fresh, as this will spoil them.

Certain herbaceous flowers which might be included in a mixed vase, tend to drop their petals very quickly when cut, and might easily spoil the appearance of an exhibit. These include the poppy, geum, and potentilla. This petal dropping may easily be prevented by dipping the bottom 2 ins. of the stems immediately after cutting in boiling water. It is only necessary to keep the stems in the water for a few seconds, but it must be boiling so that the sap is congealed in the stem.

Labelling

This is a very important point, and neat, clean labelling can make all the difference to the appearance of an exhibit. Ink which will run should be avoided, as it is very easy to get the cards damp while arranging the flowers.

The schedule must be strictly adhered to—it is useless to put, say, a dozen blooms in a vase in the hope of making a better show, if only half a dozen are stipulated, or to use greenhouse flowers in a mixed bunch when hardy ones are asked for. This will only result in disqualification.

As far as possible, flowers should be cut with as long stems as possible, and used with their natural foliage, though some of this may be stripped off if it is very thick. A crowded vase never looks so well as one in which each bloom is displayed to full advantage.

It is quite permissible to remove a diseased petal or a damaged leaf in order not to detract from the appearance of a vase, so long as this " doctoring " is not carried too far. Any kind of artificial addition to the exhibit, such as ribbons or coloured paper, should be avoided.

CHAPTER IV

Plant Propagation

SO much is written and said about propagation that the amateur is often left in such a muddle that he is afraid even to sow a radish seed without going to the shelf to consult some book on the subject. Perhaps it is the long word that impresses us, yet we all started with fine confidence when we sowed our first mustard and cress on a bit of damp flannel. Where is that confidence now? Once the gardener has done his share of the work in providing conditions favourable to germination or root formation he should be able to leave the rest to nature, sure that the results will be good.

In nature each plant is in competition with its neighbour and, to ensure the survival of its species, seeds are produced in an enormous quantity to allow for loss at all stages. Birds and animals will eat some ; others fall where they cannot germinate ; more grow so thickly that they choke each other. Only a few out of many hundreds will mature and produce more seed in their turn. In cultivation man controls these adverse factors and makes the task of the seedling much easier, hence the danger of young plants being too soft. The gardener uses paraffin, red lead, or a mercurial dressing, to make seeds distasteful to birds and resistant to disease ; he prepares seed-beds or pans with special soils to suit the plants ; he sows thinly and later thins the seedlings to reduce competition ; he puts poison for slugs that may eat the tender growth ; he protects the plants from birds with wires and nets. With all these operations done to help the plant, is the gardener not entitled to expect good results ?

When increasing plants by means of cuttings, remember that the shoot has been deprived of its root ; therefore the immediate problem is water supply. Without roots the shoot cannot take up a lot of water, therefore its water requirement must be cut down. Water is lost through the leaves by the process called transpiration ; this loss of water is slower in a still moist atmosphere, therefore cuttings are placed in frames, under bell jars or in cloches so as to reduce the water requirement until such time as a new set of roots is formed and ready to meet the full demands

Drawing out drill on the seed bed

Sowing seed in drill

9. Raking over drill after sowing

10. Pricking out seedlings

11. Planting out cuttings

of the leaves in a normal unprotected situation ; that is why more ventilation is given to cutting-frames after the rooting has started.

Plants are propagated in various ways.

SEED

This method is normally used to regenerate " old stock " and to ensure a stronger root system. Some plants are more shapely when grown from seed, many on the other hand do not come true from seed, and others do not flower as quickly from seed. Seed sowing often, however, helps with the housing problem in the greenhouse for the seedlings can be raised under cloches or frames and taken into the greenhouse later. Seeds are normally used in vegetable growing and annual flower growing.

Seeds should always be stored under the best possible conditions, i.e. neither too damp nor too dry. They should be sown in a manner as near to nature as possible. Tiny seeds, therefore, will be covered with the slightest quantity of sandy compost. Dark seeds should be whitened so as to make them easy to see when sowing (see illustration facing page 33), the alternative being to whiten the surface of the compost. After sowing and watering the pan or box, it should be covered with a sheet of glass and then a sheet of brown paper. The glass prevents the soil from drying out too quickly and the darkness encourages root formation. The exception to this rule is the primula which prefers light.

If you wish to save your own seed, it should be collected from plants of a pure strain when it is just ripe. Some seeds lose their vitality quickly and should be sown almost immediately, such as cinerarias, delphiniums and aquilegias.

Ferns are raised from spores. These must be caught just before they burst from their sporangia (spore sacs). The fronds should be cut off and placed between two pieces of paper for storing and then kept in a warm dry atmosphere. The spores should be sown in sterilised soil with a sheet of glass over the pan. The house should be kept on the damp side during propagation. When one or two fronds appear ferns may be " pricked out."

SEED SOWING OUTDOORS

The land where seeds are to be sown should be well prepared. Good drainage is required. The soil should be well dug some time before the seeds are to be sown, and well-rotted manure or compost incorporated a spit deep. In the spring, tread the surface down and rake over to produce a level surface, incorporating, if the soil is light, horticultural peat at the rate of half a bucketful per square yard. This may be damped first if the soil is dry. In addition, if the ground is poor, lightly fork in fish manure at the rate of 3-4 ozs. per square yard. Hydrated lime at 3-4 ozs. per square yard may also be applied to the surface if necessary—after raking in the fish fertiliser.

Seeds should be sown very thinly in drills. Afterwards rake over the top and firm with the head of the rake. (See illustrations facing page 64.) Annual flower seeds may be sown broadcast in groups or patches.

Most seed sowing in the open is carried out in the spring. In cold and exposed districts, sowing may be carried out in cold frames. If the soil is below a certain temperature, germination will not take place or will be very slow. Sowing should always be done in damp soil if possible, and no watering should be done until germination takes place, otherwise the seeds may rot.

COMMON CAUSES OF FAILURE

Sowing too deeply, especially in heavy soils.

Soil too wet.

Soil too dry—though less likely than the above except in the case of very shallow sowing or in frames and cloches.

Too much fresh manure which can cause the developing root to be " burnt," as can doses of inorganic fertilisers.

Soil pests such as wireworms, slugs, cutworms and leather-jackets.

CUTTINGS

All kinds of cuttings may be taken, for instance, hard wood, half-ripe, soft cuttings, leaf cuttings and root cuttings. The soil mixture used should be one containing plenty of sand. It should be slightly acid and may be watered to advantage with a solution consisting of 3 teaspoonfuls of white vinegar in a gallon of water. Keep the atmosphere close to reduce transpiration. See that the base of the cutting is firmly in the soil. Hormones will help encourage a good root system. The ends of cuttings may be dipped in a suitable solution. All cuts should be made with a sharp knife and cuttings should be taken only from healthy plants.

Hard wood cuttings are taken in October from shrubby plants. They should be 8-9 ins. long and should be removed with a small heel. They are usually placed in a narrow trench outdoors with a sandy bottom 2 ins. apart. The soil is put back and thoroughly firmed. Soft tips are pinched out.

Hardwood cuttings are also taken of blackcurrants, redcurrants and gooseberries. In the case of gooseberries, a larger proportion of cuttings will root if they are taken while the leaves are still on the bushes. Gooseberries and redcurrants should have the bottom buds removed as these bushes are grown on a " leg," but with blackcurrants all the buds are left on. The cuttings should be inserted as described above, to two-thirds of their depth.

Half-ripe cuttings are struck any time between the middle of June and the middle of September. If a shoot is bent and is left hanging by a skin then it is right. Strike such cuttings in sandy soil in a frame in the north side of the garden or round the edge of a pot filled with sandy compost—in a shady frame.

Soft cuttings are taken in June and July, and root in pure sand in a heated frame. The cuttings are pushed into the sand and watered regularly.

Root cuttings consist of portions of root 1-2 ins. long, the part of the root nearest the stem being planted uppermost. Root cuttings should be buried in light compost so that their tops are covered by about $\frac{1}{2}$ in. of soil.

Leaf cuttings can be taken of some rare plants, the leaves from the lower part of the plant being chosen. For begonias the leaf is cut through three-quarters of the way and placed on damp horticultural peat with plenty of bottom heat. With Saintpaulia the leaf is placed on its edge in the peat and a callus will be formed at the end of the stalk if it is not buried too deeply. The leaf scales of lilies are placed in a leafy compost up to their tips in October, while with lachenalias, the leaves are placed in a compost and corms appear in eight weeks' time.

Cuttings of plants filled with resin are dipped in boiling water for a second or two before being inserted in sand. Plants which contain camphor and alkaloids have to be stood in the dark for 20 days before cuttings can be taken effectively. Plants with a lot of pith are cut back 3 or 4 weeks before cuttings are required —the new side shoots are then used for propagating.

Sheets of Polythene are much used when propagating cuttings. The box or propagating frame into which the cuttings are dibbled in may be surrounded completely with Polythene with the result that no watering is required for two or three weeks by which time the cuttings should have struck.

COMMON CAUSES OF FAILURE

(*a*) *Soft Cuttings*

Placed too deeply in the sand. In a proper closed cutting-frame only the bottom inch of the cutting needs to be fixed in the sand.

Too much water during the early stages. If watered well at the time of inserting and kept closed, except for a short daily airing to ensure dryness, the frames will not need more water for a week or so.

Left in the cutting-frame after roots are formed. The best rooting medium does not generally provide plant food; thus rooted cuttings must be potted up or boxed in good soil as soon as they are well rooted or they will starve.

Moss allowed to grow on the surface of the cutting bed and " suffocating " the cuttings.

(*b*) *Hard Cuttings*

Cuttings not thoroughly firmed into the soil.

Position too dry and sunny.

DIVISION

Division can be done in spring or autumn, depending on the conditions of the plant. To encourage new growth a little soil may be worked into the centre of the clump some weeks before dividing. The outside of the clump is the youngest and most vigorous part and, therefore, provides the best pieces for replanting. Dig up the plant to be divided and insert 2 forks, back to back, right the way through the centre of the clump—open out the forks and thus split the clump up. Repeat as necessary until the portions are quite small. (See illustrations facing page 224.)

COMMON CAUSES OF FAILURE

Careless handling. Roots and young shoots cut or bruised by dividing with a spade instead of using forks or doing the work by hand.

Replanting too deeply or too shallowly.

Dividing plants which resent division.

LAYERING

Layering induces plants to produce roots artificially, but only a limited number of plants can be raised from one parent. Serpentine

12. Breaking slabs for
    crazy-paving

13. Laying crazy-paving

14. *Finished crazy path with concrete between paving stones*

15. *Preparing cement blocks*

16. *Laying cement blocks*

17. & 18. *Two ways of edging a path*

layering, however, used principally for clematis and wisteria produces greater numbers. Layers strike more easily if partially severed at a node and pegged down into a compost containing peat and sand. Part of the plant needs burying. (See Fig. 14.)

COMMON CAUSES OF FAILURE
Shoot not made firm and newly formed roots broken off.
Soil too dry to allow for root formation.

SUCKERS

Suckers may grow up from the roots of the parent plant quite naturally, and may then be severed and potted up on their own. If the plant concerned has been budded or grafted then the sucker is from the " stock "—i.e. the rootstock of a wild plant: the crab or paradise stock in the case of an apple—and should be destroyed.

BUDDING

Budding is carried out in July or August. A slit $1\frac{1}{2}$ ins. long is made in one-year-old wood with a right-angled cut $\frac{1}{2}$ in. long at the top. Remove firm buds from the current year's growth with a sharp bladed knife so as not to make a deep incision. Insert the bud the right way up in the T-shaped cut, the bark having been slightly raised for the purpose. Bind the bud with bass from the bottom upwards, leaving the actual " nose " of the bud peeping out. Loosen the binding in 3 weeks. If the leaf stalk drops off naturally, the bud has " taken," but if it withers it has not. (See Fig. 18, page 274.)

In March cut stock down to within 3 or 4 ins. above the bud and, as growth from the bud grows, tie loosely to this " snag." In June cut stock back still further to a point just above the bud.

GRAFTING

Grafting under glass is usually carried out in February or March, or even in July, August and September. Outside grafting time is usually April and May.

In all cases the stock and scion (pieces of one-year-old wood) must be in the same condition.

Whip and tongue grafting is carried out when stock and scion are of the same size; saddle grafting when the stocks are somewhat larger, while root grafting is done under glass when the plant is dormant, in a similar manner to whip and tongue grafting. The graft is covered with soil and placed in a propagating case with a certain amount of bottom heat.

Outdoors, fruit trees are grafted in late March or early April. The scions are collected in November or December and heeled in in a shady place to keep the wood from drying out until grafting time. The whip and tongue method is commonly used where the stock is the same size as the scion. Where it is larger, the scion may be placed to one side, but it is essential that the two cambium layers should come into close contact.

Other methods which are employed include side and oblique side grafting, stub grafting, rind or crown grafting, strap grafting, inverted L bark-grafting, porcupine grafting and bridge grafting. (See Figs. 29-32, pages 467-9.)

BULBS AND CORMS

Various bulbs produce offsets, either naturally or artificially. In order that other bulblets will form around the centre, their bud is sometimes destroyed. Some plants like lilies, produce bulbils on their stems which may be taken off and placed apex upwards in a leafy compost.

Gladioli have tiny corms at the base of the parent and these may be grown on and will make big plants.

Some plants have what are known as pseudo-bulbs, like orchids and thunias. The long stems of the latter when dormant may be cut into lenghts of 4 ins. and placed in a propagating case. As a result they will grow.

TUBERS

Plants having tuberous roots, like begonias for example, may be cut into pieces providing each one has an eye.

PART TWO

CHOICE OF A GARDEN

CHAPTER I

Planning Your Garden

THE day of the purely ornamental garden is almost past. Every garden, however small, is expected to produce something for use in the kitchen.

This utility aspect does not mean that a garden ceases to be a thing of beauty. The well-proportioned lay-out of paths and borders is pleasing to the eye at any season. So it is essential to have a plan for your garden before starting to work. Haphazard methods only cause extra labour in the long run.

GENERAL SCHEME

If you should happen to take a house with a neglected garden, then from the lay-out point of view it is better for the site to be treated as if it was being planned for the first time. Sometimes it is necessary to alter an over-ornamented garden so as to simplify it and make it possible to run it with the minimum amount of labour.

SIMPLICITY OF DESIGN
Labour costs and the difficulty and expense of obtaining material for the more usual garden features—such as wood for pergolas and trellis work, concrete pools and stone for paving and walls —make simplicity in the design essential as well as desirable.

EASE OF UPKEEP
Simple lines in the garden give a pleasing restful appearance with the minimum of time needed for upkeep. Complicated patterns of little beds and grass strips can look charming when kept meticulously tidy, but once the weekly clean up has to be neglected through lack of time, the little garden which was such a joy becomes a sorry wilderness of weeds, ragged verges and dead leaves.

THE PLAN ON PAPER
Before starting the drawn plan it is essential to know three things:

(1) Measurements of the boundaries in feet—not yards.
(2) Levels.
(3) Aspect.

Then proceed to plot out the main features. Decide which will be the best borders for warmth and shelter. The part of the garden which is unlikely to produce good crops will naturally be used for such things as sheds, compost heaps, incinerator and storage heaps for stakes, soils and all the other impedimenta of gardening.

Next, place the permanent features, paths, lawn, shrub borders, fruit trees, leaving as large uninterrupted areas as possible for vegetable cultivation, as this makes for simplicity in cropping schemes later.

Always consider the house and garden as a single unit and try to arrange that the best views of the garden can be had from the living-room windows, while the vegetable garden should be easily reached from the kitchen door.

PRELIMINARY WORK

Know Your Soil
Soil is the fundamental raw material of the gardener and as we must in the main accept what the site provides, the job is to do all in our power to make it as suitable for the crops we wish to grow as good cultivation and treatment can make it.

Does the Garden Need Draining ?
This will largely depend upon the type of sub-soil. Even a heavy soil seldom becomes waterlogged if it is over a porous gravel sub-soil, but where clay forms the lower levels it will be necessary to drain the ground.

This is a slow and heavy task, but well worth the trouble, as well-drained soils are warmer and will produce earlier crops than cold wet soils.

How to Drain
The first point is to decide where the drainage water is to go. If you are lucky there is a ditch already situated at the lowest point of the ground. If there is no possibility of outlet a sump pit must be dug and filled with clinker and coarse stone. The size of this must vary with the area to be drained. For further details see page 22.

LEVELLING

In the average small garden there is no need to do any levelling unless a perfectly true surface is required for any special purpose, such as a tennis court or bowling green. Formal pools and paving also require to be made on levelled sites.

At the other end of the scale is the garden which is on such a slope that a complicated system of terracing is needed. But such a site would not be the first choice of any one wanting to get high yields for little labour from the garden.

In medium-sized gardens a change of level can be pleasingly employed as a grass bank, or, if the stone is available, a dry wall planted with rock plants.

In all cases where levelling has to be resorted to it is the lower level of the soil that has to be " man handled," the top spit having been first removed and stacked ready to replace evenly over the levelled site. If this were not done the higher part of the ground would be left denuded of its fertile top soil which has been used to fill in the lower part.

COLOUR EFFECTS IN GARDENING

It is essential in a garden to plan the colour effects so that the flowers blend into a harmonious picture without discordant notes. In small beds, single colours or two harmonising colours, give a more restful effect than a mixture of all hues, such as is sometimes seen, particularly with antirrhinums. Brilliant colour schemes may be arranged with beds of annuals, while spring and summer bedding provide further opportunities for displaying individual taste.

In the herbaceous border, as far as possible, the whites and paler shades should be placed at either end so that the eye is led by degrees to the end of the border. If the brilliant oranges and scarlets are near the end they are inclined to distract attention from the main bulk of the herbaceous layout. It is better to lead up gradually through the yellows and pinks to the more brilliant colours, and then to shade down through the blues and mauves to the whites. Cream or white can be used as a foil to the brighter colours, but too many splashes of white give a broken appearance. Some of the grey-foliaged plants can also be used as a foil for the brighter colours.

Shrubs also may be planted for their colour effects, and groups of azaleas, for instance, in spring, or acers, rhus or berberis for their autumn foliage colour, will give a grand effect. It should be remembered, too, that even in the winter it is possible to have some colour by planting those shrubs and trees which have coloured stems such as the dogwoods (*Cornus*) and willows (*Salix*).

FLOWER-BEDS AND BORDERS

Flower-beds are best regarded as frames for the plants themselves, not as abstract shapes and forms. As such, a plain rectangular bed or a simple circular or curved bed is a much better choice than a complicated pattern of spirals and " star-fish " which need endless edging up and, as often as not, provide extraordinarily little space for the flowering plants for which they were intended.

When planning a long border it is important to consider the relation of length to width. A 5-ft. wide border along the side of a small lawn could look quite generous, but extend that border to twice its length and it immediately becomes a mean little strip.

Marking out the Beds

The position and shape of the flower-beds having been decided, the bed must be pegged out.

For simple straight-sided beds it is sufficient to hammer in a stout peg at each corner, with only an occasional peg down the sides. But when dealing with curved edges the more pegs used the better to get a good steady curve instead of a succession of short sides.

Preparing the Soil

On a new site the pegs round the intended flower-beds must be very well firmed into the ground. The whole area is going to be dug in one way or another and those pegs are all you have to show which areas have been specially prepared for the beds and which have been less deeply dug for a lawn. Where the beds are being prepared in established gardens this will not be so important, as the position of the new bed will be easily visible.

Soil for beds and borders must be thoroughly prepared by deep digging. In most cases double digging will be best ; with plenty of roughage and compost incorporated in the lower levels, and more well-rotted compost and slow-acting fertilisers mixed in the top spit.

This digging is best done in the autumn, leaving the surface rough to allow for frost to break down the soil, and delaying the planting until spring when the soil will have settled down.

PLANTING

Never be in a hurry to plant the new border—it only leads to disaster, for no plant can get happily rooted into soil that is still in the process of shifting and sinking.

PATHS

WALK DRY SHOD WHERE YOU CAN

The importance of paths is frequently overlooked. Yet they are in steady use all through the year. The main walks to the door from the road get attention from the builder in many modern houses, but what about that muddy little walk down to the vegetable patch? And it is the path from the kitchen door to the row of parsley or the hen run that should be the best drained, driest path in the garden, as it is here that the housewife has to run out every day regardless of weather—and generally in her thin slippers!

MATERIAL FOR PATHS

The foundation of a good path is essentially the same in every case and should be given every care, as the useful life of the path is considerably shortened when the foundation work has been badly done. (See illustrations facing pages 68 and 69.)

The most usual surfacing materials are cement, paving, gravel, asphalt, ashes and bricks. Before deciding on the material its suitability to the surroundings must be considered. Generally speaking, the paths near the house are best made the same as the walls. A red brick path which looks charming round a brick cottage would not be suitable by a stone-built house.

The surfacing of the paths leading from the garden and sheds to the kitchen and yard should, where possible, be washable, and with a slight slope down to a really efficient drain. When this is arranged it is a simple matter to give a weekly cleaning with a pail of water and stiff yard broom, thus avoiding all the bother of mud dragged into the house from garden boots.

MAKING THE FOUNDATIONS

The site of the path must be marked out and the soil removed to a depth of 18 ins. for a path 4 ft. wide or more. A narrower path can be made with only 9-12 ins. foundation.

On light soils it is sufficient to make the drainage with rubble or brushwood, but on heavy soils it is wiser to include a pipe drain in the scheme. (See Fig. 1.)

Brick, stone or broken paving paths are best set in sand. In the case of paving cut in large slabs the site must be thoroughly consolidated before laying the stone as subsequent sinking will cause the slabs to crack, and spoil the effect of a path arranged in a regular design of stone cut to a set pattern.

The finished surface of hard paths must be slightly curved to ensure a dry surface immediately after rain. A rise of an inch or so in the centre is ample; if curved too much it makes walking uncomfortable.

Mention must be made of grass paths, though these cannot be looked upon as paths proper as they are not suitable for heavy wear, and in places where there is much traffic they must have occasional " stepping-stones " set in at soil level to take the worst of the wear and tear.

Where Paths meet the Border or Lawn

The eternal problem of edgings must be solved. To give a neat edging between path and dug soil formal material is best. Tiles, bricks or low concrete walls can be recommended. (See illustration facing page 92.) Wood boarding is often seen, but is not desirable as it rots rather quickly and then is a breeding ground and refuge for many garden pests.

In kitchen gardens the old methods of rows of chives, parsley or thyme looked rather well, but that was in the days of an extra garden boy whenever needed. All the " living " edgings give extra work, and, except where low-growing tufty rock plants are allowed to grow out over a paved path, are to be discouraged.

The line between lawn and path is best trimmed with edging shears. This is not nearly such a tedious job as many people would lead one to suppose. But let it be shears that are used ; nothing is uglier than the slowly retreating lawn that is chopped back with spade or half-moon by the jobbing gardener at his fortnightly " tidy round."

When a lawn is made with a hard permanent edging be sure that the level is so arranged that a lawn mower can pass over both without leaving a little strip that has to be cut with shears. This is a far slower operation than clipping the ordinary grass verge.

Well-kept edgings are of extreme importance to the appearance of a garden. (See illustration facing page 69.) The effect of a freshly cut lawn or newly weeded path is spoiled if the edges have not been attended to at the same time.

HEDGES VERSUS FENCES

The hedge with a purpose is a good and useful occupier of the ground. But before planting a new hedge remember that, as a living boundary, it takes nourishment from the soil, and its spreading roots may starve some plant badly in need of extra food. In many cases where a barrier is needed for protection from hard winds this can better be given by fencing or hurdles rather than by a hedge. For kitchen garden work, wattle hurdles, treated as mobile units to provide shelter when and where needed, are invaluable.

In favour of the hedge we must consider its beauty as a growing plant, and the great variety of subjects that can be used for this purpose.

TYPES OF HEDGES

The hedge can be evergreen or deciduous, the former being chosen for a site where protection is important all the year round, such as hiding drains and water-tanks from the pleasure garden or screening off the main road running just too near the garden. The evergreen hedge also provides a belt of foliage through the winter when all around is bare soil and naked branches.

The deciduous hedge, on the other hand, will often provide flowers as well as protection, and as a general rule is quicker growing than the evergreen.

The hedge can be formal, that is, clipped close several times a year, of uniform height and thickness ; or it can be informal— only kept in check by an occasional trimming of the more straggling growth with a pruning knife or secateurs. It is this informal type of hedge which can be planted from a variety of flowering shrubs which will give the greatest return of bloom ; but dense growth and neatness must be sacrificed.

PREPARING THE SITE

A sickly hedge being the most miserable of sights care should be taken to make the soil which is to receive the young plants as good as possible. Remember it is your last chance to get at the lower soil to enrich it ; any subsequent feeding must be in the form of a top dressing. The soil must be double dug with as much organic matter as can be spared incorporated in the bottom spit to encourage deep rooting. Even when the hedge to be planted is of very young shrubs the dug strip should be at least 3 ft. wide.

WHEN TO PLANT

Deciduous hedges can be safely planted during the autumn until early spring, provided the ground is not frozen or waterlogged. In cold wet districts it is best to delay planting until the spring, if there has not been time to get the work done early enough in the autumn for the roots to get established in soil still warm from the sun.

Evergreens are a bit more particular about climatic conditions and should be planted in September or early October, or else left until April when they can start to grow at once in their new quarters.

In all cases, it is wise to have straw or litter handy to spread over the soil in hard weather in order to protect the newly-planted roots, and also to prevent the plants from being lifted by frost.

Care must be taken the first spring and summer to see that the soil does not dry out. An occasional soaking of water will ensure the formation of a good hedge where frequent small applications that only damp the surface of the soil are useless. In dry soils it is wise to have the hedge planted in a small trench, about an inch below the normal soil level. This will make watering a much simpler operation.

THE FIRST FEW YEARS

Patience is needed in establishing a really good evergreen hedge. If a thick solid hedge is to be formed it has to be allowed to grow slowly. The base will never thicken well when the top is taking all the nourishment and shading the lower parts. All long, vigorous shoots must be cut hard back to encourage them to branch low down, and gradually a good dense hedge will rise foot by foot, with no bare or thin patches in it.

GENERAL CARE

To keep it in good health, a hedge needs feeding as much as any other plant, and an annual top dressing of compost, leaf mould or old hot-bed manure, coupled with a sprinkling of slow-acting general fertiliser, will well repay you.

Clipping should be done with a good pair of well-sharpened shears. Always have a pair of secateurs handy for the occasional thicker shoot that will need cutting. Hedge plants with large leaves should be cut with knife or secateurs only ; larger leaves that have been clipped in half gradually die back and give an ugly brown appearance to the whole hedge.

In districts where snow is the general rule it is wisest to have all hedges cut to a pointed or curved top to allow the snow to fall off. After hard winters one sees many hedges ruined by the weight of snow that has rested on the flat cut tops and broken the branches.

Hedges near the sea, or in other very exposed places, are often helped if planted, in the first place, with an iron fence or a few spaced out strands of wire in the middle. This will give the young plants support while they are thickening up enough to stand upright on their own.

FORMAL HEDGES

*Berberis Darwinii
*Berberis stenophylla
 Carpinus betulus
*Cupressus Lawsoniana
*Cupressus macrocarpa
*Escallonia nacrantha
*Euonymus japonicus
 Fagus sylvatica
*Griselinia littoralis
*Ilex aquifolium
 Ligustrum ovalifolium
*Lonicera nitida
*Prunus Laurocerasus
*Taxus baccata
*Thuja plicata

INFORMAL HEDGES

Cydonia japonica
Cytisus, various
Forsythia intermedia
Fuchsia Riccartoni
Ribes sanguinea
Rosa rugosa
Rosa, Sweet Briar varieties
Spartium junceum
Tamarix, varieties
*Ulex europaeus flore pleno
*Viburnum Tinus

*Evergreen

FENCES

In favour of fences as a means of enclosing, dividing or giving protection in the garden we must consider several aspects of the case. Fences are dead material, and as such are more in our power—a split chestnut fencing doesn't die because it was erected in the middle of a hot summer, or because the soil is too poor; thus the jobs connected with erecting and caring for fencing can be fitted in with other work at any season.

Properly looked after, a fence is clean and should not harbour pests. The lauchlap fences are ideal. They are peep proof and last almost for ever. They don't need painting or treating in any way.

A fence frequently used now is of concrete supports with mesh wire strained between. This has the advantage of needing little care since there are no wooden parts to be treated with creosote.

As with most things, it is worth giving time and care to fences. A periodical treating with Rentokil fluid will double the life of the wooden fence and regular painting will do the same for iron railing. The time to hammer in a nail is the first time you see the first slat loose. Never wait to repair it later; the following day you may find several planks fallen down, and all the dogs in the neighbourhood trooping in and out to bury bones in your seed bed.

GARDEN WALLS

The phrase " a walled garden " always raises the picture of a well-kept kitchen garden on a sunny afternoon ; peaches are ripening against the warm red brick walls and beautifully trained cordon apples and pears line the main walks.

Are the walls an advantage ? How can they best be utilised ? These are frequent questions.

A wall in good state of repair affords support to trained fruit trees, and protection from winds. By absorbing the sun's heat it can protect early-flowering subjects from frost, and promote early ripening in the fruit season.

The borders near walls often suffer from drought, and an ample supply of water must be given to trees planted against walls if they are to grow well and give good crops. The water requirement of a tree against a wall will be higher than that of one in another position as the rate of transpiration will be higher in the warmer position.

The roughly built granite walls, so often found in the older suburbs of large towns, are the home of thousands of snails. The enthusiastic gardener would be well advised to have these walls repaired with special attention to cracks at ground level, and a little below, where slugs join the snails in the hunt for winter quarters.

New garden walls are generally constructed of precast concrete blocks and faced with cement. This makes a surface into which it is almost impossible to drive a wall nail. Where possible arrange to have a series of holdfasts built into the walls so that wires can be threaded through at regular intervals to support loganberries, roses, or fruit trees.

RETAINING WALLS

These are employed to hold up soil at the edge of a terrace or other place where a change of level occurs. In the formal parts of a garden they are constructed of brick or cut stone and generally solidly built with cement. Another method of holding in a bank of soil is to build a dry wall. (See illustration facing page 92.) This is made of roughly-shaped stone bound with soil or sand and generally planted, in the course of construction, with suitable close-growing plants. The lower course is sometimes set in cement to give a firm foundation.

LAWNS

There is something very banal about saying, " If you're going to have a lawn—have a lawn," and yet what a completely satisfying statement this is. So often you come across a grass patch that has never been properly laid, no special grass was ever sown ; like Topsy of *Uncle Tom's Cabin*, it " just grew." So, whether you are going to have a small lawn, a large tennis court or a rolling sward stretching out into the distance, give the same care and thought to preparing it as you would to any other part of the garden.

There are two ways of making a lawn, one by seeding and the other by turfing, though it is true that some people establish lawns by planting out little portions of one of the keeping grasses. However, this is a rare system. Let us take, then, the two main methods of lawn making, but before we do this it will be necessary to prepare the soil. Read on !

PREPARING THE SOIL

As a lawn does best on a medium loam, aim at producing a soil as near to this character as possible. In the case of sandy soils, dig in some moisture-holding material and, in the case of heavy clays, incorporate sand or finely ground peat. There is no need to dig very deeply—aim at preparing the top 5 ins. See that the land is well drained (see page 22) and, if it is necessary to level the ground, take care to see that the sub-soil is not brought to the surface. It may have to be dug up, but it should always be buried again on the other side to raise the level (see also page 75.) The great thing is not to put it on the top. Having prepared the ground, get the level right.

TWO METHODS OF LAWN MAKING
(a) Seed Sowing

Sow the seed either in the spring or autumn. Probably the spring in the north and the autumn in the south. Fork the land down so that the soil is really fine and then allow the ground to lie bare for a period of 3 weeks to a month. During this time the weeds will have a chance of growing, and so before the seed is sown they will be hoed down and raked off. It is most important to get rid of all the perennial weeds during the forking, and as many of the annual weeds as possible, by means of this fallowing process. Aim at having a lawn that consists of fine grasses and fine grasses only.

Rake the surface down to a fine condition. Every particle of soil should be as small as a grain of wheat. Roll the ground to get the land firm and do this when the surface is dry. Alternate rolling and raking will enable you to do the final levelling and to see the surface is fine enough.

Don't just buy " lawn seed." Buy a properly balanced mixture. A good one consists of :

    70% Chewing's Fescue

    30% Creeping Red Fescue

Increase the proportion of Fescue and reduce the amount of Agrostis should the soil be light.

Another good mixture consists of

    23% New Zealand Bent

    20% Agrostis tenuis

    57% Chewing's Fescue

Some people complain that the lawn is apt to look a little brown in the summer when the Bents are used and, in this case, it is possible to have a formula which omits the Bents, and this is :

    25% Fine-leaved Sheep's Fescue ;

    50% Chewing's Fescue ;

    25% Sea-washed Fescue.

There is no need to apply more than $1\frac{1}{2}$ ozs. of seed per square yard. It pays to divide the seed up into equal lots and to see that the right amount covers the exact area of ground it should. Sow on a still, dry day and rake the land lightly over afterwards. If the seed is soaked in a product known as Horticule, the birds will refrain from taking it.

Do not mow a newly-sown lawn quickly or you may drag up the young grasses by the roots. Wait until it is at least 2 ins. high and then either cut it with a pair of shears or scythe, or else set the blades of the mower very high and, having rolled the lawn first, cut it once.

Watch out the whole time for weeds and eliminate them the moment they are seen.

(b) *Turf Laying*

A much more expensive method and one which seldom gives as good results as seed sowing. It is very difficult to buy good turf. Turves arrive rolled up and when laid out they are 1 yd. long, 1 ft. broad and 1½ ins. thick. It is best to lay them down in January as they will not knit with the soil below if the weather is dry. Put the turf down directly it arrives, so get the land ready beforehand by preparing it as for seed sowing. Once they have been laid down, beat them by means of a turf beater (see illustration facing page 93) and, when the whole area has been treated in this way, run a roller over the ground. If any spaces are left between the sods, fill these up with equal parts of fine leaf mould and sand.

(c) *The planting of Stolons (Agrosh's Stolonifera).* See page 88.

THE MANAGEMENT OF A LAWN

Once a lawn is established, cut it once a week, directly the warm weather starts in the spring, keeping the knives as low as possible. Never cut during frosty weather, and in dry droughty weather leave off the grass-box.

Roll in the winter to encourage the young grasses to tiller out. Always brush off the worm casts first. Never use a roller heavier than 1 cwt. Do not roll lawns when the ground is sodden.

Feed the lawn by using a mixture of 3 parts of sulphate of ammonia and 1 part of calcined sulphate of iron at the rate of 2 ozs. to the square yard. Make the first application round about Easter and the next at Whitsun. Keep these *absolutely dry* before they are applied and throw the chemicals well up in the air to allow them to fall down evenly as a dust. If you attempt to apply them at knee height, you are bound to give too heavy a dressing in one patch and too little in another, and you will cause scorching as a result. Some people prefer to mark off the lawn into plots of 1 sq. yd. Place 2 ozs. of the mixture into a cocoa tin with a perforated lid and distribute this evenly over the square. This mixture will not only feed the lawn but eliminate the weeds and discourage the clovers. Those who fear that the lawn will be scorched may reduce the dressing to 1 oz. per square yard, and increase the number of applications. Lawn sand consists almost entirely of sand and the two chemicals I have mentioned. The sand merely makes the artificials easier to apply, but of course adds to the cost.

Worms do aerate a lawn but they cause worm casts, which are such a nuisance, especially on bowling greens and tennis courts. Get rid of the worms, therefore, if you wish, by applying Mowrah Meal at 8 ozs. to the square yard, preferably just before a downpour of rain and, if this is impossible, just water the meal in. The worms will rise to the surface in their hundreds and may be swept off. Where Mowrah Meal is impossible to get, dissolve 1 lb. of copper sulphate in 50 galls. of water and give the lawn a soaking with this.

Any of the prepartions containing Gammexane are found to give good results in the control of leatherjackets, and should be used in districts where this pest is causing damage to cultivated turf

When the worms are eliminated, resort to artificial aeration by spiking the lawns. Use a long five-tined fork and plunge this in as deeply as possible every 2 ft. or so all over the lawn every 3 years. (See illustration facing page 93.)

Rake the lawn with a springbok wire rake about the beginning of March in the south and at the end of March in the north. You will thus disturb the dead stolons of the Bents. (See illustration facing page 93.)

WEEDS AND WEEDING

Much is said about the control of weeds throughout this book. For instance, weed control on the lawn is given on page 85 ; the control of weeds by hoeing will be found on pages 55-56 and, in the chapters dealing with flowers, weeds are also mentioned. The great thing with weeds is to tackle them as early as possible. There are market gardeners in the Swanley district who put on extra men for the months of April and May to crawl along the rows of vegetables hoeing, thinning, and hand weeding, and they say that, if they can keep their fields quite free from weeds during those months and early in June, they need not worry much until the end of the year—and there is a lot of truth in it.

Keep the hoe going, then, in the spring and early summer. Never allow the weeds to flower and seed. In hot weather weeds may be left on the soil to wither and die, but in damp weather it is better to rake them off and put them on the compost heap to rot down. Hand weeding has to be carried out in the rows of plants ; it is better to do this after a shower of rain, because then the weeds come up more easily and the other plants are not so much disturbed.

Keep all rough grass in a garden cut before it has time to seed ; control all weeds in grass paths and grass edgings ; keep an eye on all neighbouring hedgerows and remember that there is a " Seeds and Weeds Act," so if your neighbour is a particularly dirty gardener it may be possible for you to report him to the Minstry of Agriculture and await results!

WEEDS ON PATHS

Simazine sometimes sold as Weedex can be described as a total weed killer concentrate. It can give the gardener weed-free paths and drives for 12 months. It is not poisonous—it is safe to use— it stays where applied and does not leach out. It can therefore be used on paths near flower beds without fear that the flowering plants will be damaged. It is non-corrosive and non-inflammable.

Simazine kills the weeds through their roots and then remains, so to speak, " on guard " for 12 months in order to deal with any fresh weeds that may germinate from seeds. It is effective because it stops in the top 3 or 4 inches of soil being almost insoluble in water. It is this reason that prevents if from being carried sideways or even deeper into the soil as the result of rain or overhead irrigation. It is not inflammable as is sodium-chlorate so no precautions need be taken against fire. It can be used any time from the beginning of February to September and the author finds that it gives the best results when it is applied in the spring before the weeds have had time to get established.

Not only can it be used on paths and drives but it is excellent on hard tennis courts and has been used on uncultivated land. It should not be used for shallow rooted trees or shrubs and of course never on flower beds or lawns. The watering can must be washed out very thoroughly with warm water after use.

A Flame Gun can be operated with Butane Gas. It is very light to carry and if the Gun is held in the operator's hand as he walks down the path the strong flame can be made to kill all the weeds as well as any weed seeds that may have been deposited in the top $\frac{1}{4}$ of an inch or so of the gravel or ash. This Flame Gun can be made to have a wide flame or a narrow flame at will.

Sodium chlorate (please note, not sodium chloride) may be used on paths, but it is very expensive and is better employed to control weeds in other parts of the garden where the other weed killers mentioned above could not be used.

WEEDS IN OTHER PARTS OF THE GARDEN

The Paraquat weed killer is used in flower beds, under hedges and even between vegetable rows. It is inactivated on contact with the soil. It kills by attacking the chlorophyll in the leaves. It is therefore applied, in solution, when the weeds are growing, and care must be taken not to water the plants afterwards.

Sodium chlorate is an excellent weed killer if applied to plants when they are growing well. It must be used dry as a powder and be applied on the leaves of the weeds. The leaves then pass the "poison" down to the roots which are killed. It will even destroy a very deep-rooting weed like convolvulus. After application, the weeds and soil should be left undisturbed for about 2 months. The poison enters the system of the plant through the leaves and stems. It is best applied in the afternoon on a dry sunny day. It goes further when used in solution, i.e. at the rate of 1 lb per gallon of water, but if it soaks clothing or wood it may produce a highly combustible material. I therefore never recommend Sodium Chlorate to be used as a liquid.

It can be used quite successfully to control weeds in shrub borders under the shrubs without killing the shrubs themselves. The author has also used it as a dry powder on weeds growing among fruit trees without killing the trees.

HORMONE WEED KILLERS
Latterly, there have been introduced a number of hormone selective weed killers which are quite successful at the moment on lawns, killing the weeds and not the grass. Readers may like to consult local horticultural sundriesmen on the subject. A hormone is a chemical which, in extremely small amounts, exerts an extraordinary influence on the growth of the individual cells of which the plant is composed.

PLANTING OF STOLONS
Lawns are being established to-day by planting stolons of Agrostis stolonifera Z.103 twelve inches square on level ground. The hole for them should be about 2 ins. deep, and the Stolon must be planted firmly. Plant in April, and there will be a good lawn by the late summer. If the weather is suitable and the ground not too wet the ground should be lightly rolled after planting and if the soil is dry a good watering should be given. The first growths from the offsets appear rather coarse, but these are the spreading Stolons and should not be cut. When the lawn assumes its adult characteristics, it will be covered with fine grass blades on hundreds of thousands of surface creeping stolons.

CHAPTER II

The Herbaceous Border

MAKING AND CARING FOR THE HERBACEOUS BORDER

*

STRICTLY speaking the herbaceous border is a long, stretched out bed in which hardy herbaceous perennials are grown. (See illustration facing page 136.) By that, we mean plants that will survive a normal English winter, sending up fresh shoots each spring from a rootstock that will live for many years. The herbaceous border is so popular because it is colourful almost all the year round and yet never stays the same ; it is bright and yet, even with straight outlines, manages to appear informal, almost natural if the gardener knows his art. There is, by the way, no need to be orthodox about plants used in the herbaceous border. In the very wide border some neat flowering shrubs help to shape the picture ; whilst the more sturdy growing annuals or biennials will brighten and bind together the border made of newly-purchased plants which the owner hopes to increase later on.

PLANNING THE BORDER

While this book will point out a few facts that must be considered in planning a border, no book can be a substitute for the ideal lesson on planning, which is *example*. Visit the parks, go to Kew, to Wisley, to garden parties and shows, save your bus fare and walk looking over the garden fence or hedge—look and learn ! Books and catalogues are all right in their way, but they cannot tell you what you will really like—they are like " shopping by post." This " lesson by example " business will especially help you to find out about the grouping of different plants. Not only will good example teach you—dingy or glaring borders will prevent your making many mistakes. But here are some important points to bear in mind :

WHERE SHALL THE BORDER GO ?

This depends largely on the individual garden, but there are some general points to consider.

The position for the border should be open, well drained (or at least definitely drainable), sunny, and sheltered from winds, especially the north and east winds. It is, however, possible to make very pleasing shade borders, but their effect will be rather subdued and quiet compared to the bright, infinite variety of the sunny border.

Plan the border so that the principal view point is along it rather than at it. Lastly, the usually formal outline of the border suggests for it a place near the house.

WHAT SHAPE SHALL IT HAVE ?

The border usually has straight-lined edges, but there is no reason why they should not be curved, especially if the background is also curved, e.g. consisting of an informal shrub planting. The width of the border will depend on its length and on the width of the path ; but in any case a width of more than 12 ft. would be overdoing it, whilst it is a pity to make it less than 6 ft. wide, as you then have to leave out all the really tall plants and will find it difficult to get a good succession of flowers. But even a 4-ft. border can be a success if cleverly planted.

A border is single faced when backed by a hedge, or wall, or any other structure that makes one want to walk only along the one side. A double-faced border has paths, or lawns, on both sides. Fig. 11 shows the planting in a single border. One herbaceous border may be lovely—a twin border may be twice as lovely. It consists of two parallel borders on either side of a central path or walk.

The proportions of a border that is to be long but not very wide may be improved by some interruptions of its length.

THE BEST BACKGROUND

The background to the border may be formed by some partition that is required in any case to divide one part of the garden from another, or the garden from its neighbour. It may provide shelter from wind and should help to show up the flowers in their full beauty. But the background must not compete with the border plants, either for food from the ground or for attention from the onlooker. Therefore, plant a " living background," i.e. a hedge or climbers on trellis some way back from the border, so that it will not impoverish the soil.[1] In addition, a 3-ft. deep

[1] Some space between background and border has the further advantage of allowing for freedom of movement when working at the back of the border, e.g. staking the taller plants.

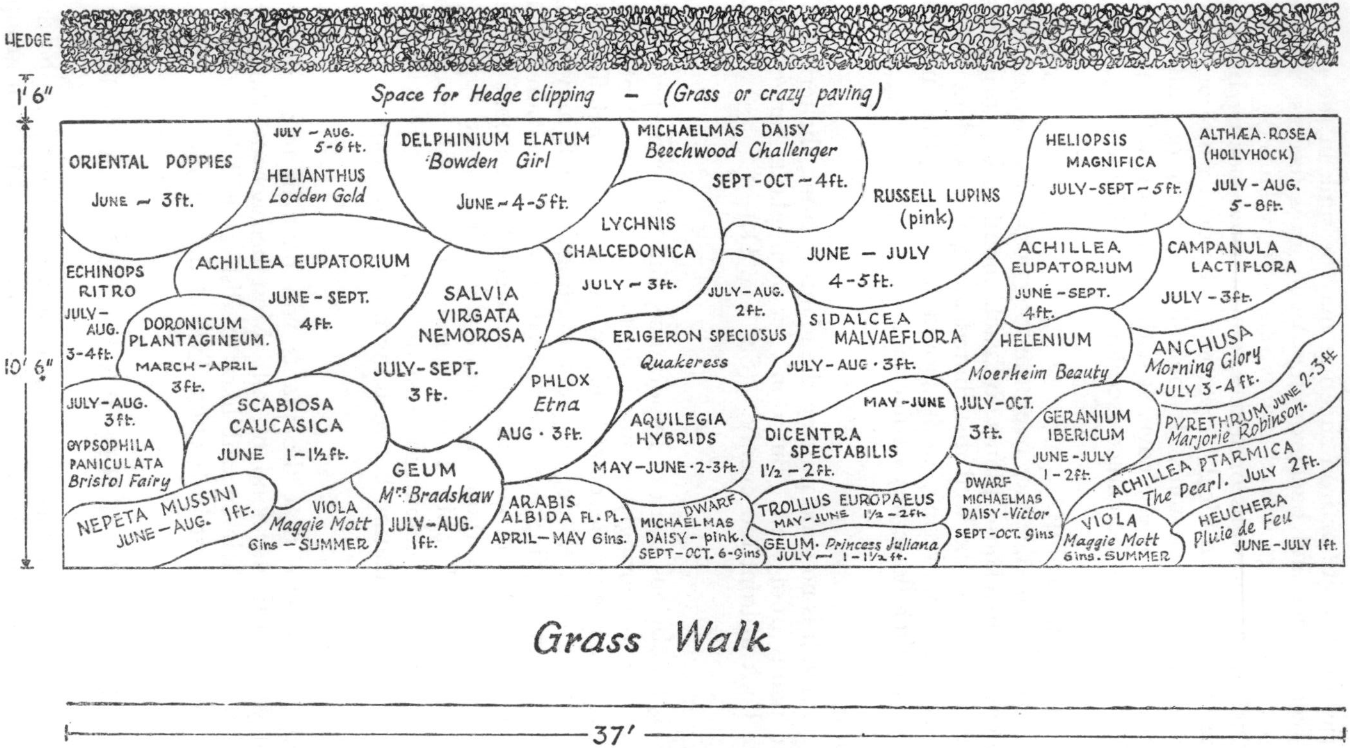

HEDGE

1' 6"

Space for Hedge clipping — (Grass or crazy paving)

10' 6"

ORIENTAL POPPIES JUNE ~ 3ft.	ALTHÆA ROSEA (HOLLYHOCK) JULY - AUG. 5 - 8ft.
ECHINOPS RITRO JULY~ AUG. 3-4ft.	HELIANTHUS Lodden Gold JULY ~ AUG. 5-6 ft.
DORONICUM PLANTAGINEUM. MARCH-APRIL 3ft.	HELIOPSIS MAGNIFICA JULY-SEPT ~ 5ft.
	DELPHINIUM ELATUM Bowden Girl JUNE ~ 4-5 ft.
ACHILLEA EUPATORIUM JUNE - SEPT. 4ft.	CAMPANULA LACTIFLORA JULY ~ 3ft.
	ACHILLEA EUPATORIUM JUNE - SEPT. 4ft.
GYPSOPHILA PANICULATA Bristol Fairy JULY-AUG. 3ft.	MICHAELMAS DAISY Beechwood Challenger SEPT-OCT ~ 4ft.
SCABIOSA CAUCASICA JUNE 1-1½ft.	LYCHNIS CHALCEDONICA JULY ~ 3ft.
	SALVIA VIRGATA NEMOROSA JULY - SEPT. 3 ft.
VIOLA Maggie Mott 6ins - SUMMER.	PHLOX Etna AUG · 3ft.
NEPETA MUSSINI JUNE - AUG. 1ft.	GEUM Mrs Bradshaw JULY-AUG. 1ft.

RUSSELL LUPINS (pink) JUNE - JULY 4-5 ft.

ERIGERON SPECIOSUS Quakeress 2ft. JULY-AUG.

SIDALCEA MALVAEFLORA JULY-AUG · 3ft.

AQUILEGIA HYBRIDS MAY-JUNE-2-3ft.

ARABIS ALBIDA FL. PL. APRIL – MAY 6ins.

ANCHUSA Morning Glory JULY 3 - 4 ft. 2·5ft

HELENIUM Moerheim Beauty MAY-JUNE

PYRETHRUM Marjorie Robinson. JUNE 2·5ft

GERANIUM IBERICUM JUNE - JULY 1 - 2ft. 3ft.

ACHILLEA PTARMICA The Pearl. JULY 2ft.

DICENTRA SPECTABILIS 1½ - 2ft. MAY - JUNE

TROLLIUS EUROPAEUS MAY-JUNE 1¼-2ft.

DWARF MICHAELMAS DAISY- pink. SEPT-OCT. 6-9ins.

MICHAELMAS DAISY-Victor SEPT-OCT. 9ins. DWARF

GEUM Princess Juliana JULY ~ 1-1½ft.

HEUCHERA Plúia de Feu JUNE-JULY 1ft.

VIOLA Maggie Mott 6ins.-SUMMER.

Grass Walk

37'

PLAN FOR THE HERBACEOUS BORDER ·

FIG. 11

barrier of concrete or iron sheeting may be sunk in the ground between border and background. Avoid gross feeders, such as privet. Avoid large leaved plants (e.g. cherry laurel)—they are too noisy. As for walls or fences, a weathered-looking brick or stone wall makes an ideal background. So does white or cream stuccoed concrete or stone. If the colour of fence or wall seems offensive, paint it, or else cover it with creepers or wall shrubs, of which there is a wide choice (see Part Four, Chapter II).

SUCCESSION OF BLOOM

To have your border gay over the longest possible season, it is not enough to choose plants for each month. The brightness must at all times be well distributed along the border. Where possible, later flowering kinds should hide those that may be unsightly after flowering earlier on.

HEIGHT

Obviously, it is no good putting the giants in front, sheltering shy little plants from view. But don't let your plants range down from back to front too evenly. (See Fig. 11.)

COLOUR

This is an obvious point of importance, and yet many people do not realise how strongly colours influence each other. A perfectly lovely colour may be completely spoilt by noisy neighbours ; whilst some other shade, not very exciting in itself, may be all important in bringing out the desired effect of a certain colour arrangement. Again, go and look at a good herbaceous border and you will get a thousand sound ideas. The same applies to shape and general habit. If you examine a successful group, you find it is not only colour contrast or harmony that pleases you, but equally the relation between the habits of the various plants.

SOIL

Lastly, make sure that the plants you have in mind do not hate your particular kind of soil. Most herbaceous plants are very tolerant. Their special likes or dislikes will be found on reading the plant list in Section Two of this chapter.

MAKING THE PLAN ON PAPER

Bearing all these things in mind, make your plan of the border (on paper) allowing 3-5 plants of the same kind to each group.

19. *Where the path meets the border and the lawn*

20. *A dry wall*

21. Beating in new t
turf-laying

22. Aerating the law

23. Raking the lawn

The Herbaceous Border

A slightly varied repetition of the groups will give rhythm to your scheme. Space the plants well, as advised individually at the end of the chapter. Now mark the names and count the numbers and order your plants from a reliable nursery in good time. But do not have them delivered till the border is ready! By the way, quite a number of plants may be raised easily from seed. You will find them pointed out individually in the above mentioned list.

PREPARING THE SOIL

The most beautifully worked-out scheme cannot be successful unless the soil is prepared properly to receive the plants. This is a very important point, especially as, once planted, the border cannot be dug for several years.

Aim at a good depth (1-1½ ft. is ideal, but less may have to do) of well-worked, well-drained soil, rich in organic matter and free from perennial weed roots. Therefore, trench to about 1 ft. depth (see pages 51-53 for method). Work in plenty of organic matter as you go along (well-rotted farmyard manure, or properly composted vegetable refuse at one large bucketful to the square yard, buried about a spade's depth), and carefully remove all visible traces of perennial weeds—the smallest bit left behind will be a cause for regrets and for much more tiresome work later on. Into the surface of the border work a liberal dressing of an organic fertiliser such as meat and bone meal or fish manure (4 ozs. to the square yard). Apply lime if the soil is inclined to be sticky or sour.

SPECIAL PROBLEMS

(a) *Virgin soil*
If pasture land has to be dug up for the border do not, for fear of wireworms, burn the turf—precious source of humus —but skim it off and bury it as if it were well-rotted farmyard manure. To kill the wireworm apply Aldrin insecticide, following the maker's directions.

(b) *Weed-ridden soil*
If perennial weeds are very bad, you can either grow a cleaning crop (none better than potatoes) the season before planting, or else apply a weed killer (see pages 87-88), following directions very carefully. Most good weed killers will

require quite some time to elapse between their application and the planting of things you do not want killed.

(c) *Ill-drained soil*

If a well-drained position is not available, a drainage system may have to be put down (see page 22). Alternatively, a raised border might be constructed, with soil held up by a low dry wall that can be planted with alpines.

(d) *Very heavy clay soil*

Very heavy clays will need a liberal addition of sedge peat to lighten them. Dressings of dry horticultural peat worked into the surface greatly improve the texture. Lime must be applied early each spring.

(e) *Very light sandy soils*

Very light sandy soils will also need a liberal addition of manure to help them hold water and plant foods. Old pig manure is suitable, but properly composted vegetable refuse is ideal.

(f) *Shallow soil*

Shallow soils, or soils with only a thin layer of good top soil, are helped by adding top soil removed from paths (see PATHS pages 77-78) to the border.

(g) *Stones*

Do not worry, they do not harm the soil, but on the contrary keep it cool and airy. If present in excess remove a certain amount which can then be used for path foundations, etc. Replace by soil.

PLANTING

If the soil is prepared early in the autumn, it will be ready for planting late in the same autumn. On very heavy soils planting is better done in spring, as the cold, water-logged winter conditions of such soils hinder root development and the ill-anchored plants will be prone to frost injury.

The ideal planting weather is a wind-still day, neither hot nor cold, with the sun lightly veiled and the earth moist but not wet. If this is not available, take the next best, but a wet soil or a gale are definitely prohibitive of successful planting.

Mark your plan on the border and lay out a small number of plants at a time. Of course, you start planting at the back or, in a double-faced border, in the middle. Make holes large enough to hold the roots spread out with any soil that may cling to them. Work fine soil between the roots, firm gently, get the soil level and porous on top. In most weathers a " watering-in " should be given, to establish contact between the water films round the root-hairs and those round the soil particles of the plant's new home. Label the groups as you proceed. Put down slug poison (see page 645), if there is any likelihood of these voracious feeders regarding your border as fresh pasture.

ROUTINE WORK ON THE HERBACEOUS BORDER

SPRING

Apply lime early in spring, especially around plants that respond particularly well, such as scabious. Young growth must be protected from slugs (see pages 645-646 for slug poisons). Delphiniums are especially popular with these molluscs.

Some protection against late frosts may be necessary with the less hardy plants if they have made rather a lot of early growth.

Divide Michaelmas daisies and, on heavy soils, other late-flowering plants, such as helenium, rudbeckia, etc.

Thin overcrowded shoots to have better quality bloom on stronger shoots. The thinnings may, in many cases, be used as cuttings if the stock is to be increased substantially.

Root cuttings may be taken (see page 67).

Seed of herbaceous border plants may be sown in cold frames.

Apply a mulch of moisture-holding material, whilst the soil is still wet. This is important. It will keep the border moist and cool and makes hoeing unnecessary and weeding easy. It is no use applying a mulch when the soil is dry. If necessary, a thorough watering will have to be given to the border before mulching. Well-rotted manure, properly composted vegetable refuse, leaf mould, lawn mowings, horticultural peat, if cheaply available, and spent hops are suitable mulching materials.

Staking must be done early so that plants will grow naturally into their artificial supports. To give this support effectively yet unobtrusively is quite an art. (See illustration facing page 137.) Bushy pea-sticks, bamboo canes and nutwands are used. With pea-sticks no tying is required ; they are useful for such plants as oriental poppy, *Anchusa italica*, erigeron, *Centaurea dealbata*. But with the taller plants, the bare, blackish pea twigs look awkward whilst they wait to be filled out or grown over by green leaves and blossoms. Bamboos and nutwands are more suitable for these. They are used with string; " Fillis " 3-ply is useful as it is soft and not too heavy. There is a special green garden twine available now which helps to make the staking inconspicuous. Bamboos are strong, but their hollow stems solve the housing problems of many a pest. They should therefore be sterilised each spring before use, with boiling water or a strong insecticide.

Summer
Continue staking attention, giving taller plants a second tie all round as required.

Water during prolonged dry spells, and remember—one thorough soaking is better than innumerable light sprinklings.

Feed taller growing plants as indicated in the list at the end of the chapter. Suitable for this purpose is liquid manufactured manure, diluted to straw colour, or else one of the available balanced organic plant foods. Feed about once a fortnight, but do not commence feeding until flower buds appear, else the plant may make much leaf-growth before producing flowers.

Cut back dead flowers.

Keep down weeds.

If a sedge peat mulch has not been given, the border should be hoed once a week.

Seed of many herbaceous plants may now be sown (see pages 97-100).

Autumn
Sowing of late-ripened seed is possible, but may be left till spring.

Plants are cut down to about 6 ins. from the ground when leaves have turned brown. These 6 in. bristly remains will protect the buds and the young growth in spring.

Most herbaceous plants may now be divided. Do not leave this work till too late in the autumn. Plants will settle back much better whilst the soil is still warm. On heavy soil division is better carried out in spring.

Winter
Fork and clean the soil when in suitable condition, and work in well-rotted manure or properly composted vegetable refuse at about 1 bucketful to the square yard.

After heavy frosts, look over the border and firm back any plants that may have been loosened by the action of frost on soil.

I. *Papaver orientale*, Olympia

II. Dahlia, Sunshine

PROPAGATION OF HERBACEOUS PLANTS

It is essential that even the amateur gardener should know how to propagate herbaceous plants.

(1) He may want to raise plants from seed as that is much cheaper than buying them from a nurseryman.

(2) He may have bought a few plants of each kind, but want to increase his stock.

(3) Though he may have all plants in plenty, he yet needs to propagate them, as after some years they will look shabby and their flowers will deteriorate, and the only cure for this lies in rejuvenation by propagation.

TWO METHODS OF PROPAGATION

These are divided into two fundamentally different sections: firstly, Seed Sowing and secondly, Vegetative Propagation. The fundamental difference between them lies in the fact that with seed sowing a truly new individual is created as the result of a fusion between the pollen of one plant and the ovule of another, whilst in vegetative reproduction, where some actively growing part is removed from the parent plant, we are merely in some way dividing up one individual and thus giving it a new lease of life. Each of the methods has its place, its advantages and disadvantages, and they will be discussed in turn.

SEED SOWING

ADVANTAGES OF SEED SOWING

It is cheap.

It produces vigorous, healthy, long-lived plants.

It is adventurous, as it may result in new varieties or colour combinations.

In many cases it will allow for plant production on a much larger scale than vegetative reproduction would.

DISADVANTAGES

It is often slow; some plants take many years from seed sowing to flowering (e.g. lily).

It is uncertain; seed taken from a particularly lovely plant is not at all likely to produce a plant exactly like its mother—many people experience disappointment by ignoring this fact.

This does not apply to true species, but a very large number of border plants are hybrids with a very complicated family history, and you can never be sure which of its ancestors is going to have a say in the appearance of the offspring.

GETTING THE SEED

Two things matter if you buy the seed : (1) It must be fresh, or few, if any, will germinate and the few will take a long time over it. (2) It must really be all the label or catalogue claims for it. So buy seed from reliable sources only. Buy it as close to the sowing time as possible.

If you collect seeds from your own plants, choose the right time, that is, the time when the plant is just going to do the scattering —only you come along and quickly snatch the seeds for yourself. Of course there is not only just this one minute at the seed collector's disposal. But leave the seeds on the plants to ripen and do not let them get sodden with rain, once they are ripe. Keep all seed in a dry, cool place.

WHEN TO SOW

Best results are usually obtained when the seed is sown as soon as ripe. In fact, with very small seeds, such as those of primulas and campanulas, this is essential, as they soon lose their germinating power. But as a general rule, any time from spring to early autumn is suitable. Those who want to sow in the open ground choose the summer months. Late ripening seed may be sown in autumn, and the seedlings will have a start on their spring-sown brothers. But adequate protection must be given to the young plants through the winter.

WHERE TO SOW

Most of the truly hardy herbaceous border plants can be sown in the open, provided—lots of things ! That the soil is well drained, moisture-holding, in excellent tilth ; not rank, nor poor ; not under dripping trees ; not exposed to the winds that blow, and not a haunt and hunting-ground for slugs. If such a place can be found, or created, it will produce seedlings that are sturdy and hardy from the very beginning, which is a great advantage. If, however, the seed-bed is not likely to be perfect, sow in boxes, pans, or frames, where you can control soil as well as winds and weather.

SEED SOWING IN THE OPEN

Choose site as indicated above.

Dig the bed to the depth of a spade, removing all weeds and breaking down the lumps of soil as you proceed. Then rake down level and fine and leave to settle for a few days. On very light soils, tread or roll lightly before raking, for the seed-bed must be firm as well as airy. Moisture will spread evenly only in a firm soil, and the young roots need a firm hold. The air is needed to set free energy in the germinating seed.

Sow in drills, not broadcast. Drills should be so deep as to allow seed to be covered with about 2-3 times its own thickness, and as far apart as to allow you to put your foot down for weeding between the rows. Seed sown too near the surface is likely to suffer from drying winds, whilst seed sown too low down will have exhausted its food fuel and building material before it has reached the light that would help it to make more. It will either never reach the surface, or reach it a worn-out, useless thing.

Sow very thinly. Thick sowing means not only waste of seed but a bad start in life for the seedlings, due to lack of light, space and air circulation. Move the soil back into the drills with the back of the rake. Firm down gently. Water with a fine spray if necessary; never flood your seed-bed, nor let it go dry and grey looking. Guard against slugs, birds, cats—or any other likely disturbers (see Part Eight, Chapter 1, page 647). Seedlings from an autumn sowing should be left in position until next spring, whilst summer-sown ones will need pricking out as soon as large enough to handle, to let them develop sooner to flowering size.

SEED SOWING IN BOXES OR PANS UNDER GLASS

The containers must be perfectly clean. They must be provided with drainage holes. Crocks are used to cover the hole or cracks. (See illustration facing page 33.) The crocks in turn must be covered with so-called " roughage," i.e. some coarse leaf-mould, or even dry leaves, peat or moss, to prevent the soil from being washed down. The soil, or compost as we call it, must contain sand for aeration and, because roots like it, peat or leaf-mould to hold moisture, and some loam to give firmness and food. The John Innes Seed Compost[1] is very suitable[2].

2 parts loam (sterilised); 1 part moistened peat; 1 part sand. To each bushel of this mixture add $1\frac{1}{2}$ ozs. of superphosphate of lime, which helps roots formation, and $\frac{3}{4}$ ozs. of ground chalk, which prevents the soil from getting sour.

Break up the loam very finely first, then add the other ingredients

---

[1] W. E. Shewell-Cooper: *The A.B.C. of Soils* English Univ. Press. P.

[2] It is possible to use the ALEX NO-SOIL compost instead.

and mix thoroughly. Add water if the compost is dry, leave to dry if the compost is wet. It should be moist but not sticky. Fill the compost evenly into the container and, in the case of boxes, make sure it is just as firm in the corners as everywhere else. For all small seeds the top $\frac{1}{2}$ in. or so will be sieved, an old label can then be used to level it and a " presser " for getting it evenly firm but not too firm (see illustration facing page 33).

With under-glass sowings, seeds are only covered with once their own thickness of soil, as there is no danger of exposure. See that the soil level in the boxes is accordingly high before sowing. Sow broadcast, fairly thinly. Cover thinly by sieving some soil on top and press down again gently, using the presser. The soil level must now not be more than $\frac{1}{4}$-$\frac{1}{2}$ in. below the rim of box or pan. If the soil level is lower, there will be much shade and poor air circulation, both factors that favour the dreaded " damping off " of seedlings. Finally, cover the box or pan with clean glass to prevent rapid drying out, and dark paper to prevent it getting too hot under the glass.

Examine frequently as, immediately the seeds begin to show, they need all the light and air you can possibly give them. Watering can in most cases be done with a syringe or a can with a fine rose, but for very small seeds it will be best to water from below, i.e. stand seed containers into shallow water or hold them suspended in a tank until a darkening of the soil shows they are moist right through.

Prick out the seedlings as soon as they get large enough to handle, for later their roots will become entangled with their neighbours' and, also, if left crowded, they will grow weak and lanky. (See illustration facing page 65.)

Soon the young plants should be moved outside and, eventually, they go to their permanent position in the border ; but there is no point in planting into the border little things barely visible to the naked eye—wait until they reach flowering size. (For soil sterilisation see pages 37-40 and for use of cloches pages 581-585.)

VEGETATIVE PROPAGATION

ADVANTAGES OF VEGETATIVE PROPAGATION
Quick results. Certainty as to the character of new plants.

DISADVANTAGES
A certain amount of wounding of tissues is unavoidable. In the case of shoot cuttings the leaves lose water, whilst there are no roots as yet to take up fresh water.

DIVISION

In most cases the easiest method of propagation. Each portion has both roots and shoots, and will speedily settle down to normal life, provided the soil is sufficiently warm, moist and airy. On light and medium soil most plants are best divided in autumn, so that they are well established before the new growing season begins. On heavy soil, divide in spring (see page 94 for reasons). The clumps are lifted for division and may be divided into several portions by 2 forks pushed back to back into the clump. (See illustration facing page 224.)

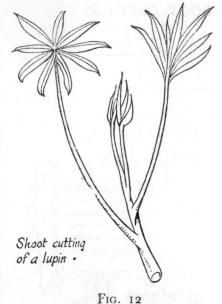

Shoot cutting of a lupin .

FIG. 12

Small portions from the outside are chosen for propagation, as they are the youngest and most vigorous. The final trimming is done with a sharp knife and the " new plants " go back into the border, or may be put into a reserve bed until required. Plants which dislike division : Anchusa (propagate by root cuttings). Anchusa does not merely dislike division, but will not survive it. *Anemone japonica* (propagate by seed or root cuttings). Geum (raise from seed) ; lupins (raise from seed or shoot cuttings); peonies (seed ; division possible, but plants will take many years to come into flower after division).

SHOOT CUTTINGS

If large numbers of new plants are required, take cuttings in spring, summer or autumn. This method requires more care and skill and the new portion cannot right away be put back into the border.

Spring thinnings of many herbaceous plants may be used as cuttings (phlox, delphinium—see illustration facing page 225 ; lupin—see Fig. 12 ; gaillardia, etc.), whilst other plants furnish suitable growth in late summer (viola, pentstemon, erigeron, pinks). The ideal cutting is a short-jointed shoot, 2-3 ins. long, neither over strong nor a weakling. If it can be taken with a " heel " all the better, but rather have a short cutting with-

ROOT CUTTINGS ·

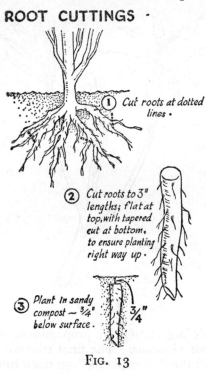

① Cut roots at dotted lines ·

② Cut roots to 3" lengths; flat at top, with tapered cut at bottom, to ensure planting right way up ·

③ Plant in sandy compost — ¾" below surface ·

¾"

FIG. 13

out a "heel" than a long wispy one with a "heel." Use a sharp knife. Trim the "heel" to a neat surface or, in case of non-heel cuttings, make a straight cut across the stem just under a node, as that is the place where roots will form most easily. Remove leaves that would otherwise be buried and reduce the size of the remainder (about half to two-thirds of the cutting will be underground). Insert cuttings in sandy compost in a cold frame or greenhouse. Plant them firmly and water them in. Help rooting by keeping a close atmosphere and by excluding strong sunlight. When well rooted, transfer to the open as soon as weather conditions permit. (See illustration facing page 65.)

For use of hormones see page 70.

Root Cuttings

When these can be taken they provide a very simple means of propagation, as there is no fear of excess water loss. Plants easily propagated by root cuttings : Anchusa, *Anemone japonica*, oriental poppy, phlox. Phlox is propagated by root cuttings only when plants are infected with eelworm (see pages 647 and 649) as the roots are the only parts not affected and so will save the stock. It is usually possible to take the cuttings without digging up the parent plant. Choose medium-sized roots (those of phlox will be much thinner than the others), and cut into lengths of 2-3 ins. Place perpendicularly in sandy compost as shown in Fig. 13. Place in cold frame or unheated greenhouse the right way up and keep moist. Shoots will appear within 2 or 3 weeks and the cuttings may then be given more room and soil. Root cuttings of anchusa taken after flowering in mid-summer, will be ready to go to their permanent position the same autumn and will make large flowering plants the following summer, so no season is missed out.

Time to take root cuttings: spring for late summer and autumn flowers; mid- or late summer for early and mid-summer flowers.

LAYERING
This method will be discussed more fully in the section on shrubs. The border carnation is the only herbaceous plant usually propagated by layering. After flowering—or not later than mid-July—surround the plant with a mound of sandy soil. The young growths that have not flowered will then be bent down to the soil. About midway along each of the shoots remove some of the leaves and make an incision (see Fig. 14) using a very sharp knife or razor blade. The cut may be kept open with a sharp grain of sand. It is gently pressed into the soil of the mound, covered over and pegged down with a wide split laundry peg or a doubled piece of wire. Firm the soil. Keep moist. Sever and transplant rooted layers in early autumn.

A LIST OF WORTHWHILE PLANTS FOR THE HERBACEOUS BORDER

*

THE following list contains a description of plants most suitable for the herbaceous border, with advice as to their cultivation and propagation. Unless any special information is required, propagation details are included under the heading Cultivation. Their species and varieties are individually described in regard to colour, height, times of flowering and natural habitat.

ACANTHUS (Bear's Foot, Bear's Breech) Order ACANTHACEÆ

Grown chiefly for their ornamental foliage which has been much used in Greek and Roman architectural design. Mauve, pink or white flowers borne in dense spikes and set off by bizarre prickly bracts. Height, 3-4 ft.

CULTIVATION : Sunny position on well-drained border. Plant near front of border, so that its foliage will not be hidden. Propagation by division.

SPECIES AND VARIETIES : *A. mollis.* White, pink, mauve, 3-4 ft., July.
A. spinosus. Purple, 2-4 ft., July, and other species and varieties mostly from S. Europe.

ACHILLEA (Milfoil, Yarrow) Order COMPOSITÆ

Grown for their bright-yellow, red or white flowers, mostly borne in flattish heads on long stiff stems.

CULTIVATION : Sunny position in well-drained soil. Propagation by division or seed.

SPECIES AND VARIETIES : *A. Eupatorium* (Syn. *A. filipendulina*). Bright yellow, 4 ft., June–September ; Caucasus.
A. millefolium, variety Cerise Queen, cherry red, 3 ft., July ; Britain.
A. ptarmica, variety The Pearl, pure white, dainty double flowers borne in loose heads, 2-3 ft., July-August ; Britain.
Other species for rock gardens.

ACONITUM (Monk's Hood) Order RANUNCULACEÆ

A cousin of the delphinium and somewhat resembling the latter in appearance, though the flower spikes are not as tall and heavy. Flowers mostly blue or bluish lilac. *Roots poisonous.*

CULTIVATION : Will grow equally well in semi-shade or full sun. No special soil requirements.

SPECIES AND VARIETIES :
A. Fischeri. Bluish lilac, 3 ft., July–October; Europe, N. America.

A. japonicum. Violet, 3 ft., autumn ; Japan.

A. Napellus. Spark's variety, deep blue, 5 ft., July–August ; Europe (England).

A. Wilsonii. Blue or purplish, 6 ft., autumn ; China.

ADONIS (Pheasant's Eye) Order RANUNCULACEÆ

The perennial adonis has very large yellow celandine flowers on feathery fresh green foliage. Height, 12-18 ins.

CULTIVATION : Both sunny and shady positions are suitable. A rich well-drained loam is required. Propagation by division or by seeds.

SPECIES AND VARIETIES :
A. amurensis, and its double form *A. a. flore pleno*, 12 ins., January; China.

A. vernalis, 18 ins., March–May; S. Europe.

The annual species are crimson and scarlet.

ALSTRŒMERIA (Peruvian Lily) Order AMARYLLIDACEÆ

Fleshy, tuberous roots, strap-shaped, bright green leaves and lily-like flowers, bright orange or yellow colour, often spotted with brown, crimson or purple.

CULTIVATION : A sheltered sunny position in a well-drained soil. After planting it may take several years before it flowers well. Propagation by division.

SPECIES AND VARIETIES :
A. aurantiaca. Orange and red, 2-3 ft., June–August ; Chile.

A. Dover Orange. Brilliant orange spotted brown, 3-4 ft., vigorous and lovely.

A. pelegrina. Lilac, red and purple, 1 ft., June–August ; Chile.

A. pulchella (Syn. *A. psittacina*). Green, red and brown, 2-3 ft., June–August ; Brazil.

ALTHÆA (Hollyhock) Order MALVACEÆ

Tall stately plants, growing up to 6 or 8 ft. high with large roundish leaves and a spike of showy flowers. Wide range of colours.

CULTIVATION : Sunny position on well-drained, moisture-holding soil required. Best grown as biennials because of the rust disease which tends to get hold of them if left to grow older. Excellent as background of border in front of wall. Propagation by seeds.

SPECIES AND VARIETIES : *A. rosea,* and many garden hybrids. White, pink or salmon, red or crimson, cream or sulphur yellow, July-August ; China.

ANCHUSA (Sea Bugloss, Alkanet) Order BORAGINACEÆ

Large plants are formed amazingly quickly after planting. The leaves are rough, the flowers a lovely bright blue, borne in profusion.

CULTIVATION : Sunny position in well-drained, moisture-holding soil. Staking required.

PROPAGATION : Do not attempt division. The fleshy roots are suitable for root cuttings, to be taken after flowering. A dozen or more new plants may thus be raised from one old plant. (See page 67.)

SPECIES AND VARIETIES : *A. angustifolia.* Deep blue, 3 ft., will flower from June to late autumn ; Europe.
A. italica. Blue, 3-4 ft., June-July ; S. France. Varieties of various shades of blue : Morning Glory, a deep, brilliant blue, probably one of the best ; Opal, a pale blue.
A. myosotidiflora. Sky blue, 1 ft., spring ; Caucasus. More suitable for the rock garden, as it does not assert itself in the herbaceous border.
A. officinalis. Deep blue, smaller flowers than *A. italica,* 1-2 ft., June ; England.

ANEMONE (Japanese Wind Flower) Order RANUNCULACEÆ

The anemone, usually grown in the herbaceous border, is very attractive with its clear, large flowers of white or pink, borne on branching stems about 3 ft. high. It also makes a good cut flower. Details of dwarf anemone species will be found in the sections on rock garden and woodland plants (see page 155), but these, of course, may be included in the herbaceous border, especially in the shady or semi-shady border.

CULTIVATION : Flowers in autumn and will do equally well in shade and in full sun.

PROPAGATION: Does not like root disturbance and is, therefore,

The Herbaceous Border

best propagated by root cuttings taken in spring. (See page 102.)

SPECIES AND VARIETIES : *A. japonica.* Pink, single, 3 ft., late summer and autumn ; Japan. Varieties : *alba*, white ; Margerete, dark pink, double ; Queen Charlotte, bright rose, semi-double ; Richard Ahrends, white, tinged lilac, single, large.

ANTHEMIS (The Garden Chamomile) Order COMPOSITÆ

The common chamomile that grows where cows tread, and is known to all by its peculiar scent, is not the one grown in the herbaceous border. The border chamomile has very showy flowers, mostly canary yellow in colour, set off by silvery, finely-cut foliage. Many flowers of the daisy type are spoilt by their tendency to be slightly ragged, but the anthemis has particularly neatly built flower heads that may, without exaggeration, be called perfect.

CULTIVATION : Full sun, well-drained soil required. Propagation by division.

SPECIES AND VARIETIES: *A. tinctoria.* Yellow, 2 ft., August ; Europe. Varieties: E. C. Buxton, lemon yellow; Perry's variety, golden yellow; Sancta Johannis, clear orange; Grallagh Gold, light yellow.

AQUILEGIA (Columbine) Order RANUNCULACEÆ

Dainty, gracefully nodding flowers with long spurs, delightfully varied in colour. Decorative foliage.

CULTIVATION : Sun or partial shade (the wild columbine is a woodland plant). The soil must be rich and moisture-holding, but very well drained. Columbines grown in dry, poor, or waterlogged soil are a pitiful sight, whilst well-grown columbines belong to the best early summer features of the border. Put later flowering plants in front of them to hide them after their flowering period.

PROPAGATION : Columbines belong to the plants that are with the least trouble raised from seed. They will flower the following season, and a great range of new colours and colour combinations may be expected. Best results are obtained if seed is sown as soon as ripe, i.e., late summer. (See pages 97-100.)

SPECIES : *A. hybrida*, 2-3 ft., June ; N. America. Varieties

107

VARIETIES: are mostly grown and may be obtained in mixed or named colours: Crimson Star, a deep crimson and white; Hensol Harebell, a pure sapphire blue; *longissima*, a long-spurred yellow.

ARMERIA (Thrift) Order PLUMBAGINACEÆ

With its neat cushions of narrow leaves and its bright pink profusion of flowers, this little seaside plant is useful for the front of the border. It also makes attractive edgings.

CULTIVATION: Sunny position on light, sandy soil required. Propagation by division.

SPECIES AND
VARIETIES:
A. latifolia. Crimson, 6-12 ins., June; Portugal.
A. maritima. Pink, 6 ins., May-June; Europe.
A. plantaginea grandiflora. Rose, 18 ins., June; Europe.

ARTEMISIA (Wormwood) Order COMPOSITÆ

Grown chiefly for its silvery grey, often finely-cut foliage, the flowers being rather insignificant.

CULTIVATION: Sunny position on well-drained, moisture-holding soil is best, though it will do quite well in semi-shade. Propogation by division.

SPECIES AND
VARIETIES:
A. lactiflora. Creamy flowers in late summer, 5 ft.; China.
A. ludoviciana (syn. *A. stellariana*). Foliage almost white, very bold and decorative, 1-2 ft.; N.E. Asia and N. America.
A. pontica. Fluffy, minutely-cut foliage, grey green, 2 ft.; Austria.

ASCLEPIAS Order ASCLEPIADACEÆ

There are several fairly hardy species of asclepias that are well worth introducing into the herbaceous border, for the interest their flowers afford as well as for their general beauty.

CULTIVATION: A sunny position in well-drained soil is required. In all but the most favoured districts some protection will have to be given in winter. Propagation by division.

SPECIES AND
VARIETIES:
A. incarnata. Red, 2 ft. summer; N. America.,
A. purpurea. Purple buds, lilac flowers, 3-4 ft.; N. America.

SPECIES AND   *A. speciosa.* Purple-lilac, fragrant, 2-3 ft. ;   N.
VARIETIES :   America.
      A. tuberosa. Orange, 1-2 ft., July–September ; N.
      America.

ASTER (Michaelmas Daisy) Order COMPOSITÆ

In large gardens, Michaelmas daisies may be given a border on their own, but normally they will be included in the herbaceous border and so will extend its flowering season well into November. The fibrous root systems send up numerous shoots each spring. Shoots are usually stiffly erect and much branched towards the top. Branches covered with daisy-like flowers in autumn. Colour varies from white, through pink and mauve, to dark red and purple. There are a few yellow species.

CULTIVATION :   To do their best, asters require a sunny position in a deep rich soil. Ordinary soil will do, if well dug and manured. Stake the taller varieties carefully —asters will be among the few tall plants left in the border when the autumn gales blow !

PROPAGA-   Divide asters into small portions every second, or
TION :   at the utmost third, spring, or else their vigour and flower quality will deteriorate.

SPECIES AND   *A. acris.* Lilac, 2-3 ft., August ; S. Europe.
VARIETIES :   *A. Amellus.* Purple, 2-3½ ft., August ; Europe. Varieties: Lac de Genève, light blue, large flowers; King George, violet blue, large flowers; Sonia, clear bright pink, large flowers.
      A. cordifolius. Mauve, 3 ft., July–August ; N. America. Varieties all bearing a profusion of small star-like flowers : Aldebaran, pale blue, very free flowering ; Edwin Beckett, clear mauve ; Silver Spray, a lovely silvery lilac.
      A. diffusus. White tinted red, 2 ft., October ; N. America. Variety Coombe Fishacre, blue, tinted rose, 3½ ft.
      A. ericoides. White, 2-3 ft., October ; N. America, sprays of tiny flower stars, heath-like foliage. Varieties : Blue Star, pale lilac, 2½ ft. ; Photograph, white ; Ringdove, rosy lavender, good cut flower, 3 ft.
      A. Novæ-Angliæ. Purple, 5-6 ft., September ; N. America. Varieties : Barr's Pink, rosy red with

SPECIES AND VARIETIES: golden eye, good cut flower; Harrington's Pink, clear rose pink, 4 ft.

A. Novi-Belgii. Blue, 4-5½ ft., September; N. America. Many varieties, all vigorous. Ada Ballard, mauve blue, 3 ft.; Carnival, cherry red double, 2 ft.; Fellowship, pink, 3 ft.; F. M. Simpson, violet-blue, 2½ ft.; Freda Ballard, red semi-double red, 3 ft.; Helen Ballard, late semi-double red, 3 ft.; Little Boy Blue, blue, 2½ ft.; Raspberry Ripple, carmine red double, 2½ ft.; Royal Velvet, violet mildew resistent, 2 ft.; Winston Churchill, ruby red, 2½ ft.

Dwarf Hybrid Asters. For the front of the border; varieties: Audrey, mauve blue, 15 ins.; Dandy, purple red, 12 ins.; Jenny, double violet purple, 12 ins.; Little Pink Beauty, clear pink, 15 ins.; Little Red Boy, rosy red, 12 ins.; Rose Bonnet, misty pink, 10 ins.

ASTILBE (False Goat's Beard) Order SAXIFRAGACEÆ

Resembles the Spiræa or Meadow Sweet with its fluffy panicles of white, pink, red or deep crimson flowers.

CULTIVATION: Suitable for woodland and wild garden as well as for the shady herbaceous border. Requires moist conditions. Propagation by division.

SPECIES AND VARIETIES: Most varieties grown belong to either of two hybrid species, *A. Arendsi* and *A. Lemoinei.* Varieties: Dusseldorf, salmon pink, 2 ft.; Fire, salmon red, 2 ft.; Mainz, lilac rose, 1½ ft.; Montgomery, deep red, 2 ft.; Venus, flesh pink, 3 ft.; Glow, glowing red spikes, 2½ ft. Betsy Cuperus, white, 5 ft.; July-August; Fanal, glowing dark red, 2 ft., June; Gertrude Brix, deep crimson, 2½ ft., June; W. Reeves, brilliant red, bronze foliage, 2½ ft., July-August.

BOCCONIA (Plume Poppy) Order PAPAVERACEÆ

Tall stately plants with amber-coloured, drooping panicles of grass-like flowers. Leaves shaped like the fig leaf, a lovely bluey-green with a bluey-white under-surface and bluey-white stems. Suitable for the large herbaceous border and the wild garden. In the herbaceous border it must be kept in check as it is a terrible spreader and as difficult to get rid of as gout weed or horse-radish. Personally, therefore, I prefer admiring it in the gardens of friends without any feeling of envy.

CULTIVATION: Likes a sunny position in rich well-drained soil. Propagation by cuttings or suckers.

SPECIES: *B. cordata.* Cream, 6 ft., summer; China, Japan.

CAMPANULA (Harebell, Bellflower) Order CAMPANULACEÆ

A large tribe providing many attractive herbaceous border flowers, mostly in varying shades of blue or white. Height from a few inches to over 5 ft. according to the species. Flowering time mostly early summer. The plants are always neat, often very graceful.

CULTIVATION: Sun or partial shade is suitable. The tallest varieties will require staking. Dwarf varieties are described in the chapter on rock gardens. Propagation by division or by seeds.

SPECIES AND VARIETIES: *C. glomerata*, variety *Dahurica*. Deep blue, 18 ins., Summer; Europe.

C. lactiflora. Pale blue, 3-4 ft., and its variety *C. l. alba*, white. These are particularly graceful, the flowers of a clear, cool, dreamy shape and colour, July; Caucasus.

C. latifolia. Blue, 4-6 ft., July; Britain. Varieties, *alba*, white; *Burghaltii*, lavender blue.

C. persicifolia. Violet blue, 2-3 ft., June; Europe. Varieties: Moerheim, semi-double white; Telham Beauty, pale blue, and many others.

C. pyramidalis. The Chimney Bellflower, 5-6 ft.; heavily laden with violet-blue flowers in July; Dalmatia.

CATANANCHIE Order COMPOSITÆ

An everlasting flower but without their usualy artificial look. Neat, erect stems bearing daisy flowers of silvery blue or white.

CULTIVATION: Full sun is required and light soil preferred. Propagation by seeds.

SPECIES AND VARIETIES: *C. alba.* White, 2 ft., July-August; S. Europe.

C. cœrulea. Blue, 2 ft. July-August; S. Europe. Variety *bicolour*, blue and white.

CENTAUREA (Perennial Cornflower) Order COMPOSITÆ

The perennial cornflowers are much heavier plants than the

well-known annual one and make shapely bushes on the herbaceous border. The flowers are usually large and may be blue, yellow, pink or white.

CULTIVATION : Prefers a sunny border. Any ordinary soil is suitable. Propagation by seeds or by division.

SPECIES AND VARIETIES : *C. dealbata*. Makes lovely showy plants with silvery pink flowers and handsome foliage, 2 ft. high, June–July ; Caucasus.
C. macrocephala. Golden-yellow flower balls, 4 ft., July ; Caucasus.
C. montana. Rather large coarse flowers in blue, pink or white, not to be recommended, 2-3 ft., July.

CENTRANTHUS (Red Valerian) Order VALERIANACEÆ

The rather magenta-red flower that looks quite cheering where it grows in masses on railway banks. In the garden it must be used with discretion as it tends to be coarse and rampant and has not much beauty of colour or shape. May look quite well on a dry wall together with silvery-grey foliage plants.

CULTIVATION : Likes a sunny position and will do well in chalky soils as well as in most others. Propagation by seeds or by division.

SPECIES AND VARIETIES : *C. ruber*. Red, 18 ins., summer ; Europe. White variety *albus*.

CHRYSANTHEMUM (Border Chrysanthemum) Order COMPOSITÆ

Sometimes used in the border to fill in gaps. For culture see pages 267-68.

CHRYSANTHEMUM MAXIMUM (Large Ox-eyed Daisy or Shasta Daisy) Order COMPOSITÆ

Very useful herbaceous border plants. Large white daisy flowers with a bright yellow centre, shown up well by glossy, deep green foliage. They make very good cut flowers. Care must be taken not to have the blossom spoilt by all sorts of insects. An imperfect daisy flower is no good at all, whilst a perfect, unspoilt one is like a beautiful dream. Therefore, give an occasional spray with liquid derris during dry spells.

CULTIVATION : A sunny position should be chosen, rich soil is appreciated. Propagation by division.

SPECIES AND
VARIETIES :
Esther Read. Large dazzling white double flowers, probably the best, 2 ft. summer species.
Other hardy species are *C. leucanthemum*, and *C. uliginosum*, the former being the Ox-eye daisy, 3 ft., flowering all summer and well into autumn ; Europe. The latter is the Grand Ox-eye or Moon-daisy and grows to 5 ft., flowering in autumn. The popular half-hardy garden Chrysanthemums are dealt with in Part Three, Chapter II.

CIMICIFUGA (Snake-Root, Bug-Bane) Order RANUNCULACEÆ

Tall, dense bushes, vigorous growth. Masses of upright, creamy white, fluffy flower spikes in summer and early autumn. Suitable for the large herbaceous border.

CULTIVATION : Sun or partial shade, moisture-holding soil. Propagation by seeds or division.

SPECIES AND
VARIETIES :
C. cordifolia. Creamy white, 4-5 ft., July–August ; N. America.
C. racemosa. Creamy white, 3-5 ft., August ; N. America.
C. simplex. White, 3 ft., August–October ; Kamtschatka. The variety Elstead has pendulous flower spikes, creamy white, 4-5 ft., September.

CLEMATIS (Traveller's Joy, Old Man's Beard) Order RANUNCULACEÆ

Most people only know the Clematis as a climbing shrub while, in actual fact, there are some very attractive herbaceous species.

CULTIVATION : Requires a sunny position and appreciates rich soil. Cut down in the autumn like other herbaceous plants.

PROPAGA-
TION :
Cuttings may be taken in summer and rooted in a close atmosphere in frame or under cloches.

SPECIES AND
HYBRIDS :
C. campanile. Pale azure blue, fragrant, 4 ft., August–September (Hybrid).
C. heracleæfolia Davidiana. Lavender blue, fragrant, 2 ft., August ; China.
C. integrifolia. Blue and silver grey, 2 ft., August ; S. Europe.
C. Oiseau Bleu. Rosy lilac, fragrant, 3 ft., August–September (Hybrid).

COREOPSIS Order COMPOSITÆ

Bright yellow daisy flowers on slender but stiffly erect, pale-green stems. The broad ray florets, the good substance and clear shape combine to make the Coreopsis a daisy of distinction.

CULTIVATION : Full sun and well-drained soil are required. Propagation by seeds or by division.

SPECIES AND VARIETIES : *C. grandiflora.* Yellow, 2½-3 ft., June–September ; U.S.A. Perry's Variety, double yellow, 2 ft., rather late flowering.

C. verticillata. Wells form. Combines golden-yellow flowers and perennial habit of coreopsis with the gracefully feathered foliage of cosmea.

CORYDALIS (Fumitory) Order FUMARIACEÆ

Dwarf and neat in habit with attractive feathery foliage and loose racemes of yellow or purple flowers. Suitable for the front of the border, if kept in control.

CULTIVATION: Sun or semi-shade and a well-drained soil. Progation by seeds or by division.

SPECIES: *C. ledebouriana.* Purple, 1 ft., summer; Altai Mountains.

C. lutea. Golden yellow, 1 ft., spring, summer; Europe.

C. ochroleuca. Creamy yellow flowers, glaucous leaves, 6 ins., summer.

DAHLIA Order COMPOSITÆ

Sometimes used in the border for filling in gaps. For culture see pages 268-270.

DELPHINIUM (Perennial Larkspur) Order RANUNCULACEÆ

One of the most beautiful herbaceous border plants. Some enthusiasts give them a border of their own, but, as they look unsightly after flowering, they are better associated with other and later-flowering types. Flowers large, closely packed in stately upright racemes, single or double, all shades of blue, mauve or violet. Pinks and white also available now. Many varieties combine several shades and colours in each flower.

CULTIVATION : Full sun ; rich, well-drained, moisture-holding soil required. When newly planted give winter protection to crowns. Keep away slugs in spring. Stake carefully, thin out shoots if too crowded.

CULTIVATION : Crowding of shoots encourages mildew. Thinnings may be used as cuttings (see illustration facing page 225) but must have the cut end dipped in charcoal to prevent " bleeding." Feed with liquid manure once a week as soon as flower buds begin to show. After flowering, cut down to just below the flowers, leaving the foliage to build up a store of food for next year's growth. A second crop of flowers may be had by cutting down lower after flowering, but this practice will soon weaken your stock and is not to be recommended. Propagation by seeds, cuttings or division.

SPECIES AND VARIETIES : The border delphiniums are hybrids of various species such as *D. elatum*, and *D. formosum*.

The hybrids may be grouped in two main types, the so-called *Elatum*, the large well-known type, and the Belladonna, which are dwarfer, daintier and suitable for the front of the border.

Elatum Varieties :

Arcadia, pale blue mauve, 5½ ft.; Blue Rosetta, lilac blue, double, 6 ft.; C. H. Middleton, medium blue, semi-double; Black Knight, very dark blue, 5½ ft.; King Arthur, royal purple, white eye, 6 ft.; Anne Page, cornflower blue, 5½ ft.; Cynthia Bishop, deep violet, 6 ft.; F. W. Smith, deep blue white eye, 6 ft.; Blue Gown, royal blue, black eye, 5 ft.; Blue Celeste, gentian blue, white eye, 5½ ft.

Belladonna varieties:

Blue Bees, light blue early, 3½ ft.; Capri, sky blue, 4 ft.; Lamartine, deep blue, 3 ft.; Naples, gentian blue, 3 ft.; Peace, intense blue, 2½ ft.; Pink Sensation, rose pink 3 ft.; Wendy, gentian blue, 3½ ft.; All of these should flower in June and July.

DIANTHUS (Carnation, Pink) Order CARYOPHYLLACEÆ

The pinks are more widely grown than the border carnations, because they are so easy to please. 1 ft. high, they are useful as an edging, or for groups in the front of the border. They look tidy all the year round with their grey-green foliage of stiff narrow leaves and are dazzling when covered with their deliciously fragrant flowers in June and July. Whilst the pinks look lovely in masses, with the border carnation each individual flower is a perfect picture. The flowers are much larger, borne on taller stems (1½ ft. high) and can be had in a large variety of colours, from white or sulphur yellow to deep mauve or the darkest of dark reds.

CULTIVATION : Any good garden soil will suit the pinks. They do best in a sunny position and can be left undisturbed for many years after planting. Border carnations do best on a well-drained soil that should not be too rich. Like the pinks, they should have a place

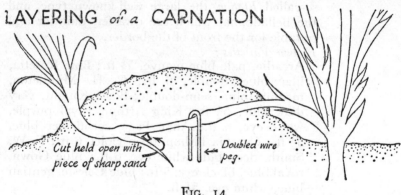

LAYERING *of a* CARNATION

Cut held open with
piece of sharp sand

← Doubled wire
peg.

FIG. 14

in the sun. Some staking will be necessary, but only light and short stakes should be used.

PROPAGA-
TION :
Both pinks and carnations can be raised from seed. But special varieties can, of course, only be perpetuated by vegetative propagation. Pinks are increased by cuttings in cold frames in summer. The plants may also simply be torn to pieces and the bits planted deeply into the permanent position as shown in the diagram. Carnations are layered in July or August in sandy soil.   (See Fig. 14.)

SPECIES AND
VARIETIES :
PINKS
D. Allwoodii. Double-flowered varieties : Alice, white with crimson eye ; Esther, mauve, shaded maroon ; Rebecca, maroon, pink, chocolate ;

SPECIES AND
VARIETIES :
Susan, lilac, black centre ; Thomas, deep red, maroon eye.

D. plumarius. Varieties : Glory, rosy red, edged deep crimson, vigorous ; Inchmery, delicate pink, free flowering ; Whiteladies, white, flowering for very long periods, very fragrant.

BORDER CARNATIONS

D. caryophyllus. Varieties : Beauty of Cambridge, pale yellow ; Bookham Clove, dark crimson, exquisite scent ; Bookham Scarlet, a vigorous, scarlet self ; Dora Spenlow, deep rose pink, large flowers ; Hyperion, very large flowers, yellow ground with fuchsia red markings ; Oakfield Clove, glowing crimson, strongly scented ; Sam Griffiths, mauve with rich red markings ; Edenside White, a very good white.

Various intermediate forms are now grown in the herbaceous border, such as :
D. Heddinsis. 12-18 ins., crimson, white-edged petals. Showy, graceful, suitable for front of border.

DICENTRA (Bleeding Heart) Order FUMARIACEÆ

A dainty, romantic, old-fashioned plant with finely-cut leaves and arching strings of hanging, heart-shaped flowers in red and white.

CULTIVATION :
Thrives in sheltered position in medium, well-drained loam. Responds well to application of liquid manure between the times of bud formation and showing colour. Propagation by division.

SPECIES :
D. eximia. Deep rose, 1 ft., all summer ; N. Carolina.
D. spectabilis. Reddish violet, 2 ft., June–August ; Siberia, Japan.

DORONICUM (Leopard's Bane). Order COMPOSITÆ

A pleasing border plant bearing large yellow daisy flowers in spring and early summer. Useful for cutting.

CULTIVATION :
Doronicum is an accommodating plant and will do equally well in sun and shade as well as putting up with almost any soil. Propagation by division.

SPECIES :
D. austriacum. Yellow, 1½ ft., March ; Europe.

SPECIES: D. *cordatum*. Large golden flowers, 6ins.
D. *plantagineum*. 3 ft., March-May. Its more striking form, **D.** *p. excelsum* flowers over a longer season.

ECHINOPS (Globe Thistle) Order COMPOSITÆ

Stiffly erect, very decorative bristly plants bearing globes of grey-green-bluish flowers which will harmonise with practically all colours in the herbaceous border, but most particularly with the so-called pastel shades of pink, pale yellow and mauve, also with white. Useful for mixed cut flower arrangements.

CULTIVATION: A sunny position in a well-drained border is required. Staking necessary. Propagation by division or by seeds.

SPECIES: E. *bannaticus*. Violet blue, 2-3 ft., summer.
E. *ritro*. Blue, 3 ft., summer; S. Europe.
E. *humilis*. Blue Cloud, 4 ft., clear blue, robust.

EPIMEDIUM (Barrenwort) Order BERBERIDACEÆ

Dwarf plants, grown chiefly for their neat green or bronzy foliage which is also useful in flower arrangements.

CULTIVATION : Does well in light soil and partial shade. Propagation by division.

SPECIES : E. *macranthum*. White and blue, 10 ins., May ; Japan.
E. *pinnatum*. Yellow, 12 ins., May ; Persia.
E. *rubrum*. Rosy red, 10 ins, April–May ; Europe.

EREMURUS (Foxtail Lily) Order LILIACEÆ

The eremurus is treasured for its stately, tall flower spikes of white, pink and yellow, borne mostly in the early summer. It is a plant for the large herbaceous border or, better still, to be planted in a setting of chiefly evergreen shrubs and trees. Needs light but rich, well-drained but moisture-holding, soil, and a sheltered, sunny position. Hates root disturbance, and so is unlikely to appear a success in the first season after planting.

CULTIVATION : Plant in autumn, covering the crowns with 6 ins. of soil. Protect with bracken or dry leaves in winter. In summer, water freely in dry weather.

PROPAGA- By division in autumn or spring or seeds sown in
TION : heat in spring, and seedlings grown in cold frames for first two or three years.

SPECIES :   *E. Bungei.* Yellow, 2-3 ft., July ; Persia.

E. himalaicus. White, 8 ft., May–June ; Himalayas.

E. Olgæ. Lilac purple, scented, 2-4 ft., June ; Turkestan.

E. robustus Elwesianus. Pink, 8-10 ft., June ; Turkestan.

ERIGERON (Flea Bane) Order COMPOSITÆ

The most usually grown erigeron looks rather like a large flowered early Michaelmas daisy and is found in similar colour shades. There are also some yellow and orange species and varieties.

CULTIVATION : A sunny position in moisture-holding soil is required. Pea-sticks should be given as support to all taller kinds. Propagation by division or by seeds.

SPECIES AND   *E. aurantiacus.* Orange, 1 ft., summer ; Turkestan.
VARIETIES :   *E. philadelphicus.* Rosy pink, 1-2 ft., summer ; N. America.

E. caucasecus. Soft mauve, 8 ins., summer.

Quakeress is a lovely variety.

ERYNGIUM (Sea Holly) Order UMBELLIFERÆ

Very ornamental, bristly plants, their thistle-like flower heads surrounded by large prickly bracts. Stems and flowers blue, leaves glaucous green. Very effective as a cut flower on its own or adding a bold note to a mixed group.

CULTIVATION: A sunny position in light soil is most suitable. Propagation by division or by seeds.

SPECIES: *E. oliverianum.* Blue, 2-4 ft., summer; Orient.

E. pandanifolium is a gigantic species that will grow from 10-15 ft. high and comes from Montevideo; summer.

E. varlifolium. Marbled leaves, 2 ft., July.

FRITILLARIA (Crown Imperial, Fritillary) Order LILIACEÆ

There are many lovely fritillaries that are best grown in the rock garden, but no herbaceous border should be without a few plants of the beautiful Crown Imperial that bears its large red, orange or yellow flower crowns in spring when the rest of the border seems hardly to have woken up from its winter sleep.

CULTIVATION: Does best in deep rich, well-drained soil, but is

CULTIVATION : fairly accommodating. Both sunny and shaded positions are suitable. Careful staking is required. Propagation by offsets or by seeds.

SPECIES AND   *F. imperialis.* Yellow, 2-3 ft., May ;   Orient.
VARIETIES :   Varieties: Aurora, orange; *lutea*, yellow; *rubra*, red. There is also a variety with the foliage leaves edged yellow (*F. Aurora marginata*), but plants with self-coloured leaves are more effective.

HOSTA (Plantain Lily) Order LILIACEÆ

Very useful plants for the front of shady borders though they will do very well in full sun too. Ornamental foliage. Leaves broadly oval with conspicuous parallel veins. Flowers white or mauve borne in close racemes.

CULTIVATION : Any soil and position, provided there is plenty of moisture. Propagation by divison.
SPECIES: *H. fortunei.* Lilac, 18 ins., July; Japan.
H. plantaginium grandiflora. White, 1 ft., August; Japan.
H. ovata. Bluish, 1 ft., May-July; Japan.
H. sieboldiana. White and blue, 1 ft., summer; Japan.
There are several varieties with variegated leaves.

GAILLARDIA (Blanket Flower) Order COMPOSITÆ

A cheerful, large, yellow and red daisy flower to be grown near the front of the border. The plants tend to be floppy and untidy but can be much improved by feeding and staking.

CULTIVATION: Grow in any ordinary soil in sunny position.
PROPAGATION: By division or by root or basal shoot cuttings.
SPECIES AND   *G. aristata.* Yellow, 18 ins., summer; N. America.
VARIETIES: *G. a. grandiflora,* 18 ins.; summer. Many varieties: Ipswich Beauty, crimson with golden edge; Mandarin, brownish red, 3 ft.; Wirral Flame, reddish brown with yellow edge; Croftway Yellow, pure yellow, 2 ft.

GALEGA (Goat's Rue) Order LEGUMINOSÆ

This is quite a pleasant feathery-leaved plant that grows tall and busy and bears clusters of vetch-like flowers in white or various shades of mauve. In masses it looks insipid, but a few clumps of it may look well with oriental poppies, irises, pæonies or other plants of bold shape and deep colour.

The Herbaceous Border

CULTIVATION : Very accommodating, will grow in any soil, in sun or light shade. Propagation by division or by seeds.

SPECIES AND VARIETIES : *G. officinalis.* Blue, 3-5 ft., summer ; S. Europe. Varieties : *alba,* white ; Duchess of Bedford, blue ; *Hartlandii,* blue ; *orientalis,* blue, 2-3 ft., summer ; Caucasus.

GERANIUM (Crane's Bill) Order GERANIACEÆ

This is not the scarlet bedding flower, pelargonium, which everybody calls by the name " geranium." There is a host of hardy geranium species useful in herbaceous borders and rock gardens. Flowers white, mauve, pink or crimson-purple. Leaves mostly very decorative, round, more or less deeply lobed, often with fine autumn tints.

CULTIVATION : A well-drained soil and a sunny position should be provided. Propagation by seeds or by division.

SPECIES AND VARIETIES : *G. argenteum.* Rose, 1 ft., summer ; Alps.
G. armenum. Purple, 2 ft., June-July ; Orient.
G. Endressii. Rose, 1 ft., summer ; Pyrenees.
G. grandiflorum. Mauve blue, 16 ins., June–September ; Himalayas. Its variety, Gravity is a deeper blue.
G. ibericum. Blue 1½-2 ft., summer ; Caucasus.
G. pratense. Blue, 2-3 ft., summer ; Britain. It has double blue and double white varieties.

GEUM (Avens, Herb Bennet) Order ROSACEÆ

These are indispensable because of their clear, bright colours (scarlet, orange or yellow) and neat habit. The rosettes of leaves continue a fresh green throughout the winter. Suitable for the front or middle of the border. The scarlets are lovely with a mauve such as that of erigeron Quakeress. Both the orange and scarlet varieties are excellent neighbours to the deep violet *Salvia virgata nemorosa.*

CULTIVATION : A sunny position in any soil. Propagation : The plants are very easily raised from seed and will flower the following season, or if sown early, in the autumn of the same year. Large clumps are divided in spring or autumn.

SPECIES AND VARIETIES : *G. Borisii.* Clear orange scarlet, with bright-green foliage, 9-12 ins., summer and autumn ; Europe. Mostly grown in rockeries.

SPECIES AND   *G. coccineum.*   Scarlet, 1 ft., summer, Asia Minor,
VARIETIES :   and its many varieties, such as Fire Opal, flame
and scarlet ; Lady Stratheden, yellow ; Mrs.
Bradshaw, dark scarlet ; Princess Juliana, double
orange.

GYPSOPHILA (Chalk Plant) Order CARYOPHYLLACEÆ

Snowdrift would be a better name, as gypsophila, when in
flower, looks like a mass of snowflakes. It brightens and lightens
the border and looks equally lovely among bright or pastel
colours. Useful cut flower for mixed vases or bouquets.

CULTIVATION :   A sunny position and chalky soil preferred. Will
do quite well in other soils. Resents disturbance.
Propagation by root cuttings taken in spring.
SPECIES AND   *G. paniculata.*   White, 3 ft., June–September ;
VARIETIES :   Europe. Varieties : *G. p. flore pleno* with double
flowers ; *G. p. flore pleno,* Bristol Fairy, a particularly good form with large double white flowers ;
G. p. flore pleno, Flamingo, with double pink
flowers ; *G. p. flore pleno,* Rosy Veil, with double
pink flowers, 2 ft.

HELENIUM Order COMPOSITÆ

Indispensable for late summer and autumn flowering. The
plants are compact and tidy and bear their large bright yellow or
orange, copper or crimson coloured daisy flowers on stiff stems.
The large flower centres are usually a deep chocolate brown.

CULTIVATION : Sun or semi-shade in well-drained, moisture-
holding soil. Thin out crowded weak shoots in
spring, stake the taller kinds with bushy pea-sticks.
Water in dry period, feed when flower buds show.
Propagation by division or by seeds.
SPECIES AND   *H. autumnale* from N. America. Varieties : Garten-
VARIETIES :   sonne, golden, brown centre, 5 ft., August-
October ; Mme. Canivet, light yellow, dark
centre, 2 ft., July-September ; Moerheim Beauty,
a deep coppery red, $2\frac{1}{2}$ ft., July-September, very
popular ; Riverton Gem, deep bronze, 5 ft.,
September–October ; *rubrum,* crimson and gold,
5 ft., August–October ; The Bishop, orange, semi-
double, $2\frac{1}{2}$ ft., August–September ; Wyndley,
bronze and yellow, $2\frac{1}{2}$ ft., July–September.

HELIANTHUS (Perennial Sunflower) Order COMPOSITÆ

Useful tall plant for the back of large borders or centre of double-sided borders. The flowers are yellow, much smaller than those of the annual sunflower, but many heads are borne on each stem.

CULTIVATION : Sun or semi-shade in any fairly rich soil. Staking not required, as strong, stiff growth is made. Water in dry weather. Propagation by division or by seeds.

SPECIES AND VARIETIES : *H. multiflorus.* Yellow, 5 ft., July–September ; N. America. Varieties : *H. m.* Lodden Gold, brilliant yellow double flower, 5-6 ft., August-September ; *H. m. maximus,* huge, single golden-yellow flowers, 5-6 ft., August–October. *H. orgyalis.* Flowers yellow in clustered heads, 7-8 ft., September–October. *H. sparsifolius* and its variety, Monarch, yellow, large flowers, 6-8 ft., September–October.

HELIOPSIS (North American Ox-eye) Order COMPOSITÆ

Big bushy plants with large, robust golden-yellow daisy flowers.

CULTIVATION : Should be treated in the same way as the perennial sunflowers described above. Propagation by division.

SPECIES AND VARIETIES: *H. lævis.* Yellow, 5 ft., autumn; N. America. *H. gigantea.* Large golden flowers, 4 ft., July-September; U.S.A. Varieties: *H. sc. incomparabilis,* a semi-double and *H. patula,* a semi-double.

HELLEBORUS (Hellebore, Christmas Rose, Lenten Rose) Order RANUNCULACEÆ

Neat, dwarf plants with tufts of large dark-green deeply-lobed leaves and interesting flowers. Their chief charm lies in the fact that some produce white " roses " at Christmas time. Suitable for the front of a shady border, but may be planted in any shady, sheltered nook, among evergreen shrubs and ferns or at the base of trees. Lovely cut flower for low vases and bowls.

CULTIVATION : Rich soil, shade or semi-shade, mulch in spring with well-decayed manure. Occasional feeding in summer is beneficial. Those that flower in winter are best protected with hand lights or cloches during that period. Propagation by seeds or by division.

SPECIES AND
VARIETIES : *H. niger.* The Christmas rose, 1 ft., white, October – April ; Europe. Varieties, *maximus*, white, tinged, purple ; *major*, large, white.
H. orientalis. The Lenten rose, white to pink, 1-2 ft., February–May ; Greece. Many good varieties, including Blue Bird, slate blue ; Darkness, red ; Eastern Queen, yellow ; Gertrude Jekyll, white.

HEMEROCALLIS (Day Lily) Order LILIACEÆ

Plants with strap-shaped leaves and large, lily-like flowers borne well above the foliage. Each flower only lasts a day or so, but many are borne on one stem, one opening as the other fades. The colours tend to be subdued shades of yellow, orange and coppery-red. It is important to get good varieties, or else the effect may be rather insipid.

CULTIVATION : Very accommodating plants, flourishing in light and heavy, deep and shallow, acid and alkaline soils, in sunny positions as well as in shade and semi-shade. But they will do their best only if they can get plenty of moisture throughout the summer. Propagation by division.

SPECIES AND
VARIETIES : *H. aurantiaca major.* Orange apricot, 3 ft., summer ; Japan.
H. citrina. Lemon yellow, large flowers, 4 ft., June–August ; China.
H. Dumortieri. Yellow and copper, 2 ft., July ; Japan.
There are many good hybrid varieties, including: Black Magic, ruby mahogany, 3 ft.; Crossus, amber and gold; Dido, ruck apricot, 3 ft.; George Yeld, canary yellow, 2 ft.; Golden Orchid, deep gold; Morocco Red, dark red, yellow cup; Negrette, purple and mahogany, golden thread; Pink charm, a pinkish shade.

HEUCHERA (Alum Root) Order SAXIFRAGACEÆ

Dainty subject for the front of the border. The compact rosettes of roundish leaves are neat all the year, but the delicate flowers borne in slender panicles suffer from lack of personality.

CULTIVATION : A light or medium soil and sunny position are required. Propagation by division.

SPECIES AND   *H. brizoides.*   Pink, 1 ft., summer (hybrid) ; N.
VARIETIES :   America.
                   H. sanguinea. Red, 1-1½ ft., summer ; Mexico.
                   Many varieties are offered in trade catalogues,
                   many with rather larger flowers, in deeper colours
                   and on longer stems.

HOLLYHOCK (*see* ALTHÆA)

INCARVILLEA Order BIGNONIACEÆ

Very attractive plants for the front of the border with showy, trumpet-shaped flowers in early summer and handsome foliage.

CULTIVATION : Light, rich, well-drained soil and sunny position
                   required. Protect crowns in winter with bracken
                   or dry litter. Propagation by seeds.
SPECIES AND   *I. Delavayi.* Bright rosy or crimson purple, 2 ft.,
VARIETIES :   summer ; China.
                   I. grandiflora, variety *brevipes.* Crimson, 1½ ft., May–
                   June ; China. There are several other species and
                   varieties.

KNIPHOFIA (Red Hot Poker) Order LILIACEÆ

Showy, very popular plants, well described by their English name. Long narrow strap-shaped leaves. The scarlet, orange, or yellow flowers look best with other brightly-coloured neighbours. They are also rather effective when grown in beds of their own.

CULTIVATION : Deep, rich, well-drained soil, sunny position.
                   Water in dry spells, feed with liquid manure
                   applied once a week in summer. Propagation by
                   seeds or by division.
SPECIES AND   *Early flowering. May–July :*
VARIETIES :   *K. præcox.* Red and yellow, 3-7 ft. ; S. Africa.
                   K. Tuckii. Scarlet and yellow, 4½ ft. ; S. Africa.
                   Some weeks later than *K. præcox.* Varieties :
                   Gold Else, with numerous pale-yellow spikes to
                   each plant, 2½ ft.; Royal Standard, bright
                   yellow and scarlet, 3 ft.; Russell's Gold,
                   yellow, 3 ft.
                   Late flowering. July—October:
                   K. aloides. Red and yellow, 4 ft. Several
                   varieties such as Mount Etna, orange-scarlet,
                   5 ft., very vigorous.

SPECIES AND   *K. corallina*. Bright green leaves and coral-red,
VARIETIES :   flowers, 2 ft.
           K. erecta. Scarlet, 5 ft.

LINUM (Flax) Order LINACEÆ

Either dainty plants with clear sky-blue or white flowers and grey-green foliage or dwarf compact plants with large radiant yellow flowers and dark-green leaves. Both are particularly lovely, the blue form being almost indispensable.

CULTIVATION : They will grow well in most soils, but must be given a place in full sun or the flowers will not open wide. Propagation by seeds or by division.
SPECIES : *L. flavum*. Yellow, 18 ins., summer ; Austria.
L. monogynum. White, 1-2 ft., June–October ; New Zealand.
L. narbonense. Blue, 2 ft., May–July ; S. Europe.
L. perenne. Blue or white, 1½ ft., summer ; Britain.
The scarlet flax, *L. rubrum*, is an annual.

LOBELIA (Cardinal Flower) Order CAMPANULACEÆ

Stately plants with tall spikes of fiery scarlet or deep vermilion flowers, set off by dark purple-bronze foliage. These dazzlingly beautiful plants should be more widely grown. A prominent position in the middle of the border is suitable. They look well, mixed with light-blue, mauve, yellow or orange flowers.

CULTIVATION : Rich, moisture-holding soil, sunny position. In all but the warmest spots it is safest to lift these plants in late autumn and house them in cold frames or greenhouses until they can be planted out the following spring when no more heavy frosts are expected. Propagation by seeds, cuttings or division.
SPECIES AND   *L. cardinalis*. Scarlet, 3-4 ft., summer ; N. America.
VARIETIES :   Has several crimson, vermilion and scarlet varieties that can be found in trade catalogues.
L. fulgens. Scarlet, 1-3 ft., May ; Mexico.
L. Gerardii. Violet, 3-4 ft., July. (Hybrid.)
L. syphilitica. Blue and white, 2-3 ft., July ; N. America.
The well-known little bright-blue lobelia is usually grown as an annual in this country, though it is a half-hardy perennial.

LUPINUS (Lupin) Order LEGUMINOSÆ

Deservedly popular border plant, flowering in early summer. Tall, close racemes of pea-flowers in an enormous range of colours. The flowers may be self-coloured or show different colours, such as cream and mauve, or yellow and red. Ornamental foliage. Glistening water drops may often be seen in the centre of the fingered fresh green leaves.

CULTIVATION : Sun or partial shade, rich soil. Mulch in spring with well-decayed manure. Water in dry spells. Cut stems down after flowering. Lupin plants are at their best only for a very few seasons.

PROPAGA-
TION :
They are easily propagated by seed sown as soon as ripe or else from April on in a good seed bed outside, or in a cold frame. Division is also possible and cuttings may be taken in spring from the young growth and rooted in an unheated frame. (See Fig. 12.) The seed method is the simplest in the case of lupins.

SPECIES AND
VARIETIES :
L. polyphyllus. Lilac blue, 3-4 ft., early summer ; California.

Most garden Lupins are varieties of the above and can be had in almost every colour: Blue Jacket, blue and white; Celandine, clear yellow, Fireglow, orange and gold; Masterpiece, purple and pink; Mrs. Noel Terry, light Pink; Susan of York, yellow and terra cotta; Thundercloud, violet purple; Riverslea, crimson lake.

The Russell Lupins are very vigorous and show particularly bold colour combinations: George Russell, coral pink and citron yellow; My Castle, brick red; The Chatelain, pink and white; The Pages, carmine; Chandelier, yellow and orange; Josephine, blue and yellow.

LYCHNIS (Campion) Order CARYOPHYLLACEÆ

Some of the Campions make very useful border plants, tidy in habit, varying in height from 2-3 ft., mostly red, pink or crimson.

CULTIVATION : Most garden soils will do. Will stand dry conditions well. Needs full sun. Propagation by seeds or by division.

SPECIES AND VARIETIES : *L. chalcedonica* (Jerusalem Cross). Scarlet flower heads, 3 ft., summer ; Russia. Varieties, *alba* and *flore-pleno.*
L. coronaria. Dark crimson flowers, pale silvery-grey foliage, tends to look artificial, 2-3 ft., summer ; S. Europe.
L. Flos-Jovis. Bright pink, 2½-3 ft., summer; Europe.
L. Viscaria (German Catchfly). Red, white, or mauve and pink varieties, 1 ft., summer; Europe

LYSIMACHIA (Yellow Loosestrife) Order PRIMULACEÆ

This must be recommended for moist shady places where it will look after itself producing its bright yellow, pleasing flower spikes year after year. Excellent cut flowers ; will continue to grow and open fresh buds in the vase, where it will look fresh for quite two weeks.

CULTIVATION : Plant in moist, shady borders, or by the banks of ponds or streams. Propagation by division.

SPECIES : *L. vulgaris.* Yellow, 3 ft., July–August ; Britain. Other yellow species are :
L. punctata. Large yellow flowers, each tinged with ochre red at the base, 2-3 ft. ; Europe.
L. thyrsiflora. Clusters of rather small flowers ; not very effective ; N. Europe.
Some white species are :
L. cletkroides, 3 ft., July–September ; Japan.
L. ephemerum, 3 ft., summer ; S. Europe.
A purple species is :
L. atropurpurea, 2 ft., summer ; Greece.

LYTHRUM (Purple Loosestrife) Order LYTHRACEÆ

Neat busy plants, bearing tall spikes of purple or rose flowers in summer. Suitable for the moist border or for water-side planting.

CULTIVATION : Sun or semi-shade, moisture-holding soil. Propagation by division.

SPECIES AND VARIETIES : *L. Salicaria.* Reddish purple, 3-4 ft., July ; Britain. Varieties : Pritchard, deep pink ; *roseum,* rose.
L. virgatum. Purple, 3 ft., summer ; Europe.

III. Dianthus, Mars

IV. Spanish Irises

MALVA (Mallow) Order MALVACEÆ

Pleasing, shapely plants, covered with rosy, white or purple flowers in summer.

CULTIVATION : Well-drained, sunny borders. Propagation by seeds or by cuttings.

SPECIES : *M. Alcea.* Purple pink, 4 ft., summer ; Europe. Mostly grown as an annual.

M. moschata, the Musk-Mallow, rose or white, 3 ft., summer ; Britain.

MECONOPSIS (Himalayan Poppy and Welsh Poppy) Order PAPAVERACEÆ

The lovely sky-blue Himalayan poppy is not as widely known as it deserves to be. It looks its best in the semi-shade of well-spaced trees, where it will be a good companion for shade-loving lilies and woodland primula species. The much dwarfer Welsh poppy with its yellow, creased tissue-paper flowers is popular in cottage garden borders and will look after itself and spread its seed rather too freely.

CULTIVATION : Himalayan poppy : semi-shady position, soil rich in humus. Needs plenty of moisture in summer and dry conditions in winter. Propagation : sow seed as soon as ripe, over-winter seedlings in cold frame or greenhouse, plant out in April.

Welsh poppy : sun or semi-shade and a moisture-holding, well-drained soil. Propagation : sow seed in position as soon as ripe, or under glass in spring.

SPECIES : *M. betonicifolia* (Syn. *Baileyi*). Blue, 3-4 ft., June-July ; Himalayas.

M. cambrica. The Welsh poppy, yellow, 1 ft. ; Europe.

M. grandis. Violet blue or slate blue, 3 ft., June ; Sikkim.

M. quintuplinervia. Lilac blue, 1-1½ ft., May ; Tibet.

M. Wallichii. Blue, 4-6 ft., summer ; Himalayas.

MIMULUS (Monkey flower, Musk) Order SCROPHULARIACEÆ

Another plant suitable for the moist, shady border. The English yellow mimulus has large, showy trumpet flowers, clear yellow with red spots, and smooth pale-green leaves. In nature it grows by the side of streams and canals.

CULTIVATION : Sun or semi-shade are suitable, plenty of moisture essential. Feeding in summer will increase the vigour of the plant. Propagation by seeds, by cuttings or division.

SPECIES : *M. cardinalis.* Scarlet, 1-2 ft., summer ; N. America. *M. guttatus.* Yellow with red spots, 2-2½ ft., summer ; Britain. *M. Lewisii.* Rose, 1 ft., July–October ; N.W. America. Many dwarf species are suitable for garden culture or edgings for shady borders.

MONARDA (Sweet Bergamot) Order LABIATÆ

Rather a showy plant for the middle of the border. Scarlet, purple or pink. The sage-like flowers are arranged in whorls around a centre that will go on growing to produce further whorls higher up. Leaves scented.

CULTIVATION : Requires sun, will do well in almost any soil. Propagation by seeds or by division.

SPECIES AND VARIETIES : *M. didyma,* variety, Cambridge Scarlet, 2-3 ft., summer ; N. America. *M. fistulosa.* Rosy purple, 2-4 ft., summer ; N. America.

MONTBRETIA (syn. *Tritonia*) Order IRIDACEÆ

The montbretia grows from corms. It is popular as an easily-grown border plant with bright orange flowers in late summer and light-green, narrow leaves that are decorative throughout the growing season. Both foliage and flowers are excellent for use in vases.

CULTIVATION : Get varieties of good flower size and colour. Almost any soil and position will be acceptable. If soil is poor, occasional feeding during summer will improve quality of bloom. Propagation by offsets.

SPECIES AND VARIETIES : *M. crocata.* Orange, 2 ft., summer ; S. Africa. *M. crocosmæflora.* Orange scarlet, 3 ft.; S. Africa. *M. Pottsii.* Orange yellow ; S. Africa. *M. rosea.* Rosy pink ; S. Africa. There are many good varieties such as : George Davidson, deep yellow ; Lord Nelson, scarlet ; Prometheus, orange and red.

NEPETA (Catmint) Order LABIATÆ

Peculiarly scented plants with neat, grey foliage and deep lavender-blue flower spikes throughout the summer. Lovely as an edging or planted in groups among other plants at the front of the herbaceous border.

CULTIVATION : Catmint does best in full sun and in light, well-drained soil. Propagation by seeds or by division.

SPECIES AND *N. macrantha.* Silvery blue, 2-3 ft., summer;
VARIETIES : Siberia.
N. Mussinii. Lavender blue, 1-2 ft., summer; Caucasus.
An *N. M.* variety, Six Hills, is much larger, very lovely in colour and habit, suitable for grouping near the front of the border rather than for an edging.

ŒNOTHERA (Evening Primrose) Order ONAGRACEÆ

Well known from the lovely display they make on railway banks. The large primrose-yellow flowers make a very good contribution to the picture of the summer border.

CULTIVATION : Sunny position in light, well-drained soil required. Propagation by seeds, cuttings, suckers, or division.

SPECIES AND *Œ. biennis.* Yellow, 4-5 ft., June–October. The
VARIETIES : Evening Primrose of the railway bank, a biennial from N. America.
Œ. fruticosa (Yellow River). Golden yellow, 1-2 ft. summer; N. America. Varieties, *major* and *Youngii.* The latter flowers over a particularly long period.

PÆONIA (Peony) Order RANUNCULACEÆ

One of the loveliest border plants. Shapely bushes of ornamental foliage, covered in early summer with flowers the size of cabbage lettuce, in deepest crimson, rose, yellow or white and many intermediate shades. They also look very lovely when grown on their own or in the front of a shrub border.

CULTIVATION : Deep, rich, well-drained soil, sun or semi-shade. The soil must be deeply worked before planting, manure being incorporated. Pæonies hate root

CULTIVATION : disturbance and should be left alone as long as possible. Water in dry spells, feed occasionally during growing season. Stake early, using short, strong canes to prevent shoots from being weighed down by the heavy flowers.

PROPAGA-
TION : There is really no truth in the story that pæonies won't divide—they take a long time to flower after dividing—though this operation must definitely not be carried out more often than every 7 or 8 years. They may be raised from seed, but can then, of course, not be depended upon as regards colour and other flower characters. Also, a seedling will take several years to reach the flowering age.

SPECIES AND
VARIETIES : Many species from many countries have contributed to the herbaceous pæonies, among them :
P. albiflora. White and pink, May. From Siberia, China and Japan ; 3 ft.
P. anomala. Bright crimson, May ; N. Europe and Asia ; 2-3 ft.
P. arietina. Dark crimson, 2-3 ft., May ; Orient.
P. Browni. A dull red flower, 1½ ft., May ; California.
P. corallina. Crimson, 3 ft., May ; Europe.
P. lutea. Yellow, 3 ft., June ; Yunnan.
P. officinalis. Crimson, 2-3 ft., May ; Europe.
P. Wittmanniana. Yellow, 2 ft., May ; Orient.
Endless varieties may be found in trade catalogues, here are some of the best :
May flowering :
Avant Garde, large flowers, creamy white, flushed pink ; *P. arietina,* Purple Emperor, bright rose, large, stamens golden ; *P. lobata,* Fire King, large deep fiery red ; Mayflower, pure silver white, flushed rose when young ; Mlokosiewiczi, lovely light - yellow flowers, bronzy-red foliage ; *P. officinalis alba plena,* pure double white ; *P. roseaplena,* crimson carmine, double ; *P. tenuifolia plena,* glowing crimson double, finely-cut foliage.
June flowering :
Adolphe Rousseau, double dark crimson with golden anthers ; Duchesse de Nemours, large white double rose scented ; Lady Alexander Duff, large, flesh pink, rose scented ; Philo-

SPECIES AND
VARIETIES :
mete, semi-double, rose pink ; *P. sinensis*, 3 ft. and its many varieties.

Late June and July flowering :
Faust, lilac guard petals, salmon-yellow centre ; Marie Lemoine, very large white with cream centre ; Moonlight, silver-white guard petals with deep red inside.

PAPAVER (Oriental Poppy) Order PAPAVERACEÆ

The most gorgeous orange scarlet of the border is provided by these. They may also be had in white, pink, salmon and dark red. Unfortunately they are untidy growers, but they may easily be screened after flowering by later-growing plants. They require rather tactful placing, or they will, so to speak, take the wind out of everything else's sail.

CULTIVATION : A sunny position in well-drained soil is required. Stake carefully before the plants have grown very large. Bushy pea-sticks are most suitable. Propagation by division or by root cuttings.

SPECIES AND
VARIETIES :
P. orientale. Orange scarlet, 3 ft., June ; Asia Minor. Varieties : Cowichan, a dazzling, huge scarlet ; Lady Haig, a deep red ; Lord Lambourne, orange scarlet with black blotches ; Mrs. Stobart, cerise pink ; Olympia, a large double red ; Perry's White ; Salmon Glow.

PENTSTEMON Order SCROPHULARIACEÆ syn. Chelone

Very graceful plants. Rather foxglove-like flowers in many colours born on slender stems. There are many species, some best grown in the rockery, others in formal beds, but some make a very interesting addition to the herbaceous border.

CULTIVATION: Sunny position, well-drained soil. In very cold districts, the plants may have to be protected in winter. Propagation by seeds or by cuttings.

SPECIES:
P. edithæ. Crimson purple, 8 ins., June-July.
P. barbatus. Scarlet, 3 ft., summer; U.S.A.
P. digitaloides. Deep rose, 2 ft., June. Rose Queen.
P. cobæa. Purple and white, 1-2 ft., August; U.S.A.

SPECIES : *P. confertus.* Purple and blue, 1 ft., summer ; Rocky Mountains.
P. glaber. Purple, 1-2 ft., summer ; U.S.A.
P. Hartwegii. Summer, 2 ft.; Mexico. This scarlet pentstemon is usually grown in beds as a biennial.
P. heterophyllus. Sky blue, 1-3 ft., July ; California.
P. ovatus. Blue and purple, 2-3 ft., autumn ; U.S.A.
There are very many varieties.
The bedding plants are usually hybrids of *P. Cobæa* and *P. Hartwegii.*

PHLOX Order POLEMONIACEÆ

One of the most popular and lovely border plants. The flowers are borne in large clusters on stiffly erect stems. Many delightful colours, sweet scent, long flowering period.

CULTIVATION : A position in full sun and a good rich, but well-aired soil required. Otherwise growth will be weak and spindly. Feed with liquid manure every 2-3 weeks as they come into flower. This makes a tremendous difference with phlox. Thin out weak shoots (the thinnings may be used as cuttings). Stake early, using 3-5 canes to each plant.

PROPAGA-TION : Healthy phlox plants are best propagated by division. But if the plants produce a lot of weak growth with the lower leaves discoloured, eelworm may be present, and such plants must be propagated by root cuttings. (See page 67.)

SPECIES AND VARIETIES : The border phlox are hybrids derived largely from 3 species, all from N. America :
Ph. glaberrima suffruticosa. Red, 1-2 ft., May–June.
Ph. maculata. Purple, July, 2 ft.
Ph. paniculata (syn. *Ph. decussata*). Purple and white, 3-4 ft., August.
Numerous other species are useful for the rockery, one, *P. Drummondii*, for the annual border and for pot culture in the greenhouse.
Some good border phlox varieties: Balmoral, rosy lavender; Endurance, salmon orange; Firefly, peach pink, red eye; Gaiety, cherry red, suffused orange; Harewood, bright carmine, 3 ft.; Harlequin, rich purple violet; Le Mahdi, deep violet; Mia Ruys, pure white; Parma Violet, fire trusses of violet; Prince George, orange, scarlet; Spitfire,

VARIETIES: orange scarlet; Windsor, carmine-rose with magenta eye.

PHYSALIS (Cape Gooseberry) Order SOLANACEÆ

These may be found some little space in the herbaceous border as their orange-scarlet " Chinese lanterns " are attractive in winter. The " lantern " is formed by the inflated calyx and encloses a tiny tomato-like edible fruit. Popular for the winter vase.

CULTIVATION : Sunny or semi-shady position in rich well-drained soil required. Propagation by seeds or by division.

SPECIES :   *Ph. Alkekengi.* Orange-scarlet inflated calyx. Summer, 1-2 ft. ; Europe.
Ph. Franchetti. Red inflated calyx. Summer, 1½-2 ft. ; Japan.
The flowers of both are white and quite inconspicuous.

PHYSOSTEGIA (False Dragon-Head) Order LABIATÆ

A very attractive plant of neat habit with bright crimson upright flower plumes born in late summer, 1-1½ ft. high, very suitable for the front of the border, or by water.

CULTIVATION : Will do well in light, well-drained soil. Prefers partial shade to full sun. Propagation by seeds, by cuttings or by division.

SPECIES AND VARIETIES :   *Ph. virginiana,* variety Vivid, is the one usually grown now, and is well described by the variety name, Crimson-Purple, 18 ins., August–September; N. America.

POLEMONIUM (Jacob's Ladder) Order POLEMONIACEÆ

P. cæruleum is a native of Britain and wins attention and praise with its clear sky-blue flowers and fresh green feathery foliage. It is suitable for the front of the border.

CULTIVATION : A sunny position in ordinary rich well-drained soil. Propagation by division.

SPECIES :   *P. cæruleum.* Blue, 18 ins., June ; Britain. Variety *P. c. album,* white.
P. carneum. Cream or rose, 1-1½ ft., summer ; N.W. America.
P. flavum. Yellow, 3 ft., summer ; New Mexico.

The Complete Gardener

POLYGONATUM (Solomon's Seal) Order LILIACEÆ

A useful plant for the shady border. Its arching stems bear pairs of smooth dark-green leaves, with clusters of white flower bells hanging down from their axils, in May and June.

CULTIVATION : Light soil rich in humus and a shady position are required. Propagation by division.
SPECIES : *P. multiflorum.* White, 3 ft., June ; Europe.
P. officinale. White, 1 ft., May ; Europe (Britain).

POTENTILLA (Cinquefoil) Order ROSACEÆ

Many pretty wild flowers and also some garden shrubs belong to this genus. But it also provides the herbaceous border with some fine plants, notably the clear crimson-scarlet *P. atrosanguinea.*

CULTIVATION: Full sun, good deep border soil required. Propagation by seeds or by division.
SPECIES: *P. argyrophylla atrosanguinea.* Scarlet with silvery foliage, 2 ft., summer; Himalayas.
Varieties: Gibson's scarlet, 2 ft. (hybrid); Master Floris, apricot with scarlet eye (hybrid).
P. nepalensis. Miss Willmott. Clear pink (hybrid), 1 ft., summer.

PRIMULA Order PRIMULACEÆ

An enormous genus, supplying our gardens with lovely species from all over the world. Some go to the greenhouse, others to rock gardens, watersides, woodlands and wild gardens. Some species are very suitable for the shady or semi-shady border.

CULTIVATION : The soil must not be too heavy and should be rich in humus and well drained, with shade or partial shade. Propagation by seeds or by division.
SPECIES : *P. Auricula.* In many colours. These have become somewhat artificial-looking in the Auricula enthusiast's hands, but are certainly interesting in their variety of colour combination within one flower and will form intensely bright groups near the front of a shady border. The species came from the Alps. 6 ins., spring.
P. Beesiana. Deep crimson, many rings of flowers above each other (candelabra type), 2 ft. high, spring, only suitable for very damp borders, where it will look splendid.

24. *Two kinds of wall and a wattle fence*

25. *A herbaceous border*

26. *Staking herbaceous plants with sticks and string*

27. *Chrysanthemums staked with wire and string*

SPECIES :   *P. Bulleyana.* Apricot yellow flowers, arranged the
same way, 1 ft. high, requiring equally moist
conditions. June–July ; Yunnan.
P. capitata. Globular heads of lilac flowers in July,
9 ins. ; Himalaya. Good winter drainage essential.
P. denticulata. Similar to *P. capitata*, but flowering
April–May ; Himalayas. Very easy to grow and a
stock of them may be increased rapidly by division
of the crowns that multiply generously year by year.
P. elatior. The oxlip, yellow, 6-9 ins. ; Britain.
P. littoniana. Deep lilac mauve, 2 ft., June–
August ; Yunnan.
P. Polyanthus. These have been improved enorm-
ously of late, and very vigorous strains in in-
numerable excellent rich colours can be obtained.
They need dividing every other year straight after
flowering. 6-9 ins., spring ; Europe.
P. pulverulenta. A candelabra type with many vivid
colours, the species crimson purple, 2 ft., June ;
China.
There is no reason why many other species should
not be grown in a cool, moist border. Further
species are described on pages 168 and 180.

PULMONARIA (Lung Wort) Order BORAGINACEÆ

Another plant for the shady or semi-shady border. Suitable for
the front. Has silver spotted leaves and 1 ft. racemes of mostly blue
flowers. Most of them change from pink to blue like their cousins,
the forget-me-nots.

CULTIVATION :   Shady position and any ordinary soil. Propagation
by seeds or by division.
SPECIES AND   *P. angustifolia azurea.* Blue, 9 ins., spring; Europe.
VARIETIES: Munstead Blue, rich blue, 6 ins.
P. officinalis English Lung Wort. Similar, slightly
dingy in colouring.
P. rubra. Brick red, 3-12 ins., spring; Tran-
sylvania.
P. saccharata. Mrs. Moon. Pink, 1 ft., April-July;
spotted foliage; Europe.

PYRETHRUM Order COMPOSITÆ

Very lovely daisy-like flowers, white, pink or glorious reds with yellow centre if single. There are doubles. The foliage is delicately feathered, the flowering stems are 2-3 ft. high. The insecticide " Pyrethrum " is obtained from its roots. Invaluable as cut flowers.

CULTIVATION : A sunny position in rich well-drained soil. They must be watered freely in dry weather.

PROPAGA-
TION : Divide and re-plant every other year or so, as the quality of the flowers will then not deteriorate.

SPECIES AND
VARIETIES : *P. roseum* (syn. *Chrysanthemum coccineum*). Red, 2-3 ft., summer ; Caucasus. There are many varieties, such as : Aphrodite, white double ; Cornet, carmine ; Eileen May Robinson, shell-pink, single ; Hamlet, bright rose, single ; Harold Robinson, large crimson, free flowering, single ; James Kelway, rich crimson, single ; Queen Mary, large, bright pink, double ; Scarlet Glow, large, deep scarlet, single.

ROMNEYA (Californian Tree Poppy) Order PAPAVERACEÆ

These are indescribably beautiful, bold, gigantic white poppies with glaucous foliage. Not absolutely hardy, they require a sheltered spot in well-drained soil. Equally lovely in the back of a large border, in beds of their own or near the front of a shrub border in a setting of dark evergreens.

CULTIVATION : If grown in the border, they should be cut down in autumn like the other herbaceous plants. If growing against a wall, they are not cut so hard, so as to increase in size year by year. Propagation by seeds or by root cuttings.

SPECIES : *R. Coulteri*. White, fragrant, 5-6 ft., late summer ; California.
R. trichocalyx. Very similar to the above, but lower growing.

RUDBECKIA (Cone Flower) Order COMPOSITÆ

A popular autumn flowering plant. Double or single yellow daisy flowers. If single, there is a distinct dark brown or purple conical centre. Height varies from 1-9 ft., according to species.

CULTIVATION : Sunny position in ordinary, rich, well-drained border soil. The tall species should be staked with bushy pea-sticks. Keep these rampant growers in their place, or they will swamp their more modest neighbours. Propagation by seeds or by division.

SPECIES AND VARIETIES:

R. californica. Yellow and brown, 4-6 ft., July–September; California.

R. grandiflora. Yellow and purple, 3 ft., autumn; N. America.

R. deamii. Deep yellow, 3 ft., summer; N. America. Variety Goldquelle, a double.

R. maxima. Yellow and dark brown, 7-9 ft., late summer; N. America.

R. Newmannii (syn. *R. speciosa*). Deep yellow with black cone, 2-3 ft., summer ; N. America.

SALVIA (Sage) Order LABIATÆ

This genus provides many lovely border plants in shades of blue, violet and red. The shapely plants are usually suited by their height for the middle of the border.

CULTIVATION : Full sun is required, dry conditions not resented. Propagation by division.

SPECIES :

S. patens. Large flowers, gentian blue, 1½-2 ft., summer ; Mexico. This most beautiful species is not quite hardy and must be lifted each autumn to be kept under glass till spring. Plant out mid-May.

S. Pitcheri (syn. *S. azurea grandiflora*). Soft sky blue, 3 ft., summer ; Mexico.

S. turkestanica. Rosy mauve with coloured bracts, 3 ft., June–July.

S. virgata nemorosa syn. *superba.* Deep violet blue, 3 ft., July–September; Europe.

SAXIFRAGA (Saxifrage) Order SAXIFRAGACEÆ

Most of the species are grown in the rock garden, but there are some very large-leaved species with dense racemes of flesh-coloured flowers, suitable for the damp, shady border. Very effective as an edging plant.

CULTIVATION : These do not require much attention. Very suitable for the town garden. Propagation by division. Divide and re-plant fairly frequently to keep them tidy.

SPECIES : *S. Bergenia cordifolia.* Flesh pink, 1 ft., spring ; Siberia.

SPECIES : *S. crassifolia.* Similar, earlier in flower, also from Siberia.

SCABIOSA (Scabious) Order DIPSACEÆ

The blue Caucasian scabious is a lovely border plant, suitable for the front of the border and excellent for cutting.

CULTIVATION : Scabious like full sun and do best in soil containing plenty of lime. On most soils a sprinkling of lime should, therefore, be given in winter or early spring. Propagation by division.

SPECIES AND VARIETIES : *S. caucasica.* Lavender blue, 3 ft., July–November ; Caucasus. Varieties, such as Clive Greaves, with particularly large flowers of deep lilac blue (it is important to get a good strain of this variety) ; *Goldingensis*, a very good lavender blue ; Isaac House, violet blue ; Miss E. Willmott, creamy white.

SEDUM (Stone Crop) Order CRASSULACEÆ

Most of the stone crops belong to the rock garden or dry wall, but there is one species growing 1½ ft. tall with large, succulent leaves of a glaucous tinge bearing plates of fluffy pink flowers. These are very decorative near the front of a sunny border.

CULTIVATION : A sunny position in ordinary border soil which may be sandy and dryish. Propagation by division.

SPECIES AND VARIETIES : *S. spectabile.* Pink, 1½ ft., autumn ; Japan. Varieties : *atropurpureum* with red flowers ; *maximum* with purple foliage, 2 ft.

SIDALCEA (Mallow) Order MALVACEÆ

Spikes of lovely deep pink, lilac or purple flowers borne in late summer.

CULTIVATION : Sunny position in ordinary border soil. Propagation by seeds and division. Needs dividing every third or fourth year.

SPECIES AND VARIETIES : *S. spicata.* Rosy purple, 3 ft., late summer ; California.

S. candida. White, 3 ft., summer; Rocky Mountains. Varieties : Crimson Glow, 3ft., July–August ; Rose Queen. Rich rose, 4-5 ft., July–August. *S. spicata.* Rosy purple, 3 ft., late summer ; California.

SOLIDAGO (Golden Rod) Order COMPOSITÆ

Yellow flowers borne in arching sprays in late summer and autumn. Must be kept in bounds, and will then be very useful. Excellent for cutting for mixed vases.

CULTIVATION : Sun or shade in ordinary border soil. Appreciates plenty of humus in the soil. Propagation by division.

SPECIES AND VARIETIES : *S. canadensis.* Yellow 4-6 ft., late summer ; N. America.

S. virgaurea. Yellow, 2-3 ft., August ; Europe (Britain). Varieties : *Ballardi*, graceful, many-branched spikes, rich golden yellow ; Golden Wings, the loveliest golden rod with rich long-arching sprays of bright yellow flowers; Golden Gates with more solid heads of flowers; brachy-stachys 9 ins.

SPIRÆA (Meadow Sweet) Order ROSACEÆ. Now called Fillipendula

Plants with neatly divided leaves and erect fluffy plumes of flowers in white, cream, pink and red.

CULTIVATION: Sun or partial shade, rich soil, plenty of moisture required. Propagation by division.

SPECIES AND VARIETIES: *S. aruncis.* White, 5 ft., June–August; Europe.

S. digitata nana. Rosy pink, 2 ft., July–August; Siberia. Several varieties of these will be found advertised in trade catalogues.

S. elegantissima. Rose, 4-6 ft., July–September; N. America.

S. palmata rubra. Rose-red, 2-3 ft., June; Japan.

STATICE or **LIMONIUM** (Sea Lavender) Order PLUMBAGINACÆ

Flowers in a wide range of pastel colours borne in oddly angular panicles. Useful as cut flowers. May be dried and used as ever-lasting flower.

CULTIVATION : Sunny position in sandy loam. Propagation by seeds and root cuttings.

SPECIES : *S. Gmelini.* Blue and rose, 1-2 ft., summer ; Caucasus.

S. latifolium. Blue, 2-3 ft., summer ; Bulgaria.

S. sinense. Yellow, 1 ft., summer ; China.

SPECIES : *S. tartaricum.* Red and white, 1 ft., summer ; Caucasus.

THALICTRUM (Meadow Rue) Order RANUNCULACEÆ

Graceful plants with very ornamental foliage and in some species also lovely feathery heads of lilac or purple flowers.

CULTIVATION : Sunny position in ordinary soil, leave undisturbed as long as possible. Propagation by division.

SPECIES AND VARIETIES :

T. adiantifolium. White, 1 ft., June–July.

T. aquilegiæfolium. Lilac, 3 ft., summer ; Europe.

T. brunonianum. Delicate lilac, bright yellow stamens, loose panicles of pendulous flowers, 2½ ft., summer.

T. dipterocarpum. Rosy lilac, 5-7 ft., summer ; W. China. Varieties : *album*, a white ; Hewitt's double, a violet, 4-5 ft.

T. delavayi. Lilac, June–July, 1½-3 ft., China.

THERMOPSIS Order LEGUMINOSÆ

A lupin-like plant bearing masses of short golden-yellow flower spikes in June or July. A rampant grower, must be restricted to its place.

CULTIVATION: Flourishes in light, chalky soil in a sunny position. Propagation by division.

SPECIES:

T. caroliniana. Golden yellow, 4-5 ft., summer; N. America.

T. fabacea. Yellow, 2-3 ft., June–July; Siberia.

T. montana. Yellow, 1-2 ft., summer; N. America.

T. lanceolata like an early Lupin, 2 ft.

TRADESCANTIA (Spider Wort) Order COMMELINACEÆ

Rather unusual plants with foliage like that of a small maize plant and with violet three-sided flowers, borne among the foliage. Useful for the town garden.

CULTIVATION : Sun or partial shade in ordinary soil. Propagation by division.

SPECIES AND VARIETIES :

T. virginiana. Violet, 1-2 ft., May–September ; N. America. Variety *rosea*, deep pink. Other varieties are : Irish Pritchard, white, marked with bright blue ; J. C. Weguelin, clear lavender blue, large flowers ; Leonora, rich violet blue.

TROLLIUS (Globe Flower) Order RANUNCULACEÆ

The "butter balls" of mountain meadows. No herbaceous border should be without them. Very useful for cutting.

CULTIVATION : Full sun or partial shade and plenty of moisture required. Propagation by seed and division.

SPECIES AND VARIETIES : *T. europæus.* Lemon yellow, 1½-2 ft., May–July ; Europe.

T. excelsior. Deep orange, large flowers, 2 ft., May–July ; Europe.

There are numerous named varieties, among them, Fire Globe, a fiery-orange, very large flowers ; Orange Globe, deep orange.

VERBASCUM (Mullein) Order SCROPHULARIACEÆ

Rosettes of crinkly, and often densely woolly, leaves from which arise tall stately spikes of mostly yellow or bronze-coloured flowers. Blue, purple and violet shades are also grown. These are found in the dwarfer kinds. The tall sorts are very useful for the back of a hot, dryish border, or centre of a double-faced border.

CULTIVATION : Sunny position in light, deep, rich soil. Propagation by division.

SPECIES AND VARIETIES : *V. longifolium.* Yellow, 4-6 ft., July-August ; Europe. Varieties : Miss Willmott, white, 6 ft. ; *Olympicum,* yellow, 6 ft. ; Cotswold Queen, pink. *V. phœniceum.* Violet and red, 3 ft., summer ; Europe. *V. thapsiformæ.* Yellow, 5 ft., summer ; Europe.

VERONICA (Speedwell, Bird's Eye) Order SCROPHULARIACEÆ

Many useful border plants. Blue, mauve or white flower spikes. Neat habit. Some of the evergreen, shrubby specimens also frequently seen in herbaceous borders.

CULTIVATION : Sun or semi-shade in ordinary border soil. Propagation by division.

SPECIES AND VARIETIES : *V. gentianoides.* Blue, 8-12 ins., early summer ; S. W. Europe. *V. incana.* Blue, 18 ins., summer ; S. Europe. *V. longifolia.* Lilac blue, 1½-2 ft., August ; Europe. Variety : *subsessilis.* Deep blue. *V. spicata.* Blue, 1-1½ ft., July ; Europe. Varieties : *alba,* white ; *rosea,* pink.

SPECIES AND VARIETIES : *V. virginica.* Pale blue, 4-6 ft., July ; N. America. Varieties : *alba*, white ; *japonica*, pale purple.

VIOLA (Pansy) Order VIOLACEÆ

Pansies are usually grown as bedding plants, whilst some viola species are suitable for the rock garden. The violas are perfectly hardy and there is no reason why some, especially the more quietly coloured ones, should not be given a place in the front of the herbaceous border.

CULTIVATION : Partial shade and a rich, moist soil are best, though pansies will also do well in full sun, provided they need not lack moisture. Cut off dying flowers and shorten straggling shoots. Propagation by cuttings in late summer as the plants will need to be replaced fairly frequently. (See page 67.)

VARIETIES : Jersey Gem, deep violet ; Maggie Mott, a lovely clear lilac mauve ; Moseley Perfection, clear yellow ; Pickering Blue, thundercloud blue ; The Swan, white.

CHAPTER III

Rock Gardens

MAKING AND CARING FOR THE ROCK GARDEN

*

NO garden is too small to have some place for growing the charming little alpine plants which give colour and interest over a very long season.

It is not the duty of this book to give detailed instructions about the construction of large rock gardens needing tons of rock, nor to describe the gradual spreading of rock gardens reclaimed from natural surroundings in which the solid rock appears at intervals, tempting the ardent gardener to extend still farther with the planting of alpines and suitable shrubby subjects.

We must deal with the problem of providing, in a small space, conditions favourable to the healthy growth of the plants we have selected.

CHOOSING THE SITE

POSITION

The first requirement is that the position should be open, well away from trees, sunny and well drained. The shaded positions required by some plants can always be provided by the arrangement of the rocks and slope of the beds.

CLIMATE

The worst enemy of alpine plants is damp. In their native habitat they endure extremes of cold, but there it is the dry cold of frost-bound soil and they are protected from icy winds by a thick layer of snow. In our climate, with its winter months of damp and fog while the thermometer hovers in the lower thirties, many a small plant rots and dies because the woolly covering that nature provides as a protection against frost, acts in exactly the opposite way at temperatures above freezing point because it holds moisture, thereby causing rotting.

145

Soil

The best soil for the purpose is a light loam to which can be added sand, limestone chippings, loam fibre or peat, granite chippings and lime, according to the individual requirements of the plants.

A lime-free soil is preferable, as many of the most beautiful alpines are lime haters. It is a simple matter to add lime to the pockets made for lime lovers, while there is a continual seeping in of lime-laden drainage water to lime-free pockets made up in a limy soil.

What Stone to Use

The choice of rock is often controlled by the supply available at a reasonable cost. But keeping the construction to one type of rock is very important. The piebald effect one sometimes sees when all the stones in the garden, even including brick-bats, are piled in a heap and called a rockery, is to be avoided at all costs.

The most usual rocks employed are limestone, granite and sandstone. These should be weathered to give an established appearance. Granite especially looks very hard and glaring when it arrives from the quarry, and the longer it can be left before being used, the better.

When ordering stone be sure to get varied sizes. A few really large rocks included in the structure give a solidity to the whole. Used as a miniature headland, or the site of a small waterfall, a single rock face gives the illusion of height that is never obtained if several pieces are built up to the same level.

TYPES OF CONSTRUCTION

Where a large area is available for a rock garden it is advisable to get help with the construction, as the lay-out in relation to its surroundings is of great importance, and decisions of that kind are best left to a specialist. This type of rock garden demands an informal setting and must be merged gradually to the formal lay-out by means of lawns, shrubberies and informal borders.

In the medium-sized garden the bank made when a lawn was levelled can be utilised for a rock slope, the rocks being firmly placed to hold up the soil, and the whole construction carried out rather on the lines of a dry wall, though less formally. (See illustration facing page 152.) The face should be broken by bays which will provide different aspects for planting.

If the garden is flat, do not try to make a high rock garden.

It will only look ridiculous, and probably be rudely called " the pudding " or " dog's grave." A slight slope can generally be made, and if backed by a judicious planting of small flowering shrubs, far enough away to avoid starving the alpines by rooting into the rock garden, the unnatural appearance of the artificial mound will be concealed.

Alpines can be utilised in other ways in the garden, always provided that good drainage is given. As an edging to borders of tall flowers the stronger growing rock plants are invaluable, and we all know the charm of a paved walk or terrace, carefully planted with suitable low-growing subjects.

THE ACTUAL BUILDING

Start with the lowest layer of rock and get the " key " stones placed. Before setting a rock, examine it carefully and decide how it will best fit in with the general scheme. An " eye for a stone " is an innate gift, but with practice a feeling for the right way to place each piece can be developed. As the work progresses be sure that the soil is well rammed into the crevices of the rocks. Air pockets left during construction will account for a large number of the deaths among the plants later on. Keep in mind the whole time that the rock garden is primarily a home for plants, and arrange pockets and crevices suitable to receive them as you go along. If you plan to have miniature precipices it is a good thing to have your plants handy at the time of building and to include them in the layers of rock as you build. In this way the roots can be spread out at full length, to connect with the main mass of soil in which the rocks are built, and get established at once.

The rocks, when in position, should look natural, not standing on end in the soil like almonds on a plum pudding. A good tip, if you are a beginner, is to let the rock drop to the ground and it will generally settle itself on a natural face and so help you to determine how best to use it.

Arrange paths and stepping stones as you go along, to blend with the general scheme, and make the job of weeding as simple as possible.

When the construction work is finished, leave it alone as long as possible for the soil and rock to settle down and consolidate. It is often necessary to add extra soil where it has sunk too low after the first rains, indicating that the job of firming each layer has been neglected. On other occasions, a whole rock face disappears under an inch of soil. In this case you have to decide whether removing the soil or raising the stone will give the finished line you desire.

PLANTING

The majority of alpine nurseries these days supply pot-grown plants and these can be planted out at any season. For the main bulk of the stuff, and for any shrubs or dwarf conifers, the best time is September, while for the tenderer subjects, or those that die down early in the season, it is wise to delay planting and dividing until the first signs of growth appear in the spring. In spite of their miniature growth, alpines have very long roots and many a tiny little cushion is sending a network of roots literally yards deep into shaly soil looking for food. Thus it will be seen that it is necessary to make really deep holes when planting, and to spread the roots out well before firming them in.

It is sometimes difficult to get plants established in the chinks of rock where they give such good effect. These position are often planted during construction, as already mentioned, but if the job has to be done later try putting in a little bunch of seedlings. Provided there is a spell of good-growing weather several little plants will generally get well rooted into the crack and form grand sturdy stuff. Another method of populating a horizontal crack is to sprinkle a mixture of seed and sandy soil along the crack and leave nature to do the rest.

The dwarf conifers, which are such a popular feature in the small rock garden, are not always easy to get established. The usual cause of failure is drought; the stiff little needles do not flag like an ordinary leaf would, and remind us of the need for watering. The first sign we have of the trouble is a browning of the growing tips, and by that time it is too late to avert the tragedy. From April, or in some seasons even earlier, right through until the soil gets its autumn rain, newly-planted shrubs will need occasional heavy waterings. In many cases the little trees are planted on sloping ground from which the water runs off before penetrating. To avoid this, arrange a stone three parts buried in the soil, on the lower side of the tree, and this will serve to hold the water and direct it down to the roots. Once well established there should be no need to bother about the water supply another year.

CARE OF THE ROCK GARDEN

As soon as growth starts in early spring, get out to your rock garden and have a general clear up. Remove the various protective devices (the glass, the twigs, the piles of cinders and leaves), and examine the new shoots for diseases and pests. Now is a good time to make war on slugs ; don't wait till the shoots have been eaten. Give a thorough application of one of the Meta slug baits at once. Many a small plant fails to reach the sunlight owing to its tender shoots being beloved by the small black slugs that work underground, and its loss is more often than not put down to frost, while the real villain of the piece is left alive to attack more treasures.

Early spring is also the best time to divide the dwarf campanulas, armerias, asperulas and dianthus. Do not be over-anxious to replace " dead " plants. It is surprising how often a very dried up little scrap will burst into leaf, long after it has been given up for lost.

After the whole garden has been thoroughly cleared give a top dressing. The material for this must vary in the different pockets. For lime lovers, nothing looks better than fine limestone chippings. These give a good setting for small saxifrages, androsace and drabas as well as helping to keep down weeds. For gentians, lithospermum, ericas, etc., a mixture of fine peat and gravel is the best top dressing. It should be gently worked in among the stems and will encourage fresh rooting.

The next main job will be a drastic cutting back of the spreading plants. This should be done immediately after flowering. Plants like aubretia are kept in good order by an annual trimming. This will prevent the appearance of lots of little seedlings of various washy shades that are so hard to throw away, and yet which spoil the general colour effects. An annual trimming also keeps the plants neat and it only takes a couple of weeks for the newly-cut-back plant to be a green cushion once more, ready to give a slight second crop of flowers.

Helianthemum and campanulas also benefit tremendously by a hard cutting back. Don't be tempted to leave this operation too late ; other plants are coming into flower all the time, and the gap left soon fills in with a new plant.

The final stage is getting ready for the winter again. Another good dose of slug bait, and at this season a sprinkle of 5% D.D.T. powder along any cracks in the rocks where woodlice collect. Then a thorough weeding and cutting back of dead shoots. Renew old labels and mark the positions of all the plants which disappear under ground for the winter. Arrange protection for the tender subjects, putting panes of glass over the woolly-leaved plants that cannot stand the wet. Dig and prepare any empty patches ready for planting in spring.

And so with the heaths still giving colour we can let the rock garden be at rest for a very short time, for the earliest saxifrages and crocuses will be flowering in a few weeks.

THE MORAINE

For those who wish to specialise in the more difficult plants that will not thrive in the ordinarily constructed rock garden, there is always the moraine. This is a reproduction, as near as we can give it, of the conditions that exist at the edge of a glacier where many exquisite small plants are found growing in what would seem to be barren shale. The humus content is practically nil and, at a good depth below the surface, there is a huge supply of water during the spring months, from the melting snows farther up

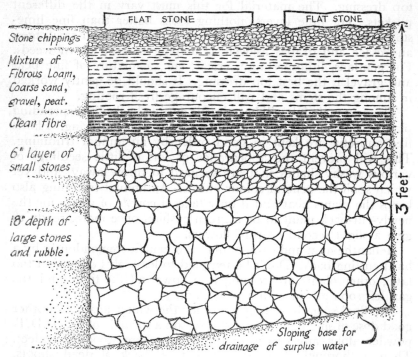

Fig. 15   Section of Moraine

the mountains. To approximate to these conditions we excavate the soil to a depth of about 3 ft., leaving the base sloping to drain off surplus water. (See Fig. 15.) Then fill in 18 ins. with large stone and rubble. Over this comes a layer of finer stone about 6 ins. deep. Next, a covering of the clean fibre from good loam or some peat fibre ; this is to prevent the finer topping layer from falling between the stones and hindering drainage. Now comes a layer of a mixture of sieved fibrous loam, coarse sand, gravel and peat. Finish off with a layer of small stone chippings—ones that pass through an inch-gauge sieve are a good size. Let a few large flat stones appear on the surface. As well as being useful for walking on they also afford a favourable root run for many of the plants.

In the early days of artificial moraine construction, complicated and costly systems of underground irrigation were included in the schemes, but it has gradually been ascertained that these are quite unnecessary and that an ample water supply is maintained by the natural rise of water from the average subsoil, and retained by the drainage stones to provide the cool root run which is the ultimate end of the whole moraine. For a deep-water supply with a dry surface condition is what is aimed at for the plants.

INCREASING YOUR PLANTS

In the rock garden many of the most popular and colourful plants are readily increased by division. In fact many of them only give the best results when divided annually to avoid overcrowding. Others produce little rooted side shoots which can be pulled off and planted straight out in the open, with a little extra sand in each case. More can be treated as layers and a side shoot is pegged down into sandy soil and a flat stone laid over the stem to preserve moisture, later this rooted shoot can be cut off and planted out in its new site.

An unheated frame with 4 ins. of sharp, clean sand over a layer of coarse drainage stones will provide a suitable place for the striking of cuttings of most of the rock plants in common use to-day.

The cheapest way of raising a large batch of plants is undoubtedly by seed. This must be treated in a spartan fashion to get the best results. Most of the seed is very small indeed, and the tiny seedlings damp off easily if allowed to get soft by being grown in a heated house. Sow the seed thinly and prick out as soon as the seedlings are large enough to handle. Where space permits it is always worth while to keep pans of seed a second year if they have failed to germinate the first. Quite often if the pan has stood out all winter in the frost and snow, the tiny seedlings will appear early in the spring and make fine sturdy little plants very quickly.

A FEW CONIFERS AND SHRUBS SUITABLE FOR THE SMALL ROCK GARDEN

Abies balsamea Hudsonica. A neat little " Christmas tree " with short needles.

Cistus crispus, Sunset. A true rock rose. Sage-green leaves. Mauve-pink flowers.

Cistus purpureus, Brilliancy. Huge pink flowers with chocolate blotches.

Cotoneaster horizontalis perpusilla. Prostrate growth covered with sealing-wax berries each year.

Cupressus pisifera plumosa pygmæa. A slow-growing little tree, soft, green rounded appearance.

Daphne Blagayana. Fragrant white flower. Needs a lime-free soil.

Daphne Cneorum. Clusters of pink scented flowers on low green bush.

Erica carnea, and all its varieties. Has the advantage of giving colour during the winter months.

Erica mediterranea. Upright growing heath useful as a background in lime-free soils.

Genista tinctoria flore pleno. Very low-growing little broom, bearing double yellow flowers.

Juniperus hibernica compressa. Dwarf pyramids of blue-green. The slowest growing of the Junipers.

Juniperus sabina tamariscifolia. Spreading branches of grey-green, a lovely feature in the winter garden.

Potentilla fruticosa. Silvery leaves. Large yellow " strawberry " flowers.

Rosa spinosissima. The Scotch rose.

28. *A rock garden showing natural stratification*

29. *A wild garden*

30. *Preparing a garden pond*

31. *A water garden*

A LIST OF WORTHWHILE ROCK PLANTS

*

ACÆNA Order ROSACEÆ

Suitable for paving and steps.

CULTIVATION : Ordinary soil. Sun or shade. Increased by division.

SPECIES : *A. Buchanani.* Pale silvery-green leaves. Inconspicuous flowers in July and August, 2 ins.
A. microphylla. Bronze leaves, very decorative scarlet spiny seed heads, in July and August, 3 ins.
A. microphylla inermis. Bronze leaves. Flowers inconspicuous, 3 ins.

ACANTHOLIMON (Prickly Thrift) Order PLUMBAGINACEÆ

CULTIVATION : Light sandy soil. Well-drained, sunny position. Flat-rooted side shoots.

SPECIES : *A. glumaceum.* Forms a rounded clump like a green hedgehog. Flowers light rose in June, 6 ins.

ACHILLEA (Yarrow, Milfoil) Order COMPOSITÆ

CULTIVATION : Apart from the flowers the silver-leaved forms make excellent carpeters between bulbs. Soil ordinary. Sun or half-shade. Increased by division.

SPECIES : *A. argentea.* Silvery leaf. Flowers white in June, 6 ins.
King Edward. Grey-green leaf. Flowers pale yellow from May till September, 9 ins.
A. tomentosa. Green ferny leaf. Flowers strong yellow in July, 9 ins.

ÆTHIONEMA Order CRUCIFERÆ

CULTIVATION : A neat little bushy plant. Light well-drained soil Full sun. Seed. Cuttings of named varieties.

SPECIES : *A. armenum.* Long spikes of pale pink flowers. May, 9 ins.
Warley Rose. Covered with round heads of deep pink, April–May, 6 ins.
Warley Ruber. Deeper colour than the above, but not quite such a good habit. May, 6 ins.

AGATHÆA Order COMPOSITÆ

CULTIVATION : A shrubby blue daisy. Sandy soil. Full sun. Not quite hardy, but easily propagated by cuttings. Excellent near the sea.

SPECIES : *A. cælestis.* Clear blue daisies produced over a very long season, June–August, 12-18 ins.

AJUGA (Bugle) Order LABIATÆ

CULTIVATION : A useful carpeter for sun or shade, in any soil. Increase by division.

SPECIES : *A. reptans purpurea.* Leaves a reddish purple. Flower spikes blue, May–June, 6 ins.

ALYSSUM (Gold Dust) Order CRUCIFERÆ

CULTIVATION : Light limy soil. Full sun. Also suitable for dry walls. Increased by seed, or cuttings of double-flowered forms.

SPECIES AND VARIETIES : *A. idæum.* Dwarf prostrate silver leaves. Yellow flowers. May–June, 2 ins. Suitable for moraine. *A. saxatile.* Strong yellow flowers, in April–May. The well-known Gold Dust, 9 ins. Varieties : *citrinum*, lemon-yellow form of the above, 9 ins. ; Dudley Neville, apricot flowered hybrid ; *flore pleno*, double flowered form, 9 ins. *A. spinosum roseum.* An uncommon little shrublet. The flowers, a dirty pink, fall off and leave a close network of spines which remain silvery white all through the winter, June, 12 ins.

ANDROSACE Order PRIMULACEÆ

CULTIVATION : Well-drained soil, with ample supply of sharp stones. Full sun. Winter protection with a pane of glass. Suitable for moraine. Increase by cuttings, division or seed.

SPECIES AND VARIETIES : *A. lactæa.* Green rosettes. Flowers pure white, 3 ins., June–August. *A. lanuginosa.* Silvery prostrate foliage. Flower heads pink, 6-in. stem, July. Variety : *Leichtlini*, as above. Flowers white with red eye. *A. pyrenaica.* Miniature grey-green hummocks. Flowers white, borne close to the leaves in April, 1 in. ; moraine or alpine house.

SPECIES AND VARIETIES : *A. sarmentosa.* Hairy rosettes, umbels of pink flowers, May–July, 4 ins. Varieties : *Chumbyi*, as above. Rosy red ; *Watkinsii*, as above, deep pink. *A. sempervivoides.* Rosettes of leaves free from hairs making the plant a little more tolerant of damp. Flowers brilliant pink, April, 3 ins.

ANEMONE Order RANUNCULACEÆ

CULTIVATION : Well-drained soil rich in humus. Sun. Increased by seed.

SPECIES AND VARIETIES : *A. Pulsatilla.* Ferny foliage. Rich purple flowers in April and May, 12 ins. Varieties : *alba*, white form of the above ; *rubra*, wine red ; and several named hybrids. Always select the best forms when raising from seed.

A. vernalis. Large silver-grey flower, the outer petals covered with silky hair. May–June, 4 ins. Best grown in the moraine.

ANTENNARIA Order COMPOSITÆ

CULTIVATION : A useful carpeter. Soil ordinary. Sun or half-shade. Increased by division.

SPECIES : *A. dioica rosea.* Neat green foliage, flowers small pink, June, 6 ins.
A. tomentosa. Foliage silvery. Flowers white, summer, 6 ins.

AQUILEGIA (Columbine) Order RANUNCULACEÆ

CULTIVATION : Ordinary well-drained soil. Sun or semi-shade. Seed.

SPECIES : *A. alpina.* Clear blue flowers, May–July. Suitable for naturalising where there is plenty of space, 18 ins.
A. escalcarata. Ferny leaf. Small flowers of an unusual brown purple, 6 ins, May–June.
A. pyrenaica. Like *alpina* only dwarf, 6 ins. Suitable for moraine.

ARABIS Order CRUCIFERÆ

CULTIVATION : Useful for carpeting, edging, dry walls and banks. Ordinary well-drained soil. Sun. Cuttings and division.

SPECIES AND
VARIETIES :
A. albida flore pleno. Low green leaves. Heads of double white flowers. April–June, 9 ins. Variety : *variegata*, leaves liberally marked with yellow. Flowers single, white.
A. blepharophylla. A doubtful perennial easily raised from seed. Flowers rich purplish pink, 8 ins., May–June.

ARENARIA Order CARYOPHYLLACEÆ

CULTIVATION : Increase by seed and division.

SPECIES :
A. balearica. A carpet of little green leaves starred with white flowers. May–June, 1 in. Moist positions in semi-shade where it will clothe bare rock face.
A. montana. Light soil and sunny position on the rock garden. Forms a mat of wiry leaves. Large white flowers. June–July, 6 ins.
A. purpurascens. Shiny green leaves, lilac starry flowers in June, 2 ins. Rock garden or moraine.

ARMERIA (Thrift) Order PLUMBAGINACEÆ

CULTIVATION : Light sandy soil. Full sun. Increase by division in spring.

SPECIES AND
VARIETIES :
A. cæspitosa. Neat little tufts. Pink flowers in April–May, 3 ins. Suitable for moraine.
A. corsica. An unusual terra-cotta flowered Thrift. June–August, 6 ins.
A. maritima var. *Laucheana.* Bright pink free-flowering form of the common Thrift, 6 ins., June–July. Variety Vindictive, flowers strong red, 6 ins.

ARTEMISIA Order COMPOSITÆ

CULTIVATION : Light soil. Full sun. Cuttings and division.

SPECIES :
A. lantana pedemontana. Silver-grey finely-cut leaves. Flowers inconspicuous. Form a lovely carpet 3 ins. deep.

ASTER Order COMPOSITÆ

CULTIVATION : Ordinary soil, sunny.

SPECIES AND
VARIETIES :
A. alpinus. Mauve daisy flowers, May–June, 6 ins. Variety : Nancy Perry, pink flowered.
A. diplostephioides. Strong green basal rosette. Large

purple flower with distinct yellow eye. June, 9-12 ins.

A. Thompsoniana. Sprays of clear mauve-blue flowers. Late summer to autumn, 9 ins. Slow growing.

Many of the *Aster amellus* and *Aster pygmæus* included in herbaceous lists are invaluable in the rock garden where space is available.

ASTILBE Order SAXIFRAGACEÆ

CULTIVATION : Moist soil rich in humus. Partial shade. Division.

SPECIES : *A. chinensis pumila.* Ferny leaves, stems covered with reddish-brown hairs. Flower spikes of rosy mauve. July–September, 12 ins.

Peter Pan. Neat little hybrid. Flowers pink, 9 ins.

A. simplicifolia. Shiny leaved feathery heads of bluish-pink flowers. July–August, 9 ins.

AUBRIETIA Order CRUCIFERÆ

CULTIVATION : The well-known carpeter. Spring, 2-3 ins. Light well-drained soil. Full sun. Excellent for walls and paving. Cuttings of named varieties. Seed : a mixture will do.

SPECIES AND
VARIETIES : Carnival. Very large deep violet purple.

Church Knowle. Pale blue with white eye.

Crimson King. Large red purple.

A. deltoidea. Purple.

Dr. Mules. Still one of the best real purples.

A. gloriosa. Very large pale pink.

Gurgedyke. Strong red purple.

Mikado. Strange dusty rose purple.

Red Carnival. Good strong red.

A. variegata argentea. Leaves marked with white, very neat grower.

A. variegata aurea. Leaves edged with golden yellow. Flowers pale mauve.

Vindictive. Vigorous grower, good crimson.

BELLIS Order COMPOSITÆ

CULTIVATION : Soil well-drained, good loam. Sun or half-shade. Needs frequent division to give best results.

SPECIES AND
VARIETIES : *B. perennis* with its varieties : Alice, soft double pink, 4 ins. ; Dresden China, double pink, 3 ins. ;

VARIETIES : Rob Roy, double crimson, large flowers, 4 ins. ;
Rose Queen, double deep rose, 4 ins, June.

CALAMINTHA Order LABIATÆ

CULTIVATION : Soil ordinary, well drained. Full sun. Cuttings
and division.

SPECIES : *C. alpina.* Neat little sub-shrub with aromatic
leaves. Flowers purple in June, 6 ins.
C. grandiflora. Larger than the above. Flowers pink,
June, 12 ins.

CALANDRINIA Order PORTULACACEÆ

CULTIVATION : Well-drained gritty soil. Sun. Seed.

SPECIES : *C. umbellata.* Showy magenta flowers with brilliant
yellow anthers, 9 ins., moraine. Only a biennial,
but worth planting for its brilliant colour from
July–September.

CALCEOLARIA Order SCROPHULARIACEÆ

CULTIVATION: Well-drained but not dry soil. Shade. Division.

SPECIES : *C. biflora.* Flat rosette from which rises golden
yellow flower on 6-in. stems, in spring.
C. polyrrhiza. Creeping roots. Deep yellow flowers,
July–August, 6 ins.
C. tenella. Bright green carpet on rocks in semi-
shade. Yellow flowers speckled with crimson,
summer, 2 ins.

CAMPANULA Order CAMPANULACEÆ

CULTIVATION : Good well-drained soil. Though some will flower
in shady positions they do better in sun. Division.

SPECIES AND
VARIETIES :
C. Allionii. Prostrate plant. Large deep, purple
bells, June–August, 3 ins., moraine.
C. arvatica. Upstanding starry flowers of deep
violet, July, 2 ins., moraine.
C. Bellardii (pusilla). Low mat of leaves with blue
harebell flowers, 4 ins., spring. Specially suitable
for paving or moraine. Variety : Miranda, large
flowers of pale silvery blue.
C. carpatica. Varieties : Isobel, big flat saucers of
dark purple-blue, June–August, 9 ins. Strong

SPECIES AND
VARIETIES : grower ; Riverslea, deep blue erect cups ; White Star, pure white cup.

C. garganica. Prostrate trailing stems covered with starry blue flowers for a long season, 3 ins. Varieties: *hirsuta*, a grey-leaved form, with pale flowers ; W. H. Paine, beautiful violet-blue stars with white eye.

C. kewensis. A small-growing wiry little plant with dark blue flowers, July, 3 ins., moraine.

C. Portenschlagiana (muralis). One of the most popular campanulas, and deservedly so having a very long flowering season and giving a show of blue flowers even in shady positions, 6 ins.

C. Poscharskiana. Makes strong clumps of green leaves. Long trailing reddish stems of lavender-blue stars. Summer into autumn, 8 ins. Excellent in walls.

C. pulla. A charming little plant with 3-in. stems, bearing pendulous blooms of a metallic purple in June, moraine.

C. turbinata. Hairy greyish leaves. Large blue saucers. Summer, 9 ins. Variety : *albescens*, silvery counterpart of the above.

C. warleyensis. Very double-flowered china blue, July, 6 ins. Scarce in commerce. Worth a place in the moraine.

CERASTIUM Order CARYOPHYLLACEÆ

CULTIVATION : The well-known Snow-in-Summer. Admirable for covering walls and dry places in full sun, where its rampant growth will not smother more delicate plants.

SPECIES : *C. tomentosum.* Leaves more covered with white hairs than the commoner *C. Biebersteinii*, and not quite so rampant. Flowers white, June–July, 6 ins.

CHEIRANTHUS Order CRUCIFERÆ

CULTIVATION : Ordinary soil. Sun. Cuttings from named varieties.
SPECIES AND
VARIETIES : Harpur Crewe. Double golden-yellow flowers in spring, 15 ins. If cut back will give second bloom. Moonlight. Clear lemon yellow, 9 ins.

C. mutabilis. Mixed bronze and purple, 9 ins.

Rufus. Beautiful fiery red-orange, 9 ins.

CHRYSANTHEMUM Order COMPOSITÆ

CULTIVATION : Well-drained loam. Sun. Cuttings or seed.

SPECIES : *C. Mawii.* Silver-grey ferny leaves. Flowers in shades of pink, borne on delicate stems over a long season. Summer and autumn, 12-15 ins., moraine.

CODONOPSIS Order CAMPANULACEÆ

CULTIVATION : Gritty soil. Sun. Seed.

SPECIES : *C. ovata.* Prostrate stems bearing pale blue bells, interestingly marked on the inside with dark veining, June–July, 8 ins.

CONVOLVULUS Order CONVOLVULACEÆ

CULTIVATION : Light, well-drained soil. Sun. Cuttings.

SPECIES : *C. mauritanicus.* Though only hardy in very sheltered positions, this plant is worth its place in the garden for its clear blue flowers borne on trailing stems, July–September, 9 ins.

COTULA Order COMPOSITÆ

CULTIVATION : A useful carpeter, growing as it does in almost any position. Division.

SPECIES : *C. squalida,* 2-3 ins. Even the name tells that it has no claim to beauty, but it does cover the soil, and that very quickly.

COTYLEDON Order CRASSULACEÆ

CULTIVATION : Sandy. Sun or semi-shade. Division and cuttings, seed.

SPECIES : *C. simplicifolius.* Fleshy leaves. Pendulous racemes of clear yellow flowers, April–June, 6 ins.

CYANANTHUS Order CAMPANULACEÆ

CULTIVATION : Lime-free soil, with extra peat and sand. Out of the full glare of the sun. Seed or cuttings.

SPECIES : *C. Farreri.* Soft green mat of small leaves. Terminal deep blue flowers, July–August, 6 ins.
C. lobatus. Leaves deeper green. Flowers large dark

SPECIES :   blue, 4 ins., August. Both plants much beloved by
slugs. Lime-free moraine.

DELPHINIUM Order RANUNCULACEÆ

CULTIVATION : Rich loam. Sun. Seed. Although the Belladonna
types are suitable for the large rock garden they
will be found too tall in most places.
SPECIES :   *D. nudicaule.* Orange scarlet, June–July, 12 ins.
Disappears completely in winter.
D. tatsienense. A wonderful brilliant blue in its best
forms, 18 ins., summer.

DIANTHUS Order CARYOPHYLLACEÆ

CULTIVATION : Gritty soil. Sun. Division, cuttings, seed.
SPECIES AND   It is impossible to include all the lovely little plants
VARIETIES :   in this huge family of which so many are suitable
for rock garden work.
D. Allwoodii alpinus, var. Apollo. A neat-growing
free-flowering little hybrid blooming continuously
all through the summer. Good pink, 4 ins.
Another variety is Mars. As the above with strong
crimson flowers. Both do well in rock garden or
moraine.
D. alpinus. Deep rose, June–July, 3 ins., moraine.
D. arvernensis. Grey mat. Pale pink flowers, May–
June, 3 ins. Lovely hanging over a wall.
D. cæsius. The Cheddar pink, and all its many
hybrids, named and otherwise, make welcome
patches of neat grey green all the year round with
the brave summer show of flowers both double and
single in a full range of colour from pure white to
darkest red, 3-6 ins.
D. deltoides. And its many varieties. Green or
brownish-green leaves. Flowers white, pink, or red,
summer, 4-6 ins.
D. neglectus. Narrow leaves. Flowers carmine,
reverse of petal buff. June–July, 4 ins., moraine.

DOUGLASIA Order PRIMULACEÆ

CULTIVATION : Well-drained position in the sun. Division and seed.
SPECIES :   *D. vitaliana.* Fine leaved grey-green mat. Golden
flowers in spring, 3 ins., moraine.

DRABA Order CRUCIFERÆ

CULTIVATION : Light sandy soil. Full sun. Seed and division.

SPECIES : *D. aizoides*. Green thorny rosettes. Golden-yellow flowers in spring, 3 ins., moraine.

D. pyrenaica. Low-growing tufts. Green leaves covered with pale lilac-scented flowers in spring, 1 in., moraine.

DRYAS Order ROSACEÆ

CULTIVATION : Sandy soil. Sun or semi-shade. Cuttings and division.

SPECIES AND VARIETIES : *D. octopetala*. Prostrate mat of shiny dark-green leaves. White flowers, June–August, 6 ins. Fluffy seed heads prolong the interest until later in the season. Variety *grandiflora* is a freer flowering form of the above, cuttings root more readily.

EDRAIANTHUS (syn. *Wahlenbergia*) Order CAMPANULACEÆ

CULTIVATION : Well-drained stony soil. Sun. Seed and cuttings.

SPECIES : *E. serpyllifolia*. Prostrate small stems ending in large satiny purple campanula-like flowers. May, 3 ins., moraine.

ERIGERON Order COMPOSITÆ

CULTIVATION : Ordinary light soil. Sun. Seed and division.

SPECIES : *E. leiomerus*. A really dwarf little daisy. Pale violet flowers, June, 3 ins.

E. mucronatus. A wiry little plant covered all summer with pink and white daisies, 6-12 ins. Excellent for seeding itself into cracks of rock or paving.

ERINUS Order SCROPHULARIACEÆ

CULTIVATION : Light soil. Sun. Seed.

SPECIES AND VARIETIES : *E. alpinus*. A useful little plant in all rock-work, walls and paving. Seeds itself freely, but never becomes a nuisance. Rosy pink flowers, 3 ins. Varieties : *albus*, white form of the above ; Dr. Hanele, rich ruby red.

ERITRICHIUM Order BORAGINACEÆ

CULTIVATION : Lime-free soil. Sun. Seed.

SPECIES :   *E. strictum.* Glaucous green leaves. China-blue flowers, 2-3 ins., summer. Difficult to cultivate, moraine.

ERODIUM Order GERANIACEÆ

CULTIVATION : Light soil. Sun. Seed and cuttings.

SPECIES :   *E. chamædryoides roseus.* Flat rosettes of green. Covered all summer with pink starry flowers, 2 ins. *E. chrysanthum.* Ferny grey-green leaves. Pale yellow crane's bill flowers. June–September, 6 ins. *E. macradenum.* Pink flowers with dark blotches on the lower petals, 6 ins., summer.

GAZANIA Order COMPOSITÆ

CULTIVATION : Sandy soil. Full sun. Seed and cuttings. Although these plants are not hardy except near the sea their brilliant colour over a long period justifies their inclusion in this list. Cuttings strike freely and a supply of duplicates can be kept in a frame to replace winter losses. New named varieties are being produced all the time.

SPECIES :   *G. splendens.* Trailing shoots of thick green leaves, large daisy flowers of clear orange with black and white disc. May–September, 6 ins.

GENTIANA Order GENTIANACEÆ

CULTIVATION: Varied soils, well drained. Sun and shade. Seed and division.

SPECIES :   *G. acaulis.* Close pale foliage. Huge trumpets of prussian blue, April–May, 4 ins. *G. Farreri.* Grass-like leaves. Trumpets of sky-blue, September–October, 3 ins. Lime-free soil, rich in humus. *G. septemfida.* Prostrate shoots ending in clusters of lavender-blue flowers, August–September, 6 ins. *G. sino-ornata.* Narrow shiny leaves. Trailing stems bearing large brilliant blue trumpets late into the autumn, 3 ins. Lime-free soil and good water supply. *G. verna.* The little gentian that figures in all Swiss pictures. Upstanding flowers of clear blue in spring, 2 ins., moraine.

GERANIUM Order GERANIACEÆ

CULTIVATION : Sandy soil. Sun. Seed and cuttings.

SPECIES AND VARIETIES :
G. argenteum. Beautiful silver foliage. Large rose-pink flowers in June, 6 ins.

G. napuligerum (G. Farreri). Pale pink flowers with large black anthers, June–July, 4 ins., moraine.

G. sanguineum. Magenta flowers on spreading stems, May–September, 9 ins. Variety : *lancastriense,* pale pink variety of the above.

G. subcaulescens. Brilliant carmine flowers with black anthers, July–October, 6 ins., moraine.

GEUM Order ROSACEÆ

CULTIVATION : Any garden soil. Division.

SPECIES : *G. Borisii.* Brilliant orange flowers produced in succession all through the season, 9-12 ins. Well worth a place in the larger garden, but too coarse growing for the small bed.

GLOBULARIA Order GLOBULARIACEÆ

CULTIVATION : Sandy soil. Sun. Division.

SPECIES : *G. bellidifolia.* Neat carpet of shiny dark-green leaves. Round heads of powder-blue in June, 3 ins.

G. trichosantha. As the above in a size larger—the flower stems being 6 ins. Does best in semi-shade.

GYPSOPHILA Order CARYOPHYLLACEÆ

CULTIVATION : Light loam. Sun. Cuttings.

SPECIES : *G. fratensis.* An invaluable little trailing plant, clear pink flowers, June–July, 3 ins.

HELIANTHEMUM Order CISTACEÆ

CULTIVATION : Light good loam. Sun. Cuttings of named varieties and seed. The " Rock Rose " is too well known to need description.

SPECIES : Many lovely hybrids include : Ben Alder, terracotta ; Ben Dearg, rich flame ; Ben Lawers, pale orange ; Ben Lomond, rose madder ; Ben Nevis, yellow, orange eye ; Ben Venue, huntsman pink. Also various double-flowered forms, 3-4 ins., June.

HELICHRYSUM Order COMPOSITÆ

CULTIVATION : Shady soil. Sun. Division.

SPECIES :   *H. frigidum.* Green leaves. Tiny " everlasting " flowers, July–August, 3 ins., moraine.

HEUCHERA Order SAXIFRAGACEÆ

Where space allows, the inclusion of these herbaceous plants is more than justified. For details, see pages 124-125.

HYPERICUM Order HYPERICACEÆ

CULTIVATION : Light soil. Full sun. Seed. Cuttings.
SPECIES :   *H. Coris.* A fine-leaved little bushlet, bearing golden flowers all summer, 6 ins.
H. cuneatum. Trailing brittle stem, covered with brilliant red flower buds opening in yellow flowers. June–September, 1 in., moraine.
H. fragile. A neat little shrublet if kept well cut back after flowering. Large golden-yellow flowers. June–September, 9 ins.
H. reptans. Trailing. Yellow flowers, June-August, 3-4 ins. Half-shade.

IBERIS Order CRUCIFERÆ

CULTIVATION : Ordinary soil. Sun. Cuttings.
SPECIES AND   *I. sempervirens.* Varieties : Little Gem, neat little
VARIETIES :   evergreen. White flowers, May–June, 6 ins. ; Snowflake, larger than the above, makes a pure white patch from April–May, 12 ins.

IRIS Order IRIDACEÆ

CULTIVATION : Good loam. Sun. Division.
SPECIES :   *I. cristata.* A dwarf, bearing blue flowers marked with gold. April–May, 3 ins., moraine.
I. pumila. All its named hybrids are excellent for the rock garden, April 3-8 ins., Lilac-purple.

LEONTOPODIUM Order COMPOSITÆ

CULTIVATION : Well-drained soil. Sun.
SPECIES :   *L. alpinium.* The well-known Swiss Edelweiss or " Flannel Flower," white, June–August, 6 ins.

LINARIA Order SCROPHULARIACEÆ

CULTIVATION : Sandy soil. Sun. Seed.
SPECIES AND   *L. alpina.* Violet and orange flowers, May–July,

VARIETIES :   3 ins. Variety : *rosea*, pink and orange. Both seed freely in rocks or moraine.

L. origanifolia. Upstanding growth, mauve flowers all summer, 6 ins.

LINUM Order LINACEÆ

CULTIVATION : Well-drained soil. Sun. Cuttings.

SPECIES :   *L. alpinum.* A prostrate little blue flax, May–June, 2 ins.

L. arboreum. Neat little bushlet, covered with large yellow flowers, May–July, 12 ins. One of the best rock plants.

LITHOSPERMUM Order BORAGINACEÆ

CULTIVATION : Well-drained lime-free soil. Sun. Cuttings.

SPECIES AND VARIETIES :   *L. intermedium.* Shrubby growth not unlike lavender, bearing 6-in. stems of bright blue flowers in May. *L. prostratum*, Heavenly Blue, 2-3 ins. Continuous succession of blue flowers where it is happy. Hates lime. Variety : Grace Ward, slightly larger form of the above.

LYCHNIS Order CARYOPHYLLACEÆ

CULTIVATION : Well-drained soil. Sun. Seed and cuttings.

SPECIES :   *L. Lagascæ rosea.* Little pink flowers, May–August, 4 ins.

L. Viscaria flore pleno. Free flowering. Strong pink, May–June, 12 ins.

MORISIA Order CRUCIFERÆ

CULTIVATION : Dry, poor soil. Sun. Root cuttings.

SPECIES :   *M. hypogæa.* Flat rosette. Yellow flowers, March–April, 1 in., moraine.

NEPETA Order LABIATÆ

Included in herbaceous plants (see page 131), but frequently useful in rock garden, wall and paving.

ŒNOTHERA Order ONAGRACEÆ

CULTIVATION : Good loam. Sun. Cuttings.

SPECIES :   *O. riparia.* A lovely spreading net of wiry stems covered with large yellow flowers all summer, 9 ins.

Rock Gardens

OMPHALODES Order BORAGINACEÆ

CULTIVATION : Good loam. Sun and shade. Seed and cuttings.
SPECIES :   *O. cappadocica.* Clear blue forget-me-not flowers in
succession over a long season, 9 ins.
O. Luciliæ. Leaves blue green. Flowers pale china
blue, 4 ins., summer. Well-drained position in
moraine.

ORIGANUM Order LABIATÆ

CULTIVATION : Light soil. Sun. Division.
SPECIES :   *O. hybridum.* Purple hop-like flowers on 9-in. stems,
August–September.

OROBUS Order LEGUMINOSÆ

CULTIVATION : Light soil. Sun. Seed.
SPECIES :   *O. vernus.* A useful little pea-flower. Purple, April–
May, 9 ins.

PAROCHETUS Order LEGUMINOSÆ

CULTIVATION : Moist well-drained soil. Sun. Seed and runners.
SPECIES :   *P. communis.* A little clover-like steel-blue pea-
flower in summer, 4 ins. Needs winter protection
in some districts.

PENTSTEMON Order SCROPHULARIACEÆ

CULTIVATION : Well-drained light soil. Sun. Cuttings.
SPECIES :   *P. Roezlii.* Dwarf shrublet. Clear red flowers in
May–June, 6 ins. Hard to obtain the true plant.
Moraine or rock garden.
P. Scouleri. Small bush. Clear lilac flowers, May–
June, 12 ins.
Six Hills Hybrid. Lower growing. Rosy-purple
flowers, May–June.

PHLOX Order POLEMONIACEÆ

CULTIVATION : Well-drained soil. Sun. Cuttings.
SPECIES AND   *P. amœna.* Low growing. Pink flowers, April–May,
VARIETIES :   4 ins. Protect from slugs.
P. Douglasii. Neat cushions of spiny leaves covered
with lilac stars in May, 2 ins.
P. subulata. Of its many-named varieties the best

VARIETIES : are : G. F. Wilson, mauve blue ; Margery, good pink ; Samson, rose pink, red eye ; The Bride, white, pink eye, May, 4-6 ins.

POLYGALA Order POLYGALACEÆ

CULTIVATION : Lime soil. Sun. Division.

SPECIES : *P. calcarea.* Prostrate. Brilliant blue flowers in May, 3 ins.
P. chamæbuxus purpurea. Little bushlet. Crimson and yellow gorse-like flowers in May, 9 ins.

POLYGONUM Order POLYGONACEÆ

CULTIVATION : Ordinary soil. Sun or shade. Division.

SPECIES : *P. vaccinifolium.* A neat-growing carpeter. Spikes of pale pink in autumn, 6 ins. Not so rampant as the other varieties, which are not advised.

PRIMULA Order PRIMULACEÆ

CULTIVATION : Ordinary soil. Sun or half-shade. Division or seed.

SPECIES AND VARIETIES : Another huge genus of which only a few can be mentioned :
P. Juliæ. Its hybrids are all worth growing. Specially the well-known Wanda. Magenta, 3-4 ins., Spring.
P. marginata. A lovely little alpine primula with clear lavender flowers in April, 4 ins.
P. pubescens. Varieties : Mrs. Wilson, lilac purple ; The General, rich crimson, May–June, 3-6 ins.

PULMONARIA Order BORAGINACEÆ

CULTIVATION : Ordinary soil. Sun or half-shade. Division.

SPECIES : *P. angustifolia azurea.* The best. Bright blue flowers, March–April, 8 ins.

RAMONDIA Order GESNERIACEÆ

CULTIVATION : Lime-free, well-drained soil. North aspect. Division.

SPECIES : *R. pyrenaica.* Flat rosettes. Bearing lilac-blue flowers with golden centres. Early summer, 6 ins. Does best planted on its side in a shaded crevice.

RAOULIA Order COMPOSITÆ

CULTIVATION : Sandy soil. Sun. Division.
SPECIES :   *R. australis.* Dwarf carpeter. Foliage quite silver, cannot tolerate winter damp.

ROSA Order ROSACEÆ

CULTIVATION : Good loam. Sun. Cuttings.
SPECIES :   The miniatures can find a home in the rock garden.
Oakington Ruby. Ruby-red flowers, 8 ins, June–July.
Peon. Red with white centre, semi-double, free flowering, 6 ins., June.
R. pumila. Pale pink, 18 ins., June.
R. Rouletti. Very double pink, 6 ins., June.

SAPONARIA Order CARYOPHYLLACEÆ

CULTIVATION : Sandy soil. Sun. Seed.
SPECIES :   *S. ocymoides.* Trailing. Covered with small pink flowers, May–August, 6 ins.

SAXIFRAGA Order SAXIFRAGACEÆ

This huge genus must be divided into sections for cultural purposes. Cultivation will be dealt with under the headings of individual sections.

The Encrusted

The Encrusted section includes those with large rosettes bearing tall spires of flowers. They require a gritty soil well supplied with lime.

SPECIES AND
VARIETIES :   *S. cochlearis.* Neat foliage. White flowers, May, 4 ins.
S. Cotyledon pyramidalis. Tall spires of pure white, 24 ins., June.
S. longifolia, variety. Tumbling Waters. Sprays of white flowers, 15 ins., July.

The Mossy

The Mossy section needs a leafy loam and semi-shade.

SPECIES AND
VARIETIES :   *S. decipiens Bathoniensis.* Crimson, May, 6 ins.
Varieties : Crimson King ; Sir Douglas Haig, deep red.

The Kabschia

The Kabschia section needs very gritty soil. May do well in the moraine. The earliest flowers are in this section, many showing colour in February.

SPECIES :   *S. apiculata.* Easily grown. Yellow. Feb.–March, 2-3 ins.

S. burseriana, variety Gloria. Lovely large white flowers. March, 2 ins. Moraine.

Faldonside. Citron yellow.

S. Jenkinsii. Pink. March–April, 2-3 ins. Easily grown.

Lady B. Stanley. Deep cerise. Moraine.

Myra. Bright rose pink. Moraine.

S. oppositifolia. Quite prostrate trailing growth ; purple flowers. March–April, 1 in. Not in full sun.

SEDUM Order CRASSULACEÆ

CULTIVATION : Sandy Soil. Sun. Division.

SPECIES :   *S. acre.* The common golden stonecrop, June, 3 ins. Watch out in case it becomes a pest and too free-growing.

S. Sieboldii. Lovely pink flowers in August, 6 ins.

S. spathulifolium atropurpureum. Chiefly grown for its lovely red leaves. Flowers yellow, May–June, 3–4 ins.

S. spectabile. Handsome upstanding heads of pink. September, 12 ins.

S. spurium coccineum. Low growing with large heads of ruby-red flowers in July–August, 6 ins.

SEMPERVIVUM Order CRASSULACEÆ

CULTIVATION : Sandy Soil. Sun. Division.

SPECIES :   The well-known house leek comes in so many varieties that none but the collector would need more than a few different kinds.

SOLDANELLA Order PRIMULACEÆ

CULTIVATION : Leafy or peaty shale. Shade. Division and seeds.

SPECIES :   *S. alpina.* Violet blue, March–April, 3 ins. Though difficult to establish it is worth a place in the moraine.

S. montana. Like the above but larger.

Rock Gardens

SOLIDAGO Order COMPOSITÆ

CULTIVATION: Good loam. Sun. Division.
SPECIES: *S. brachystachys.* A dwarf golden rod. Flowers yellow, September, 8 ins.

THYMUS Order LABIATÆ

CULTIVATION: Light soil. Sun. Seed and division.
SPECIES AND VARIETIES: *T. citriodorus.* Silver Queen. A lovely lemon-scented bush of variegated silver leaves. Flowers pale mauve. July, 9 ins.
T. serpyllum. The perfect carpeter. Mauve flowers, May-June, 1 in. Varieties: Annie Hall, flesh pink; *coccineus,* crimson; *lanuginosus,* silver-grey leaves, pink flowers.

VERBENA Order VERBENACEÆ

CULTIVATION: Light soil. Sun. Cuttings.
SPECIES: *V. chamædryfolia.* Prostrate. Intense scarlet. Needs winter protection.

VERONICA Order SCROPHULARIACEÆ

CULTIVATION: Light soil. Sun. Division.
SPECIES: *V. incana.* Grey leaves. Spike of blue flowers in summer, 8 ins.
V. rupestris. Prostrate, green leaves—covered with tails of clear blue flowers in summer, 3 ins.

ZAUSCHNERIA Order ONAGRACEÆ

CULTIVATION: Light soil. Sun. Division.
SPECIES: *Z. californica.* Orange-scented flowers in August-October, 12 ins. A valuable patch of colour at this season.

CHAPTER IV

Water Gardens

MAKING AND CARING FOR THE WATER GARDEN

*

HAPPY the man who has a stream running through his pleasure garden. His chief problem will be to select which of his hundred and one schemes for it can be put into practice. Shall he dam the stream and form a pond and bog garden, or, given slope on the ground, make a series of small waterfalls through rock work?

Failing a natural supply of water from stream or spring, any one intending to construct some form of water garden must first be sure of a continuous supply of water. It is useless to plant an artificial pool with choice water lilies only to discover that the local water supply is such that the use of water for your pool is prohibited during a drought. It is at such times that water requirement will be at its greatest, and the dwindling supply of water in the pool will be a sad sight in place of the beautiful cool vista you had anticipated.

THE NATURAL POOL

Under this heading I intend to deal with a contradiction in terms and include the pool that has been artificially made but in a natural setting.

The natural pool must be situated in a low-lying part of the garden and blend well with the rock and wild garden. Its form should suit the site. A very irregular outline will look just as unnatural as a straight-sided one. Study the way water settles in deep puddles and use the knowledge thus gained to make your pool fit into the contours of the slope of ground to be submerged. The natural small pool is frequently a straggling affair and a certain amount of tidying up of the margins will be needed. Boggy land must be controlled to occupy definite areas, and at least a third of the water's edge should be clear of high vegetation or there will be little chance of an uninterrupted view of water. Beds to be planted with bog plants should have large firm stepping-stones placed at convenient intervals. A paved approach to the water will be welcome after a spell of heavy rain.

THE ARTIFICIAL POOL

This name is here used for those pools, tanks and waterways so often found in formally laid out gardens, situated near the house. These are of necessity frequently on the higher levels of the site and make no attempt to conceal their artificial origin. Constructed as they are of concrete these pools should have very definite edges, and any planting of subjects requiring less depth of water than the main pool should be allowed for within the general plan.

Though in their natural habitat many plants will be found in 5-6 ft. of water they will do equally well in less, and it is found that a pond 2½-3 ft. at its deepest point will provide all the water needed.

CONSTRUCTION

In either case, for both the natural and the artificial setting, the construction of the water-retaining part of the pond will be similar. (See illustration facing page 153).

The site should be marked out with pegs, and the levels also marked with distinctive pegs ; ones that have been painted a bright colour are easily distinguished.

Excavate the soil to a depth of 3 ft., barrowing the soil well away from the cut edges or it will fall in later and cause endless bother.

Now examine the site. If the " floor " is hard and consolidated it need only be rammed to make a good foundation, but if it is still soft a further 6 ins. should be taken out and the space filled with clinker, brickbats, etc., and made solid and quite level. The firm level foundation is essential ; uneven sinking later on is the cause of most leaky pools.

The concrete should be made of 1 part cement, 2 parts washed sand, 2 parts aggregate, and mixed thoroughly. Sea sand must not be used as it has a bad effect on the plant and fish life in the pond later.

The concrete base of the pond should be 6 ins. thick for small and medium-sized pools, and up to 9 ins. for larger ones. Make the layer firm with a builder's trowel and scratch the area where the sides will rise to ensure a firm grip.

In dry, crumbly soil it will be necessary to use shuttering each side of the walls, but if the soil is heavy the concrete can be put against it direct and in that case only the inner side will need wooden shuttering. Unless there are plenty of boards available for shuttering, the sides will have to be made in several layers. In this case, leave the top of each layer as rough as possible so that the next layer will unite with it to form a solid wall.

Where one wants to allow for a shallower trough for bog plants an inner wall, 6 ins. lower than the outer one, is built, or, alternatively, made outside the area of the main pond.

Some methods of emptying must be made for all but the smallest ponds. An ordinary bath waste-pipe and stopper can be built in, with some sort of strainer to prevent the pipe getting clogged with weed. Also an overflow pipe so that the surrounding soil does not get water-logged in bad weather is necessary.

After the cementing of the pool is finished an even coating of " Glasol " should be applied. This stops the caustic action of fresh cement, which is injurious to fish and plant life. As a result of using such a finishing coat, the pool should be ready for planting and stocking in a week. " Glasol " can be purchased from any good horticultural sundriesman.

It is now possible to buy Plastic pools ready to sink into the ground. These are very simple to use and are most effective.

PLANTING

The soil for aquatic plants should be a good strong loam, and unlike the general composts should not have much organic matter in it. Some well-rotted cow dung can be mixed with the lower layers, but this should always be covered with an inch of pure loam and made very firm. Organic matter, such as leaf mould, peat, or horse manure, is undesirable as it ferments and rises to the surface of the water, polluting the whole pond and doing no good to the plants.

The larger plants, such as water lilies, are planted into the soil and the pond then filled slowly. Do not add the whole of the water at once, but fill gradually, allowing the plants to grow to the surface before adding more water. This method has the added advantage of allowing the water to warm up more quickly than would happen if the whole pond were filled at one time.

Another method of planting is to fill baskets with loam and plant the lilies into these and then lower them into the water. In very large ponds the plants are often wrapped up in sacking with a ball of soil and then dropped over the side of a boat into the desired position. By the time the sacking has rotted away the plant will be well established in the soil at the bottom of the pond.

In the small garden it is possible to derive great pleasure from aquatics grown in tubs sunk into the ground. Be sure the tubs are watertight; any cracks should be filled with clay. Ram the soil firmly round the outside of the tub, leaving no air-pockets which may cause uneven shrinking of the wood. General treatment of plants in tubs is the same as for larger areas.

CARE OF THE WATER GARDEN

The chief work connected with growing aquatics is keeping the more rampant subjects under control. Drastic thinning must be done continually or the whole surface will become covered with foliage and the general effect spoiled, as well as preventing the growth of submerged plants. If fish are to be allowed a place in the pond they also need to have plenty of light and air, so much of the surface must be kept clear of plant growth.

Steps must be taken to keep the water as clean as possible, and this is done by keeping a right balance of growth. The underwater plants are useful purifiers, also water snails and fish. Where fish are not included it is possible to keep down the smothering flannel weed by adding small quantities of copper sulphate, $\frac{1}{8}$ ozs. of copper sulphate being enough for 1,000 gals. of water.

Unless a lot of time can be devoted to caring for the pond it is best to plant only the hardy plants, of which there is an ample choice, and leave the tender forms to the specialist.

There should be little trouble from insects. Various types of aphis will attack water plants, but provided there are fish in the pond the aphis should not become a serious pest ; a strong jet of water from hose or syringe will dislodge the insects and enable the fish to find them more easily. Snails can also become too numerous ; these are best trapped by leaving a lettuce or cabbage floating on the water at night. In the morning it will be found with many of the snails on it. These can be killed and the process repeated.

FISH IN POOLS
Fish are useful in the garden pool not only because of their ornamental value but also because they help to keep the pool clean and keep down mosquito and gnat larvæ.

Suitable types of fish

Goldfish. There are many varieties of different colours—pale yellow, pink, orange, red and black.

Golden Orfe. A very hardy fish, salmon pink in colour.

Golden Tench. Old gold in colour, marked with black or chocolate.

Dogfish. A hardy little fish with brown markings.

Gudgeon. A spotted fish which is an excellent scavenger.

BOG PLANTS

There are many moisture-loving plants which make useful subjects for planting in moist parts of the garden, or at the margins of pools and streams. Plants suitable for this purpose, though not all of them are strictly speaking bog plants, include : *Trollius, Iris sibirica, I. Kæmpferi*, the yellow loosestrife (*Lysimachia*), the purple loosestrife (*Lythrum*), *Rodgersia*, astilbes, funkias, monkshood, and many of the primulas such as *P. beesiana, P. bulleyana, P. cashmiriana, P. Florindæ, P. helodoxa, P. japonica, P. pulverulenta, P. sikkimensis* and *P. Veitchii.*

Larger plants and shrubs which make a suitable background in the bog garden include bamboos, some of the dogwoods, including *Cornus sanguinea* and *C. alba*, willows, alders, gunnera, rheum (the ornamental rhubarb), the swamp cypress (*Taxodium distichum*), and Osmunda ferns.

A LIST OF WORTHWHILE PLANTS FOR THE WATER GARDEN

*

IT seems that in any list of water plants it is the Nymphæas or Water Lilies that are placed first, while all the rest await their turn in alphabetical order, a sure tribute to the high position they hold in favour and importance.

NYMPHÆA (The Water Lily) Order NYMPHÆACEÆ

Varieties for Tubs and Shallow Pools that can be grown in less than 12 ins. of water

SPECIES AND VARIETIES :

N. Froebelli. Deep crimson, orange stamens, medium-sized foliage.

N. Laydekeri fulgens. Crimson, carmine stamens, spotted foliage. Scented.

N. L. lilacea. Pink and white, fading to pink and crimson. Scented.

N. L. purpurata. Deep carmine, fiery stamens.

N. Marliacea chromatella. A hybrid with primrose and rose-coloured flowers.

N. odorata minor. White with yellow anthers, starry flowers. Very fragrant.

N. tetragona alba. White, very neat growth.

N. t. Helvola. Delicate yellow. Leaves spotted maroon.

Varieties needing 12 ins. of water and over

SPECIES AND VARIETIES :

N. amabilis. Salmon shading to deep pink in the centre. Young leaves reddish.

N. atropurpurea. Purple crimson with yellow stamens. Leaves purple turning dark green.

Escarboucle. Huge, wine crimson flowers.

N. Indiana. Yellow orange shading to coppery red. Leaves spotted maroon.

James Brydon. Rich crimson pink, golden stamens. Young leaves purple.

N. Moorei. Soft canary yellow. Leaves pale green, spotted purple.

Paul Hariot. Copper rose, inner petals sulphur flushed pink. Leaves spotted maroon.

SPECIES AND VARIETIES : Princess Elizabeth. Peach, golden anthers.
Robinsoniana. Yellow overlaid crimson orange. Leaves dark green, maroon spots.
Sunrise. Clear yellow. Very large flowers.
Willie Falcoult. Crimson, tinged ruby red, golden stamens. Flowers very large. Young leaves dark red.

Acorus Calamus (Sweet Flag) Order ARACEÆ

Suitable for planting in the marshy borders of the pond. 3 ft.

Alisma Plantago-aquatica (the native Water Plantain) Order ALISMACEÆ

Delicate rose-coloured flowers. 3 ft., for the pond side.

Aponogeton distachyus (Water Hawthorn) Order APONOGETONACEÆ

White fragrant flowers on a forked flower head. Large floating leaves. Plant in shallow water, but will grow just as well in depth up to 2 ft.

Astilbe Order SAXIFRAGACEÆ

Not an aquatic, but invaluable for the damp border by water. Height and range from 4 ins. to 4 ft., and colour from deep red to white. Many named varieties are listed by nurserymen.

Butomus umbellatus (Flowering Rush) Order BUTUMACEÆ

Charming native plant, bearing umbels of pink flowers. 2-3 ft. high. Likes to be planted in a few inches of water.

Calla palustris (Bog Arum) Order ARACEÆ

Small white flowers followed by red berries. Boggy margin and shallow water.

Caltha palustris (Marsh Marigold) Order RANUNCULACEÆ

Clear golden flowers and large leaves. Plant in shallow water or wet margins. Very rampant grower.

VARIETIES : *C. p. flore pleno.* Double flowered marsh marigold. Flowers make a blaze of gold over the leaves which are neat growing and do not smother blossom.

Water Gardens

Hottonia palustris (Water Violet) Order PRIMULACEÆ

Foliage submerged, pale green finely divided leaves. The lilac and white flowers are borne 8-10 ins. above the water.

Iris Kæmpferi (Clematis-flowered Iris) Order IRIDACEÆ

A beautiful plant for the border by the water's edge. Many named varieties in shades of white, blue, red, violet, yellow and crimson.

Iris Pseudacorus (Fleur-de-Lis) Order IRIDACEÆ

Fine sword-shaped leaves and bright yellow flowers. Will grow in a little water or at the water's edge.

Iris sibirica Order IRIDACEÆ

Charming spikes of flowers which look well grouped by water and are equally useful as cut flowers. Growing 3-4 ft. Several shades of blue and purple, also pure white.

Lysichitum americanum (Skunk Cabbage) Order LEGUMINOSÆ

Huge yellow arum-like flowers, followed by enormous green leaves. Boggy land at the water side.

Lysimachia vulgaris (Yellow Loosestrife) Order PRIMULACEÆ

Showy yellow spikes. 3-4 ft. for wild garden and water side.

Lythrum Salicaria (Purple Loosestrife) Order LYTHRACEÆ

Graceful spikes of blossom. Best grown in a border by the water side. Several good named hybrids in shades of pink and purple. Growing 3-5 ft. high.

Mentha aquatica (Water Mint) Order LABIATÆ

Whorls of lilac flowers. Very hairy leaves.

Menyanthes trifoliata (Bog Bean) Order GENTIANACEÆ

Vigorous grower for shallow water. The pink buds open into white flowers.

Mimulus cardinalis (Musk) Order SCROPHULARIACEÆ

Invaluable for giving colour to the margins of pools. Many named varieties in reds and orange scarlet.

VARIETIES :   *M. luteus.* Taller growing, yellow flowers frequently spotted with red.

Monarda didyma

See for description, page 130.

Myosotis palustris (Water Forget-me-not) Order BORAGINACEÆ

This well-known native needs no description. Thrives at the water's edge or in a few inches of water. Clear pale blue flowers.

VARIETIES :   *M. p. semperflorens.* Has a prolonged flowering season and neater habit than the above.

Nuphar luteum (the wild or native Water Lily)
Order NYMPHÆACEÆ

Only recommended for large spaces as its yellow flowers are small and not very showy.

Nelumbium (Lotus Flower) Order NYMPHÆACEÆ

Not entirely hardy, but looks well in tubs where the leaves, held above the water, are seen to advantage.

Pontederia cordata (Pickerel Weed) Order PONTEDERIACEÆ

Shiny olive-green leaves. Spikes of closely-packed blue flowers. Plant in 4 ins. of water.

Primula Order PRIMULACEÆ

Several species are invaluable for the water's edge where they will seed freely.

SPECIES AND   *P. bulleyana.* Buff-orange whorls of flowers.
VARIETIES :   *P. denticulata.* Round head of lilac.
                P. denticulata alba. Round head of white.
                P. Florindæ. Head of soft yellow flowers. Leaves large and handsome in damp positions.
                P. japonica, and its many named varieties in white, pink and crimson. Tall whorls of flowers.
                P. Waltoni. Heads of large pendulous flowers of deep crimson stems covered with white farina, making a contrast to the green leaves.

Water Gardens

Ranunculus aquatilis (Water Crowfoot) Order RANUNCULACEÆ

Finely-cut leaves, submerged in running water. Flowers, which have small, white petals with yellow stamens, float on the surface.

VARIETIES :   *R. lingua grandiflora.*   (Great Spearwort.)   Large yellow buttercup flowers.

Senecio clivorum Order COMPOSITÆ

Big orange daisy flowers. Large round leaves. Very handsome for the water side.

Typha latifolia (Reed Mace) Order TYPHACEÆ

Commonly called Bulrush. Too tall for the small pool, but very handsome in a few inches of water and given shelter from the wind.

CHAPTER V

The Wild Garden

WHAT IS A WILD GARDEN?

WHAT is the Wild Garden, where does it begin, where end, and which plants are at home in it ?

All these questions are very hard to answer, the secret of the charm of a wild garden being its freedom from hard and fast rules. (See illustration facing page 152.) It can be a woodland in which spring flowers and bulbs are naturalised to give colour before the shade of the opening leaves prohibits growth ; or it may be a bare rocky stretch where heathers, gorse and rock plants mingle with colourful natives that would be called weeds elsewhere. Large borders of flowering shrubs with strong-growing herbaceous plants that need little attention can be combined to make a perfect wild garden with stretches of rough grass that is scythed at intervals.

In actual fact it is simpler to define what the wild garden is not, or should not be ; and that is, a home for all the bits and pieces which overflow the other parts of the garden. Nor is the shady, dry slope where nothing can grow an ideal site for a wild garden. One often sees a neglected little strip of ground between a country road and small modern house that is full of dead leaves, match boxes and lengths of rusty wire ; in all probability the owner still sees it as the attractive bit of real wood, complete with bluebells and primroses, which was there when the house was built. The change for the worse has been so gradual that only the passer-by sees it for what it is, wild perhaps, but certainly not a garden.

PLANTING

Planting in the wild garden should be on broad lines. Large sweeps of a single variety give the desired effect.

Many of the most suitable plants are not beautiful as specimen plants but when massed together have definite charm. Of these, *Anchusa myosotidiflora* is a good example. In the herbaceous border its coarse leaves seem too heavy for its delicate flower heads. But when seen in a large drift in semi-shade the haze of clear pale blue benefits from the carpet of its rough foliage.

Beware of planting the more specialised florist flowers in a wild setting, they look out of place, and demanding generous treatment they only become straggly and weak when left to fend for themselves. In a few cases the named hybrids can be used to blend with wild forms and add interest. Of these, the coloured primroses take a high place. Planted in groups of a single colour, or colours so graded as to look like a single family, they fit into the scheme without any appearance of artificiality. Some of the hybrid aquilegias can be used in the same way, also foxgloves. In every case keep the planting to blocks of single colours. A harlequin appearance, looking like patches of confetti, is not natural and will strike a discordant note in the well-arranged wild garden. A shrub clipped into a round ball is another out-of-place feature that is sometimes seen. Any clipping and pruning to be done must leave the shrubs looking natural. Keep all close clipping for the formal parts of the garden.

CARE OF THE WILD GARDEN

The wild garden is planted with the intention of giving little labour, but that does not mean neglect. The removal of seed heads from the more vigorous subjects will give the delicate plants a better chance of seeding themselves. Cut out all broken and dead branches. Be drastic in the pulling up of the more rampant plants that try to smother their neighbours. If all these things are attended to the wild garden will be a pleasantly ordered part of the garden at all seasons.

SOME WORTHWHILE PLANTS FOR THE WILD GARDEN

Aconitum Napellus millefolium
Ajuga reptans purpurea
Allium Moly
Anchusa myosotidiflora
Anemone apennina
Anemone nemorosa
Aquilegia vulgaris et var.
Artemisia lactiflora

Astilbe Arendsii
Buphthalmum salicifolium
Calluna vulgaris
Cardamine pratensis
Centaurea montana
Chionodoxa Luciliæ
Chionodoxa sardensis
Clematis heracleæfolia Davidiana

SOME WORTHWHILE PLANTS FOR THE WILD GARDEN (CONT'D)

Colchicum agrippanum
Colchicum autumnale
Colchicum speciosum
Convallaria majalis
Crocus biflorus
Crocus pulchellus
Cyclamen europæum
Cyclamen neapolitanum
Cyclamen repandum
Digitalis purpurea
Doronicum plantagineum
Echinops Ritro
Epilobium roseum
Eranthis hyemalis
Erica arborea
Erica carnea
Erica mediterranea
Eryngium planum
Erythronium dens-canis roseum
Fritillaria imperialis
Fritillaria meleagris
Galanthus nivalis
Galega officinalis
Gentiana asclepiadea
Geranium armenum
Geum rivale
Helianthus sparsifolius
Hemerocallis aurantiaca
Hemerocallis citrina
Hieracium aurantiacum
Hosta lanceolata
Hosta subcordata
Hypericum balearicum
Iris fœtidissima
Iris fulva
Iris sibirica
Kniphofia erecta
Kniphofia uvaria
Leucojum æstivum
Leucojum autumnale
Lilium auratum

Lilium croceum
Lilium formosanum
Lilium Hansoni
Lilium longiflorum
Lilium pardalinum
Lilium regale
Lilium testaceum
Lilium tigrinum
Lilium umbellatum
Lupinus arboreus
Lupinus polyphyllus
Lysimachia vulgaris
Lythrum virgatum
Meconopsis cambrica
Mentha citrata
Monarda didyma
Montbretia (Tritonia)
Muscari botyroides
Myosotis sylvatica
Narcissus spp.
Oenothera biennis
Omphalodes cappadocica
Ornithogalum umbellatum
Orobus verna
Oxalis floribunda
Pæonia officinalis
Phormium tenax
Polygonatum multiflorum
Polygonum campanulatum
Primula Bulleyana
Primula Beesiana
Primula denticulata
Primula Florindæ
Primula japonica
Primula vulgaris
Rheum palmatum
Rodgersia pinnata
Rudbeckia nitida
Saxifraga megasea
Scilla nutans
Senecio Clivorum

SOME WORTHWHILE PLANTS FOR THE WILD GARDEN (CONT'D)

Senecio tanguticus
Solidago canadensis
Thalictrum aquilegifolium
Thalictrum glaucum
Tritonia crocosmæflora
Tulipa Sprengeri
Tulipa sylvestris
Valeriana officinalis

Veratrum album
Veratrum nigrum
Verbascum longifolium
Vinca difformis
Vinca major
Vinca minor
Viola odorata
Viola sylvestris

CHAPTER VI

Window Box, Balcony, Roof and Room Gardening

MAKING THE BOX

WINDOW boxes are most often made of wood, though concrete, lead, zinc and pottery are used. If a wooden box is to be made, oak and teak are the most lasting, but any other timber obtainable may be employed. The wood used should be $\frac{5}{8}$-$1\frac{1}{2}$ ins. thick. The box should be 7 ins. deep and 6 ins. wide and long enough to fit closely to the window frame. If possible, dove-tail the wood together ; otherwise use screws. Nails are not reliable. (See Fig. 16.)

When made, the inside of the box should be charred with a blow lamp or red-hot iron, or soaked in a solution of copper sulphate, to preserve the wood. Never treat with creosote or tar as these are injurious to plant roots.

The outside of the box should be painted. The simpler the style of the box the better, but some people like to have the front decorated with virgin cork, tiles or miniature garden fences with gates.

DRAINING THE BOX

Good drainage is most important and holes should be bored in the bottom of the box. (See Fig. 16.) If drips are likely to cause trouble a wedge may be inserted so that the box slopes towards the back of the sill. Drainage holes are then made at the back of the box, a shallow tray being placed under them which is emptied periodically. Alternatively, the box may be made to slope to one corner and a tin placed under the main drainage hole made

——MAKING A WINDOW BOX——

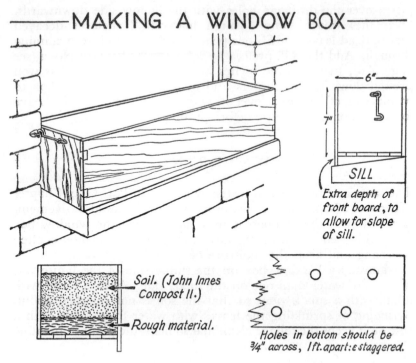

Extra depth of front board, to allow for slope of sill.

Soil. (John Innes Compost II.)

Rough material.

Holes in bottom should be ¾" across, 1ft. apart:&staggered.

FIG. 16

there ; and removed when the drips have ceased. Another method is to have the window box as a framework and to grow the plants in pots standing in saucers on the window sill.

The ideal window box is one supplied with two interior-fitting tins, the second one kept filled and ready to take the place of the one in position as soon as the plants have finished flowering. The tins must be properly perforated and painted, with rust-preventing paint, inside and out.

Where there is no window sill, brackets may be inserted in the wall to support the box. In this case it is equally important to prevent the drips from falling on passers-by.

PAINTING THE BOX

When the box has been made or bought, place in position, as it is easier to handle before the soil is put in. Then place a layer of crocks over the bottom of the box, being sure to place concave pieces over the drainage holes with the hollow side downwards. Over these place some " rough materials," such as decayed turves, dead leaves, or fibrous peat, to keep the soil from running through. Add the soil, preferably John Innes Compost No. 2 (see page 576), two or three inches at a time, seeing that it is well pressed down in the corners and at the edges. Fill the box to within 1 in. of the top ; level off with a flat piece of wood. Leave for a week or two to settle before putting in the plants.

WATERING

The same general rules on watering as seen in Part One, Chapter III, pages 57-58, apply to watering window boxes also. Remember, however, that though it may have rained the window box may still need watering because the eaves of the house often overhang and keep the moisture off.

Naturally a window box on the sunny side of the house will need more water than one on the shady side. Always water with a can with a small spout so that the soil is not splashed about. Syringing or sprinkling the leaves with water from a can with a rose on it keeps the foliage clean and so helps the plant to breathe.

PLANTING

It is not advisable to sow seeds in window boxes as the conditions are far from ideal, and the plants take some time before they flower. It is better to buy plants which are about to flower. If possible, obtain them in pots, remove them carefully from the pots and plant in the boxes ; by doing this they have the minimum check to their growth. If buying them in boxes, get them when they are young plants so that they feel the move less and are able to become well established before they flower.

Trailing plants, such as ivy leaf geraniums and nasturtiums, may be planted towards the front of the box and taller plants, such as antirrhinums, towards the back. The planting scheme must be left to the taste of the owner and there are many possible and lovely combinations with a wide choice of plants known to do well in window boxes, the names of some of which are given below.

GENERAL CULTIVATION

Dead flower heads and yellowing leaves should be removed once a week regularly, and the surface of the soil pricked over with a small hand fork. Feed the plants with a good liquid manure which can be obtained in bottles and has only to be diluted to the required strength according to the directions on the label. Should the soil show signs of greenness sprinkle a little hydrated lime on the surface and fork in.

VEGETABLES IN WINDOW BOXES

Some town dwellers will wish to use any available space to increase their food supply by raising a few vegetables and herbs.

For example, the window box by the kitchen window can be used to grow such herbs as parsley, mint, rue, sorrel, tarragon, basil, thyme and chives ; salad plants such as corn-salad, lettuce and radishes. Dwarf stump-rooted carrots will also grow in the window box. Dwarf peas and beans may be tried, also spinach.

For the roof-garden, or the balcony, runner beans may be used to climb up the posts or trellis. Some excellent tomatoes have also been grown in pots and boxes on verandas and roofs. For details of varieties and culture see pages 545-548.

A LIST OF PLANTS FOR AUTUMN AND SPRING PLANTING

Autumn Planting	Spring Planting
Sunny Aspect	*Sunny Aspect*
Aubrietia	Antirrhinum
Alyssum saxatile	Geranium
Cheiranthus	Dwarf dahlia
Chionodoxa	Lobelia
Crocus	Hydrangea
Daffodil	Marguerite
Hyacinth	Petunia
Scilla	Salvia
Muscari	Stock
Tulip	Verbena
Wallflower	Polyantha rose

PLANTS FOR AUTUMN AND SPRING PLANTING

Shady Aspect	*Shady Aspect*
Clipped Box	Begonia (fibrous)
Creeping Jenny	Calceolaria
Crocus	Creeping Jenny
Dwarf conifers	Fern
Olearia	Fuchsia
Variegated ivy	Tobacco plant
	Viola

TRAILING PLANTS (PLANT AUTUMN OR SPRING)
Campanula isophylla
Ivy leaved geranium
Periwinkle
Tradescantia
Variegated ivy

BALCONY GARDENS

★

WHAT TO DO WITH A BALCONY

Occasionally one finds a balcony which can be used for growing plants and here larger window boxes are used, 9 ins. wide, 9 ins. deep, and any length required to fit in the space. They may be used to grow climbing plants such as Virginia creeper, ivy, clematis, roses and the Russian vine, which will serve to clothe the railings or pillars, and are perennial plants. Annuals like Canary creeper, nasturtiums, and *Cobæa scandens* are very colourful but must be planted each year.

If the balcony is surrounded by a wall several of the top bricks may be removed and boxes put in their place and these filled with plants. All the plants given as suitable for growing in window boxes may be grown with equal success on the balcony.

BOXES, TUBS AND HANGING BASKETS

Tubs and boxes are popular containers used extensively in towns where the available space for growing plants is very restricted.

They may be placed in the front porch, courtyard, veranda or on flat roofs. Any size or shape will do, provided that the same rules are observed as those given for the preparation of window boxes. In addition, it is usual for the tub or box to be placed on bricks, or provided with legs, as this helps to give perfect drainage. A box or tub may be raised on a pole to give variation in height and to allow the full beauty of a trailing plant to be seen. A hollowed-out old tree stump may be used to grow plants to great effect. In addition to the lists of plants already given, the following plants and shrubs are also suitable for planting in tubs and boxes:

Agapanthus	Hosta
Campanula	Iris
Carnation	Retinosporas, various
Cupressus Fletcheri	*Veronica Traversii*
Cupressus Lawsoniana	Yew
Geum	Windsor Hybrid Chrysanthemum
Gladiolus	

A few words must be said about hanging baskets, which can be used most effectively for growing plants and adding to the colourful decoration of the town house porch, veranda, or garden. If none of these are available baskets may even be hung indoors, in a window. They should be prepared and planted as advised in Part Seven, Chapter I, pages 577-578.

From the lists of plants suitable for planting in baskets many lovely combinations of colour may be made:

FOLIAGE PLANTS	PLANTS FOR SUMMER
Asparagus Sprengerii	Begonia
Fern	Calceolaria
Golden-veined honeysuckle	Fuchsia
Ivy, various	Geranium
	Heliotrope
PLANTS FOR SPRING	Mignonette
Arabis	Nasturtium
Dwarf tulip	Lobelia
Grape hyacinth	Petunia
Polyanthus	Salvia
Primrose	Verbena
Wallflower	

32. *Chrysanthemum, Goldfinder*   33. *Sweet Pea, Gigantic*
34. *Rose, Fashion*   35. *Rose, Bridget*

36. *Chrysanthemum
August Red*

37. *Charm Chrysa.
themums*

ROOF GARDENS

★

That very successful gardens may be made on roof tops has become a firmly established fact since the first large-scale garden was made on the roof of Adelaide House in 1923. Roof gardens have been on view where lawns, perennial flowers, alpines in rock gardens, aquatics in pools, trees and shrubs, and even some fruit trees, have been seen growing happily.

In some respects a roof garden has definite advantages over a garden on ground level. There is more light and purer air, freedom from pests and diseases and weed seeds. On the other hand, there is greater exposure to the wind and to extremes of heat and cold.

Before attempting to start a roof garden it is essential to consult a builder and to be sure that the structure of the roof will support the weight of soil that is to be placed upon it. Also, an adequate and effective system of drainage must be devised.

Start to make the border by placing inverted turves for the base. Upon these place 2-in. drains of broken bricks across the border connecting with the drains beneath. Good soil to the depth of 9 ins. should be used and " tear holes " every 6 ft. should be made in the wall of the border.

SHELTER

Attention must now be paid to providing shelter from the prevailing winds. This is often no simple matter, as on a roof the angle of the walls and surrounding buildings may cause the wind to blow from the most unexpected quarter. The screen should be firmly fixed and the method of fixing not too obvious. Climbing plants should be grown up any supports necessary. The screen may be painted with a garden scene to give an idea of distance and continuation of the garden. Trellis may be used where the wind is lighter and a solid screen is not necessary. Do not, however, completely surround the roof with screens so that the sun and air are excluded.

LAY OUT

All kinds of schemes can be devised and modified forms of larger plans may be used. In the chapter on the Flower Garden details will be found for the making and planting of herbaceous, annual, and shrub borders. The same general principles apply to the roof garden.

GENERAL INSTRUCTIONS

It must always be remembered that the roof garden is artificial and a certain amount of fresh soil must be introduced every year, plus the addition of organic matter to the soil already there. Weeding, watering, spraying and syringing must be regularly carried out. Remember, that the roof garden is likely to need more watering than an ordinary garden in a hot, dry summer as the heat on the roof will be greater, also it will be more exposed to drying winds. In the winter it will be more exposed to cold conditions and the more tender subjects should receive protection, in the way of screens, mulches and, where appropriate, cloches.

ROOM GARDENS

*

MINIATURE GARDENING

A miniature garden may be made in any room in a large tray or flat bowl. Porous pottery is to be preferred to glazed pottery.

Much can be done to get landscape effects in a small area. Baby rocks and pebbles give height and represent mountains, a mirror used to give the effect of water, moss for grass, etc. Tufa is the best stone to use as it is porous and the roots of the plants can get a hold of it.

With an ordinary bowl it is a good thing to have a layer of charcoal at the bottom covered with some stones to act as drainage, then a layer of some light compost, John Innes No. 1, for instance. To this may be added ground-up, broken flower pots which help to keep the soil porous. Some alpines like granite chips around them. When planning a little miniature garden be sure to try and keep each feature in proportion to the others.

The bowl should be placed where the maximum amount of light and air are obtainable.

A list of suitable plants for these tiny gardens is given below :

Dwarf Trees	*Shrubs*	*Plants*	*Succulents*
Cherry	Ivy	Arenaria	Agave
Cypress	Picea	*Bellium minutum*	Aloe
Juniper	*Pinus montana*	*Calamintha alpina*	Cotyledon
Maple		Cotula	Echeveria
Oak		Dryas	Gasteria
Plum		*Erica carnea*	Haworthia
		Festuca glauca	Sedum
		Helxine	Stapelia
		Oxalis	
		Saxifrage	
		Sempervivum	
		Thymus	

ROOM PLANTS

For those who prefer something larger and more showy, there are many delightful foliage and flowering plants that will flourish in the house, providing certain conditions are given. Plants need plenty of daylight and fresh air but cannot stand draughts. Plants do not like direct heat from a fire, but appreciate a moderate, equable temperature during the cold weather, with cooler conditions during the night than the day. Do not, however, leave plants close to the window during severe frosty weather as they are liable to be frosted.

Give the plants sufficient water, but do not keep them standing in a saucer of water. Syringe and wash the leaves of foliage plants regularly once a week and sponge the leaves of flowering plants.

Cut off the dead flowers, yellowing leaves and broken stems. Stake the plant when necessary using a split bamboo, tying with raffia or green string. Take care to use a tie for each shoot. Do not bunch all the stems up together tied to one stake. Never tie so tightly that the stems are damanged. Aim to have the plant looking as well shaped and natural as possible.

Pot plants do not need heavy manuring and a good liquid manure, as advised for window boxes, should be used. Keep the surface of the pots clean by scrubbing. The surface of the soil should be kept pricked over with a small hand fork and, if it appeared to be at all green or sour, a little hydrated lime should be sprinkled over it and forked in.

An electric propagator, which consists of a cloche, or cloches, over a container in which boxes of soil are placed, could easily be kept in the house and would provide an endless source of interest in the raising of small plants for growing in any of the ways suggested in this chapter.

LIST OF PLANTS SUITABLE FOR ROOM CULTURE

Early-flowering bulbs:
   (For cultural detail see Part Three, Chapter IV, page 279.)
   Crocus, hyacinth, narcissus, tulip, snowdrop, scilla.

Late-flowering bulbs and corms:
   Cyclamen, freesia, lily.

Room Gardens

Flowering plants:
(For cultural details see pages 587-619.)

Azalea	Cineraria	Hydrangeas
Begonia	Clivia	Lily
Campanula	Fuchsia	Oxalis
Chrysanthemum	Geranium	Primula

Foliage plants:

Aralia Sieboldii	*Cyperus diffusus*
Araucaria excelsa	*Fatshedera Lizei*
Asparagus plumosus	*Ficus elasticua*
Asparagus Sprengeri	*Maranta leuconeura*
Aspidistra lurida	*Pilea Caderei*
Carex Morrowii variegata	*Tradescantia Zebrina pendula*
Cordyline australis	

Ferns:

Adiantum cuneatum (difficult)	*Nephrodium molle*
Aspidium Lonchitis	*Pteris cretica Wimsettii*
Asplenium	

Palms:

Cocos weddelliana	*Livistona borbonica*
Geonoma gracilis	*Phœnix canariensis*
Kentia	

PART THREE

THE GARDEN BEAUTIFUL
FLOWERS AND FOLIAGE

CHAPTER I

Annuals and Plants Grown as Such

SECTION ONE

ANNUALS AND PLANTS GROWN AS SUCH

★

ANNUALS are plants that complete a whole life cycle within a year. They start from a seed, build up a structure of roots and shoots, and then put their entire energy into the production of flowers and the ripening of seed. Exhausted they die. They have laid their lives down to secure a next generation. This is the botanist's definition of an annual, and a typical example is the giant sunflower. The gardener is apt to include other plants under this term, any plants that may easily be treated as annuals—sown, flowered and discarded in one season. Many of these are half-hardy perennials that would not survive our winter in the open, but flower so readily from seed sown the same season, that we do not bother to take them up and house them. We save our valuable greenhouse or frame space for more needy applicants and get vigorous flowering plants fresh from seed. Typical " gardeners' annuals " are the bedding begonias, the little blue lobelias, the scarlet sage and many other popular bedding plants.

This chapter deals with both types, their uses and culture. Both will be referred to as annuals, but their true nature will be indicated in the description of individual plants. (See page 209.)

USES OF ANNUALS

Annuals have many uses in the flower garden. To mention some :

BEDS
A formal feature usually found near the house. A garden bed is a patch with geometrical outlines (i.e. not pretending to be natural), planted closely with one or more kinds of " bedding plants," so as to get a mass effect. Applicants for employment in bedding schemes must be sturdy growers and will be required

to produce a brilliant show of blossom. Decorative foliage may, however, be offered as an alternative. Most bedding schemes are renewed several times a year so as to maintain a bright show throughout the season. Many of the plants thus used are annuals, but biennials, perennials, even shrubs, may be chosen. Further details on bedding schemes are given in Chapter II, pages 259-262.

BORDERS

These are long stretched-out beds with straight or curving outlines, according to their position. Here you can let yourself go ! You can try dozens of annuals in one season, can make the most brilliant or the most delicate colour schemes. The arrangement of plants will be similar to that in the herbaceous border, i.e. you group the drifts according to height and colour. Flowering time is not such an important factor here as the majority of plants will bloom from late June into September. Like the individual annual plant, the annual border reaches the height of its glory in one season and then sinks to nothingness. Information on preparing the soil, seed sowing and routine work on the annual border will be found later in this chapter, pages 203-208.

EDGINGS

Edgings to paths, beds, borders and shrubberies are often made up of the dwarf annuals, such as ageratum, alyssum, lobelia, sanvitalia, *Tagetes signata pumila*, " Tom Thumb " tropæolum, etc. Of course, many perennial herbaceous plants and sub-shrubs are also useful for this purpose.

CUT FLOWER BORDERS

Their usefulness is emphasised later, on page 263, and many annuals make first-class cut flowers, among them cornflower, annual gaillardia, love-in-a-mist, marigold, nasturtium, zinnia, etc. Suitability for cutting is indicated in the description of individual plants. (See pages 209-258.)

WINDOW BOXES

A stroll up Parliament Street and Whitehall in London would convince any one of the usefulness of window boxes. Stern government buildings are here " humanised " by a cheerful display of flowers under the windows.

Plants for window boxes may be true annuals, like candytuft and nasturtiums, " gardener's annuals," like lobelias, petunias and sweet Wivelsfield, or downright perennials, like marguerites and pelargoniums.

CULTIVATION OF ANNUALS—SOIL

Soil requirements are usually not extravagant. The soil should be well drained and moisture holding, not too rich nor very poor. It must be well worked and, especially where seed is to be sown outside, the surface must be in good tilth.

PREPARING THE SOIL

If possible dig the soil in autumn, incorporate organic matter if the soil needs it, and remove all perennial weeds. Give a light dressing of lime sometime after Christmas to facilitate crumbling. Further enlightenment on the subject of soil preparation in general will be found in Part One, Chapters I and III, pages 22-40 and 51-55. The special needs of some plants, such as sweet peas, are pointed out in the individual descriptions that follow. Where summer bedding plants are rushed in, immediately the spring bedding is out, the soil will get nothing but a light forking over, but this will be quite adequate if it has had the necessary attention before the spring.

SEED SOWING

Obviously, annuals are raised from seed. But where, when, how, do we sow?

(1) WHERE TO SOW
Under Glass
    (*a*) All half-hardy annuals, unless you are willing to postpone sowing till late May, when plants would flower very late and tend to be of poor quality. Examples : schizanthus, tagetes, zinnia.
    (*b*) Hardy annuals that are wanted early. This applies especially to summer bedding flowers which have to be shapely plants by the end of May, when the spring bedding is turned out to make room for the summer bedding.
    (*c*) Perennials grown as annuals, that will only flower in their first season if given a good long-growing period.

In the Open
    (*a*) All hardy annuals that dislike transplanting. Examples : All types of poppies.

(*b*) All hardy annuals that are required to flower particularly early and whose outdoor quarters are unoccupied in winter.

(*c*) Half-hardy annuals.

(2) WHEN TO SOW

Under Glass

Sow early (January–early February) all plants that need an extra long-growing season before they will flower. Many of the " pretend " annuals belong to this group : antirrhinum, begonia, petunia, salvia.

Sow late (end of March–early April) plants that develop quickly and if sown earlier would crave transplanting before weather conditions make this possible : nemesia, phlox, zinnia, belong to this group.

Most of the sowing under glass will be done in February and early March, when clarkia, *Centaurea candidissima*, salpiglossis, stocks, tagetes and many others are sown.

Note.—If continuous cloches can be made available for the purpose, plants may be sown under glass and yet in their outdoor flowering position. Place cloches over soil 2 weeks before sowing, to warm and dry soil. After sowing close up ends of cloche row with sheets of glass to avoid draught.

In the Open

In the spring, all hardy annuals not sown in autumn or under glass. Actual time varies according to soil, climate and season. You must wait until the soil is ready, i.e. dry enough to work down to a fine tilth. To sow before the soil is ready, is to violate nature. The punishment is " no flowers for your labours." Even where conditions are favourable it is rarely wise to sow before the last week in March, whilst in cold districts, clay soils, severe seasons, you may have to wait till the second half of April.

(3) HOW TO SOW

Under Glass

Sowing of annuals differs in no way from the sowing of perennial herbaceous plants under glass. Therefore see pages 99-100 and follow instructions carefully.

In the Open

If the soil has been dug in autumn, give it a light forking over in spring, a week or so before you want to sow. The soil surface should be level and fairly fine after forking. Immediately before sowing, rake the soil surface to a very fine tilth. On light soils it is advisable to consolidate the seed-bed by gentle treading or rolling, to ensure adequate water circulation. On heavy soils do not tread or roll, as this would make the soil too hard for the small roots to penetrate. At sowing time, the soil should be moist but must not be wet and sticky.

For cut flower borders sow in straight rows just as if you were sowing carrots. The smaller the seed, the shallower the drill, so that the seed is covered with about twice its own thickness of soil.

For annual borders the procedure is more elaborate. Let us assume you have planned the border in winter, when the seed catalogues come. Now you transfer your plan on to the border, marking the outlines of each drift with a pointed stick and placing the appropriate label. For a large border it pays to mark the outlines more lastingly, in case the sowing cannot be completed in one day ; drills are taken out with a hoe and some silver sand is run in to show them more clearly. Either of two methods may be adopted for the actual sowing :

METHODS OF SOWING IN THE OPEN

BROADCASTING

The drifts are sown one by one. The top ½ in. or so of soil is gently raked to one side. The patch is made quite level. Now the seed is spread. Sow thinly. Flower seed is expensive and crowded seedlings will be weaklings from the start. The soil that has been raked to one side is then made to fly back over the sown patch by a quick light push with the back of the rake. Firm the soil lightly with back of rake. Finish drift by fairy-light raking over the top, only just touching the soil with teeth of rake. This last raking helps air circulation. Proceed in this way until the entire border is sown, leaving a label in each drift as you go along. The one disadvantage of this method is that it needs great care to avoid bare little alleys between neighbouring drifts.

SOWING IN DRILLS

Shallow drills are drawn parallel to each other and very close together across each drift. They may run at angles to the drills of the neighbouring drift (see Fig. 17.) Seed is sown in much the same way as radish seed. The idea is that these lines will not be

PLAN FOR SEED SOWING IN THE ANNUAL BORDER •

PATH

Dotted lines show direction of seed drills

FIG. 17

noticed much, once the plants cover the surface, especially if thinnings can be transplanted into the spaces between the lines. The advantage of this method is that gaps between drifts are easily avoided. Altogether it requires less skill than the first method. But the first method, if really well executed, will give the most natural-looking appearance to the border.

AFTER-CARE OF SEED BEDS

Never allow the seed bed to get dry. A greyish look indicates that watering is required. Use a can with a fine rose for the job. If birds are troublesome, use fish-netting, black cotton or scarecrows to keep them off. Protect the small plants against slugs by little heaps of metaldehyde and a spreader (see page 645) placed here and there on the border.

THINNING

However thinly you may sow, it will practically always be necessary to thin the seedlings. Do this early, so that those you leave in can stretch to all sides whilst they are young. Once drawn up by lack of space and light, they will never become sturdy and bushy. Space the plants according to height and habit. Many failures in annual borders are due to insufficient thinning, resulting in weak plants that bear poor quality flowers over a short period, whereas properly thinned-out plants would have grown stately and bushy, producing fine flowers for many weeks. Thinning is best carried out in showery weather when the plants pull readily. If desired, thinnings can be transplanted to fill gaps.

PRICKING OUT

Plants raised under glass are sown much more closely than their outdoor colleagues. Therefore they are in danger of overcrowding much sooner. Prick out seedlings as soon as large enough to handle. (see illustration facing page 65.)

HARDENING OFF

This means that plants are gradually exposed to less protected conditions before being finally planted out in the open. The stress is on " gradually." This is a full hardening programme :

(1) Turn off heat during daytime, ventilate freely.
(2) Turn off heating altogether, ventilate freely.
(3) Transfer plants to cold frames, ventilate freely.
(4) Take lights off during daytime.
(5) Take lights off altogether.
(6) Stand boxes of plants outside in sheltered position.
(7) Stand boxes in position as exposed as their final position will be.
(8) Plant !

This process takes about 3 weeks. If interrupted because of severe weather, it will have to be repeated all over again.

With the present labour shortage, few gardeners will be able to follow all the 7 steps conscientiously, but the need for careful hardening cannot be too strongly emphasised. Supposing even that a rashly exposed plant will survive, it will yet be put weeks back in its development so that the advantage it had, by being sown under glass, is nullified and all the labour therefore wasted.

PLANTING

The planting of annuals really does not differ much from lettuce planting. Be careful to disturb the roots as little as possible. Make holes large enough to hold the roots and the soil that clings to them. Plant firmly—that means, as always, firm soil against roots to establish contact between soil water and water film around root hairs, but do not press the soil surface down tightly or air circulation will be disturbed. When planting out in drifts in the annual border, or into gaps in the herbaceous border, the spacing is done " casually " ; whilst for cut flower borders or bedding you plant in definite rows. More on the planting of flower beds will be found in Chapter II, page 260.

Always water after planting and, if the seedling boxes are at

all dry, water them before you lift the plants, or you are bound
to injure the roots seriously.

"PINCHING" (OR "STOPPING")

Many plants will give much better results if the growing point
is pinched out when they are about 6 ins. high. This will cause
stronger side shoots to form. The plant will be sturdier and carry
more flowers.

STAKING

Several of the taller annuals require staking. In most cases this
may be done by placing a few bushy pea-sticks among the plants
whilst they are still young. Then they will settle naturally among
the supports. Where more elaborate staking is needed, instructions
are given in the list of individual plants.

GENERAL CULTIVATION

Water liberally in dry spells.

Weeding and hoeing is easy enough where annuals are planted
in straight rows, but in the annual border it is difficult to carry
out. Weed thoroughly at thinning time. If the border was
prepared well, there should not be much trouble from weeds
later. Try to keep the soil surface loosened by using a very
pointed hoe or a Dutch hoe in an upright position.

Many annuals will appreciate occasional feeding with liquid
manure (see individual descriptions). Liquid manure can now
be bought in bottles. It is important to dilute the liquid, as
directed on the bottle. Never feed plants before they are
thoroughly established.

REMOVAL OF DEAD FLOWERS

Removing dead flowers prolongs the blossom period. If for some
reason it is desired to delay flowering, all flowers and flower buds
may be cut off. The plants will be covered with new blossom
in 2 or 3 weeks' time.

A LIST OF WORTHWHILE ANNUALS

★

THIS is a descriptive list of annuals which, whilst by no means complete, contains all the plants usually grown as annuals in gardens—and many more that would be worth growing.

All annuals are raised from seed. For further details about propagation, see under Cultivation in the list below. Unless it states definitely to the contrary all annuals flower during the summer months.

ADONIS (Heart's Blood, Pheasant's Eye) Order RANUNCULACEÆ

Perennial species are described on page 105.

Very lovely plants with erect stems bearing pale-green, finely-cut foliage and brilliant red flowers of the lesser Celandine type.

CULTIVATION : Sow where to flower, in March or April.

SPECIES :   *A. æstivalis.* Crimson, 1 ft, June–July ; S. Europe.
              A. annuus. Blood red, 1 ft., June–August ; Europe.
              A. autumnalis. Scarlet, 1 ft., May–September ; Britain.

AGERATUM Order COMPOSITÆ

Half-hardy annuals of compact, bushy growth, bearing a profusion of small fluffy flowers in pleasing shades of lilac. A useful bedding plant.

CULTIVATION : Sow in gentle heat in March, and plant out when all danger of frost is past.

SPECIES AND   *A. mexicanum.* Lilac blue, 1½-2 ft., summer; Tropical
VARIETIES :   America. The various types advertised in trade lists are much dwarfer : Blue Cap, a compact, free-flowering variety, suitable for edging ; Imperial Dwarf Blue, Imperial Dwarf White, well-known, sturdy varieties, larger flowers.

ALONSOA Order SCROPHULARIACEÆ

Dainty half-hardy perennial shrubs, often grown as annuals for beds and borders or as pot plants. The upright racemes of orange-scarlet flowers are very useful for cutting too.

CULTIVATION : As for half-hardy annuals.

SPECIES :   *A. incisifolia.* Scarlet, 18 ins., summer ; Chile.
A. Warscewiczi. Rosy scarlet, 1½-2 ft., summer ; Chile. And several others including some whites and yellows.

ALTHÆA Order MALVACEÆ

Strictly speaking, these are perennials grown as biennials usually, but " Annual Hollyhocks " are now being advertised, i.e. kinds that will flower the same season as sown.

CULTIVATION : As for hardy annuals.

SPECIES :   *A. rosea* (Indian Summer). Coppery-pink, 5-6 ft., late summer.

ALYSSUM (Sweet Alyssum) Order CRUCIFERÆ

Dainty little plants with heads of small, white, sweetly-scented flowers. There is a lilac-coloured variety. Suitable for edgings, carpeting, groups in the front of the border or to grow among stonework of paved paths, steps or rockery.

CULTIVATION : Sow in April in the open where it is to remain.
SPECIES AND   *A. maritimum.* White, 6-10 ins., summer ; Europe
VARIETIES :   (Britain). Numerous varieties, such as : Little Dorrit, white, very sweetly fragrant, only 4 ins. high; Royal Carpet very similar, but violet-purple in colour. There also is a variegated variety.

AMARANTHUS (Love-lies-Bleeding) Order AMARANTHACEÆ

Half-hardy annuals with pale green leaves and long, languidly dangling " cords " of dark velvety red flowers. Rather artificial looking.

CULTIVATION : As for all half-hardy annuals. Soil should be fairly light and not too rich.
SPECIES :   *A. caudatus.* Crimson, 2-3 ft., summer ; Tropics.
A. hypochondriacus (The Prince's Feather). Taller and bears its flowers in erect plumes. A number of other species are grown for their attractively-coloured foliage.

ANAGALLIS (Pimpernel) Order PRIMULACEÆ

Very neat and attractive hardy annuals and perennials. The latter may also be grown as annuals. Plants mostly dwarf, compact or trailing. Flowers, very clean in shape and clear in colours.

CULTIVATION: Treat as hardy annuals. Best sown where intended to flower.

SPECIES AND *A. fruticosa.* Brilliant red, 2 ft., summer; Morocco.
VARIETIES: *A. indica.* Blue, 1 ft., July; India.
A. linifolia (syn. *A. grandiflora*). Blue, perennial, 1 ft., July; Europe. Numerous varieties, including pinks and reds.

ANCHUSA Order BORAGINACEÆ

These are perennials and biennials.

CULTIVATION: The biennial *A. capensis* can be treated as a hardy annual. Flowers like a giant forget-me-not.

SPECIES AND *A. capensis,* bright blue, 1-1½ ft., July; S. Africa.
VARIETIES: Variety Blue Bird, which is dwarfer and makes an excellent bedding plant.

ANTIRRHINUM (Snap-dragon) Order SCROPHULARIACEÆ

These perennials are often grown as biennials or annuals, because as such they are among our very best summer bedding plants. The widespread Antirrhinum rust disease usually attacks older plants, so that we do not often find these plants included in the perennial borders.

CULTIVATION: Give these a long-growing season by sowing early. Sow under glass January-March for a succession of bloom from June to October. Give seedlings plenty of space at all times, to obtain vigorous plants. For bushy plants pinch our growing points when 6 ins. high. You can sow in late summer or early autumn in the open. Plants raised this way will be sturdy and frost-resisting and come into flower about the same time as those sown in January under glass.

SPECIES AND *A. majus.* Pink 1-2 ft., July; S. Europe. Numerous
VARIETIES: hybrids and varieties including a wide range of lovely colours that may be most delicate or most brilliant. Special large-flowered strains and dwarf strains will be found advertised in the seed catalogues.

ARCTOTIS Order COMPOSITÆ

Half-hardy perennials usually grown as annuals. Their purity of shape and colour makes these large daisy flowers most strikingly beautiful.

CULTIVATION : Grow as half-hardy annuals. They will do equally well in full sun or in semi-shade ; in fact when grown in shady places such as an enclosed court or quadrangle all the light that is there seems to emanate from them.

SPECIES AND
VARIETIES :
A. breviscapa. Orange, 6 ins., summer ; S. Africa. Variety, *aurantiaca*, which is more brilliant still.
A. grandis. Ray florets snow white with delicate lavender blue reverse, disc florets deep smoky blue, 1½ ft., summer ; S.W. Africa.
A. scapigera. Wide range of colours, including delicate pink and white as well as brilliant orange and crimson scarlet, 1½ ft., leaves dark green with white woolly underside.

ARGEMONE (Prickly Poppy, Devil's Fig) Order PAPAVERACEÆ

Hardy annuals and perennials. The latter are also grown as annuals. Large white, yellow or purple poppy flowers borne in great profusion throughout the summer months. The plants grow rather large, and the stiffly erect stems and leaves are covered with bristly rough hairs.

CULTIVATION : Sow in March or April where intended to flower. Earlier flowers may be obtained from sowings under glass in February, but like all members of the poppy family, the Argemones do not like transplanting. This would have to be done with great care.

SPECIES :
A. grandiflora. White, 2-3 ft., summer ; Mexico.
A. mexicana. Lemon yellow, 2 ft., June ; Mexico and Tropical America.
A. platyceras. White or purple, 1-4 ft., summer ; N. and S. America.

ASPERULA (Woodruff) Order RUBIACEÆ

Dainty plants with whorled fragrant leaves and terminal clusters of starry white, blue or pink flowers.

CULTIVATION : Sow in April where intended to flower. Sun or shade suitable.

SPECIES :   *A. azurea setosa* (syn. *A. orientalis*). Blue, 6-10 ins., summer ; Syria.

BEGONIA Order BEGONIACEÆ

A large tribe of greenhouse perennials, some of them grown like half-hardy annuals for the summer bedding.

CULTIVATION : Sow bedding Begonias in February in heated greenhouse and grow on under glass till June. Then harden to plant out late in June. Begonias require a compost that is well drained and rich in moisture-holding matter. They resent firm potting and all harsh treatment.

TYPES :   Two types are used for bedding, the tuberous-rooted and the fibrous-rooted.

The tuberous-rooted produce enormous flowers shaped like flat giant roses in an amazing variety of colours, including delicate pinks, lemon yellow, white, apricot, as well as the most fiery orange, scarlet or deepest blood red. Foliage dark green, handsome.

Parent species of tuberous-rooted begonias :
B. boliviensis, B. Clarkei, B. Davidsii, B. Pearcei, B. rosæflora, B. Veitchii, all hailing from Peru and Bolivia, 1-2 ft.

The fibrous-rooted type bears a profusion of small flowers in various shades of pink and red as well as white. The leaves are shiny and pale green often tinged or edged red. Height, 1 ft.

B. semperflorens from Brazil is the fibrous-rooted species usually seen in summer bedding.

BRACHYCOME (Swan River Daisy) Order COMPOSITÆ

Half-hardy annual with delicate sky-blue daisy flowers, too dainty for formal bedding but lovely in the annual border.

CULTIVATION : Treat as half-hardy annual, does best in full sun in well-drained border.
SPECIES :   *B. iberidifolia.* Blue, 1 ft., summer ; W. Australia.

CALCEOLARIA (Slipperwort) Order SCROPHULARIACEÆ

These showy and very pretty plants are not so often seen now, as over-attention to them in the Victorian days has brought them into disgrace. There is, however, no reason why we should not give them a turn in our beds and borders from time to time. The slipperworts are tender and half-hardy perennials but for bedding purposes are grown as annuals.

CULTIVATION : The smaller types are grown like any half-hardy annual. The large-flowered hybrids are sown in August and planted out early the following summer.

SPECIES AND VARIETIES : *C. hybrida* is the large-flowered hybrid grown as a pot plant and bedding plant. Several good strains can be had with colours including yellows, coppery oranges, scarlet and dark reds and browns. Height, 18 ins.-2 ft.

CALENDULA (Pot Marigold) Order COMPOSITÆ

One of the easiest and hardiest annuals that brighten our gardens. Choose a good strain. Excellent as cut flowers as well as in narrow beds on their own, and together with other brightly-coloured flowers in larger beds and borders.

CULTIVATION : Treat as hardy annuals. May be sown outside in autumn for early flowering ; once established, marigolds will come again from seed—often only too much so ! Seed may also easily be collected, though the seedlings will not be true to type.

SPECIES AND VARIETIES : *C. officinalis.* The parent of the garden calendulas. Orange yellow, 2 ft., summer ; S. Europe. Good varieties include : Chrysantha, a double buttercup yellow ; Lemon Queen ; Orange King ; Radio, a brilliant orange with quilled petals.
The old-fashioned singles with dark centres and a great range of variations are not so often seen now.

CALIFORNIAN POPPY (*see* ESCHSCHOLTZIA)

CALLIOPSIS (*see* COREOPSIS)

CALLIRRHOE Order MALVACEÆ

Showy and attractive hardy annuals and perennials that deserve to be grown more widely. The perennial species may also be grown as annuals.

CULTIVATION : Treat as hardy annuals. For early flowering, sow under glass in March and transplant in May.

SPECIES AND   *C. Papaver.* Deep violet-red, white eye, 2-3 ft.,
VARIETIES :   perennial.
             C. pedata. Cherry-red, 2 ft., summer ; Texas.
             Variety, *compacta*, is crimson with a white centre.

CALLISTEPHUS (China Aster) Order COMPOSITÆ

Hardy annual. Very popular for late summer and autumn flowering. Excellent for beds, banks, borders, as well as for house decoration. These many-coloured daisy flowers can be had in several types, each type including hosts of varieties.

CULTIVATION : Best treated as half-hardy annual, sown under glass in March and planted outside in May. The quality of the flowers will be greatly improved by occasional feeding with liquid manure. China asters are often destroyed by a disease known as black leg. Where this occurs do not plant asters in the same place for several seasons, or else sterilise the soil or use resistant varieties.

SPECIES AND   *C. chinensis.* Several colours, 1-2 ft., summer ;
TYPES :   China. Many garden types, among them : Anemone-flowered, a 2 ft. mid-season, good cut flower.
             Chrysanthemum-flowered, which can be had dwarf (9 ins.), or fairly tall (18 ins.) in brilliantly-coloured double flowers of various shades. Mid-season. Good bedder.
             The Comet type has more loosely streaming ray florets and can be had tall or dwarf; various colours.
             Giant of California, 2 ft., large-flowered, very late ; various colours.
             Leviathan, grows to $2\frac{1}{2}$ ft. with very large double flowers in various colours.
             Ostrich Plume is very popular because the very large flower heads are feathery and graceful, borne on $1\frac{1}{2}$-2 ft. stems ; various colours.

CAMPANULA (Harebell, Bell Flower) Order CAMPANULACEÆ

There are some very pretty annual harebells, most of them dwarf but large flowered and very easy to grow.

CULTIVATION : Grow like half-hardy annuals, sowing under glass in March, transplanting into the open in late May or early June.

SPECIES : *C. drabæfolia.* Blue, 3 ins., July ; Greece.
C. kewensis. Deep blue, 3 ins., June–July, hybrid.
C. Loeflingii. Blue, 1 ft., July ; Portugal.
C. macrostyla. Blue, 18 ins., July ; Asia Minor.
C. sulphurea. Pale yellow, 9 ins., July ; Syria.

CELSIA Order SCROPHULARIACEÆ

Half-hardy biennials that may well be grown as annuals for beds or borders. In appearance they are compact somewhat " refined " mulleins.

CULTIVATION : Sow in March under glass, transplant to flowering position in May.
SPECIES : *C. Arcturus.* Yellow, 2-4 ft., July ; Crete.
C. cretica. Yellow, 3-5 ft., July ; S. Europe.

CENTAUREA (Cornflower) Order COMPOSITÆ

Perennial species are described on page 111. But several annual species are worth growing, among them the ever-popular cornflower, *C. cyanus.*

CULTIVATION : Sow in autumn or spring where intended to flower. To prevent weedy growth, start thinning early. A sunny position is required.
SPECIES : *C. americana.* Pink or purple, 2-5 ft., August ; N. America.
C. cyanus. Blue, pink or white, 3 ft., summer ; Britain.
C. moschata. Sweet Sultan. Yellow, white or purple, 2 ft., summer ; Orient.

CERINTHE (Honeywort) Order BORAGINACEÆ

These are popular with the bees and one annual species is worth cultivating for its wealth of pretty yellow and violet flowers.

CULTIVATION : Treat as hardy annuals, sowing in position in the open in April.
SPECIES : *C. retorta.* Yellow and violet, 1½ ft., July ; Greece.

CHRYSANTHEMUM Order COMPOSITÆ

The annual Chrysanthemum is popular in beds and borders and especially as a cut flower. The flowers are showy and interesting in their great variety of shades and markings.

CULTIVATION : Grow as any hardy annual, sowing in the open in

CULTIVATION : March or April, or for early flowering under glass in March and transplant into flowering position in May.

SPECIES AND VARIETIES : *C. carinatum.* White, yellow, purple, 2 ft., summer ; N. Africa.
C. coronarium. Yellow and white, 3 ft., summer ; S. Europe. Many varieties, such as Coronet, lemon and cream bands round dark centre ; Eastern Star, lemon with chocolate centre ; Eclipse, buff, brown or bronze, with crimson markings.

CLARKIA Order ONAGRACEÆ

These very showy annuals are easy to grow and do well on a heavy soil.

CULTIVATION : Treat as hardy annuals. For earlier' flowering, seed may be sown under glass early in March and transplanted to the open in May.

SPECIES AND VARIETIES : *C. elegans.* Pink, 1-4 ft., July ; N. America. Varieties : Crimson Queen ; Dorothy, brilliant rose ; Enchantress, salmon pink ; Firefly, rose crimson ; Snowball, white ; Vesuvius, orange scarlet.
C. pulchella. Several colours, 1-1½ ft., June–July. Varieties : Mrs. Langtry, white with crimson eye ; Tom Thumb, a dwarf variety, useful for the front of the border.

COBÆA Order POLEMONIACEÆ

A pretty blue-flowered climbing annual of easy cultivation. useful for training along arches, fences, balconies.

CULTIVATION : Treat as half-hardy annual.

SPECIES : *C. scandens.* Lilac-blue, 10-30 ft., summer ; Mexico.

COLLINSIA Order SCROPHULARIACEÆ

Hardy annuals of easy culture, some of them very showy and lovely.

CULTIVATION : Treat as hardy annuals, sowing seed in position in autumn or spring. Thin seedlings to 6 ins. apart when 2 ins. high.

SPECIES :   *C. grandiflora.* Blue and white, some forms purple,
1 ft.; N.W. America.
C. verna. Blue and purple, 9 ins. ; N. America.

COLLOMIA Order POLEMONIACEÆ

Hardy annuals worth growing because of their brilliant scarlet
flowers.

CULTIVATION :   Treat as hardy annual, sowing in autumn or spring
where the plants are intended to flower.
SPECIES :   *C. coccinea.* Bright red, 18 ins., June ; Chile.
There is also a salmon or buff species from
California (*C. grandiflora*).

CONVOLVULUS Order CONVOLVULACEÆ

The troublesome bindweed has a very lovely cousin in the
flower garden, a compact bushy plant, smothered with deep blue
or light blue flowers with white or yellow centres. Equally
excellent on their own in narrow beds or as edgings or forming
clumps in the mixed annual border. Also quite suitable for
filling gaps among herbaceous plants.

CULTIVATION :   Treat as hardy annual, sowing in March or April
in the open where intended to flower. For early
flowering, outdoor sowings may be made in
autumn. Sowing under glass in February or
March may also be done to bring about earlier
flowering. The thinnings will transplant well. A
sunny position is required, as the flowers only open
fully when the sun shines on them. Collect seed
for future sowings.
SPECIES AND   *C. minor* (syn. *C. tricolor*) and several varieties which,
VARIETIES :   however, do not seem an improvement on the
species ; various colours, 1 ft.

COREOPSIS (syn. *Calliopsis*) Order COMPOSITÆ

This genus has some very fine annual species. Their delicate
daisy flowers have wide ray florets of contrasting colours. Foliage
feathered, habit graceful.

CULTIVATION :   Treat as hardy or as half-hardy annuals.
SPECIES AND   *C. coronata.* Orange and purple, 2 ft., summer ;
VARIETIES :   Texas.

SPECIES AND   *C. tinctoria.* Yellow and purple, 2 ft., summer;
VARIETIES :   N. America.
                  C. tinctoria atrosanguinea. Purple, 1-2 ft. Many
                  varieties : Crimson King, dwarf; Fire King, bright
                  scarlet, semi-dwarf ; Garnet, crimson scarlet, semi-
                  dwarf; Sultan, crimson, dwarf; Tiger Star, brown,
                  mottled yellow, dwarf.

CORNFLOWER (*see* CENTAUREA)

COSMOS (Mexican Aster) Order COMPOSITÆ

This lovely, graceful, hardy annual has the broad ray florets in common with the coreopsis, but cosmos has much larger flowers and a different colour range, including white and all shades of pink, also pale yellow, cream and lilac.

CULTIVATION : Best grown as half-hardy annual if the flowers are
                  to be had fairly early.
SPECIES AND   *C. bipinnatus.* Various colours, 3 ft., August ;
VARIETIES :   Mexico.
                  C. diversifolius. Lilac, 3 ft., September ; N. America.
                  C. diversifolius atrosanguineus. An improved strain
                  of the last.
                  C. sulphureus. Pale yellow, 3-4 ft., July–August ;
                  Mexico.

CREPIS (Hawksbeard) Order COMPOSITÆ

Their deep rosy-pink flowers make these little cousins of the crimson hawksbeard worth having. They are suitable for the edge of a border.

CULTIVATION : Treat as hardy annual, sowing in April where
                  intended to flower.
SPECIES :   *C. rubra.* Rosy red, 6-12 ins., summer ; S. Europe.

CYNOGLOSSUM (Hound's Tongue) Order BORAGINACEÆ

A wealth of deep true blue flowers covers the hoary shoots of this hardy perennial—which is usually grown as an annual. It may be had at its best right until the really heavy frosts cut it down. Excellent in the annual border as well as for filling gaps in the herbaceous border. A grand cut flower that will grow and last in the vase for a long time.

CULTIVATION : Treat as hardy annual, sowing in spring where

CULTIVATION : intended to flower. For late flowering, to brighten autumn border and autumn vases, delay sowing until late May or early June. True blues are rare and very valuable in the autumn garden.

SPECIES : *C. amabile.* Blue, 2 ft., June–October ; S.W. China.

DELPHINIUM (Annual Larkspur) Order RANUNCULACEÆ

Annual Larkspur can be had in many lovely colours, bright or gentle and being a tall annual of good shape, it is very important both for cutting and for the back of an annual border.

CULTIVATION : Sow in the open in autumn for sturdy plants and early flowers. A succession is obtained by seed sown in March or April where the plants are intended to flower. Thin early and vigorously.

SPECIES AND VARIETIES : *D. Ajacis.* Violet, blue, 1-1½ ft., summer ; Europe. This, the rocket larkspur, has given rise to many garden varieties.
D. cardinale. Scarlet, 3 ft., late summer ; California.
D. consolida. Blue, 2½ ft., summer ; Europe. This, the stock-flowered Larkspur, is parent of the Giant Imperial varieties, which include a wide range of lovely colours, such as deep violet, bright rose, lavender and white. The varieties grow much taller than the species, some reaching 5 ft., and many of them have double flowers, which in the annual Larkspur are an asset.

DIANTHUS (Carnation, Pink) Order CARYOPHYLLACEÆ

These are best known as perennials and biennials, but some types may be successfully grown as annuals. They are very showy and often sweetly scented and so make a valuable contribution to the annual border.

CULTIVATION : Sow under glass in February or March and transplant to sunny borders in April or May.

TYPES, SPECIES AND VARIETIES : There are three main types :
(1) Those rather resembling a border carnation, but with small, less heavy flowers. They are the Marguerite and Chabaud carnations, hybrids of *D. caryophyllus* with various other species. Wide colour range including crimson, scarlet, pink, pale yellow and white, sweet scent, height 1-1½ ft., flowers late summer.

Annuals and Plants Grown as Such

SPECIES AND VARIETIES :
(2) Those resembling pinks. Varieties of :

D. sinensis. Various colours, 6-12 ins., summer; Central Asia.

D. s. Heddewigii. The Japanese Pinks. Probably the most popular of the dianthus. They can be had single or double in white and all shades of pink and red, 6-12 ins.

(3) These resembling the Sweet William, which is one of their parents.

D. hybridus, Sweet Wivelsfield. In range of colour as well as flower arrangement resembles the Sweet William, but has much larger flowers and does well as an annual, 1-1½ ft.

D. hybridus, Delight, often called the annual Sweet William, 1-1½ ft., various colours.

DIASCIA Order SCROPHULARIACEÆ

Half-hardy annual, fine rose-pink flowers well spaced on graceful, upright racemes. Suited for bedding or borders of annuals. Also a good pot plant for the greenhouse.

CULTIVATION : Sow under glass, March or April. Transplant to open end of May.

SPECIES : *D. Barberæ.* Rose pink, 1 ft., summer ; S. Africa.

DIMORPHOTHECA (Star of the Veldt) Order COMPOSITÆ

This S. African genus contributes a number of strikingly beautiful daisy flowers to annual beds and borders. Most of them are good cut flowers, but must be given a sunny position, as flowers will otherwise not remain fully open.

CULTIVATION : Best treated as half-hardy annuals, sown under glass in March and transplanted to the open in May.

SPECIES AND VARIETIES :
D. aurantiaca. Brilliant orange, 1-2 ft., summer. Various hybrid varieties, white, yellow, orange or red.

D. Ecklonis. White with deep smoky-blue disc, 1½-2 ft. A lovely bedding plant. Very suitable where a sombre place needs quiet, radiant brightening.

D. pluvialis. White with golden-yellow disc. Ray florets reversed with delicate lavender blue, 1-2 ft.

D. p. ringens. Has a striking zone of deep lavender blue at the base of the white ray florets, 1-2 ft.

221

SPECIES AND   *D. p. flore pleno.* A double form in which all the
VARIETIES :   radiant beauty of the species is lost, 1-2 ft., white
and lavender.

DOWNINGIA (syn. *Clintonia*) Order CAMPANULACEÆ

Dainty yet compact little hardy annuals, suitable for edgings and rockeries. Also used for pots and hanging baskets in the cool greenhouse.

CULTIVATION : Sow in April in sunny position where intended to
flower. Thin to 6 ins. apart.

SPECIES :   *D. elegans.* Blue with white lips, 6 ins., summer ;
N.W. America.
D. pulchella. The flowers are a neat pattern of light and dark violet blue with white and yellow markings, 6 ins., summer ; W. America.

DRACOCEPHALUM (Dragon's Head, Moldavian Balm)
Order LABIATÆ

Bushy plants with long spikes of deep violet-blue, sage-like flowers, loved by bees.

CULTIVATION : Sow this hardy annual in April where intended to
flower. Will do quite well in partial shade.

SPECIES :   *D. Moldavica.* Violet-blue, 1-1½ ft., July–August ;
E. Siberia. There are a number of perennial species.

ECCREMOCARPUS Order BIGNONIACEÆ

This lovely, not quite hardy, perennial climber is sometimes grown as an annual. Its full description will be found under FLOWERING SHRUBS, page 333.

ECHIUM (Viper's Bugloss) Order BORAGINACEÆ

Hardy annuals, biennials and perennials, some of them well worth including in the annual border. Loved by bees.

CULTIVATION : Seeds may be sown where plants are intended to
flower, but earlier flowering is assured by raising plants under glass and transplanting to open in May.

SPECIES AND   *E. creticum.* Deep violet, 1-1½ ft., July–August ;
VARIETIES :   S. Europe. This is a fine annual.
E. plantagineum. Lavender blue, 2-3 ft., summer ; S. Europe. This biennial is much grown as an

VARIETIES :　annual and a number of varieties in shades of mauve, pink, blue, even white, are offered " Blue Bedder " is a popular, showy variety.

EMILIA (syn. *Cacalia*) (Tassel Flower) Order COMPOSITÆ

Its clusters of vivid scarlet little daisy flowers make this fairly hardy annual a welcome summer guest.

CULTIVATION : Sow outdoors in April or raise under glass in February or March, and transplant to the open in May.

SPECIES :　*E. flammea.* Scarlet, 1-1½ ft., summer ; Tropical America.

ERYSIMUM (Alpine Wallflower) Order CRUCIFERÆ

This genus includes one showy annual, whilst some of its biennial and perennial members may also be grown as annuals.

CULTIVATION : Sow in April where intended to flower, in sunny, well-drained position.

SPECIES :　*E. asperum.* Orange or yellow, 1-2 ft., spring and early summer ; N. America.

E. muralis. Golden yellow, 1-1½ ft., early summer ; Europe.

E. perofskianum. Deep orange red, 1 ft., all summer ; Caucasus.

This latter is a true annual, sweetly scented and worth having for making a good show over a long period.

ESCHSCHOLTZIA (Californian Poppy) Order PAPAVERACEÆ

These deservedly popular hardy annuals require no introduction. They may be had in many lovely colours, frequently combining several shades in one flower. Suitable for beds and borders as well as for cut flowers, if they can be given a sunny position. Children delight in watching them " take off their cap " as they burst into flower.

CULTIVATION : Choose a sunny well-drained position. Sow in autumn for early flowering or in March or April for late summer flowering. Seed may be collected or the plants allowed to re-seed themselves. Occasionally, plants refuse to die after flowering, as an

CULTIVATION : orthodox annual should, and will continue for several years if given the chance.

SPECIES AND VARIETIES : *E. californica.* Orange yellow, 1-1½ ft., summer; California. Varieties include dwarfer types, which are useful as edgings, and doubles—doubleness being, however, a doubtful asset in the case of Eschscholtzia : *alba,* creamy white, single, 1 ft. ; Aurora, cream, suffused peach pink, single, 1 ft. ; Carmine King, a brilliant red, dwarf single ; Cherry, red, single, 1 ft. ; Dazzler, brilliant orange red, dwarf, single; Flame, brilliant orange red, tall. Monarch Art Shades. The most beautiful semi-double frilled flowers in glorious colours.

Popular double varieties, all about 9 ins. high : Autumn Glory, semi-double, coppery orange ; *crocea flore pleno,* deep orange ; Robert Gardiner, orange with fluted petals.

EUCHARIDIUM Order ONAGRACEÆ

A Californian genus of very showy hardy annuals that deserve to be grown more widely. Somewhat resemble Clarkia.

CULTIVATION : Sow in autumn, spring and early summer where intended to flower.

SPECIES : *E. Breweri.* White, lilac and purple, 9-12 ins., summer, sweetly scented.
E. concinna. Rosy purple, 1 ft., summer.
E. grandiflorum. Rosy purple, 1 ft., summer.

EUPHORBIA (Spurge, Poinsettia) Order EUPHORBIACEÆ

An enormously varied genus of wide distribution in temperate, sub-tropical and tropical regions. See also page 603, for greenhouse-grown Euphorbias. One, the Annual Poinsettia, is a delightful and unusual plant for beds and borders of annuals as well as for pot culture in the cool greenhouse.

CULTIVATION : Sow in April where intended to flower.

SPECIES : *E. heterophylla.* Red and orange, 2 ft., summer ; Mexico. As with all euphorbias the true flowers, small and orange, are not very showy, but the surrounding brightly-coloured bracts form the real attraction.

38. *Dividing with forks*

39. *Divided Michaelmas daisies*

40. *Taking cutting from a delphinium*

41. *Taking side shoot from a Wallace chrysanthemum*

Annuals and Plants Grown as Such

FELICIA Order COMPOSITÆ

Dainty daisy flowers of liveliest blue. The genus includes biennials and perennials as well as annuals, but all are best grown as annuals.

CULTIVATION : Sow under glass, February–March, and transplant to the open in May.

SPECIES : *F. adfinis.* Large blue flowers, 8-9 ins., summer ; S. Africa.
F. fragilis (syn. *F. tenella*). Blue, 6 ins., summer ; S. Africa.
F. rotundifolia. Blue, 1 ft., bushy and very free-flowering.

GAILLARDIA Order COMPOSITÆ

Apart from herbaceous perennials, this genus also gives us some particularly beautiful annuals that produce large brightly-coloured daisy flowers over a very long period.

CULTIVATION : Sow under glass in March, transfer to sunny position outside in May. Gaillardias like a rich soil.

SPECIES AND VARIETIES : *G. amblyodon.* Brilliant red, 2-3 ft., autumn ; Texas.
G. pulchella. Crimson and yellow, 2-3 ft., summer ; N. America. This has very large flowers and has given rise to a number of good varieties, the best of which include *G. p. picta albo-marginata*, ray florets deep bronzy red tipped white ; *G. p. picta Lorenziana*, a double form with fluted ray florets, may be had in many colours and colour combinations.

GAURA Order ONAGRACEÆ

This hardy perennial is often grown as an annual. Its tall graceful spikes of white and pink flowers make a good background for an annual border.

CULTIVATION : Sow in April where intended to flower.

SPECIES : *G. Lindheimeri.* White and rose, 3-4 ft., July–October ; Texas.

GILIA Order POLEMONIACEÆ

A genus of dainty, free-flowering annuals, biennials and perennials. The annuals are hardy, mostly dwarf and particularly suitable for the front of the annual border.

CULTIVATION : Sow in autumn or spring where plants are to flower. Thin to 3 ins. apart. Sunny position required.

SPECIES : *G. achilleæfolia.* Violet, 1 ft., August ; California.

G. androsacea (syn. *Leptosiphon parviflorus*). Lilac, pink and white, 1 ft., August ; California.

G. densiflora (syn. *L. densiflorus*). Lilac, 6 ins., June ; California.

G. dianthoides (syn. *Fenzlia dianthiflora*). Lilac or rosy purple with white or yellow, 6 ins., July ; California.

G. micrantha (syn. *Leptosiphon roseus*). Rose, 9 ins., summer ; California.

G. tricolor. Orange and purple, 1 ft., June ; California.

The last two are particularly popular both for beds and borders.

GLAUCIUM (Horned Poppy) Order PAPAVERACEÆ

These poppies have glaucous foliage and long, curved pods that gave them their name of Horned Poppy. Though quite decorative, these plants tend to sprawl and should only be used in the really large border or in the wild garden. They are actually biennials but may be grown as annuals.

CULTIVATION : Sow in early autumn or spring where the plants are to flower. The seedlings will not transplant well.

SPECIES AND VARIETIES : *G. corniculatum.* Crimson with black, 1 ft., summer ; Mediterranean.

G. flavum (syn. *G. luteum*). Yellow, 1-3 ft., summer ; Europe (Britain).

There are several varieties in both species, showing variations of colour, including shades of yellow, orange and red.

GODETIA Order ONAGRACEÆ

Deservedly popular hardy annuals. Flowers large, densely packed ; many lovely colours including rich and delicate shades. Suitable for beds and borders as a cut flower or pot plant.

CULTIVATION : Sow where plants are to flower, in autumn or spring. Early flowering plants may also be raised from sowings under glass in early spring.

SPECIES AND   Parents of our garden varieties are :
VARIETIES :   *G. amœna.* Lilac crimson, graceful, 1-2 ft., summer ;
California.
G. grandiflora (syn. *Œnothera Whitneyi, Godetia
Whitneyi*). Red, crimson or white, 1-2 ft., sum-
mer; California, and several others. Good
varieties: Cherry Red, a tall double; Flam-
ingo, crimson-scarlet, 1 ft., single; Kelvedon
Glory, salmon pink, 1 ft., single; Lavender
Queen, clear lavender, 18 ins., single; Lilacina,
tall double; Monarch Dwarf Bedding Mixed.
Uniform compact single flowers, brilliant col-
ours.

GYPSOPHILA Order CARYOPHYLLACEÆ

The annual Gypsophila resembles its perennial cousin, but is,
if anything, still more airy and feathery. Used with discretion, it is
a lovely " lightener " of borders and vases.

CULTIVATION : Sow in April where plants are intended to flower.
SPECIES AND   *G. elegans.* White, 1-1½ ft., June–October ;
VARIETIES :   Caucasus. Varieties : *carminea,* with pink flowers ;
grandiflora, with extra large flowers.

HEBENSTRETIA Order SELAGINACEÆ

Half-hardy perennial, treated as annual. Though it is both
showy and sweetly fragrant, it is not often seen in gardens
to-day.

CULTIVATION : Sow under glass in March, transplant to open in
May. Outdoor sowings may also be made end of
April or early May.
SPECIES :   *H. comosa.* White, spotted scarlet, 1½-2 ft., summer ;
S. Africa. The flowers are fragrant and are borne
in long, dense spikes.

HELENIUM (Sneeze-wort) Order COMPOSITÆ

The perennial Heleniums are invaluable in the herbaceous
border. But there is also an annual species well worth cultivating,
as it is graceful, compact and showy. The yellow daisy flowers are
well shown up by the finely cut light-green foliage.

CULTIVATION : Sow in April where plants are to flower, or raise
plants from sowing under glass in March, seedlings
to be planted out in May.

SPECIES : *H. tenuifolium.* Yellow, 1½-2 ft., summer ; N. America.

HELIANTHUS (Sunflower) Order COMPOSITÆ

The old-fashioned giant sunflower is a lovely thing if given the right place. It must be planted where its extreme boldness and brightness will be an asset—perhaps against a wall or fence, perhaps with dark shrubs as a background. Don't ask it to partner any of the more delicate annuals. Several varieties are available now, differing from the original type in colouring and flower size.

CULTIVATION : Sunny, sheltered position required. Sow in April where plants are to flower. Seeds are best planted in stations of 3 with about 15 ins. between the stations. Thin to one plant to each station, keeping the strongest of each trio, water freely in dry weather. Feedings with liquid manure will bring out the true giant character in these flowers. Stakes should be given in all but the most sheltered positions.

SPECIES AND VARIETIES : *H. annuus.* Yellow, 6-10 ft., summer ; N. America. Varieties include : *flore pleno,* a large double form (not to be recommended) ; Primrose Perfection, pale yellow with black centres ; Sutton's Red, with a wide chestnut-brown band at the base of the ray florets, and many others.

H. argyrophyllus. Yellow, 6 ft., summer ; N. America. Has its leaves densely covered with a down of silky white hairs.

H. debilis (syn. *H. cucumerifolius*). Yellow, 3-4 ft., summer ; N. America. The miniature sunflower, more dainty in habit, bears numerous smaller flowers on each plant.

HELICHRYSUM (Immortelle, Everlasting Flower)
Order COMPOSITÆ

Of these everlasting flowers, the best known ones are annuals. The chief use of these many-coloured strawy daisy flowers is for winter decoration in the house. They are also much used for cemeteries.

CULTIVATION : Raise under glass in early spring to transplant to the open in May, or sow in April where intended

CULTIVATION : to flower. Cut flowers as soon as fully opened
Sunny position required.

SPECIES AND   *H. bracteatum.* Various colours, 2-3 ft., summer ;
VARIETIES :   Australia. A number of varieties with named
colours can also be had.

HELIOPHILA Order CRUCIFERÆ

A genus of graceful and showy hardy annuals, natives of S.
Africa.

CULTIVATION : Sow under glass in March and transplant to the
open ground in May. Alternatively sow in April
where the plants are intended to flower. When
thinning have clumps of 3 to 5 plants, treating
them as one.

SPECIES :   *H. amplexicaulis.* White and purple, 9 ins., summer.
H. coronopifolia. Bluish white, 2 ft., summer.
H. leptophylla. Bright blue, white eye, 9 ins.,
summer.
H. linearifolia. Blue, 1 ft., summer.

HELIPTERUM (Australian Everlasting, Immortelle Flower)
Order COMPOSITÆ

These everlasting flowers seem more alive than most of their
colleagues. The genus now includes those formerly talked of as
Acroclinium and *Rhodanthe*. Some of them are well worth including
in a mixed border of annuals. All are natives of Australia.

CULTIVATION : Sow under glass, March or April, transfer to open
May or early June. Sunny well-drained borders
required.

SPECIES AND   *H. humboldtianum* (syn. *H. Sandfordii*). Yellow, 1 ft.,
VARIETIES :   summer.
H. Manglesii (syn. *Rhodanthe Manglesii*). Rose-pink
with yellow disc, 1-1½ ft., summer. This is a very
lovely species and several varieties are obtainable,
including dark red and white forms.
H. roseum (syn. *Acroclinium roseum*). Rose, 2 ft.,
summer, and several beautiful varieties of this fine,
large-flowered species. Some of these are double,
which in this case is an improvement, as they are
more showy at all times, but especially in dull
weather, when the single form tends to close its
flowers.

HIBISCUS (Musk Mallow, etc.) Order MALVACEÆ

A widely distributed genus of hardy and tender annuals and perennials. The flowers resemble those of their cousin the hollyhock.

CULTIVATION : Sow under glass in February or March. Transplant to sheltered, sunny border in June. *H. Trionium* may be sown in April outdoors, where intended to flower.

SPECIES : *H. esculentus*, yellow and reddish, 6 ft., summer ; Tropics. The fruits of this species grow to 1 ft. long and are edible when immature.
H. Manihot. Yellow and purple, 6-8 ft., summer ; Tropics. This is a half-hardy perennial, but very suitable for cultivation as an annual. A fine species.
H. Trionium. Yellow and purple, 2 ft., summer ; Africa.

IBERIS (Candytuft) Order CRUCIFERÆ

A very popular annual, accommodating and useful for a variety of purposes, such as edgings, borders, cut flowers. The genus also supplies us with some widely-grown hardy perennials (see section on Rock Gardens, page 165).

CULTIVATION : Sow where the plants are intended to flower. Autumn sowings for early summer flowering, spring sowings for summer and early autumn flowering. Thin to 3-4 ins., when 1-2 ins. high.

SPECIES AND VARIETIES : *I. coronaria* (Rocket Candytuft). White, 1 ft., summer.
I. umbellata (Common Candytuft). Purple, 1 ft., summer ; S. Europe. There are several varieties of the rocket candytuft, all white, and very many good varieties of the common candytuft, representing a wide range of colours, including violet and crimson, lilac, pink, cherry red and white. Fairy Mixed. Excellent mixture of dwarf types about 6 ins. high.

IMPATIENS (Balsam) Order GERANIACEÆ

A genus of annuals and perennials, some hardy, some half-hardy or tender, several suitable for treatment as annuals.

CULTIVATION : Differs for various species and is therefore given in detail below.

SPECIES AND   *I. amphorata.* Purple, 5 ft., August ; Himalayas.
THEIR   A hardy annual, suitable for a moist, shady
CULTIVATION : position in the wild garden. Sow in April, where
the plants are intended to flower.

I. balsamina. Rose-scarlet and white, 2 ft., summer;
Tropical Asia.

Garden balsam is also one of the plants to which
the name of Lady's Slipper is given. A greenhouse
annual that may with success be used for summer
bedding. Sow under glass in March or early April.
Transfer to the open ground in June.

The dwarf bush-flowered balsam is a much more
showy form of the above, bearing large double
flowers.

I. Roylei (syn. *I. glandulifera*). Purple, 6 ft., summer ;
Himalayas. Treat like *I. amphorata.*

IPOMÆA (Morning Glory, Moon Creeper) Order
CONVOLVULACEÆ

A genus of beautiful climbing plants with large blue, red,
purple or white convolvulus flowers. Some of them half-hardy
annuals, suitable to cover fences, pillars, etc. Others are stove
and greenhouse species, including the Morning Glory and the
Sweet Potato.

CULTIVATION : Sow under glass in March. Harden off towards
end of May, plant out in June. Supports are
required.
SPECIES :   *I. hederacea.* Various colours, 6-8 ft., summer ;
Tropical America.

I. purpurea (syn. *Convolvulus major*). Purple, 6-8 ft.,
summer; Tropical America.

I. versicolor (syn. *Mina lobata*). Buds rosy crimson,
opened flowers yellow, fading to cream, 6-8 ft.,
summer ; Tropical America.

Some of the greenhouse species have been successfully flowered outdoors in sheltered positions and
favoured districts.

JACOBÆA (*see* SENECIO)

JASIONE (Sheep's Bit Scabious) Order CAMPANULACEÆ

Unassuming little plants, their lavender-blue flower heads resembling those of the scabious. The annual species is widespread throughout Britain and may be used as an edging or in groups near the front of the annual border.

CULTIVATION : Sow in autumn or spring where the plants are intended to flower. Sunny position required.

SPECIES : *J. montana.* Lilac-blue, 1 ft., summer ; Europe (Britain).

KOCHIA (Summer Cypress) Order CHENOPODIACEÆ

Look at these before you decide to have them as they are not everybody's taste. They are like miniature cypresses, with insignificant flowers and feathery bright yellow-green foliage, turning a vivid bronzy purple, in autumn. Rather formal, slightly artificial appearance.

CULTIVATION : Sow under glass March or April. Water carefully to avoid damping off. Plant outside, end of May or beginning of June.

SPECIES AND VARIETIES : *K. scoparia trichophylla.* 2-3 ft., Europe. The more compact variety, *K. sc. tr. Childsii,* is usually offered.

LARKSPUR (*see* DELPHINIUM)

LASTHENIA Order COMPOSITÆ

Hardy annuals with showy bright yellow daisy flowers. Useful for front of borders or as edging.

CULTIVATION : Sow in autumn or spring where plants are intended to flower.

SPECIES : *L. glabrata* (syn. *L. californica*). Yellow, 1 ft., summer ; California.

LATHYRUS (Everlasting Pea, Sweet Pea) Order LEGUMINOSÆ

The sweet pea is loved by all and deserves it. It is a grateful plant that will repay any extra trouble taken over its cultivation. Here are some sign-posts on the road to success :

POSITION : A sheltered, sunny position and good soil are required. Don't put sweet peas in a showy place— the plants as such are rather unsightly. The cut flower section is ideal. Groups grown up bushy sticks in the back of a flower border are possible.

PREPARING THE SOIL : A rich soil is required. To obtain this, special trenches with manure and good garden soil are

42. *Daffodils*

43. *Tulips*

44. *Planting a rose bush*

45. *A well-planted rose bush*

46. *Disbudding a rose*

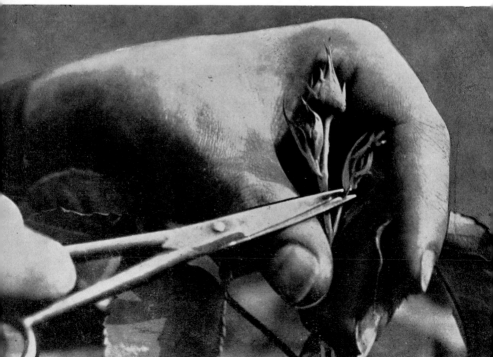

PREPARING THE SOIL : prepared. This is best done in autumn. Take out a trench 2 ft. deep, 2-2½ ft. wide. In its bottom put 6 ins. of well-rotted manure or properly composted vegetable refuse. A 1-ft. layer of equal parts of soil and manure (or compost), thoroughly mixed follows. Fill up with good soil to 3-4 ins. above surrounding ground level, thus allowing for soil to settle down. A top dressing of bone meal (2 ozs. per square yard) and wood ashes (½ lb. per square yard) is raked into the surface, followed in spring by a light application of lime (6-7 ozs. per square yard).

SEED SOWING : A long-growing season will give best results. Therefore sow in autumn if some protection by cloches, cold frame or greenhouse can be given.

Spring sowing under glass or, later, in the open is also possible but the resulting plants are not quite as magnificent and flower later. Autumn-sown plants must be kept as hardy as possible—don't pretend to them that it is not winter, but keep severe frost out of their way.

Autumn sowing is usually best in 3-in. pots filled with John Innes seed compost, 1 seed to each pot, placed about ¾ in. down. In mild districts or where cloches are employed sowing can be done in the open ground. Plants grown singly in pots will not suffer from root disturbance at transplanting time. When 4-6 ins. of growth have been made, pinch out growing point of central shoot to encourage growth of laterals from base. Give some twiggy sticks as support when required. Protect from slugs. When severe frosts set in, give the necessary protection as indicated above. Give plenty of air whenever possible.

Plant in late March or early April.

GENERAL CULTIVATION : Good staking is essential. The supports are best fixed before the sweet peas are planted out. There are several methods to choose from. By far the best is to stretch one or two wires between two strong posts at either end of the row and tie to these wires one bamboo or nutwand per plant. In very sheltered positions, string may be used instead of bamboos or nutwands. The bamboos

GENERAL
CULTIVATION :
are sometimes put on a slant which wastes space but makes for particularly fine straight flowering stems. Regular tying up will be required with all the above-mentioned methods. Sweet pea enthusiasts attend to the tying every third day. A method that requires no tying whatsoever is often used in cottage gardens : tall bushy pea-sticks are pushed into the ground, forming a sort of hedge which will later be covered by sweet peas and will then look very lovely. The quality of flowers obtained in this way will, however, be inferior to those grown on bamboos or nutwands.

Flowers must be cut regularly. If seed pods are allowed to develop, ready production of new flowers will soon cease. Protect against slugs at all times (see page 650), against greenflies if and when these appear. (For diseases and pests of sweet peas (see pages 647-650 and 668-670.) Tie up as required. For best quality blooms only one main shoot is retained and all tendrils are removed to prevent any entangling flowering stems. To lengthen flowering period, some quick-acting fertiliser may be applied once a fortnight from midsummer onwards. Some people retie their plants in September thus encouraging formation of more flowering growth.

SPECIES,
TYPES AND
VARIETIES :
L. odoratus. The Sweet Pea. Various colours, 6-10 ft. ; Italy.

Late Flowering

The late-flowering type is the one most generally used in gardens. There are countless varieties, and new ones are being added to the list constantly. You can probably not do better than go to a good flower show in summer, noting the varieties you like. Here are some in the list to date :

White

Majesty, very large flowers; Snocap, sweetly scented; Gigantic, very large; Swan Lake, huge snow-glistening flowers.

Cream

Cream Gigantic; Hunters Moon.

Pink

Mrs. R. Bolton, deep rose pink; Modesty, china-pink suffused with salmon on white ground.

VARIETIES: *Pink and Rose*
Carnival, cyclamen rose with white; Sally
Patricia, golden rich salmon pink; Princess
Elizabeth, salmon pink on creamy buff—
charming.

Salmon
Melodie, warm shell pink and soft salmon;
Sun Dance, bright orange salmon, cream base.
Red
Air Warden, crimson; Firefly, scarlet, Mollie,
cerise.

Maroon
Midnight; Warrior, sweetly scented.
Purple
Royalty; Saturn.

Lavender and Mauve
Elizabeth Taylor, large clear mauve; Mabel
Gower, good deep mauve; Leamington, lilac,
vigorous, sweet scented.
Blue
Stylish, mid blue; Mrs. Tom Jones, delphinium
blue; Blue Veil, pure lavender blue.

Early or Winter Flowering
The early or winter-flowering Spenser sweet peas
make a fine winter display when grown in the
cool greenhouse.
The dwarf cup type of sweet pea may be used
for bedding or as a pot plant.
L. sativus azureus. Blue, 2 ft., summer; S. Europe.
L. tingitanus. Purple and red, 4-6 ft., summer;
Tangier.
Both these species have little garden value, as
the flowers are small and not very conspicuous
among the prolific foliage.
There are several perennial climbing species.

LAVATERA (True Mallow) Order MALVACEÆ

A genus of hardy shrubs and annuals. The annuals have very
large, showy flowers, pink or white and resembling those of the
hollyhock. They set seed freely and so can be raised again and
again without additional expense.

CULTIVATION: Sow in September or April where plants are

CULTIVATION : intended to flower. Thin seedlings to 9-12 ins., apart. Collect seed when ripe.

SPECIES AND VARIETIES : *L. trimestris.* Rose, 3-4 ft., summer ; S. Europe. Varieties : *L. t. alba splendens,* a good white form ; *L. t. rosea splendens,* an improvement on the species that has given rise to the deservedly popular variety Loveliness, which is now mostly grown.

LAYIA Order COMPOSITÆ

Hardy annuals, useful as edging or groups in the front of the annual border. These yellow daisy flowers are natives of N.W. America; most of them came to us from California.

CULTIVATION : Plants may be raised under glass by sowing in April and transplanting to open ground end of May, or sown in April where intended to flower.

SPECIES : *L. calliglossa.* Yellow, 1 ft., summer ; California. *L. chrysanthemoides.* Yellow and white, 1 ft., summer ; California. *L. elegans.* Yellow, white tipped, 1 ft., summer ; California. This is the most showy of the species ; flowers large and freely produced. *L. glandulosa.* White, sometimes tinged rose, $\frac{1}{2}$-$1\frac{1}{2}$ ft., summer ; N. America. *L. platyglossa.* Yellow, 1 ft., summer ; California.

LEPTOSYNE Order COMPOSITÆ

Hardy annuals and perennials. Their delicately feathered foliage and showy yellow flowers make the annual species well worth having in the annual border.

CULTIVATION : Sow under glass in March. Transfer to open ground late in May.

SPECIES : *L. calliopsidea.* Golden yellow, $1\frac{1}{2}$ ft., September ; California. *L. Douglasii.* Yellow, 1 ft., autumn ; California. *L. Stillmanii.* Golden yellow, $1\frac{1}{2}$ ft., late summer and autumn ; California. The last named is a much hardier species and may be sown in April in the open.

LIMNANTHES Order GERANIACEÆ

A genus of dwarf hardy annuals, useful as edgings or for the front of the annual border.

CULTIVATION : Sow in September or April where intended to flower. Sunny position required.

SPECIES : *L. alba.* White, 6-8 ins., summer ; California.
L. Douglasii. Yellow and white, fragrant, 1 ft., spring to autumn ; N.W. America.

LINARIA (Toad-flax) Order SCROPHULARIACEÆ

This genus provides us with some very dainty annuals for the border. They can be had in a great variety of colours and colour combinations.

CULTIVATION : Sow in August or April where the plants are intended to flower. Sunny beds and borders. The dwarf species are useful in the rock garden.

SPECIES AND VARIETIES : *L. bipartita.* Red, violet, purple, rose, white and yellow, 1 ft., summer ; Algeria.
L. Brousonetti (syn. *L. multipunctata*). Orange with black spots, 6 ins., summer ; Algeria.
L. heterophylla. Straw and yellow, 1-2 ft., summer ; Morocco.
L. maroccana. Violet rose, 9-12 ins., June ; Morocco. This species has given rise to many lovely varieties, all of them bushy and compact. Colours very varied, including blood red, white, yellow, purple and many colour combinations.
L. reticulata. Purple and yellow, 2-3 ft., summer ; Portugal.
L. tristis. Yellow and purply brown, 1 ft., July ; Spain.

LINUM (Flax) Order LINACEÆ

A genus of graceful, most attractive annual and perennial herbs. Delicate foliage, flowers usually large, clear in shape and colours, which include lovely deep sky blue, cherry red, chrome yellow and white.

CULTIVATION : A sunny position must be provided for the flowers to open fully. Sow in April where the plants are intended to flower. Thin to 3 ins. apart.

SPECIES AND VARIETIES : *L. grandiflorum.* Rose, 1 ft., summer ; Algeria. Its more usually grown varieties : *coccineum,* scarlet, *rubrum,* blood red, a most desirable variety ; *splendens,* rose.
L. usitatissimum. Sky-blue, 1½ ft., June ; Europe.

VARIETIES : This is the common flax from which linseed oil and linen fibre are obtained. A very dainty annual.

LOASA (Chile Nettle) Order LEASACEÆ

Some of these S. American annual climbers may be flowered in the open. They have stinging leaves and rather showy flowers in several colours.

CULTIVATION : Sunny, sheltered position required. Sow under glass in February or March, transplant in June to foot of sunny wall or fence.

SPECIES : *L. lateritia.* Coral red, 10-20 ft., August ; Chile. *L. vulcanica.* White, yellow and red, 2-3 ft. ; Ecuador.

LOBELIA Order CAMPANULACEÆ

These flowers are really perennials (see also page 126), but many of the dwarf kinds are grown as half-hardy annuals. Though the blue bedding Lobelia may have been used too much in the past there is no reason why it should not now lend its lovely intense blue to edgings, borders and window boxes.

CULTIVATION : Sow under glass in February, transplant to the open in June. It is also possible to take cuttings in spring from plants that have been lifted in the autumn and grown on in pots in the greenhouse.

SPECIES AND VARIETIES : *L. Erinus.* Blue or blue and white, 6 ins., summer ; S. Africa.
From this species the bedding varieties are derived, some of which are : Cambridge Blue, a lovely light blue ; Crystal Palace, deep blue with dark foliage ; Emperor William, clear light blue ; Mrs. Clibran, deep blue with white eye ; Snowball, a compact, large-flowered white ; there are also double varieties, but they are not so popular.
L. tenuior. Bright blue, 1-1½ ft., September ; W. Australia. This lovely large-flowered species is generally more successful when grown as a pot plant than when grown in the open.

LOVE-IN-A-MIST (*see* NIGELLA)

LUPINUS (Lupin) Order LEGUMINOSÆ

The annual lupin is a smaller edition of the perennial kinds, but it retains their colourful brightness and much of their stateliness. A very desirable plant for the annual border and a welcome change from the many daisy-type species.

CULTIVATION : Sow in April where intended to flower. Thin 10-12 ins. apart in May. Do not allow seed pods to form on plants, as this would shorten the flowering time. The annual lupin appreciates occasional feeds with liquid manure when in flower.

SPECIES AND VARIETIES : *L. densiflorus* (syn. *L. Menziesii*). Yellow, fragrant, 2 ft., August ; California.

L. Hartwegii. Blue, white and rose, 2-3 ft., August– September ; Mexico. A very popular species that has given rise to many lovely brightly-coloured varieties.

L. hirsutissimus. Reddish purple, 1 ft., July ; California.

L. hirsutus. Blue and white, 1½-2½ ft., July–August, Mediterranean.

L. luteus. Yellow, 1-2 ft., June–August ; S. Europe.

L. mutabilis. White, blue and yellow, fragrant, 3-4 ft., summer ; Colombia. Variety *Cruckshanksii*, violet and purple.

L. nanus. Lilac and blue, 1 ft., summer ; California. A showy compact species.

L. pubescens. Violet blue and white, 1½-3 ft., July– September ; Mexico and Guatemala. This species has given rise to many valuable varieties of various shades and colour combinations.

L. subcarnosus. Blue and yellow, 1 ft., summer ; Texas.

LYCHNIS (Campion) Order CARYOPHYLLACEÆ

This genus supplies one very lovely hardy annual to our beds and borders. Many varieties—usually still offered as Viscaria— can be had, mostly in light shades of blue, mauve and pink.

CULTIVATION : Sow in April where intended to flower. In favoured localities autumn sowing for spring flowering is possible.

SPECIES AND VARIETIES : *L. Cœli-rosa* (syn. *Agrostemma Cœli-rosa*), Rose of Heaven. Red and purple, 1 ft., summer ; Levant. Its many lovely varieties include : *alba* and *candida*, both white ; Blue Bouquet, Blue Pearl, *cærulea*, all

SPECIES AND
VARIETIES :
blue ; *cardinalis* and Fire King, both brilliant crimson ; *oculata*, rose with purple eye ; there is also a dwarf form, with similar colours.

MALCOMIA (Virginian Stock) Order CRUCIFERÆ

A cheerful little annual, much used for edgings and groups in the front of the mixed border. Perhaps they resemble " hundreds and thousands " rather more closely than a " nice " annual should.

CULTIVATION : May be sown in autumn for spring flowering, and from March to June for summer and autumn flowering. A sunny position is best.

SPECIES : *M. maritima*. Various colours, 6 ins., summer ; S. Europe. Varieties in distinct colours are obtainable.

MALOPE (Large-flowered Mallow Wort) Order MALVACEÆ

Hardy annuals, forming tall bushy plants that will bear large hollyhock-like flowers over a long period.

CULTIVATION : Sow in April where plants are intended to flower. Gradually thin to 1 ft. apart. Appreciates feeding with liquid manure when flower buds begin to show.

SPECIES AND
VARIETIES :
M. malacoides. Rose and purple, 1-2 ft., summer ; S. Europe.
M. trifida. Purple, 2-3 ft., summer ; Spain. This is a fine, large-flowered species which has given rise to several good varieties : *alba*, a white ; *grandiflora*, rosy-red with crimson venation ; *rosea*, a good pink.

MALVA (Mallow) Order MALVACEÆ

Annuals, biennials and perennials, some of these may be worth growing as annuals ; either for their decorative foliage or their flowers.

CULTIVATION : Sow under glass in March or April, transplant to flowering position end of May or early June.

SPECIES : *M. crispa*. White and purple, 3-6 ft., summer ; Europe. This is a true annual grown for the sake
M. sylvestris. Rosy purple, 2-3 ft., summer ; Europe. of its foliage, the flowers are small and not showy. A biennial species usually grown as an annual.

240

MARTYNIA (Elephant's Trunk, Unicorn Plant)
Order MARTYNIACEÆ

These half-hardy annuals are not much seen in English gardens. Their name is derived from the curiously horned fruit.

CULTIVATION : Sow thinly under glass in February or March, transfer to the open in June. Water freely in dry periods.

SPECIES : *M. fragrans.* Unicorn Plant. Crimson purple, 2 ft., summer ; Mexico.

M. proboscidea. Elephant's Trunk. Pale mauve with purple, 1-3 ft., summer ; N. Mexico.

MATHIOLA (Stock) Order CRUCIFERÆ

Easily among the loveliest of all annuals, both for their unequalled, almost intoxicating scent and their many beautiful colours. Their sturdy habit and pleasingly simple grey foliage add significantly to their merits. Stocks range among those plants with which " doubleness " is a real asset—in fact here it makes all the difference. Several of the types are suitable for pot culture.

CULTIVATION : The Ten-Week Stock is sown under glass in February or March and transplanted to the open in May.

The Intermediate Stock may be treated in the same way but is more usually grown as a biennial, being sown in a cold frame in June or July and later transplanted to where it will flower next year. The seedlings may also be potted up singly in small pots, over-wintered in cold frames and transplanted next March to flowering position.

The Brompton Stock and Wallflower-leaved Stock are dealt with in the same way.

The Night-scented Stock is treated as a hardy annual and sown in April where it is to flower.

SPECIES, TYPES AND VARIETIES : *M. annua* (syn. *Incana annua*). Various colours, 1-2 ft., summer ; S. Europe. Parent of Ten-week Stock and Intermediate Stocks.

M. bicornis. Lilac purple, fragrant, 1 ft., spring ; Greece ; the Night-scented Stock. Its flowers remain closed during day-time but open wide in

SPECIES, TYPES AND VARIETIES :

the evening, when they also emit their lovely sweet scent.

M. fenestralis. Scarlet or purple, 1 ft., summer ; Crete. This biennial, parent to the giant Cape-type of stock, has given rise to many brightly-coloured varieties.

M. incana. Mauve, purple or violet, 1-2 ft., spring or summer ; Levant. This biennial is parent of the Brompton and Wallflower-leaved Stocks.

M. sinuata. Purple or reddish, night fragrant, 1-2 ft., summer ; Europe (Britain). This annual has contributed to the make-up of the Intermediate and East Lothian Stocks.

Each type can be had in a wide range of lovely colours. Stock variety names usually just indicate the type and colour. Beauty of Nice is a very popular group of winter-flowering varieties.

MAURANDIA Order SCROPHULARIACEÆ

Half-hardy perennial climbers. Well worth growing as half-hardy annuals. Suitable for covering fences, trellis, etc., during the summer months.

CULTIVATION : Sow under glass February or March, transplant to sunny position in the open in June.

SPECIES : *M. barclayana.* Violet purple, summer ; Mexico.
M. erubescens (syn. *Lophospermum erubescens*). Rose and white, summer ; Mexico.
M. scandens (syn. *Lophospermum scandens*). Purple and violet, summer ; Mexico.

MENTZELIA (syn. *Bartonia*) Order LOASACEÆ

A genus of very lovely hardy annuals, dwarf with very large flat flowers radiant yellow or white. The petals make a neat and unusual pattern.

CULTIVATION : Sow in April or May where the plants are intended to flower.

SPECIES : *M. bartonioides.* Yellow, 1 ft., summer ; U.S.A. Often grown as pot plant in cool greenhouse.
M. Lindleyi (syn. *Bartonia aurea*). Yellow, 1 ft., summer ; California.
M. ornata. White, fragrant, 1 ft., August ; N. America.

MESEMBRYANTHEMUM (Fig Marigold, Ice Plant, Livingstone Daisy) Order AIZOACEÆ

A very large genus of sub-tropical plants of very varying characteristics. Most of them have three-edged succulent leaves. The " Livingstone Daisy " is a delightful annual with fairy-tale flowers in many lovely shades of pink, crimson, pale or golden-yellow or apricot. There are also many colour combinations, such as white with crimson, rose-pink or buff edges. The plants are dwarf and spreading and, though mostly seen in rockeries or on top of dry walls, they look lovely in any sunny bed or border.

CULTIVATION : Sow the Livingstone Daisy under glass in March, transplant to sunny, well-drained position in June. Chalky soil or a dressing of lime appreciated.

SPECIES : *M. criniflorum.* Many colours, 4 ins., creeping, summer ; S. Africa.
As indicated above, there is a host of further species, mostly for greenhouse culture. Some are hardy, others may be treated as half-hardy annuals, such as *M. crystallinum*, the Ice Plant, which has white, inconspicuous flowers, but all the more striking foliage with silver glistening hairs.

MIGNONETTE (*see* RESEDA)

MIMULUS (Monkey Flower, Musk) Order SCROPHULARIACEÆ

This genus is an asset to the garden in many ways (see page 129 and 179) and some of its showy species are annuals, particularly useful for shady and moist positions. They will also do well in full sun, provided there is plenty of moisture.

CULTIVATION : Sow under glass in March, transplant to the open late in May or early June. Keep well watered in dry spells.

SPECIES : *M. brevipes.* Yellow, 1½-2 ft., summer ; California.
M. cupreus. Copper red, 6-8 ins., summer ; Chile.
M. Fremonti. Crimson, 6-8 ins., summer ; California.
All species have large two-lipped flowers, beautiful in shape and colour.

MINA LOBATA (*see* IPOMÆA VERSICOLOR)

NASTURTIUM (*see* TROPÆOLUM)

NEMESIA Order SCROPHULARIACEÆ

Whilst even the thought of these delightful S. African annuals is a joy, one wonders why they are not grown much more widely. Each plant is covered with a mass of prettily two-lipped flowers. There are good large-flowered forms, and there is an unending variety of colours, including blazing orange, rich crimson, true sky blue, pale yellow, pink, cerise, white, self-coloured flowers, as well as some that are mottled or patterned in several colours.

CULTIVATION : Sow seeds under glass in March, transplant to the open in late May or early June. Outdoor sowings in May are possible but somewhat risky. Some recommend placing the seed containers in a cold frame rather than a greenhouse for germination. A sunny position is required.

SPECIES AND VARIETIES : *N. strumosa*. Various colours, 1 ft., summer. This is the parent of the popular garden varieties. *N. versicolor*. Many colours, 8-12 ins., summer. There are other species, such as *N. barbata*, *N. floribunda*, *N. lilacina*, but they are rarely seen in gardens. The large-flowered varieties are the best to grow. Dwarf forms are available. The loveliest effect is probably produced by planting varieties containing many colours.

NEMOPHILA (Californian Bluebell) Order HYDROPHYLLACEÆ

These dwarf or trailing annuals are well worth having for the lovely deep blue found in some of the species. The flowers are bell-shaped.

CULTIVATION : Sow in March or April where plants are intended to flower. Autumn sowing for spring flowering possible.

SPECIES : All from California, all summer flowering :
N. aurita. Purple and violet, 1 ft.
N. insignis. Blue or white, trailing. The blue form of this is the most popular.
N. maculata. White and purple, 6 ins.
N. Menziesii (syn. *N. atomaria*). Blue or white, trailing.

NICOTIANA (Tobacco Plant) Order SOLANACEÆ

Groups of these fragrant plants are well worth having in the annual border or the night-scented border. Often grown as a pot plant. The flowers open more widely and the scent is intensified at dusk.

CULTIVATION : Sow under glass in March, transplant to the open late May. The genus includes annuals and perennials, but the treatment given is always as for annuals.

SPECIES AND VARIETIES : *N. alata grandiflora* (syn. *N. a. affinis*). White, fragrant, 3-5 ft., summer ; Brazil. This species has given rise to the most popular garden varieties, including many colours and some dwarf forms : Crimson Bedder, 15 ins. ; Crimson King and Scarlet King, 2-3 ft. ; Miniature White, 18 ins., covered with small white flowers. Shades of rose pink, lilac and cream are also available.

N. sylvestris. White, 3-4 ft., summer ; Argentine.

N. tabacum. Rose, 4 ft., summer ; S. America. This is the commercial Tobacco Plant. It has also given rise to some forms of garden merit, including : *N. t. macrophylla*, red. Varieties, *atropurpurea* and *rubra.*

N. tomentosa (syn. *N. colossea*). Pale pink, 10-20 ft.; S. America.

N. Sanderæ. Shades of rosy red, 2-3 ft., summer ; hybrid. From this again we have obtained a number of good garden varieties in several colours, much the same range as *N. affinis.*

NIEREMBERGIA Order SOLANACEÆ

Half-hardy perennials that are often grown as annuals, suitable for edgings, carpet bedding, semi-shady places in the rock garden, etc.

CULTIVATION : Treat as half-hardy annuals.

SPECIES : *N. cærulea* (often called *N. hippomanica*). Violet blue, 9-12 ins., summer ; S. America.

N. frutescens. White with lilac and yellow, 1-2 ft., summer ; Chile. Best treated as biennial.

NIGELLA (Love-in-a-Mist) Order RANUNCULACEÆ

Popular, lovely, hardy, accommodating. Excellent in the border and as a cut flower. The large flattish flowers in shades of blue are embedded in the delicate lacework of pale-green foliage.

245

CULTIVATION : Sow where intended to flower, in autumn or spring. Seed may easily be collected or the plants may be left to re-sow themselves.

SPECIES AND VARIETIES : *N. damascena.* Blue, 1-2 ft., summer ; S. Europe. Varieties : Miss Jekyll, semi-double, deep sky-blue ; Miss Jekyll Dark Blue ; Miss Jekyll White, and *nana,* a dwarf form, useful for edging.

NIGHT-SCENTED STOCK (*see* MATHIOLA)

ŒNOTHERA (Evening Primrose) Order ONAGRACEÆ

A genus of hardy annuals, biennials, perennials (see page 131). The annual species closely allied to Godetia.

CULTIVATION : May be sown in April where intended to flower or under glass in March to be transplanted to open in May.

SPECIES AND VARIETIES : *Œ. amœna.* Rose and crimson, 1-2 ft., summer ; California.

Œ. a. rubicunda. Lilac purple.

Œ. bistorta. Yellow and red, 1 ft. ; California.

Œ. Drummondii. Yellow, 1-2 ft., June-October.

Œ. odorata. Yellow, sweetly scented, 1-2 ft. ; Chile.

Œ. tetraptera. White, 1 ft. ; Mexico. Pink variety, *Œ. t. rosea.*

PAPAVER (Poppy) Order PAPAVERACEÆ

The poppy needs no introduction. There are some perennial species and many lovely annuals for beds, borders and cut flowers.

CULTIVATION : Poppies dislike transplanting. Therefore sow thinly where intended to flower. Autumn or spring. To make poppies last as cut flowers, cut when just about to open, dip end of cut stem into a flame or in boiling water for the fraction of a minute. This will prevent the latex (milky juice) blocking entrance to water pipes. Seed may easily be collected for re-sowing.

SPECIES AND VARIETIES : *P. glaucum.* Crimson, 18 ins., summer ; Syria. The Tulip Poppy, well described by its name. *P. lævigatum.* Scarlet, black and white, 2 ft., summer ; Greece. *P. pavonium.* Scarlet and black, 18 ins. ; Afghanistan. The Peacock Poppy.

SPECIES AND
VARIETIES :

P. Rhœas. Various colours, 18 ins. ; Britain. The Corn Poppy and its host of lovely garden varieties, tall and dwarf, double and single and of innumerable colour shades. The Shirley Poppy is the most widely grown of the garden forms of *P. Rhœas.*

P. somniferum. Opium Poppy, various colours, 3 ft. ; Europe and Asia. Many lovely garden forms include the Carnation-flowered and Pæony-flowered, both very double, in a wide range of beautiful colours and well described by their name. Many named single varieties are available : Admiral, white with a broad band of scarlet ; Dainty Lady, pale lilac ; Danebrog, a white cross on red ground, etc.

PERILLA Order LABIATÆ

Half-hardy annual grown for its rather ornamental foliage. Its bronzy-purple leaves look well with salmon, lilac, sulphur yellow, orange and a variety of other shades.

CULTIVATION : Sow under glass in March, transplant in sunny border in late May or early June.

SPECIES : *P. arguta atropurpurea,* commonly referred to as *P. nankinensis.* Leaves bronzy purple, flowers inconspicuous, 1-3 ft. ; China, Japan, Himalayas.

PETUNIA Order SOLANACEÆ

These half-hardy perennials are often grown as annuals for bedding, edgings, window boxes. Dwarf, large-flowered forms in many colours are now available, singles and doubles, frilled and plain flowers.

CULTIVATION : Sow in heated greenhouse in pans of John Innes compost (see page 576) late January or early February. Transfer to a sunny position in the open late in May. Propagation by cuttings taken in July and inserted under glass in sandy soil may be practised instead of raising from seed each year.

SPECIES AND
VARIETIES :

The garden varieties are hybrids between :

P. hybrida grandiflora includes most of the garden varieties, doubles as well as singles.

All Double Mammoth Pæony-flowered has huge, very double flowers in white or shades of pink and

SPECIES AND VARIETIES : rosy purple ; Carmine Glory is a crimson self-coloured one ; Giant of California, large flowers of many shades, veined in the throat with different colours.

P. hybrida pendula. The window-box varieties.

P. nana compacta. Includes the famous bedding varieties : Lavender Queen, Rose Queen, Snow Queen and Violet Queen.

P. nyctaginiflora. White, 2 ft., August ; Argentine and

P. violacea. Purple, 6-10 ins., summer ; Argentine.

PHACELIA Order HYDROPHYLLACEÆ

Lovely little annuals with true blue, violet or mauve flowers. Very suitable for edgings or groups in the annual border.

CULTIVATION : Sow in April where plants are intended to flower. Sun or partial shade.

SPECIES AND VARIETIES : *P. campanularia.* Blue, 8 ins., summer ; California.

P. ciliata. Lavender blue, fragrant, 1 ft.

P. congesta. Lavender blue, 1-3 ft., June ; Texas or New Mexico.

P. Parryi. Violet, 1 ft., summer ; California.

P. tanacetifolia. Lilac blue, 1½-3 ft. ; California, Flowers small and numerous, liked by bees.

P. viscida (syn. *Eutoca viscida*). Blue, white eye, 1-2 ft. ; S. California.

P. Whitlavia (syn. *Whitlavia grandiflora*). Blue, 1 ft., September ; California.

A number of varieties may be found in trade catalogues.

PHLOX DRUMMONDII Order POLEMONIACEÆ

Here we have one of the most delightful of annuals, equally excellent for beds, borders, cut flowers, pot culture. The annual phlox is not as tall or robust as its perennial cousin but probably excels the latter in variety and beauty of colours, which include the deepest blood red and crimson, rich violet, primrose yellow and endless colour combinations within each flower, as well as all the shades found in the perennial phlox, white, pink, mauve, salmon red. The annual phlox flowers from June to October. As a cut flower it lasts in the vase for an unusually long time.

CULTIVATION : Sow under glass in March, plant out late May.

47. *Rose bush before pruning*

48. *Rose bush after pruning*

49. (left) *The yellow Bartonia aurea*

50. (above right)   *Using grafting tape*
for wrapping round a bud when budding

51. (below) *Potting on ferns*

CULTIVATION : Never let the plants get root-bound. For bushy plants pinch out growing point when plants are 6 ins. high. Alternatively, the plants may be pegged down along the ground, when many upright flowering shoots will be produced from the leaf axils. A sunny position, fairly rich, moisture-holding soil appreciated.

SPECIES AND VARIETIES : *P. Drummondii.* Various colours, 1 ft. ; Texas. Many varieties are offered. For outdoor cultivation I would probably go for something like Large-flowered Mixed, though separate colours may look lovely, e.g. an edging of crimson or scarlet *Phlox Drummondii* to a bed of mauve stock or godetia. For pot culture, separate colours are more suitable. Dwarf strains (9 ins.) are also available.

PINK (*see* DIANTHUS)

PLATYSTEMON (Cream Cup, Californian Poppy)
Order PAPAVERACEÆ

Showy, dwarf annuals, with pale yellow poppy flowers.

CULTIVATION : Sow in April where plants are to flower, thin to 2-3 ins. apart. Water freely in dry periods.
SPECIES : *P. californicus.* Yellow, 1 ft., July ; California.

POLYGONUM (Knot Weed) Order POLYGONACEÆ

A large genus of herbaceous annuals and perennials and shrubby climbers. There are some very useful species (see also page 168).

CULTIVATION : Raise under glass in spring and transfer to the open in May or sow in the open in April, 1½ ft. distance between plants.
SPECIES : *P. orientale.* Rosy purple, 4-6 ft., August ; Tropics. Several varieties white, pink or red, tall or dwarf. dwarf.

POPPY (*see* PAPAVER, ARGEMONE; *also* ESCHSCHOLTZIA, GLAUCIUM, PLATYSTEMON, RŒMERIA.)

PORTULACA (Purslane, Sun-Plant) Order PORTULACACEÆ

Showy little annuals with brightly-coloured flowers.

CULTIVATION : Sow under glass in March, transfer to well-drained sunny beds or borders in the open late in May.

SPECIES AND   *P. grandiflora.* Red, yellow, rose or white, 6 ins. ;
VARIETIES :   Brazil. Varieties of many dazzling colours.
                  P. oleracea. Purslane, a salad plant.

RESEDA (Mignonette) Order RESEDACEÆ

A perennial, but usually treated as an annual, 18 ins. It is
grown for the sake of its unusual fragrance and is not a showy
plant in spite of useful efforts made on its behalf by the plant
breeders.

CULTIVATION : Work some old mortar rubble or hydrated lime
              into soil surface before sowing. Sow in April in
              sunny position outdoors where intended to flower.
              Water freely in dry periods. Appreciates occasional
              feedings with liquid manure when in flower.
SPECIES AND   *R. odorata.* Yellow and white, 1-2 ft. ; N. Africa.
VARIETIES :   Has a number of varieties, all with rather small
              flowers in white or shades of yellow and red.

RICINUS (Castor Oil Plant) Order EUPHORBIACEÆ

Looking at this noble foliage plant, it is hard to believe that
it rears in its seeds the nasty castor oil—yet it does. A tree in
its African home, it is here grown as a half-hardy annual for
more pretentious bedding schemes and will reach a height of
4-7 ft.

CULTIVATION : Sometime in March soak seed in tepid water for a
              few hours, then sow in heated greenhouse. Transfer
              hardened plants to sunny warm bed in June.
SPECIES AND   *R. communis,* 3-6 ft. ; Tropical Africa. Has a
VARIETIES :   number of varieties. In its native home the
              Ricinus will make a tree up to 40 ft. high.

RŒMERIA (Purple-horned Poppy, Wind-Rose)
Order PAPAVERACEÆ

Cousin of the poppy, some very showy, all very graceful.

CULTIVATION : Sow in spring where the plants are to flower.
SPECIES :   *R. refracta.* Scarlet with white, 2 ft. ; Mediter-
              ranean.
              R. violacea (syn. *R. hybrida*). Pale violet blue, 1 ft. ;
              Mediterranean. It is found as a weed in cornfields
              in Central Europe, very rarely also in England,
              e.g. in Norfolk and Cambridge.

RUDBECKIA (Cone flower) Order COMPOSITÆ

This genus not only brightens the herbaceous border in late summer but also gives us several very showy annuals useful for the border and as cut flowers.

CULTIVATION : Sow in March under glass, transfer to the open in May. Alternatively, sow where to flower late in April.

SPECIES AND VARIETIES : *R. bicolor.* Yellow and maroon, 1-2 ft., July–September; N. America. Has many good varieties. *R. hirta.* Yellow and brown, 1-3 ft. ; N. America. Varieties of *R. hirta* include crimson, bright yellow and bronze shades, often several colours in one flowerhead, with the disc a dark blackish brown. *R. triloba.* Similar, both these may be annual or biennial.

SALPIGLOSSIS Order SOLANACEÆ

An unusually beautiful annual that should be more widely grown. The large trumpet-shaped flowers show a never-ending variety of colours and colour combinations, such as copper red with violet venation, mauve suffused with lemon yellow, scarlet with brown and gold, etc., etc. Excellent cut flowers.

CULTIVATION : Raised under glass in March, plant out early June, water freely, feed occasionally. Where greenhouse space is available, plants might be sown in autumn to set out in spring for extra fine specimens.

SPECIES AND VARIETIES : Various colours, 2 ft. ; Chile. Many strains and varieties grown in gardens.

SALVIA (Sage, Clary) Order LABIATÆ

Hardy and half-hardy annuals and perennials. Many of them very showy. Several of the perennial species are often grown as annuals.

CULTIVATION : Most kinds are best sown in heated greenhouse January or early February to be planted in the open in late May or early June. *S. Horminum* may be sown in April where intended to flower. All require sunny position and do best in fairly rich soil.

SPECIES AND VARIETIES : *S. coccinea.* Deep scarlet, 2-3 ft., autumn ; N. America. *S. farinacea.* Lavender blue, 2-3 ft. ; Mexico.

SPECIES AND VARIETIES : *S. Horminum.* Purple bracts, 18 ins., summer; S. Europe. Has several varieties mostly with very richly coloured bracts, such as : Blue Beard (bright purple) ; Oxford Blue (deep blue) ; *S. H. purpurea* (various shades of red). This is a true annual.

S. patens. Gentian blue, 2 ft., summer ; Mexico. One of the loveliest blue flowers grown in gardens. Cambridge Blue is a good light-blue variety (see also page 617).

S. splendens. Scarlet, 2-3 ft. ; Brazil. The popular Scarlet Sage used in formal beds, stone vases, tubs, etc.

Almost all the species mentioned are greenhouse perennials that are easily flowered in their first year from an early sowing and will do well in warm positions in the open throughout the summer (see also pages 616-617).

SANVITALIA Order COMPOSITÆ

A sweet-faced little bright yellow daisy flower with a dark disc. Its dwarf, trailing habit makes it suitable for the front of the annual border, top of dry walls, sunny position in the rockery.

CULTIVATION : May be sown under glass in early spring to be moved to the open later on or else sown in April or May where to flower.

SPECIES : *S. procumbens.* Yellow and purply black, trailing, summer and autumn ; Mexico.
There is a double form, *S. p. flore pleno.*

SAPONARIA (Soapwort) Order CARYOPHYLLACEÆ

Apart from the popular rock-garden trailers, this genus also supplies some particularly lovely annuals for our beds and borders.
CULTIVATION : Sow in autumn or spring where plants are to flower.

SPECIES AND VARIETIES : *S. calabrica.* Rose, 6-12 ins., July–September ; Italy. A number of varieties in pink, white or red.

S. Vaccaria (syn. *Lychnis Vaccaria*, *Vaccaria vulgaris*). Pink, 2-3 ft., summer ; Europe. Several fine varieties of white and various shades of pink. A good cut flower.

Annuals and Plants Grown as Such

SCABIOSA (Scabious) Order DIPSACEÆ

The biennial scabious is mostly grown as an annual and is liked for its wide range of colours. Makes a very good cut flower.

CULTIVATION : For summer flowering sow under glass in early spring and transplant to the open in May. For late summer and autumn flowering, sow in the open ground in April.

SPECIES AND VARIETIES : *S. atropurpurea.* Various colours, 1-3 ft., July ; S. Europe. Many large-flowered varieties in all shades of pink, mauve, red, crimson, and purple. There are also white and sulphur yellow varieties. Height varies from 9 ins.-3 ft.

SCHIZANTHUS Order SOLANACEÆ

These half-hardy annuals of exotic, indescribable beauty are usually grown in the cool greenhouse for spring display, but they will do quite well in sheltered sunny borders in the open. The delicate bushy plants bear pale green finely-cut foliage and will be covered with masses of butterfly-like flowers self-coloured or spotted and edged in many colours. White, yellow, brown, red, pink, lilac—an enormous range of colouring.

CULTIVATION : Sow under glass in March, transfer to the open in late May or early June. Water and feed liberally and give a stake to each plant.

SPECIES AND VARIETIES : *S. Grahami.* Lilac and orange.
S. pinnatus. Rose, purple and yellow.
S. retusus. Rose, crimson and orange.
All these come from Chile, are 1½-2 ft. high and are parents of many beautiful garden varieties and hybrid forms.
S. wisetonensis. One of the most widely grown hybrid strains. The flowers are mostly many-coloured and frilled, but in the Danbury Park strain they are self-coloured and smooth-edged ; 2 ft.

SENECIO (syn. *Jacobæa*) Order COMPOSITÆ

The groundsel and ragwort belong to this genus. But here we are referring to a lovely daisy-flowered annual that has some resemblance to the perennial Pyrethrum. Makes a good cut flower.

CULTIVATION : Sow in April where the plants are to flower. Thin seedlings to 6 ins. apart.

SPECIES AND VARIETIES : *S. elegans* (syn. *Jacobæa elegans*). Various colours, 1-2 ft., summer ; S. Africa. Single and double varieties.

SILENE (Catchfly) Order CARYOPHYLLACEÆ

This genus contributes some pleasing showy annuals for the border. The dwarf kinds are suitable as edging.

CULTIVATION : Sow in autumn or spring where required to flower. May also be sown under glass in autumn or spring and transferred to flowering position in April or May.

SPECIES AND VARIETIES : *S. Armeria.* Pink, 1-2 ft., summer ; S. Europe.
S. Asterias. Rosy purple, 1-2 ft., summer ; Macedonia, Rumania.
S. pendula. Rose, 6-8 ins., spring ; Mediterranean. Many single or double varieties in white or numerous shades of pink.

SOAPWORT (*see* SAPONARIA)

SPECULARIA (Venus's Looking Glass) Order CAMPANULACEÆ

Dainty hardy annuals with lilac, purple or lavender-blue bell flowers.

CULTIVATION : Sow in April where to flower. Support plants with a few slender, bushy sticks put among them.

SPECIES : *S. hybrida.* Lilac, 1 ft., July ; Europe.
S. pentagonia. Bluish purple, 1 ft., summer ; Asia Minor.
S. perfoliata. Lavender blue, 1-1½ ft., June ; N. America.
S. speculum-Veneris. Venus's Looking Glass. Purple, 1 ft., summer ; Europe.

STATICE (Sea Lavender) Order PLUMBAGINACEÆ

A genus of everlasting flowers, some of them annuals. They are rather " a matter of taste "—fairly bright but somewhat papery and certainly not very graceful.

CULTIVATION : Sow under glass, February or March. Transplant to the open in May. The flowers may be cut when

CULTIVATION : fully opened, bunched and hung up to dry for use as winter decoration.

SPECIES AND VARIETIES : *S. Bonduelli.* Yellow, 1-2 ft. ; Algeria.

S. sinuata. Mauve and cream, 1-2 ft. ; Mediterranean. Really a perennial, but usually grown as an annual. Many varieties are derived from this, including pink, white and various shades of blue. *S. Suworowi.* Lilac or pink, 1½ ft.; Central Asia. The genus is also referred to as *Limonium.*

STOCK (*see* MATHIOLA *and* MALCOMIA)

SUNFLOWER (*see* HELIANTHUS)

SWEET PEA (*see* LATHYRUS)

SWEET SULTAN (*see* CENTAUREA)

SWEET WIVELSFIELD (*see* DIANTHUS)

TAGETES (African, French and Mexican Marigolds)

Order COMPOSITÆ

Half-hardy annuals, carrying on stiffly-erect stems brilliant orange, yellow, or orange and maroon daisy flowers, often " very double," the larger types rather coarse.

CULTIVATION : Sow under glass in March, plant out in late May or early June. Sunny position, fairly rich soil appreciated.

SPECIES AND VARIETIES : *T. erecta.* Yellow, 2-3 ft., summer ; Mexico. The African marigold with many orange and yellow varieties.

T. lucida. Yellow, 1 ft., summer ; Mexico.

T. patula. French marigold. Orange, red and brown, 1-1½ ft., Mexico, and a number of good varieties, among them the dwarf *T. p. nana* which makes a very neat and showy edging.

T. signata. Yellow and red, 1 ft. ; Mexico. Its lovely little variety, *T. s. pumila,* is about 6 ins. high. It will be noted that all the tagetes come from Mexico, in spite of their suggestive names.

TOADFLAX (*see* LINARIA)

TROPÆOLUM (" Nasturtium ") Order GERANIACEÆ

The tropæolum should find a place in every garden, as it makes such intensely bright colour splashes and produces no end of flowers for cutting over a long period. Leaf and flower of attractive shape. Doubles now rather popular, but not nearly as beautiful as singles.

CULTIVATION : Soil must not be rich, else luxuriant foliage will hide the flowers. Climbing kinds are grown to cover fences, trellises or to trail over banks. Sow in April where required to flower. Thin to 9 or 12 ins. apart. Water in dry spells. Control insect pests by spraying with liquid derris.

SPECIES AND VARIETIES : *T. majus.* Orange and yellow, climbing, summer ; Peru. Many varieties, climbers or dwarf, double or single, ranging from lemon-yellow via scarlet to the deepest crimson and maroon. Some varieties have variegated leaves.

Gleam varieties are double semi-dwarfs, can be had in separate colours as well as in mixture. Globe varieties are double dwarfs. Tom Thumb (or *nanum*), single dwarfs in many colours, are probably still the best to grow.

T. peregrinum, yellow, climbing ; Peru. The Canary Creeper, less hardy than the above, may be sown under glass in March and planted out in May.

Other species will be found in other sections, as they are more definitely perennial.

URSINIA Order COMPOSITÆ

These half-hardy annuals grow about 1 ft. high and bear large daisy flowers of exceptional brightness, usually orange, marked with red, purple or black. Foliage feathery. Good cut flowers. From South Africa and Abyssinia.

CULTIVATION : Sow under glass in March, plant out in the open in May. Or sow outdoors in late April or early May.

SPECIES : *U. anthemoides.* Yellow and purple, 1 ft., summer. *U. pulchra.* Orange, marked black, 9 ins., summer, a compact bushy plant, useful for edging or pot culture. There are several other species of minor importance.

Annuals and Plants Grown as Such

VENIDIUM Order COMPOSITÆ

Another genus of S. African daisies. Strictly speaking some of these are half-hardy perennials, but they are usually treated as annuals. The foliage is more substantial than with Ursinia and in some species is covered with a silvery fur of hairs.

CULTIVATION: Soil must not be rich, or else flowers may be mis-shapen. Sow under glass in March or April, transplant to open late in May.

SPECIES *V. decurrens calendulaceum.* Yellow and purplish-brown, 2 ft., summer.

V. fastuosum. Orange, marked brown, centre black, leaves furry, 2-2½ ft., summer.

V. macrocephalum. Lemon yellow and black, 2-3 ft., summer.

VERBENA (Vervain) Order VERBENACEÆ

Hardy and half-hardy perennials, some of them grown as annuals, making very attractive bedding or edging plants. Their clean, bright colours and neat habit recommend them.

CULTIVATION: Sow under glass January or February, plant out late in May. Either stop plants when 6 ins. high to obtain bushy growth, or plant 1 ft. apart and peg shoots down, stopping them as they meet each other. Sunny position, rich well-drained soil required. If desired, the plants may be propagated by cuttings taken during summer.

SPECIES: *V. Aubletia.* Purple or lilac, 1 ft. summer; N. America.

A number of species have contributed to the popular hybrid strain, among them:

V. hydrida. Various colours, 1 ft. Small-flowered and large-flowered, self-coloured or white-eyed, dwarf or taller—an enormous range to choose from. Colours from white to deepest violet and crimson.

V. chamædryfolia. Scarlet, trailing, 2-3 ins., summer and autumn; Peru.

V. teucrioides. Pale yellow or pink, 1 ft., summer; Brazil.

WAITZIA Order COMPOSITÆ

Australian everlasting flowers of the daisy type, not usually seen in gardens now. Various species, yellow or white, 1-1½ ft.

XERANTHEMUM (one of the Immortelles) Order COMPOSITÆ

Everlasting hardy annuals from Southern Europe. Pink, purple or white.

CULTIVATION : Sow under glass in March, transfer to open in April or in May. Flowering shoots may be cut and dried for winter decoration.

SPECIES AND VARIETIES : *X. annuum.* Purple, 2 ft., upright habit. Some pink, white, double and semi-double varieties.

ZINNIA Order COMPOSITÆ

Half-hardy annuals from Mexico and tropical America. Stems sturdy, stiffly erect. Flowers very large. Substantial, single, double or semi-double in a wide range of unusual and beautiful shades from pale yellow via orange, scarlet, blood red to crimson and from white to cream, pink, apricot, mauve, etc. There are interesting in-between shades, such as copper, salmon scarlet, old rose.

Excellent cut flowers. Will last well over a week if the water is changed occasionally.

CULTIVATION : Sow under glass March–April, transfer to open end of May, beginning of June. Sunny position in deep, rich, moisture-holding, well-drained soil required. Zinnias appreciate mulching, generous watering and feeding.

SPECIES AND VARIETIES : *Z. elegans.* Various colours, 1-3 ft. ; Mexico. Many types and varieties from Lilliput to Giant, in colours as indicated above.

Z. mexicanum haageana. Orange scarlet, 1 ft., Tropical America.

Z. linearis. Orange, marked maroon, 9 ins.

Z. tenuiflora. Scarlet, 2 ft.; Mexico.

CHAPTER II

Bedding Plants and Plants for Cutting

SECTION ONE

BEDDING PLANTS

*

THE much maligned bedding plant still holds its own after years of being scorned by nearly every type of gardener. Bedding as such is likely to be used so long as gardens are planted and tended. No other type of planting gives such a blaze of colour over such a long period, with so little labour compared with the orderliness of the result.

Bedding is the best treatment for town front gardens, public parks and ornate formal schemes.

The plants are grown to a considerable size in nursery beds, frames or houses, and only moved into their flowering quarters when the previous occupant's flowering season is over. Thus a strong plant is formed in good soil and healthy conditions, able to give a fine show of bloom even if moved into a city garden where it could not possibly be grown from the start.

Bedding also solves the problem of those who do not enjoy having to " potter " in their garden constantly but prefer to get the job done and be finished with it. With two major operations each year the beds can be kept trim with the minimum of intermediate work. Against the reduction of labour must be put the increased expenditure. Bedding plants are not cheap, and to look well they must form a solid mass in the bed. Economy in the number of plants bought is a great mistake. Most of them only last one season, and even the perennials used for bedding need more care to prepare them for the next year than can generally be provided in the small garden. They must be regarded as finished once the flowering season is past.

PREPARING THE SOIL

The usual programme for bedding is to dig the ground thoroughly in autumn, generally late September or early October, and give

259

the beds a heavy dressing of well-rotted manure or compost. Consolidate the soil by treading ; then rake the bed and edge it up, using a line whenever possible. A really level surface and neat edges make the difference between a good and bad final result. If there has not been enough rain to wet the soil thoroughly since the hot weather it will be necessary to give the beds a good watering, if possible with a sprinkler. After watering leave the beds a couple of days before planting.

PLANTING

Plot the planting distances before starting work so that the spacing will be uniform throughout. Leave enough room for the plants to develop without overhanging the edge of the grass and making clipping difficult. Always use a line when measuring out the distances.

GENERAL CULTIVATION

Keep a few spare plants to replace casualties, and during the winter look over the beds occasionally and firm in any plants that have been lifted by frost or loosened by wind.

By May the spring bedding will be looking shabby, and the plants for the summer display ready to put out when the chances of late frost are past. The beds are cleared, dug and replanted as before with suitable plants to carry on the succession of colour until the cycle starts again in autumn.

Bedding schemes can consist of a single colour of one variety of plant with, perhaps, an edging of some lower-growing subject, or simple colour patterns of one kind of plant. An arrangement of tall dot plants over a carpeting of low-growing ones is also effective. For summer bedding taller growing tender shrubs, such as fuchsia and heliotrope, can be interplanted with medium-height flowers and edged with neat little foliage plants. Bulbs interplanted with tufty plants make a good combination in spring, while geometrical patterns of multi-coloured succulents have a charm of their own, provided they are put in with perfect precision and are in a very formal setting.

Bedding Plants
SOME WORTHWHILE PLANTS

SPRING BEDDING

(a) Flowering Plants

Achillea argentea
Alyssum saxatile compactum
Alyssum saxatile citrinum
Arabis albida flore pleno
Arabis albida variegata
Aubrietia (many shades)
Aubrietia variegata argentea
Aubrietia variegata aurea
Bellis perennis (large-flowered
  varieties)
Cerastium Beibersteini
Cheiranthus Allioni (Siberian
  Wallflower)

Cheiranthus Cheiri (Wallflower)
Iberis sempervirens
Myosotis (Forget-me-not)
Pansy (winter flowering
  selection)
Primula vulgaris cœrulea (Blue
  primrose)
Primula Juliæ hybrids
Primula polyantha (good
  named varieties)
Viola (many shades)

(b) Bulbs and Corms

Anemone St. Brigid
Chionodoxa
Crocus
Hyacinth
Iris, Dutch

Iris, Spanish
Muscari
Narcissus
Tulip

SUMMER BEDDING

(a) Foliage Plants

Artemisia arborescens
Centaurea candidissima
Cineraria maritima
Echeveria

Kochia
Sedum
Sempervivum

(b) Flowering Plants

Ageratum mexicanum
Alyssum maritimum, Little Dorrit
Alyssum maritimum, Lilac Queen
Antirrhinum (tall and dwarf
  varieties)
Begonia semperflorens (and
  varieties)
Calceolaria
Calendula
Chrysanthemum frutescens
Clarkia

Coreopsis
Dahlia (use dwarf bedding
  varieties)
Gazania
Geranium
Godetia
Heliotrope
Lobelia
Nicotiana
Pentstemon
Petunia

Salpiglossis
Salvia patens
Salvia splendens
Scabiosa (annual)
Tagetes

Tropæolum nanum
Verbena hybrida
Verbena venosa
Zinnia elegans

(c) *Corms*
Gladiolus

BIENNIALS

A biennial is a plant which completes its life's cycle, i.e., grows flowers and seeds, all within two years. Usually the gardener sows his biennials in May, June, or July to flower the following year. Some plants are commonly treated as biennials though they are really perennials, for instance, the Hollyhock and the Pentstemon.

Three plants, however, are commonly grown by the gardener as biennials. They are Forget-me-nots, Sweet Williams and Wallflowers.

FORGET-ME-NOT (*Myosotis alpestris*)

Very suitable for spring bedding; will grow in any ordinary soil. Seeds are usually sown out of doors in May, the drills being quite shallow at 8 ins. apart. When the seedlings are big enough to handle they should be thinned and transplanted 6 ins. square. They can be planted out in their flowering positions in October, 8 ins. square. They should flower in April, May and June. Good varieties are Royal Blue, Indigo Blue and Express. Express is the earliest.

SWEET WILLIAM (*Dianthus barbatus*)

Will grow in almost any soil. Seeds should be sown in May in rows 8 ins. apart in a prepared seed bed. Transplant early in July—6 ins. square into a reserve border. Plant into the flowering beds in August or early September—1 ft. square. Can be had in many colours, white, pink, red, salmon and " mixtures." Holborn Glory is a very large-flowered Auricula-eyed strain

WALLFLOWER (*Cheiranthus cheiri*)

Will grow in any ordinary soil, providing it is well drained and not too heavy. Appreciates a good dressing of lime because it is subject to the club root disease. (See page 681) Plants do well in sunny borders and beds and even on old walls. Sow in drills outdoors in May or June, drills 12 ins. apart and ½ in. deep. When the plants are 2 ins. high, transplant either into their permanent quarters or into a temporary bed. By September or early October the plants must be in their flowering positions at 1 ft. square. They should flower in April and May the following year. It helps if the growing points are pinched out when the plants are 6 ins. high. Good varieties are Golden Monarch, Golden Queen, Scarlet Emperor, Giant Fire King (a red orange), and Vulcan Improved (a velvety crimson).

SECTION TWO

FLOWERS FOR CUTTING

*

WHERE there is a heavy demand for cut flowers for the house it is as well to have a special border at the bottom of the garden to supply this demand, thus the " pukka " flower garden can be left with a full display of colour.

Grown for cutting, the plants should be in straight rows and kept in blocks of single varieties, in fact grown as you would grow vegetables. Long beds, to hold four lines of plants with two-foot paths between them, make cultivation and gathering easy. Staking and tying will be needed in most cases and a good method is to place strong posts at each corner and at intervals down the sides of the beds, and run a network of strings around and across the bed. By adding a new tier in good time the plants grow up between the strings themselves and a lot of breakage is saved.

FLOWERS FOR CUTTING—ANNUALS

Annuals for cutting may be divided roughly into two natural divisions: (1) those which may be sown out of doors in September and over-wintered, and (2) those which have to be sown in the spring, or that can only be sown in the autumn if they are covered with continuous cloches. The site chosen should be an open but fairly sheltered sunny spot. The soil should not be too rich or there will be a tendency for the plants to make too much growth and not flower properly. The normal preparation will be digging a month before sowing, so as to allow the land to settle. Then, when raking the surface down level, damped horticultural peat should be incorporated at half a bucketful to the square yard.

SEED SOWING

The seed will be sown very thinly in shallow drills drawn out 1 ft. apart, though with the taller annuals like larkspur 18 ins. may be given. Despite thin sowing it will be necessary to thin out the plants when they are 1 in. or so high to about the same distance apart as given for the rows (see page 206). Support should always be provided for the plants as already suggested.

SELECTION OF SUITABLE FLOWERS

The best annuals for cut flowers are: cornflower, candytuft, larkspur, calendula, nigella (love-in-the-mist). All these may be sown out of doors in September and will normally live through the winter. Other annuals are: annual chrysanthemums, clarkia, godetia, annual gypsophila, linaria, lychnis, sweet sultan. These may be sown in the autumn if covered with continuous cloches. The half-hardy annuals, which are often grown as cut flowers, are the China asters, the stocks, zinnias and cosmos, together with a number of everlasting flowers, like helichrysum and statice. These are raised, either in a greenhouse or frame, from sowings made at the end of March, or are sown *in situ* under continuous cloches at about the same time.

FLOWERS FOR CUTTING—BULBS

The flowers from most bulbs are excellent for indoor decoration and irises, anemones, gladioli, montbretias, daffodils, tulips, narcissi, lilies and lily of the valley are used for this purpose. It is always advisable to grow first-class blooms because when flowers are massed in a border even quite small specimens make a brave show, but only the best blooms can stand the close-up scrutiny of indoor conditions.

The bulbs are usually planted in rows 1 ft. apart, though in the case of the anemones and irises, 6 ins. apart will do. The bulbs may be put in almost touching one another in the rows and the planting should be carried out at the right time of the year for each particular type of bulb. It is better to get in the narcissus by the end of September. Tulips may be left until October. Irises can go in at the end of November. Anemones are usually planted in October, and again in February or March so as to provide succession. Gladioli usually go in about mid-March.

FLOWERS FOR CUTTING—PERENNIALS

There are a very large number of perennials which are excellent as cut flowers. They again have to be planted in serried rows and in beds no wider than 4 ft. for ease of picking. For perennials of a normal height, rows 1 ft. apart suit admirably, but for the taller types, like delphiniums, rows 2 ft. apart are preferable. It is always worthwhile choosing the particular varieties which are known to flower well and which are of a particularly good colour in the artificial light. The following perennials are easy to grow and make excellent cut flowers: achillea, alstrœmeria, aquilegia, Michaelmas daisies, *Chrysanthemum maximum*, delphiniums, doronicums, gaillardia, geums, gypsophila, heleniums, heuchera, the Iceland poppy, pæoines, the Christmas rose, pyrethrum, scabious, statice, thalictrum, and trollius.

Once planted, these perennials may be left down for two or three season before being disturbed. The site on which they are to grow should be thoroughly dug and manured (see pages 259-260) and when raking the surface level, 4 oz. of a good fish manure should be applied per square yard. With stronger-growing perennials, it is necessary to thin out the growths when they appear in the spring. This can be done by cutting out the weaker shoots on each plant when they are a few inches long. The very strong-growing types, like the Michaelmas daisies and heleniums, are best divided every second year. The plants should always be supported as advised on pages 95-96 (see illustration facing page 137), and it will be necessary to water well, preferably by overhead irrigation (see page 57), during the dry summer weather.

SECTION THREE

SPECIAL FLOWERS FOR CUTTING

*

SOME plants do not fit into any of the usual classes for cultural directions yet have many uses in the garden. Among the most important of these are border carnations, early-flowering chrysanthemums and all varieties of dahlia. All are invaluable for planting in mixed borders and can be used to follow spring bulbs in spaces reserved for them in perennial flower borders. In beds on their own they make a brave show, though the flowering season makes them unsuitable for fitting into the regular bedding routine.

OUTDOOR CARNATIONS

Carnations can be grown in a variety of soils, provided there is good drainage and a sufficiency of lime. All but the heaviest of garden soils should produce good results.

The plants are not very long lived, as they tend to get too woody after three or four years, so a few new plants should be raised each year for replacements. This is best done by layering parts of the old plants in June or July.

When planting a young rooted cutting in the border remember the size it will eventually attain, also the tendency to grow forward, and place it well back, at least 15 ins. from the edge.

Small twigs to support the flower heads will be sufficient staking. After flowering cut the whole stems right back.

To get the best blooms all the side buds should be removed, leaving only one on each stem, but for general border work it is more usual to let a number of the buds develop.

Border Carnations
> Border Orange, an attractive orange Self.
> Border Crimson, a rich crimson with wiry stem.
> Imperial Clove, a violet carmine, good grower.
> Downs Cerise, a rich growing cerise pink.
> Bookham Spice, pure white clove, strong aroma.
> Beauty of Cambridge, sulphur yellow, large size.

Cottage Carnations
    Cottage Apricot, rich apricot.
    Cottage Coral Pink, a coral salmon pink.
    Cottage Mauve, a really deep mauve.
    Cottage Pink, a large flesh pink.
    Cottage Primrose, a hardy yellow.
    Cottage Ruby, a wine or ruby shade.
    Cottage Scarlet, a good red, rich in perfume.
    Cottage Vivid, a gorgeous scarlet, compact grower.
    Cottage White, a beautifully formed highly fragrant white.

EARLY-GROWING CHRYSANTHEMUMS

Chrysanthemums are one of the most popular flowers for cutting as they last for such a long time in water.

CULTIVATION: *Soil and Preparation*
    The best soil for chrysanthemums is a good medium loam. It should be well dug in the autumn, and plenty of well-rotted organic matter incorporated —say, one good barrowload to 10 sq. yds. If desired, a good complete organic fertiliser such as fish manure may be added in the spring at the rate of 4-5 ozs. per square yard.

    Propagation
    The usual method is by cutting (see illustration facing page 225), though it is also possible to carry out division of the roots. The cuttings should be made from strong basal shoots about 3 ins. long, and should be taken in late February or early March. They are inserted 4 or 5 round the edge of a 3-in. pot and placed in a greenhouse (temperature 50° Fahr.) till rooting takes place, when the young plants may be potted singly into 3-in. pots. As soon as weather permits, the young plants may be placed in cold frames, where they should receive as much air and light as possible.

    Planting out
    This may be done as soon as danger of frost is over, the plants being put in rows 12-14 ins. apart each way.

    Staking
    Some system of staking will be necessary. If only

CULTIVATION: a few plants are grown, they may be staked individually with bamboos, otherwise a system of wires and cross-strings may be employed (see illustration facing page 137).

Stopping

This consists of the removal of the growing point on a certain date, which varies according to the variety. Most outdoor varieties are only stopped once, about the beginning of June, and this causes the plant to produce side growths and encourages it to flower earlier than it would normally.

Feeding

When the plants are established, weekly feeding with dilute liquid manure may commence, and this should continue until the plants come into bloom.

Disbudding

Chrysanthemums may be either grown as sprays, or, if large single blooms are required, disbudding should be carried out in accordance with the instructions on page 596.

VARIETIES: Amy Shoesmith, clear pink, satin sheen, September.

Ashover Supreme, clear yellow, incurved, mid-September.

Buccaneer, bright red, reflex, late August.

Evelyn Bush, large incurving white, early September.

Golden Harvest, rich golden yellow, September.

Hotspur, bright maroon, silver reverse, September.

Lilac Moon, pale lilac, incurved, silver reverse, August.

Merry Lass, shell pink, upright grower, mid-September.

Peter Shoesmith, rich orange bronze, September.

Salmon Una, beautiful salmon, late September.

Supersonic, brilliant crimson scarlet, September.

Westfield Flame, flaming red, dark foliage, late August.

DAHLIAS

Dahlias are officially divided into eleven big groups: Single, Star, Anemone-flowered, Collarette, Pæony-flowered, Decorative,

Double Show and Fancy, Pompon, Cactus, Miscellaneous, and Dwarf Bedding.

CULTIVATION: *Soil and Preparation*

The Dahlias will grow in most soils provided they have been previously well dug and enriched with organic matter such as well-decayed compost or manure. Alternatively, the organic matter may be applied as a top dressing early in June as soon as the plants become established. No nitrogenous fertilisers should be given, but some bone meal may be applied at 3-4 ozs. per square yard, and sulphate or muriate of potash at 2 ozs. per square yard.

Propagation

Dahlias are usually propagated either by division of the tubers or by cuttings, though it is possible to raise the small bedding varieties from seed. Division is a very simple method of increasing stock, the separate tubers merely being split up and planted out singly. If cuttings are to be taken, the tubers should be started into growth in a heated greenhouse in February, the resulting shoots being severed when 3-4 ins. long, and placed 4 round the edge of a 3-in. pot. When the cuttings are rooted, pot them singly in further 3-in. pots.

Planting out

This should not be done before the end of May in the south, or the beginning of June in the north. The tall Decorative and Cactus types will need to go 4 ft. apart, the smaller Decoratives, Collarettes and Pæony-flowered kinds at 3 ft., and the Dwarf Bedding kinds 18 ins. each way.

Staking

The large kinds will need staking with strong bamboos or wooden stakes soon after planting. Even the smaller kinds may require some support in windy situations.

Winter treatment

The tubers must be lifted at the first sign of frost and stored in a dry frost-proof shed with a little sand or dry soil over them.

VARIETIES: Croydon Masterpiece, reddish bronze, four and a half feet, Large Decorative.

Salmon Glory, salmon apricot, yellow centre, 5 feet, Large Cactus.

Second Century, brilliant scarlet, 4 feet, Large Cactus.

Golden Heart, flaming orange, scarlet, 4 feet, Medium Cactus.

Tango, salmon and rose, 4 feet, Medium Cactus.

Ballego's Glory, crimson, edged golden, 4½ feet, Medium Decorative.

Crimson Flag, bright crimson, 3½ feet, Small Decorative.

Gerrie Hoëk, shell pink, 4 feet, Small Decorative.

Jescot Jim, pure yellow, 4 feet, Small Decorative.

Jescot Tandra, lilac and white, 3½ feet, Small Decorative.

Willy den Ouden, cardinal red and orange, 3½ feet, Small Decorative.

Andries Orange, clear orange, 3½ feet, Small Decorative.

Sheila Brunton, scarlet and yellow, 4 feet, Small Cactus.

Mima Richardson, carmine rose, 2 feet, Dwarf Bedding.

Northern Gold, golden yellow, 2 feet, Dwarf Bedding.

Shirley Orange, pale orange, Dwarf Bedding.

Little Prince, clear yellow, 3½ feet, Pompon.

Mars, bright scarlet, 3½ feet, Pompon.

Pride of Berlin, pale mauve pink, 3½ feet, Pompon.

CHAPTER III

Roses

SECTION ONE

GROWING ROSES

★

GREAT BRITAIN is noted for its roses. Most gardens have special beds set aside for growing roses, and all the larger estates have definite rose gardens. Fortunately, there are roses to suit almost every condition.

GROUPING

Tea roses (T.) do better in France than in England. Most people prefer the Hybrid Teas (H.T.) which bloom over a long period.

The Pernetianas, or Pernets, came to us through a crossing made with the Austrian briars, and they have largely become lost through ill-breeding. It is the Pernets which produce the glorious oranges and bronzes now seen to-day in the H.T.'s. The Wichuraiana (W.) is the rambler rose group and the hybrid Wichuraianas are really a cross between the W.'s and the H.T.'s. The Multiflora Rambler is sometimes called the Climbing Polyantha, but is described in catalogues as M.R. Crimson Rambler is typical of this class. The Floribundas can be described as " crosses " between *Rosa multiflora* and the H.T.'s.

SOIL

Most soils can be made to grow good roses; they dislike water-logging so the land must be drained.

PREPARING THE SOIL

They like rich ground, so when preparing the soil it is advisable to dig in well-rotted composted vegetable refuse at the rate of 1 bucketful to the square yard. The digging should be done as early as possible, say a month or so before planting, so as to allow the soil to settle. Work organic fertilisers into the top 2 or 3 ins. at 3 or 4 ozs. to the square yard, prior to planting. A good fish manure is ideal, providing it has had potash added to it during its manufacturing process. Finely-divided wood ashes may be given in addition at ½ lb. to the square yard, or sulphate or muriate of potash at 2 ozs. to the square yard.

FEEDING

In addition to the manures given during preparation some kind of organic matter must be given yearly, preferably in May in the south and in June in the north. The dung or compost will be applied at one good forkful per bush as a surface dressing. In addition, the fish fertiliser, or the meat and bone meal, will be applied at 3-4 ozs. to the square yard in April, plus the sulphate or muriate of potash at 2 ozs. to the square yard. During the summer, Liquinure (Flower Special) may be applied once a fortnight in June and again in August, if necessary.

PLANTING

When the trees arrive, put the roots into a bucket of water. They should never be allowed to dry up. Always plant in the autumn if possible. If planting has to be delayed until March cut the trees back quite hard. Prepare a good hole so as to be able to spread out the roots evenly from the centre. (See illustration facing page 233.) Plant at about the same depth at which the tree was growing in the nursery. It is generally quite easy to find the soil mark. Plant very firmly. Never plant in wet weather when the soil is likely to be sodden. When planting climbers close to a wall, or fence, do not make the hole too close to the structure or the roots will not get sufficient rain. The hole should be at least a foot away.

Normal varieties of bush roses will be planted 20 ins. apart and the dwarfer kinds 18 ins. apart. It is convenient to plant in square or rectangular beds because these are easier to cope with, the front row of bushes being 1 ft. away from the pathway and the other rows 20 ins. away from each other. A convenient sized bed is one that is 5½ ft. wide and this takes 3 rows of bushes.

PRUNING

Rose pruning may be divided into two main operations : (1) the complete removal of dead and diseased wood, weak wood and misplaced and crossing branches, and (2) the cutting back of shoots in order to produce strong growths the following season. This is usually done in April. Always prune with a sharp pair of secateurs or knife.

The various types of roses are pruned in different ways. The H.T.'s (bush roses) are pruned in early April, the shoots cut back to within 4 buds of their base. (See illustrations facing page 248).

The climbing roses are pruned in March and a sufficient number of growths over 2 years of age are cut away to prevent overcrowding. Side growths may be pruned back to within 3 or 4 buds of their base.

In the case of ramblers (or Wichuraianas) the main pruning is done directly after flowering ceases when the wood that has flowered is cut back to its base. It is possible to leave in some of the older growths if they are needed to furnish the upper part of a pole or pergola.

Provence or Moss roses should have their vigorous growths cut back to within 4 buds in March and the laterals, on the 2-year-old wood, should be pruned back to a similar length also.

With the Austrian briars you just cut out the dead wood in the winter and, with the Pernetianas, you usually prune when the winter is over, cutting back all the dead wood. These bushes are very liable to frost damage.

In the case of standard roses, except Gloire de Dijon and W. H. Richardson, when you only remove the superfluous and worn-out shoots and shorten slightly, you prune as for H.T.'s or for H.P.'s.

With weeping standards you shorten the growths that actually trail on the ground and cut back the older wood as near to the head as possible. There should be plenty of new wood each year. This work is usually done in March.

GENERAL CULTIVATION

Keep the beds hoed regularly and give top dressings of lawn mowings as mulches no deeper than 1 in. (see page 35). These will not only keep the roots cool and supply organic matter, but they will do much to help in the control of the Black Spot disease.

Dis-shoot in April by removing any young growths that look as if they are going to overcrowd the centre of the bushes. Pinch them out with the thumb and forefinger. Disbud (see illustration facing page 233) by removing the side flower buds and thus giving the terminal or central bud the chance of getting all the plant food available. Watch out for suckers coming up from the roots and keep these cut down at a low soil level. They can easily be recognised because their leaves are smaller and they are more spiney or thorny. Cut back the faded blooms in June, or early July, by about 6 ins. and you will help the second blooming in September. Do not cut back any harder or you may encourage basal buds to break into growth and the young shoots may be killed by the frost in the winter.

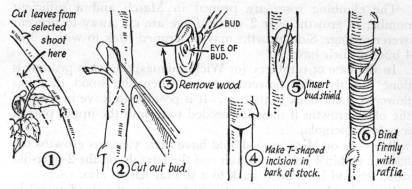

FIG. 18 ROSE BUDDING

Water the beds thoroughly in the summer if the weather is dry, by means of an overhead whirling sprinkler (see page 47). Mildew is always bad when the soil is allowed to get dry. Rake up all fallen leaves in the autumn and put them on the compost heap to rot down. If a proper accelerator is used on the heap, disease spores and insects' eggs will be killed.

PROPAGATION

There are very few amateurs who will take the trouble to bud their own roses, so only very brief instructions on this operation will be given.

Budding is done in July or August. (See Fig. 18.) The buds

should be chosen from the current year's growth, and the leaves removed, but the leaf stalks left. The bud is cut together with a shield-shaped piece of bark about an inch in length. Some growers remove the thin sliver of wood at the base of the bud. The stock is prepared by making a T-shaped cut through the bark—not any deeper—and slipping the bud shield into this so that it fits closely against the stock. It should then be firmly tied up with raffia, leaving only the bud exposed. The following spring the stock should be cut back to just above the bud.

Roses can also be raised from cuttings, taken in the autumn. The cuttings should be made 10-12 ins. long, choosing well-ripened young shoots which have not flowered. Cut just below a bud at the base and remove the bottom leaves. A narrow trench should then be made with a spade in a shady border, say 4-6 ins. deep, and the cuttings inserted 6 ins. apart, the soil being made very firm around them. They should be left in position for 12 months, i.e. until the following autumn.

SHOWING

Roses are one of the most popular flowers for exhibition, and there are few flower shows which do not have a special class for roses. Roses intended for show must be well grown ; the bushes should receive as much manure or compost as can be spared. They should be very severely pruned, and the aim should be not to allow more than six shoots per bush. Disbudding should be carried out, allowing only one bud per stem. The flowers may be given a very light tie with wool just before cutting in order to keep the flower in shape and to prevent it from opening too quickly.

A LIST OF WORTHWHILE ROSES

MENTION has already been made (page 271) of the various kinds and types of roses. It will only be necessary now to describe them briefly and mention a few of the best varieties. The most important groups of roses are:

H.T. Roses

These rose bushes are probably the most consistent flowerers and they are quite easy to prune because you can hardly overdo it.

The following are good varieties that should give satisfaction in most gardens: Apricot Silk, sheened apricot; Beaute, apricot yellow shading; Blue Moon, soft lilac, scented; Chicago Wonder, orange salmon; Duke of Windsor, luminous orange; Ena Harkness, crimson and scarlet; Fragrant Cloud, deep coral red; Grandpa Dickson, lemon yellow; Isobel Ortez, deep pink; Lady Sylvia, rose pink scented; Mischief, coral salmon; Ophelia, light pink blush; Papa Meilland, rich crimson; Piccadilly, scarlet and gold; Red Devil, crimson, fragrant; Shot Silk, cherry cerise; Spek's Yellow, bright yellow; Summer Holiday, orange red; Super Star, bright vermilion; Wendy Cussons, deep cerise; Whisky Mac, golden amber.

Floribunda Roses

This group of roses produces compact clusters of flowers throughout the season.

Good Floribundas are: Alec Rose, brilliant red; All Gold, unfading golden yellow; Charles Dickens, double salmon; Copper Pot, copper orange; Dearest, rosy salmon; Dickson's Flame, pure dazzling scarlet flame; Elizabeth of Glamis, salmon pink; Hylo, soft pink; Irish Mist, orange salmon; Lili Marlene, crimson scarlet; Masquerade, yellow, salmon and red; Merlin, yellow overlaid pink; Oberon, soft salmon apricot; Paint Box, a highly coloured larger Masquerade; Princess Michiko, coppery orange; Red Gold, red and gold; Scented Air, rich carmine pink; Sea Pearl, peach pink; Summer Song, orange and lemon; Queen Elizabeth, pink and carmine rose; Zambia, pure orange and yellow.

Roses

Bourbons

These have smooth, thick leaves, large curved thorns and beautiful seed pods form after the flowers. They need on the whole very little pruning. Good varieties are: Kathleen Harrop, a pale pink; Souvenir de Malmaison, a double rose pink; Zephyrine Drouhin, a silver pink.

China Roses

Very free-flowering over a very long period; excellent for massing and for hedges; should be thinned by cutting out one or two of the strongest shoots late in April or in July. Good varieties are: Common China, a vigorous pink; Fabvier, a crimson and white; Laurette Messimy, a rose-shaded yellow; Queen Mab, a soft apricot.

Climbers

Climbers are more suitable for training against walls than Ramblers because they don't have to be cut down each year, and because they stand the heat given off by walls far better. The following climbers spread themselves well over a wall and give little trouble; Climbing Etoile d'Hollande, a dark crimson; Climbing Madame Butterfly, a pink apricot and gold; Madame Alfred Carriére, a fragrant white; Mermaid, a yellow.

Damasks

Very old roses with fragrant flowers borne in clusters; flowers almost all through the summer.

Moss Roses

Very attractive roses because on the outside of the buds there grows a moss-like calyx. Good varieties are: Blanche Morreau, a white; Crested Moss, a pink; Golden Moss, a yellow; Old Pink, a pale rose.

Musk Roses

The lovely scent of the Musk roses comes from the stamen. They make good hedges or look well as isolated bushes. Just thin out some of the old wood in late March. Good varieties are: Aurora, a canary-gold; Cornelia, a strawberry flushed with yellow; Pax, a white; Penelope, a pink.

Provence Roses

The old-fashioned cabbage roses; gross feeders but their blooms are very fragrant. There is a red Provence and a white Provence.

Ramblers

The following ramblers may be recommended as being easy to grow: Dr. Van Fleet, a pale pink with deeper pink centre; Emily Gray, a deep golden buff; Lady Godiva, a flesh pink; New Dawn, a deep flesh pink; Paul Crampel, a deep orange scarlet; Princess of Orange, an orange; Shower of Gold, a yellow. Wichuraiana ramblers can be budded on to tall briar stems and made into attractive weeping standards: the most suitable varieties are the tree wichuraiana hybrids of the ' Dorothy Perkins ' class.

Rose Species

There are a number of botanical species of roses which can be planted in shrub borders. Many have brightly coloured fruits, others have attractive crimson foliage; some are very fragrant; others are decorative thorns. Some nurserymen specialise in these species. Ones that fascinate me are: *Rosa Moyesii*, which has ruby-red flowers, followed by sealing-wax red, pitcher-shaped fruits; *Rosa acicularis*, which is highly scented and bears red pear-shaped fruits; *Rosa pomifera*, bears red apple-like fruits, and *Rosa Wilemottiæ* which has orange-red fruits plus fragrant foliage. There are many other delightful species to choose from and interested planters should consult one of the specialist catalogues.

Rugosas

A hardy free-flowering group which produces large blooms during the whole summer. They have brilliant red seed pods in the autumn. They make good bedding plants. Choice varieties are: Blanc Double de Coubert, a white; Golden King, a clear yellow; Grooten Dorst Supreme, a bright red; Picardy, a red and yellow bi-colour.

CHAPTER IV

Bulbs

GROWING BULBS

★

BULBS are used in so many ways in the garden, in the greenhouse and in the house that they have become almost a necessity. As a group they are fairly easy to grow and, as they will last for a number of years, they prove to be a good investment. For the purpose of this section the term " bulb " ,will be used in a somewhat loose manner. This all-embracing term will have to include the corms and any tubers that are normally grown as bulbs. The true bulb, of course, exhibits, when cut horizontally across, those layers of flesh which overlap one another in a similar manner to the onion.

PLANTING IN THE OPEN

Bulbs are much used in formal beds. They are generally planted in lines running parallel to the edges of the bed and they are interplanted with what are known as the carpeting plants, for instance, forget-me-nots, wallflowers or alyssum. Tulips are much used for this purpose, the planting being done in October. The single and double earlies will make a show during the month of April and the May-flowering tulips, the Cottage and Darwin tulips, during the month of May. Daffodils may be used for bedding also while crocuses are often planted 2 ins. apart and are used as edgings. Hyacinths are planted fairly close together, say 9 ins. square, but some gardeners prefer them at 6 ins. because they say that they help to hold one another up. For bedding, always use the hyacinths with short stalks and plant with a trowel so that the bulbs are about 4 ins. deep. Always use the medium-sized bulbs because these produce one large flower only. Irises are sometimes used for late bedding ; the Dutch irises flower from mid-May to the end of May, and the Spanish irises towards the end of May. The English irises which flower later still are too late for bedding.

Some gardeners prefer a green background to their flowers and so use saxifrages, prostrate thyme and Gibraltar mint in order to produce a nice thick carpet of foliage.

The common carpeting plants are wallflowers, forget-me-nots, aubrietia—both the mauves and blues—double arabis, variegated arabis, polyanthus, coloured primroses, double daisies, yellow alyssum, winter-flowering pansies and the Siberian wallflowers. Two good bedding schemes, which may be given as an example are : the double early tulip Tea Rose, interplanted with the single tulip Mrs. Moon, and carpeted with the double aubrietia Dr. Mules ; and the King of the Blues hyacinth, planted 9 ins. apart and carpeted with the double-white arabis.

NATURALISING

One of the best ways of growing bulbs is to naturalise them in grass. This means that they are planted in a lawn, in a grass bank or in any wild or semi-wild portion of the garden. Here there must be no serried rows, no straight lines, and no complete circles. A good plan is to take the bulbs and throw them nonchalantly on to the grass and then plant them exactly where they fall. It is in this way that natural drifts can be produced. Do not make the mistake of planting too few bulbs. You want a hundred or so to make a good show. Take up a little circular piece of grass, plant the bulb 1-3 ins. deep, according to its size, replace the turf and tread down. Do not cut the grass until all the foliage has died down so that the leaves can have a chance of passing back the plant food they have manufactured. For this reason it is better not to plant bulbs in the main lawn, but only in the surrounds.

Daffodils are much used for this purpose but in addition trilliums, scillas, hardy cyclamen, snowdrops, colchicums and ornithogalum may be used.

PLANTING INDOORS

Many types of bulbs can be grown in bowls or pots in the greenhouse or living-room. These include hyacinths, tulips, narcissi (daffodils), irises, scillas, snowdrops, crocuses, cyclamen, gladioli, freesias and lilies. The simplest way of growing them is in moistened fibre, which not only holds the moisture well but does not damage the most delicate china. The moistened fibre must be pressed firmly around the bulbs so that the pots or bowls are filled to within half an inch of the rim. Directly the bulbs arrive they may be planted so that they are just not touching one another, and it is always better to plant one type of bulb per bowl to ensure that all the bulbs are flowering at the same time.

GENERAL CULTIVATION

A general rule is to place the pots or bowls on a concrete yard or hard path and then to cover them with sand or fine ashes to a depth of 3 or 4 ins. so that they are in the dark, and yet undergo the normal climatic conditions. They should be removed at the end of 8 weeks when a really good root system should have formed. It is then that they can be brought into the greenhouse or dwelling-house for forcing, as it is called. After flowering, there is no reason to throw away the bulbs—they may be planted in the garden.

ROCK GARDEN BULBS

There are a number of miniature plants, like, for instance, *Narcissus minimus*, which only grows 3 ins. high, which are grown almost entirely in the rock garden.

CULTIVATION

Some of them, like the baby irises, prefer a rather alkaline soil ; others are not a bit particular. A good general rule with regard to planting is to multiply the length of the bulb from tip to toe by three and plant at that depth.

A LIST OF WORTHWHILE BULBS

*

VARIETIES suitable for forcing or growing in bowls for the house are marked (F).

ACONITE (*See* ERANTHIS)

ALLIUM Order LILIACEÆ

A member of the onion family which flowers in May or June.

CULTIVATION : Plant the bulbs 2 ins. deep, and a similar distance apart.

SPECIES : *A. acuminatum.* Grows about 8 ins. high and bears deep rose-coloured flowers in July.
A. Moly. One of the best, bearing yellow flowers in May on stems 1 ft. high.
A. Karataviense. A rosy lilac which blooms in May, 6 ins. high.
A. neapolitanum. Bears lovely dark glossy green leaves with pretty white flowers. Blooms in May, 6 ins. high.
A. pedemontanum. A red which blooms in July, 12 ins. high.
A. triquetrum. A white and green which blooms early in July, 15 ins. high.

ANEMONE Order RANUNCULACEÆ

There are four main types : St. Brigid, which has semi-double flowers in all colours ; the French type, which has single self-coloured flowers ; the *fulgens*, which bears bright scarlet flowers, and the Dutch group which has extra large flowers. The De Caen differ from the St. Brigid in that they are semi-double and not quite so robust. The *apennina*, *blanda* and *nemorosa* types naturalise well in the wild garden or may be grown in the rock garden. They are the dwarf types.

CULTIVATION : The taller types of anemones are good cut flowers. They do best in a medium loam and are usually planted in October for flowering in March and April, and in March for flowering at the end of August onwards ; the wild and rock garden types

CULTIVATION : are best planted in October. Plant the larger
corms 2 ins. deep and the smaller ones 1 in. deep.
Cut-flower growers usually plant the corms 9 ins.
apart between the rows and 2-3 ins. apart between
the corms.

SPECIES AND   *A. apennina.* (Rock or wild garden.) Sky blue,
VARIETIES :   6 ins. high. Blooms in March.
               A. blanda atro-cœrulea. (Rock or wild garden.)
VARIETIES :   Blue, 6 ins. high. January–March.
               De Caen. Giant French Mixed.
               Dutch Double. Broumer, dark blue.
               Dutch Double. Rose.
               Dutch Double. Violet.
               Dutch Single. Rose.
               Dutch Single. The Bride, white.
               A. fulgens. Single, scarlet, black centre.
               St. Brigid. Mixed, all colours.
               All these varieties bloom in late spring and are 1 ft.
               high.

BLUEBELL (*see* SCILLA)

CAMASSIA Order LILIACEÆ

Bears star-shaped blossoms in light blue, purplish-blue or pure
white colours. A lover of shade. Blooms in May and June. Bulbs
may be left down for a number of years.

CULTIVATION : The bulbs should be planted 3-4 ins. apart, 4-5 ins.
deep. They prefer a heavy type of soil.

SPECIES :   *C. esculenta.* Looks something like a very large blue
hyacinth. 2 ft. high.
               C. Leichtlinii. Not to be recommended because of
its habit of holding its flowers, which gives it an
untidy-looking appearance; 2 ft., dark blue.
               C. Quamash. A purplish blue, and the most
common of all of them; 2-2½ ft.

CHIONODOXA (Glory of the Snow) Order LILIACEÆ

Bears starry lavender-blue flowers on 6-in. stems in the spring.

CULTIVATION : Plant 2-3 ins. deep in September in a sunny
position and well-drained soil.

SPECIES :   *C. Luciliæ.* Blue and white, 6 ins. March.
               C. sardensis. Deeper blue.

CROCUS Order IRIDACEÆ

These do particularly well in towns and cities.

CULTIVATION : When planted in a warm sunny spot they will often flower three weeks earlier than in another part of the garden. Plant them 3 or 4 ins. deep and 2 or 3 ins. apart early in October. The birds usually go for the yellow ones and not so much for the mauve varieties.

There are autumn-flowering crocuses which are very attractive and, curiously enough, almost unknown to many amateurs. These should be planted in July.

SPECIES AND VARIETIES : *Dutch or named Crocuses* (usually flowering in February) :

Baron von Brunow. Purple feathered violet.

Grand Maître. Indigo blue.

Kathleen Parlow. White striped lilac.

Paulus Potter. Ruby purple.

Snowstorm. Pure white.

Yellow Mammoth. Yellow.

Spring-flowering Crocus Species :

C. Fleischeri. White striped violet with red stigmata.

C. Korolkowi. Golden yellow inside, bronze outside.

C. tommasinianus. Pale lavender and silver grey, orange stigmata.

Autumn-flowering Crocus Species :

C. lævigatus. White, orange throated, purple feathered.

C. pulchellus. Lavender with paler veins and golden throat.

C. sativus (Saffron Crocus). Purplish violet, long red stigmata.

C. speciosus. Violet blue, veined deeper violet, orange-red stigmata.

All these species and varieties grow 4-6 ins. high.

ERANTHIS (Winter Aconite) Order RANUNCULACEÆ

Eranthis look something like buttercups and have very attractive foliage.

CULTIVATION : They prefer a half-shady place. Plant the bulbs 2-3 ins. deep and the same distance apart.

Bulbs

SPECIES :   *E. cilicica.* Large yellow flowers. January–March, 4-6 ins.
                 E. hyemalis. The usual variety grown. Golden-yellow flowers from January–March, 4-6 ins.
                 E. Tubergeni. Bears clear primrose-yellow flowers, in February and March, 4-6 ins., sweetly scented.

GALANTHUS (Snowdrop) Order AMARYLLIDACEÆ

These can be planted in little wandering groups anywhere in the garden. To get the best effects have twenty or thirty bulbs together.

CULTIVATION : Plant 3 ins. deep and 1 in. apart.

SPECIES AND   *G. Elwesii.* Said to be the giant snowdrop. It is
VARIETIES :   perhaps best grown in cultivated land for it does not naturalise as well as the common type. Grows 8-9 ins. high and flowers in January and February.
                 G. flavescens. Sometimes grown in the rock garden. It has a " flavour " of yellow in it, and because of this is not liked by those who insist on a snowdrop being white. Grows 4-6 ins. high and flowers in January and February.
                 G. nivalis. The common snowdrop usually planted. Grows 4-6 ins. high and blooms from January–March. A better type is the variety *Melvillei*, because it throws fine spikes and bells.

GLADIOLUS Order IRIDACEÆ

There are three main groups : the early flowering, the Grandiflora and the Primulinus. The early flowering are principally used for forcing under glass but make quite a good cut flower out of doors. The Grandiflora, or large flowering type, blooms in the autumn and is tall and stately. The Primulinus and Primulinus hybrids are much more dainty in appearance.

CULTIVATION : They all seem to do well in a sandy loam which has been enriched with plenty of moisture-holding material. The larger corms may be planted 4 ins. deep and the smaller ones 3 ins. deep. It is usual in the south to plant in mid-March and in the north towards the end of April.

SPECIES AND   *Early Flowering* (June, 2-3 ft.)
VARIETIES :   Peach Blossom. Delicate pink.
                 The Bride. White.

SPECIES AND VARIETIES : *Grandiflora Gladioli* (August, 3-4 ft.)

Albatross. White.
Apple-blossom. Pink.
Ave Maria. Blue.
Baron van Wynbergen. Salmon rose.
Flaming Sword. Scarlet.
Gold Dust. Butter-flower yellow.
Holland's Glory. Large sunflower yellow.
Lady Boreel. Light rose, darker blotch.
Rising Sun. Yellow novelty.
Yvonne. Pure white, wine-red blotches.

Primulinus Gladioli (August, 3-3½ ft.)

Athalia. Orange scarlet.
L'Innocence. White.
Maiden's Blush. Soft pink.
Souvenir. Yellow.

GRAPE HYACINTH (*See* MUSCARI)

HYACINTH Order LILIACEÆ

Quite useful in the formal bed. Grand for the pot or bowl in the house.

CULTIVATION : Hyacinths are not tolerant of badly-drained soils and they seem to prefer light land. They do not like shade ; may be planted in October out of doors, the smallest bulbs 3-4 ins. and the largest 5-6 ins. deep.

For the house the early Roman hyacinth should be potted in August so as to be ready for Christmas. The Italian hyacinths must be potted in September and the Dutch hyacinths in October or early November

SPECIES AND VARIETIES : *Double Hyacinths*

Chestnut Bloom. Chestnut pink.
General Kohler. Parma violet.
Sunflower. Buff yellow, salmon.

Dutch Hyacinths

White and Blush

(F.) Argentine Arendsen. Pure white.
Grande Blanche. Ivory white, tinged rose.
(F.) L'Innocence. Pure white.

Red, Pink and Rose

(F.) Garibaldi. Carmine-scarlet.

Bulbs

SPECIES AND
VARIETIES :

(F.) Lady Derby. Light rose pink.
Queen of the Pinks. Cerise pink.

Blue and Lavender
King of the Blues. Indigo blue.
(F.) Myosotis. Lavender blue.
(F.) Queen of the Blues. Cambridge blue.

Mauve and Purple
King of the Lilacs. Rosy violet.
Prince of Wales. Violet, white eye.
Queen of the Violets. Rosy violet, purple.

Yellow and Orange
(F.) City of Haarlem. Deepest of the yellows.
King of the Yellows. Primrose yellow.
(F.) Yellow Hammer. Canary yellow.

Roman Hyacinths
(F.) White. Early.

Italian Hyacinths
(F.) White, blue, pink, early.

All these varieties flower in spring and grow about 9 ins. high.

Iris Order Iridaceæ

Iris bulbs are quite small and the foliage which comes up in the spring is grass-like. The flowers look well in a mixed border in groups and they are grand when grown in rows for cut flowers.

CULTIVATION : When grown for cut flowers the rows are usually 1 ft. apart and the bulbs are planted 6 ins. apart in the rows. Planting is normally done in October ; the bulbs 3-4 ins. deep. The three main groups are the Spanish, the Dutch and the English. The Dutch flower first, the Spanish follow and the English come on last, and thus you can get a succession sometimes from May to July. There are a number of dwarf irises which are grown in rock gardens. These flower on the whole in the winter.

SPECIES AND
VARIETIES :

Dwarf Iris
I. alata. 1 ft., white, violet and blue. October.
I. histrioides. 1 ft., blue purple, white and yellow. January.
I. reticulata. 6 ins., violet purple. February.

Dutch Iris (Flower in early June, 1-2 ft.)
A. van Wiel. Bronze.

SPECIES AND VARIETIES :	Hart Nibbing. Soft blue.
	Jacob de Wit. Deep blue.
	Woerman. White.
	Spanish Iris (*I. Xiphium*) (Flower in June, 1-2 ft.)
	Cajanus. Canary yellow.
	Golden Wonder. Yellow.
	Royal Blue. Deep blue.
	Thunderbolt. Bronze.
	English Iris (*I. Xiphiodes*) (Flower in late June, 1-2 ft.)
	Bleu Celeste. Sky blue.
	Lamartine. White, with carmine-rosy flakes.
	Mont Blanc. White.
	Thackeray. Purple-maroon.

LEUCOJUM   (Snowflake) Order AMARYLLIDACEÆ

This is usually called the snowflake and is much confused with the snowdrop. It bears white flowers with green tips on stems 8 ins. tall.

CULTIVATION : Plant 3 ins. deep and 3-4 ins. apart.

SPECIES : *L. æstivum.* Does not often flower till May.

L. Hernandezii. The only one that likes to be planted around a pond or swamp. It seems to like tremendous moisture.

LILY Order LILIACEÆ

There are four hundred so-called species of the lily family and probably many more types and kinds. Most do well among shrubs ; others are grown in the wild garden ; some are excellent as cut flowers.

CULTIVATION : All lilies seem to thrive in partial shade and they like an open, well-drained soil. Most lily bulbs arrive in time for autumn planting ; the bulbs should be out of the ground for the minimum amount of time. Most people plant dormant bulbs In November. Types that have been brought on in frames they put out in March. A good rule is to plant them about three times as deep as their greatest diameter. The smaller growing types may be planted as close as 6 ins. and the taller varieties at least 1 ft. apart. It is a good plan to place a little sand just below the bulb at planting time.

v. Rose, Mrs. Henry Bowles

vi. *Nymphaea Marliacea chromatella*

Bulbs

CULTIVATION : The bulbs of the non-stem-rooting kind may remain dormant a whole season after planting and not begin to show until the second summer.

It is impossible in a book of this type to deal with all the lilies that may be planted, which may be divided roughly into three groups : the earliest, the mid-season and the late-flowering types. In the list below will be found a few varieties which are quite easy to grow.

SPECIES AND VARIETIES :

L. candidum and varieties. June. White, 4-5 ft.

L. dauricum. May–June. Yellow, 2-3 ft.

L. Hansoni. June. Yellow, 3-4 ft.

L. Henryi. July–August. Orange-yellow, 6-8 ft.

L. Martagon and varieties. June. Purple, 3 ft.

L. pardalinum Parryi. June–July. Yellow and brown, 3 ft.

L. p. giganteum. July. Orange-crimson, 4-6 ft.

L. pyrenaicum. May. Yellow, 3 ft.

L. regale. June–July. White banded with rosy-purple, 3-6 ft.

L. Thunbergianum. Variety, Orange Queen. June. Orange, 1-2 ft.

L. tigrinum Fortunei. August. Orange, red and black, 3-5 ft.

L. t. splendens. July. A larger-flowered variety.

L. umbellatum and varieties. June. Red, 3 ft.

L. Willmottiæ. June–July. Orange-red and brown, 4 ft.

MUSCARI (Grape Hyacinth) Order LILIACEÆ

These look well in drifts among shrubs, as edges to borders, or in the woodland garden.

CULTIVATION : Plant in September or early October with the bulbs 3-4 ins. deep and 3-4 ins. apart. The variety Heavenly Blue is particularly popular.

SPECIES :

M. armeniacum. A violet-coloured grape hyacinth and perhaps one of the most handsome. March, 6-8 ins.

M. comosum monstrosum, sometimes called *M. plumosum.* This is an extraordinary type which sends up a mauvy-blue flower more like a tousled feathery plume than anything else. It looks like a large distorted flower and always causes comment

The Complete Gardener

SPECIES :from those who do not know it. Blooms in April and grows 8 ins. high.

M. hyacinthus azureus. One of the earliest to flower and has been called the Snowdrop's Companion. Deep blue, flowers in early spring, 6 ins.

M. h. amethystinus. The latest type to bloom. Bears pale blue flowers and looks very dainty. April, 6 ins.

NARCISSUS (Daffodil) Order AMARYLLIDACEÆ

One of the best bulbs for naturalising and makes an excellent cut flower ; the baby types do well in the rock garden. Most of the daffodils bloom in March and the narcissi varieties in April and May. All grow 1-1½ ft. high except the baby types, which only reach a height of 6-9 ins.

CULTIVATION : Out of doors the bulbs must be planted by the end of September ; large bulbs 4-5 ins. deep, smaller bulbs 3 ins. deep. Each bulb must be placed upright and be well seated in the soil.

I. TRUMPET DAFFODILS

Trumpet in this division is as long, or longer, than the perianth.

Trumpet yellow, perianth yellow
- (F.) Emperor.
- Golden Goblet.
- (F.) Golden Spur. Good for bowls.
- (F.) King Alfred. Very handsome moonlight yellow.
- (F.) Olympia. Handsome frilled trumpet.

Trumpet white, perianth white
- (F.) Mrs. E. H. Krelage. Excellent.
- White Emperor.

Trumpet yellow, perianth white or whitish
- Madam de Graaff. Lovely.
- (F.) Oliver Cromwell. Early.

II. LARGE-CUPPED NARCISSI

This division includes the varieties which have a cup or crown more than one-third, but less than equal to the length, of the perianth.

Yellow shades, with or without red on cup
- (F.) Crœsus. Strong free bloomer.
- Damson. Deep red cup.
- Fortune. Giant flower, perfect form.

290

Red Cross. First-class exhibition.
St. Ives. Good for cutting.
Bi-colour, self-yellow, red-stained or red cup, white perianth
Chancellor. Good for cutting.
Great Warley. Large flower.
John Evelyn. Very handsome and striking.

III. SMALL-CUPPED NARCISSI

These flowers have the cup or crown not more than one-third of the length of the perianth.
Yellow shades, with or without red on cup
Bath's Flame.
Bonfire. Rich orange-scarlet cup.
Bi-colour, self-yellow, red-stained or red cup, white perianth
Caryeth. Very fine.
(F.) Lady Moore. Extra fine.
Sacrifice. Very late flowering.

IV. DOUBLE NARCISSI

Argent. Creamy white.
Inglescombe. Sulphur yellow.
Mary Copeland. Primrose yellow.

V. TRIANDRUS HYBRIDS

Baby types. Yellow.
Moonstone. Creamy white.

VI. CYCLAMINEUS HYBRIDS

These are so called because the perianth is reflexed like a cyclamen.
Golden Cycle.
Orange Glory.

VII. JONQUIL HYBRIDS

These have several flowers on each stem and are much prized for their sweet scent. They are excellent for garden or cutting.
Buttercup. Golden-yellow perianth and cup.
Golden Sceptre. Naturalises. Golden yellow.
Orange Queen. Orange yellow.

VIII. TAZETTA NARCISSI

Cheerfulness. Double, creamy-white.
Elvira. White, bright yellow cup.

IX POETICUS

This group is popularly known as the Pheasant's Eye Narcissus.
Excellent varieties have been produced which can be used for

forcing, for cut flowers, for naturalising and for planting in garden borders.

(F.) Horace. Very good. White with bright red eye.

(F.) Glory of Lisse. Purest white.

Recurvus. Latest to flower. Naturalises well. White.

ORNITHOGALUM (Star of Bethlehem) Order LILIACEÆ

This may easily become a weed in the garden so it is best given the go-by. It is for this reason that no cultivation notes are given.

SPECIES : *O. arabicum.* Flowers often 2 months later than other varieties, with stems 18 ins. high. White.

O. nutans. Has orange-coloured flowers in spring and grows 6 ins. high.

O. pyramidale. Even taller than *O. arabicum,* bearing white flowers with a greenish stripe, in early summer.

RANUNCULUS Order RANUNCULACEÆ

These look something like little pom-pom dahlias when growing. They are rather susceptible to weather damage and should be grown in a warm border.

CULTIVATION : Plant the tubers with claws downwards, 2 ins. deep and 6 ins. square. If planted in March, they flower in June, if planted in the autumn, they will flower in May. All grow 6-12 ins. high.

SPECIES AND VARIETIES : *Ranunculus asiaticus superbissimus*

(a) French Ranunculus, double flowers.

Emperor of China. Gold.

Primrose Beauty. Pale yellow.

Veronica. Carmine pink.

(b) Paris Ranunculus, single flowers. Mixed colours.

Ranunculus asiaticus vulgaris

(a) Persian. Mixed colours.

(b) Turban. Double mixed, various shades.

Ranunculus sanguineus

Pæony-flowered, rose pink.

SCILLA (Bluebell) Order LILIACEÆ

The bluebells fall into this section.

Bulbs

CULTIVATION : The secret of success is early planting, so get the bulbs into position in September. The bigger bulbs can be planted 5 ins. deep and 4 ins. apart, and the smaller bulbs 3 ins. deep and 2-3 ins. apart.

SPECIES AND VARIETIES : *S. festalis*, sometimes *S. nutans*. It is really the true English bluebell. Has blue flowers in May, 8-12 ins. *S. hispanica*, or *S. campanulata*. This is the Spanish bluebell. It often grows 1 ft. or more in height and is very vigorous indeed. Blue, white or pink, May.

S. sibirica. Dwarf with flower spikes only 4 ins. high. Blooms usually in February. The best variety of this is *atro-cærulea*, which is the tallest of the family and bears very large deep blue bells. The bulbs of this variety may be difficult to get.

SNOWDROP (*see* GALANTHUS)

SNOWFLAKE (*see* LEUCOJUM)

STAR OF BETHLEHEM (*see* ORNITHOGALUM)

STERNBERGIA Order AMARYLLIDACEÆ

Looks like a large crocus and flowers in the autumn. *S. lutea* is my favourite.

CULTIVATION : Plant the bulbs in August, 3-4 ins. deep and 6 ins. apart.

SPECIES AND VARIETIES : *S. Fischeriana*. Flowers in the spring. Yellow, 6 ins. *S. lutea*. The flowers are of a peculiarly beautiful yellow. October, 6-8 ins.

TULIP Order LILIACEÆ

Tulips are often used for bedding, are grand as a cut flower, but do not do well as a whole in grass or in bowls. There are 15 main groups, which flower over a period from late March to May.

CULTIVATION: They do well in almost all types of soil, though they hate badly-drained land. They should be planted out of doors in October, the early varieties 3-4 ins. deep and the later varieties 5-6 ins. deep. The *Kaufmannuanas* and *Clusianas* can be planted 8 ins. deep.

SPECIES AND
VARIETIES:

Early Flowering Tulips, Single. Christmas Marcel, cherry pink; Keizerskroon, scarlet edged yellow; Van der Neer, plum purple.

Early Flowering Tulips, Double. Electra, cherry red; Garanza, deep peach-blossom pink; Hoangho, pure yellow.

Mendel Tulips. Apricot Beauty, salmon-rose tinged red; Krelage's Triumph, crimson red; Olga, violet-red edged white; Pink Trophy, pink flushed rose.

Triumph Tulips. Bandoeng, mahogany red flushed orange; Crater, carmine-red; Madame Spoor, mahogany red-edged yellow; Topscore, geranium-red, yellow base.

Darwin Tulips. La Tulipe Noire, purple-black; Mamasa, bright buttercup-yellow; Pink Attraction, silvery violet-rose; Stylemaster, cochineal-red.

Darwin Hybrid Tulips. Beauty of Apeldoorn, flushed magenta edged yellow; General Eisenhower, orange red; President Kennedy, yellow flushed rosy scarlet; Yellow Dover, buttercup yellow.

Lily-Flowered Tulips. Aladdin, scarlet edged yellow; Lilac Time, intense violet-purple; Mariette, deep satin rose.

Cottage Tulips. Balalaika, turkey red; Golden Artist, golden-orange striped green; Princess Margaret Rose, yellow edged orange-red.

Rembrandt Tulips. Black Boy, dark chocolate-black on garnet brown; Insulinde, violet on yellow ground; Paljas, white flamed blood-red.

Parrot Tulips. Black Parrot, purplish-black; Erna Lindgreen, bright red; Orange Favourite, orange with green blotching.

Double Late Tulips. Bonanza, carmine-red edged yellow; Golden Nizza, golden-yellow feathered red; Orange Triumph, orange-red edged yellow.

Tulipa Species. Tulipa griegii. Mottled or striped foliage. Later than kaufmanniana. *T. kaufmanniana.* 6 ins., white, golden base, red stripe. Variety Primrose, 8 ins. sulphur yellow. March. *T. Fosteriana.* Large early flowering, some with mottled or striped foliage.

WINTER ACONITE (*see* ERANTHIS)

CHAPTER V

Ferns and Grasses

FERNS

*

THERE are a number of plants which are grown almost entirely for the beauty of their foliage, and this applies particularly to ferns and ornamental grasses. Most of the grasses are very graceful ; others are compact in growth. Some may be said to be majestic ; others to look curious. It much depends on their height and size as to where they are planted in the garden. They are often used by the sides of ponds and streams and in the wild garden, and some of the more graceful types are often included in the herbaceous border. Ferns differ tremendously in their forms and habits of growth, and even in range of colour.

Ferns are divided into two main groups : (1) Greenhouse Ferns and (2) Hardy Ferns. They are generally classified according to the shape of their spores called sori, or sporangia, some being round ; some kidney-shaped ; some naked ; some covered. In the maiden-hair fern and brackens, the edges of the ferns actually fold over to cover the sori.

PROPAGATION

Ferns are propagated by means of spores which are particularly fine. These are usually found in dots or lines or in marginal patches on the underside of the fronds. They normally ripen in July and can be collected and stored in tiny bags until March or April. Then, amply crocked pots are prepared with a good depth of sterilised soil. The spores are scattered thinly over the surface and are not covered. A piece of glass is put over the pots and the pots are placed, in earthenware saucers containing water, in a shaded house at a temperature of 60-70° Fahr. Where it is not possible to shade them, the pots, with their saucers, should be placed under the staging.

In one week, or maybe as long as two months, the spores will grow into prothallus, and fronds will grow on the underside of the prothallus. These fronds are first of all pricked out in clusters into a sandy compost 1 in. apart. Later on, when they are big enough to prick out, they will be divided up in patches. As the ferns grow the temperature is reduced. Overhead watering should never be given during the young stages.

Some ferns can be propagated by division in March. They are then re-potted (see illustration facing page 249) and put out in cold frames until established. Hardy ferns will of course be planted out after division. Some types may be increased by layering, those, for instance, that have long rhizomes which can be pegged down into the ground and thus form new plants. Some ferns, like the *Asplenium bulbiferum*, can be propagated from bulbils on the fronds. These are removed and placed flat on a sandy compost and will quickly produce roots when in contact with the damp soil.

GREENHOUSE FERNS

The greenhouse ferns consist largely of the genera and species which like a high temperature. Some, which like a very high temperature, say 60-65° Fahr., are known as Stove ferns ; others which will do with a temperature of 45° Fahr. are known as greenhouse ferns. During the first year or two in the greenhouse, after being propagated from spores, the plants may need two pottings per annum. But, when they are established in their final pots, say 6 or 7 ins. in size for the normal types, they will only be re-potted in March each year, the aim being to pot them back into the same sized pots. A good compost consists of 2 parts loam, 1 part peat, $\frac{1}{8}$ part sand. For the vigorous varieties add a little bone meal. It is usual to warm this compost to the same temperature as the house before using it.

Ferns need plenty of water in the growing season and a minimum of water in the winter. On the whole they dislike being syringed over, but they do like a dampish atmosphere. Some plants grow well in hanging baskets and the way to water these is to submerge them in a trough of rainwater.

SOME GOOD KINDS TO GROW
There are a very large number of types and varieties which may be grown in the greenhouse, but only a few that are easy to grow are mentioned :

Adiantum cuneatum. The maiden-hair fern, often used for room decoration.

A. Farleyense. Pink when young and very, very graceful.

Asplenium bulbiferum. Bears tough pretty foliage and an abundant crop of young plants on its fronds. It is easily propagated.

A. Nidus. The birds' nest fern, a Stove type.

Davallia and its many species and varieties, known as the hare's foot fern, usually need an 8-in. pot. It has brown felted rhizomes.

Gymmogramma. A Stove genus which comprises a number of beautiful ferns including the so-called silver and gold fern, the plant being covered with silvery-white or golden-yellow powder.

Nephrolepis exalta. The ladder fern, quite a popular type of which there are many " varieties " or sports. Easy to propagate from stolons ; likes a temperature of 65° Fahr. The variety *Scottii* has very frilly fronds.

Platycerium. The stag's horn fern, is usually grown on bark suspended from the roof.

Polypodium. A large and varied genus ; the variety *cristata* is much used for pot plants or hanging baskets.

Pteris cretica and *P. tremula*, the trembling fern, are often used for house decoration.

P. scaberula. The New Zealand lace fern.

HARDY FERNS

There are a number of hardy ferns in Great Britain which will grow out of doors without protection. The number of sports and varieties may easily be 5000. They all need damp conditions and shade, but they like to have a certain amount of drainage so that there is no stagnant water in the winter. They love deep beds containing plenty of humus, and in the case of *Asplenium* and *Scolopendrium*, the hart's tongue fern, a little lime or mortar rubble may be worked into the soil before planting.

The ferns may be planted in March, either in beds on their own or round deciduous types of evergreens. Firm planting is important, plus a really good watering in. Water well in the spring and summer when necessary and feed with Liquinure once a month. Give top dressings of damped horticultural peat or leaf mould in droughty weather.

SOME GOOD KINDS TO GROW

It is impossible to mention any but a few kinds.

Asplenium Trichomanes. The maiden-hair spleenwort. It has black stems and grows 6 ins. high.

Asplenium viride. Has bright green stems. 6 ins.

Athyrium Filix-Fœmina. The lady fern. It grows about 3 ft. high, but its height may be cut by frost in the spring.

Blechnum spicant. An evergreen little fern 6 ins. high, very hardy and pretty.

Dryopterix Filix-Mas. The male fern. It is very free-growing and does well under almost any conditions. It is deciduous and grows about 3 ft. high.

Osmunda cinnamonea. A beautiful American variety of the *O. regalis*, the royal fern which is often planted near the water-side and may grow 10 ft. in height. It can be killed by frost.

Polypodium Phegopteris. The beech fern and *P. Dryopteris*, the oak fern. Both like sheltered positions and plenty of leaf-mould. 6 ins.

Polystichum angulare. The soft shield fern which thrives in any ordinary garden. It has produced many beautiful sports. 1-2 ft.

Scolopendrium vulgare. The hart's tongue fern. It is very hardy indeed. It will grow in exposed positions and has many garden forms and sports. 9 ins.

GRASSES

★

THE grasses can be roughly divided into three main groups :
(1) the annuals ; (2) the perennials, and (3) the very tall
kinds.

ANNUALS

These are definitely graceful and charming, and some people
like to cut them when growing and, having dried them, use them
for floral arrangements. Even before drying, the grasses are
sometimes used for making up bouquets. The seed is best sown
where the plants are to grow in April, or May in the north.
It is possible, at any rate in the south, to sow seed in August and
get the plants to over-winter. They are thus at their best much
earlier in the summer. The half-hardy varieties have to be
sown under cloches in April, or in boxes under glass, and after
hardening off the plants they can be put out late in May, or early
in June.

Some good varieties are :

Agrostis laxiflora. A Cloud Grass which grows much taller than
A. nebulosa.

A. nebulosa. The Cloud Grass ; grows about 18 ins. high.

A. pulchella. A miniature type ; only grows about 6 ins. high.

Avena sterilis. The Animated Oat ; grows about 2 ft. high with
large, drooping spikelets.

Briza gracilis. The Quaking Grass ; grows 9 ins. high.

B. maxima. The Pearl Grass ; grows about 18 ins. high and
bears large, fascinating seed heads.

Coix Lachryma-Jobi. Usually known as Job's Tears ; is definitely
half-hardy. It grows about 2 ft. high and bears peculiar greyish
round seeds which hang in clusters.

Eragrostis elegans. The Love Grass ; grows about 2 ft. high
and is sometimes used in bouquets.

Hordeum jubatum. The Crested Barley Grass, sometimes called
the Squirrel Tail Grass ; grows 2 ft. high, bearing long, hairy,
gracefully curved spikes.

Lagurus ovatus. The Hare's Tail Grass, grows about 1 ft. high.

Milium effusum. The pretty Millet Grass. 2 ft.

Panicum Teneriffæ. The Teneriffe Grass. 3-4 ft.

There are, in addition, a number of variegated maize known as

Zea Mays variegata which, with their reddish and golden-striped leaves, look very pleasing when planted among other subjects. These are half-hardy. 3-12 ft.

PERENNIALS

These may be propagated by the division of roots in April or October, or by the sowing of seeds in May, or early June, in a seed bed out of doors. The plants thus raised are put into their positions in October. Half-hardy types are usually sown under glass in March or under cloches in April and are then ready for planting out in the open in October. It is always necessary to thin these grasses out very early if well-grown bushy specimens are desired. Most of the perennials like well-drained, open, sunny positions.

Good types are :

Elymus arenarius. The Lime grass. 4-5 ft.

Festuca glauca. Silvery foliage. Feather grass, often used as an edging plant. 6 ins.

There are various species of *Miscanthus* and their varieties which grow to a height of 3-5 ft. and are useful for mixing in herbaceous borders. There is one exception, *Miscanthus saccharifer*, which grows to a height of 10 ft.

There are a number of *Stipas* such as *S. splendens* and *S. pennata*, which are delightful Feather grasses and which usually grow up to 4 or 5 ft. in height.

THE VERY TALL KINDS

Into this group we should put the Pampas grass, *Cortaderia argentea*, and the variety *C. a. elegans*, as well as the silvery reed-grass from New Zealand now known as *Cortaderia conspicua*.

The Pampas grasses often grow 4 and 5 ft. across and they need planting on their own, so as to be allowed plenty of room to develop. They have to be protected in very severe winters by having straw hats put over them, or by covering them with a " tent " of boughs and sacking. It is possible to raise plants by sowing seeds in March in boxes or pots under glass and planting out the seedlings in seed beds in May. It is also possible to propagate by division in April or October.

PART FOUR

THE GARDEN BEAUTIFUL
FLOWERING SHRUBS AND TREES

CHAPTER I

The Culture of Flowering Shrubs and Trees

SPECIMEN flowering shrubs, and beds of these, are increasingly grown now because permanent effects can be obtained from them with much less upkeep.

Formerly, the " shrubbery " was merely a screen to shut off ugly objects or a windbreak to provide shelter. The shrubs used were mostly laurels, privet, cotoneasters, conifers, etc., which were not worth looking at. The modern flowering shrub cult is quite another matter. At first, mixed beds were mostly planted with many different species singly interspersed. But this was found to be very unsatisfactory, because either the bed had to be planted so as to leave ample room for the ultimate size of the plants without crowding their neighbours (thus leaving bare spaces for some years) or, with closer planting, the shrubs had to be constantly pruned to prevent their interfering with the symmetry of their neighbours. The latest method, however, is to mass shrubs of the same species (in different coloured varieties) in large groups, with not more than two or three kinds in each bed. Thus a real display of colour is secured from each bed during two or three parts of the flowering season. The beds can be closely planted at the start, and so secure a quick return in blossom. And there is little or no need for pruning as, the shrubs being all of the same kind, no distortion takes place ; instead the bed rapidly forms a mass, or thicket, which discourages weeds and forms a harmonious picture.

GENERAL DESIGN

To look well, flowering shrubs require a somewhat informal grouping. Consequently, in order to break the lines of the beds, specimen shrubs are set in the turf near the margins and, as shade is required by a large proportion of the better shrubs, groups of flowering trees are planted to the southward of the beds. In the past a great number of exotic shrubs, which reached this country owing to the work of plant collectors in foreign lands,

303

has been planted and tried out but, as might be expected, comparatively few of these can really challenge the older favourites for practical planting, colour effect and reliability. Selection is gradually eliminating the less effective kinds, as the modern, small, flowering shrub garden requires subjects with flowers of rich and brilliant colourings which it can rely on to produce in abundance. There is no room for plants of doubtful decorative value.

It is important to select species which will bloom in succession so as to cover the whole summer flowering season, at least, when gardens are most lived in and enjoyed. Fortunately, there is an ample selection from which to choose, with flowering times ranging from April to September, whilst for those able to afford the space for effects in late autumn, winter or early spring, as well as in summer, there are a number of species flowering in these seasons which are hardy enough to withstand our climate.

LAYOUT

As regards the design of the layout, one of the best general schemes is to form a glade of lawn, with a slight serpentine curve, to the farthest point possible and then plant flanking beds, also specimens set in individual small circular beds, about the margins. Behind the flanking beds a winding grass path may be placed, with a planting of flowering trees on the farther side. In this way, the largest area of garden lies open to the view from the house, or other viewpoint, and the flowering trees lift up the effect and provide a much greater area of bloom than is possible when the flowers are set approximately on one plane. In such a position, too, the trees form an effective background, windbreak, and screen.

PROPORTIONS

The proportions of the beds and the size of the specimen plants or trees depend upon the area of ground available, but it is easy to overstress this. It is sometimes thought that in very small gardens, such as, for example, a small courtyard, only very small subjects should be planted. This is a mistake as, in actual fact, the miniature plants only emphasise the smallness of the space. A lesser number of full-sized shrubs would provide a much more pleasing composition, and there would be, actually, more flowering surface visible to the eye. The more or less flat plane of the flowering surface of the miniatures, obviously, covers a much smaller area than the mounded, or towering, surfaces of larger flowering shrubs and trees. It will be found, too, that the possession of a few fine specimens, of a size well able to take care of themselves, gives greater satisfaction than the continual labour necessary to defend tiny shrubs against pests, weeds and animal marauders.

In the smaller gardens, flowering trees of small size, such as robinias, cherries, crabs, rowans, thorns, magnolias, eucryphias, etc., are in keeping and give a good return in blossom. A garden without a tree of any kind always lacks interest. In larger places trees of full forest size are capable of colour effects hardly yet realised because few of the new kinds have had time to grow to their full stature. Ice-blue cedars, maples, cryptomerias, golden elms, incense cedars, etc., offer superb colour harmonies for the planter of parks and pleasure grounds. In the arrangement of flowering trees use can be made of the fact that some species unfold their leaves before others; for example, a robinia can be planted almost in front of an early-flowering cherry. The cherry will have completed flowering before the leaves of the robinia appear, and the latter will remain brilliantly green long after those of the former have had their colour dimmed by high summer suns.

BACKGROUNDS

Where flowering shrubs are planted it is important to have, as far as possible, a living or naturalistic background. The material used for this purpose varies in accordance with the space at command and the type of soil. With a rich soil, in a garden reasonably sheltered from wind, the various species of hardy bamboo make an original and beautiful background. In an acid, sandy soil rhododendrons, with their dense, evergreen leafage and their useful quality of taking very little from the soil, are ideal. In a windswept place where shelter and screen of greater height are needed, pines and other conifers are best.

In planning the beds it is important to select a good proportion of evergreens, otherwise the effect is very dreary for a great part of the year. The best garden pictures are made when the evergreens are planted first, making an arrangement that is satisfactory to the eye before the deciduous (or leaf-losing) shrubs are planted in the foregrounds of the beds. The value of these, it will be found, will be doubled in effectiveness by being shown up clearly to the eye in contrast to the dark background behind.

PLANNING

In planning the layout of the beds (assuming that the glade design has been chosen), a good method is to form them in curved, island-like shapes, leaving grass paths between and at the back.

Curved paths are best as they do not form miniature wind tunnels but tend to temper the force of the wind which is very bad for most flowering shrubs. If inspiration is lacking a good plan is to secure a quantity of cut evergreen branches and stick these into the ground to imitate shrubs until a satisfactory picture is made.

Some useful evergreens for background planting are camellias, rhododendrons, *Choisya ternata*, *Fatsia japonica*, etc. (See alphabetical list in Chapter II, page 319.)

In most cases a mere " spine " of evergreen planting will be sufficient to give a bed the necessary solid look in winter and thus there will be ample space in the foregrounds, and at either end, for the deciduous kinds. In choosing these we have to look for certain characteristics. In the first place, we want a shrub which can be relied on to produce a brilliant and beautiful effect of massed flowers ; next, we require a compact, bushy habit and a nature that does not object to our particular soil and climate. Examples of flowering shrubs which are effective for massing are : Evergreen Japanese azaleas ; hybrid deciduous azaleas (*mollejaponicum*, Ghent, *occidentale*, and Knap Hill) ; *Chaenomeles japonica* ; rhododendron hardy hybrids of the more low-growing varieties ; helianthemum varieties ; brooms (varieties of *Cytisus scoparius*) ; hydrangeas (varieties of *H. macrophylla* and *H. serrata*) ; fuchsias (*F. magellanica*, variety *Riccartonii*) ; roses of bush varieties, etc.

BOLD EFFECTS

In general the boldest effects are obtained where a bed is planned to give only two seasons of bloom, for example, a background planting of *Rhododendron* Britannia, scarlet ; *R.* Mrs. John Clutton, white ; *R.* Lady Clementine Mitford, peach blush, to flower in early June, and, in the foreground, a planting of *Hydrangea macrophylla* varieties such as Bluewave, Générale Vicomtesse de Vibraye, both blues, with *H. macrophylla* variety *macrosepala*, white, as a contrast, to flower in late July and in August. To bring the bed into the scheme of the main garden landscape during its off season one or two " diversifications " may be added. These may either take the form of an odd plant or two of quite a different flowering time, and preferably of a quite distinct habit of growth from the principal occupants planted in the bed, such as, for the example give above, say, a small tree of *Prunus incisa*, and a dwarf cherry tree giving a cloud of pale pink blossom in spring. Again, this effect may be achieved by placing a single specimen, of a species which flowers at a different time, in the turf nearby.

The Culture of Flowering Shrubs and Trees

As a rule, it is best to have the evergreen background plants flowering first, so that they are clearly seen before the later flowering, deciduous shrubs come into leaf and flower. Early-flowering rhododendrons, such as *R. venustum* variety *Jacksonii*, in the background with roses, such as Betty Prior, with pink flowers from late June onward, are an example. Limy soils will not grow rhododendrons, azaleas of any kind or blue hydrangeas (see section on soils, page 308), so substitutes have to be found (see plants suitable for limy soils in the alphabetical list, Chapter II, page 319).

Certain times during the summer months are more difficult to cater for than others, such as the well-known "June-gap." Fortunately a number of most decorative flowering shrubs do flower at precisely that moment. Examples are *Cornus Kousa*, *Rhododendron indicum*, *Philadelphus* Belle Etoile, and most important of all, the shrub roses.

SUCCESSION OF BLOOM

With flowering shrubs, rather than rely upon one bed to give a succession of bloom in sections (as one does with the herbaceous border by draping, tying and pruning away), it is best to make the halves, either foreground or background, of the different beds succeed one another in bloom. Usually it will be found sufficient, when planning, to divide the flowering season into four periods only, i.e., spring, early summer, midsummer and late summer. The most important shrubs and trees typifying these periods for the main effects being : for spring, magnolias, cherries, crabs, evergreen Japanese azaleas, quinces, early rhododendrons, etc. ; for early summer, hybrid azaleas, brooms and hardy hybrid rhododendrons ; for midsummer, the "June-gap" species mentioned and roses, philadelphus, helianthemums, etc. ; and for the late summer, hydrangeas, eucryphias, fuchsias, hypericums, heaths, etc. More often than not, too much planting space is given over to spring-flowering shrubs with consequent dullness during the real summer months when more time is likely to be spent in the garden. It is, of course, a matter for personal choice ; the essential in planning is to decide which periods of the summer are to be selected for the best show of bloom and then plant accordingly.

WINTER EFFECT

It will be found that the " off-season " of the winter months yields a surprising show of attractive colour and form when flowering shrubs are planted. Although selected for flower display primarily, most of the species and varieties mentioned as the most important have a high decorative value when out of flower as well. For example, the evergreen azaleas form mounds of rich green ; the flowering cherries turn their leaves to rich shades of crimson and orange in autumn ; the roses have attractive red, or rose-coloured, young growths in spring ; the hydrangeas retain their flowers in good shape all winter and the sepals turn to various green and maroon tints and finally to quite a pleasing buff colour, very effective against the dark background of evergreens. *Eucryphia glutinosa*, also, after its tremendous display of large white blossoms, turns its leaves to fine shades of orange and yellow before they fall. It is much more fun to adventure with a few of these really fine kinds than to buy the old humdrum sorts that are quite outclassed to-day.

Drawing up the Plan
Having decided, therefore, on the times when the best flower displays are wanted, or when to plant so as to cover the whole of the summer, a scheme may be got out on paper. Assuming that the four main periods of bloom suggested are desired, four copies of a sketch plan of the proposed beds will be required. If each of these is filled in *only as regards the shrubs blooming at one particular period* it will be easy to see just what the display will be at any one of the seasons mentioned. In the section dealing with the different species and varieties the flowering time will be mentioned so that, if desired, a selection can easily be made to reinforce a weak period.

SOIL

Preparing the Soil
Flowering shrubs differ widely in their requirements as to soil, but nearly all do better in a soil rich in humus (or decaying vegetable matter). Sometimes, however, it is not desirable to give a shrub a too favourable soil. The brooms, for example, are longer-lived, more floriferous and shapely in a poor soil with full exposure. The heaths, too, are more compact and better in every way on poor ground. On the other hand, no one can expect to grow fine azaleas, roses or hydrangeas on poor soils insufficiently worked and manured with the particular fertilisers required. Lime, so useful in the kitchen garden owing to the fact that its presence discourages certain pests of the brassica (or cabbage) family, is fatal to the well-being of most of the choicer shrubs and

is needed by none. If it is present in quantities beyond the neutral point, azaleas, rhododendrons, heaths, eucryphias, etc., cannot be grown and hydrangeas will grow poorly and their flowers will not assume the splendid blue shades generally admired. Artificial lime is even more poisonous than the natural chalk and even a small quantity can do great damage. The practice of digging in rotted humus is, with flowering shrubs, less advantageous than the easier method of merely covering the surface of the soil, after planting, with a mulch of fallen leaves. The mulch feeds the soil in Nature's way, from above, without lowering the nitrogen content of the soil, which is what happens when rotting material is dug in. The moisture does not evaporate because the direct rays of the sun are prevented from acting on the bare soil, and frost is also kept away from the delicate root system by the insulation provided by the coating of dead leaves. In addition to these benefits, the leaf-mulch inhibits the growth of weeds and there is, therefore, no need to hoe the ground at all. The roots of most of the members of the valuable rhododendron and azalea families feed right on the soil surface, just below the mulch. Hoeing is therefore *fatal* to these plants. In digging-in material to improve the soil for flowering shrubs exception must be made in favour of inverted turves, kept to a minimum of a foot's depth for roses and hydrangeas, and for fresh fallen oak leaves or bracken to improve heavy clay soils for rhododendrons or azaleas. Briefly, the best system of digging the ground is that known as bastard-trenching (see page 51.) In this method the top spit of soil is turned over and the lower spit merely broken up with a pick or mattock. The subsoil, therefore, remains in its old position, at the bottom.

In preparing the ground for specimen shrubs, which, it will be found, are among the most important decorative elements in the garden, a circular bed 6 ft. in diameter should be dug. If the specimen is small when first planted some turf may be replaced, if thought absolutely necessary, to leave a smaller circle, but the initial work is essential to rapid and satisfactory growth. It cannot be done later.

Good cultivation is the secret of good results with flowering shrubs. It is a fallacy to think that they will grow properly without it. The attentions necessary to ensure good cultivation are, however, of a very simple nature. Provided that the ground has been properly loosened by bastard-trenching and, for roses and hydrangeas, enriched with inverted turves as described, it is merely necessary to keep the earth of the beds mulched. Lawn mowings are not very satisfactory as a mulch, except for roses or hydrangeas, and even then care must be taken not to mulch too thickly with them or the coating ferments in such a way that it heats up the ground and is likely to kill the young annual growth necessary to renew these shrubs from the base. Bracken is perfectly satisfactory and, if cut in June, feeds the ground very beneficially.

SPECIAL SOIL PROBLEMS

The most serious soil problem for the grower of flowering shrubs is the presence of lime. No effective treatment has yet been found, although experiments are continually being made. If the soil has a high lime-content the only thing to do is to concentrate on growing shrubs which will tolerate it.

A very poor sandy soil will require enrichment with moisture-holding organic matter, such as peat. When planting, several shovelfuls should be mixed in with the sand round the young plant. If the beds are kept well mulched with bracken or leaves, however, no difficulty will be found in growing any of the shrubs mentioned.

A very dense clay soil will require loosening up by digging in long bracken or vegetable refuse, best of all fresh fallen oak leaves, etc., and, where a bed is set in a hollow, a drain should be made to prevent standing water drowning the plants in winter. Roots have to have air, hence plants die if flooded for long.

Excessively stony soils often grow flowering shrubs very well, provided that if there is a " pan " of impervious soil below the surface, as is often the case, this is well broken up before planting.

WEEDS

Provided that a mulch of fallen leaves or bracken, about 6 ins. thick, is kept on the shrub beds and around the specimens no ordinary weeds of the annual type will appear. Perennial weeds should, of course, have been eradicated in the initial preparation of the soil. An occasional bramble or tree seedling will push up through the mulch, but these are very easily pulled up from the loose soil. It will be found that the mulch keeps the earth permanently loose and moist as earthworms pull the leaves down gently among the roots of the shrubs and none of the caking of the surface, which demands hoeing, takes place. To hold the leaf mulch in position in windy places a thin preliminary layer of long bracken and a few sticks with twigs or small branches laid on top, will be found effective. Extra supplies of dead leaves are usually obtainable from local authorities who will often be glad to dump leaves collected from the roads, especially if the gardener arranges a convenient place alongside a firm roadway.

PLANTING

The care taken in the initial planting of a flowering shrub often affects its entire life and makes all the difference between healthy and abundant growth or a standstill followed by dwindling and subsequent death. Dig a large shallow hole, rather than a small deep one, when planting. The roots *must* be spread out evenly in all directions without intercrossing and, preferably, at two different depths by filling in earth over the lower ones first, pressing this firmly down and then spreading out the upper layer of roots. These are then covered with earth, too, and the ground firmly pressed down with the foot until it is impossible to pull the plant up without breaking the roots. (See illustration facing page 328.) Most important factor of all is the depth in the soil at which the young plant is set. Failure to attend to this point is the cause of suckering from the briar stock by roses, because the plants have been set insufficiently deep in the soil. It is also the cause of the death of hundreds of azaleas annually, owing to these being set too deep in the soil. When planting, then, observe the soil mark which shows the depth at which the plant's roots were set previously, and take care that this mark is again just at soil level when the shrub is replanted. At the same time, judgment must be used. Plants are often roughly transplanted in nurseries so as to accustom them to re-establishing themselves easily. In the case of roses make sure that the union of the briar stock (or root system) and the true rose is 2 ins. below soil level. With azaleas and rhododendrons see that the top of the ball of fibrous roots is only 1 in. below soil level and do not place any soil over this. Put only a sprinkling of peat (ordinary peat moss litter thoroughly soaked beforehand will serve) on top of these roots, and then the mulch of leaves. It is not only necessary that these roots should breathe and feed just under the surface but, particularly in the case of azaleas, the growing point (or base where the branches spring from the roots) must be exposed to air. If this is buried in earth new shoots, which are necessary annually to maintain the plant's youth and vigour, will not grow. Thus the shrub dwindles away as the old wood becomes feebler and feebler. When azaleas are grafted or budded on the *ponticum* azalea stock suckers of this plant are likely to emerge unless the plant is set too deep in the ground for health. Consequently "layers" (or rooted branches, of the true azalea variety) are infinitely preferable. Nurserymen specialising in these species are usually able to supply such plants at slightly increased cost, and this is well worth while.

STAKING AND TYING TREES

In the case of flowering trees the same care should be used to insure that the roots are spread out straight in all directions, without curls or inter-crossings, and the earth over these should be carefully rammed down tight. A strong stake should be firmly inserted, too, when planting, and driven in tight, so that it comes parallel to the stem of the tree at a distance of two or three inches. *After* the tree is planted, and the ground firmed, a tie may be fixed to secure the stem against wind-rocking. The best tie is made from a 6-in. length of old rubber hosepipe and a 12-in. length of galvanised iron wire. Thread the wire through the pipe ; place the rubber-covered portion of the tie round the tree stem ; cross the ends over and then twist up the wire ends round the stake with three or four neat twists. The tree is then firm and safe from galling and the tie can easily be adjusted at any time by re-twisting the wire as required.

ROUTINE WORK, SPRING

PRUNING

In spring, when growth restarts, we can see what damage, if any, plants have sustained during the winter and any dead wood can be cut away. If desired, the old flowers, which will have been decorative during the winter and done much to protect the branches from frost, can be pruned off hydrangeas. Bush roses can have one or two of the older branches removed at the base although, if these are grown as flowering shrubs, that is to say as large permanent bushes, little need be done in this direction provided that young shoots are coming from the base. Members of the philadelphus (sometimes called syringa) family can be treated in much the same way, merely removing a few of the older branches. Where it is desired to keep the bush small the magnolias of the *Sieboldii* (*parviflora*) section can be similarly dealt with without harm. Brooms will be improved by shearing back the thinner twigs to aid compactness, but it is risky to cut into the old wood. (See illustration, page 329.) *Spartium junceum*, the Spanish broom,

The Culture of Flowering Shrubs and Trees

should have the rush-like upper twigs shorn back in the same way or it soon gets leggy and prematurely aged. No pruning is required for rhododendrons, azaleas, or camellias, and flowering cherries are better tied into position rather than cut, as gumming and brown rot are encouraged by the wounds. Heaths may be clipped over with the shears to make them more compact and the same treatment is good for helianthemums. Apart from these exceptions pruning is not necessary, as a routine, but young trees need looking over to ensure that a side branch is not challenging the mainleader. If it is found that this is so, the side branch should be cut off about one-third of the way from the stem directly above a branchlet pointing outwards.

In some cases the protective mulch will have been disturbed by winter gales. This should accordingly be renewed to prevent drying out of the soil and the growth of weeds.

CARE OF NEWLY-PLANTED SUBJECTS
Sometimes newly-planted specimens of the Prunus family will set a heavy crop of blossom, and this would take too much sap from the wood before the roots are sufficiently re-established to make good the drain. In such cases the only thing to do to save the tree is to pinch off the blossom buds. They are no loss as, in any case, they would only have shrivelled before they were fully open, but the damage would have been already done. Ties should also be looked to and stakes made firm, wind-rocking is fatal to good growth and must be avoided at all costs.

PESTS
Slug killer should be placed near hydrangeas as these pests destroy many a promising shoot as it pushes through the ground. A watchful eye should be kept for caterpillars on roses, cherries and azaleas. Dusting with a pocket-type dust-gun using fresh Derris powder is highly effective. (See PESTS, Part Eight, Chapter I, pages 647-650.)

" WINDOW DRESSING '
Faded flowers on camellias and early-flowering rhododendrons should be nipped off both for effect and to save the plant's sap for succeeding flowers.

ROUTINE WORK, EARLY SUMMER

" WINDOW DRESSING "

The full tide of blossom on the later azaleas, the brooms and the Japanese quinces, rhododendrons, etc., will be at its peak now and much " window dressing " and " dead-heading " will be needed to keep the display free from faded flowers.

WEEDS

Few weeds will be found to push up through the mulch of dead leaves or bracken. An occasional bramble seedling will do so, but is easily pulled out by grabbing it by the unarmed portion of the stem below the mulch. Bracken in woodland sections should be cut and carefully stored in a stack as, at this time of year, the fronds are rich in plant foods which will not have descended yet to the underground rhizomes where they are stored in winter.

LAWNS AND SUBSTITUTES

Lawns will require constant mowing and edging. In fact they require far more maintenance labour than all the flowering shrubs in the garden. Where such labour can ill be spared it may be well to study the alternatives. Moss, encouraged by sweeping and firming the ground is one of these, but it requires the shade of large trees, such as beeches, to come readily. White sand, in sandy districts, is another alternative. It requires occasional treatment with sodium chlorate weed killer and erodes untidily on slopes, but otherwise is fairly satisfactory for places where the labour for grass mowing cannot be spared. In times of crisis and difficulty new systems to meet the circumstances are worth trying out.

ROUTINE WORK, MID-SUMMER

The spring and early summer flowers will be over and the scheme devised for this period will be coming into bloom. If it is insufficiently effective its reinforcement at the expense of some period which is over-catered for may be considered. This is a good time to visit the great gardens open in aid of the District Nursing Association, taking notes of effective shrubs in bloom at this season. Nurseries should also be visited, this is a far more effective way of choosing new material than giving orders at a flower show where many subjects are forced forward or retarded so as to be in bloom at the required date.

LAWNS

These will still require continuous attention, but the flowering shrubs will need little maintenance work provided that the initial work has been effectively done.

WEEDS

Where the mulch system is objected to, and perhaps herbaceous subjects are mixed up with the shrubs in the beds, weeds will require much labour in hoeing and forking with consequent damage to the roots, and consequently the growth, of the flowering shrubs. Certain subjects, however, are ideally suited to a life among the shading branches and leafy floor of the shrub beds. Of these the lilies are pre-eminent, and in particular *L. regale* among azaleas and hydrangeas, and *L. auratum,* in its various forms, among the deeper shades of the rhododendron beds. The various varieties of *L. umbellatum,* valuable for their quality of blooming in the " June-gap," are also useful and " at home " along the verges of the groups. It is hardly possible to eradicate established perennial weeds by merely planting shrubs and applying a heavy mulch, but there is no doubt that, starting with clean land, invasion can be prevented.

ROUTINE WORK, LATE SUMMER

PROPAGATION (*see also* LAYERING, *page* 317).

This is the season when cuttings of most flowering shrubs can be taken. The principle, in propagating plants from cuttings, is to keep a shoot, cut from the parent plant, alive long enough for it to make roots for itself and so start an independent existence. The best material is obtained by slicing off side-shoots at the junction with the branch when these are " half-ripe " (or partly matured). These are then three-parts buried in the soil of a prepared frame. To prepare the frame a good plan is to fill it with about 9 ins. of sandy loam or, better still, a mixture of three-parts good turf loam, one part sharp silver sand and one part screened leaf mould. Before putting in the cuttings this soil is well watered and then a layer of about a quarter of an inch of sharp sand, in a dry state, is put on. A stick is used to make the slightly slanting hole required and the stem of each cutting is measured each time so as to bury about two-thirds of its length. As the stick is withdrawn from the hole made, a trickle of sand finds its way in, and this assists the cutting to form roots quickly. When the cuttings are in position they are watered overhead with a rose-can to prevent wilting of the foliage and a piece of burlap is used to cover the light and so temper the sun's rays.

An even simpler method which is usually very successful is to put in cuttings in similar fashion merely under a north wall in the open ground. Among the kinds often successfully propagated in this way are hydrangeas, roses of the hybrid polyantha and rambler types, cistus of most species, *Senecio laxifolius*, *Fuchsia magellanica* variety *Riccartonii*, ceanothus species, etc.

ROUTINE WORK, AUTUMN

In autumn the leaves which fall from the trees and shrubs should be swept off the lawns and paths and used to mulch the beds in the manner already described. If the soil is in good moist condition evergreen shrubs may be moved with safety in October. Where berried shrubs are a feature, black cotton may be strung about between the branches to keep off birds. If the leaf-fall from the garden itself is insufficient for mulching all the shrubs, further supplies can often be got from neighbours, and local authorities are frequently glad of the offer of a place to dump the leaves collected from the roads and pavements of the district. In this way a goodly store of leaf-mould can be built up which will ensure the healthy growth of the flowering shrubs.

ROUTINE WORK, WINTER

The worst time for planting is undoubtedly the dead of winter, that is to say during December and January. Rather than plant at that time many growers merely " heel " the plants in until the turn of the season in February. The plants are laid with their roots in trenches which are then filled in so that they are covered completely with moist soil and, if the species is one that is on the tender side, straw, leaves, etc., are also used as additional covering against frost on the branches. In severe weather tender shrubs may have extra protection against frost given them by placing bracken or spruce branches over them temporarily. But, as winter cold is less harmful than is generally supposed (it being late spring and early autumn frosts that do the worst damage), and as the coverings have to be removed the moment the frost is over, it is really best to rely upon a good mulch permanently protecting the roots. Much can also be done to mitigate the effects of the deadly late spring frost by attention to katabatics. This is the name given to the study of the laws governing the incidence of frost in accordance with air drainage. (See Fig. 20.) Briefly, the cold air is heavier than warmer air and so tends to drain away to a lower level unless trapped by some obstruction. The removal of such obstacles to free airflow in a downward direction away from the site is often attended with very marked improvement. Winter temperatures are not affected but the exasperating spring frosts come less frequently.

LAYERING

During mild spells the opportunity can be taken to increase many shrubs by layers. To do this choose a low, outward-growing branch that can easily be made to touch the ground. Make a small hole, about 6 ins. deep, with a trowel, and gently bend the part of the branch that is about a foot from the tip so that it enters and leaves the hole in a U-shape. Then fill up the hole again firmly, leaving the tip of the branch and about 6 ins. of stem emerging from the soil looking rather like a young plant. The great thing is to choose young shoots and to make the stem bend sharply in the hole so as to check the flow of sap and encourage rooting. After a growing season the branch will probably have rooted and can then be cut off where it enters the ground. The young plant formed by the rooted tip can be moved wherever wanted. Choose something easy, first, like a forsythia, rhododendron or hydrangea. For rhododendrons it is usually enough to weigh a branch down with a large stone, about four times the size of a brick, and tie up the outer end of the branch with a stick.

TYPES of CLIMBERS·

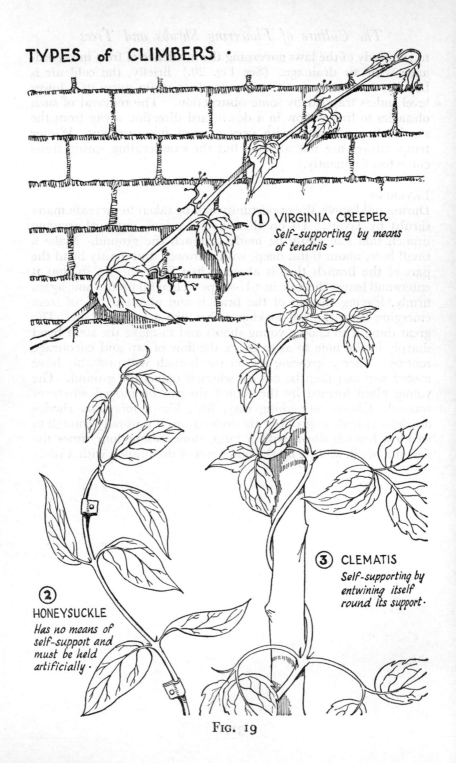

① VIRGINIA CREEPER
*Self-supporting by means
of tendrils·*

② HONEYSUCKLE
*Has no means of
self-support and
must be held
artificially·*

③ CLEMATIS
*Self-supporting by
entwining itself
round its support·*

FIG. 19

CHAPTER II

A List of Worthwhile Flowering Shrubs

THESE lists have been carefully compiled so as to include only flowering shrubs and trees of *real garden effectiveness* which can be grown in small gardens by amateurs without difficulty and have proved reasonably hardy by surviving recent very hard winters. Many of the finest hardy flowering shrubs have remained unknown to the majority of gardeners who have thus had to be content with old material long outclassed. It is hoped that these lists will stimulate them to try some of the new kinds described which they have not grown before.

BERBERIS Order **BERBERIDACEÆ**

Mostly spiny bushes having small yellow flowers and ornamental fruits. Both evergreen and deciduous species cultivated. Useful owing to their tolerance of limy soils unable to grow more decorative flowering shrubs. The wood and inner bark are usually yellow in colour. The name is derived from the Arabic name of the fruit. Some species are alternate hosts of wheat rust.

B. Darwinii. Evergreen upright shrub up to 10 ft. high. Leaves shining, and relatively large and bright yellow flowers in spring, fruits dark purple. This species grows easily anywhere but the colour is somewhat harsh and the flowers do not provide a very solid mass of colour. Habitat, Chile.

B. stenophylla. Evergreen shrub up to 9 ft. in height. Flowers golden yellow in spring. Fruits are black, bloomy. A useful shrub for poor limy soils but surpassed by the hybrid following.

B. stenophylla var. *corallina nana.* Evergreen of compact rounded form with decorative apricot flowers opening in spring from scarlet buds. About 4 ft. Not hardy, badly damaged in severe winters.

B. Thunbergii. This is the most effective of its family, over a short period—not for the flowers, which are not conspicuous, nor for the fruits which are seldom numerous, but for the reliably brilliant red of its leaves in autumn. It is particularly good in the bays of beds of evergreens. It is a shrub of about 4 ft. or more, of compact and bushy habit and strikes easily from cuttings. The variety *purpurea* is a form with purplish-red leaves.

B. vulgaris. A native shrub up to 10 ft. in height, with attractive hanging racemes of yellow flowers in spring followed by red fruits in autumn. In the opinion of many it is more decorative than many of the exotic species. The variety *purpurea* has deep purple leaves.

B. Wilsonæ. A low spiny shrub with attractive translucent red berries in autumn. These do not last very long and the shrub is intensely prickly. 2-3 ft.

B. polyantha. A deciduous shrub from western China, distinct in its large panicles of deep yellow flowers in spring. Height up to 10 ft. Also decorative in autumn with red fruits and valuable for flowering in July when shrub bloom is less common than in spring.

OTHER SPECIES AND VARIETIES : About forty in cultivation, mostly grown for autumn effects. Easily grown from seeds which are freely produced. Being well armed, berberis make effective ornamental hedges but should not be pruned more than the minimum necessary, as flowers and succeeding fruits are sacrificed when the young growth is cut away.

CULTIVATION : No special requirements but an open position preferred.

BIGNONIA Order BIGNONIACEÆ

One species cultivated.

B. capreolata. A climbing evergreen with handsome trumpet flowers of red-orange colour in June, from the Southern States of America. This species is reasonably hardy and should be more freely planted. Not often damaged on walls by winter cold. Unfortunately the form in commerce in England is one with unusually dull flowers. It is self-clinging and the evergreen leaves, of long, pointed shape are decorative. Up to 30 ft.

CULTIVATION : Requires a south wall and a moist soil enriched with leaf-mould. Plant in spring.

BUDDLEIA Order LOGANIACEÆ

The Buddleias tolerate a limy soil.

B. alternifolia. A vigorous willow-like species up to 16 ft. with dense clusters of small lilac-purple flowers. Quite attractive for a dry bank. Flowers July–September.

VII. *Rhododendron Loderi*, Pink Diamond

VIII. Rose, Betty Prior

CULTIVATION : A dry sunny position suits this species which is best grown as a specimen as it is apt to grow rank and sprawling when too near other shrubs. (See illustration facing page 329.)

B. Davidii. A greyish-leaved somewhat ungainly shrub with lilac spikes of small fragrant flowers, valued for its late-blooming quality. This buddleia will grow almost anywhere and is easily propagated from seed or cuttings. Owing to its success as a coloniser of blitzed sites it has become common and almost naturalised in some localities. A native of China, it grows up to 15 ft. in height, and is particularly attractive to butterflies. Unfortunately its decorative qualities are not of a high order as the flower spike usually carries a number of browned old flowers as well as those freshly opened. The variety *magnifica* is the best form, it has finer flower spikes. Flowers July–October.

CULTIVATION : Any ordinary garden soil will serve but an open, well-drained position is best.

B. globosa. This is a semi-evergreen species from Chile with globular orange-yellow flower heads in May. Unfortunately these are of small size in proportion to that of the large, ungainly shrub which grows up to 15 ft. It is hardy and easily propagated.

CULTIVATION : A warm and sunny position is required. No special soil treatment necessary.

CALLUNA (Heather) Order ERICACEÆ

This is the common heather, as distinct from heath, and only the one species is known.

C. vulgaris. The wild heather has given rise to a number of garden forms characterised by brighter or larger flowers. As garden plants these heathers are, however, somewhat dull in tone compared with the heaths. (See ERICA.)

VARIETIES :   *C. v. alba.* Flowers white.

C. v. atro-rubens. With greyish, downy leaves and crimson flowers.

C. v. aurea. With gold-yellow leaves.

C. v. cuprea. With yellow leaves in summer and bronzy-red leaves in winter.

C. v. decumbens. A prostrate form with pink flowers.

C. v. Foxii. Forming dense, dwarf tufts.

C. v. Hammondii. Tall with bright-green leaves and large white flowers.

VARIETIES :   H. E. Beale. Pale pink.

C. v. nana. Dwarf, purple flowers.

C. v. plena. With double pink flowers.

C. v. purpurea. With dark purple flowers.

C. v. Searlei. Tall, branching, with late, white flowers.

C. v. serotina. With downy leaves, flowers white, late September to November.

C. v. variegata. With leaves variegated with white. The majority of these heathers flower from August onwards. Their chief value is for covering rough banks on sandy and peaty soils where they make an attractive trouble-free ground covering.

CULTIVATION : Unlike most shrubs, heathers require a poor soil or they soon become tall and gangling. They are best clipped fairly closely after the flowers are over. They are not suitable for mixing with other species except as ground cover under flowering trees which are benefited by the root protection that they afford. They will not grow well where there is much shade.

CAMELLIA Order THEACEÆ

These are mostly shade-loving evergreen shrubs with large and beautiful flowers of the highest value for gardens. For a long time the varieties of *C. japonica* were thought not to be hardy and were cultivated in greenhouses. Actually they are perfectly hardy in the British Isles although their early opening flowers (April) are, of course, often damaged by spring frosts.

C. japonica. The wild form has red single flowers which are greatly surpassed by the many garden varieties. In nature it grows in the Japanese forests under taller trees.

VARIETIES :   Adolphe Audusson. A fine single red of strong, semi-upright growth.

C. j. alba plena. A white with very symmetrical formal, rosette-shaped, double flowers, dense habit.

C. j. Chandleri elegans. A large-flowered semi-double rose flower with white flecks and a good habit of growth.

C. j. Donckelaarii. A cherry-red semi-double with white marblings and prominent golden stamens in a compact central boss.

Lady Clare. A beautiful single of rich pink colour

A List of Worthwhile Flowering Shrubs

VARIETIES : and large size, superb for floating in bowls for house decoration; the shrub is, however, of somewhat sprawling habit.

C. j. latifolia. A strong, shapely bush with semi-double crimson flowers.

C. j. magnoliæflora. A lovely, semi-double, magnolia-like flower of pearly white, compact habit of growth. There are a very large number of florists' varieties produced during the last century when the camellia was a popular greenhouse plant. To modern tastes many of these are too formal in shape. They are ideal subjects for a cold greenhouse as under these conditions the flowers can be enjoyed from January onwards.

C. reticulata. The form of this lovely camellia which is most commonly seen is a Chinese garden form with very large carmine flowers. One of the most beautiful of all flowering shrubs it requires the protection of a greenhouse except in particularly favoured gardens in the south-west.

C. saluenensis. This camellia has flowers somewhat resembling a wild pink dog rose. Only comparatively recently introduced to cultivation, it is still somewhat rare. It has, however, already produced hybrids with other species which will undoubtedly be among the choicest garden shrubs of the future. One, *C. J. C. Williams*, is already to be seen in a few gardens with laden sprays of exquisite wild-rose-like blossoms in early spring.

OTHER SPECIES : *C. cuspidata, C. maliflora, C. Sasanqua, C. Thea.* The last is, of course, the plant which produces tea.

CULTIVATION : The camellia likes a calm, shady position with moist soil generously enriched with leaf-mould. The plant will grow well in dark courtyards or under quite dense trees provided that the soil is kept rich and moist. To lessen the effects of spring frosts camellias are best placed where the early morning sun does not strike in. The north wall of a house is an ideal position and there is nothing nicer than a pair of good camellias flanking a front door. When well grown, camellias will eventually reach a height of 10 ft. or even more. They are not fast growers and so easily kept in bounds, although pruning is to be deprecated unless necessary for this purpose. They can be moved when quite large, provided that care is taken to secure the root

CULTIVATION : system intact in a ball of soil. The ground under camellias should be kept mulched with fallen leaves, and faded flowers should be removed so as to conserve the sap for the succeeding buds which will open over quite a long period. Single camellias can be struck from cuttings inserted in July.

CAMPSIS (Trumpet Vine) Order BIGNONIACEÆ

C. grandiflora. A superb climber with divided leaves and large scarlet flowers produced in late summer. A Chinese plant, it requires a south wall and is not hardy enough for the northern counties. In a cold, wet summer it does not open its flowers freely, but in a hot one it is a gorgeous sight.

CULTIVATION : A warm sunny position is essential and good loamy soil. If pruning is necessary to keep it in bounds this should only be done in spring.

C. radicans. An American plant hardier than the preceding but with much smaller, duller flowers.

C. Tagliabuana. A hybrid between the two preceding species sufficiently hardy to be preferable to the latter on account of its much larger and brighter flowers.

CARYOPTERIS Order VERBENACEÆ

C. clandoniensis. The wild species are somewhat tender but this hybrid is reasonably hardy. It is a deciduous shrub of bushy habit up to 2 or 3 ft., with greyish-green leaves and soft blue flowers in late summer.

CULTIVATION : A warm and sheltered position, will tolerate limy soil. Can be grown from cuttings.

CEANOTHUS Order RHAMNACEÆ

American shrubs mostly from the Pacific coast. Not hardy, but valued for their blue flowers. The species are seldom seen, but a number of hybrids are commonly grown. They will grow on a limy soil.

C. Veitchianus. This hybrid is one of the best of the May-flowering group. It is often planted against walls but is more decorative in a sunny spot in the open. It is not long-lived and is liable to be damaged in severe winters. The small blue flowers are clustered so thickly on the branches that it is quite an effective shrub. 8 ft.

CULTIVATION : Ordinary garden soil and a sunny position. Strikes easily from cuttings. Liable to be killed by wind-rocking so stake firmly or layer outer branches with stones. Will grow on limy soils.

C. Gloire de Versailles. This is one of the best hybrids of the late-summer flowering group. The flowers are an attractive greyish-blue and freely produced until frosts come, but it is not really hardy even against a wall. 5 ft.

CULTIVATION : Similar to the preceding species.

CERATOSTIGMA Order PLUMBAGINACEÆ

C. Willmottianum. The rich royal-blue flowers in late summer make this a useful shrub, but its habit is thin and it is liable to be cut to the ground in winter. 2-3 ft.

CULTIVATION : A warm sunny position is required. The cerato-stigma is easily struck from cuttings or grown from seed. It will grow on limy soils.

CHÆNOMELES ("Japonica") Order ROSACEÆ

Under this awkward name are now grouped two most valuable and long-cultivated flowering shrubs that are to be commended for gardens both large and small. They were at first thought to be quinces, but later research has shown that they are a family to themselves. They will grow on limy soils.

C. speciosa. This is the well-known, red-flowered Japanese quince often called merely the japonica. It was long known as Pyrus japonica, then as Cydonia japonica and now, it is to be hoped, its name will remain firmly fixed as the above. Often grown against a wall, which is quite unnecessary in the south of England as there it makes a fine lawn specimen. Every one knows its handsome red flowers in early spring wreathing the branches before the leaves appear. Against a wall the plant will run up to 12 ft. or more, but if grown in the open is seldom more than 8 ft. with a spread of nearly as much.

VARIETIES :   C. s. Aurora. Flowers rose and yellow.
C. s. cardinalis. Salmon crimson.
Knap Hill Scarlet. Brilliant scarlet flowers.
C. s. Mœrlœsii. White flowers faintly blushed.
Phyllis Moore. Large, double, scarlet flowers but poor habit.
C. s. sinica. Flowers double, deep red.
C. s. sulphurea. Flowers yellowish.

CULTIVATION : No special soil required. Suckers may be trouble-some and these may be dug out with a piece of root attached to form a new plant or cut-off. Any pruning required should be done after flowering. The shrub flowers on the old wood so new shoots may be shortened back to within a couple of inches of the old branches with advantage. It may be propagated from seeds or layers.

C. japonica. This is the shrub which used to be called *Pyrus* or *Cydonia Maulei*. It is like a dwarf bush of the preceding, but is, if anything, an even more valuable plant. Seldom more than 2 ft. high, the scarlet, orange, or blood-red flowers are borne from April to June and followed by scented fruits which make quite good jam. It is quite hardy and is one of the finest, but most neglected, of flowering shrubs. A bed in an open position with a foreground planting of this shrub and evergreens at the back makes a fine feature of any garden.

VARIETIES : *C. j. alba.* White.
C. j. atro-sanguinea. Deep red.
C. j. rosea. Rose.
C. j. Simonii. A lovely hybrid with abundant dark-red flowers.
C. j. superba. Large blood-red flowers, taller growth.

CULTIVATION : A warm and sunny spot is required for free flowering and the soil should not be too rich or too much leafage is made. Propagated from seed or pieces with a little root attached such as can often be secured from the base of the plants. Both the chænomeles will grow on limy soil.

CHIMONANTHUS (Winter Sweet) Order CALYCANTHACEÆ

C. præcox. A winter-flowering shrub often grown against warm walls for its extraordinarily fragrant flowers. These are not showy, being small and yellow and purplish brown, and the shrub takes some years to reach flowering size, generally 6-9 ft. high.

CULTIVATION : Sunny position and poorish soil. Easily grown from seed, but it takes some years to flower.

CHOISYA (Mexican Orange) Order RUTACEÆ

C. ternata. This most useful evergreen comes from Mexico but is reasonably hardy. It has divided leaves and fragrant white flowers in spring and often again in late summer. Although it will grow in the shade of trees it flowers better and grows more compactly in full sun. The usual height is about 4-5 ft.

CULTIVATION : Sunny position, ordinary garden soil. Cuttings strike well in the sand frame.

CISTUS (Rock Rose) Order CISTACEÆ

Often known as rock roses, cistus are tender but fast-growing shrubs suitable for warm slopes with poor soil. They are seldom long-lived, and mostly evergreen but hard winters destroy much of the foliage. They come from the Mediterranean region.

C. albidus. Up to 4 ft. high, rosy-lilac flowers with a yellow blotch at the base. The leaves are covered with a whitish felt. Flowers May–June.

C. corbariensis. A good hybrid cistus with white flowers with a yellow stain at the base. The shrub is bushy and compact and usually about 4 ft. high. Flowers May–June. Less free-flowering than some others.

C. crispus. This cistus is usually only about 1 ft. high with deep pink flowers and sage-green leaves with crisped edges. Like the other members of this family it flowers in June and continues over quite a long period.

C. ladaniferus (the Gum Cistus). A sticky plant to handle and apt to become leggy, but the flowers are beautiful being large and white with a red blotch at the base of the petals. Up to 6 ft. Flowers May–June.

C. laurifolius. A good grower and perhaps the commonest, it will reach 6 or 8 ft. high with white flowers in bunches. It often produces self-sown seedlings. Flowers May–June.

C. lusitanicus decumbens. A hybrid with white flowers with a crimson blotch at the base of the petals. Good for a poor soil on a warm bank. Flowers May–June.

C. purpureus. One of the finest hybrids, it has large rosy-red flowers with a rich brown blotch. Usually about 4 ft. high but of rather sprawling habit.

Silver Pink. A delightful hybrid cistus, perhaps the best of all. The shrub is compact and shapely with large shrimp-pink flowers produced from June onwards. Unfortunately it is no hardier than the others so cannot be counted on as a permanency.

CULTIVATION : All the cistus require much the same treatment, this is a poor soil in a sunny position with sharp

CULTIVATION : drainage, such as a bank affords. They are easily propagated from seed or cuttings and are most useful to furnish new gardens in exposed, sunny places quickly. By the time the cistus are killed by hard winters the more permanent plants will have established themselves. They do not object to a limy soil.

CLEMATIS Order RANUNCULACEÆ

Clematis are climbing plants supporting themselves by twining their leaf stalks (see Fig. 19) round taller plants or other supports. They are seldom long-lived and do best in a limy soil. Often grown on trellis on walls they really do better if allowed to twine into other growth. An ideal host for this purpose is *Euonymus radicans* as it is a good wall climber and its beautiful leaves set off the clematis flowers nicely. Much of the endless bother of training in and tying the clematis is then avoided. Another good method is to grow the plant in the open border and give it a few pea-sticks to ramble over. There are a considerable number of species, but the garden hybrids and the varieties of the spring flowering *Clematis montana* give the better return.

Comtesse du Bouchard. Another fine hybrid with carmine rose flowers from July to October.

C. *Jackmanii*. This late summer-flowering hybrid with its masses of blue-violet flowers is one of the most showy of all climbers and therefore repays the trouble of training and pruning it. There is also a reddish-crimson flowered variety—C. *Jackmanii rubra*—which is also very effective.

VARIETIES :   C.*J*. Lasurstern. Deep blue. July–October.
            C.*J*. Perle d'Azur. Pale blue, smaller, freely borne. July–October.
            C.*J*. Ville de Lyon. Crimson. July–October.

CULTIVATION : The above hybrid clematis like to grow in full sun but with their lower stem and roots in the shade, and they do much better in a limy soil. In early spring the old growth may be cut away to within a foot of the ground. If a support, such as a twiggy bush, is available the plant may be allowed to make its own way up this, but it is usually necessary to spend quite a lot of time spreading out and tying in the growths in a fan shape, otherwise the clematis tangles itself up and gets nowhere. This is the chief drawback to an otherwise fine plant.

52. *Planting an evergreen shrub*

53. *Nailing up a shrub*

54. *Protecting wall shrubs*

55. *Pruning clematis*

56. *Pruning broom*

57. *A pruned buddleia*

CULTIVATION : Another is that the old leaves do not turn a nice colour and then fall off, as with so many shrubs, but remain in unsightly blackened masses all through the winter. If grown up another shrub these are less evident so this is a further reason for adopting the advice given in the preamble.

C. Armandii. This is an evergreen clematis with fine white flowers in spring. It comes from China and is not altogether hardy.

C. montana. This is the popular spring-flowering clematis with white or pale pink flowers in great masses which often cover a whole house. It loses its leaves in winter and then looks somewhat untidy, but the spring effect is superb.

VARIETIES :   *C. m. grandiflora.* Larger flowers.
  C. m. lilacina. Flowers lilac.
  C. m. rubens. Leaves purplish, flowers rosy red.

CULTIVATION : As with all climbers planted against walls be sure to plan at least a foot away from the wall as the actual wall-foot is too dry to give a plant a fair chance. Tie in carefully at first and spread out the branches fanwise. Once a good start is made the plant can look after itself. Pruning is only necessary to keep it in bounds and is best done in spring before growth starts.

CORNUS (Cornel) Order CORNACEÆ

There are a large number of species of cornus, but only a few of these are worth growing, although *C. Kousa* is one of the most spectacularly beautiful of all white-flowered shrubs.

C. florida. The flowering dogwood of America is one of the most beautiful wild shrubs of that country when it is covered with its large white flowers in May. It forms a large bush up to 15 ft. high and the leaves turn to attractive shades of red and orange in autumn. In this climate, however, it does not make much of a display, although it grows freely enough. The variety *rubra* has pink flowers instead of white.

C. Kousa. This is one of the finest of all flowering shrubs and quite hardy. It comes from Japan and China but grows well and flowers extraordinarily abundantly, once it has reached flowering size, which is about 7 ft. Like the one preceding, the true flower is a small button in the centre, but it is surrounded by large white, petal-like bracts which form a beautiful pearly flower. These are produced so freely on the branches, right down to the ground, that one can hardly put a pin between them. *C. Kousa* flowers in June when shrub bloom is scarcer than at other times, so is particularly valuable. In autumn the leaves turn to fine shades of red and the round red fruits, about the size of a walnut, are also decorative. Usually about 15 ft. it may, eventually, reach a height of over 20 ft.

VARIETIES :   As this plant is often raised from seed some poor forms, either with ragged bracts which make the flower unattractive or types of a shy-flowering nature, are sometimes produced. So be sure to get a good form. Variety *sinensis*, a Chinese form, usually has larger flowers but, as those of the Japanese form are quite large enough, this is of little advantage, especially as there are more forms with badly shaped flowers than of the Japanese type. But it has the advantage of growing on limy soil which the other does not.

CULTIVATION : This cornel is best grown as a lawn specimen in an open, sunny position ; if crowded in with other shrubs it does not flower so well and the natural, graceful shape of the shrub is apt to be distorted. The dwarf rhododendron, *R. indicum*, also known as *Azalea macrantha*, makes a fine foil for it having its red flowers open at the same time. A good loam and a sunny position are desirable. It can be grown from seed or layers.

COTONEASTER Order ROSACEÆ

Cotoneasters are a large family with dull flowers but notably fine red berries. They are mostly hardy and will grow anywhere. Care should be taken not to plant too many where their dullness in summer will spoil the effect of the garden at that time. A few of the best, only, therefore, are mentioned here.

C. conspicua. One of the newer species with more attractive flowers in June and more freely produced berries, in autumn an excellent evergreen for covering a bank. 2-3 ft.

C. Dammeri. This cotoneaster is a carpeting species that covers itself with bright red berries in autumn and does not ramp unduly. The only species suitable for the rock garden.

C. frigida. This is the largest of the family, making a small tree of about 20 ft. The hybrid known as *Watererii* is a better investment with brighter and more freely-borne berries, in autumn.

C. Henryana. One of the best of the larger species. It is an evergreen bush up to 10 ft. in height with arching branches laden in autumn with red berries.

C. horizontalis. The Fishbone cotoneaster is one of the commonest and has a mass of red berries which last from September until the birds take them. The flat, fishbone-like branches are easily trained against a wall but it grows perfectly in the open. Self-sown seedlings come up everywhere.

CULTIVATION : No special requirements. Easily grown from seed. When it is desired to cover a north wall the larger cotoneasters might be used with advantage. They grow well in limy soils.

CYDONIA (*see* CHÆNOMELES)

CYTISUS (Broom) Order LEGUMINOSÆ

This is the family of the common broom, useful yellow-flowered shrubs of quick growth suitable for poor soils and exposed positions. About 6 ft.

C. scoparius (Common Broom). Has many garden varieties. Some, with two colours which cancel one another out at a slight distance, are to be avoided. Flowers May.

VARIETIES : Cornish Cream. Creamy white.
C. s. sulphureus. Moonlight Broom, low habit, sulphur-yellow flowers.
Donard Seedling. Red and gold.
Firefly. Scarlet and yellow.
C. s. fulgens. Crimson, not good at a distance.

C. Battandieri. A tall, lanky broom lately introduced from Morocco, with silvery foliage and yellow spikes in June. Will grow in limy soils.

C. Beanii. Dwarf, yellow flowers, not long-lived. May.

C. emeriflorus (glabrescens). An attractive compact little broom about 2 ft. high, flowering very freely in May. It comes from the Alps and is quite hardy.

C. kewensis. Dwarf, creamy-white flowers. April.

C. multiflorus (White Portugal Broom). An attractive white-flowered broom for spring effect.

C. nigricans. This broom flowers in July with erect, slender, branches studded with the usual yellow pea flowers of the family. The flowered wood is best pruned away to prevent seed formation.

C. præcox. Pale yellow flowers, unpleasant smell, but very beautiful. April–May.

CULTIVATION : The brooms need a poor soil, an open situation and stern clipping of the young growths when young to induce a firm, bushy habit. They do not do well on very limy soils but *C. Battandieri* is an exception. Most kinds are particularly at home on dry, sunny banks.

DAPHNE Order THYMELACEÆ

The daphne family is a large one and they are mostly rather difficult and uncertain plants in the garden, but their lovely scent makes them well worth while.

D. Cneorum. This daphne grows only about a foot high with sweet-scented pink flowers in May. The leaves are evergreen. Not long-lived.

D. Mezereum. A common species well known in cottage gardens. The fragrant lilac-purple flowers appear with the first hope of spring and, later, red berries make the plant attractive. Easily grown from seed. 3-4 ft.

D. japonica. An evergreen from Japan, needing a sheltered, warm spot. It has rosy-purple flowers of delicious scent throughout the winter if the weather is mild. So attractive that it is worth risking in any southern garden. 2-3 ft.

CULTIVATION : Daphnes are always liable to die off when least expected, so they cannot be counted on as permanencies. Ordinary good garden soil and an open but sheltered position. They will grow on limy soils.

DEUTZIA Order SAXIFRAGACEÆ

The deutzias are mostly white or pale pink flowered deciduous shrubs useful for blossoming fairly late in the season. The garden hybrids are more effective, on the whole, than the pure species.

D. magnifica. Dense panicles of pure white flowers in June, shrub about 6 ft. high.

D. elegantissima. Rose-pink flowers in June.

D. longifolia, var. *Veitchii.* Deep lilac-pink flowers during last half of June. Not a colour that makes much effect, but useful for flowering during a difficult period of the summer.

D. Monbeigii. An attractive species with arching sprays laden with small white flowers in June.

D. rosea, var. *carminea.* Scented flowers of rose purple in June.

D. scabra. A Japanese species that is very hardy with fringed bell-like white or pale pink flowers in June and July. Shrub about 6 ft.

CULTIVATION : Ordinary garden soil, sunny position. They will grow on limy soils.

DIERVILLA (*see* **WEIGELA**)

ECCREMOCARPUS (Chilean Glory Flower) Order **BIGNONIACEÆ**

E. scaber. An attractive half-hardy climber, requiring a sheltered position against a south or south-west wall. The scarlet and yellow flowers are produced in summer, and the plant may grow to a height of 15-20 ft.

CULTIVATION : Plant June in light rich soil. Protect in winter by covering roots with ashes.

ERICA (Heath) Order **ERICACEÆ**

This is the heath family which gives us many invaluable garden shrublets *for a lime-free soil.* Often known as Bell-heathers, they are really called heaths. In sandy and peaty gardens they may be used to carpet the ground instead of grass.

E. carnea. This is the winter-flowering heath of the Alps. It forms low evergreen mats, bright with colour, in the different varieties, from December to April, and is remarkably hardy ; will grow on limy soils. White, pink or purple, 6 ins.

VARIETIES : James Backhouse. Large pale pink flowers, late.
King George. Early, rose crimson.
E. c. Vivellix. Very dwarf, purplish crimson.

E. ciliaris (Dorset Heath). Is of trailing habit, about 9 ins. high with purplish-pink flowers in late summer. It needs a slightly better and moister soil than the preceding.

VARIETIES : *E. c. alba.* White.
E. c. Maweana. Larger flowers of rich crimson.

E. cinerea. This is the brightest flowered of the family, but will not grow where there is any lime in the soil at all. It forms an evergreen carpet about 9 ins. high, from which the spikes, set with deep pink bells, arise in August. Poor soil is essential for compact growth.

VARIETIES : The garden varieties are richer in colour than the wild one.
Apple Blossom. Delicate blush pink.
E. c. atro-purpurea. Purple crimson.
E. c. coccinea. Very dwarf, intense blood crimson.
Frances. Cerise.

E. vagans (Cornish Heath). This is a taller grower, up to 3 ft., with rich pink flowers in late summer. A good plant for poor, sandy banks, it sprawls in too rich a soil.

VARIETIES : Lyonesse. A fine white.
Mrs. D. F. Maxwell. Deep cerise flowers, superb
St. Keverne. Rose-pink flowers.

CULTIVATION : Poor, peaty soil, open position. Can be increased by burying the plants with only the tips showing, in sandy peat, and dividing next season.

ESCALLONIA Order SAXIFRAGACEÆ

The Escallonias are mostly small-leaved evergreens of wispy habit with small flowers in late summer. They are not hardy, coming from South America. Quite successful in mild coastal districts. They vary in height from 6-12 ft.

VARIETIES : C. F. Ball. Tall, crimson flowers.
Donard Brilliance. Rich red flowers, one of the most attractive.
Donard Seedling. Blush-white flowers.
E. Iveyi. A fairly dense evergreen with abundant white flowers.
E. Langleyensis. One of the hardiest, 6 ft. high, rose-pink flowers in June, good.
E. macrantha. An evergreen with fairly dense growth much planted around our coasts. Flowers small, rose pink, from June to August.

CULTIVATION : Escallonias do best in warm positions, no special soil needed. They will even grow on chalk. Can be increased by small cuttings in a frame.

FATSIA Order ARALIACEÆ

F. japonica. A handsome evergreen with huge fig-like leaves and white flower-heads in October. Often known as the Parlour Fig and grown as a pot plant, this makes a good evergreen for the southern counties with a most imposing and tropical appearance. Up to 9 ft.

CULTIVATION : Sunny position, loamy soil.

FORSYTHIA Order OLEACEÆ

Shrubs with bright yellow flowers in early spring very commonly planted, 5-8 ft. high. Showy enough at that time, they are somewhat dull furnishing at all other times.

F. intermedia, var. *spectabilis.* This is the finest forsythia, with rich yellow flowers in profusion in early spring. It is a hybrid.

F. suspensa. This shrub has a pendulous habit, and the branches root freely when they touch the ground.

CULTIVATION : Forsythias look best in groups where they will not be too prominently before the eyes in summer, but can be appreciated when in flower in early spring when little else is in bloom. Ordinary garden soil. They strike very easily from open-ground cuttings. Will grow on limy soils.

FUCHSIA Order ONAGRACEÆ

F. magellanica, var. *Riccartonii.* This, and the new Lynewood variety of it, are the hardiest fuchsias for outdoor planting and most decorative late summer-flowering shrubs. Cut down by frost in winter, or by pruning in spring, it makes long arching growths from which hang the curious flowers with their red calyx and violet petals. The best effect is obtained when a bed is stuck full of cuttings which are allowed to flower where they stand. This fuchsia is quite reasonably hardy in the southern counties. Flowers June–October. About 4 ft.

F. gracilis. A slenderer shrub in all its parts and not nearly so effective as the foregoing. Flowers June–September. About 3 ft.

CULTIVATION : A good loamy soil and a sunny position preferred. Strikes easily from cuttings. Will grow on limy soils.

GENISTA Order LEGUMINOSÆ

This is an important family of garden shrubs, giving us several valuable late-flowering kinds. They all have yellow, pea-shaped flowers and rather small leaves. The taller kinds mentioned make particularly lovely lawn specimens.

G. ætnensis. This is a very attractive broom with slender green branchlets almost devoid of leaves and covered in late summer with little yellow pea-flowers, up to about 10 ft. It is somewhat untidy if left alone and the best way to grow it is to prune it from early youth to a single stem and make it form a weeping standard. Grown in this way it makes one of the most beautiful specimens it is possible to have.

CULTIVATION : This broom can be easily grown from seed, but like all members of this family it often dies if moved except when very small. Sow one or two seeds only, in small pots, and be sure to plant it out before the seedling gets pot-bound.

G. cinerea. This lovely species grows up to about 8 ft. high with long slender branches. The leaves are small and grey-green covered with silky hairs when young. The countless yellow flowers appear in clusters in July ; they are delightfully fragrant. It does not set seed.

CULTIVATION : A sunny spot with a well-drained soil suits this beautiful broom.

G. hispanica (Spanish Gorse). A dense low-growing, spiny shrub, making a fine display of tightly-packed bright yellow flowers in May. 1-2 ft.

CULTIVATION : Poor soil and a sunny position are necessary or it grows rank and tender. Propagated by seed or cuttings. Grows well on chalk.

G. lydia. A lovely dwarf species from S.E. Europe making a dense bushlet profusely covered with bright yellow flowers in June. 1 ft.

CULTIVATION : A well-drained raised position in full sun is best. No soil preference.

G. virgata (Madeira Broom). Very like *G. cinerea*, it flowers a little earlier, is leafier in habit and produces plenty of seeds which are easily grown. If anything the scent is even more delightful than that of *G. cinerea*. This species will grow well in a more shady situation and is one of the great beauties of midsummer. It appears to be quite hardy. Flowers June–July.

CULTIVATION : An open sunny situation is perhaps the best of all and a light soil is desirable although the foregoing genistas do not object to lime, as the varieties of the common broom do.

A List of Worthwhile Flowering Shrubs

HELIANTHEMUM (Sun Rose) Order CISTACEÆ

This is a valuable family of tiny shrubs with brightly-coloured flowers admirable for the small garden. They are particularly suitable for the foreground of raised beds or rockwork. Their chief drawback is that one cannot mulch them, so that they have to be weeded frequently.

H. vulgare. The native wild yellow sun-rose. This is only of interest as one of the parents of the excellent garden varieties. 6-12 ins.

VARIETIES : These are innumerable and range in colour through yellow, pink, crimson, scarlet and orange. Particularly good are those of the Scottish named group such as Ben Affleck, Ben More, etc. Although the sun-roses like lime they will, like other lime-lovers, do just as well without it. A delightful scheme with dwarf evergreen shrubs is thus possible by interplanting groups of helianthemums of the single-flowered varieties with groups of alpine dwarf rhododendrons or Japanese azaleas. The sun-roses flower in June and July.

CULTIVATION : Helianthemums need sharp drainage, full sun and clipping with the shears after flowering to keep them bushy. They are easily grown from cuttings.

HIBISCUS Order MALVACEÆ

H. syriacus (Tree Hollyhock). A deciduous, slow-growing Chinese shrub with three-lobed leaves and convolvulus-like flowers in August and September. Perfectly hardy, but it needs warmth to flower well. The hibiscus grows up to about 8 ft., but can be kept smaller by pruning.

VARIETIES : *H. s. cœlestis.* Blue-lilac flowers.
Hamabo. Pale blush with a crimson blotch, one of the most beautiful.
H. s. Leopoldii plenus. Double pink, good.
H. s. totus albus. White.
Woodbridge. Crimson.

CULTIVATION : A well-drained soil and a sunny warm corner are the requirements. The hibiscus can sometimes be struck from cuttings ; it does not object to a limy soil.

The Complete Gardener

HOHERIA Order MALVACEÆ

There are several species but only two of the hoherias are hardy enough to be worth planting in the small garden.

H. Lyallii. Formerly known as *Plagianthus Lyallii*, this is such a beautiful thing that, although it is not hardy enough for very cold districts, it is very well worth growing anywhere in the south of England. It came through recent hard winters without appreciable damage. It is a deciduous shrub about 8 ft. high with grey green, toothed leaves and cherry-blossom-like white, fragrant flowers in July. A plant of great refinement and charm, which comes from New Zealand.

H. glabrata. Similar to *H. Lyallii*, but flowers ten days later. Has larger greener leaves which sometimes partly hide the flowers. It is best to have both kinds so as to secure a succession of blooms.

CULTIVATION : Best in a sunny corner and it is wiser, perhaps, to prune a young plant so that it forms a shrub of several stems rather than a tree on one stem. Thus, if it should be cut to the ground by frost in a hard winter it will be more likely to shoot up again. A mulch of long bracken about the roots in autumn will make them safer against a deep frost. It will grow on limy soils and can be propagated from seeds.

HYDRANGEA Order SAXIFRAGACEÆ

The hydrangeas are among the most important flowering shrubs for small and large gardens. Almost alone they can provide us with the masses of colour in late summer that so many other shrubs are ready to provide in spring. Hardy, accommodating, striking very easily from cuttings, they are everybody's plant and no garden should be without them, except those in frost-holes where spring frosts perpetually wreck everything.

H. macrophylla (the common Hortensia). Every one knows the globular heads of sterile flowers of pink, white or blue, appearing from July to October, but few are aware of the *best varieties* of this Japanese plant for outdoor planting. The best blue colouring is only attained by certain varieties, and then only when the soil is acid. In limy soils the flowers do not attain the blue colouring as the plant cannot obtain the required iron and aluminum. In good conditions hortensias reach from 4-6 ft. or more in height, depending on the variety.

338

A List of Worthwhile Flowering Shrubs

They are best massed in the foreground of beds backed by earlier flowering evergreens such as rhododendrons, camellias, *Choisya ternata*, etc. On the other hand they will make fine lawn specimens or decorate the foot of a north wall. Besides the hortensia type there is another type of *H. macrophylla*, the Lacecaps, which have a flat head with small fertile flowers in the centre and a ring round the outside formed by the larger sterile flowers. This shape is preferable in many ways, giving a very pretty outline as opposed to the rather lumpish shape of the hortensias. Both kinds are reasonably hardy having suffered little damage in past severe winters when many common shrubs were killed.

VARIETIES :   The choice of variety should depend on whether the natural soil of the garden is limy or not, as the red and orange kinds will not be a good colour in acid soil and the blue varieties will only be a washy pink in limy soil.
Hortensia varieties for a limy soil :
Carmen. Red.
Hatfield Rose. Pure crimson.
Mme Mouillière. White.
Munster. Crimson.
Parsifal. Pure pink.
Vulcan. Salmon pink.
Lacecap varieties for a limy soil :
H. m. Veitchii.   White with very large flowers around the head.
H. m. Mariesii. Pink.
(See also varieties of *Hydrangea serrata*.)
Hortensia varieties for an acid soil :
Générale Vicomtesse de Vibraye. Purest Cambridge blue.
Mme Mouillière. White.
Maréchal Foch. Deep blue.
Mousseline. Pale blue.
Lacecap varieties for an acid soil :
Bluewave. Blue.
H. m. Veitchii. White.
(See also varieties of *H. serrata*.)

CULTIVATION : The wild hydrangea flowers in Japan in the overcast and rainy month of July, and the main parent of these hybrids is a sea-coast plant growing close to the waves. Consequently it really requires a

CULTIVATION : little shade for its flowers to last well in this climate but it likes an open sky above. The hydrangea has a great need for iron in the soil and this is easily enough provided by watering it, during the time the flowers are being formed, with a solution of a quarter of an ounce of sulphate of iron to a gallon of water. With this treatment the leaves will become a deep healthy green and the plants will make good growth and set plenty of flower buds. To attain the blue flower colour a further treatment is necessary if the soil is not naturally favourable, i.e. acid. Water weekly from the time growth starts until the time when the blooms commence to open with a solution of $\frac{1}{4}$ oz. aluminium sulphate to 1 gal. of water. Some varieties are more obdurate than others owing to hybrid parentage of species whose flowers are never blue. In a really acid soil, rich in humus the flowers of the blue varieties mentioned will be a good blue, but it may spoil the colour of the orange-pink Vulcan. A good acid loamy soil, preferably on the heavy side, and well enriched with rotted turves is the best. A watch must be kept for slugs which destroy many young shoots (see PESTS AND DISEASES, page 650). Cuttings strike readily if taken in July. Do not prune hydrangeas unless necessary to keep in bounds and then only in spring by removing one or two of the older branches. It is best not to remove the old flower heads as they look nice in the winter and keep a lot of frost off the branches.

H. serrata. This is a Japanese hybrid race of the woodland species. 1-8 ft., according to variety. It is even hardier than the preceding. The wild forms have not been introduced but we have had the garden varieties for a great many years. It is a smaller and slenderer plant than *H. macrophylla* with long pointed leaves with a dull surface instead of a shining one. *H. serrala* requires shade.

VARIETIES : Grayswood. A great improvement on *H. s. intermedia* with twice as many individual flowers on the head and of much brighter colour and lasting twice as long. One of the most beautiful of the hydrangeas and quite hardy. The white flowers

340

VARIETIES :   turn a rich red and then crimson, remaining attractive for many weeks. Height 4 ft.

H. s. intermedia. A coarse, strong-growing variety very close to *H. japonica.* The flowers open pure white and then turn crimson. It grows up to 6 ft. in rich soil. The flowers twist downwards and so only last a short time.

H. s. rosalba. A slight improvement on the preceding, more elegant in habit and with slightly larger and more numerous flowers.

CULTIVATION : The varieties of *H. serrata* are suited by the same soil conditions as *H. macrophylla*, but quite dense shade is tolerated without their going lanky, soft and flowerless. Cuttings strike fairly freely.

H. acuminata. This species is quite a distinct type. The flowers are a beautiful blue in suitable soil. An excellent plant for the small garden. Height about 3 ft.

CULTIVATION : As for *H. serrata.*

HYPERICUM (St. John's Wort) Order GUTTIFERÆ

The St. John's Wort family provides us with two or three fine late-flowering shrubs whose large yellow flowers contrast effectively with the hydrangeas and fuchsias of August.

H. calycinum (the Rose of Sharon). A low, creeping shrub very easily grown from any rooted piece. The flowers are large and yellow with a big tuft of stamens in the centre. Very useful for forming a foot-high carpeting for rough banks and odd corners where it would be troublesome to cut grass. It revels in a chalky soil.

H. patulum. In itself this is of little value, but it has two varieties which are first rate. July–August.

VARIETIES :   *H. p. Forrestii.* Far the finest form with yellow flowers 2 ins. across and autumn-tinting leaves July–October, 5 ft.

H. p. Henryi. A valuable shrub growing about 4 ft. high with golden-yellow salver-shaped flowers in late summer.

CULTIVATION : A good loam and a warm position. Cuttings or seed.

IBERIS (Candytuft) Order CRUCIFERÆ

I. sempervirens. This little evergreen with its hard white flowers will make an attractive little shrub if sheared to a rounded shape after flowering. It needs careful placing or the effect is too staring. Flowers spring.

CULTIVATION : A well-drained spot and full sun.

JASMINUM Order OLEACEÆ

The jasmines are well known climbing shrubs notable for their fragrance.

J. nudiflorum (Yellow Jasmine). This flowers in winter and is quite hardy. A sunny spot yields the most flowers but it will grow on a shady wall, or better still up a berry-bearing bush or tree. When well arranged such a combination makes a pleasant winter picture.

CULTIVATION : Easily propagated from layers which root freely.

J. officinale (Common White Jasmine). The scented white flowers are borne in clusters from June to October. It will, by pruning, make a self-supporting bush in the south, but farther north needs the protection of a wall.

CULTIVATION : A sunny wall is best. Care should be taken to train out the growths fanwise at the start.

KALMIA Order ERICACEÆ

The kalmias are quite attractive but need a lime-free soil suitable for azaleas and rhododendrons which are much brighter coloured garden shrubs.

K. glauca. A small evergreen shrub of under 2 ft. with attractive rose-purple cups in spring.

K. latifolia (Calico Bush). An evergreen up to 15 ft. with pink, cup-shaped flowers in bunches, borne in June. Attractive on close inspection but makes no effect at a distance.

VARIETIES : *K. l. myrtifolia.* More dense and dwarf in habit with pale crimson flowers. The best for small gardens, it makes a fine effect.

CULTIVATION : All kalmias mentioned need a moist, peaty soil, but require sun to flower freely.

KERRIA Order ROSACEÆ

K. japonica. A bushy deciduous shrub up to 5 ft. high, with yellow flowers in spring. Best known in the double-flowered form commonly seen against walls. The single-flowered form is much the better shrub as it is more compact and bushy in habit, and the flowers do not look so artificial. It flowers in April and May.

VARIETIES: *K.j. aureo-variegata.* Yellow-margined leaves.
K.j. picta. Leaves edged white, flowers most of summer.
K.j. pleniflora. The double form with a gaunt habit and pom-pom flowers.

CULTIVATION: Any good garden soil will serve, but a sunny position is required. Cuttings of half-ripe shoots can be struck under a bell-glass in July.

LAVENDER Order LABIATAE

VARIETIES: *Lavendula officinalis* (Syn. *L. spica*, *L. vera*). 3 ft. Leaves white and woolly when young, flowers lavender.
L.o. atropurpurea. Dark lavender-purple flowers.
L.o. compacta. A low and compact type.
L. Staeches. Up to 3 ft. Dark purple. The French lavender.

CULTIVATION: Will grow in any ordinary light soil, in a warm, dry, sunny position. Prune straggly plants into shape in March or April. Plant March or September.

LITHOSPERMUM Order BORAGINACEÆ

L. diffusum. A charming little evergreen, prostrate shrublet with gentian-blue flowers in May and June.

VARIETIES: Grace Ward, the true variety is more compact in growth and freer flowering.
Heavenly Blue. This older variety is still the best for dry sandy soils.

CULTIVATION: Lime-free soil, open position and sharp drainage are essential. Best, perhaps, grown as a rock plant or with helianthemums and alpine rhododendrons.

LUPINUS (Tree Lupin) Order LEGUMINOSÆ

L. arboreus. A lovely shrub with yellow, white or mauve flowers, like small editions of those of the herbaceous lupin. It grows up to 6 ft. high and is one of the handsomest of the " June-gap " flowerers. It makes a fine lawn specimen. Not long-lived and apt to die in winter by getting wind-rocked unless carefully looked after. Named varieties with flowers of different colours are badly wanted.

CULTIVATION: A poor, sandy, but well-drained, soil in full sun is the best, but this lupin will grow almost anywhere. Snip off all seed pods as soon as flowers fade and nip back when young to induce compact growth. Cuttings with a heel attached and seed are both easy ways of making new plants.

MAHONIA Order BERBERIDACEÆ

The mahonias or evergreen barberries are handsome shrubs with fragrant yellow flowers and decorative divided leaves.

M. Aquifolium (the Holly-leaved Barberry). A useful hardy ever-green with yellow flowers in April, growing about 2 or 3 ft. high.

M. Bealii. This has fine upright spikes of yellow flowers often as early as February. The leaves are much larger than those of the preceeding but it is not as hardy. Up to 8 ft.

M. japonica. Large flower spikes and a bushier habit with very handsome foliage. Up to 8 ft.

VARIETIES: *M. Moseri.* A very beautiful but scarce variety with rose-tinted foliage and fine habit.

CULTIVATION: No special soil requirements. The two latter species do not move well. Increase by seeds.

OLEARIA (Daisy-bush) Order COMPOSITÆ

Commonly called Daisy-bushes, these shrubs are not completely hardy in Britain.

O. Haastii. The most commonly grown and hardiest species. Has small, dark-green leaves and clusters of small, white daisy-like flowers.

O. macrodonta. The leaves are somewhat holly-like, grey-green, silvery on the underside. The clusters of small white flowers are sweetly scented.

CULTIVATION: Any good garden soil will serve. Cuttings of half-ripe wood can be struck under a bell-glass in July.

58. Japanese cherry, Shirotae

59. Viburnum macrocephalum

60. *Magnolia obovata*

61. *Magnolia stellata*

A List of Worthwhile Flowering Shrubs

PÆONIA (Moutan) Order RANUNCULACEÆ

P. suffruticosa. The tree pæony, or moutan, is a gorgeous shrub though somewhat scarce and dear. The large flowers are pink, red, white, lilac, salmon or violet according to variety. The plant is hardy but apt to make growth too early and get the young shoots killed back and the flowering thus spoiled. It is, therefore, not worth while trying in a low-situated garden where spring frosts are bad, although it will be one of the glories of a high-lying garden where such visitations seldom come. It takes three years from planting to flower freely. Flowers in April-May.

CULTIVATION: Enrich the bottom " spit " well with rotted manure, so the roots can find it later. Give an occasional top dressing of rotted manure. Plant in a north-facing situation where early morning sun does not shine on frosted growth, see that the spot has air-drainage (see page 374) as spring frosts are the one serious enemy. No pruning needed. Will grow on limy soils if well manured.

PEROWSKIA Order LABIATÆ

P. atriplicifolia (Bluesage). Thin twigs with white powdered leaves and violet-blue flowers in August and September.
CULTIVATION: A warm spot is needed. Prune away any winter-killed growth in spring. Increased by cuttings with a heel in July.

PHILADELPHUS (Mock Orange) Order SAXIFRAGACEÆ

These are the mock oranges, or syringas as they are sometimes called, though this name is really that of the lilac family. Their strongly-scented white flowers in June and July are much appreciated. There are a great many kinds. The following is a selection of some of the best hybrids. 3-12 ft. according to variety.
P. Belle Etoile. Perhaps the loveliest of the mock orange, this variety has large, single flowers with a faint purple stain at the base of the petals. The habit of the shrub is good and bushy and the fragrance spicy and enjoyable. Flowers in June or July.
P. Conquête. Flowers nearly 3 ins. across with very little scent.
P. Virginale. This variety has large, double white flowers which are pleasantly fragrant. The foliage and habit are not very attractive but the flowers largely make up for this.

345

OTHER
SPECIES:
P. microphyllus. A dwarf-growing species making a dense shrub, eventually 3 ft. high, with flowers appearing singly in June.
P. pubescens. This is the large, tall mock orange often seen in old gardens with masses of fragrant white flowers at the end of June.

CULTIVATION: Though they will tolerate a limy soil, being shallow rooting the mock oranges like a moist, or at least a well-mulched soil. Pruning should consist of removing a few of the oldest branches at ground level occasionally so as to keep the plant on young wood, but they grow quite well left to themselves.

PIERIS Order ERICACEÆ

P. Forrestii. An evergreen from Yunnan, up to about 8 ft. in height with brilliant salmon-coloured young leaves in spring followed by panicles of fragrant, white, urn-shaped flowers. It is not very hardy but beautiful enough to be worth the risk of an occasional set-back from spring frosts.

CULTIVATION: Lime-free soil essential, propagation by seed or layering.

PONCIRUS (Hardy Orange) Order RUTACEÆ

P. trifoliata (Ægle sepiaria). This hardy Chinese orange is armed with ferocious spines but has pretty white, fragrant blossoms in May, and in a hot summer will produce its small orange-like fruits which are quite useful for flavouring purposes. It grows about 6 ft. high and is reasonably hardy.

CULTIVATION: A lime-free soil and a sunny spot are required. It can be grown from seed.

PONTENTILLA (Cinquefoil) Order ROSACEÆ

The Cinquefoils are hardy shrubs flowering over a long period throughout late summer, mostly with white or yellow flowers. They are most valuable for the small garden.
P. fruticosa. Native of Britain, rounded bush 2-4 ft. high with deciduous, divided leaves and inch-wide buttercup yellow, strawberry-like flowers.

VARIETIES:
P. f. Farreri (parvifolia). Dwarf habit and large bright yellow flowers.

346

A List of Worthwhile Flowering Shrubs

P. f. nana argentea (*Beesiana*). Silvery leaves, paler yellow flowers.

P. f. Veitchii. Grey-green leaves, white flowers.

P. f. Vilmoriniana. Silvery leaves, creamy flowers.

CULTIVATION: An open position and sandy soil is best but Potentillas are not particular. Some " manicuring " of dead leaves and seed pods may be done with advantage to the appearance of the bushes. Propagation by seeds, cuttings, or even division.

PYRACANTHA (Firethorn) Order ROSACEÆ

The firethorns are usually grown against walls but this is not really the best way. When grown as specimens in an open position they form dense, rounded bushes covered with flowers followed by the bright red or yellow berries. On walls, too often the necessary pruning removes flowering growth so that berries are only seen at the top.

P. coccinea (Common Firethorn). Makes a fine lawn specimen with coral red berries in autumn.

VARIETIES: *P. c. Lalandii.* Freer flowering with larger berries but more upright habit, requiring some pruning in early stages to make a compact bush.

CULTIVATION: Sunny, open position, ordinary soil. Sometimes attacked by fungus discolouring the berries. Cure is spray with Bordeaux Mixture in early spring as the buds burst. Grows from seed.

P. crenato-serrata (*P. Gibbsii*). Larger leaves, very free.

P. crenulata Rogersiana var. Aurea. Yellow berries, fruits well when small.

CULTIVATION: As for *P. coccinea.*

RHODODENDRON Order ERICACEÆ

Under this " umbrella " name are grouped families ranging from creeping alpine plants to forest trees; the deciduous azaleas and forest evergreens with immense leaves are all included. It is, therefore, simpler to divide the rhododendrons into sections according to their garden use (1) Dwarf evergreens suitable for small gardens and rock gardens; (2) deciduous azaleas; (3) evergreen shrub rhododendrons suitable for the average garden. Most of the best garden plants are hybrids or picked forms of species. People can often be heard saying that their gardens are too small for rhododendrons, but this is hardly possible because many of the most attractive are little shrublets hardly bigger than a mole-heap. The only thing which *should* stop people growing them is a limy soil; under such conditions one must make do with such substitues as *Chænomeles japonica*, *Genista hispanica*, helianthemums, berberis, etc., but no lime-free garden can do without azaleas and rhododendrons and there is *no difficulty* in growing them well, provided that a little trouble is taken at the start.

I. DWARF EVERGREENS
Suitable for the smallest gardens or rock gardens.

(a) Evergreen Azaleas
These dwarf evergreen azaleas are among the oldest cultivated garden plants, having been grown in Japanese gardens for hundreds of years. It is difficult to find more ideal subjects.

R. *obtusum* (Japanese Azalea). A small, dense evergreen shrub covered in spring with red, white, pink, crimson or orange flowers according to variety. Planted in beds with yellow dwarf forms and blue alpine rhododendron species and perhaps helianthemums for midsummer effect, and varieties of *Erica cinerea* for late summer effect, it is difficult to imagine a more pleasing arrangement. There is some variation in the size of the varieties and allied species, but most are of low, mounded habit and can be kept to 2 or 3 ft. or less by clipping after flowering if necessary. They bloom in late April or early May.

VARIETIES: Hinomayo. Pink.
Hinodegiri. Crimson.
R. *o. Kæmpferi*. Orange.
Kure-no-Yuki. White.

ALLIED SPECIES: R. *indicum*. Flowers in June with similar large azalea flowers on a small evergreen bushlet. There are red, salmon and pink forms.
R. *mucronatum*. White, with large azalea flowers in masses in May.
R. *pulchrum* var. *Maxwellii*. Flowers at the same time with crimson-red flowers.

(b) Alpine Rhododendron species and hybrids
A short selection. Height up to 3 ft.
Blue Tit. Blue flowers opening in early April.
R. *chryseum*. Bright yellow flowers early in April.
R. *impeditum*. A low shrublet with purplish-blue flowers in June.
R. *Ledoides*. Fragrant little daphne-like blush bells. Charming. Flowers April and May.
R. *scintillans*. Bright royal-blue flowers, in best forms. Flowers March and April.

CULTIVATION: These little shrubs all like a little peat put around the roots when planting (peat moss litter is obtainable cheaply) and to be planted in a cool rather than a sun-scorched position. A few sandstone rocks over their roots seem to help them greatly. The alpine rhododendron species mentioned all grow easily from cuttings and will flower in eighteen months from seed so, although they may be expensive plants to buy in the first instance, they can easily pay their rent if a little trouble is taken. Those mentioned are reasonably hardy.

II. DECIDUOUS HYBRID AZALEAS

The garden azaleas are the most gorgeously coloured of all flowering shrubs and the brilliant oranges, scarlets, yellows, reds and salmon-coloured flowers all harmonisc easily. They are divided into sub-sections here depending on race and time of flowering:

(a) Mollis Azaleas.

These have large pink, orange, yellow, buff or salmon flowers and flower in April which is too early for most gardens. They will reach 4 or 5 ft. in time, but are usually broader than high.

R. Kosterianum. Brilliant red, reddish-orange.

VARIETIES: Floradora. Orange pink, late.
J. C. van Thol. Very large orange-red flowers.
Mrs. L. J. Endtz. Vivid yellow.
Mrs. Oliver Slocock. Orange yellow.

CULTIVATION: Most of these azaleas die merely from being planted deeply in heavy soil. Plant with the ball of roots *barely covered* with peaty soil and mulch with fallen leaves. Grafted plants are seldom satisfactory, so get either seedlings or layers of named varieties.

(b) Knap Hill Hybrid Azaleas

This is a new type of strong, hardy, large-flowered azalea in a most brilliant colour range. They flower later, in May, and are perhaps the cream of flowering shrubs. 6 ft.

VARIETIES: Fire Glow. Orange vermilion.
Gog. Tangerine, very vigorous.
Harvest Moon. Pure pale yellow.
Knap Hill pink. Rich salmon pink.
Persil. White with a yellow blotch.
Pink Delight. Warm peach with a yellow eye.

VARIETIES: Satan. Brilliant scarlet.
                    Seville. Orange red.
                    Tunis. Red and orange.

CULTIVATION: As for the *Mollis* types. Some shade is desirable for otherwise the rich colours are soon faded by the hotter suns of May. Increase by layers. Seed germinates well but the seedlings are, of course, variable, as the parents are hybrids.

(c) Ghent and Occidentale Hybrid Azaleas

These flower later still, in early June, so their flowers are seldom interfered with by frost, even in cold districts. The Ghents are the best azaleas, therefore, for cold gardens and, being hardy, seldom fail to give a good account of themselves. Their colour range is similar to that of the previous sub-sections. Shade is wanted to preserve the bright colours from the hot mid-summer sun. Many varieties are delightfully fragrant. The hybrids of *R. occidentale*, on the other hand, are of rather pale pastel shades but stand up to the sun much better. A good plan is to use them, therefore, in the sunnier parts of the azalea scheme when these pale shades will be found to set off the more fiery colours of the Ghents most excellently. Up to 8 ft.

VARIETIES: Aurore de Royghem. Orange-pink.
                    Fanny. Pink.
                    Graf Alf von Nipping. Orange red.
                    Pallas. Soft red.
                    Vesuvius. Red, late.

CULTIVATION: A warning must again be given not to plant these azaleas too deep; no soil, only a scattering of peat or leaf-mould, should be put over the ball of roots when first planting and a mulch of dead leaves should be kept over the ground *at all times*. No pruning is needed but it is a good plan to remove the seed pods after flowering as this saves the plants' sap for new growth and next year's flowers.

III. EVERGREEN RHODODENDRON HYBRIDS FOR THE GARDEN

The hardy hybrid rhododendrons are invaluable for the bright colours of their massed flowers in spring or early summer and for the evergreen background they afford which doubles the effectiveness of other shrubs. Properly planted in lime-free soil in semi-shade and kept mulched with fallen leaves they are no trouble at all and layer so easily that they can pay their way handsomely if desired.

A List of Worthwhile Flowering Shrubs

(a) Early-Flowering Semi-hardy and Hardy Hybrids

This sub-section is typified by the well-known Pink Pearl, flowering in late April or early May. This is somewhat early for many gardens; spring frosts spoil the flowers too often. Shade is helpful in keeping the flowers in good condition much longer and in warding off a certain amount of frost where the trees form a light canopy overhead. Betty Wormald, carmine; A. C. Kenrick, pink; Corona, cerise; Mrs. Stirling, pale blush; Raoul Millais, salmon pink, are examples. All these ultimately make sturdy bushes 10 ft. high or more, under good conditions. When properly grown the leaves are about 6 ins. long and the new shoots of the year about twice the thickness of a pencil.

Allied to these is *R. Loderi*, probably the finest in flower of all the hybrids. The flowers, white or pink according to the variety, borne in May, are often six inches across and delightfully fragrant. It succeeds well against a north wall in the colder districts provided that poor soil is removed and replaced with an acid mixture of peat, sand and leaf-mould. Pink Diamond is a beautiful rose pink variety.

CULTIVATION: Light shade, lime-free soil enriched with leaf-mould and an annual mulch of 6 ins. of fallen leaves are required for healthy growth. Increased by layers. Shelter from wind is necessary or the big leaves get broken off and growth therefore is held up.

R. Jacksonii, rose; Cunningham's Blush, pink; Cunningham's White, white. These are three low-growing ultra-hardy early flowerers suitable for exposed positions. The first-named does not grow more than about 3 ft. high and the others are easily kept low by pruning if desired. Very good background plants for a bed in the open and about the easiest of all rhododendrons to grow.

CULTIVATION: As for ultra-hardy hybrids below.

(b) Later-Flowering, Ultra-Hardy Hybrids

The rhododendrons in this sub-section are some of the best for general planting as their smaller, tougher leaves can stand more wind and their flowers, opening later, are usually safe from the destructive spring frosts. Examples are: Britannia, red; Doncaster, dwarfed; Lord Roberts, crimson; Lady Clementine Mitford, peach blush; Lady Annette de Trafford, pink with a crimson blotch; Mrs. John Clutton, white with a yellow blotch; Purple Splendour, violet; Midsummer, pink with a yellow blotch. There are hundreds of these named varieties. They are usually grafted on the common purple *R. ponticum*, naturalised in many parts of the south of England. Such plants often give trouble by the *ponticum* stock coming up and robbing the variety. People speak of it as " reverting," but all that has to be done it to take a sharp spade and chop out the *ponticum* suckers as one would a briar on a rose. These hardy hybrids are ideal garden shrubs to provide the evergreen background and play their part in the early summer flower display. The crimsons and pinks " fight " the azalea colourings so, where these are grown near, it is best to keep to true reds, purples and whites for the rhododendrons. Otherwise the crimson, pink, white and purple rhododendrons harmonise perfectly together.

CULTIVATION: Many of these old hardy hybrids will stand a good deal of sun and wind, but all are better with some wind-break and light shade. Mulching is important as their growth in sun-baked, naked soil is poor. In exposed places it is best to start with low, bushy plants; leggy specimens, unable to shade their roots, only dwindle at the top and make little progress until fresh shoots grow from the base. Feed annually with a mulch of fallen leaves kept in position with branches, long bracken or sandstones. *With such proper attention* the hardy hybrids grow very fast, making 7 or 8-in. shoots, with leaves at least 5 ins. long, annually. The size of these hybrids varies according to situation and variety, but an average would be about 8 ft. high in an open situation. Rather than cut off branches, the best way to shape them, when necessary, is to bend down the outer branches and layer them with large stones. All members of the rhododendron and azalea family can be perfectly safely moved, however large they may be, *provided that* the ball of roots is secured entire. To assist this it is a good plan to place peat, with a little soil mixed with it, round the ball when first planting. The plant roots into this in preference to the ordinary soil and thus a compact, easily-moved ball of roots is obtained. October and March are good months to move rhododendrons, but be sure the ball of roots is well soaked beforehand and that the plant does not get dry during the spring following.

A List of Worthwhile Flowering Shrubs

RIBES (Flowering Currant). Order SAXIFRAGACEÆ

R. sanguineum. A common shrub with pink flowers in spring. Very hardy and easily grown. 6 ft.

CULTIVATION: Easily rooted from cuttings.

ROSA (Rose) Order ROSACEÆ

The rose, quite apart from the bedding and climbing roses grown in every garden, is an important flowering shrub. Up to now no varieties have been expressly bred for use as specimen shrubs so we have to make the best of the most suitable for this purpose. The rose is at its best just in the " June-gap," which makes it particularly valuable. Well-grown specimen bushes, alight with blossom, can " carry " the garden at that time as few other shrubs can, and the mock oranges, genistas and tree lupins in flower at the same time complete the picture very nicely.

(a) Garden Rose varieties specially suitable for growing as Shrubs:
Betty Prior. A fine strong bush, about 5 by 4 ft. when grown up as a specimen, rich rose-pink, single flowers, very long lasting.
Betty Uprichard. Pale coppery pink.
Billy Boy. Buttercup yellow, semi-single.
Blanc Double de Coubert. A Japanese (*rugosa*) type with very fragrant white flowers.
Catalonia. Huge orange and scarlet flowers.
Cuba. Red and orange.
Cupid. A big fierce rose with large, single, pale peach-coloured flowers all at once.
Donald Prior. A shapely bush with beautifully presented semi-double red flowers.
Felicia. A hybrid Musk with double blush-pink flowers delightfully scented, will make a bush 10 × 10 ft. like a huge basket of roses if well grown.
Grüss an Teplitz. Bright crimson, fragrant.
Irish Elegance. Single, pale apricot pink.
Isobel. A lovely cherry orange, single.
Kirsten Poulsen. Cherry red, single flowers.
Moonlight. A very strong white hybrid Musk.
Zephyrine Drouhin. The rose without a thorn, deep pink fragrant flowers.

CULTIVATION: The aim is different to that for growing bedding types; what we want is not just a few large flowers but a great, round, permanent bush densely set with a great number of smaller flowers on stalks weak enough to let them bend over and look at *us*.

CULTIVATION: To achieve this we must go about the pruning in quite a different way, and we must take a certain amount of trouble at the start. In the first place the rose has got to *really grow*. This means an open position, as a specimen, or at any rate not mixed up with other tall plants in a bed. Also, it means that we have got to feed the plant and the best way to do this is to make a hole a yard across and 18 ins. deep and cover the bottom with two or three layers of inverted turves and then put back the best of the top soil. Now we plant the rose in this and take particular care that the union between the briar and the rose itself is a couple of inches below the surface of the soil. We do not want any trouble with suckers from the briar roots. Then as to pruning, we must prune the nursery-grown wood hard at first as we need new, strong stems from the base to build up a permanent framework for our large bush. The first season it will not do a great deal, but by the second the roots will be enjoying the turfy loam. The only further pruning needed is to cut away the old flower stems *just to the nearest dormant bud*, and occasionally to remove the oldest branch of the shrub at ground level. On the whole it is best not to use manure in solid form but a little rich liquid will not come amiss if the plant seems to check at any time. Practically all Roses will grow on limy soils, though research has shown that they do best on rather acid soils.

(*b*) *Rose species suitable as shrubs.*
A short selection:

R. Hugonis. A single yellow, flowering in spring, rather liable to " die-back." Pretty, arching sprays.

R. Moyesii. A tall shrub, up to 9 ft. in height, with handsome foliage and scarlet hips in autumn and lovely rich red roses of heraldic shape in summer. Not a compact bush, having an open habit and liking some shade.

R. spinosissima (Burnet Rose). Variety *lutea* is a fine yellow. The variety *altaica* has large creamy-white flowers.

R. xanthina. Attractive yellow flowers in June. A small, twiggy bush.

CULTIVATION: Ordinary garden soil will serve, but turf-loam (not clay as is sometimes recommended) is best.

CULTIVATION: *R. spinosissima* grows naturally on sandy soils. Some species may be grown from cuttings taken of flowered shoots in early September.

SENECIO Order COMPOSITÆ

S. laxifolius. Too tender to be really safe in any but coastal or southern gardens, but the beautiful silver-green foliage with white underside and masses of yellow daisy-flowers in late June make it worth trying in a warm spot. 3 ft.

CULTIVATION: Any soil, open position. Strikes very easily from cuttings.

SIPHONOSMANTHUS Order OLEACEÆ

S. Delavayi (Osmanthus Delavayi). An evergreen with small-toothed leaves and small, fragrant white flowers in April. 6 ft.

CULTIVATION: Sunny position. Will grow in limy soil. Cuttings can be rooted in a frame.

SOPHORA Order LEGUMINOSÆ

S. viciifolia. An attractive Chinese shrub with pinnate (divided into leaflets) leaves and blue pea-flowers in June. It grows up to 6 ft., but is often much less in the open. It is hardy and valuable for flowering in the "June-gap."

CULTIVATION: Full sun, will grow on sandy or limy soils, can be propagated from cuttings in the sand frame.

SPARTIUM (Spanish Broom) Order LEGUMINOSÆ

S. junceum. Rush-like branchlets and spikes of fragrant yellow pea-flowers from July to frost. Very beautiful in warm and coastal gardens. 4-8 ft.

CULTIVATION: An absolutely open position and well-drained poor soil, no matter if limy, are best. Prune the soft growth firmly when the plant is young and shear back the thin twigs every spring to make it form a dense low bush, otherwise it grows up gaunt and ugly and does not live long. Easily grown from seed.

SPIRÆA Order ROSACEÆ

There are a great many species but few of much distinction. Perhaps the three best are the following:

S. *arguta* (Bridal Wreath). A bushy shrub with small leaves and masses of small white flowers in April and May. Grows about 6 ft. high. Hardy, free-flowering and easily increased by layers.

S. *canescens*. Has arching branches clustered their whole length with little bunches of white flowers in June and July.

S. *nipponica* (*bracteata*). Clusters of white flowers in June.

CULTIVATION: These spiræas like a fairly rich soil. Occasionally prune away one or two of the oldest branches at ground level.

SYRINGA (Lilac) Order OLEACEÆ

The lilacs are very commonly planted but though first-class for cut flowers they are somewhat outclassed as flowering shrubs for garden decoration. The foliage is ugly, the habit of growth unattractive, and the colouring, except for some white varieties like S. *vulgaris*, variety Vestale, does not show up decoratively in comparison with brighter-coloured species.

S. *vulgaris* (Common Lilac). A deciduous bush up to 20 ft. high with pale lilac flowers in short, blunt spikes in May.

VARIETIES: *Singles*
            President Lincoln. Light bluish lilac.
            Reaumur. Reddish purple.
            Souvenir de Louis Spath. Deep purple.
            Vestale. A fine white of good bushy habit.
            Doubles.
            Condorcet. Lilac blue.
            Emile Gentil. Almost blue.
            Miss Ellen Wilmot. Snow white.
            President Loubet. Dark purple.

CULTIVATION: The lilacs like a rich soil, though they grow well on limy soils, and a warm position. Remove faded flowers to prevent seed formation. Grafted plants are troublesome owing to suckers. Layers are better. Possibly the best are the tree-like specimens, free from suckers, obtainable by grafting on privet.

VIBURNUM Order CAPRIFOLIACEÆ

Mostly white-flowered, deciduous shrubs comprising a great number of species. The following are outstanding among them for garden value. The viburnums tolerate a limy soil.

356

V. Carlesii. A rounded shrub up to 3 ft. high with dull, rather ugly leaves and clusters of exquisitely scented white flowers, pink outside, in April. Unfortunately the clusters are often spoiled by some of the flowers composing them being brown and withered before the others open.

CULTIVATION: A spot sheltered from the north-east winds and where spring frosts seldom come is the one to choose. No pruning needed. Keep a look out for suckers as plants are sometimes grafted on the native *V. lantana* which otherwise soon overwhelms the Korean plant. Cuttings in July sometimes strike.

V. opulus (the Guelder Rose). A native shrub with white flowers in May, red berries and good autumn colour.

VARIETIES: *V. o. sterile.* The Snowball Tree. Instead of the flat flower-head with only a few sterile, showy flowers round the margin this has a round ball of sterile flowers. It does not, of course, produce berries. 10 ft.

V. tomentosum. An oriental species flowering in May, best in its two special varieties.

VARIETIES: *V. t. Mariesii*, a very beautiful white-flowered shrub with flat heads of lace-like blossom in early June, recalling the wild Guelder rose but much finer. The leaves turn a rich claret colour in autumn. It makes a fine lawn specimen. Up to 10 ft.
V. t. sterile (Japanese Snowball). This has a round head of sterile flowers and is one of the finest white-flowered shrubs. Requiring a little care to start off, once well established it is quite hardy. Up to 6 ft.

CULTIVATION: The above repay a good soil, well enriched, although tolerant of lime. No pruning required. They need some care to strike from cuttings but fairly easily layered.

V. macrocephalum sterile has very large white flower-heads in May like a Hydrangea, grows up to 8 ft.

CULTIVATION: In most districts it requires the protection of a wall and well enriched soil, either limy or acid.

WEIGELA Order CAPRIFOLIACEÆ

The weigelas are hardy and accommodating shrubs with

357

funnel-shaped flowers which are not very showy. Often known as diervillas. Really the small garden requires better furnishing but they are useful for limy soils, where better shrubs will not thrive. The garden hybrids are more effective than the true species. Most of them flower in June. 6-8 ft.

Hybrid: Abel Carrière. Rose carmine flowers.
Espérance. Pale pink.
Eva Rathke. Dull crimson flowers, July.
Le Printemps. Large peach-pink flowers.
Mont Blanc. White.

CULTIVATION: Except for the variety Eva Rathke, the weigelas mentioned will grow on limy soils, although a rich soil is preferred. Increase by cuttings in sand frame in February.

WISTERIA Order LEGUMINOSÆ

The wisterias are beautiful climbing shrubs often grown against walls, but really the long racemes of flower are best seen on a pergola or on an old tree where they can hang down and display themselves better. By frequent nipping-back they can be made to form self-supporting shrubs. The Japanese grow them on a framework of poles over water or up trees which bend over water and this is the most spectacular way of all.

W. floribunda (*W. multijuga*) (Japanese Wisteria). This is the plant with the longest mauve racemes, but not the brightest in colour. They are sometimes over 3 ft. long. It is too strong a grower to be suitable for house walls unless there are large spaces for it to cover and much time can be spent in training and tying. A framework of poles or an old tree are really the best supports. Flowers in June successionally.

W. sinensis (Chinese Wisteria). This has richer-coloured mauve flowers in shorter and chubbier racemes. Flowers in May, opening all together; better, perhaps, for a house wall than the preceding.

CULTIVATION: Both wisterias like plenty of moisture at the roots, and a sunny space to climb in. Layering is not always successful and those grown from seeds are often inferior plants.

CHAPTER III

A Select List of Flowering Trees

ACER (Maple) Order ACERACEÆ

The Japanese Maples are really the best trees grown for autumn colour alone.

A. palmatum (Japanese Maple). The purple flowers are not noticeable. It is for the gorgeous colours of its autumn leaves that this little tree is prized in our gardens. Though hardy, its early leafage is apt to be cut by spring frosts. Ultimately about 20 ft. high, but slow growing.

VARIETIES :   *A. p. atro-purpureum.* Leaves purple.
     A. p. aureum. Leaves yellow.
     A. p. dissectum. Dwarf with much divided leaves.
     Osaka-Suki. Invariably turning to brilliant red in autumn.

A. japonicum. A slightly differing species with broader leaves.

VARIETIES :   *A. j. aconitifolium* (*filicifolium*). A richly colouring form with large, much-divided leaves.
     A. j. aureum. Has handsome yellow leaves.

CULTIVATION : Good soil and a sunny but sheltered position or the leaves are blown off as soon as they colour. Grows easily from seed.

AMELANCHIER Order ROSACEÆ

A. canadensis (the Mespilus or June Berry). A slender tree up to 25 ft. high, with white blossom covering the tree in April and fine red colouring of the leaves in autumn, but neither effect lasts very long. The fruit, which is black when ripe, is very good to eat.

CULTIVATION : Best on light acid soils. Easily grown from seed.

CATALPA Order BIGNONIACEÆ

C. bignonoides. This is a handsome tree growing up to 40 ft. with decorative large leaves and white horse-chestnut-like flowers in August. There is a fine group near the Houses of Parliament. It is a most desirable garden tree, but not long-lived.

CULTIVATION : Plant in ordinary garden soil and stake very firmly as otherwise the tree is likely to be blown over. Once established it stands wind well.

CRATÆGUS (Thorn) Order ROSACEÆ

The hawthorn family is a large one but few members are showy enough to be worth while growing in the small garden.

C. Oxyacantha. The common pink and white mays are too well known to need description.

C. Crus-galli. The Cockspur Thorn is a fine little tree for the garden, having white blossom in spring. The leaves colour superbly in autumn and, lastly, the large bright red fruits remain on the tree all the winter.

C. Lavallei (*C. Carrieri*). A fine hybrid thorn, with white flowers and conspicuous orange fruits throughout the winter.

CULTIVATION : Ordinary soil and an open position. Lime is not objected to.

EMBOTHRIUM Order PROTEACEÆ

Embothrium is included here as, although not absolutely hardy, it is the most brilliantly coloured flowering tree which can be grown in our climate. As regards its hardiness, it survived the severe winters which killed hundreds of ceanothus, cistus, escallonias and other shrubs commonly seen in our gardens, so the chance is well worth taking by the adventurous.

E. coccineum (the Chilean Fire-Bush). A somewhat thin, evergreen small tree from South America, the largest specimens being nearly 30 ft. high in the south-west of Britain. The best form, the variety *longifolium*, flowers when only 5 or 6 ft. high as a rule. The flowers are individually formed of brilliant scarlet tubes, but they appear in such numbers in a bottle brush, or raceme, formation that they make a positively dazzling effect.

VARIETIES : The botanical situation is still obscure, but there are two distinct forms available : *E. coccineum* with rounded leaves and short racemes of flower, reasonably hardy and long-lived, and the form *longifolium* with lance-shaped leaves, much freer flowering with longer racemes.

CULTIVATION : A warm, sunny spot sheltered from cold winds and a lime-free soil with plenty of leaf-mould is required.

360

A Select List of Flowering Trees

EUCRYPHIA Order **EUCRYPHIACEÆ**

The eucryphias are mostly evergreens from the southern hemisphere. They are among the most beautiful of white-flowered small trees when covered with their amazing profusion of large and shapely blossoms in August. They are indispensable for southern or coastal gardens.

E. glutinosa. This is a Chilean plant, growing to about 20 ft. at the most but flowering freely from about 8 ft. high. The beautiful flower is about 2½ ins. across and shaped like a St. John's Wort as to the mass of stamens, but with petals rather recalling the wild rose. The evergreen-looking leaves are divided and turn to fine colours before they fall in late autumn. Flowers in early August. A lovely shrub worthy of every care. Such is the freedom of flowering of a mature bush that the branches are weighed down by the mass of flowers.

E. nymansensis. A hybrid between the preceding and *E. cordefolia.* This makes an upright, pyramidal tree at first, then broadens out into a tower 15 ft. high. The white flowers, borne about the middle of August, are rather firmer than those of *E. glutinosa,* which is reasonably hardy, whereas the hybrid, which is evergreen, is apt to have its leaves killed in a really hard winter. Owing to its stronger habit it is perhaps even more beautiful than *E. glutinosa.* The pyramid, or tower, of densely set white blossom soaring up to a blue summer sky makes an unforgettable picture.

VARIETIES :   Unfortunately when *E. glutinosa* is grown from seed most of the seedlings come with a dwarf habit and ugly, misshapen, double flowers ; others have unusually small single flowers. It is best to insist, therefore, on a layer from a good plant.

CULTIVATION : Eucryphias like plenty of leaf-mould and mulch. Sunny position. Increase by layers. They do not grow well in limy soils or in cold districts.

LABURNUM Order **LEGUMINOSÆ**

The laburnums are showy but perhaps a little commonplace and difficult to harmonise with other flowering trees and shrubs.

L. anagyroides (Common Laburnum). Flowers in late May with short racemes of yellow flowers. It certainly does not make a pleasing colour scheme with the pink hawthorns so often grown near it. A late white cherry such as the Morello or the Japanese " Shiro-fugen " makes a prettier contrast.

L. alpinum (Scots Laburnum). This is a better species, being hardier, flowering a fortnight later, and having longer racemes of flower. Very pretty grown on a pergola with wisteria or making a shapely tree 30 ft. high.

VARIETIES :   *L. Watererii* (or *L. Vossii*), a still finer flowering variety of the above, but inferior as a tree.

CULTIVATION : Almost any soil, even chalk, seems to suit the laburnums, but a sunny position is best. The seeds are poisonous.

MAGNOLIA Order MAGNOLIACEÆ

The magnolias are probably the most spectacularly beautiful of flowering trees. Unfortunately many of the loveliest species take ten or more years to grow big enough to flower freely. A selection has therefore been made of the kinds which give a reasonably quick return. With most magnolias a dark evergreen tree as background is valuable to show up the beauty of the flowers.

M. obovata. This large species is included as it makes such a beautiful tree and its great creamy flowers with a red rosette in the centre come in early June and have a lovely scent. It takes some years to flower. In Japan it grows nearly 100 ft. high and is hardy in this country, though usually less than half this height.

CULTIVATION : Rich soil with leaf-mould. Prune hard when first received to encourage a new shoot from the base, and grow that up quickly instead of the old wood.

M. denudata (the Yulan or Lily Tree). A tree up to 20 ft. or more, this is one of the most spectacularly beautiful of all. The large scented white flowers are of the most exquisite shape and borne in great profusion in March and April on the naked branches. It is better as a tree in a sheltered spot than on a wall. Hardy, but the flowers, of course, are sometimes spoiled by spring frost.

CULTIVATION : This species will grow on a limy soil.

M. grandiflora. A magnificent evergreen tree or wall plant. Poor seedling forms take many years to grow or flower. Flowers white, July–September.

VARIETIES :   Exmouth. This form grows quickly and flowers early in life. The scented white flowers come in August and are 6 ins. across and the large evergreen leaves are felt with rusty down on the underside.

VARIETIES :   Goliath.   A free-flowering variety with rounded leaves, green instead of rusty underneath. Hardy enough for the south only.

CULTIVATION : A south wall with ample space needed. Rich soil. Increased by layers, but this is not easy.

M. salicifolia. An attractive slender little tree, the fragrant white flowers are borne in April, on the naked shoots. Grows up to 20 ft. Flowers freely when quite young. The bark has a scent like lemon verbena.

CULTIVATION : The magnolias all do best in a rich, moist soil. Shelter from wind is desirable to save the flowers getting knocked about. They are not easily propagated by the amateur.

M. Sieboldii (parviflora). This is a good magnolia for the small garden because it flowers when fairly young and can be kept in bounds by pruning if necessary. The deliciously scented white flowers with a crimson boss in the centre are borne successively from May to August. Height about 6 ft., usually with several stems.

CULTIVATION : As with the preceding kinds, the aim of pruning is to get rid of the stems that have suffered moving and grow it up from the ground on new wood. But, unlike the last, this magnolia is best grown as a shrub with several stems. The oldest may be cut away at ground level whenever it gets too big. A good rich soil and a sunny position. Increase by seeds. Spring frosts often damage its flowering.

M. Soulangeana. A hybrid of *M. denudata.* The most commonly planted. It flowers April–May and is not so spectacular, as some leaves are already showing by the time the white flowers, flushed purplish pink, open. None the less, it is a very beautiful small tree for the average garden.

CULTIVATION : As for *M. salicifolia.*

M. stellata. Also with white flowers rather similar to *M. salicifolia,* but this species is more of a bush and will flower when little more than a foot high, so is suitable for the very smallest gardens. Flowers March–April.

CULTIVATION : As for *M. salicifolia.*

M. Watsonii. A hybrid between *M. Sieboldii* and *M. obovata,* with the good points of both, but unfortunately very scarce. Flowers white, flushed pink with red central rosette, May–July. 12-15 ft.

CULTIVATION : As for *M. salicifolia.*

MALUS (Crab Apple) Order ROSACEÆ

The flowering crabs are among the best of small garden trees. Most flower in May and grow up to 20 ft. They have not the refinement of the cherries or the brilliance of colour of the peaches but will put up with bad conditions better than either. There are a large number of species and hybrids. The following is a selection of the best.

M. baccata (Siberian Crab). A fine tall crab with white blossom in April followed by red fruits lasting well on the tree.

M. Eleyi, and *M. aldenhamensis* and *M. Leminei.* These all have reddish-purple leaves, vinous-red flowers and dingy purplish-red fruits. They are really somewhat overrated. Much superior in its brighter flowers is *M. purpurea* which is otherwise somewhat similar.

M. floribunda (Japanese Crab). One of the finest in blossom covering itself completely with the red buds and pink open flowers. Fruits dingy and scarce.

M. hupenensis (*M. theifera*). A beautiful crab that forms a taller and more shapely tree than most. The flowers, almost as finely formed as cherry blossom, are pale pink at first, changing to white, and appear in April. There is also a pink-flowered variety.

M. John Downie. A fine crab with white blossom and red and yellow fruits.

M. Sargenti (Sargent's Crab). A bush crab which is one of the best for small gardens. Charming white blossom in May, followed by red, cherry-like fruits. With pruning it can be kept to a bush about 3-4 ft. high, or grown up as a small tree.

CULTIVATION : The crabs are not particular as to soil, but like a sunny position. Stake carefully when first planting (see page 394). Spray as advised for apples (see page 391).

PRUNUS Order ROSACEÆ

The prunus family is a very large one, the most important for garden purposes being the members of the peach and almond section, the cherry section and the plum section. Most do well on limy soils and are admirable flowering trees for the small garden.

PEACHES AND ALMONDS

P. Amygdalus (the Common Almond). Every one knows the pink blossom in early spring. Too often there is wanting the dark background of pine or fir which doubles the effectiveness of the picture. Grows up to 15 ft.

VARIETIES :   *P. A. Pollardii.* Possibly a hybrid with the peach, but with larger, brighter flowers.

P. persica (the Peach). The peach and its garden varieties like a hotter sun than we can usually give them. Seedling peaches grown from stones often make attractive trees with pink blossom in early April, and excellent fruit, but they do not move well. On the other hand such seedlings are longer-lived and healthei̇r trees than the named varieties which are grafted on plum root-stocks. The peach grows about 15 ft. high.

VARIETIES :   Clara Meyer. Double pink flowers.
Russell's Red. Charming red flowers.

CULTIVATION : Choose a warm, sunny spot, stake carefully and spray in March, with a colloidal copper wash to avoid the leaf-curl fungus which will otherwise ruin the growth of any grafted peach.

CHERRIES

The flowering cherries are, perhaps, the best of all ornamental trees for the small garden, admirable for spring effect and providing the light shade necessary for azaleas, hydrangeas, etc. They are best planted singly, as lawn specimens south of the beds in which shade-loving shrubs are grown, and, preferably, with a dark background of pines beyond.

P. serrulata (the Japanese Cherry). The garden forms with large flowers have many fine varieties. The following is a selection (with other species also) :

(*a*) *Early Cherries* (*early April*)

P. incisa (Cutleaf Cherry). A delightful dwarf tree or large bush. One of the finest for the small garden. Masses of small white or pale pink blossoms.

P. Sargentii. A species flowering at the same time as the above with beautiful pink flowers on short stalks, and fine autumn colour.

P. serrulata var. *mutabilis.* This makes a tall tree eventually up to 40 ft. or more, but flowers when 7 or 8 ft. high. The small flowers are beautifully shaped and produced in great masses among the young, copper-coloured leaves. Good autumn colour.

Tai Haku. Has very large single white flowers that appear among the bright copper-coloured young leaves. Also early flowering. Perhaps the finest of the cherries.

Yoshino. One of the most beautiful early-flowering sorts covering itself with single white blossoms in early April on the naked branches.

P. subhirtella (Spring Cherry). Masses of blush-pink or white blossom.

(b) Mid-season Cherries (late April, early May)

P. avium flore pleno (Double Gean). A double form of our wild cherry, makes a tall tree.

P. serrulata Ama-no-gawa. Upright, like a Lombardy poplar on a small scale, the branches smothered with fragrant pink, single or semi-double blossoms.

Hokusai. Shapely double blush-pink blossoms in picturesque clusters very effective against the dark wood of the branches.

P. s. rosea (Cheal's Weeping Cherry). Double pink flowers on a fine weeping tree. Requires some skill in training to make it form a good head.

Shirotæ. Shrubby but vigorous habit with double white blossom

(c) Late Cherries (May)

Kanzan. The large-flowered, double, pink cherry of spreading habit, much used for street planting.

Shirofugen. A tall-growing cherry with pendent white blossoms, very attractive as a standard.

Sho-get-su. So free flowering that it often fails to grow much, this cherry has very long-stalked, pendent, very double, white flowers. It makes a lovely little tree for the small garden.

CULTIVATION : The cherries like a sunny position in the open and do well on limy or acid soils. Spray against caterpillars and aphis (see Pests, page 644). It is best not to prune cherries but to tie any misplaced branches into better positions until they harden. With a little tuition any amateur can bud most of them on to young geans which make good stocks. Bull-finches strip the buds wholesale in the early mornings unless dealt with. Cherries can be moved safely even when quite large.

PLUMS

The flowering plums are lovely in early spring but rather dull trees for the rest of the year. The two best unfortunately have reddish-purple foliage which is apt to make a sudden blob of sullen maroon in the garden landscape, difficult to harmonise.

P. cerasifera (Cherry Plum). Usually seen as the variety *Pissardii* with reddish-purple foliage and white blossom in earliest spring. 15-20 ft.

P. Blireiana. A very pretty double pink blossom in early spring, reddish-purple leaves. Grows to about 8 ft.

CULTIVATION : No objection to limy soil, sunny position.

ROBINIA (Locust) Order LEGUMINOSÆ

R. pseudoacacia. One of the best of the larger garden trees with rich green leaves brighter than most, enjoying town atmosphere and having racemes of scented white flowers in early June.

VARIETIES : *R. p. Decaisneana.* Fragrant light rose-coloured flowers.
CULTIVATION : A poor soil is best. Prune when young by shortening long shoots and encouraging a definite leader as any wind breaks the branches easily.

SORBUS Order ROSACEÆ

This is the whitebeam and rowan family. There are many exotic kinds of rowan, but our own native is hard to beat.

S. aria (Whitebeam). A small tree growing up to 40 ft., with plum-like leaves with a silver-white underside attractively displayed in a wind. Red berries in autumn.

S. aucuparia (Rowan or Mountain Ash). A small tree growing up to 30 ft., with pinnate leaves and large heads of red berries from August to November.

CULTIVATION : Not particular as to soil. Easily grown from seed.

STYRAX Order STYRACACEÆ

S. japonica. A graceful little tree about 10 ft. high, or more, with charming small white flowers hanging down from the branches in June. To show its full charm it should be grown up as a standard so that the flowers may be seen from below when it makes a very attractive feature for any garden.

CULTIVATION : Sandy or loamy soil and a position likely to avoid spring frosts. Can be grown from seed, but is not a fast grower.

PART FIVE

FOOD PRODUCTION
FRUIT

CHAPTER I

Fruit Growing in General

HOW fortunate it is that fruit can be grown in almost all parts of Great Britain. Hardy fruits seem quite happy over a wide range of soils, providing they are given the necessary care and attention. The great thing is to ensure the right balance between growth on one hand and fruit bearing on the other. No one wants a stunted tree or bush and yet, on the other hand, when the tree grows too fast it will produce too much leaf and wood growth and, in consequence, little fruit. A tree that makes a tremendous amount of soft, succulent growth is very subject to both parasitic and functional diseases.

Unfortunately to-day there are a large number of pests and diseases out to attack fruit trees and bushes, and though it is probably true to say that if the soil is correctly manured and is rich in humus these troubles are never so severe, yet there are always insects to fight and fungoid spores to kill which come in from the garden next door or from the neighbouring copse or wood. Most fruit growers find it necessary to carry out a definite spraying programme and details of the control of pests and diseases will be found in Part Eight.

Be very careful when planting fruit trees and bushes. They are going to be down for a long time and so it is worth while taking a great deal of trouble in the choice of varieties, and in the forms of the trees and bushes—in the selection of the kinds of fruit that are to be planted, and of course in the selection of the soil. There is the site and aspect to be considered, together with the problems concerning cultivation, pruning and manuring. It isn't sufficient just to buy a fruit tree and then to stick it in the ground, so follow the instructions given in this section, with care.

SOIL

More detailed suggestions with regard to suitable soils are given in the chapter devoted to individual fruits. It must be made quite clear here, however, that a much deeper examination of soil is necessary, for even the most dwarfing trees may send down roots 10 ft. and gooseberry bushes are known to send their roots down 8 ft. The soil surveyor, therefore, uses the special soil augur to test the soil. It is sufficient, however, to dig down at least 3 ft. so as to see whether the subsoil is impenetrable or consists of sodden clay. Under such conditions the roots of deep-seating trees and bushes would, of course, perish. It isn't that the richest soil is the most suitable, because over-rich land will cause a tree to make overmuch growth. As a matter of fact, rich soils are more suitable for blackcurrants and raspberries than they are for apples and pears. Sometimes you get a soil in which the surface layer is very disappointing indeed and then find better layers of soil lower down. Such land is quite suitable and the tree roots do not take long to get into the good strata and do well.

No one wants a stunted tree or bush and yet, on the other hand, when the tree grows too fast it will produce too much leaf and wood growth. The point to remember, therefore, is that it makes a tremendous amount of soil, succulent growth is very subject to

PREPARING THE SOIL

When preparing land for fruit trees bastard trenching should be carried out as advised in Part One, Chapter III, pages 51-52. During the operation all perennial weeds must be removed, but no farmyard manure or compost need be added. It is always better to apply the organic manure as a top dressing on the surface of the ground all round the fruit trees and bushes after they have been planted. Such organic matter, be it dung or properly composted vegetable refuse, will act as a mulch and ensure that the moisture is retained in the soil. Further, the worms will come up and pull the organic matter into the ground bit by bit and, in this way, the necessary humus content of the soil will be built up.

When trees are to be planted in grass there is no need to dig the whole of the area over. All that is necessary is to dig out holes 3 ft. square, and 9 ins. deep, and then to break up the sub-soil below with a fork, without bringing it to the surface in any way. The trees should always be planted shallowly and soon after the hole is dug. It never does to prepare a large number of holes beforehand because when this is done the earth becomes dried out in droughty weather or water-logged in wet.

After the bastard trenching is done, in the normal manner in the autumn, and the trees are in the ground, no cultivations will be necessary until the spring when the first hoeing will be carried out. Further hoeings will proceed during the summer. It is well worthwhile, in the case of strawberries and bush fruits, to keep the ground clean all through the season, but once the top fruits are established, say after the first 5 or 6 years, it is possible to allow weeds to grow after the end of June and then, having cut these down in the autumn, to dig them in very shallowly. The weeds will take out of the soil any excess nitrogen and so help with the colouring and ripening, especially of dessert apples. It is a good plan to sow the orchard with Chewing's Fescue grass seed, using ½ oz. per square yard.

MANURING

Whole books have been written on the manuring of fruit trees, and those who want the fullest details on the subject should consult the work of the late Dr. T. Wallace in the Long Ashton Research Station. It can, however, be stated quite broadly that the main plant food required by gooseberries, redcurrants and dessert apples is potash in some form or other. In the case of cooking apples, blackberries, raspberries, pears and strawberries, the main manurial requirement is potash plus a fair quantity of nitrogen. But with peaches, nectarines, damsons, plums, black-currants, cherries, apricots and cob nuts the main requirement is undoubtedly nitrogen, if a regular supply of annual shoot growth (on which the fruit is borne) is to develop. This group likes to have a little potash, but they are primarily nitrogen lovers.

It is, however, important to keep up the organic content of any soil and, if possible, the nitrogen should be given in a bulky organic form such as dung, wool shoddy or properly composted vegetable refuse, especially in the cases of the trees and bushes that have to produce luscious fruits in the summer, i.e. plums, peaches, raspberries, blackcurrants and the like. Trace element deficiencies too often appear when soils have been fed, or over-fed, with certain types of chemical fertilisers year after year. The humus content of the soil must always be considered.

There are, however, a number of factors which must be borne in mind. Clean cultivations and severe or hard pruning, for instance, have a similar effect to an application of nitrogen. It is not advisable, therefore, to feed heavily with a nitrogenous fertiliser if you are going to prune heavily. Trees growing in grass orchards are often short of nitrogen because the grass takes up this plant food and the trees suffer in consequence. Here, if the leaves of the trees show starvation symptoms, it is often necessary to give doses of nitrogen. These symptoms are, incidentally, a yellowing of the foliage. (For further details see *The Diagnosis of Mineral Deficiences in Plants*, by Dr. T. Wallace, published by H.M. Stationery Office.)

Trees on vigorous root stocks naturally make strong growth.

But if the grower allows his trees to be badly eaten by cater-pillars or ruined by aphids or scab then, of course, the leaves cannot carry out their normal function and so the trees tend to be starved of elaborated, or leaf-manufactured, sap. Thus the manurial programme is made more difficult.

What general advice, then, can be given ? (1) Apply mulches of composted vegetable refuse, well-rotted manure or spent hops once a year, giving heavier dressings to the trees that need nitrogen. (2) Feed right from the start land known to be poor by applying a dressing of an organic fertiliser like fish manure, meat and bone meal, or hoof and horn meal, at 4-5 ozs. per square yard. (3) Give the trees and bushes which ask for potash, wood ashes at $\frac{1}{2}$ lb. per square yard or, if these are unobtainable, purchase one of the proprietary flue dusts and apply it at 5 ozs. to the square yard every December.

Lime should be applied as a precaution, for it will help to lighten the heavier soils and to correct acidity in light land. Apply hydrated lime at 7 ozs. to the square yard in January, after planting the fruit trees and bushes, and give a further dressing, say every 5 years, except, of course, in the case of chalky or limestone soils. Lime will help to release the potash present in the soil.

SITUATION

SHELTER

Shelter is quite important so that the trees may be protected from cold winds in April and May, when they are blossoming, and so that similar protection may be given to the fruits in the summer and autumn. There is nothing worse than having a good crop blown down by a gale. Most gardens have the necessary pro-tection, and care has always to be taken never to plant trees and bushes in draughts, caused, say, by paths leading to the front garden, or from back gates and the like.

FROST

Care must be taken never to plant fruit trees and bushes in low-lying spots, or frost holes as they are sometimes called. The great thing is to try and arrange for the " frozen " air to be able to flow away somewhere lower down (see Fig. 20). " Frozen " air moves very much like water, that is to say it finds its lowest level and then fills up any valley or area where it cannot get away. Then, when the height of the layers of " frozen " air reaches the branches of the trees and bushes, of course the blossoms are killed. Sometimes walled-in gardens are great frost traps though designed in the first place to give extra warmth and protection. It is therefore as important to have free air drainage as it is to have good soil drainage.

SUN

Another important consideration must be sunshine, especially in districts around towns and cities where the smoke and soot are likely to diminish sunlight. Don't choose a site over-shadowed by tall buildings or trees. You cannot ensure healthy fruit bud formation unless the sun can get in to the trees and help to ripen the wood, let alone the fruit of course, later on.

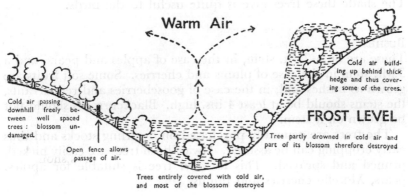

Warm Air →

Cold air building up behind thick hedge and thus covering some of the trees.

Cold air passing downhill freely between well spaced trees : blossom undamaged.

Open fence allows passage of air.

FROST LEVEL

Tree partly drowned in cold air and part of its blossom therefore destroyed

Trees entirely covered with cold air, and most of the blossom destroyed

FIG. 20   A FROST HOLE

WATER

It is always necessary to have plenty of water available so that efficient spraying may be carried out. It is nothing to use 5 or 6 gals. of diluted wash all over the tree in the winter or summer, and bigger specimens need far more. With 300 trees to the acre, as you may get in the case of bush types, it will be seen that a large gallonage of water must always be " on tap."

TYPES AND SHAPES OF TREES

It is possible to obtain trees and bushes in all kinds of shapes. (See Fig. 21). The garden owner should study the space he has available and should determine to grow the types and shapes of trees which will give him the best results and yet take up the minimum amount of room. It is seldom advisable in small gardens to plant standards or half-standards. The greatest advantage should always be taken of walls and fences.

STANDARDS

Suitable only for the grass orchard, the trees being very slow in coming into bearing. They are on a stem 6-7 ft. high, and need 30-40 ft. of room.

HALF-STANDARDS

These have stems 4-6 ft. high and are usually used in poultry runs, so that the birds cannot easily get up into the branches. The shade these trees give is quite useful to the birds.

BUSHES

These are on a $2\frac{1}{2}$-ft. stem, in the case of apples and pears, and a $3\frac{1}{2}$-ft. stem in the case of plums and cherries. Some soft fruits are grown as bushes and, in the case of gooseberries and redcurrants, the stems should be at least 4 ins. high. Blackcurrants should not be grown on a stem.

The trees are generally purchased on dwarfing stocks and thus early cropping can be assured. Dwarf bush trees are easily picked, pruned and sprayed. This form of tree is suitable for apples, pears, Morello cherries and plums.

CORDONS

This is a tree with only a single stem. The side growths are pruned back hard and thus short-fruiting spurs are encouraged right up the stem. A cordon takes up very little room. It enables a large number of varieties to be grown in a small garden. It produces high quality fruit. It is usually planted upright and then, a year later, is trained to an angle of 45°. Two or three years after that the cordon may be " lowered " once more so as to be at an angle of 30°. It is possible, of course, to train a cordon parallel to the ground or to have double or treble stem cordons.

DWARF PYRAMIDS OR FUSEAU

These trees may be likened to an upright cordon on which the side branches have been allowed to develop. The tiers of short branches spring from the main stem, the lowest being 2 ft. above soil level.

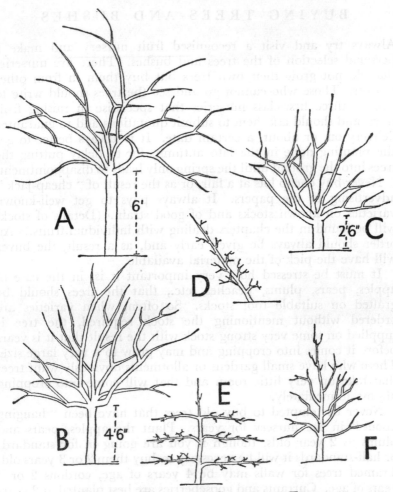

FIG. 21   TYPES AND SHAPES OF TREES
A, *Standard*—B, *Half-standard*—C, *Bush*—D, *Cordon*—
E, *Espalier*—F, *Dwarf Pyramid or Fuseau*

ESPALIERS AND FANS

In the case of espaliers, 5 or 6 tiers of horizontal branches are
trained so as to grow 1 ft. apart from each other at right angles
to the main stem.   They are suited to apples and pears.

In the case of fan-shaped trees, the main stem will be 18 ins.
or so high and the branches will grow out shaped like a fan.
This system is adopted for apricots, cherries, figs, nectarines and
plums.

BUYING TREES AND BUSHES

Always try and visit a recognised fruit nursery and make a personal selection of the trees and bushes. There are nurseries that do not grow their own trees but buy them in from other sources. Those who cannot go and see the trees should write to two or three first-class nurseries that specialise in raising fruit trees, and should ask them to submit quotations and to guarantee delivery on, or about, a certain date. It is always better to get the planting done in the late autumn, for to delay putting the trees into the ground until the spring only leads to disappointment.

Never buy cheap lots at a fair, or as the result of " cheap-jack " advertising in the papers. It always pays to get well-known varieties on known stocks and of good strain. (Details of stocks will be found in the chapters dealing with individual fruits.) An order should always be given early and, as a result, the buyer will have the pick of the material available.

It must be stressed how very important it is, in the case of apples, pears, plums, peaches, etc., that the trees should be grafted on suitable root stocks. So often, when varieties are ordered without mentioning the stock required, the tree is supplied on some very strong stock with the result that it is years before it comes into cropping and may grow to a very large size. Those who have small gardens or allotments obviously want trees that take up very little room and that will come into cropping almost immediately.

Never be tempted to buy old trees that have been " hanging about " in the nursery for years. Plant the apples, pears and plums as 2 year olds, though if you are going in for standards or half-standards it will be necessary to buy them 2 or 3 years old. Trained trees for walls may be 4 years of age, cordons 2 or 3 years of age. Currants and gooseberries are best planted at 2 years of age, but blackberries, loganberries, raspberries and strawberries should always be planted as 1 year olds. People imagine that by buying an old tree they will get quicker results, but an old tree or bush is usually stunted and invariably leads to disappointment.

FIVE TYPES OF FRUIT GROWING

Many readers may only be able to have one or two fruit trees in their garden and they will plant them where they can. It is useful to have an apple at the corner of a small lawn, or to plant plums or pears against walls or fences. A blackberry or loganberry can be trained up the netting surrounding a tennis court while pergola posts, originally designed perhaps for rambler roses, could be used for cordon apples or pears, or even for the attractive Japanese Wineberry. The usual fruit-growing attempts however may be divided up into 5 main groups :

(1) THE MODEL FRUIT PLOT

I have purposely called it the model fruit plot, because this is an ideal way of growing and producing the best fruit. In the first place the fruit is grown on its own. No vegetables or flowers are grown in between and so there is no interference with spraying, manuring or whatever cultivations may be necessary. The planning is carefully done so that the plums and cherries, which love lots of nitrogen in an organic form, can be interplanted with blackberries, loganberries and blackcurrants, which need similar food. Apples on the other hand (particularly dessert types) seem to need large quantities of potash, and these can be interplanted with gooseberries and redcurrants which ask for similar treatment. Later, such an area may have to be grassed down to reduce the amount oi nitrogen in the soil and then, of course, it will be necessary to plant the gooseberries and redcurrants on their own. For this reason most people will prefer to have another part of the fruit plot devoted to strawberries, raspberries, redcurrants and gooseberries, which ask for good cultivation, plus a certain amount of nitrogen and ample potash. Thus it is seen that the fruit plot is divided up into 3 parts : (1) What might be called the nitrogen plot ; (2) the potash plot, and (3) the nitrogen plus potash plot.

It is usually advisable to plant trees on dwarfing or semi-dwarfing stocks so that they take up the minimum amount of room. Few gardens to-day can cope with large standard and half-standard trees.

(2) THE GRASS ORCHARD

This will suit the man who owns a grass field next to his house and wants to plant it up with standard or half-standard trees. He will probably keep the grass down with poultry and/or geese, or he will cut it two or three times a year, say, in June and September. The cut grass is then piled around the trees and will thus supply the necessary humus to the soil. (See illustration facing page 32.) It is often necessary to apply nitro-chalk in addition, at about 2 ozs. to the square yard, in order to give a little extra nitrogen, and to encourage the

379

bacterial activity in and among the cut grass. This is especially necessary in soils that tend to be acid.

Standard trees take a long time to come into bearing ; they produce large unwieldy trees which are difficult to spray properly and some people consider such an orchard a "white elephant." Where, however, efficient spraying facilities are available, and where the branches are just thinned and no attempt is made to spur prune, such a system may suit garden owners in the country.

(3) THE WALLED-IN GARDEN

In the past most fruits were planted in the walled-in garden and, as a result, it either meant that the other crops, be they flowers or vegetables, had to play second fiddle or vice versa. It is impossible to manure trees correctly if they are to be grown in ground which is fed with large quantities of dung, needed to produce good vegetables. Furthermore, it is impossible to spray fruit trees as they should be sprayed if there are all kinds of valuable crops below them that would be injured by the spray fluid.

In the olden days, when there was plenty of labour, compromises were possible. The trees were dug up every few years to be root pruned and so the excessive vigour induced by the feeding given to the vegetables was checked. When spraying was carried out all the crops below were carefully covered up with tarpaulin sheets. To-day labour is the great problem, and so it is obviously better to keep the fruit and vegetables apart. By all means if you have a walled-in garden use the walls for fruits, but do not attempt to plant the centre of the garden with fruit trees of any kind. If there are any there already it will be better to remove them, if only to plant them in a corner of the walled-in garden on their own.

Furthermore, as has already been pointed out on page 375, walled-in gardens may be frost traps, while land that, because of its shallowness, is quite suitable for growing vegetables may be quite unsuited for fruit production. The main advantage of the walled-in garden is that it is sheltered from the wind and that its walls, being warm, do make the production of the more " delicate " type of fruit possible.

(4) THE LARGE PLANTATION

The term plantation is generally used to describe a unit of fruit trees, say, of 5 acres or more. In this case the owner usually becomes a commercial fruit-grower and sells his fruit and as this is not a commercial book, no further details need be given. It is, however, worthwhile stating that the term plantation, when applied to fruit production, implies that the soil is to be cultivated intermittently. The plantation, therefore, may be described as the cultivated orchard, and the orchard as the grassed down plantation !

(5) THE NORMAL KITCHEN GARDEN

Many readers will only be able to use their kitchen gardens for fruit tree planting, but if they do find it possible to plant the trees and bushes in a little plot on their own so much the better. It is always very difficult to keep trees growing at their normal rate and to keep them free from pests and diseases if vegetables have to be the main consideration. The one advantage of a kitchen garden is that it is likely to be more sheltered than an open field.

IMPORTANCE OF STOCKS

It is possible to-day to produce trees which will suit the requirements of the individual. This information is available as the result of the work of the East Malling Research Station. The varieties chosen are grafted, or budded, on to stocks which may be described as the root system of the trees. It is the stock that largely determines whether the tree is going to be weak growing and crop early in its career or whether it is to be a strong grower, with the result that cropping may be delayed for a large number of years. It is, therefore, very important to get a guarantee when purchasing a fruit tree with regard to the stock, as well as to the variety.

Details of the various stocks used for different species of fruit trees will be found in the chapters dealing with each fruit individually (see chapter II, page 397).

PROPAGATION OF FRUIT STOCKS

It is necessary to propagate the numbered, or named, Malling stocks vegetatively and this means that the work has to be done by stooling, layering or cuttings. Occasionally root cuttings are used, but at present only in the case of certain plums and cherries.

STOOLING

Most stocks are propagated by stooling. (See Fig. 22.) The

named, or numbered, root stocks should be planted upright (A) in rows 3 ft. 6 ins. apart, with the parent stocks 12 ins. apart in the rows. They are then allowed to grow for one year without being pruned (B) and, early in the winter, are cut down to within 1 in. of ground level (C). The following summer 5 or 6 shoots should develop and, when these are 5 ins. high, soil is drawn up to them to a height of $2\frac{1}{2}$ ins. (D). A further earthing up is done when the growths are 9-10 ins. high, this time to a height of 4-5 ins. Another earthing should be done in July, when the growths are 18 ins. high, though if this month is a very dry one it may be better to

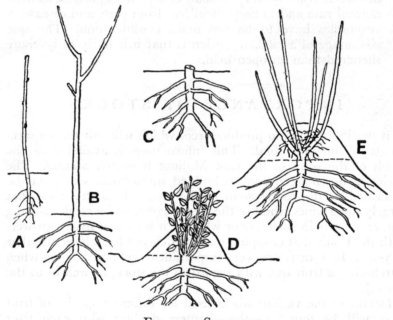

FIG. 22   STOOLING

wait till August. At this final earthing, the soil should be drawn up 7-8 ins. At the second earthing up it is worthwhile placing a spadeful of soil into the middle of each stool to cause the shoots to bend outwards a little. This is said to assist rooting.

In November, the soil is drawn away from the stools and it will be found that each shoot has developed a separate root system (E). Each one is then cut off and is planted out in nursery rows ready for budding or grafting. Budding may be done the following summer and grafting the following March or April twelve month.

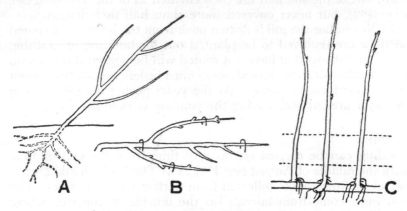

FIG. 23 LAYERING. (Dotted lines show progressive
earthing up of young growth)

After the newly-rooted shoots have been removed the parent
stool is left exposed until fresh young shoots start to develop the
following spring. The earthing-up process commences once more
and thus a further batch of stocks are produced with a minimum
amount of labour. Stock stool beds should remain productive
for 15-20 years.

LAYERING
This is widely used for plum and cherry root stocks. (See Fig. 23.)
The stocks are planted at an angle of 45° along the rows,
pointing towards the south (A). Rows are 4 ft. 6 ins. apart and the
stocks 1½-2½ ft. apart in the rows. The following winter (January
or February) the parent stocks are pruned. All weak laterals are
cut back to ½ in. from their base, while strong laterals are tipped
lightly. A shallow trench is then made along each row and the
parent stocks are pegged down into this, so that they are lower
at the tip of the stem than at its base. Stout wire or pieces of fairly
elastic wood are used for pegging (B). The layers are then covered
with a good inch of fine soil.
In April, young growth will appear on the layers. This should
be covered with further soil (C). When growth again appears above
this, a further earthing is given, and another, and the last, when
the green growth shows once more. This process of earthing
ensures that the base of each shoot is grown in darkness. This
makes it more ready to develop roots later on.
Following these initial earthings the shoots are allowed to grow

3 ins. out of the soil and are then earthed as in the stool-bed (see page 382), but never covered more than half their length.

In November the soil is drawn back from the layers. All rooted portions are removed to be planted out for budding or grafting, whilst any shoots that have not rooted will be pegged down again. Even if all shoots have rooted, some must be left, say, one every foot of row, for future layering. As the years go by, the old parts of the layer are cut out, leaving the younger ones to carry on.

BUDDING

Budding can be carried out at any time from the end of June until the middle of August (see Fig. 24). The buds should always be taken from shoots collected from perfectly healthy trees. The best buds come from laterals on the outside of the tree where there is plenty of light. Immediately the shoot is severed from its parent, cut off the leaves (to prevent further transpiration) leaving at least ¼ in. of stalks (A). Cut off the soft tip of the shoot and, if the buds are not going to be used immediately, put the stripped lateral into water.

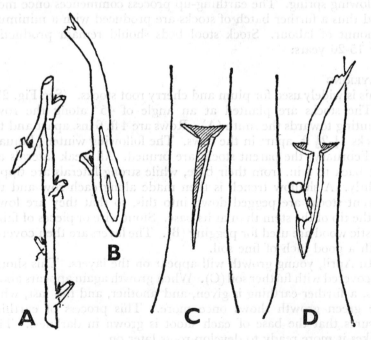

FIG. 24   BUDDING

62. Planting a fruit tree. (Note soil laid on sacking, pruning of roots, and planting board with bamboo in the nick where tree will stand)

63. A well-planted fruit tree. (Note tree planted and staked, and turf being replaced upside down)

64. A well-pruned blackcurrant

65. Raspberry canes pruned and thinned

66. *Pruning and nailing up a wall cherry tree*

67. *Protecting fruit with a screen*

Extract the bud which is to be inserted into the stock by placing the edge of the knife blade ½ in. below the bud and its leaf stalk and, by making a shallow slicing movement, pass the knife blade beneath the bud so that it emerges 1 in. above it (A). Do not complete the cut but grip the sliced portion and tear away the bark in a strip. This strip is used as a handle (B). Cut the shield of bark which holds the bud thinly so that it will be pliable and mould itself to the curved surface that lies beneath the bark on the stock. There is no need to try and remove the wood at the base of the bud as so many gardening books advise.

Make a T-shaped cut in the stock (C). The upper part of the T should be ½ in. in length and the vertical cut of the T about ¾ in. long. Raise the edges of the bark or rind, as it is called, by inserting the thin wedge-shaped end of the budding knife and then slide the bud the right way up into position (D), so that the bud shield lies just underneath the raised surface of the downward part of the T. Cut off the rough end or top strip, just at the top of the T cut, and press the rind or bark back into position. Bind firmly round with damped raffia or adhesive tape. Work round as though putting on a puttee, just leaving the bud exposed. There are proprietary adhesive tapes which give excellent results.

When raffia is used it will be necessary to release the tie in 4 weeks and, if the bud has " taken," the leaf stalk should come away naturally. If the stalk remains on the bud and looks dry and shrivelled then the budding has failed, and if the season is not too advanced another bud could be inserted in its place. Some people insist that it is worthwhile smearing the buds and the incisions with petroleum jelly immediately after tying.

The following February the stocks should be cut down to within 4 ins. of the bud and it is to this " snag," as it is called, that the bud growth is tied.

The snag should be removed at the end of August by a cut made at an angle of 45°, just above the new bud growth. This cut surface should then be smeared with vaseline.

GRAFTING

Grafting usually takes place in March or April. The stone fruits are grafted first and the apples and pears afterwards. Pears if anything should be worked before apples. The one-year-old pieces of wood should be collected during the winter pruning. These " scions " should be the stouter prunings and the shoots should be left at full length and be buried 6 ins. deep in moist sand or soil, in a spot where protection can be given from drying winds. In this way the wood keeps alive until the grafting season.

At grafting time this scion wood is cut into lengths of 3 or 4 buds, discarding the unripened tips. The upper end of each scion should be cut close above a bud. The stock should then be cut down to within 3 ins. of soil level and, on one side of the stock, a slanting cut should be made upwards, 1 in. or so long. A similar slanting cut of the same length should then be made in the scion wood and, in order to ensure that these two cut surfaces fit nicely together, a little tongue is made about one quarter of the way down the cut surface of the stock and a similar tongue in about the same position in the cut surface of the scion. These tongues then fit into each other and hold the stock and scion together while the grafter gets on with the tying. It is absolutely necessary to see that the cambium layer (which lies just underneath the bark) on one side of the cut surface of the stock lies exactly underneath the cambium layer on one side of the scion.

Tie with raffia or tape in such a way that the cambiums are not separated. See that the stock bud, which should lie mid-way between the top and the bottom of the cut surface of the scion is covered and not left exposed as in the case of budding. When raffia is used it is necessary to paint over all the cut surfaces with grafting wax. The following formula makes a good wax mixture : resin 5 lbs., burgundy pitch 1 lb. 10 ozs., tallow 1 lb. 4 ozs., paraffin wax 1 lb. 4 ozs., venetian red 1 lb. 8 ozs. and, of course, *pro rata*. Heat the resin and burgundy pitch together till melted then add the paraffin wax and 1 lb. of the tallow. When melted and just boiling take the pot off the fire and stir in the venetian red. Grease the hands well with the spare tallow. Pour a portion of the mixture into a bucket of cold water and then pull the material about as though making toffee. Re-heat this wax over a flame when it is to be used and paint over the raffia while hot with a small brush. Ready-made grafting wax can also be obtained now in tins of various sizes.

When adhesive tapes are used for tying in the grafts, waxing is not necessary. Constriction may occur the following early June and it is then that the raffia or tape may be cut. The following early May, the newly-grafted scions should be gone over and any growths that have developed from the stocks should be cut off. In early June the growths from the scion should be examined, the end one being left and the side growths being pinched back to 5 leaves. It is after this that the tension on the ties is usually released. Most gardeners like to stake the scions at this stage, and they push into the ground near the stocks a cane or wand about 2 ft. in length. The root stock is then tied to this below the union, and the scion growth lightly tied to the support 6 ins. above the union. With plums it is often necessary to have taller canes and to make more ties as they grow rather quickly and remain slender.

PROPAGATION OF BUSHES

Soft fruit bushes can be propagated quite easily by means of cuttings. These hardwood cuttings are best taken in the autumn, or early winter, and should be inserted into well-aerated, well-drained " open " soil which retains sufficient moisture throughout the summer. All cuttings should be taken from healthy bushes only. Further details, however, with regard to the propagation of soft fruits will be found under the headings dealing with each individual fruit. Gooseberries don't root as easily as blackcurrants or redcurrants, but the tip is to strike them before the leaves have fallen.

PRUNING FRUIT TREES

It is never easy to write about pruning. It is far better to demonstrate it in the orchard. But it is possible to give general rules, and this is the aim of the notes given below.

Pruning must be divided into two main parts : (1) winter pruning, and (2) summer pruning. In addition, there are the various sub-divisions : (*a*) the pruning of hard fruits like apples and pears ; (*b*) the pruning of stone fruits, like plums and cherries ; (*c*) the pruning of soft fruits, like gooseberries and blackcurrants ; (*d*) the pruning of cane fruits, like loganberries and raspberries, and (*e*) the pruning of wall fruits which ask for special treatment. In addition, of course, there are special types of pruning such as the delayed open centre, usually known as D.O.C., and the modified pruning methods carried out by those who like the dwarf pyramid or fuseau system.

To Prune or not to Prune ?
If trees or bushes are planted in November it is quite safe to cut back the leaders in the early spring of the following year. Trees, however, that are not planted until the turn of the year and that have weak root systems are better left until the following winter before being pruned hard back.

In the case of raspberries and blackcurrants it is always necessary to cut the canes or branches back to almost ground level at the time of planting.

WINTER PRUNING

The whole point of winter pruning is to build up a strong framework in the early stages of the tree on which the future fruit can be borne. It is also necessary to shape the framework according to the form required, so that a certain amount of wood may be removed to let in light and air, or to ensure that a branch grows in a certain direction.

Once the framework has been built up, and this usually takes 5 years, winter pruning can be reduced to a minimum so as to get the young tree into bearing. The principle to bear in mind, of course, is that the less winter pruning is carried out the more quickly will the tree come into bearing. Winter pruning does not promote fruiting as so many people believe. It encourages wood growth.

There can be a third stage in the life of a tree and that is when it is, say, 15-20 years of age. It has been cropping for some time and, because of the heavy cropping, the amount of wood produced has been reduced considerably. At this stage it may be necessary to start pruning fairly heavily again, with the idea of restoring the balance of growth. This applies particularly to apples and pears and not so much to plums and cherries. When trees are very old, of course, say, 50 years of age, it may only be necessary to thin the tree out, cut out a branch here and there, and to shorten any branches that are tending to droop down too close to the ground. It is never wise to do too much to an old tree in one year. It is better to spread what pruning is necessary over 3 or 4 winters.

Some may not quite understand what is meant by hard pruning and it is, therefore, necessary to explain that a gardener prunes a tree hard when he cuts back the leaders by, say, three-quarters. Leaders are the lengths of wood of the current year's growth (i.e. one year old only)which will be found at the ends of each branch in the winter. Light pruning, on the other hand, is when the leaders are only reduced by about one-quarter.

It will be noted that cuts are always made just above a bud at an angle of about 30°, the particular bud being selected in accordance with the direction in which one wants the new leaders to grow from that bud.

The other term used in pruning which refers to 1-year-old wood is " the lateral." This is the current year's side shoot, or side growth, which develops as the result of leader pruning (for that always encourages side growths to develop, especially when severe leader pruning is carried out), and this may be pruned back to within 3 or 4 buds of its base (this would be regarded as hard lateral pruning) or to within, say, 7 buds of the base (which would be regarded as moderate lateral pruning).

SUMMER PRUNING

Summer pruning is as a rule only carried out in the case of apples and pears, though there is a special type of summer pruning known as brutting, used for redcurrants (see page 451). Some exhibition growers of dessert gooseberries summer prune their bushes or cordons also. Normally, however, the summer pruning systems are two-fold. (1) The normal English method which is to cut back the laterals, or 1-year-old side growths, about half-way, i.e. to within 6 or 8 buds of their base, during August or September. The object of this is to improve the colour and appearance of the fruit, particularly dessert apples, as a result of the increased amount of light and air let into the tree.

(2) What I call the Anglicised Lorette system, which aims at encouraging the formation of fruit buds and at checking and directing the tree's growth. This system necessitates continued pruning during the summer months, but obviates any pruning during the winter. All laterals not required for the extension of growth are pruned back to within $\frac{1}{8}$ in. of their base, with a pair of secateurs, when they have reached a stage of semi-maturity. This usually means when they are 6 or 7 ins. long. The earliest and strongest laterals usually reach this state by the middle of June. Therefore, every fortnight or 3 weeks from this date until end of September, the bushes or cordons will be gone over and the laterals that have reached the right length and maturity will be pruned back hard. No shoot will be cut back, however, until it is the right length.

Any shoots that do not become semi-mature, or reach the 6-in. length by the end of September, should be left on the trees un-pruned until the following summer. The leaders or end growths (1 year olds) are never pruned back in the summer. They are left until May when they are cut back by about half if they are 12 ins. long or more, and by about three-quarters if they are only about 7 or 8 ins. long. The object of such pruning is to encourage the buds at the base of the leaders to break out into growth as well as to form a good strong leader that season.

This Anglicised Lorette system of pruning is always considered most revolutionary, but it does work well, especially in the south, and is excellent when used on cordons. In the north-west, where the rainfall is high, this system may prove unpractical because of the secondary growths that are sometimes produced. However, in the north-west it is always a good idea to grass down any orchard so as to reduce the amount of nitrogen pumped up into the trees.

HARD FRUITS
(See under APPLES and PEARS, pages 399 and 428.)

STONE FRUITS
Stone fruits are particularly susceptible to the silver leaf disease, *Stereum purpureum* (for further details see page 678). Experiments have shown that it is always better to prune during the summer when rapid formation of a gum barrier can be assured. Prune all stone fruits if possible in June, July or August, when the wounds will not allow spores of the silver leaf disease to enter. It is possible to tip leaders in the spring, however, when the sap is rising.

BUSH-LIKE SOFT FRUITS
As these have to be pruned differently the whole question is dealt with carefully under the heading of the individual fruits. (See pages 448-453.)

CANE FRUITS
Here the pruning largely consists of cutting down to ground level the canes that have borne fruit the previous season. (See illustration facing page 384). Occasionally with blackberries it is possible to retain some of the old wood and to cut back the laterals that have developed on them. (For further details see the instructions regarding individual cane fruits, page 446.)

WALL FRUITS
Wall trees are usually espalier or grid-iron in the case of apples and pears, and fan trained in the case of stone fruits. The shaping of the trees is usually done in the nursery in the early years and, in consequence, the trees are not usually bought until they are 4 or 5 years of age, or even older. The general treatment of espaliers is similar to that of cordons, that is to say, the Anglicised Lorette summer pruning is carried out as detailed on page 389.

The framework of the fan tree is usually completed in the third or fourth season, but it is a complicated process and needs the skill and practice of a good nurseryman or gardener. Once the fan has been established the object each winter is to cut out some of the old wood and retain the new, tying it against the wires provided. The experienced man is able to do much of this work in the summer.

ROUTINE SPRAYING

The spraying programme for the year should start with the application of a tar oil wash in December, using a 7½% solution, and applying it with plenty of force so that the tree is covered and soaked from top to toe. Apples, pears, plums, cherries, currants, gooseberries, blackberries, peaches, nectarines, apricots, raspberries and loganberries should all receive this spray.

WINTER PETROLEUM

Where bad attacks of woolly aphis, red spider or capsid bug occur, a 7½% solution of a D.N.C. petroleum wash should be applied early in March.

LIME-SULPHUR

For scab control, apply a pre-blossom lime-sulphur spray to apples and pears, using a strength of 1 part lime-sulphur in 30 parts of water. Follow this with a post-blossom spray, this time using a concentration of 1 in 80. A further spraying with lime-sulphur may be made 3 weeks later at 1 in 100. In the case of "sulphur-shy" varieties, Captan should be used instead.

Nicotine, or lead arsenate, may be incorporated with the second lime-sulphur spray to control apple sawfly and codlin moth respectively.

Raspberries, blackberries and loganberries should receive a spraying of liquid derris at blossoming time to keep down the raspberry beetle.

Gooseberries should be sprayed or dusted with derris to control sawfly and wilt, with lime-sulphur to control mildew.

Blackcurrants should be sprayed with lime-sulphur, 1 in 20, when the bulk of the leaves are the size of a two-shilling piece, i.e. just before the blossoms open, to check the big bud mite.

PLANTING CONSIDERATIONS

There are several things to bear in mind when planning out a home orchard, in addition to the manurial considerations mentioned on pages 373-374. Most trees need to be sprayed with a tar distillate wash in the winter but this will injure flowering shrubs, or green vegetables, if they be near at hand. A tar oil spray will, however, damage the cherry plum or myrobalan, all nut trees and strawberry plants. These will then have to be planted on their own.

Lime-sulphur spraying has to be carried out, particularly in the case of apples and pears, to control fungus diseases. There are, however, certain apples like Stirling Castle, St. Cecilia, Belle de Boskoop, Newton Wonder, Beauty of Bath and Duchess Favourite, which are susceptible to lime-sulphur damage ; the last three only in a very dry summer. Most yellow varieties of gooseberries are sulphur-shy and should, therefore, never be interplanted among trees that have to be sprayed with lime-sulphur in the spring and early summer. Davison's Eight blackcurrant is also sulphur-shy. Those who want to pick any kind of gooseberry early should not interplant bushes between apples or pears because a deposit of lime-sulphur may remain on the berries. In the case of sulphur-shy varieties Captan should be used.

POLLINATION

There are two kinds of fruit trees : (1) those which will set fruit with their own pollen—the self-fertile or self-compatible ones, and (2) those which produce little or no fruit unless the blossoms are fertilised by pollen from another variety—these are the self-sterile or self-incompatible ones.

Some of the self-compatible varieties produce very little good pollen and so are useless as pollinators.

When planting an orchard, care must be taken to see that varieties which will pollinate each other are chosen, and that these are planted together. It is useless, as a rule, to plant single trees or large blocks of a single variety. For instance, for a Cox's Orange Pippin plant a Worcester or James Grieve ; for a Coe's Golden Drop plant Oullin's Golden Gage ; or for Early Rivers cherry plant Governor Wood. Full pollination tables will be found on pages 401, 412, 429 and 438.

ACTUAL PLANTING

It is always better to plant a young tree than an old one, except of course in the case of specially trained trees such as espaliers and fans. A young tree gets over transplanting much more quickly than an old one for it quickly accustoms itself to the new position. In the case of top fruits the bush trees should be 1 or 2 years of age, the half-standard trees 3 years old, the standard trees 3 or 4 years old and the cordons 2 years old. Currants and gooseberries may be bought as 2-year-old bushes or cordons. Blackcurrants can be 1 or 2 years of age, while with blackberries and loganberries 1-year-old rooted tips are generally purchased. With raspberries nice young canes are needed, and with strawberries, recently struck runners which should be ready to put out in late July, August or early September.

Always make a rough plan on paper before ordering the trees and bushes so that you know exactly the number you require. It is a great mistake to order more than you need. Buy from a reliable nurseryman and when the trees arrive unpack them immediately, checking them over with the order to see that they are correct. If you are not satisfied write immediately and complain. If the weather is very frosty when the trees arrive, leave them in the bale in a shed and drop a post card to the nurseryman advising him that you are doing this. If you can unpack the trees, see that you cover the roots with soil in some odd corner of the garden until you are ready to plant them in their permanent position. It is quite easy to dig out a trench for this purpose. This is known as hecling the trees in.

Though it is possible to plant any time between November and the beginning of March it is always better to get the job done during November if possible. This gives the trees a chance of getting established before a hard winter sets in.

Do not dig very deep holes. In normal soil one 9 ins. deep will do. In very heavy clay land a hole 3 ins. deep is ample. The hole need not be wider than 3×3 ft. for top fruits, and no wider than 18 ins. for soft fruits. These, by the way, needn't be planted deeper than 6 ins.

With the top fruits that are budded or grafted, take great care to see that the union of stock and scion is not buried. If the nurseryman has grafted low down this may force the grower to plant particularly shallowly. It is silly to purchase a tree on a definite stock and then to plant so deeply that the scion, i.e. the variety itself, starts to make its own roots and so ruins the growth-regulating effect of the stock. Trees that scion root usually " leap " into strong growth and cropping is delayed.

Do not dig out holes weeks beforehand or they will either become dried out, or water-logged. Put a little mound in the bottom of the hole on which the base of the stems may sit, and then spread the roots out evenly like the rays of the sun, keeping them in the right position if necessary, by putting half a spadeful of earth over them at a time and treading it well down. It does help matters to use a planting board with a fairly large "nick" in it (see illustration facing page 384). The tree then fits into the nick and the soil is put into position under the board to start with. This ensures that the tree is exactly where it should be. Cut back any damaged portions of the roots with a sharp knife. Put the soil back into the hole, treading firmly all the time, easing the tree up and down very slightly from time to time so as to encourage the soil to trickle between the roots. When the hole is filled there should be a slight mound towards the centre, so as to allow for settling down afterwards. If the tree is planted on grass the same procedure may be carried out, except that the turf will be buried upside down above the roots and not below them, a little more soil being placed on top to level up the hole. (See illustration facing page 384).

STAKING AND WIRING

Bush trees should be given a diagonal stake, i.e. this should be driven into the ground at an angle of about 45°. Cordons will be tied to wires ; standard and half-standards will be provided with double stakes with a cross-bar nailed in position to which the stem of the tree is tied. Bands of sacking 3 ins. wide and 9 ins. long are wrapped around the stem and, at this point, the trees are tied to the stake or cross-bar with tarred string. In this way the tree itself is not injured. These ties must be released in the summer when the stem swells, and tied up again.

In areas where rabbits and hares may do harm (and it is surprising what harm they can do in a night) wire netting should either be placed around the stem of each tree or preferably around the whole fruit plot. The mesh should be no larger than 1 in. but there is no need for the netting to be wider than 4 ft. 6 ins., the extra 6 ins. being needed for burying in the ground. Turn it outwards away from the orchard, to prevent the rabbits from burrowing under. In grass orchards where sheep are to graze, or even geese, it is better to wire each tree separately.

HOW MANY TREES TO PLANT

In order to discover the number of bushes, canes or trees that can be planted per acre multiply the distance between the trees or bushes by the distance between the rows and then divide that sum into the number of square feet in an acre, i.e. 43,560. For instance, if you are going to plant an acre of blackcurrants 6 ft. apart between the rows and 4 ft. apart in the rows, the sum would be 43,560 divided by 24, which equals 1815.

The following chart will give a very good idea as to the planting distances.

PLANTING DISTANCE

Form	Distance apart to plant		Best age to plant	Years to come into bearing	Useful life of tree
	Between Rows	Between Trees or Bushes in the Row			
APPLES					
STANDARD	40 ft.	40 ft.	3 yrs.	10 yrs.	100 yrs.
HALF-STANDARD ..	30 ft.	30 ft.	2 yrs.	8 yrs.	100 yrs.
PYRAMID	15 ft.	15 ft.	1 yr.	2 yrs.	50 yrs.
DWARF PYRAMID					
(FUSEAU) ..	8 ft.	3 ft.	1 yr.	2 yrs.	50 yrs.
ESPALIER	6 ft.	15 ft.	1 yr.	2 yrs.	50 yrs.
BUSH	15 ft.	15 ft.	1 yr.	2 yrs.	50 yrs.
CORDON	6 ft.	2 ft.	1 yr.	2 yrs.	50 yrs.
DOUBLE VERTICAL	6 ft.	5 ft.	1 yr.	2 yrs.	50 yrs.
PEARS					
STANDARD	25 ft.	25 ft.	2 yrs.	6-8 yrs.	50-60 yrs.
HALF-STANDARD ..	18 ft.	18 ft.	2 yrs.	4-5 yrs.	50-60 yrs.
DWARF PYRAMID					
(FUSEAU) ..	8 ft.	3 ft.	1 yr.	4-5 yrs.	50-60 yrs.
BUSH	12 ft.	12 ft.	1 yr.	4-5 yrs.	50-60 yrs.
ESPALIER	5 ft.	15 ft.	4 yrs.	4-5 yrs.	50-60 yrs.
GRID-IRON, WALL OR					
WIRE TRAINED ..	5 ft.	6 ft.	4 yrs.	4-5 yrs.	50-60 yrs.
CORDON (SINGLE)	6 ft.	2 ft.	1 yr.	4-5 yrs.	50-60 yrs.
CORDON (DOUBLE)..	8 ft.	5 ft.	2 yrs.	4-5 yrs.	50-60 yrs.
PLUMS					
STANDARD (STRONG)	20 ft.	20 ft.	2 yrs.	5 yrs.	50 yrs.
HALF-STANDARD ..	15 ft.	15 ft.	1 yr.	5 yrs.	50 yrs.
(MODERATE) ..	15 ft.	15 ft.	2 yrs.	5 yrs.	50 yrs.
BUSH	15 ft.	15 ft.	1 yr.	5 yrs.	50 yrs.
FAN	6 ft.	15 ft.	4 yrs.	5 yrs.	50 yrs.
CHERRIES					
STANDARD	40 ft.	40 ft.	2 yrs.	8 yrs.	50 yrs.
FAN	8 ft.	20 ft.	2 yrs.	8 yrs.	50 yrs.
APRICOTS					
FAN	6 ft.	15 ft.	2 yrs.	6 yrs.	20 yrs.
PEACHES					
FAN	6 ft.	18 ft.	2 yrs.	6 yrs.	20 yrs.
NECTARINES					
(*See* PEACHES)					

PLANTING DISTANCE (CONT'D)

Form	Distance apart to plant		Best age to plant	Years to come into bearing	Useful life of tree
	Between Rows	Between Trees or Bushes in the Row			
FIGS					
FAN	18 ft.	15 ft.	4 yrs.	5 yrs.	80 yrs.
GRAPES (*See page* 421)					
NUTS	15 ft.	15 ft.	3 yrs.	10 yrs.	80 yrs.
WALNUTS ..	50 ft.	50 ft.	3 yrs.	10 yrs.	100 yrs.
GOOSEBERRIES					
BUSH	5 ft.	5 ft.	2 yrs.	3 yrs.	15 yrs.
ESPALIER ..	5 ft.	5 ft.	2 yrs.	3 yrs.	15 yrs.
FAN	5 ft.	5 ft.	2 yrs.	3 yrs.	15 yrs.
CORDON (SINGLE) ..	5 ft.	1 ft.	2 yrs.	3 yrs.	15 yrs.
„ (DOUBLE) ..	5 ft.	3 ft.	2 yrs.	3 yrs.	15 yrs.
„ (TREBLE) ..	5 ft.	4 ft.	2 yrs.	3 yrs.	15 yrs.
CURRANTS					
(BLACK)					
BUSH	5 ft.	5 ft.	1 yr.	3 yrs.	8 yrs.
(RED AND WHITE)					
BUSH	5 ft.	5 ft.	2 yrs.	3 yrs.	15 yrs.
ESPALIER	6 ft.	5 ft.	3 yrs.	3 yrs.	15 yrs.
CORDON (SINGLE) ..	6 ft.	1 ft.	2 yrs.	3 yrs.	15 yrs.
„ (DOUBLE)	6 ft.	3 ft.	2 yrs.	3 yrs.	15 yrs.
„ (TREBLE)	6 ft.	4 ft.	2 yrs.	3 yrs.	15 yrs.
RASPBERRIES ..	6 ft.	2 ft.	1 yr.	2 yrs.	8 yrs.
BLACKBERRIES ..	6 ft.	12 ft.	1 yr.	2 yrs.	15 yrs.
LOGANBERRIES	7 ft.	8 ft.	1 yr.	2 yrs.	15 yrs.
STRAWBERRIES	2 ft. 6 ins.	1 ft.	1 yr. runners	2 yrs.	5 yrs.
MEDLARS ..	20 ft.	20 ft.	2 yrs.	2 yrs.	50 yrs.
MULBERRIES ..	30 ft.	30 ft.	2 yrs.	8 yrs.	100 yrs.
QUINCES	12 ft.	12 ft.	3 yrs.	8 yrs.	50 yrs.

CHAPTER II

Fruits in Particular

TREE FRUITS

★

APPLES

UNDOUBTEDLY apples are the most important fruit of the country. They have been grown in England from the earliest times and though it is true to say that originally they were planted for making cider, to-day there are a large number of delicious dessert and cooking varieties. Fortunately apples can be grown on a very wide range of soils, though where the soil is likely to cause trees to grow strongly it is better to plant cookers rather than eaters.

STOCKS

The stock is a very important part of the apple tree for it is the root system which controls the growth and fruitfulness. A weak stock will cause the tree to come into cropping early and generally keep it dwarf. A strong stock will produce a much larger tree and cropping may be delayed a number of years. Naturally a strong variety on a weak stock will not be such a small tree in 5 years' time as a weak variety on the same stock. Be sure, therefore, to purchase the tree which is not only true to name but which is grafted on to the correct stock. Mention of the various types of stocks was made on pages 381-384 when dealing with the propagation of fruit stocks.

Originally the East Malling classified 16 stocks, and latterly they have included a number of Malling Merton Stocks.

(a) *The Very Vigorous*
In this group you have Malling XVI, Malling XXV, and Malling-Merton 109. Malling XXV is an outstanding vigorous root stock, excellent for light soils and dry areas.

(*b*) *Vigorous Stocks*

Malling No. II is a very popular root stock used for bush trees, Espaliers, and Dwarf Pyramids, also used for weak varieties in the case of cordons.

Malling-Merton III very similar to Malling II, causes trees to yield slightly heavier crops.

Malling-Merton 109 much like Malling II, but stands drought better and produces larger trees.

Malling-Merton 104 makes good anchorage but staking is unnecessary.

(*c*) *Semi-Dwarfing Stocks*

Malling VII makes a vigorous tree in the first four or five years and then settles down to heavy cropping.

Malling-Merton 106 not as heavy cropping as Malling VII, but has given double the crop of Malling IX.

(*d*) *Very Dwarfing Stocks*

Malling IX a very weak stock, too weak for sandy soils, bears very early, needs staking all its life, produces small quickly cropping trees, good for Cordons.

MANURING

Apple trees need feeding regularly like other plants. In the case of trees growing in grass it is usual to cut the grass twice a year, in June and September, and to pile this around the trees in a circle 2 or 3 ft. across. (See illustration facing page 32.) When the trees do not seem to be growing sufficiently well it is usual to apply nitro-chalk at 2 ozs. to the square yard after the September cut.

For trees that are growing in cultivated land, good general advice will be to try and give some form of potash, preferably sulphate of potash, each winter at 2 ozs. to the square yard. Until this is readily available it may be necessary to use a proprietary flue dust, 6 or 7 ozs. to the square yard, instead. As a precaution it will be wise to give a good fish manure at 3-4 ozs. to the square yard at the same time.

Do not allow trees that are growing in cultivated land to suffer from lack of humus. To prevent this the weeds may be allowed to grow from 1st July onwards, and in the late autumn these should be cut down and very shallowly dug in.

Tree Fruits

PLANTING

It is always better to plant in the autumn than to delay planting until the spring. Do not plant in the rich soil of a vegetable garden, though if this is absolutely necessary select cooking apples only. Do not plant on soil infested with perennial weeds. Clean the ground first by having a bare fallow or by taking a crop of potatoes. Be very careful in choosing the right stocks and the right varieties and see that the graft or bud union is planted well above soil level. (See page 393.)

DISTANCES TO PLANT

For distances, see Chart on page 395.

PRUNING

It is always better to under- than over-prune. Generally speaking it is better not to prune at all than to hack the trees back anyhow. The aim of pruning should be to see that the branches are evenly spaced ; to see that they are strong enough to bear the weight of the crop ; to ensure that light and air can get to all parts of the tree ; to help produce fruit spurs where they are required, and to maintain fruit size in the mature tree.

The object of pruning during the early stages is to produce a tree with 8-10 good strong branches equally spaced, or even 15, in the case of a very strong variety. The one-year-old end growths, or leaders as they are called, are therefore cut back by about half their length to a point just above a bud which faces the direction in which it is intended that the next year's leader should grow. Any laterals or side growths that are not required for the extension of the branches should be pruned back to within 5 or 6 buds of their base, with the idea of trying to cause the tree to form a fruit spur.

After the first 5 years it should be possible to reduce the amount of pruning that has to be done. This means that the leaders of one-year-old end growths of the branches would only be cut back by about one-third, and the one-year-old side growths or laterals to within 5 or 6 buds.

When the tree is about 10 years old there may be no need to prune the leaders at all, and if the fruit-bud-bearing spurs have got too long these may have to be cut back so as to reduce the number of fruit buds on each spur. Any laterals or side growths that are still developing will be pruned back to within 4 or 5 buds of their base.

Regulating or the Thinned System

A very popular method of pruning to-day is the regulating system. The trees are pruned, as already advised for the first

5 years or so, and are then allowed to grow almost naturally. The crossing wood, rubbing wood and diseased wood is cut out and entire branches are removed, as and when necessary, in order to let in light and air.

Shoot Circling

Instead of cutting back the one-year-old side growths or laterals in the winter these are curled round to form an almost complete circle, the tips being tied to the main branch. This operation causes fruit buds to develop low down on the curl and the following winter these laterals may be pruned back to just above one of the recently-formed fruit buds. Dessert varieties like Laxton's Superb, Ellison's Orange and Laxton's Exquisite respond particularly well to this treatment.

Delayed Open Centre Pruning

The Delayed Open Centre system is so complicated that it is impossible in a book of this character to do more than explain the principles. These are that the branches are so pruned as to leave them evenly balanced—so that one side of the tree has a branch corresponding to a similar branch on the opposite side of the tree. To ensure that branches develop in this way on either side of a " maiden " or one-year-old tree, "notches" or " nicks " should be made just above selected buds. As a result the "nicked " buds grow out and produce branches. The top of the maiden is then cut away, one foot above the nicked buds, at a bud, and the bud just below this one is completely removed with a sharp knife. The effect is that the top buds grow and produce a centre stem while the other 4 buds produce branches which are well balanced.

As the tree grows older leader-tipping is not as a rule carried out. Branches which grow too low are removed, and those that grow too tall are shortened back.

The system does ensure that big trees are formed quickly and that blossom buds are readily formed because of the way the branches lie almost flat. The D.O.C. system is very difficult to explain on paper, but is dealt with in detail in a special book, *Modern Apple Tree Pruning*, by C. R. Thompson, published by Headley Bros. Thompson " invented " the method.

Summer Pruning

Apples respond well to summer pruning, particularly dessert kinds. For details, see page 389.

POLLINATION

There are some varieties of apples which will not set any fruit with their own pollen ; others are moderately self-fertile, but all give better crops with cross-pollination. The variety Bramley's Seedling can set quite a good crop of fruit with its own pollen, for example, but better results are obtained by interplanting with another suitable variety. It must be remembered that apples are of two kinds, the diploids, which have good pollen, and the triploids, with bad pollen. Varieties such as Blenheim Orange and Bramley's Seedling are triploids, therefore these cannot be expected to be good pollinators for others. If any of the triploid varieties are to be planted, it is necessary to plant at least two diploids with them so that they can fertilise one another as well as the triploid.

CLASSES OF APPLE VARIETIES[1]

Diploids	*Triploids*
1. ADAM'S PEARMAIN	BELLE DE BOSKOOP
BAUMANN'S REINETTE	GENNET-MOYLE
BEAUTY OF BATH	GRAVENSTEIN
BISMARCK	RIBSTON PIPPIN
BROWNLESS RUSSET	WASHINGTON
CARLISLE PIPPIN	
DEVONSHIRE QUARRENDEN	
DUCHESS FAVOURITE	
DUCHESS OF OLDENBURG	
EGREMONT RUSSET	
GOLDEN SPIRE	
IRISH PEACH	
KENTISH CODLIN	
KESWICK CODLIN	
LORD LAMBOURNE	
MANX CODLIN	
MARGIL	
RED ASTRACHAN	
REV. W. WILKS	
ROYAL SHOW	
ST. EDMUND'S RUSSET	
STUMER PIPPIN	
WAGENER	
WHITE TRANSPARENT	

[1] This pollination chart is included by the courtesy and permission of Dr. Cyril D. Darlington, the Director of the John Innes Horticultural Institution, Merton, and is taken from the book "The Fruit and the Soil" (*Oliver and Boyd, 1948*). Also see pages 402 and 403.

CLASSES OF APPLE VARIETIES (CONT'D)

Diploids	Triploids
2. ALFRISTON	BALDWIN
ALLINGTON PIPPIN	BLENHEIM ORANGE
BETTY GEESON	BRAMLEY'S SEEDLING
BLUE PEARMAIN	CRIMSON BRAMLEY
CALVILLE BLANCHE	KING OF TOMPKINS' COUNTY
CALVILLE ROUGE	WARNER'S KING
CHARLES ROSS	
CHELMSFORD WONDER	
CORONATION	
COX'S ORANGE PIPPIN	
DELICIOUS	
DUKE OF DEVONSHIRE	
EARLY VICTORIA	
ECKLINVILLE	
ELLISON'S ORANGE	
ENCORE	
GRENADIER	
JAMES GRIEVE	
KING OF THE PIPPINS	
KING'S ACRE PIPPIN	
LADY SUDELEY	
LANE'S PRINCE ALBERT	
LAXTON'S SUPERB	
LORD DERBY	
LORD GROSVENOR	
MONARCH	
NEWTON WONDER	
NORFOLK BEAUTY	
ONTARIO REINETTE	
PEASGOOD'S NONSUCH	
POTT'S SEEDLING	
RIVAL	
ST. CECILIA	
ST. EVERARD	
STIRLING CASTLE	
WEALTHY	
WINTER BANANA	
3. ANNIE ELIZABETH	REINETTE DU CANADA
CELLINI PIPPIN	
COX'S POMONA	

CLASSES OF APPLE VARIETIES (Cont'd)

Diploids	Triploids
Crawley Beauty (v. late)	
Edward VII	
Gascoyne's Scarlet	
Mother	
Northern Greening	
Northern Spy	
Orleans Reinette	
Royal Jubilee	
Winter Majetin	
Worcester Pearmain	
4. Antonowka	Rhode Island Greening
Golden Russet	

1. Early flowering.
2. Mid-season flowering.

3. Late flowering
4. Flowering season not recorded.

The apples in each group fail with their own pollen and with that of any other in the same group, but fruit well when pollinated by one from another group.

CULTIVATION

The work that has to be done in and among apple trees may be divided into two main groups : (1) trees growing in grass ; (2) trees growing in cultivated land. In the case of the orchard the grass must be kept down, either by being eaten by ducks, hens, geese or goats (I hate goats, because they usually get loose and ruin the trees) or by being cut as advised on page 398, in June and September. The grass should never be carted away but should always be allowed to lie on the cut sward and rot down. The worms will then pull it back into the soil and so keep up the humus content of the soil. Putting the grass in a circle around the trees is a good thing, with an application of nitro-chalk at 2 ozs. to the square yard in September to help rot down the grass and provide extra nitrogen.

This artificial need not be given till the trees are, say, 15 years of age, or until growth slows down considerably, or the leaves show signs of being golden yellow in colour and so lacking in nitrogen.

In cultivated land the soil will be dug over shallowly in the autumn, the weeds will be buried and the soil left in a cloddy condition so that the winds and frost can pulverise these lumps and make the soil workable in the spring. During the spring and early summer, hoeing will be carried out regularly so as to keep down weeds and provide a dust mulch. It will be possible to stop hoeing in the case of dessert apples at the end of June, and to allow the weeds to grow. It can be done also in the case of cooking apples, though in the dry parts of England it is sometimes necessary to keep on hoeing among cookers in order to ensure that the apples grow really large. The weeds of course take up a good deal of nitrogen and moisture from the soil. This is an advantage in the case of dessert fruits because it helps to colour up the apples.

ROUTINE WORK

Winter pruning will be carried out in November if possible, and this will be followed by a good tar distillate washing in December or January (see page 391). The fertilisers will be applied in December, and the land will be dug over and left rough. In areas where capsid bugs and red spiders abound it will be necessary to spray the trees late in February or early in March with di-nitro-ortho-cresol and to give a thorough soaking. To control scab lime-sulphur will be applied just before the blossoms open, at a strength of 1 pint of the liquid to 30 pints of water. Lime-sulphur will again have to be applied immediately after all the petals have fallen at a strength of 1 in 80. Where apple sawfly maggots give trouble, nicotine will be added to this wash at the rate of 1 oz. to 10 gals. of wash. In " scabby " districts a further spraying with lime-sulphur will be given 14 days later, the strength being reduced to 1 in 100. There are some sulphur-shy apples (see page 405).

The apples will be thinned in June. In the case of dessert varieties no apples will be left closer than 4 ins. apart, and in the case of cooking varieties none closer than 8 ins. apart. The king apple, or centre apple of the cluster, should always be removed first.

If it is found impossible to pick all the apples at the right time, owing to lack of labour, the trees may be sprayed with a special hormone wash, and the apples may thus be prevented from falling for three weeks or so.

VARIETIES

SELECTED LIST FOR SMALL GARDEN:

Eaters	Cookers
Tydemans Early Worcester	Arthur Turner
Cox's Orange Pippin	Edward VII
Ellison's Orange	Encore

Tree Fruits

Eaters	Cookers
Fortune	Grenadier
Laxton's Advance	Lane's Prince Albert
Laxton's Exquisite	Lord Derby
Laxton's Superb	The Rev. W. Wilks
Worcester Pearmain	Wagener

To be Grown as Standards and Half-Standards:

Eaters	Cookers
Allington Pippin	Annie Elizabeth
Blenheim Orange	Bramley's Seedling
Charles Ross	Early Victoria
Laxton's Superb	Newton Wonder
Worcester Pearmain	Warner's King

Varieties for Eating or Cooking—Dual Purpose:

Allington Pippin	Herring's Pippin
Barnack Beauty	Newton Wonder
Blenheim Orange	Rival
Charles Ross	Wagener ⎰Cooker Dec.–Apr.
Duke of Devonshire	⎱Eater Apr.–July

Common Sulphur-shy Varieties

Beauty of Bath	*Stirling Castle
Lane's Prince Albert	†Blenheim Orange
Newton Wonder	†Charles Ross
Cox's Orange Pippin	†James Grieve

* Very subject to scorch
† May suffer in some districts and on some soils

GOOD VARIETIES OF APPLES

Variety	Cooker or Eater	When to Pick	When to Use
Allington Pippin	E	1st week September	Oct.–Dec.
American Mother	E	3rd ,, September	Oct.–Nov.
Annie Elizabeth	C	3rd ,, October	Dec.–April
Arthur Turner	C	1st ,, September	Sept.–Oct.
Barnack Beauty	E	2nd ,, October	Dec.–March
Beauty of Bath	E	1st ,, August	Early Aug.
Belle de Boskoop	E	3rd ,, October	Dec.–April
Blenheim Orange	E	2nd ,, October	Nov.–Jan.
Bramley's Seedling ..	C	2nd ,, October	Nov.–March
Charles Ross	E	1st ,, October	Oct.–Dec.
Christmas Pearmain ..	E	2nd ,, October	Dec.–Jan.
Claygate Pearmain ..	E	2nd ,, October	Dec.–Jan.
Cornish Gilliflower ..	E	2nd ,, October	Dec.–May
Court Pendu Plat ..	E	3rd ,, October	Jan.–April

GOOD VARIETIES OF APPLE (CONT'D)

Variety	Cooker or Eater	When to Pick	When to use
COX'S ORANGE PIPPIN	E	1st ,, October	Nov.–March
CRAWLEY BEAUTY	C	3rd ,, October	Feb.–April
CRIMSON COX	E	1st ,, October	Nov.–March
D'ARCY SPICE	E	3rd ,, October	Jan.–May
DUKE OF DEVONSHIRE	E	3rd ,, October	Feb.–March
EARLY VICTORIA	C	3rd ,, July	July–Aug.
EASTER ORANGE	E	2nd ,, October	March–Apr
EDWARD VII	C	2nd ,, October	Dec.–April
EGREMONT RUSSET	E	3rd ,, September	Oct.–Dec.
ELLISON'S ORANGE	E	3rd ,, September	Sept.–Oct.
ENCORE	C	3rd ,, October	Dec.–June
GOLDEN NOBLE	C	1st ,, October	Sept.–Jan.
GRENADIER	C	2nd ,, August	Aug.–Sept.
HERRING'S PIPPIN	CE	1st ,, October	November
HEUSGEN'S GOLDEN REINETTE	E	2nd ,, October	Mar.–April
IRISH PEACH	E	2nd ,, July	July–Aug.
JAMES GRIEVE	E	2nd ,, September	Sept.–Oct.
KING OF THE PIPPINS	E	1st ,, October	Oct.–Dec.
LANE'S PRINCE ALBERT	C	1st ,, October	Jan.–March
LANGLEY PIPPIN	E	1st ,, August	Aug.–Sept.
LAXTON'S ADVANCE	E	1st ,, August	Early Aug.
LAXTON'S EPICURE	E	2nd ,, September	September
LAXTON'S EXQUISITE	E	4th ,, August	Sept.–Oct.
LAXTON'S FORTUNE	E	2nd ,, October	Oct.–Nov.
LAXTON'S PEARMAIN	E	4th ,, October	Dec.–April
LAXTON'S SUPERB	E	4th ,, October	Nov.–March
LORD DERBY	C	4th ,, September	Nov.–Dec.
LORD LAMBOURNE	E	4th ,, October	Oct.–Dec.
MAY QUEEN	E	2nd ,, November	Jan.–May
MONARCH	C	1st ,, October	Oct.–April
NEWTON WONDER	C	3rd ,, October	Oct.–March
ORLEANS REINETTE	E	4th ,, October	Jan.–Feb.
OWEN THOMAS	E	1st ,, August	August
RIBSTON PIPPIN	E	3rd ,, October	December
RIVAL	E	1st ,, October	Oct.–Dec.
ROYAL JUBILEE	E	2nd ,, October	Oct.–Dec.
ST. CECILIA	E	1st ,, October	Dec.–March
ST. EVERARD	E	4th ,, August	September
SUNSET	E	2nd ,, October	Oct.–Feb.
STURMER PIPPIN	E	2nd ,, November	March–May
THE QUEEN	C	1st ,, October	Oct.–Jan.
THE REV. W. WILKS	C	1st ,, September	Sept.–Nov.
THOMAS RIVERS	E	1st ,, September	Sept.–Dec.
UNDERLEAF	C	2nd ,, November	Nov.–Feb.
UPTON PYNE	E	2nd ,, October	Dec.–March
WAGENER	E	3rd ,, October	April–June
WARNER'S KING	C	4th ,, September	Oct.–Nov.
WEALTHY	E	2nd ,, October	Oct.–Dec.
WELLINGTON	C	4th ,, October	Dec.–April
WORCESTER PEARMAIN	E	2nd ,, September	Sept.–Oct.

APRICOTS

These are trees which are used to the warmth of a south European summer, and so insist on having a sunny south wall. They are likely only to do well in the south of England, though there are warm spots in the north where they may flourish.

STOCKS
Here it is difficult to advise. Some nurserymen swear by common mussel which they say has a dwarfing effect. Other nurserymen prefer Brussels or St. Julien stocks, while it has been stated that you must use Myrobolan as a stock if planting in heavy soil.

Curiously enough there are a number of people who have done well with apricots raised from stones. In this case it is only necessary to save 2 or 3 stones from good fruits, put them in a pot of soil until early May and then plant them out 18 ins. apart and 2 ins. deep. At the end of a year the trees can be dug up and be planted in their permanent position against a sunny wall.

MANURING
Do not attempt to plant apricots on rich land. Add ground chalk to clay soils at the rate of $\frac{1}{2}$ lb. to the square yard and dig ample, well-rotted compost into sandy soils. Some take the trouble to dig out a hole 2 ft. deep and 3 ft. wide and about 4 ft. long, and bury in the bottom a 6-in. thickness of broken brickbats and old mortar rubble. This is said to discourage tap-rooting and ensure good drainage. It is, therefore, often used in the case of heavy clay soils.

When the trees are 10 years of age and over, give nitro-chalk at 2 ozs. to the square yard each March and mulch with farmyard manure or compost each early June.

PLANTING
Buy fan-shaped trees or train your own seedlings into fan shapes. Buy your fans at 4 years old or the cordons at 2 years of age. Plant during the month of November.

DISTANCES TO PLANT
Fan-shaped trees must be planted 15 ft. apart, while cordons may be put at 3 ft.

PRUNING
The apricot produces plenty of fruit spurs on the old wood and bears also on the season's growth. Unfortunately trees often

suffer from " die back " and this may necessitate the removal of a whole branch. It is therefore advisable to induce plenty of branches.

Try and do the bulk of the work in the summer. Pinch back, with thumb and forefinger, shoots growing on the fronts of the branches at 90°. Weakly shoots may be removed when they are 4 or 5 ins. long and any thinning done to prevent overcrowding. Strong " watery " shoots should be cut out entirely, i.e. right to their base.

Growths that are needed to form further branches should be tied into the wires in between the older growths. Any dying or exhausted wood seen in the summer should be cut away immediately.

In the case of young trees slightly tip the leaders, or end growths, in order to shape the tree. Never cut an apricot too hard, however, for this may encourage unnecessary soft growth.

POLLINATION
Titillate the blossoms with a rabbit's tail on the end of a bamboo or with a camel's hair brush so as to transfer the pollen from the anthers to the stigmas.

Large orchards of one variety are planted in South Africa without any pollinators. The South African Horticultural experts say, " It would seem that our varieties do not require inter-pollination."

CULTIVATION
Apricots grown against walls often suffer from lack of water. Flood the borders in the summer during hot dry weather. Follow the flooding by mulching. Some gardeners swear by syringing the trees with clean water night and morning, except when the fruits are ripening.

As the flowers appear early give the trees some protection with sacking or fish netting during cold nights at this time.

Thin so as to leave not more than one fruit to each 4 in. of branch.

Keep the green fly or aphids in check by regular sprayings with nicotine (see page 644). It is better not to spray with a tar distillate wash in the winter.

ROUTINE WORK
Do what pruning is necessary when the leaves have fallen in November, training new growth in place. If red spider is bad, spray with dinitro-ortho-cresol in January (see page 391). Spray

with nicotine and suitable spreader in April to control greenfly (see page 391). Mulch in May, or early June. Thin the fruits in June. Flood the ground, if and when necessary, in June and July. Pick directly the fruits are ripe in August or September.

VARIETIES

Breda. Small roundish fruit. Orange, shaded red. Mid-August. Very hardy.

Early Moor Park. Flesh orange. Rich flavour. Mid-July. Hardy.

Hemskerk. Flesh tender. Pronounced greengage flavour. Early August. Hardy.

Moor Park. Orange yellow. Red-brown side. Early September. Hardy.

Shipley (sometimes called Blenheim). Deep yellow. Excellent for jams. Beginning September. Hardy.

Royal. Large, dull yellow, tinged red. Beginning September. Hardy.

CHERRIES

The cherry insists on having well-drained soil and preferably one with a natural lime content. That is why it does well on soil that has a chalk or limestone subsoil. Cherries hate wet, heavy clays.

They must be planted above the " frost line," so never plant in dips or frost holes, and they must be given protection from the prevailing winds of the district, so that the bees and other pollinating insects may fertilise the flowers. These can only work methodically when the atmosphere is free from strong winds.

STOCKS

It is difficult to be dictatorial in regard to root stocks for cherries. The East Malling Research Station are still working on this problem. The Mahaleb stock, which was once recommended for fan-trained trees, now seems to be passing out of use. The Wild Cherry seedlings, known as Gean or Mazzard, are generally used, but being seedlings they are mixed. East Malling have at least one stock which they now raise vegetatively, known as Malling XII/I, and it may be that this will be used largely by nurserymen in future. This stock has the valuable property of resisting bacterial canker and, as its leaf colour is very dark, it enables it to be distinguished from the normal popular sweet varieties of cherries. It is excellent for standard trees as well as for bush trees of the acid or morello varieties.

MANURING

It is never advisable to try and feed cherries, especially during the first 8 or 9 years. If they are given any " forcing " nitrogenous feeds such as blood, poultry manure, nitro-chalk or sulphate of ammonia they tend to rush into growth and, as a result, cropping is postponed and diseases encouraged. Potash might be given each December, as an insurance—sulphate of potash being preferred at 2 ozs. per square yard. Wood ashes or flue dust may be used as a substitute at 6 ozs. to the square yard. Hydrated lime may be applied in January every 3 years at 6 ozs. to the square yard, if the soil is known to be lime-free.

When the trees are planted in grass orchards (and sweet cherries like this because they hate root disturbance) see that the grass is grazed regularly or cut three times a year and allowed to remain on the ground to rot down. This cut grass should never be removed for hay. When the trees are well established and cropping well, apply nitro-chalk to the grass each November at 2 ozs. to the square yard, plus basic slag at 4 ozs. to the square yard. Sulphate of potash may be given in addition at 1 oz. to the square yard.

The great thing is never to feed cherries until they have started carrying a crop.

PLANTING

Always plant cherries if possible in November. Plant sweet cherries where they will be undisturbed by deep cultivation. You can plant straight into a grass field if you keep a 3-ft. circle cultivated around the trees for the first 4 or 5 years.

Plant standard trees when they are 4 years old, bush trees at 2 years old, and be prepared to root prune them regularly if they are to be kept small. Plant fan-shaped trees when 4 years old, trained against a wall or fence. It is possible to plant sweet cherry cordons and these should be 2 or 3 years of age when planted.

DISTANCES TO PLANT

Standard cherries need to be 40 ft. apart for they grow tremendously, while fan-shaped trees will need to be 20 ft. apart. Sweet cherry cordons can go in at 3-4 ft.

PRUNING

Sour cherries bear their fruit on the previous year's wood and sweet cherries and the " Duke " types bear their fruit on short spurs on the old wood. In the case of both sweet and sour varieties, young trees should be pruned fairly hard for the first 3 or 4 years so as to establish strong branches. (See Fig 25.) This

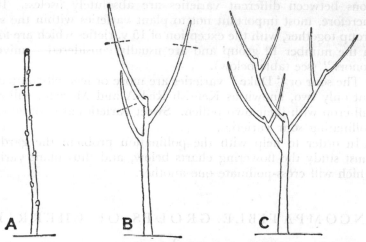

FIG. 25   PRUNING YOUNG CHERRY TREE

usually means cutting back the leaders, i.e. the one-year-old end growths of each branch, by half for the first 2 years after planting, and, say, one-quarter for the next 2 years. It is important to leave the tops fairly level at pruning time.

After this, sweet cherries need very little pruning at all except for the removal of dead wood, diseased wood, crossing and rubbing branches. Much of this kind of pruning may be done in the summer. Any cuts that have to be made in the winter should be cleaned up with a sharp knife afterwards, and be painted over with thick white lead paint immediately.

In the case of the sour cherry group a certain amount of old wood will be cut away each year in order to encourage the production of young wood. This applies whether the sour cherries are grown as bushes, or as wall trees.

Sweet cherries growing on walls are usually summer-pruned in July—the laterals or one-year-old side growths being cut back to within 5 leaves of their base. (See illustration facing page 385.) In the early autumn, these pruned laterals are usually pruned back again to within 3 buds of their base. Any young shoots that develop inwards towards the wall or fence should be rubbed out with the thumb and forefinger when first seen.

POLLINATION

All varieties of sweet cherries are self-sterile. The flowers must be fertilised by pollen of a different variety of cherry. Varieties of sweet cherries fall into definite groups within which even pollinations between different varieties are absolutely useless. It is, therefore, most important not to plant varieties within the same group together, with the exception of 15 varieties which are found in the number 12 group and are usually considered " universal donors " (see table below).

The sour or " Duke " varieties are more or less self-compatible but only two, known as Kentish Red A and Morello, will set a full crop with their own pollen. Sweet varieties are not good for pollinating sour varieties.

In order to help with the pollination problem the gardener must study the flowering charts below, and thus plant varieties which will cross-pollinate one another.

INCOMPATIBLE GROUPS OF CHERRIES[1]

I

1. BAUMANN's MAY
   BEDFORD PROLIFIC
   BLACK DOWNTON
   BLACK TARTARIAN A *

2. BLACK EAGLE
   CARNATION
   EARLY RIVERS
   KNIGHT's EARLY BLACK
   LEICESTER BLACK
   RONALD's HEART

3. BLACK CIRCASSIAN
   ROUNDEL HEART

4. BLACK TARTARIAN B *

II

1. BLACK HEART B
   SEMIS DE BURR

2. WINDSOR
   BELLE AGATHE
   BIGARREAU DE SCHRECKEN
   BLACK ELTON
   WATERLOO
   MERTON BIGARREAU

3. BLACK CLUSTER
   FROGMORE EARLY
   MAIDEN's BLUSH
   VICTORIA BLACK

[1] This pollination chart is included by the courtesy and permission of Dr. Cyril D. Darlington, the Director of the John Innes Horticultural Institution, Merton, and is taken from the book " The Fruit and the Soil " (*Oliver and Boyd, 1948*).

INCOMPATIBLE GROUPS OF CHERRIES (Cont'd)

III

1. Emperor Francis	3. Bigarreau Napoleon
2. Mezel 1 and 2 Ohio Beauty	

IV

1. Merton Premier	3. Late Amber Kentish Bigarreau
2. Ludwig's Bigarreau White Bigarreau	Yellow Spanish
	4. W. Midlands Bigarreau

V

1. Late Black Bigarreau Turkey Heart	2. Bohemian Black

VI

2. Early Amber Stark's Gold Merton Heart	3. Elton Heart Governor Wood Turkish Black

VII

2. Hooker's Black Mezel No. 3 *	3. Bradbourne Black Hedelfingen

VIII

1. Peggy Rivers	2. Noir de Schmidt

IX

1. Red Turk	2. Red Cluster Ursula Rivers

INCOMPATIBLE GROUPS OF CHERRIES (CONT'D)

X

1. BIGARREAU JABOULAY RAMON OLIVIA	4. BLACK TARTARIAN D *

XI

1. CRYALL'S SEEDLING
 GUIGNE'S D'ANNONAY
 KNIGHT'S BIGARREAU

XII

	3. CAROON NEWINGTON LATE BLACK NOBLE

GROUPLESS
(UNIVERSAL DONORS)

1. BEEVES HEART BELLE D'ORLEANS BLACK OLIVER EARLY PURPLE GEAN GOODNESTON BLACK NOIR DE GUBEN SMOKY DUNN	2. GUIGNE TRÈS PRÉCOCE MUMFORD BLACK ORD 3. BIGARREAU GAUCHER FLORENCE SMOKY HEART

1. Early flowering.
2. Mid-season flowering.
3. Late flowering.
4. Flowering season not recorded.

For example, EARLY RIVERS fails with its own pollen and with the pollen of BEDFORD PROLIFIC, and all varieties in Group 1 ; but it fruits abundantly when pollinated by any variety in the other eleven groups. Similarly the pollen of EARLY RIVERS is effective on any variety outside its own group.

* Under the name Black Tartarian and also under the name Monstrueuse de Mezel, three distinct varieties are distributed in commerce. Ask your nurseryman which one he sells.

414

The following are the fertility rules to observe in planting :

(i) No sweet cherry variety must be planted alone but always with a second variety.

(ii) The two varieties must always be of a different group unless they are both groupless.

(iii) The two varieties should also overlap amply in flowering season.

Thus the failure to obtain fruit from self- and cross-pollination in cherries is not due to the female or male organs, the ovules and pollen, being sterile or bad, but simply to their being brought together in the wrong combinations. The same ovules and pollen in the right combinations will give an abundant set of fruit. These right and wrong combinations are such as provide *compatible* and *incompatible* pollinations respectively.

CHERRIES—MORELLO

As Morellos are so much grown it is well worthwhile devoting a special section to them. The advantage of the Morello is that it is never so badly attacked by birds as the sweet cherry. The Morello, however, is very liable to the Brown Rot Fungus disease and it is necessary to cut out, and to burn immediately, any branches which die when this occurs, even in the summer. The Morello will do well on any wall and is often planted on the north wall because it is the best fruit to put up with that sunless spot.

PRUNING

The Morello is a difficult fruit to prune for it bears its cherries on the young wood which grew the previous season, thus it is always the leader or extension shoot which bears the fruits while the old wood at the base of this will be quite bare in the summer. As a result you get long whippy branches and if you are not careful the tree becomes too thick. The best way to deal with the problem is to cut out a few of the older branches each October, and thus not only thin, and so let in light and air, but, in addition, encourage the production of further young wood which eventually will take the place of the older wood. When you want a lateral to develop at a particular place always cut back to a pointed single bud at the base of a shoot. This is known as a growth bud.

When Morellos are growing on walls the same type of pruning should be carried out. A proportion of the older wood should be cut away each year and the young shoots will be tied up in its place. A nice fan-shaped tree should be aimed at. Never summer prune a Morello cherry, always retain the young wood for tying-in in the winter.

It is always possible at the end of March to saw off the whole of the top of a Morello cherry that has got into a neglected condition. The saw cut thus made should be smoothed over with a sharp blade of a knife and painted with a white lead paint. As a result strong new growth will develop and with careful subsequent pruning a heavy cropping tree can be assured.

CULTIVATION

As for plums ; see page 440.

ROUTINE WORK

Grease band the trees late in September in order to trap the females of the winter moth. Delay pruning until March, except in the case of dead wood. It is better to cut this out in the late summer when it can easily be seen, i.e. before the leaves fall. Pick off and burn all " mummied " fruits in November.

Spray in December with a good tar distillate wash using a 7% solution. Apply a good fish manure, to which some potash has been added during preparation, in December or early January, at 3-4 ozs. to the square yard. Cultivate lightly in order to bury the weeds in the case of Morello cherries. (Sweet cherries will prefer to be grown in grassland.)

Look for withered tips in the spring and if these occur cut them off and burn them. Spray the trees with lime-sulphur, 1 pint to 100 pints of water immediately before blossoming and again immediately after it. This is to control brown rot and red spider. If there is a bad insect attack owing, say, to omitting the tar oil wash in December, spray with nicotine immediately after the blossoms have fallen. Dissolve $\frac{1}{4}$ oz. of nicotine in $2\frac{1}{2}$ gals, of water, plus $\frac{1}{4}$ lb. soft soap or a proprietary " spreader." The nicotine may be added to the second lime-sulphur wash.

Give a mulch of rotted manure in late May or early June and hoe regularly in between the trees to keep down weeds and provide a mulch. In the case of grassland see that the grass is kept mown or grazed so that it is always short. Do not summer prune, but do cut out any dead wood seen in June or July. During the ripening of the fruits, protect the trees with nets to prevent the fruit being eaten by birds. Scarers may be used. In big orchards it is usual to employ a man with a gun known as a " bird minder."

8. Propping up heavily
fruited branches

9. Tree with branches
propped

70. *A ringed tree*

71. *Removing basal growth from a standard apple tree*

72. *Pegging down a strawberry runner*

GOOD VARIETIES OF CHERRIES

Variety	When to pick	Colour	Habit	Description
SWEET CHERRIES				
AMBER HEART	Mid-July	Yellow, red streak	Strong	Hardy
BIGARREAU NAPOLEON	August	Yellow, red streak	Very strong, spreading	Liable to Silver Leaf. Heavy cropper
BLACK EAGLE	July	Black	Strong, quick grower	Sweet
BLACK TARTARIAN	Early July	Black	Very strong, spreading	Large fruit, hardy
EARLY RIVERS	Late June	Deep red	Strong and spreading	Very hardy Good variety for all methods
ELTON	Early June	Light red	Fairly upright	Tender variety
EMPEROR FRANCIS	July–Aug.	Deep red	Spreading	Late cherry, good in north
FLORENCE	Late July—Early Aug.	Deep yellow deep red flush	Fairly upright	Liable to bacteria " die back "
FROGMORE BIGARREAU	Late June–Early July	Yellow, red flush, tender	Fairly upright	Reliable
GOVERNOR WOOD	Early July	Yellow slightly red	Fairly upright	Fruit rots easily, sweet
MONSTRUEUSE DE MEZEL	Early July	Black	Strong, spreading	Large
NOBLE	End July	Purplish-red	Fairly upright	Fair
NOIR DE GUBEN	Late June	Black	Fairly upright	Good cropper
ROUNDEL HEART	Early July	Reddish-black	Strong upright	Sweet
SOUR CHERRIES				
FLEMISH RED	End July	Bright red	Fairly strong	Grow as standard or bush, self-fertile
KENTISH RED	Early July	Deep red	Spreading	Bears well with Flemish Red as pollinator
MORELLO	Aug.–Sept.	Deep red to black	Whippy	Best cooker, self-fertile, good on north wall
TURK	Early Aug.	Shiny black	Strong	Best late sour, good for jam, bottling, etc.

SELECTED LIST OF SWEET CHERRIES TO PLANT IN A SMALL GARDEN

Variety	Pollinator
Bigarreau Napoleon	Frogmore Early
Early Rivers	Noir de Guben
Emperor Francis	Early Amber
Frogmore Early	Late Amber
Monstrueuse de Mezel	Governor Wood
Noble	Bigarreau Napoleon
Noir de Guben	Black Tartarian A

VARIETIES OF SWEET CHERRIES FOR WALLS

Variety	Pollinator
Amber Heart	Florence
Black Eagle	Governor Wood
Early Rivers	Roundel
Elton	Kentish Bigarreau
Napoleon Bigarreau	Frogmore Bigarreau

FIGS

Figs generally speaking need more heat and light than they get in the normal English summer. It is probably true to say that they should only be grown outdoors in the south and preferably against south walls—and near the sea. Figs do well also in Anglesey and North Wales.

Figs will grow on almost any soil providing it is well drained. This is the reason why they quite like a soil overlying chalk and under such conditions deep-seating tap roots are discouraged. It is important to try and restrict the rooting space, for this reason some growers cement in a hole 4 ft. square and 3 ft. deep while others sink a 12-in. pot in the ground and plant the fig in this. It is possible just to get out a hole 4 × 4 ft. and bury plenty of broken brickbats and stones in the bottom. On the top of 8 ins. of this rubble, good loamy soil may be placed together with a fair " dash " of ground chalk.

STOCKS

The fig does well on its own roots. It can, therefore, be raised by cuttings, by lifting suckers, or by layering. Cuttings 1 ft. long are taken in September and are planted 9 ins. deep in a warm spot. If watered occasionally during a dry period, they will root and then will be ready to plant out 2 years later.

Rooted suckers may be dug up in the autumn and be planted in their permanent quarters.

In the north it is possible to plant the tree, pot and all, out of doors in the spring and then dig it up, pot and all, in the late autumn for storing in the cellar " dugout " or greenhouse, and thus protecting from frost.

MANURING

The main feed for figs would seem to be bone meal at 2 ozs. to the square yard applied in December. In sandy land, sulphate or muriate of potash may be applied in addition at 1 oz. to the square yard. In heavy land, where there is no chalky subsoil, ground chalk or hydrated lime should be applied to the surface of the ground in January at 4 ozs. to the square yard. In dry seasons and on dry land, mulches of well-rotted farmyard manure or compost should be placed round the stems early in the summer.

PLANTING

Plant any time during the dormant period, preferably November. Do not dig in manure. Two-year-old trees will do, but some prefer to purchase 4-year-old fan-shaped trees for walls.

DISTANCES TO PLANT

Plant 18 ft. apart on walls and 15 ft. apart as bushes. It is only possible to grow figs as bushes out of doors in very warm situations in the west and south-west.

PRUNING

Grow the fig on the wall on the fan-trained system. Spread out the shoots fan-wise and tie them in to the wires. Allow ample room so that the branches get all the sunshine and warmth they need. This means they must be about a foot apart.

The figs are borne on the well-ripened wood of the previous year. Aim therefore at producing sturdy, short-jointed shoots. Never prune hard as this encourages rank growth and little fruit. Each year cut out the weakly crowded branches and the old wood which seems to be " spent," as well as removing bodily any rank shoots that seem to be unnecessary.

In the summer, trim back a certain number of the side-growths so as to let in the sunshine. This usually means pinching back the overstrong lateral growths when they are about 8 ins. long.

Always remove the suckers coming up from ground level, and

when the trees grow too vigorously, dig up and root prune during the winter months.

POLLINATION

The flowers are on the inside of the immature fruit and so are not normally visible. In this country good fruit is usually produced without pollination. Failure to bear is, therefore, undoubtedly bound up with exuberant growth. Check excessive vigour and fruit will appear the following year.

CULTIVATION

Keep the surface of the soil hoed in spring and summer. Water thoroughly in the summer when the fruits are developing. Cease watering when the figs start to colour.

A potential fruit-bearing shoot may be divided roughly into three sections. At the tip you get the embryo figs which will produce next year's crop. Half-way down you may get three or four small figs which will never mature in an English climate. Lower than this appear the large figs which will ripen in the summer. It is always better to remove the very small figs in the middle section so as to divert the sap to the bigger figs.

ROUTINE WORK

Do what winter pruning is necessary the moment the majority of the leaves have fallen. Grub up the suckers. Do not winter wash, but apply the fertilisers needed in December.

If it is necessary to protect the tree in the winter, either dig it up and take it under cover or untie the branches from the wall, pull them down close to the ground and cover them with straw. Tie the branches back into position in the spring. Fork shallowly around the tree to work in the organic fertilisers or, if there is excessive growth, dig the tree up, root prune and re-plant. This operation may be necessary every 5 years.

Spray with a petroleum white oil emulsion to which nicotine has been added—at the rate of $\frac{1}{4}$ ozs. to 5 gals. of the diluted solution—in April to control mussel scale and mealy bug.

Pick the figs directly they are soft and ready to use. Eat within a week after picking.

It is possible to cover the fig with branches of spruce, and then by April when the tree needs more sunshine and warmth, most of the needles will have been shed and yet the branches will still give some protection against the spring frosts in late April and mid-May.

VARIETIES

Brown Turkey. Mid-season. Large fruits. Hardy. Fertile. Rich flavour.

Brunswick. Mid-season. Fruits green with dark blue—brown flush. Hardy. Bears one of the largest fruits. Good flavour.

Negro Largo. Mid-season, August. Black fruits, thin skinned. Vigorous grower. Not so hardy as Brown Turkey. Rich sweet flavour.

White Marseilles. Late August, early September. Pale green. Flesh inside opal tinted. Hardy. Said to be richest and sweetest-flavoured fig grown.

GRAPES

Grapes have been grown out of doors in England since the time of the Romans. Even as late as 1875 there were quite large out-of-door vineyards for the purpose of making wine. Grapes are grown against the south and south-east walls of many houses, even in London. Grown outdoors they are on the whole more a fruit for the southern half of England than the north.

The vine seems to do well in any ordinary garden soil and succeeds in quite heavy land providing the drainage is good. It is possible to dig out a hole 4 ft. square and 3 ft. deep and, having buried 6 ins. of broken brickbats and stone in the bottom for drainage, a compost (consisting of 2 parts soil, $\frac{1}{8}$ part ground mortar or ground chalk and an $\frac{1}{8}$ part bonfire ashes or burnt earth) may be mixed together and placed therein.

STOCKS

Vines are not grafted or budded on stocks. They are propagated as a rule by cuttings made in October. These should be 12-16 ins. long and all the buds, except the two or three upper ones, should be removed. The cutting should be inserted about two-thirds of its length in the soil, 8 ins. away from the wall where it is to grow. Insert the cutting in November and protect it during the winter with some strawy litter.

MANURING

The roots of a vine usually get all the food they need from crops nearby. The great thing is to prune hard and this is as good as a dose of nitrogen. In the young stages, a little fish manure may be given at 4 ozs to the square yard when the border is forked and cleaned for the winter.

The Complete Gardener

PLANTING

Get the planting done any time between the middle of October and the beginning of February. The earlier the better. If the vine arrives in a pot, knock it out, unravel the roots and spread them out evenly in the hole. Plant firmly 1 ft. away from the wall and 6 ins. deep. Give the young rod a stake.

You can grow the vine as a cordon, you can grow it as an espalier, or you can let it grow almost naturally on the fan-spreading system. Some people like to grow it on the grid-iron system.

DISTANCES TO PLANT

Single cordons, 4 ft. apart ; horizontally trained espalier types 18 ft. apart ; grid-irons 15 ft. apart.

PRUNING

A young tree should be cut back to within 1 ft. of its base in order to encourage a strong rod to develop. When growing as a cordon, allow about 4 ft. of growth each year, pruning back in the winter the main shoot to just above a bud. All the side shoots or laterals that develop should be pruned back to within one eye of their base.

When growing as an espalier, cut the main rod back to within 8 ins. of soil level after planting and, if 3 shoots grow out at the top in the summer, train the 2 lower ones left and right and the upper one vertically. Cut back the vertical shoot to half its length in the winter, and the 2 side shoots in a similar manner. Train 2 further side shoots growing out of the vertical shoot left and right about 18 ins. above the lower branch layer. Continue on this system for 3 or 4 years until the requisite layers of branches have been formed.

Once the horizontal branches have been formed, their leaders, or 1 year-old end growths, may be pruned back hard each winter. Any side growths that appear will be cut back each December to within one bud of their base. When the allotted space has been filled, the end or extension growth of each branch should be stopped by repeatedly pinching it back in the summer.

Summer Pruning

If more than one lateral grows out at a spur in the spring, retain the stronger and rub out the weaker. Cut back the growths at 2 leaves beyond the place where the bunches of young fruit are forming. If no fruit develops, prune to the fourth leaf from the base of the young laterals.

POLLINATION
Vines are self-fertile.

CULTIVATION
The normal cultivation carried out in the garden is all that is necessary.

Do not allow the vine to over-crop in its early years, allow 1 good bunch at the third season, 5 bunches at the fourth season, 8 bunches at the fifth season, and so on.

Apply liquid manure once a fortnight in the summer and mulch the soil with dung or compost.

Thin the fruits so as to clear the centre of a cluster of its little fruitlets and space the other forming berries evenly round the outside. Use a pair of scissors with pointed blades.

ROUTINE WORK
Winter prune each November, cut hard, spray the rods with a 5% solution of a good tar distillate wash in December.

Flood during dry weather when the vine is young; when older this is not necessary.

Thin the berries when the size of sweet pea seeds and thin again when the fruits are the size of marrowfat peas. Few beginners thin bunches of grapes properly. They always underdo it.

Mulch in June with grass mowings, rotted leaves or compost.

Give protection to ripening grapes before harvesting.

VARIETIES
Muscat de Saumur, early cropping golden muskat.
Noir Hatif de Marseilles, a fine early black outdoor grape.
Pirovano 14, reddish black grapes, very prolific.
Brant; small black grapes; very regular crop.
Chasselas 1921, golden grapes, early and large.
Muscat Hamburgh, large black muskat, rather delicate.

PEACHES AND NECTARINES

For the purpose of this book peaches and nectarines are regarded as one and the same thing, the nectarine merely being a peach without the velvety skin.

A peach will grow in any soil where the drainage is perfect. It prefers a soil containing plenty of lime and does well on any wall between, say, the south-east and south-west.

STOCKS

As in the case of apricots, many people have grown excellent peach trees through planting stones. They seem to do well on their own roots. It is only necessary to keep the stones in damp soil over the winter. In March crack them slightly by hand and plant them 2 ins. deep. Good seedlings usually result.

Very often definite varieties of peaches are budded on to plum stocks and it is said that, for medium-sized trees, the common mussel stock is best. The Brompton stock seems to be the best stock for larger trees. Peaches have been budded on the St. Julien C and Pershore stocks with success.

MANURING

Mulch with farmyard manure or well-rotted compost early in June. Apply a good fish manure to which potash has been added at 3-4 ozs. to the square yard each November. After the fruit has stoned, water with weak liquid manure that can now be obtained in bottles ready for dilution. Apply ground chalk in January once every 3 years at the rate of $\frac{1}{2}$ lb. to the square yard; this is especially necessary on heavy soil.

PLANTING

Fan trees may be planted at 4 years of age. Try and get them into the ground early in November and see that there is a space of 4 ins. between the trunk of the tree and the brickwork of the wall. Plant shallowly. In the open plant 2-year-olds. Dig a hole big enough to contain all the roots when they are spread out properly. Ram the soil over the roots so that the tree cannot possibly move. If any big roots appear broken, cut them back with a sharp knife so that the cut surface faces downwards.

DISTANCES TO PLANT

Fan-trained trees should be 18 ft. apart, bush-trees planted in the open are usually planted 20 ft. apart either way.

PRUNING

(a) *Wall Trees*

The peach flowers on the wood produced the previous year, as well as on the few short spurs. Aim to furnish the tree with equal-sized branches radiating from the main stem. When training a young tree, see that it is well furnished with lower branches first of all and allow the centre of the fan to be filled up afterwards.

Fix the growths to wires secured 4 ins. away from the wall, have these wires 12 ins. apart. In the winter, remove much of the older wood and retain much of the growth that has been made that season. Aim at having well-ripened young growths spaced 4 ins. apart all over the area occupied by the fan. Trees that crop heavily naturally make less wood than trees that are not bearing a crop.

From each shoot retained in the winter, numbers of laterals or side growths will grow out in the spring and summer. Only allow 2 or 3 of these to remain on each lateral, rub out the surplus when they are ½ in. long. Leave a good shoot at the base of each fruiting wood and use this young shoot to take the place of the fruiting one after the peaches have been picked.

(b) In the Open

Do all pruning in April when the trees are in leaf. Cut out the old hard wood and encourage young growths to develop on which the fruit will be borne the following year. Aim at producing a round, ball-shaped tree. Keep the centre cut back and, as the growths bear their fruits, they will tend to droop and thus give the trees a flattish-looking head.

POLLINATION

It is possible to help with hand pollination by tickling the blossoms with a camel-hair brush, or a rabbit's tail tied on the end of a short bamboo. All varieties are self-fertile. Protect wall trees during frosty nights when blossoming by hanging fish netting or hessian in front.

CULTIVATION

Keep the ground hoed round and about the trees. Be prepared to water well in a dry summer especially in the case of wall trees, as the walls themselves absorb much of the moisture and evaporate it. Some gardeners bury three or four 6-in. land drains 2 or 3 ft. away and around the tree in such a manner that the tops are a few inches above soil level. It is thus possible to pour water into the drain pipes and so ensure that it reaches the subsoil. In addition to watering or flooding the ground around the trees, put mulches of well-rotted vegetable refuse on the surface of the ground for 2 or 3 ft. around the stem of each tree.

In the winter, if it is thought that the tree is making too much growth, it may be lifted and the thicker roots cut back, the cuts being made so that they face upwards and not downwards. On strong land, root pruning may be necessary every third year. Root pruning is not advisable in the case of wet clay land and is not necessary in light sandy soil if sufficient water is given in the summer to ensure fibrous root growth. Trees that suffer from lack of moisture often send out deep foraging roots in search of it.

ROUTINE WORK

Prune the wall trees as early as possible in November, then if any big cuts have to be made clean them smooth and paint with lead paint. Spray with a 5% solution of tar-distillate wash in December. Soak the trees thoroughly. In bad cases of red spider spray with D.N.C. mixed with petroleum oil in January (see page 391). Apply fish manure in November and ground chalk in January. When the fruit is swelling give liquid manure at 10-day intervals.

Spray with nicotine if aphids appear in April. Mulch with compost or farmyard manure in May or early June. Water thoroughly if necessary in June and July. Syringe the leaves of the trees night and morning on hot days, omit when the fruit is ripening but continue after the fruit has been picked.

Thin the fruits so that they are at least 1 ft. apart or, if you don't mind smaller peaches, 6 ins. apart. Never allow fruits to set in pairs. Always leave the fruit on the top side of a branch in preference to one on the bottom side. Start thinning when the fruits are the size of a thimble and continue until they are the size of a horse chestnut.

Pick carefully ; if birds and wasps are a nuisance cover the fruits with little muslin bags tied to the branches.

VARIETIES

(a) Peaches

Bellegarde. Considered by some the best-flavoured peach there is, ripens early to mid-September.

Duke of York. Good flavour, ripe mid-July, does well on a wall or as a bush.

Hale's Early. Ripens early August, medium size, delicious, bush or wall tree.

Peregrine. Good quality, medium to large, ripens early August, bush or wall.

Prince of Wales. Good flavour, regular cropper, ripens end September.

Rochester. Excellent quality, good size, ripens mid-August.

(b) Nectarines

Early Rivers. Very large, excellent, ripening end July.

Elruge. Hardy, very popular, medium sized, good quality, ripens end August.

Humboldt. Large, good quality, very decorative, ripens mid-August.

John Rivers. Good flavour, heavy cropper, for walls, ripening mid-July.

Lord Napier. Large, excellent, regular cropper, ripe early August.

PEARS

Pears grow on similar soil to apples, the ideal soil being deep, warm and moisture-holding. Pears do best in districts where there is an equable temperature. This usually means in the southern half of England and Wales, or in areas alongside large stretches of water. The late-keeping pears, like Winter Nelis, need a sunny position and perfect shelter, plus a dry ripening season. They really, therefore, need a nice sunny wall. In most parts of England it is better to grow the hardy types like Williams, Conference and Laxton's Superb.

As pear blossom is out earlier than apple, it is more likely to be damaged by frost and, as pollination may be said to be a matter of minutes, it is important to provide shelter to encourage the visitation of bees and other pollinating insects.

STOCKS

For gardens it is always advisable to buy pears grafted on to quince stocks. These are divided into 3 types : (1) Malling Quince A, a good general purpose stock for bushes, dwarf pyramids and cordons. This stock produces good anchorage roots and much fibre ; (2) Malling Quince B seems to be a little more dwarfing than A, while (3) Malling C makes a smaller tree on the whole, and usually brings varieties into bearing early. It is a very useful root stock for shy cropping kinds and is grand for cordons.

Unfortunately there are some varieties of pears which will not make a satisfactory union with a quince stock. This means that it is necessary to carry out what is called " double working "— a variety like D'Amanlis or Pitmaston Duchess is grafted on to the quince stock, and the scion or graft of the incompatible variety is then worked on to the intermediate variety. Such trees usually cost more. The varieties which are incompatible with quince stocks are Dr. Jules Guyot, Marguerite Marillat, Jargonelle, Souvenir de Congrés, Joséphine de Malines, Thompson's, Marie Louise, and Williams' Bon Chrétien. The following three varieties are usually used as intermediates between the incompatible variety and the stock ; Beurré D'Amanlis, Pitmaston Duchess and Uvedale's St. Germain.

The large trees used in pear grass orchards are usually raised on wild pear stocks, or pear seedlings.

MANURING

Generally speaking pears should be manured in a similar way to apples (see page 398). On the whole, however, they suffer less from potash starvation and like regular applications of composted vegetable refuse each May. Such organic matter is usually put around the trees as a mulch. Bone meal may be given in the case of heavy soils at the rate of 4-5 ozs. to the square yard every December.

PLANTING

Pears are often grown as espaliers and cordons against walls, or even as cordons in rows. They are popular as pyramids on 2-ft. stems and sometimes they are grown as half-standards or standards in grass orchards. As the fruits require full sun exposure, if they are to be fully flavoured, the dwarfer types of trees are usually preferred. On the whole pears are slower than apples in coming into bearing.

In the case of bushes or cordons, plant 2-year-olds, and in the case of standards and half-standards, 3-year-olds ; with espaliers plant 4-year-olds. Get the planting done in the autumn rather than very early in the spring.

Plant as advised on pages 392-394, taking the greatest care that the union of the stock and scion is well above soil level, for pears scion-root quickly.

DISTANCES TO PLANT

See page 395, where the distances are clearly given in a chart.

PRUNING

The main principles of pruning are those outlined for apples on page 399.

Fortunately most varieties of pears throw fruit spurs readily and so the spurring system is generally successful. When the trees get old it is necessary to thin the spurs out by removing, say, every other one and, in addition, to cut back a long spur to a plump fruit bud lower down. Some varieties of pears need fairly hard pruning, if their vigour is to be maintained. Where trees are making little growth the leaders, or end growths, may be pruned back quite hard. When branches tend to droop down to the ground, owing to a heavy weight of crop in the summer, it is necessary to saw the branch back to just above a strong lateral, or side growth, growing in the right direction.

Some varieties are apt to grow rather too upright, for instance, Marguerite Marillat, Dr. Jules Guyot and Conference in the early stages, and in such cases it is essential to keep the centre of the tree open. Other varieties tend to be too spreading and the pruning will help to keep them upright. When it is seen that fruit buds are being produced on the tips of laterals, as they are, for instance, in the case of Jargonelle and Joséphine de Malines, it will not be advisable to cut these back. Otherwise, of course, all the fruit buds would be removed.

POLLINATION

A very large number of pears are what is called self-sterile, i.e. their flowers need the pollen of another—often special—variety, flowering at the same time, if the blossoms are to set and produce fruit. Most self-fertile varieties crop more heavily when cross-pollinated. It is, therefore, important to plant more than one variety in a garden, and to see that the varieties that are planted will pollinate one another. Full details as to the varieties that will pollinate each other will be found in the John Innes Pollination Charts that follow.

CLASSES OF PEAR VARIETIES[1]

Diploids	Triploids
1. BEURRÉ GIFFARD	BEURRÉ ALEX. LUCAS
COMTESSE DE PARIS	BEURRÉ D'AMANLIS
LOUISE BONNE DE JERSEY	BEURRÉ DIEL
MARGUERITE MARILLAT	DOYENNÉ BUSSOCH
PASSE CRASANNE	VICAR OF WINKFIELD
ST. LUKE	

[1] This pollination chart is included by the courtesy and permission of Dr. Cyril D. Darlington, the Director of the John Innes Horticultural Institution, Merton, and is taken from the book " The Fruit and the Soil," (*Oliver and Boyd, 1948*). See also page 430.

CLASSES OF PEAR VARIETIES (CONT'D)

Diploids	Triploids
2. BARONNE DE MELLO	CONSEILLER A LA COUR
BEURRÉ BEDFORD	JARGONELLE
BEURRÉ BROWN	ST. GERMAIN
BEURRÉ CLAIRGEAU	
BEURRÉ FOUQUERAY	CATILLAC
BEURRÉ SIX	PITMASTON DUCHESS
BEURRÉ SUPERFIN	
CHALK	RATEAU GRIS
CONFERENCE	
DURONDEAU	
EMILE D'HEYST	
FONDANTE DE THIRRIOTT	
GANSELL'S BERGAMOTE	
LE BRUN	
LE LECTIER	
NAPOLEON	
OLIVIER DE SERRES	
ORANGE BERGAMOTE	
SECKLE	
SOUVENIR DE CONGRÈS	
WILLIAMS' BON CHRÉTIEN	

Diploids	Tetraploids
3. BEURRÉ BOSC	
BEURRÉ DUMONT	DOUBLE WILLIAMS
BEURRÉ HARDY	FERTILITY IMPROVED
BEURRÉ MORTILLET	
CLAPP'S FAVOURITE	
DR. JULES GUYOT	
DOYENNE DU COMICE	
FERTILITY	
GLOU MORCEAU	
LAXTON'S SUPERB	
MARIE LOUISE	
NOUVEAU POITEAU	
TRIOMPHE DE VIENNE	
WINTER NELIS	

4. EARLY MARKET	No good pollen

1. Early flowering. 3. Late flowering.
2. Mid-season flowering. 4. Flowering season not recorded.

Pears are diploid, triploid and tetraploid. No diploid or triploid pear sets a satisfactory crop with its own pollen. When a triploid pear is grown it is again advisable, as with apples, to interplant it with two or more diploid varieties. MARGUERITE MARILLAT, though a diploid, has no good pollen and is therefore, like the triploids, useless as a pollinator.

The tetraploids are in a class by themselves : FERTILITY IMPROVED sets a full crop with its own pollen.

The following two groups have been recognised :

INCOMPATIBLE GROUPS OF PEARS

I	II
BELLE LUCRATIVE	BEURRÉ D'AMANLIS
LAXTON'S SUPERB	CONFERENCE
LOUISE BONNE DE JERSEY	
SECKLE	
WILLIAMS' BON CHRÉTIEN	

Note.—Group I has not been tested by all possible pollinations. In Group II BEURRÉ D'AMANLIS, which is a triploid, fertilises CONFERENCE but fails with CONFERENCE pollen.

CULTIVATION

As pears are frequently grown against fences and walls the roots often find difficulty in getting enough moisture as such situations are dry. It is necessary, therefore, to give the soil around pear trees a good drenching with water during droughty periods in the summer. Mulchings of lawn mowings or composted vegetable refuse must be applied around the stems of the trees for 3 or 4 ft. in May or June. Mulching may be done immediately after a good watering.

Other cultivations will be carried out as advised for apples, except that it is seldom that pears will be grown in grass, other than in the north.

When pears bear unusually heavily it is necessary to thin the fruits out.

431

ROUTINE WORK

Prune the trees in the winter directly the leaves have fallen, cleaning up any cuts made and painting over afterwards with thick white lead paint. Spray in December with a tar distillate wash and immediately afterwards dig over the ground shallowly, burying the weeds and leaving the ground rough and applying the fertilisers advised on page 428 at the same time.

If the leaf blister mite is troublesome, spray with lime-sulphur during February using 1 part of lime-sulphur to 30 parts of water ; spray again with this brown liquid just before the blossoms open, and again immediately after the blossoms have fallen ; formula : pre-blossom 1 in 30 ; post-blossom 1 in 80. If caterpillars are present in the post-blossom stage, add lead arsenate to the wash (for formula see page 652).

During the summer, hoe the ground regularly and carry out any summer pruning necessary. Remove any fruits seen to be affected by pear midge maggots in June. If any trees are bearing very heavy crops thin out the pears in June so that no fruit is closer than 5 ins. from the next. This is particularly necessary in the case of varieties like Fertility and Hessle, which normally bear small pears. It need not be done in the case of Conference.

Even after thinning, some pears crop so heavily that the branches are apt to break ; therefore, give such branches support in July and August by driving a pole into the ground and tying the branches up to this.

Where wasps and birds do damage, protect the individual fruits by tying paper or muslin bags around them ; the mouth of the bag should be tied to the spur or branch so that even if the fruit falls it cannot drop to the ground.

It is most important to pick pears at the right time and to know the varieties that will not keep. If the fruits are mealy in taste then they have been left too long on the trees. Pick the early and mid-season kinds just as the base colour of the fruits turns yellow. Lift a pear in the palm of the hand and, if it comes away naturally from the spur without pulling or tugging, it is ready. The earlies can be picked in the south in late July or early August and the mid-seasons three weeks later. The chart on page 434 gives the approximate picking time.

Try and store pears separately from apples. Pears like a storage temperature of from 40-45° Fahr. Store separately on trays if possible, and do not let the fruits touch one another.

Tree Fruits

SELECTED LIST OF VARIETIES FOR SMALL GARDENS:

Eaters	*Cookers*
Conference	Catillac
Dr. Jules Guyot	Uvedale's St. Germain
Doyenne du Comice	
Durondeau	
Joséphine de Malines	
Laxton's Superb	
Marie Louise	
Williams' Bon Chrétien	

TO BE GROWN AS STANDARDS AND HALF-STANDARDS:

Beurré Diel	Jargonelle
Doyenne du Comice	Louise Bonne de Jersey
Emile d'Heyst	Souvenir de Congrès
Hessle	Williams'

VARIETIES FOR EATING OR COOKING:

Beurré de Capiaumont	Pitmaston Duchess
Beurré Diel	Williams'
Durondeau	

DESSERT VARIETIES FOR CORDONS OR ESPALIERS, FOR SUCCESSION:

Doyenne d'Eté	July
Laxton's Superb	August
Williams' Bon Chrétien	August
Souvenir de Congrès	September
Dr. Jules Guyot	September
Beurré Hardy	October
Doyenne du Comice	October
Conference	October–November
Durondeau	October–November
Emile d'Heyst	October–November
Charles Ernest	November
Fondante de Thirriot	November–December
Joséphine de Malines	January

433

GOOD VARIETIES OF PEARS

Variety	Cooker or Eater	When to Pick	When to Use
Beurré d'Amanlis	E	1st week September	Early Sept.
Beurré de Capiaumont ..	E	3rd „ September	October
Beurré Diel..	E	1st „ September	Oct.–Nov.
Beurré Hardy	E	3rd „ September	October
Beurré Superfin	E	2nd „ September	October
Bristol Cross	E	3rd „ September	October
Catillac	C	3rd „ October	Feb.–April
Charles Ernest	E	2nd „ October	Oct.–Nov.
Clapp's Favourite	E	4th „ August	September
Conference	E	4th „ September	Oct.–Nov.
Dr. Jules Guyot	E	3rd „ August	Early Sept.
Doyenne du Comice ..	E	1st „ October	November
Doyenne d'Eté	E	3rd „ July	July–Aug.
Duchesse de Bordeaux ..	E	2nd „ October	Jan.–March
Durondeau	E	4th „ September	Oct.–Nov.
Emile d'Heyst	E	4th „ September	Oct.–Nov.
Foremost	E	2nd „ September	Late Sept.
Glou Morceau	E	2nd „ October	Dec.–Feb.
Jargonelle	E	1st „ August	August
Joséphine de Malines ..	E	1st „ October	Dec.–Jan.
Laxton's Superb ..	E	4th „ August	Early Sept.
Louise Bonne de Jersey ..	E	3rd „ September	October
Marie Louise	E	3rd „ September	Oct.–Nov.
Packham's Triumph ..	E	2nd „ October	November
Pitmaston Duchess	CE	4th „ September	Oct.–Nov.
Roosevelt	E	4th „ September	Oct.–Nov.
Souvenir de Congrès ..	E	1st „ September	September
Thompson's	E	3rd „ September	Oct.–Nov.
Uvedale's St. Germain ..	C	4th „ September	Oct.–March
Vicar of Winkfield ..	C	4th „ September	Nov.–Jan.
Williams' Bon Chrétien ..	CE	4th „ August	September

PLUMS

Plums will grow in grassland once they are established but they prefer, on the whole, to grow in cultivated ground. They are happy in most soils but they naturally hate land that is droughty in the summer as it is then they have to produce luscious fruits. They can put up with a little bad drainage, but they hate water-logging. As they flower early they must not be planted in low-lying places liable to spring frosts. In a district that is subject to spring frosts, the two best varieties to grow are probably Giant Prune and Czar. Plums like to be in a sheltered spot so that the insects that do the pollinating in the spring can do their work.

STOCKS

Unfortunately the classification of plum stocks isn't as simple as it is in the case of apples and pears. There are numerous varieties which are incompatible with certain stocks. This incompatibility may not appear for several years which is very serious, for a variety grafted on to an unsuitable stock may do well for a few years and then become stunted, and quite unprofitable ; or it may easily snap right off at the union of the stock and scion.

The chart given below (which appears by kind permission of the Ministry of Agriculture) shows which combinations of root stock and variety seem to be suitable and compatible.

PLUM ROOT STOCKS AND THEIR USES

Some suggested combinations of root stock and scion which appear suitable and compatible.
X=Combinations for large to medium trees.
O=Combinations for medium to small trees.

Scion Varieties	Myrobalan B	Brompton	Damas C	Common Mussel	Marianna	Pershore	St. Julien A	Common Plum
BELLE DE LOUVAIN		X		X	X			
BULLACES	X							
BUSH (KENT)	X							
CAMBRIDGE GAGE (*See* GAGE PLUMS)								
CHERRY PLUM	X							
CZAR	X	X		O				
DAMSONS	X							
GAGE PLUMS IN GENERAL		X	X	O			O	O
GIANT PRUNE	X	X		O	X			
GREEN GAGE (*See* GAGE PLUMS)								
MONARCH		X		O		O		O
MYROBOLAN (*See* CHERRY PLUM)								
OULLIN'S GOLDEN GAGE		X	X				O	O
PERSHORE (YELLOW EGG)	X	X			X	O		O
POND'S SEEDLING	X	X		O		O		
PRESIDENT	X	X		O				
PURPLE PERSHORE	X				X			O
RIVER'S EARLY PROLIFIC	X	X		O	X			O
UTILITY (LAXTON'S)	X			O	X			O
VICTORIA	X	X	X	O	X	O	O	O
WARWICKSHIRE DROOPER	X	X		O				

435

Some stocks seem to be perfectly satisfactory with all varieties, i.e. Common Mussel, Damas C, St. Julien A, and Pershore. Common Mussel is used for peaches, nectarines, apricots and all kinds of ornamental plums, but unfortunately it suckers badly and the fruit produced doesn't always maintain its size. Damas C and St. Julien A are similar in their behaviour and the latter will probably replace Common Mussel in time. It induces medium growth coupled with early cropping not only with plums but with peaches and apricots also. Pershore is useful for the production of small trees. This stock brings them into cropping early. The reason it is not more used is that it is difficult to propagate in the nursery.

MANURING

Young trees usually need little food and good soil. The great thing is to give well-rotted farmyard manure, or properly composted vegetable waste, each May as a mulch. What remains of this in the autumn after the worms have pulled the material in can be dug into the ground shallowly. When the trees come into bearing, apply a good fish manure or a good meat and bone meal, at the rate of 4 ozs. to the square yard during the autumn cultivations. On light land, trees may suffer from lack of potash and, as an insurance, sulphate of potash should be applied each season at 1 oz. to the square yard. When this is not obtainable, muriate of potash may be used instead at a similar rate, or a proprietary " flue dust " at 4 ozs. to the square yard.

Lime

All the old text-books tell you that stone fruits need quantities of lime. Actually this is not true, and a good dressing would be 7 ozs. of hydrated lime per square yard applied once every 5 years in January. Even this would not be necessary in cases where the trees grow in land with a chalky subsoil.

PLANTING

With plums, it is usual to plant standards or half-standards, even in small gardens, and then to grow soft fruits, especially blackcurrants, beneath. Many plums tend to droop and so are not suitable to grow as bushes.

It is necessary with plums to plant very firmly and, if the bark looks dried out after planting, release the bark tension in April by slitting the trunk vertically from top to bottom with a sharp knife, on the north side of the tree. The tension will thus be relieved and a good rise of sap assured. Always plant in the late autumn if possible rather than in spring. Do not, of course, plant during a frosty period. Stake afterwards as advised on page 394.

Standard and half-standard trees are usually bought as 3-year-olds and fan-shaped trees as 4 or 5-year-olds. Plums do not seem to mind being moved late in life, and it is possible to plant standards 6 or 7 years of age. In fact, when the trees in a 20-year-old orchard had to be thinned out recently, the plums were re-planted in another position and did quite well.

DISTANCES TO PLANT

For distances apart see Chart on page 395. It is always better to give more room than the distance suggested if possible.

PRUNING

As plums and damsons form spurs naturally, there is no need to prune back the laterals as is often done in the case of apples and pears. In the first 5 years aim to build up a strong framework of branches on which heavy crops of fruit may be borne later. Cut back all leaders, or 1-year-old end growths, by about half (see Fig. 25), the only exception being in the case of very strong growing varieties planted on very rich land ; hard cutting back in such cases tends to delay cropping.

Once the trees are established, say, at the end of the 6-year period, no further leader pruning should be necessary and the trees should be allowed to grow naturally. Crossing and rubbing branches and any diseased wood will of course be removed, and any branches that tend to droop on to the ground will be cut back to just below a more upward-growing branch.

Because the plum is particularly liable to silver leaf disease, and because the spores of this fungus are abundant in winter, it is always advisable to prune plums when established, in the summer, for then the silver leaf spores cannot get in. All large saw cuts, which have to be made either in the summer or winter, should be made smooth afterwards with the sharp blade of a knife and then painted over with a thick white lead paint. It is always better with plums to make a few large cuts than many small ones.

There are some varieties that tend to have an upright habit of growth and so need to be pruned with an eye to keeping the tree open. They are Belle de Louvain, Blaisdon Red, Czar, Gisbourne's Prolific, Monarch, President and Utility. There are others that have a drooping habit of growth and, when pruning, every attempt should be made to keep the branches off the ground. Natural "droopers" are Bountiful, Early Laxton, Merryweather, Purple Pershore, Rivers Early Prolific, Victoria and Warwickshire Drooper.

Summer pruning is not carried out in the normal way but, where trees are grown against walls as "fans," any breast wood (that is, wood that grows out at an angle of 90° from the wall) not required for tying in in the autumn is usually cut back to within 1 in. of its base. The winter pruning, in the case of fan-trained trees, is concerned with cutting out some of the old wood each winter and tying some of the new in its place.

POLLINATION

As large numbers of plums are self-sterile, and many are only partially self-fertile, it is most important, before planting, to study the John Innes Pollination Chart below. Too often one or two varieties are planted in a garden which cannot set their own flowers and then people wonder why they do not get fruit. Plums fall into three classes :—(*a*) those which entirely fail to set a crop with their own pollen ; (*b*) those which partly fail ; and (*c*) those which will set a crop with their own pollen. The rules to follow are : plums in class (*a*) and class (*b*) must be interplanted, either with suitable varieties from these classes, or with varieties from class (*c*). Plums in class (*c*) may be planted in large blocks of one variety.

CLASSES OF PLUM VARIETIES[1]

CLASS A entirely fail to set with their own pollen	*CLASS B set a poor crop (2-5% of the total number of blossoms produced) with their own pollen*	*CLASS C set and develop a full crop (15-30% of the total number of blossoms produced) with their own pollen*
1. Coe's Golden Drop Coe's Violet Gage Comte d'Althan Crimson Drop Diamond Early Greengage Frogmore Damson Grand Duke Jefferson Late Orleans Mallard President Primate	Blue Rock Early Favourite Early Laxton River's Early Prolific Utility	Bountiful Brahy's Greengage Denniston't Superb Early Transport Goliath Guthrie's Late Monarch Prince of Wales Prosperity Warwickshire Drooper
2. Allgrove's Superb Black Prince Bryanston Gage Golden Esperen Late Orange McLaughlin's Gage Old Greengage A & B Transparent Gage	Old Greengage C & D Reine Claude Violette	Bastard Victoria Blaisdon Red Brandy Gage Cropper [Damson Merryweather Prune Géante Reine Claude de Bavay Victoria

438

CLASSES OF PLUM VARIETIES (CONT'D)

CLASS A entirely fail to set with their own pollen	CLASS B set a poor crop (2-5% of the total number of blossoms produced) with their own pollen	CLASS C set and develop a full crop (15-30% of the total number of blossoms produced) with their own pollen
3. DELICIOUS KIRKE'S BLUE LATE TRANSPARENT LAWSON'S GOLDEN GAGE POND'S SEEDLING PRUNE D'AGEN	BELGIAN PURPLE CAMBRIDGE GAGE COX'S EMPEROR FARLEIGH DAMSON GOLDFINCH	BELLE DE LOUVAIN BELLE DE SEPTEMBRE CZAR GISBORNE'S GOLDEN TRANSPARENT JUBILEE KEA KING OF THE DAMSONS LAXTON'S GAGE MARJORIE'S SEEDLING OULLIN'S GOLDEN GAGE PERSHORE PURPLE PERSHORE SUPREME WHITE MAGNUM BONUM
4. BLACKBIRD DECAISNE WHITE DAMSON YELLOW MAGNUM BONUM		EARLY MIRABELLE

1. Early flowering.
2. Mid-season flowering.
3. Late flowering.
4. Flowering season not recorded.

Note.—GOLDEN ESPEREN has no good pollen, and is therefore useless as a pollinator.

INCOMPATIBLE GROUPS OF PLUMS

(from Classes A and B)

I	IIa	IIIa
JEFFERSON COE'S GOLDEN DROP COE'S VIOLET GAGE CRIMSON DROP ALLGROVE'S SUPERB	PRESIDENT LATE ORANGE	RIVERS' EARLY PROLIFIC
	IIb	IIIb
	OLD GREENGAGE CAMBRIDGE GAGE	BLUE ROCK

Note.—The *a* and *b* sub-groups are not completely compatible.
IIa pollinated by IIb sets a full crop.
IIb pollinated by IIa sets a very poor crop.
Similarly for IIIa and IIIb.

Four varieties, perhaps bud sports, are distributed as OLD GREENGAGE. They all belong to Group II. The differences are mainly in flower and leaf characters.

[1] This pollination chart is included by the courtesy and permission of Dr. Cyril D. Darlington, the Director of the John Innes Horticultural Institution, Merton, and is taken from the book " The Fruit and the Soil " (*Oliver and Boyd, 1948*). See page 438.

CULTIVATION

Plums do best on land that is regularly cultivated and, as they are surface rooters, winter digging must be shallowly done, and so must summer hoeings.

If it is absolutely necessary to grow plums in grassland, care must be taken to see that the trees receive sufficient nitrogen. Keep the grass regularly grazed with poultry or, if mowing has to be done, allow this to lie on the ground and apply nitro-chalk at 3 ozs. to the square yard in June and September just after mowing.

It is never advisable to allow grass to grow among plum trees until they are 6 years or so old.

ROUTINE WORK

Spray the plums with a good tar distillate wash in December ; a 5% solution will be sufficient. Dig or fork the ground over shallowly afterwards to bury weeds and apply bone meal at 3-4 ozs. to the square yard at the same time, plus sulphate of potash at 1 oz. to the square yard. When this latter is not available, use a proprietary flue dust about 3 ozs. to the square yard. It is often simpler to use a good fish manure to which potash has been added by the manufacturer at 4-5 ozs. to the sqare yard.

Prune the trees as late as possible, preferably in March, if winter pruning be necessary. Remove any dry " mummied " plums seen on the trees at the same time. These mummied plums are a perfect curse and spread the brown rot disease that ruins a crop. While doing this, look for dead shoots and cut these off and burn them. They will probably have been killed by the wither tip or brown rot disease.

Spray with lime-sulphur, formula 1 in 100, immediately after flowering, to control red spider and rust. If aphids are present, add nicotine to the wash or use nicotine alone in cases where there is no red spider or rust, formula $\frac{3}{4}$ oz. liquid nicotine to 10 gals. of water.

Apply lawn mowings, composted vegetable refuse, damped horticultural peat, or some similar material around the trees in May as far as the branches spread and to a depth of 1 in. This is particularly necessary in the case of young trees and on dry soils.

Hoe regularly throughout the summer, and in July, if it is seen that the mulchings have disintegrated, a further top dressing may be applied.

Be careful to thin the heavy cropping varieties, spacing the plums out to 2 ins. apart. This not only encourages annual bearing because it prevents a tree exhausting itself one year, it also prevents the branches from breaking. Do this work in June.

Be prepared to support the branches of plums early in July because with a heavy crop they are apt to break. A broken branch may not only ruin the shape of the tree and cause a reduction of crop afterwards, but the wound thus formed may let in the Silver Leaf disease. There are various ways of supporting branches :

(1) A wooden prop, or pole, may be tied to the trunk of the tree, with the top of it 3 or 4 ft. above, and from this top strings or old telephone wires may radiate down to the branches so as to take the weight.

(2) Strong, long, double-ended wire hooks may be used, one end of the hook going round a branch on one side of the tree and the other end of the hook round a branch on the opposite side of the tree, so that the one branch supports the other.

(3) Eyelet screws are screwed into the branches so that old telephone wire or strong string may be inserted and one branch made to support another.

(4) It is possible to use poles with a V top like a laundry prop, each to support one branch. (See illustrations facing page 416.)

Pick plums immediately they are ready. Go over the tree several times for this purpose. Don't pick carelessly for, if the stalks are pulled out of the plums when picking, the fruit rots. When wasps are a great nuisance hang a jam jar in the tree $\frac{1}{4}$ filled with a little sugary liquid. The washings of a jam jar will do. Cover the jar with thick paper, and make a hole in the centre, with a pencil. The wasps will go in, but can never get out.

SELECTED LIST OF VARIETIES FOR A FAIR-SIZED GARDEN

Coe's Golden Drop	Jefferson
Czar	Monarch
Denniston's Superb	Rivers' Early Prolific
Early Laxton	Victoria

SELECTED LIST FOR A SMALL GARDEN

Czar	Jefferson
Giant Prune	Victoria

TO BE GROWN AS STANDARDS OR HALF-STANDARDS

Belle de Louvain	Monarch
Bryanston Gage	Oullin's Golden Gage
Coe's Golden Drop	Pond's Seedling

To be Grown as Standards or Half-Standards (Cont'd)

Czar
Denniston's Superb
Early Laxton
Giant Prune
Jefferson

Purple Pershore
Reine Claude de Bavay
Rivers' Early Prolific
Victoria
Wyedale

Varieties for Eating or Cooking

Coe's Golden Drop
Denniston's Superb
Jefferson

Rivers' Early Prolific
Victoria

Damsons and Bullaces for Half-Standards or Bushes

Farleigh
Merryweather

Shropshire Prune

GOOD VARIETIES OF PLUMS

Variety	When to Pick	When to Use
Belle de Louvain ..	Late August	Will keep a little after picking
Burbank's Giant Prune	Late September	Will keep a little after picking
Cambridge Gage ..	Mid-August	Use on picking. Dessert
Coe's Golden Drop ..	Mid-late Sept.	Use on picking. Dessert
Czar	Early August	Good for bottling
Denniston's Superb ..	Mid-August	Use on picking. Dessert
Early Laxton	Mid-July	Will keep a very little after picking
Early Transparent Gage	Mid-August	Use on picking. Dessert
Greengage	Late August	Will keep a little after picking
Jefferson Gage ..	Early September	Use on picking. Dessert
Laxton's Gage ..	Late August	Will keep a little after picking
Oullin's Golden Gage..	Mid-August	Good for bottling if picked early
Pershore	Late August	A good variety for jam
Pond's Seedling ..	Late September	Will keep a little. Good for dessert when ripe
Purple Pershore ..	Mid-August	Will keep a little after picking
Rivers' Early ..	Late July	Culinary or dessert
Victoria	Mid-August	Culinary or dessert, preferably the latter when fully ripe
DAMSONS		
Merryweather ..	Mid-late Sept.	Culinary
Shropshire Prune ..	Mid-September	Culinary

NUTS

★

FILBERTS AND COB NUTS

FILBERTS and cob nuts are so similar that they are being dealt with in one group. They will do quite well on almost any soil if well drained but, as they tend to make too much growth on " strong " land, this should be avoided. Choose a sunny open position where there is protection from the north and north-east.

TYPES OF TREES
Grow as bushes on a 15-in. stem. Plant 2 or 3-year-olds 15 ft. square.

MANURING
Apply fish manure each February at 3 ozs. to the square yard, and each autumn apply 1 good barrowload of well-rotted vegetable compost per 10 sq. yds., and dig in very shallowly. Lime is usually given every third year, say, hydrated lime, at 7 ozs. to the square yard.

PRUNING
When the trees are young, prune very much like young apple trees. After 7 or 8 years, delay winter pruning until early in March, cutting back the laterals or side growths by about ¾ and removing ¼ from the ends of each leader.

Cut off all suckers coming up from the roots. Do not cut back the short laterals that look rather spindly. The bulk of the best fruit is often borne on such laterals.

In the summer in August, prune back the laterals by half. They can be broken off. This is known as brutting. Once the branches have got to be about 6 ft. in height, cut the leaders back hard.

POLLINATION
The female flowers bloom early in the season, from mid-February onwards. This is the reason why pruning is delayed until March, so that there may be ample pollen from the male catkins.

CULTIVATION AND ROUTINE WORK
Apply manure in the winter and lightly dig or fork in. Prune the

443

leaders and laterals in March. Spray in April with lime-sulphur to control the nut gall mite (formula, 7 parts lime-sulphur to 93 parts of water). Spray with arsenate of lead early in June to kill nut weevil. Use arsenate of lead and a suitable spreader.

Wait until the husks are quite hard before gathering the nuts.

VARIETIES

Cosford. Upright tall tree; nuts very thin shelled. Sweet flavoured.

Kentish Cob. Crops heavily in clusters of from 2-5. Excellent flavour.

White Filbert. A slender grower. Upright. Kernel skin pure white.

WALNUTS

Walnuts must always be planted where they are not likely to be damaged by frost in the spring. They prefer a deep heavy loam containing a sufficient quantity of lime.

STOCKS

More uniformly growing trees can be produced on the two stocks, *Juglans nigra* and *Juglans regia*.

MANURING

Apply meat and bone meal at 2 ozs. to the square yard in the spring. Work this into the ground.

PLANTING

Normally half-standards or standards are planted and it is possible to-day to get good results with bush trees. Standards should be 50 ft. square and bush trees 18 ft. square. Plant early winter, trees to be 3 years old.

PRUNING

If standards, allow the small side shoots up the main stem to develop for the first 4 or 5 years, pruning them back in the summer to a length of 9 ins. The 1-year-old growths at the ends of these branches known as leaders should be pruned back the first 2 years by about half.

Bush trees are usually kept dwarf by pinching out the tips of the young shoots when not more than 5 or 6 leaves have formed. Half-inch of the tip is removed, and this causes the buds below to plump up and form female flower buds. Thin, weak shoots are not touched as these bear pollen catkins. If a tree persists in making too much wood, lift it in October and re-plant in the same spot. It is unwise to prune walnuts at any time between Christmas and May.

POLLINATION
Male and female flowers are produced separately. Therefore, to get trees to crop early, it is necessary to plant varieties that throw male catkins during the first few years of their life. Plant as a pollinator a variety that bears catkins freely when the tree is young.

CULTIVATION AND ROUTINE WORK
Cultivate around the trees for the first 5 or 6 years for at least 4 ft. Winter fork, therefore, each December to clean the ground. Apply meat and bone meal in February. If bacterial blight occurs spray the trees when they come into leaf with Bordeaux Mixture, and again a fortnight later.

Hoe regularly around the trees during the summer and summer prune the bush trees in June and July, to keep the branches dwarfed. Pick the nuts directly the leaves start to fall, or pick them up from the ground when they fall.

VARIETIES
Franquette; produces leaves late. Less susceptible to May frosts. Nuts large, and easily cracked.
Mayette; produces large rounded nuts, well filled. Easy to crack.
Perasienne; very hardy, almost frost resistant, produces nice round large nuts of good flavour.

N.B.—There are some first-class English varieties recommended by the East Malling Research Station, Kent. I cannot find a nurseryman, however, who stocks them.

SOFT FRUITS

★

BLACKBERRIES, LOGANBERRIES AND HYBRID BERRIES

ALL these cane fruits like to be liberally treated. They appreciate plenty of organic matter and the soil should be bastard trenched properly before they are planted. They all dislike badly-drained soils and are all gross feeders.

MANURING
Give well-rotted farmyard manure or properly composted vegetable refuse as a mulch each May. In addition give the organic fertilisers advised for raspberries (see page 453).

PLANTING
Plant 1-year-old bedded plants in the spring, rows 6 ft. apart, plants 15 ft. apart in the rows. They may be grown against fences or walls, up pergolas or against a trellis.

Where a special structure is erected this may consist of posts 7 ft. long, driven 18 ins. into the ground, with 3 wires stretched tightly between; the bottom wire 18 ins. from soil level, the second wire 2 ft. above this and the third wire at the top of the post.

PROPAGATION
Select young canes during the third week of August and layer these with the terminal bud intact. Bury the tip of the cane 4-6 ins. in the ground. Put a 1-in. layer of damped horticultural peat in the bottom of the hole made for the purpose and take care not to damage the tip when covering over. (See Fig. 26.) Tips layered the third week in August may be severed from their parents the third week in November and transplanted into their new position in April. Sever from the parent plant 6 ins. above the ground.

PRUNING
Cut away old canes a month after they have finished fruiting. With some of the stronger berries, like Himalaya Giant, a few of the older canes may be left till the second year. These have their side growths pruned back to within 2 ins. of the main stem. Pick from August to mid-October as the berries turn ripe. Never allow them to become over-ripe and drop to the ground.

CULTIVATION AND ROUTINE WORK
Dig ground over shallowly to bury manure, or other organic matter, in winter. Spray with liquid Derris when blossoms are open to prevent maggots in fruits. Hoe shallowly during the summer to keep down weeds.

SPECIAL NOTES
Boysenberry
> Very heavy cropper, bears very large loganberry-like fruits, very dark red in colour. Often takes 2 years to settle down in new position.

King's Acre Berry
> Like a large blackberry but parts from its core like a raspberry.

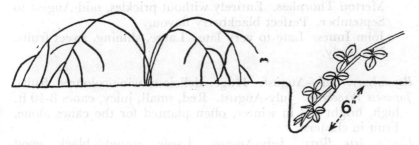

FIG. 26. LAYERING LOGANBERRY WITH DROOPING STEMS

Loganberry
> This is picked with the plug inside the fruit and not like the raspberry where the plug is left on the cane. It is worthwhile buying a good strain of loganberry. There are several poor types on the market.

Nectarberry
> Produces a huge blackberry-like loganberry, three times the size of a normal loganberry fruit. Very delicious, both for dessert or jam.

Newberry
> Similar to the phenomenal berry.

Phenomenalberry
> A kind of loganberry that throws larger fruits and ripens later.

Cane tipping is usually not necessary because phenomenal berries are not strong growers.

Veitchberry

The veitchberry is used in August and is of a mulberry colour.

Youngberry

Intermediate between loganberry and what is usually called dewberry. May be damaged by winter frosts.

VARIETIES
Blackberries

Bedford Giant. Early, say, end July. Large, excellent flavour, sweet.

Himalaya Berry. Mid to late. Strong canes. Black shiny fruits.

Merton Thornless. Entirely without prickles, mid-August to September. Perfect blackberry flavour.

John Innes. Late to very late. Large, shining, sweet fruits. Not seedy.

Boysenberry. July-August. Huge, delicious wine-coloured fruits.

Japanese Wineberry. July-August. Red, small, juicy, canes 8-10 ft. high, bright red in winter, often planted for the canes alone. Fruit in clusters.

King's Acre Berry. July-August. Large, round, black, good flavour fruits.

Loganberry. July-August. Strong good croppers, claret colour, acid.

Lowberry. July-August. Jet black. Good fruits, not acid.

Nectarberry. July-August. Very large black, long-shaped fruits, excellent flavour.

Phenomenalberry. August. Purplish-red firm fruit. Sweet.

Veitchberry. August. Mulberry colour. Culinary.

White Blackberry. Mid-August-September. Sweet, white, juicy, transparent fruits.

Worcesterberry. Mid-August-September. Grows like a strong gooseberry and should be treated as such. Bears oval fruits, very dark, with currant-like flavour.

Youngberry. July-August. Large sweet wine-coloured fruits.

CURRANTS, BLACK

Blackcurrants are so rich in vitamin C that they should be grown in every garden. They succeed on most kinds of soils, though

ix. *Campsis Tagliabuana*

x. Nemesias

they prefer one that is deep and contains plenty of humus. They will put up with wetter conditions than most other soft fruit. They like shelter from east winds at the time of blossoming.

MANURING

Apply one good barrowload of properly composted vegetable refuse to every 6-yd. length of row each autumn, and give mulchings with similar material in June. Apply a good organic fertiliser, like fish manure, meat and bone meal or hoof and horn meal, at about 4-5 ozs. to the square yard, each December. In January or February dried blood may be applied at 4 ozs. to the square yard on light soil, and nitro-chalk on heavy land at 2 ozs. to the square yard. The great thing is to give plenty of organic matter.

PLANTING

Plant 1- or 2-year-olds, either 5 ft. square or in rows 6 ft. apart, the bushes 3 ft. apart in the rows.

PROPAGATION

Make cuttings 9 ins. long, from 1-year-old wood, cut just above a bud at the top and below a bud at the bottom. Prepare trenches 6 ins. deep, and lay the cuttings in these, upright, 4 ins. apart, with the rows 1 ft. apart.

PRUNING

After planting, cut all branches down almost to ground level. In subsequent years remove 2 or 3 branches each winter so as to keep the bush furnished with plenty of new growths. (See illustration facing page 384.)

POLLINATION

Many blackcurrant varieties depend on the visitation of insects for pollination, particularly Boskoop Giant, French Black and Seabrook's Black. Therefore give protection from cold winds at blossoming time.

CULTIVATION AND ROUTINE WORK

Prune bushes in November. Spray in December with a 5% solution of a tar distillate wash. Then apply the compost and dig the land over shallowly. In April, when the leaves are the size of a two-shilling piece, spray with lime-sulphur, at 1 in 20 (i.e. 1 pt. to 20 pts. of water) to control big bud mite. (For sulphur-shy varieties, see page 450.) Apply a mulching of compost in June.

Examine the bushes in July for reversion. Cut out affected branches or grub whole bushes. (See page 674.) Spray with Bordeaux Mixture in August if necessary to control the leaf spot fungus. Any leaves affected by leaf spot may be collected and burned in October.

Varieties

Amos Black; large delicious berries, compact bushes, very late.

Cotswold Cross; berries moderately large, easy to pick, heavy cropper. Late.

Malvern Cross; berries moderately large, trusses compact, upright grower. Late.

Mendip Cross; very heavy cropper, large berries, long trusses, bush slightly spreading. Early.

Welling XXX; best mid-season kind, heavy cropper, fine flavour, good quality.

CURRANTS, RED AND WHITE

On the whole red and white currants prefer a light soil and a sunny situation, plus shelter from strong winds. They may easily suffer from lack of potash.

Manuring

Apply 2 large forkfuls of well-rotted compost or dung to each bush each spring. Apply sulphate or muriate of potash each December at 2 ozs. per bush. Use fine wood ashes at $\frac{1}{2}$ lb. per bush, if these are not available. Every other year give, in addition, an organic fertiliser, such as fish manure, hoof and horn meal, meat and bone meal, or poultry manure, at 5 ozs. per square yard.

Planting

Plant bushes on a 6-in. leg, or short stem. Half-standards may be planted in a border, or cordons trained up wires, fences or walls. Plant 2- or 3-year-olds in November or December if possible though the half-standards may be 4-year-olds. Bushes are planted 5 ft. square, though with weak varieties like Fay's, 4 ft. square will do.

Propagation

Take healthy 1-year-old growths in November and cut them up into lengths of 15 ins. Remove all buds, with the exception of the top 3 or 4. Dig out a trench 7 ins. deep, with 1 straight side, and lay cuttings against this side, 6 ins. apart, and 7 ins. deep. Put the soil back and firm it thoroughly against base of cuttings.

Soft Fruits

PRUNING

Aim to build up a bush with 6 or 7 main branches " goblet-shaped." For the first 4 years, cut the leader or end growth back by about half. After this, prune leader back by $\frac{1}{4}$ in each case to just above a bud. Try and leave the tops of the leaders level. Cut back laterals (side growths) each winter to within 1 in. of their base. With cordons, the end growth is pruned back by about half each year and the side growths cut back to within 1 in. Half-standards are pruned as for bushes except that the main stem is allowed to carry short fruiting spurs.

The laterals are broken off by half in the summer to let the sunshine in to ripen the fruit. This is known as brutting.

HARVESTING

Pick directly the currants are of a good clear colour. A whole bunch should be gathered at a time, and the branches gone over 2 or 3 times.

CULTIVATION AND ROUTINE WORK

Prune in November. Spray with a tar distillate wash in December and, afterwards, add organic manures and fork over. In bird-infested districts, cotton the bushes with black cotton to prevent buds being ruined.

If capsid bugs have caused trouble the previous year, spray with D.N.C. (see page 391) in March. If aphids give trouble in May, spray with nicotine. They should not do so if tar distillate washing was properly done in December. Hoe shallowly during the summer. Apply mulches of well-rotted compost in June. Summer prune in mid-June and, in July, cut off any dead wood there may be and burn it.

VARIETIES

Earliest of Fourlands. The earliest, regular cropper. Large berry.

Fay's Prolific. Early. Heavy cropper. Wood rather brittle.

Laxton's No. 1. Early to mid-season. Lovely colour. Regular heavy cropper. Large berry.

Laxton's Perfection. Mid-season. Excellent colour. Good cropper. Very large berries.

River's Late Red. Late. Bright red. Heavy cropper. Large berries.

White Champion. Late. Good clear colour. Large berries.

White la Versaillaise. Early. Very pale yellow. Heavy cropper. Large berries.

Wilson's Longbunch. Mid-season. Long truss. Large berries.

GOOSEBERRIES

Do best on a medium-type soil. Insist on good drainage.

MANURING
Give one good barrowload of well-rotted vegetable compost to each 12 bushes every year. In December apply 2 ozs. of sulphate or muriate of potash per bush.

PLANTING
Buy bushes on a 6-in. leg, as this prevents suckering and discourages mildew. Plant 5 × 5 ft. before the turn of the year, rather than after the New Year. Choose a 2- or 3-year-old bush. Cordons may be planted 2 ft. apart.

PROPAGATION
Choose healthy 1-year-old wood 15 ins. long. Cut with a sharp knife just above a bud at top end and just below at bottom end. Remove all the buds on the cuttings except the top 3. Insert the cuttings in the soil 6 ins. deep and 6 ins. apart.

PRUNING
The simplest method of pruning is to remove the crowding and rubbing branches, together with any growing too near the ground. Such little pruning makes for ease of picking and a minimum of strong growths which may otherwise be difficult to handle. Varieties which tend to droop should be cut back to an upward-growing bud. For the first 3 or 4 years the leaders will need cutting back by half to form a good strong framework.

Cordon trees are usually spurred ; the side growths are cut back to within 1 in. of their base and the leaders reduced by half. Most winter pruning is left until late, say, March, because birds often come and peck out the buds when pruning is done earlier— as the bush is more open. Further, if the pruning is delayed, and birds have attacked, you can at least see what buds are left !

THINNING
When gooseberries are grown for dessert, the berries should be thinned out from Whitsun onwards, to leave the berries spaced out 1 or 2 ins. apart.

HARVESTING
Pick dessert gooseberries when ripe, and green gooseberries any time from May onwards.

Soft Fruits

Cultivation and Routine Work

Spray the bushes with a tar distillate wash in December. Fork over the ground and add the compost in December or January. Carry out the pruning in March and, if red spider and capsid bugs are bad, spray at the end of March with a white oil D.N.C.

To control mildew spray with lime-sulphur or washing soda immediately after flowering, in April. (For sulphur-shy varieties see below.) Mulch if necessary with compost or lawn mowings in June.

In gardens where birds abound, protect bushes during winter by intertwining black cotton between the branches.

Varieties

Careless. Mid-season. Heavy cropper. White.

Lancashire Lad. Mid-season. Dark red. Resistant to mildew.

Leveller. Mid-season. Excellent dessert. Yellow. Susceptible to lime-sulphur spray.

Ringer. Mid-season. Yellow. Exhibition variety.

Warrington. Late. Makes excellent jam. Red.

Whinham's Industry. Mid-season. Sweet flavour. Hardy. Red.

White Lion. Late. White. Picks well green. Early.

Whitesmith. Mid-season. White. Upright grower. Popular for small gardens.

RASPBERRIES

There are both summer and autumn fruiting types. They love moisture in the summer when they are trying to produce their berries. They prefer the loams but will grow in clay if well drained. Plenty of organic matter must be added to the soil before they are planted and this may be done when bastard trenching the ground. Aim to give 1 good barrowload to 10 sq. yds.

Manuring

Apply well-rotted dung, or compost, along the rows each May, to act as a mulch. Other organic substances, like spent hops, may be used instead. Each autumn, apply a good fish manure, meat and bone meal or hoof and horn meal, at 4 ozs. to the square yard and give sulphate or muriate of potash, in addition, at 2 ozs. to the square yard. Apply these all over the ground rather than along the rows.

Propagation

Be very careful only to save suckers or spawn (see Fig. 27) from

453

healthy canes. Dig up the suckers (or spawn, as it is called) in November and plant out in separate rows.

PLANTING
Plant as early as possible in the winter, preferably November or December. Buy canes of medium length and vigour with a good root system. Virus-free stocks are available in some varieties. Plant no deeper than 2 ins., or on very sandy soils, 3 ins. Rows 4 or 5 ft. apart ; canes 18 ins. apart in the rows. In the February after planting, cut the canes down to within 6 ins. of ground level.

Have a stout post at either end of the rows and stretch two wires, one 3 ft. 6 ins. and the other 4 ft. 6 ins. from ground level. Tie canes to wires.

PRUNING
Cut canes that have fruited, down to ground level each autumn.

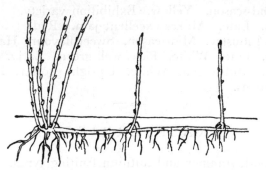

FIG. 27   RASPBERRY PLANT AND SUCKERS

(See illustration facing page 384.) Cut out all weak canes, leaving 5 or 6 strong ones per " stool." Tip tallest canes back to 5 or 6 ft., or bend them round and tie tips to top wire. Do either in February.

Autumn fruiting varieties should be cut down to ground level early in March.

HARVESTING
Pick directly the berries are ready. Do not allow ripe berries to fall to the ground or useless seedlings may arise and cause trouble.

CULTIVATION AND ROUTINE WORK
Never cultivate deeply near raspberries. Give mulches of well-rotted dung or well-rotted compost each May or June. Be liberal with organic matter. Do not use a thick mat of fresh grass

mowings, or the heat engendered may damage base of canes and newly-forming shoots.

Look out for cane spot or spur blight and spray with lime-sulphur at 1 pint to 15 pints of water, late in April and early in May. Late in May, pick off and burn any dying laterals. These may contain red caterpillars.

Spray with liquid Derris in June when the flowers are open, to prevent maggots in the fruits.

Prune in September, removing old canes and dead wood. Burn these and apply the ash along the rows.

VARIETIES

Lloyd George (New Zealand strain), red firm berry, summer and autumn fruiter, good for jam.

Malling Exploit, long bright red berries, very showy, ripens early.

Malling Jewel, very heavy cropper, stiff erect canes, early, good for dessert or jam.

Malling Landmark, very heavy cropper, bright coloured fruit, somewhat soft.

Malling Notable, a good northern variety, berries large bright and easy to pick.

Malling Promise, large fruits, blossoms resistant to frost, ripens early and yields heavily.

Norfolk Giant, a very late variety resistant to frost, makes lovely jam.

STRAWBERRIES

Strawberries love to grow in soil rich in organic matter. Land must be properly drained and the ground free from perennial weeds.

MANURING

Take great trouble in preparing the ground, so as to " push up " the organic content. Bastard trench the ground, digging in well-rotted dung or properly composted vegetable refuse at one good barrowload to 8 sq. yds. When forking over the surface to level it and work it down fine, add damped horticultural peat at the rate of half a bucketful per square yard. In addition, apply a high-grade fish manure, hoof and horn meal or meat and bone meal, at 4-5 ozs. to the square yard, and sulphate or muriate of potash at 2 ozs. to the square yard. A good flue dust, with a high potash content, might be given instead at 4-5 ozs. to the square yard.

Each season after the strawberries have been planted, apply an organic fertiliser such as those mentioned above, at 2-3 ozs. to the yard run in late February or early March.

PLANTING

Obtain a good virus-free stock. See that the land is level, clean and firm. Always plant late in the summer or early in the autumn. July and August plantings invariably succeed better than those put in later. Plant with a trowel. Spread the roots out, never allow them to be bunched up. Plant so that the crowns are just above soil level.

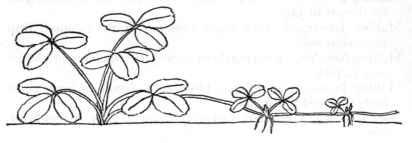

FIG. 28   STRAWBERRY PLANT AND RUNNERS

POLLINATION

Most varieties are self-fertile, but three of the usual varieties are self-sterile, i.e. Huxley's Giant, Oberschlesien and Tardive de Leopold. Royal Sovereign is a good pollinator for almost any variety.

PROPAGATION

Only save runners (see Fig. 28) from virus-free plants. It helps to peg the runners down with bent wires shaped like hairpins. (See illustration facing page 417.) These should be pushed into the ground just behind the plantlets as they form. It is possible to sink 3-in. pots filled with a John Innes compost (see page 576) into the ground to rim level, and strike the runner plantlets in them. Large numbers of runners may be saved from 1-year-old plants, but it is not advisable to save runners from 2-year-olds.

Soft Fruits

PROTECTION

Straw put along the rows does not give protection from frost, but rather " encourages " frost damage. Continuous cloches are ideal for giving the right protection. They ensure earlier fruiting. Fish netting put over the beds does keep away birds and may help in preventing frost damage.

HARVESTING

Pick early in the day, though during very hot weather it may be necessary to gather twice a day.

CULTIVATION AND ROUTINE WORK

Clean the ground thoroughly after fruiting, removing the straw, and putting it on the compost heap. Keep the rows clean by hoeing and earth up to the plants rather than away from them, for new roots are formed higher up the plants each season.

Remove any stunted small-leaved plants seen and burn them.

Apply fish manure or other organic fertilisers in February or early March.

Spray in March with lime-sulphur solution (see page 645) to keep down tarsonemid mites and red spiders.

Put down straw or peat (I prefer sedge peat) along the rows to keep the berries clean.

Spray early in June with nicotine to keep down aphids (see page 644). If mildew or red spider is bad that month, dust with a proprietary sulphur dust.

VARIETIES

Cambridge Favourite (Shewell-Mauditt Strain) very heavy cropper, fruits large, salmon scarlet, plants compact. Second-Early.

Cambridge Late Pine, flowers late, resistant to frost. Fruits excellent sweet flavour. Late.

Cambridge Prize-winner; berries light scarlet, firm, appreciates wood ashes. Early.

Cambridge Rival. Good for wet parts of England, resistant to Red Core, fruits conical crimson. Early.

Cambridge Rearguard. Hates poorly drained soil, prefers light land. Very late. Poor colour.

Crusader; fruit solid, firm, superb flavour, resistant to frost. Early.

Red Gauntlet; vigorous grower, fruits medium, scarlet, flavour excellent. Mid-Season.

Templer; v. vigorous grower, medium sized fruits, scarlet. Flavour first class.

Royal Sovereign; (East Malling 50 Strain), very delicious, fruits scarlet, large, the epicure's variety. Mid-Season.

Talisman; vigorous and heavy cropping; large crimson berries, resistant to mildew. Mid-Season.

ALPINE STRAWBERRIES

These are raised by sowing seed in spring or autumn, either in a rich, warm seed bed in the open or in a John Innes compost in the greenhouse. Put plants out in rows 1 ft. apart, plants 1 ft. apart in the rows. It is advisable to raise new plants from seed every other year.

VARIETIES

Alpine Improved. Mid to late. Deep red. Small, good flavour. Hardy.

Belle de Meaux. Mid to late. Red. Medium. Long fruits. Good flavour. Forms runners.

Gaillon Rouge Amélioré. Mid to late. Pale red. Sweet. Strong grower. Heavy cropper.

REMONTANT STRAWBERRIES

These crop in the summer and throughout the autumn to December, if grown in a nice sunny sheltered situation. The autumn crop is produced on the rooted runners. The rows should be $2\frac{1}{2}$ ft. apart, the plants 2 ft. apart in the rows. When the runners develop in the summer, peg them down around their parents, only allowing one plant to develop on each runner. Make new beds annually in September by planting out the best of the runners.

VARIETIES

Hampshire Maid; deblossom May and June so that it fruits from July to November. Very heavy cropper.

Red Rich; dark red juicy berries, dark green leaves, strong grower and heavy late cropper.

Sans Rivale; very heavy cropping; vigorous grower. Large trusses. Fruits late September to Christmas, if covered with glass Ganwicks.

St. Claude; vigorous grower, disease resister. Berries juicy and sweet. Picks September to late November.

SPECIAL FRUITS

★

CRAB APPLES

GROW in just the same way as ordinary apples, usually as half-standards or standards. May be planted on grass or cultivated land if required.

VARIETIES

Probably the best varieties are :

Dartmouth. Deep crimson fruit, very pretty. Makes good preserves.

John Downie. Oval-shaped fruit, scarlet. Heavy cropper. Decorative.

Siberian Yellow. Small golden-yellow apples. Very prolific.

Transcendent. May be used as dessert variety. Yellow with crimson cheek.

Veitch's Scarlet. Can be used as dessert. Flushed crimson. Oval fruits.

MEDLARS

Medlars are not much grown nowadays, but will do quite well in almost any soil, though rather moist loam is preferable.

MANURING

Medlars should be manured in a similar manner to pears (see page 428).

PLANTING

Two- or three-year-old trees are best in the case of bush types and 3- to 4-year-olds as standards. Plant any time between November and March, the earlier the better. Stake properly.

PRUNING

When a tree is established, after 6 or 7 years, cut out dead and diseased wood each year, removing all crossing and rubbing branches and any misplaced growths, to let in light and air.

HARVESTING

If trees are growing on grass the fruit may be allowed to fall to the ground, and be collected. Otherwise they should be picked in November and stored, calyx downwards, on sheets of clean paper in a cool, light, airy room or on a shelf in a greenhouse. In 3 weeks or so the fruit will have turned brown and begun to decay. This is known as " bletting," and means the medlars are ready to eat.

VARIETIES

Dutch. Large, good-flavoured fruits. Spreading habit. Good cropper.

Royal. Prolific cropper. Crops when quite young. Suitable as bush or pyramid.

MULBERRIES

Only one variety of mulberry is grown in this country, but it is very decorative.

They like deep soil, especially a loam which will retain moisture. The best fruit is obtained from trees in cultivated soil.

PLANTING

Plant during late spring. Do not break roots when planting, and do not shorten the roots, as may be done in the case of apples, pears and plums.

PRUNING

Retain as much as possible of the previous year's wood. Aim at forming short spurs to make for ease of picking, and better-sized fruit. Shorten the leaders back to half their length, when the tree is young. After this the leaders should only be tipped and the laterals spurred back to, say, a length of 3 ins.

HARVESTING

The fruit usually ripens late in August and early in September. Pick it when it is a blackish-purple. If preferred, cloths can be laid on the ground and the fruit shaken from the tree on to these, but the cloths will be much stained by the juice. Thus only the really ripe berries will fall off and they can be used for dessert. For culinary purposes gather berries when bright red.

CULTIVATION

Apart from pruning and general cultivation there is little to be done. In dry seasons flood the ground well and give mulchings regularly.

VARIETY
Black. Originally a native of Persia. Crops heavily and is of excellent flavour.

QUINCES

The quince will grow well on rich, loamy soil, near a pond or swampy ground, though it does fairly well in dry areas.

MANURING
Manure as for pears (see page 428).

PLANTING
Plant standards 3 or 4 years old, or bush-trees 2-3 years old. Plant before Christmas if possible.

PRUNING
Little pruning need be done once the tree is established. Just thin out the branches sufficiently to let in the light and air.

THINNING
Thinning should be done if the tree bears very heavily, but is not generally necessary.

HARVESTING
The fruits are usually picked in October. Do not store quinces near any other fruit, as they will taint anything with which they come into contact. Keep in boxes filled with bran or chopped straw, etc.

CULTIVATION
Grease-band in October. This will prevent the flowers being damaged. Cultivate shallowly, during the winter. Hoe around the tree in the summer and give thorough floodings with clean water in dry weather.

VARIETIES
Bereczki. Good flavour. Heavy cropper. Large tender fruits. Crops early.

Common Quince. Apple-shaped fruits. Good grower. Flesh turns red when cooked.

Portugal. Bears large pear-shaped, mild-flavoured fruits. Vigorous grower. Medium cropper.

Smyrna. Vigorous grower. Large mild-flavoured fruits.

CHAPTER III

Additional and Helpful Information

REASONS FOR TREES NOT FRUITING

FRUIT trees are sometimes planted that never fruit. Garden owners are disappointed and want to know why. When this happens there are several probable reasons.

(1) POLLINATION
It is no good planting a self-sterile variety on its own. Either plant a self-fertile variety or put in a self-sterile kind with its mate. (Details of the pollinators needed will be found in the Charts, pages 401, 412, 429 and 438.)

(2) OVER PRUNING
A bush or tree that is not pruned will come into cropping far quicker than a tree that is pruned. Over-pruning delays cropping and therefore is often the reason for non-bearing.

(3) PESTS AND DISEASES
There are both pests and diseases which can ruin the blossoms. It is necessary, therefore, to carry out a definite spraying programme and suggestions are given under the heading Routine Work towards the end of the information given on each individual fruit in Chapter II.

(4) STARVATION OR OVER-MANURING
A tree may fail to set because it is overfed. On the other hand, starvation may prevent the blossoms from setting. Care must be taken, therefore, to follow the suggested systems of manuring given in the text dealing with individual fruits.

(5) BIRDS EATING BUDS
Birds may peck out the fruit buds during the winter. They are particularly fond of the buds of gooseberries, greengages, plums, redcurrants, damsons and opening pear buds. There is no simple method of control. Three things are suggested : (a) to plant a

Prunus Pissardi which the birds prefer to the others ; (*b*) to spray the trees all over with a thick solution of lime and salt ; (*c*) to string black cotton in between the branches. Some people grow their soft fruits in specially built " cages."

(6) Frost
When gardens lie low the blossoms may be frozen every spring. The tip is to plant late-flowering varieties.

(7) Cold Winds
In exposed gardens blossoms may be damaged by gales in the spring. The answer is to provide permanent or temporary shelter in the form of a windbreak.

(8) Dryness at Roots
Sometimes, during a droughty period, flowers will fail to set owing to lack of moisture. Wall trees are perhaps more affected than trees growing in the open. Answer : Lightly fork over the soil and flood it a week or so before the blossoms are due to open.

FRUIT THINNING

It is usual to thin apples, pears and plums when they are quite small. Dessert apples, say, to 4 ins. apart, cookers to 6 ins. apart, plums to 2 ins. apart, and the small-fruited varieties of pears, like Hessle, Fertility and Doyenne D'Eté, to 5 ins. apart. The thinning is done by hooking the first two fingers around the little fruit and then pushing it off its stalk with the thumb. The centre of each cluster of apples, known as the King Apple, is usually abnormal and should always be removed first when thinning.

Peaches and nectarines are thinned as described on page 426.

Gooseberries are thinned, when about $\frac{1}{2}$ in. in diameter, to 2 ins. apart where large dessert fruit is required.

BEARING METHODS

Apricots, blackberries, blackcurrants, bullaces, figs, gooseberries, loganberries, nectarines, peaches, plums, raspberries, walnuts, Morello cherries and the hybrid berries bear their fruits on 1-year-old wood.

Apples, cobnuts, damsons, filberts, medlars, mulberries, pears, quinces, redcurrants and sweet cherries, generally bear their fruits on wood of more than 1 year old.

This gives the key to pruning, very largely.

BARK RINGING

The leaves manufacture the elaborated sap. The roots send up the crude minerals to be manufactured. These are carried up to the foliage through the wood vessels, and the manufactured sap flows downward through the cells which are just under the bark.

Bark ringing encourages the setting of fruit and the formation of fruit buds, by preventing the manufactured plant food from passing down below the ring. The simplest method of ringing is to remove a ring of bark just down to the wood about $\frac{1}{4}$ in. wide, a few inches below the level of the lowest branch. The work should be done at blossoming time, the wound being covered over with thick white lead paint or adhesive tape.

Some people prefer to use 2 half-rings, one 4 ins. above the other, on the opposite side of the trunk from one another. (See illustration facing page 417.)

Bark ringing is usually carried out only in the case of apples and pears.

SLITTING THE BARK

If the wood of the trunk grows and swells, and the bark fails to keep pace with it, it is necessary to release the bark by making a slit right the way down the trunk on the north side of the tree. The reduced tension allows the passage of far more sap. The symptoms of a tree being bark-bound are : (*a*) flowering and non-cropping ; (*b*) the top of the tree seeming too big for the stem ; (*c*) an audible cracking when you put your knife into the bark and move it downwards.

ROOT PRUNING

The effect of root pruning is to cut off much of the food and water and so to check exuberant growth. A tree should never be root pruned unless it is making too much growth to the detriment of its fruiting capacity. Root pruning must be carried out late in the autumn when the leaves have fallen. Soft fruits are not root pruned.

Trees under 6 or 7 years of age are not normally root pruned. The scheme is to dig a trench 2 ft. wide, 3 ft. away from the trunk of the tree, and to cut off all the roots met with during this excavation. It may be necessary to dig down 4 ft. or so. The old-fashioned idea that trees have one tap root must not be believed. A tree has a number of anchorage roots and a greater number of fibrous roots.

KNIFE NOTCHING

If a little notch is nicked out of the bark $\frac{1}{8}$ in. above a wood bud on 1-year-old wood that particular bud will break out and form a strong shoot. If a similar notch is made just below a wood bud on 1-year-old growth the bud will plump up and form a fruit bud.

HEADING BACK

When trees get too tall the branches may be cut back to just above a point where there is a young strong branch to carry on the growth.

Equally, when branches are drooping down to the ground owing to heavy cropping, these may be sawn back to a suitable growth growing in an upward direction. All saw cuts should be made at an angle of about 45°, the wound being smoothed over with a knife and painted over with a thick lead paint.

GRAFTING METHODS

Sometimes it is necessary to convert one variety into another when it does not prove profitable because it is self-sterile, or because the variety is not popular. The fullest details of various grafting methods will be found in *The A.B.C. of Fruit Growing*, published by the English Universities Press. Here, however, is a brief summary.

Special Note.—It is quite possible to carry out a number of different methods of grafting on the same tree.

(1) RIND GRAFTING
The tops of the branches are sawn off to a suitable level in the winter. Early in April a further 2 ins. is sawn off and the top is then trimmed with a sharp knife. A cut from the top is made

vertically **2 ins.** long in the side of the bark. At this point the bark is opened up and the scion or graft is inserted until the top of the cut is just over the level of the sawn branch. The scion is prepared by making a long oblique cut at the base of the piece of grafting wood (see Fig. 29), the top cut of the graft being made just above a bud at an angle of 45°. The scion is usually about 4 ins. long. When the graft is inserted, it is bound round tightly with raffia, just leaving the bud exposed on the graft which may be seen through the slit bark. The cut surfaces should be painted over with grafting wax. (See page 386.)

RIND GRAFTING

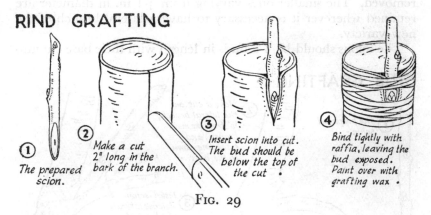

① The prepared scion.

② Make a cut 2" long in the bark of the branch.

③ Insert scion into cut. The bud should be below the top of the cut.

④ Bind tightly with raffia, leaving the bud exposed. Paint over with grafting wax.

FIG. 29

(2) PORCUPINE GRAFTING

The main branches are not sawn down, but all the lateral growths are removed plus the spurs. Scions are cut into lengths of 4-6 buds, each one having a slanting cut 1½ ins. long on one side and a cut ¼ in. long at the base on the opposite side. (See Fig. 30.) An

PORCUPINE GRAFTING ·

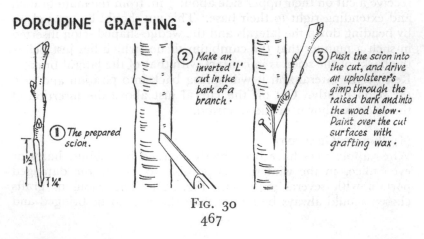

① The prepared scion.

1½"
¼"

② Make an inverted 'L' cut in the bark of a branch.

③ Push the scion into the cut, and drive an upholsterer's gimp through the raised bark and into the wood below. Paint over the cut surfaces with grafting wax.

FIG. 30

467

inverted L-shaped cut is made in the bark of a branch, so that it penetrates right down to the wood. The bark is then raised and the scion pushed into position. An upholsterer's gimp pin is driven through the edge of the raised bark and scion and into the wood below. The cut surfaces are then waxed over. It may be necessary to insert 200 grafts or more, equally spaced all over the various branches.

(3) STUB GRAFTING

The branches are not cut down, nor are all the lateral growths removed. The smaller ones varying from ¼-1 in. in diameter are retained wherever it is necessary to have a lateral branch of the new variety.

The scions should be 4-6 buds in length with their base cut into

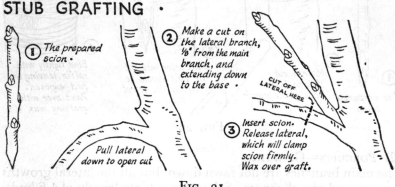

STUB GRAFTING ·

① The prepared scion ·

② Make a cut on the lateral branch, ⅛" from the main branch, and extending down to the base ·

CUT OFF LATERAL HERE

③ Insert scion. Release lateral, which will clamp scion firmly. Wax over graft.

Pull lateral down to open cut

FIG. 31

the form of a wedge (see Fig. 31). The lateral branches should receive a cut on their upper side about ⅛ in. from the main branch and extending right to their base. This cut should be opened up by bending down the laterals and the wedge-shaped scion inserted in such a manner that the cambium tissue (which lies just below the bark) of the scion is in contact with that of the lateral branch. Release the lateral and it will spring back into position and grip the scion tightly. Cut off the lateral just above the insertion of the scion as shown in the diagram.

(4) BRIDGE GRAFTING

When apple trees have been badly marked by rabbits, hares or even mice, in the winter, it is possible to bridge the damaged portion with several grafts (see Fig. 32). The scions or grafts chosen should always be longer than the part to be bridged and should be prepared so that they have long oblique cuts at either end. T-shaped cuts are then made in the bark above and below the wounds and the sloping cuts are thrust under the bark of the trunk so that a bridge is formed. Three or four grafts are usually used.

BRIDGE GRAFTING

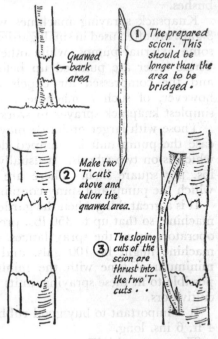

FIG. 32

(5) INARCHING
This is done where the rootstock is found to be unsatisfactory. A suitable young rootstock is planted close to the tree that needs it. Its top is given a wedge-shaped cut. A corresponding cut is made just under the bark in the tree trunk and the wedge-shaped end is pushed in. It is best to use 2 inarching stocks to a tree, else future development may be lopsided.

SPRAYING AND DUSTING MACHINES

There are those who believe that if you work sufficient organic matter into the ground, and the humus content is high enough, the time will come when your fruit trees and bushes will not suffer from pests and diseases. My trees and bushes have not reached that stage as yet, and so it is still necessary to carry out a spraying programme.

In order to apply the sprays, washes and dusts efficiently it is necessary to have adequate machinery for the purpose. For the small garden a double-acting syringe type of pump is often sufficient. The Solo sprayer is a typical example. It gives a continuous spray at a pressure of about 60 lbs. per square inch.

Bucket pumps of the A.R.P. stirrup type have been much used since the 1939-45 war. They usually apply the wash at a pressure of 75 lbs. to the square inch. It is best to have someone to pump and a second worker to direct the spray fluid on to the trees and bushes.

Knapsack spraying machines with a tank capacity of about 3 gals. are often used in small gardens. Some have internal pumps, some external pumps, while others are of the pneumatic type. These latter are pumped up before being carried on the back and the compressed air expels all the spray. The pressure, however, of such a machine is relatively low. Probably the simplest knapsack sprayer to work is the internal pump type.

Those with larger orchards may use barrel pumps and in this case the pump unit is clamped down on to the tank or barrel which is on two wheels. It usually gives a pressure of about 200 lbs. per square inch. There are quite large barrel pumps in which the pump and spray container are all in one unit.

It is a great thing when the gardener can have a motor spraying machine, so that up to 350 lbs. pressure can be assured, with two operators using the spray lances. The tank capacity of such a machine might be 100 gals. and the spraying is done in the minimum of time with the minimum of effort. To-day it is possible to fit these spraying units to various types of mechanical cultivators.

It is important to buy good rubber hose and light lances about 4 ft. 6 ins. long.

The new multiple nozzles save labour and speed up spraying. An expert should always be consulted when buying a spraying machine.

What has been said of spraying machines is equally true of dusting machines. There are hand-operated rotary blowers which give excellent results and ensure a uniform distribution of dust in the minimum of time. These rotary dust guns are somewhat expensive for the small garden, but they are well worth every penny.

There are smaller hand-dusting machines, but these are not satisfactory for fruit trees and bushes : better not to dust at all, unless it can be done properly.

Note.—Where a good water supply is available, spraying rather than dusting should be carried out as it gives a more uniform coating of fungicide or insecticide.

PICKING AND STORING

All fruits are delicate and must be handled with care. Just a slight bruise and fungus spores may enter. Picking should therefore be done very carefully. In the case of some fruits—for instance, peaches—it may be necessary to extend the picking over several weeks, on each occasion only the really ripe specimens being gathered.

With keeping apples it is inadvisable to pick too early, because they may shrivel in store. With pears it is often necessary to pick early for many a pear comes to full ripeness in the store. Never take a fruit between the finger and thumb or there will be a slight pressure, and so two bruises. Lift the fruits up with the palm of the hand. The stalk should come away from the spur without any pulling at all. The later varieties of cooking apples and pears may be left on until the leaves start to fall. The earlier varieties of cooking apples may be picked long before they are ripe so that they may be used. Gooseberries also are picked directly they are large enough for cooking. The time of picking will, of course, depend on many factors, including the soil on which the trees are growing, the stock on which the trees are grafted, the district, the season and so on. It is very difficult, therefore, to be dictatorial.

Where it is necessary to delay the picking of early or late varieties owing to shortage of labour it is possible to spray the trees with a special hormone solution which will cause the fruits, particularly apples, to cling to the trees, for, say, 3 weeks longer.

Always pick into a smooth container, like a bucket, which has been painted inside with enamel paint—or into a basket which has been lined with material of some sort. Place the fruit in such a container. Never drop it in. Use whatever ladders are necessary to reach the fruits. It is never wise to pull down branches or climb up into the tree.

When picking, never leave diseased fruits on a tree or the trouble will be carried over to another year. If birds are attracted by the pleasant odour of ripening fruit, and cause damage, it is possible to pop little muslin or paper bags over the fruits and tie the mouth of the bag to the spur or branch. The fruits will colour and ripen as if they were completely exposed.

SPECIAL NOTES ON PICKING

APPLES
Dessert apples may be left on the tree till they are ripe. Cooking apples may be picked immature. Keepers need not be picked until late.

CHERRIES

Gather cooking cherries when they are coloured deep red. Pick dessert cherries when ripe.

CURRANTS, BLACK

Often turn black 10 days before they should be picked.

CURRANTS, RED AND WHITE

Pick when all the berries of the individual bunch are properly coloured.

GOOSEBERRIES

Pick when fit to cook. Gather dessert varieties when fully ripe.

LOGANBERRIES

Go over the canes once or twice a week and pick those that are ripe.

NECTARINES

Gather very carefully just as ripe. Daily inspection is necessary.

PEACHES

See Nectarines.

PEARS

Pick early and mid-season varieties when ripe. Gather later varieties before fully ripened and bring to maturity in store.

RASPBERRIES

Pick when ripe. Never allow fruits to fall to the ground or useless seedlings may arise that will smother out the original variety.

STRAWBERRIES

Pick with the stalk when ripe.

N.B. Gale Warning.—It is always worthwhile, in the case of apples and pears, trying to get the bulk of the picking done before the autumn gales.

THE STOREHOUSE

The main thing is to use a structure in which the temperature keeps at round about 40° all the time. The atmosphere must not be too dry or the fruit will shrivel. The floor must be absolutely clean and free from disease spores before the fruit is put in. It may be necessary to spray with a 2% solution of formaldehyde.

An earth floor is quite suitable, providing wire netting is let into the ground to prevent vermin from burrowing in. There is no need to have windows. Light can be provided by slides covering ventilators, or electric light can be installed. Over the large ventilators $\frac{1}{4}$ in. mesh wire netting should be tacked to prevent the entry of birds. Double walls are useful, match-boarding inside and weather boarding outside, the 3 ins. space between them being filled in with cork chippings or asbestos wool, to provide the necessary insulation. A good roof would be weather boarding covered with tarred felt, covered in turn with thatch. A double door should be provided, one opening inwards and the other outwards. It is not much use having insulated walls without double doors.

METHOD OF STORING

The apples or pears to be stored will be allowed to sweat outside first for a fortnight. They will then be brought into the store in boxes or trays made in such a way that the air can circulate easily. Special orchard boxes may be purchased for the purpose. When in the store the ventilators and the doors will be closed, so that the temperature will remain constant. If it is not possible to allow the fruit to " sweat " out of doors it may be put into the store with full ventilation for a fortnight.

It is possible to convert barns, sheds, attics and cellars into suitable storehouses—providing the above ideals are borne in mind.

ALTERNATIVE SYSTEMS

It is possible in glut years to store apples in clamps out of doors in a similar manner to potatoes (see page 521). It is usual to allow the apples to sweat for a fortnight, the straw being put into position at night time but removed during the day. After 3 weeks the straw is put back into position and covered with a 6-in. layer of soil, and the necessary twisted straw ventilators made.

Commercial fruit growers store their apples in cold stores at a temperature of just above 32° Fahr., or in gas stores where the carbon dioxide given off by the apples is collected and stored, and given off in fixed amounts. The higher percentage of carbon dioxide in the air slows down breathing, i.e. internal combustion, in the apple and so gives the fruit a longer lease of life.

PART SIX

FOOD PRODUCTION
VEGETABLES

CHAPTER I

Growing Vegetables

ROTATIONS AND CROPPING

ROTATION is a system whereby vegetables of the same character are *not* grown on the same piece of ground year after year. For instance, the deep-rooting vegetables can be classed together, or the shallow-rooting ones. Vegetables like peas and beans that enrich the soil with nitrogen may go together. Each of these groups needs a particular type of cultivation and requires certain manures.

The first step towards rotation is to classify the crops to be grown into groups and then to see that one particular group does not remain on the same plot of land year after year. Land that gets the same treatment year after year tends to deteriorate. Crops that need shallow cultivation, for instance, would only receive shallow cultivation and the land in which they were grown would never be really deeply worked. Rotation prevents the exhaustion of a particular plant food in the soil. Some crops take from the soil large quantities of plant foods and so the growing of one particular type of crop on the land year after year would result in impoverishment of the soil in some directions.

Then again, some crops can leave the land in better condition than others. Celery needs deep cultivation and thus ensures excellent soil for crops that are to follow. Peas and beans leave nitrogen in the soil and members of the cabbage family can make much use of this.

Pests and diseases can be kept down by rotation—one example is club root. When cabbages are grown on the same plot year after year this trouble gradually gets worse and worse until, in some cases, members of the cabbage family cannot be grown there at all. Pests, too, like the carrot fly, find it easier to damage a crop if the carrot seeds are sown directly on the top of the spot where the chrysalids are buried after the previous year's attack.

It is said that some plants secrete " toxins " which accumulate if the same plants are grown on the land year after year, but these toxins may be quite harmless to other plants, e.g. land that is

" cauliflower sick " will grow good peas and beans. Rotations are a saving of labour for they save the gardener from digging the whole plot deeply every year. They make for the keeping down of weeds and allow for green manuring to take place.

Examples of Rotations are as follows :

3-course (1) Cabbage family.
(2) Root crops.
(3) Group consisting mainly of potatoes.

Deep-rooting crops thus alternate with shallow-rooting ones.

4-course (1) Early potatoes, second earlies, and main crop if necessary.
(2) Pea and bean family and if necessary leeks and celery.
(3) Root crops.
(4) Cabbage family.

Lettuce, spinach, etc., may be grown as catch-crops.

SUCCESSIONAL CROPPING, CATCH CROPPING AND INTERCROPPING

SUCCESSIONAL CROPPING

This term can be taken as having two meanings. (1) to provide a succession of one crop for as long as possible, and (2) to keep up a succession of different crops throughout the year, so that the land is never idle.

For example, a succession of peas may be had by starting to sow a first early variety in late February, followed by second early and maincrop varieties in March, April and May, then making further sowings of early varieties for a late crop.

Land occupied by early potatoes during the early months of the year may be kept in cropping by putting in winter greens as soon as the potatoes are harvested.

CATCH CROPPING

A catch crop is one which matures quickly and can be sown between other slower growing crops and harvested when the room is required. Examples are French beans, radish or lettuce sown on the ridges of celery trenches ; summer spinach or early turnips sown on land which is only vacant for a few weeks between two crops, and so on.

INTERCROPPING

A scheme by which the maximum use is made of ground by allowing two crops to grow in the same piece of ground at the same time. For instance, lettuce, turnips or radish may be sown between rows of peas or beans; small types of quickly maturing summer cabbage may be planted between the Brussels sprouts, and these must be cut before the sprouts require the additional room. I have sown runner beans in between rows of Brussels sprouts (in fact before the sprouts were planted). Then the bean plants were kept cut back to dwarf them and when the sprout plants needed the room the beans were cut to ground level and piled around the Brussels sprouts to act as a mulch.

AVERAGE YIELDS OF VEGETABLES

These figures are, of course, only a rough indication of the crops which can be expected from a given area. The yield is bound to be affected by weather conditions, soil, situation and so on.

The figures are for main crops which have been allowed to grow to maturity, worked out to the nearest figure and not mathematically.

VEGETABLE	*YIELD*		
	Per foot of row	*Per sq. yd.*	*Per acre*
BEANS, BROAD	½ lb.	2 lbs.	4 tons
BEANS, FRENCH	¼ lb.	1½ lbs.	3 tons
BEANS, HARICOT	—	½ lb.	15 cwts.
BEANS, RUNNER	4 lbs.	5 lbs.	10 tons
BEETROOT	1 lb.	6 lbs.	12 tons
BROCCOLI	1 lb.	4 lbs.	8 tons
BRUSSELS SPROUTS	½ lb.	2 lbs.	4 tons
CABBAGE (Autumn and Winter)	1 lb.	7 lbs.	15 tons
CABBAGE (Spring)	¾ lb.	4 lbs.	9 tons
CARROTS (Early)	¼ lb.	4 lbs.	8 tons
CARROTS (Maincrop)	¾ lb.	7 lbs.	14 tons
CAULIFLOWER	1 lb.	3 lbs.	6 tons
KALE	1 lb.	5 lbs.	10 tons
LEEKS	¾ lb.	5 lbs.	10 tons
LETTUCE	2 heads	12 heads	—
ONIONS	¾ lb.	6 lbs.	12 tons
PARSNIPS	¾ lb.	5 lbs.	10 tons
PEAS	½ lb.	2 lbs.	3 tons
POTATOES	1½ lbs.	5 lbs.	10 tons
SAVOYS	1 lb.	7 lbs.	15 tons
SHALLOTS	¾ lb.	8 lbs.	—
SPINACH (Summer)	¼ lb.	4 lbs.	8 tons
SWEDES	1 lb.	6 lbs.	13 tons
TURNIPS	1 lb.	6 lbs.	13 tons
TOMATOES (Outdoor)	4 lbs. per plant	10 lbs.	20 tons
TOMATOES (Under glass)	6 lbs. per plant	15 lbs.	30 tons

CONTINUITY CHART FOR PRINCIPAL VEGETABLES

	Jan.	Feb.	Mar.	Apr.	May	June	July	Aug.	Sept.	Oct.	Nov.	Dec.
ARTICHOKES	——										——	
BEANS, BROAD	....	....	....	....					....	....	....	....
BEANS, FRENCH										....	....	....
BEANS, HARICOT	....	....	....									....
BEANS, RUNNER	....									....	....	....
BROCCOLI												
BROCCOLI, SPROUTING												
BRUSSELS SPROUTS												
CABBAGE												
CARROTS	....	....	....								....	....
CAULIFLOWER												
CELERY												
ENDIVE												
KALE												
LEEKS												
LETTUCE												
ONIONS	....	....	....	....						....	....	....
PARSNIPS	....	....	....									
PEAS	....	....	....									
POTATOES	....	....	....	....							....	....
SAVOYS												
SHALLOTS							....	....	....	....		
SPINACH												
SWEDES	....	....	....	....								
TOMATOES	....				....						....	....
TURNIPS	....	....	....									....
TURNIP TOPS												
VEGETABLE MARROWS	....	....									....	....

In the above chart the continuous lines indicate the times at which vegetables are available from the open ground, while the dots show how the season may be extended by the use of stored crops or continuous cloches. It may be possible, with care and management, to extend the season of some of the crops even further.

SEED SOWING

SELECTING THE SEED

Under the Seeds Act of 1920 all seeds named under this Act have to be tested in accordance with the provisions of the Act. Germination of peas, for instance, must be up to 70% and broad beans to

XI. Freesias

XII. Lupins

75%. The following table gives the required germination, and from it one can ascertain whether the particular seed in question can be sown thinly or fairly thickly :

Beans, dwarf and broad	75%	Kale ..	..	70%
Beans, runner..	.. 60%	Kohl Rabi	..	70%
Beetroot ..	.. 50%	Onions ..	..	68%
Broccoli ..	.. 60%	Parsnips ..	..	45%
Brussels sprouts	.. 70%	Peas ..	..	70%
Cabbage ..	.. 70%	Swedes ..	..	75%
Carrots ..	.. 50%	Turnips ..	..	75%
Cauliflower ..	.. 60%			

Although the law demands that good seed be sold there is no law preventing seedsmen from marketing poor varieties or types not suited to certain conditions, so care should be taken when selecting seeds, and they should be purchased from a reputable firm. Some seeds last longer than others, but to get the best results it is safest to get new seed every year.

THE SEED BED
One of the first things to do is to get a good seed bed. This needs three things—air, warmth and moisture—to be really successful. In order to produce these conditions a good deal of forking, raking, etc., has to be done. (See illustration facing page 489.) After the bed has been prepared, each particle of soil should be no larger than a grain of wheat. If land is left rough, small seed may fall into the crevices formed and large portions of soil may bury them.

Seed beds may be improved by the use of horticultural peat. This helps to retain moisture and gives a good medium into which the roots may grow.

SOWING THE SEED
A general rule when sowing seed is that it should be sown to a depth of three times its own width. Some seeds have to be sown almost on the surface of the soil.

It is far better to sow the seed in rows, or drills, than to broadcast it. The rows should be marked out by means of a line, and then the drills drawn out with a triangular hoe or the edge of a draw hoe. (See illustration facing page 64.) The seed should be taken in the palm of the hand and gently pushed out by means of the thumb and forefinger. (See illustration facing page 64.) With dark-coloured seeds it is a good plan to mix

C.G.   481   Q them with a little hydrated lime first of all so that they can be easily seen and thin sowing can be ensured. (See illustration facing page 33.)

When the seed is sown it can be covered up either by raking the soil over, using a rake in a backwards and forwards movement, or, if the seeds are very small, by a sprinkling of soil.

On light land the rows should be trodden down lightly, or beaten down gently with the back of a spade. This induces the moisture to rise to the surface and so helps early germination of the seed.

Once the plants are through hoeing should be carried out regularly.

STATION SOWING

The seeds may be sown at points so many inches apart along the drills, 3 seeds per " station " and then thinned down to one if all 3 seeds germinate.

THINNING

Thinning should be carried out as soon as it is possible to handle the seedlings. They should be thinned with great care and the best plants left in position. The soil must be firmed again along the rows after thinning. If the weather is very dry a watering through a fine rose should be given beforehand, and hoeing should be done afterwards.

It is customary to thin at two periods, first, to half the ultimate distance required, and later, to the final distance apart. In many cases the second thinnings may be used for the table.

Often thinned seedlings may be transplanted to form other rows.

TRANSPLANTING

PLANTING OUT

Planting out should be done with care, if possible during a showery period, but otherwise a good watering should be given afterwards or the hole filled up with water as the plant is put into position. A mud puddle may be made in a bucket and the roots swished about in this if preferred.

The seed bed from which the plants are taken should have a good watering the previous day if the weather is dry. For small seedlings or plants a dibber is a very good transplanting tool, but, naturally, for larger plants a trowel is more satisfactory. Holes should be made large enough to take the whole root system without cramping it in any way. The plant should go in so that the bottom seed-leaf rests on the surface of the soil. Planting should be done firmly.

PRICKING OUT

This term really means transplanting the little seedlings in their *very early* stages. Lettuces, for instance, are often " pricked out " as soon as their seed-leaves are large enough to handle. Small holes can be made with a pencil for this purpose.

Everyday Vegetables

ARTICHOKE, GLOBE

GROWN for its large flower buds which are used as a vegetable.

SOIL
This crop does best in a deep, rich moist soil, and better heads are produced if the plants are grown in a sunny situation. Artichokes may die out on wet soils during severe weather if they are not protected or if the soil is not lightened in some way. It is in the summer that artichokes need moisture and not in the winter.

MANURING
Before planting, dung or compost should be applied to the ground at the rate of 1 good barrowload per 12 sq. yds. In addition, give fish manure at 4 ozs. to the square yard. Every year compost may be forked in between the rows during the spring, and a similar quantity of fish manure given as well.

PROPAGATION
Propagate by suckers, which should be cut off the old plants when they are about 9 ins. high. Each sucker should have a portion of root attached to it. Do this during November. Pot up the suckers, standing them in a cold frame for the winter.

It is possible to remove suckers in April and to plant them out immediately in rows 4 ft. apart, with the plants 3 ft. apart in rows. Plant 4 in. deep and water well.

Take precautions against slugs. In May, should the weather be dry, mulch with peat or straw, and water well. Flowers should not be allowed to grow the first year.

GENERAL CULTIVATION
Hoe and weed regularly. The lateral heads may be removed when they are about the size of an egg.

After all the heads have been cut in the autumn, stems should be cut down, together with some large leaves. The central leaves should not be touched, as these protect the crown.

Where severe frosts are expected, draw soil up to the plants and throw a little dry straw over them. Remove this litter in the spring and draw the earth back level again. Don't leave a plantation of artichokes down longer than 5 years.

HARVESTING

The main flowering heads should be cut while they are still young and tender. If left on the plant too long they become coarse. Cut with a stem 6 ins. long. Stand in water under cover until required. The main heads are best. If the laterals are not removed in the early stages they produce a second crop.

VARIETIES

Camus de Grande Bretagne, and Green Globe which is devoid of prickles.

ARTICHOKE, JERUSALEM

A more popular vegetable than the globe artichoke.

SOIL

Grows in almost any soil. Will produce crops under indifferent treatment.

Produces the finest samples when grown in an open situation in a deep friable loam and when liberally manured.

PREPARING THE SOIL

Bastard trench in the autumn, adding farmyard manure or compost. Leave rough during the winter, and in the spring fork down level.

MANURING

In addition to organic manure add a good compound organic fertiliser, like fish manure, at 4 ozs to the square yard.

PROPAGATION

Save tubers from the previous year's crop. The seed tubers should be about the size of a pullet's egg.

PLANTING

Rows should be 2 ft. 6 ins. apart and the tubers 12 ins. apart and 6 ins. deep.

GENERAL CULTIVATION

After the plants are through the ground hoe regularly. When the growths are above the soil earth up as for potatoes. Cut down the stems to within 1 ft. of the ground in November.

HARVESTING

Lift the whole crop up at one time and store the tubers in sand, or lift a few roots as they are required. When lifting care should be taken not to damage the artichokes, and suitable-sized tubers should be selected for planting the following season. Tubers may be stored in a clamp (see Potatoes).

VARIETIES

New White has a delicate flavour.
Fuseau is free from awkward "knobs" and is smooth skinned.

ASPARAGUS

An asparagus bed is comparatively easy to lay down and costs little to maintain.

SOIL

This crop will grow in almost any soil if good drainage is provided.

PREPARING THE SOIL

The land where asparagus is to be grown should be bastard trenched. Bury well-rotted dung or compost at the rate of 1 good barrowload to 10 sq. yds. during the digging. Be particular about removing every trace of perennial weed.

MANURING

Farmyard manure or compost should be applied every year in the autumn, after the asparagus foliage has been cut down. In addition, use 4 ozs. of fish manure per square yard. Apply dried blood each spring at 3 ozs. per square yard.

On the sandy soils apply salt at the rate of, say, 1 oz. to the square yard, in the north near the end of April and in the south towards the middle of April. Another dressing may be given 3 weeks later.

Calcium cyanamide, if used at 2 ozs. to the square yard all over the rows in the spring, just after the weeds have started to show, will give complete control of chickweed and drastic scorching of other weeds.

PROPAGATION
It is possible to raise plants from seed, but those who wish to get quick returns should purchase plants.

PLANTING
It was once customary to have raised beds, but most gardeners now prefer the flat bed provided the drainage is perfect. The beds may be 3 ft. wide, and in large gardens a series of such beds is made with temporary pathways 2 ft. wide between them. It is better to plant in single rows 4 ft. apart, the plants being 2 ft. apart, or in rows 3 ft. apart with the plants 18 ins. in the rows.

On the 3 ft. bed two rows of plants are planted 9 ins. in from the edges of either side. Plant early in April on a mild day. Take out a trench 9 ins. wide and 9 ins. deep and spread the spidery-looking roots out. If the plant is set upon a little mound of soil, it is easier to get the roots into position. The crown (or the growing bud part) of the plant should be about 4 ins. below soil level after covering in.

The roots of young plants should not be exposed to dry winds or sun but be planted immediately. If this is impossible cover with a damp sack. Get the bed ready so that when the plants come they can be put in immediately.

GENERAL CULTIVATION
It is possible during the first year or two to grow radishes, lettuces and onions between the rows if necessary. The first season, towards the middle of June, look for blank spaces in the rows. If these occur obtain further plants and gap up immediately. Hoe regularly and shallowly throughout the season.

In the late autumn cut the foliage down close to the ground. Never allow the berries to ripen and drop on the soil.

As the stems are fragile it is usual in windy situations to give the feathery growth some support. Bamboos may be pushed in at either end of the rows and string or green twine be run between them. In the south earth up in February, and in the north in late March. It is usually necessary to put a little extra soil over the crown so as to give a good length of branch stem. As the crowns grow larger they naturally need more soil to cover them and so the ridges tend to be higher, but in the summer the soil from the ridge may fall away owing to cultivation, and by the time the foliage is cut in the autumn the ridges may have practically disappeared.

HARVESTING

Cutting will not normally take place until the plants are 3 years old. Every year cutting should cease by the end of June, and during harvesting the thinnest shoots should be left to grow. When cutting ceases, all shoots are left. Cut the sticks just below the ground, being careful not to injure younger shoots coming through at the same time. Cut when the green tips are 4 ins. above soil level.

VARIETIES

Connover's Colossal. The large "commonly grown" variety.

Early Argenteuil. Said to be one of the earliest, cuts from the beginning of April.

K.B. Strain. A new type of pedigree asparagus which is very popular.

Mary Washington. An American type valued because it resists asparagus rust.

BEANS, BROAD

SOIL

Not particular as to soil, will grow almost anywhere.

PREPARING THE SOIL

Bastard trench the ground. Bury whatever organic manure is going to be used. In the case of autumn sowings which follow previously well-manured crops, only plain digging is necessary.

MANURING

Dig farmyard manure or well-rotted compost into the ground a spade's depth at the rate of one bucketful to the square yard 3 weeks before sowing the seed. Rake into the ground when levelling it at seed-sowing time, 3-4 ozs. of a good fish fertiliser containing potash; or use meat and bone meal at 3 ozs. to the square yard plus wood ashes at 5 ozs. per square yard.

SEED SOWING

Sow in November for over-wintering, or sow from early to mid-March. January sowing is possible where continuous cloches are

73. *A well laid-out kitchen garden*

74. *Forcing seakale*

75. *Onions ready for harvesting*

76. *Breaking down earth with a fork*

77. *Bean poles for runners*

78. *Growing leeks in a trench*

79. *Draw hoeing*

used. The November sowings may be covered with continuous cloches also during exceptionally bad weather.

It is possible to sow in frames in December or January and put out the plants thus raised into rows in the open about the second or third week in March. Never sow or plant out unless the soil is in good condition; it is better to delay sowing a few days than try to plant in sodden land. The rows should be 2 ft. 6 ins. apart, the drills 5-6 ins. wide, a double row of beans should be sown staggered (zig-zag fashion) so that they are 6 ins. apart, in drills 3 ins. deep. In addition, sow 12 beans in a group at the end of each row and use the plants that appear for gapping-up later.

GENERAL CULTIVATION
Hoe regularly to keep the soil clean, look out for the black aphid, or dolphin, and spray as soon as it is seen, with liquid Derris. Directly the crop is over cut the tops down and put them on to the compost heap to rot down for manure. Leave the roots in the ground.

HARVESTING
Pick regularly, never allowing the beans to become old and leathery.

VARIETIES
Sow the long pod types in November and January and the Windsors in March.
(a) *Long Pods*
Aquadulce. An early, tall-growing variety.
Longfellow. Bears large well-filled pods, good flavour.
(b) *Windsors*
Get any good seedsman's strain of Windsor.
(c) *Small Pods*
There are 2 or 3 varieties which produce very small pods.
Royal Dwarf Fan. Grows 1 ft. high. Quick maturing. If sown in July crops same year.

BEANS, DWARF
(FRENCH OR KIDNEY BEANS)

The French bean can be sown in pots under glass, in pots in frames, in the south border (to get a crop early in the season), under cloches in April and in the main garden as late as June in order to get a picking towards the end of September.

SOIL

This bean prefers a light soil rather than a heavy one. It enriches the soil. It withstands drought better than any other vegetable crop.

PREPARING THE SOIL

Dig the land a spade's depth and bury farmyard manure or compost. This digging will help to warm up the soil ; do it in the autumn if possible. In the spring inter-crop with lettuces. These give some protection to the young plants as they come through. Cut the lettuce as the French beans grow.

MANURING

When preparing the land for the " nurse " crop, fork in artificial manures in addition to organic manures. Superphosphate is applied at 1 oz. per square yard and sulphate of potash at ½ oz. per square yard. Should bad weather affect the plants after coming through, apply potassic nitrate of soda along the rows at ½ oz. to the yard run ; water this in. Lime is necessary for the pea and bean families and may be applied to the surface of the ground after forking in the artificials, at from 4-7 ozs. per square yard, depending on the acidity of the soil.

SOWING THE SEED

Provide for a succession of pods by sowing in various ways. A sowing may be made in frames about the middle of March, seeds being placed 3 ins. apart in rows 1 ft. apart. When the plants are through, thin out to 6 ins. apart and transplant thinnings into other frames. Do not give air until the seed has germinated, after which ventilation may be given. To prevent freezing cover the frames with sacking or mats. As the plants grow give them more air, until by mid-May the lights can be removed during the day. These beans need regular watering and picking should commence after the 15th June.

Early in April sow again in a cold frame protected from frosts. Whenever possible, air may be given to the seedlings, and these, when hardened off, may be planted outside in a sheltered border the second or third week of May. When lifting and transplanting French beans, leave plenty of soil around the roots. When in position they should be watered and shaded. Protect early crops from frost when outside by putting straw along the rows or covering with continuous cloches until the end of May.

Outside, the first sowing may be done during the first week of May. The " nurse " crop should by then be growing well. Draw drills 2 ins. deep, 4 ins. wide and from 2-3 ft. apart depending on the variety. In each drill, plant the beans " staggered " so that they are 6 ins. apart. Rake over to cover, firm over the top and sow 6 or 7 beans in a circle at the end of the row so as to raise plants for gapping up later should any blanks occur.

Make another sowing the first week of July with the rows 2 ft. apart and the beans spaced out 10 ins. apart along a narrow drill 2 ins. deep. This sowing will be harvested in mid- or late September and in the north should be covered with cloches at that time.

GENERAL CULTIVATION
Hoe regularly between the rows, drawing the soil up to the plants rather than away from them. Clear the " nurse " crop as soon as the plants are growing well. Give the taller varieties some support with twiggy sticks.

HARVESTING
Always pick when the beans are young, never let them get old and coarse.

VARIETIES
Feltham Prolific. A dwarf variety.
Lightning. Extra early forcing.
Mont D'or. Bears golden French beans.
Processor. Best for canning and bottling.
Phoenix Claudia. Quite stringless, tender and delicious.
The Prince. Early for the garden.
There are some strains of French beans which climb like runner beans :
Prince of Wales. A climber and a heavy cropper.
Tender and True. Usually considered the best climber.

BEANS, HARICOT

These are grown for the white, dried beans which can be stored for use during the winter.

SOIL
Prepare the soil as for French beans and cultivate and grow in a similar manner.

SEED SOWING
Try and sow the seeds early to give the plants a chance of ripening the seed before the autumn sets in. Sow if possible at the beginning of April under cloches, and then the pods will mature late August or early September and may be ripened off under cloches. Those who haven't cloches should sow about the end of April and dry off the pods under cover.

HARVESTING
The simplest way of harvesting is to pull the plants up whole, put them in sacks and beat them with sticks to thrash out the beans.

VARIETIES
Comtesse de Chambord. Tallish and rather spreading.
White Countess. Much dwarfer.

BEANS, HARICOT VERTS

These are the beans which are harvested green like peas from the fresh green pods. Sow as for French beans, but harvest when the green beans in the pods are still fresh, it is these that are cooked.

VARIETIES
Green Flageolet. Extended season.
Green Gem. Heavy cropper, shorter.

BEANS, RUNNER

SOIL
Do well in practically all soils. Like to have a deep root run.

PREPARING THE SOIL
For really big beans of the exhibition type it is usual to take out trenches 2 ft. wide and 2 ft. deep and to fork over the bottom of these trenches, incorporating well-rotted compost or farmyard manure at the rate of 1 good bucketful to the yard run. Some gardeners even use an 18-in. thickness of such material. Trenches are then filled in and allowed to settle down, further soil being

placed over the top a month later, if necessary to bring the surface to the level of the surrounding ground. The beans are then sown directly over the top of the trench in a row.

In the ordinary way the ground is just bastard trenched (see page 51) and liberally manured. This work may be done late in March or early in April, if necessary, but is better carried out in the autumn.

MANURING

Use the dung or compost as already advised. In addition work a good fish manure at 4 or 5 ozs. to the square yard, plus sulphate or muriate of potash at 1 oz. to the square yard. Apply this a fortnight before the seed is sown. Dust the surface of the ground before seed sowing with hydrated lime at 3 ozs. to the square yard.

SEED SOWING

Runner bean seed will not germinate unless the soil is warm. Except under continuous cloches, it is not possible to sow until the second week in May. Make another sowing at the beginning of June.

Make the rows 5 or 6 ft. apart when the beans are to grow up poles. Where the beans are to be kept cut back or grown on the flat as it is called, make the rows 4 ft. apart. Sow the seed in both cases 2 ins. deep and either sow in 6-in. wide flat-bottom drills, with the beans staggered at 9 ins. apart, or sow in V-shaped drills with the seed $4\frac{1}{2}$ ins. apart. Some gardeners dibble in 1 seed near the bottom of each pole. Where the $4\frac{1}{2}$ ins. sowing is done it is usual to thin out later to 9 ins. apart if all the beans grow, and to transplant any of the seedlings for gapping-up, if necessary. It is equally possible, as with French beans, to sow a number of " runner " seeds in a group at the ends of the rows to provide plants for gapping-up later.

Some sow the seeds in boxes under glass early in April and then plant out the seedlings thus raised early in June, so getting an earlier crop. Those with continuous cloches just put cloches in position early in April so as to warm a strip of land and will then sow the beans about mid-April.

STAKING

Put two rows of poles into position either just before or just after sowing. It is usual to have them 9 ins. apart and just between the 2 drills. Make the poles cross at the top end at, say, 6 ins., and lay cross poles along the top, lashing them all together at this point. (See illustration facing page 489.)

Where it is impossible to get poles, stretch wires along the level of the ground from stout posts driven in at either end of the row with a top wire running 6 ft. above. Stretch strands of string in between, up which the beans can climb. Tall wire netting is sometimes used instead.

GENERAL CULTIVATION

Beans that are to grow on the flat should have the growing tips nipped back when they are 18 ins. high; further cutting back being necessary every few weeks.

Hoe regularly along the rows and in between the plants when the " runners " are 4 ins. high; draw a little soil up to them.

Give a mulch of lawn mowings, straw or compost early in July. If the weather is dry give a really heavy watering first of all. Syringe the plants over in the evening after a hot day.

HARVESTING

Pick regularly, never allow any of the pods to mature.

VARIETIES

The Czar. White seeded, white flowered kind. Delicious. Excellent for canning and bottling.

Princeps. A dwarfish variety which crops 14 days earlier than any other. The best for "growing on the flat."

Crusader. A large podded variety. Not coarse. Delicious.

Hammond. A real dwarf type. Does not need "stopping."

BEETROOT

Don't allow beetroots to grow too large or they get coarse. Use them served hot with white sauce as well as served cold in salad.

SOIL

They will grow on most soils but prefer a light loam of good depth.

PREPARING THE SOIL

Don't dig in dung, grow the crop on land that was well manured the previous year. Fork the ground over deeply early in May, then rake down finely.

MANURING

On very light land finely divided compost or seaweed may be dug in at the rate of 1 barrowload to 10 sq. yds.; in addition salt may be worked in to the top 2 ins. at 2 ozs. to the square yard.

Normally, a good fish manure will be applied at 4 ozs. to the square yard 10 days before sowing the seed.

SEED SOWING

Sow at the end of April, or at the beginning of May, depending on the weather and district, in rows 15 ins. apart, drills 2 ins. deep. In the north it may be necessary to wait until May 15th.

With the smaller globe varieties rows may be as close as 1 ft. apart. In this case, sowings are often made in a south warm border about the end of March. Protection is given from birds and frosts with pea-sticks laid along the rows or with fish net. Continuous cloches are ideal, of course, and may be used instead. Make another sowing of a globe variety in July for harvesting in the autumn and winter.

Sow one large seed (it is really a " capsule " containing a number of seeds) every 4 ins. along the drill and cover over. Thin down to one per station if more than one seedling should appear, and when the roots are half-grown thin out every other plant, leaving the beetroots 8 ins. apart in the row. These second thinnings are delicious when used as a vegetable.

It is possible to transplant young beetroot seedlings if necessary, to fill up gaps.

GENERAL CULTIVATION

Hoe regularly, taking care never to damage a root or it may bleed.

HARVESTING

Lift the roots as required for use or lift in the autumn and store in a clamp as for potatoes (see page 521). Twist off the tops before storing, but not too near the crown. Beetroots may be stored in sand or dried off in a shed. It is possible to leave some roots in the ground until they are needed provided they are covered with continuous cloches, straw or bracken.

VARIETIES

Globe or Round

> Detroit. Dark red, excellent for canning or bottling.
> Egyptian Turnip Rooted. The best for shallow soils.
> Empire Globe. Dark crimson, free from white rings.
> Model Globe. The earliest strain. Does well under cloches.

Intermediate

> (May be said to be a cross between the round and globe beet.)
> Obelisk. Delicious, tankard shape. Very popular with chefs.

Long Shaped

> Bell's Non-Bleeding. Retains its colour even when cut into slices before cooking.
>
> Cheltenham Greentop. Very popular, excellent colour.
>
> Dell's Crimson. Excellent flavour, medium size.

BROCCOLI
(WINTER CAULIFLOWER)

Produces white curds in the winter. Has been so " inter-married " with the cauliflower that it is now considered as good. It is possible to produce broccoli for the table from Michaelmas one year to the middle of June the next.

SOIL

Will grow on most soils, seems to prefer a heavy loam. Light soils must be made firm.

PREPARING THE SOIL

Broccoli prefers firm land so plant on ground that has been well manured for a previous crop.

MANURING

Only give really well-rotted compost or farmyard manure to poor light land, and see that the ground is really firm afterwards. Apply bone meal at 3 ozs. to the square yard, plus muriate or sulphate of potash at 1 oz. to the square yard when the land is being got ready for planting.

SEED SOWING

Succession with broccoli can be assured through sowing a number of varieties which will turn in at different periods of the year. Most sowings will be made about the second week in April, though it is usual to delay the sowing of the main varieties until the middle of May.

Sow seeds thinly in drills $\frac{1}{2}$ in. deep and 6 ins. apart in a narrow bed where the surface soil has been made really firm. Protect from flea beetles by dusting the area 10 days later with Gammaxene.

Before the seedlings get too long, thin out and, if necessary, transplant them into further seed beds 6 ins. between the rows, and 3 or 4 ins. apart in the row.

PLANTING

Plant after early potatoes, French beans or early peas. Have the rows 2 ft. 6 ins. apart, and the plants 18 ins. apart in the rows. In the case of smaller varieties, plant at 2 ft. by 18 ins. Gap up if necessary a fortnight after planting out.

GENERAL CULTIVATION

In November take a little soil away from the north side of the plants, push them over and place the soil on the other side. This helps to give them extra protection.

Hoe regularly until the weeds cease to grow.

HARVESTING

Cut the curds directly they are ready and if too many seem to turn in at one time, break 1 or 2 leaves over the curds, cover them and so help keep them back.

VARIETIES

Autumn

Extra Early Roscoff. Turns in November and December, only suited for south and south-west.

Veitch's Self-protecting. Pure white, close heads.

Winter and Early Spring

Early Feltham. Turns in mid-January and beginning of February.

Mid Feltham. Turns in March and April.

New Year. Turns in late December and early January.

Roscoff No. 2. Cut January, only for south and south-west.

Roscoff No. 3. Cut February and March only for south and south-west.

Winter Mammoth. A favourite in the south.

Spring

Roscoff No. 4. Cut March–April, only for south-west.

Satisfaction. Good northern variety, hardy, pure white.

Late Spring, Early Summer

Clucas's June. Very hardy, dwarf grower, June.

Late Feltham. Hardy, cut in May.

Late Queen. Very hardy, cut May, early June.

May Blossom. Mid-May, good southern variety.

Whitsuntide. Southern variety, very late.

497

BROCCOLI, SPROUTING

Sprouting broccoli does not throw a pure white curd, but produces a large number of elongated flower-heads. It is hardier than its cousin the ordinary broccoli, and there is no need to protect plants during the winter.

Seeds may be sown in April. Plants are put out in rows 2 ft. square in July. The purple variety is preferred to the white, and there are both early and late kinds. The purple is the hardiest and is seldom attacked by pests.

HARVESTING
Do not cut sprouting broccoli until flower-shoots are growing from in between the axils of the leaves. The main leaves are not cut until the sprouting tops have been removed as they protect the tender shoots.

VARIETIES
Calabrese. Good flavour. One of the earliest to turn in. Sow in March. Use during September.

Early Purple Sprouting. Compact grower, fit to cut from December to February. Shoots should be cut when 9-12 ins. long.

Late Purple Sprouting. Withstands severe frosts and grows quickly in mild weather. Cut in April.

White Sprouting. Comes in at same time as Early Purple, but not so hardy.

BROCCOLI, STAR

This is a peculiar type of sprouting broccoli which throws a large number of small cauliflowers on one stem. It is plain that it is a cross between a sprouting type and an ordinary variety. It is possible to cut as many as a dozen small cauliflowers from one plant.

Grow as for Sprouting Broccoli.

BRUSSELS SPROUTS

To grow this vegetable successfully 5 main points must be borne in mind : (1) it needs a long season of growth ; (2) it requires plenty of room for development ; (3) it should be heavily manured; (4) it insists on firm ground ; (5) it asks for deep cultivation.

PREPARING THE SOIL

It is always better to plant sprouts on land that has been deeply cultivated for a previous crop, thus all that is necessary is to level the ground and plant the sprouts.

MANURING

Manure heavily the crop that precedes the sprouts. Just before planting apply a good fish manure or "meat and bone" meal at 4-5 ozs. to the square yard, plus sulphate or muriate of potash at 1 oz. to the square yard. Wood ashes could be used instead at 6 ozs. to the square yard.

SEED SOWING

So as to ensure a long season of growth sow the seeds either the previous August in a sheltered border or under continuous cloches in January. A later sowing may be made at the end of February or early in March in a frame, or even in early April out of doors. It is impossible, however, to get the best sprouts from the last sowing mentioned.

Sow in a seed bed in rows 6 ins. apart and thin out the plants to 3 ins. apart when they are fit to handle. It is possible to transplant the thinnings to a further seed bed if necessary.

PLANTING

Plant during late May or early June, for the early crops, and as late as mid-June for the later varieties. For the tall, heavy-cropping types plant 3 ft. square and for the dwarf varieties $2\frac{1}{2}$ ft. between the rows and 2 ft. apart in the rows. It is possible to take an inter-crop of spinach, radish or lettuce between the rows put out in May.

GENERAL CULTIVATION

Hoe throughout the summer, remove the big leaves as they turn yellow. Firm in plants that have been loosened by wind, drawing soil up to the rows.

HARVESTING

Cut the sprouts off leaving a short stalk on the main stem and further loose sprouts will result. Cut systematically from the bottom of the stem upwards.

VARIETIES

Cambridge Early No. 1. The best early of medium height.

Cambridge Main Crop No. 3. An excellent general purpose variety.

Claucas's Favourite. A good tall northern variety.

Dwarf Gem. Produces small sprouts liked by French chefs. A dwarf type.

Harrison's XXX. An excellent strain for the Midlands.

Peer Gynt. Early, medium-sized dark green sprouts.

Prince Askold. Delicious vigorous growing, uniform in size.

King Arthur. Very heavy cropping.

CABBAGE

May be divided into three main groups : (1) spring cabbage ; (2) summer cabbage, and (3) winter cabbage.

I. SPRING CABBAGE

Usually planted out after an early crop like potatoes or peas, and in that case no special preparation of the ground is needed.

SEED SOWING

Seeds should be sown during the month of July. The ground should be raked down finely, the drills made ½ in. deep and 9 ins. apart. Thin sowing is desirable ; the plants should be put out into their permanent position, in September. In the south, August sowing is sometimes made for planting in October.

PLANTING

Plant 18 ins. between the rows and 12 ins. between the plants. Stronger varieties may need 18 ins. by 18 ins.

GENERAL CULTIVATION

On heavy land nitro-chalk may be used in March to hurry cabbages along but, on other soils, Chilean potash nitrate will be more suitable. Stalks of cabbages should be removed and put on the compost heap to rot down as manure.

VARIETIES

(Buy good seed from a first-class seedsman.)

Clucas's First Early. One of the earliest varieties. Dark green in colour forming a good heart.

Durham Early. Earlier than First Early, but not so hardy.

Flower of Spring. Compact variety with few outer leaves. Produces full-sized hearts.

Harbinger. Hearts make delicious eating and heads mature early.

II. SUMMER CABBAGE

SEED SOWING

Seeds are usually sown in March outdoors or in frames in February, and further sowings made at 14-day intervals. Plants may be put out whenever the land is free.

MANURING

Use a liberal dressing of farmyard manure or compost. Artificials to use during preparation of soil should be fish manure at 4 ozs. to the square yard and sulphate of potash at $\frac{1}{2}$ oz. to the square yard. During the growing season, Chilean potash nitrate may be applied at 1 oz. to the yard run if necessary. Apply 7-8 ozs. of hydrated lime to the surface of the ground before planting out.

VARIETIES

Suitable for sowing under cloches in February
> Harbinger. Pointed heart, moderate firmness.
>> (When sown in July and covered with cloches in October, can be cut in December.)
>
> Velocity. Round-headed. Will cut in 12 weeks if not transplanted.

Quick Maturing Varieties
> Early Paragon Drumhead. Does well from February or March sowings.
>
> Golden Acre. Produces heads 6 ins. across and 5 lbs. in weight.
>
> Primo. If sown in frames in February ready 4 months later. Firm, tender and excellent flavour.
>
> Primata. Early, uniform, ball shaped.

Mid-Season Types: All sown in March
> Cotswold Queen. Most delicious spring-sown cabbage. Ready in July.
>
> Greyhound. Quickest growing variety there is. Ready in July.
>
> Fillgap. Earlier than Primo. Round hearts remain in perfect condition for weeks. Ready in August.
>
> Standfast. Dark green, very uniform, solid ball-shaped hearts, last well.

Winnigstadt. Popular for showing. Remains in condition for a considerable time. Ready in September.

Autumn Queen. To follow Winnigstadt. A drumhead of moderate size. Ready in September.

III. WINTER CABBAGE

SEED SOWING

Sow seeds of summer varieties in March if desired. This is usually done in the north and south midlands. Two sowings are normally made in the south, one in the first week of April and the second early in May.

PLANTING

Rows should be 2 ft. apart with plants 2 ft. apart. Compact types, however, may be as close as 18 ins. in the rows. Watering is advisable in dry weather. Draw out shallow furrows and plant in these ; then give them a good soaking.

GENERAL CULTIVATION

Continue hoeing throughout the season. Dust or spray plants with Derris directly there is any sign of pests.

VARIETIES

Christmas Drumhead. Large and very " hearty " variety, needs plenty of room.

Early Paragon Drumhead. Throws a drum-like heart, firm and of good flavour.

January King. Sown in May, cuts in February, extremely hardy.

CABBAGE, RED

This is usually grown for pickling, though in some districts it is stewed.

SEED SOWING

Sow in March on a seed bed and, when planted out, it will come in for use in the autumn. Those who like it stewed may make a sowing in April. For huge heads in the north, sow previous August. Plant October, cut the following August.

VARIETIES

Danish Stonehead. Can be used for pickling or cooking. Throws heads of a deep red colour with a firm heart.

Lydiate. One of the largest red varieties. Throws a firm heart, is late and quite hardy.

Ruby Red. One of the earliest and should be sown in the spring. Is a good variety for the north.

CARROTS

You can have carrots as a vegetable all the year round. The main crops are stored and used in the winter and " frame " varieties very early in the spring. There are many types :

(1) Forcing types for frames on hot-beds.
(2) Shorthorns for early sowings in warm borders and for shallow soils.
(3) The Intermediate, used as a " main " crop.
(4) The Long. Grown by the acre on the deep sandy soils to store.

Soil
Carrots do best on a deep sandy loam.

Preparing the Soil
Try and get the land dug over early in the winter and leave so that the frost and winds can break down the clods. It is a great advantage with heavy soil.

Manuring
Do not dig in farmyard manure as this tends to make the roots fork. Well-rotted compost may be dug in for light soils to provide moisture-holding material and finely-divided compost into heavy soils to help open them up. In addition, use 4 ozs. of a good fish manure to the square yard.

Seed Sowing
Sow the earlies in March in a warm spot. Drills 6 ins. apart. If the soil is wet, cover with continuous cloches for a fortnight beforehand. Sow the seed of the main crop in April in drills ¾ ins. deep and 12-18 ins. apart, according to variety. Sow 3 seeds every 3 ins. along the drill and thin down to 1 per station 3 weeks later, if necessary. Carrots can be grown in cold frames. In this case the seed is usually sown in mid-February. Make the frame face south.

Make another sowing of the early varieties in July so that nice young roots will be available in the autumn and winter.

If the seed of the early varieties is sown very thinly there should be no need to thin out, as it is after thinning that the carrot fly invariably attacks the roots (see page 663).

GENERAL CULTIVATION
Hoe between the rows. Carrot seeds will not germinate if there is not sufficient moisture present. Water thoroughly if necessary.

HARVESTING
Lift the main crop before the winter frosts appear. Store in sand.

CAULIFLOWER

A very popular summer vegetable.

SOIL
Does best on a rich loamy soil with a fair moisture content. You can't grow good cauliflowers unless you take a great deal of trouble in preparing the soil.

PREPARING THE SOIL
Bastard trench incorporating dung or well-rotted compost at the rate of 1 barrowload to 10 sq. yds.

MANURING
A week before planting, fork the ground down level and add a good fish manure or meat and bone meal at 4-5 ozs. to the square yard. Give sulphate of potash at 1 oz. to the square yard, or wood ash at 5 ozs. to the square yard. Finally, apply hydrated lime to the surface of the ground 5-6 ozs. to the square yard.

SEED SOWING
It is possible to get a supply of good white curds from early June to late autumn. To achieve this, make an autumn sowing late in August or early in September. The plants thus raised are those pricked out into frames 4 ins. square, where they live throughout the winter, to be planted out early in April in a sheltered part of the garden. January and February sowings can be made in boxes in frames or greenhouses or under continuous cloches and when the young seedlings come through, the plants are pricked out 4 ins. apart into further frames, or under further cloches. These plants are put out early in April. Another sowing is often made out of doors late in March or early in April, in rows 6 ins. apart, the seedlings being thinned out to 3 ins. apart in the rows, when

80. *Planting : making earth firm with the trowel handle*

81. *Planting out sweet corn*

82. Sowing peas in a drill

83. Peas sown for succession of supply

they are well through. Still later sowings may be made late in April or early in May in a similar manner. It is necessary to take the utmost care to keep down the club-root disease, and the cabbage-root maggot (see pages 662 and 681).

PLANTING

The autumn sowings are often planted in March in a sheltered position, 1 ft. square. For the later sowings the rows are usually 2 ft. apart, the plants being 18 ins. apart in the rows. For the later summer sowings the rows should be $2\frac{1}{2}$ ft. apart, the cauliflowers being 2 ft. apart in the rows. Plants should always be put out before they get too big.

GENERAL CULTIVATION

Hoeing must be done regularly between the plants. During the dry weather give copious waterings. When the plants are producing their white curds, two of the inner leaves should be bent over the flower to prevent it from turning yellow.

HARVESTING

The curds should be cut as early in the morning as possible. If too many heads turn in together, the plants may be pulled up with soil attached to the roots and hung up in a shed. (See BROCCOLI.)

VARIETIES

Very Early Summer Cauliflowers

   Sown in the autumn and over-wintered in frames, or for sowing in the greenhouse in January and February.

   (1) For growing in the greenhouse or deep frame throughout: Feltham Forcing. Delicious, quick growing. Snow-white curd.

   (2) For sowing in the autumn and planting out in April for cutting in early June :
   All the Year Round. Sow in early September. Neat, compact growth.
   Early London. The earliest type. Sow September.

Early Cauliflowers

   For sowing mid-February ; for cutting mid-June–early July.
   Early Snowball. Quick growing, small, very early.
   Dominant. Well protected, pure white, first class quality.
   Cluseed Major. An excellent early, snow white, good size and quality.

Late Summer and Autumn Cauliflowers
(1) For sowing in March to crop in August and early
   September:
   Early September. Solid white heads—exceptional
   quality.
   Silver Fox. Very popular with exhibitors. Delicious
   flavour.
   Majestic. Very large and fine type of cauliflower.
(2) For sowing in April to crop in October, November:
   Royal Swan. Firm white heads, first-class quality;
   Australian raised.
   Veitch's Autumn Giant. Produces huge white heads of
   excellent quality.

CELERY

A crop that leaves the land in a grand condition for another.

SOIL
A peaty soil is ideal, a soil which retains moisture is important.

PREPARING THE SOIL
It is usual to grow celery in specially prepared trenches 16 ins.
deep and 18 ins. wide. The preparation of the trenches makes it
easier to plant the celery afterwards. As the trenches are being
dug, the soil taken out is piled equally on either side making ridges.
If more than one trench is being dug the next one should be 2 ft.
6 ins. away. The ridges are usually flattened at the top so that
catch-crops can be grown.

MANURING
Dig well-rotted dung or properly composted vegetable refuse
into the bottom of the trench using one large bucketful per 2-ft.
run. Fill in 3 or 4 ins. of top soil over this. Sprinkle fish manure,
meat and bone, or hoof and horn meal into the bottom of the
trench at 4 ozs. per yard run. Add sulphate or muriate of potash
at 1 oz. to the yard run or 5 ozs. of fine wood ashes instead. If
trouble with celery heart rot has been experienced in the past,
apply $\frac{1}{2}$ oz. of borax crystals per 5 yd. run also. Further feeds may
be given with liquid manure every 10 days or so when the celery
is growing well.

SEED SOWING
Obtain formaldehyde-treated seed (see page 682). Make the first

sowing about the middle of February so as to have sticks to use at the beginning of September. The main sowing will be done in March for the normal winter use. The February sowings are made in John Innes Compost in boxes in the greenhouse at a temperature of 60° Fahr. The March sowing is usually made in a frame or under continuous cloches. The seed must be sown thinly and shallowly.

It is possible to sow as late as early in April out of doors if it is not desired to dig celery until February or March the following year.

PLANTING
When the plants are 3 or 4 ins. high they may be lifted carefully with a trowel and planted in the specially prepared trenches 1 ft. apart. The weaker-growing varieties may be as close as 9 ins. Plant firmly and soak the trench well afterwards.

GENERAL CULTIVATION
Keep the bottom of the trenches moist, feed with liquid manure every 10 days. Keep the ridges hoed, harvest the catch-crops as soon as possible. Remove the side growth from the base of the celery.

Spray the leaves with nicotine to keep away celery fly maggots early in June, again in August and yet again in September.

Earth up when the plants are over 1 ft. high, about the middle of August. Earth up again 3 weeks later and undertake a further earthing up in October. (See illustration facing page 513.) Fork the soil over first to make it fine before using it for earthing, be very careful to see that no earth gets between the stems. For exhibition sticks, wrap the stems with brown or corrugated paper before earthing.

Protect the celery from frost in a hard winter by covering the tops with either straw or bracken.

HARVESTING
Eight weeks must be allowed between the first earthing up and the first harvesting. When one stick is removed replace the soil to prevent the other sticks from greening.

VARIETIES
White
> Cluseed New Dwarf White. Very solid dwarf white for late cropping.
> White Perfection, strong growing. Solid, firm sticks. Good flavour.

Pink

Clayworth Prize Pink. Early. Excellent quality. Keeps well.
Clucas's White Pink. Though a pink, blanches nearly white.
Stem very wide.
Resistant Pink. Resists celery blight. Tall, late, good flavour.

Red

Covent Garden Red. Good flavour, very crisp.
Standard Bearer. Solid sticks, good size, good flavour.

CELERY, SELF-BLANCHING

PREPARING THE SOIL
The soil should be bastard trenched and enriched with plenty of farmyard manure or well-rotted compost.

MANURING
In addition, the following artificials should be forked into the top 3 or 4 ins.; 4 ozs. fish manure or hoof and horn meal and 1 oz. sulphate of potash per square yard.

SEED SOWING
Sow the seed in boxes placed on the staging of the greenhouse in a temperature of 60-65° Fahr. in February. A fortnight later, prick the seedlings out into further boxes, 3 ins. apart. Those who have not got a greenhouse may sow the seed in a frame or under continuous cloches.

Obtain seed that has been treated with formaldehyde so that it is not infected with celery rust.

PLANTING
Plants may be obtained from a nurseryman.

Put them out in rows 9 ins. apart and 9 ins. apart in the rows about the third week of May. Dwarf varieties need be only 1 ft. square. The ground should be well soaked afterwards. The following day the bed should be given a good hoeing, so as to leave the surface rough.

GENERAL CULTIVATION
Though the celery is self-blanching, and can therefore be grown " on the flat," it is better to place straw among the plants in the autumn to ensure that the stems are really white. Some people cover them with whitewashed cloches.

HARVESTING
Dig up and use when sufficiently blanched ; is not frost resistant.

VARIETIES
Doré. Perhaps the best pure white dwarf. Of good flavour.
Golden Marvel Blanching. Very solid ; blanches easily.

COLEWORT

A small, very hardy type of cabbage.

PROPAGATION
Sow in seed beds in the spring as for cabbage, or sow thinly in
rows 18 ins. apart where the plants are to grow.

PLANTING
Put the plants out 1 ft. square, or if sown in situ, thin out first to
6 ins. apart, and later on to 1 ft. apart, using the second lot of
thinnings as a vegetable.

VARIETIES
Rosette. Has rosette-shaped heads which are very crisp.
Hardy Green. Has larger hearts and is very hardy.

KALE

Invaluable in an emergency. Kale ensures a good supply of greens
in the winter. Improved by frosts.
   Make no special preparations for kales, they follow another
manured crop.

SEED SOWING
Sow the first week in May in the north and towards the end of
May in the south. Prepare a fine seed bed by raking the soil
down. Make the drills 9 ins. apart. Thin the plants to 6 ins.
   Sow asparagus kale as late as June and July.

PLANTING
Put the plants into their permanent positions at the end of June
or the beginning of July. They follow early potatoes, early peas,
lettuce, spinach, or French beans, etc.

The Complete Gardener

General Cultivation

If dry, pour water in the holes at planting time. Prevent club-root and cabbage-root maggot (see pages 662 and 681).

Harvesting

Allow the kales to grow and build up a good plant, then keep cutting them. Remove the heads of the kales early in the new year and then dozens of side growths will break out. These are first-class.

Varieties

Asparagus Kale. A hardy late. Can be sown where it is intended to grow.

Extra Curled Scotch. Robust and compact.

Hardy Sprouting. Withstands the most rigorous winter.

Hungry Gap. Withstands drought, wet and frost.

Russian Kale. Very hardy, dense head in November, followed by young shoots in January and February.

Thousand-headed. Very hardy, strong, and branching.

LEEKS

A very valuable vegetable used in the winter when other vegetables are scarce. May be dug up as required. Does not have to be lifted and stored.

Soil

The leek can be grown on practically any soil provided it has been deeply worked. It prefers a soil in which there is plenty of organic matter.

Preparing the Soil

Trenches should be got out a spade's depth, plenty of manure or compost placed in the bottom, and 3 ins. of good soil put on top. This, after treading, should leave the trenches about 6 ins. deep. The trenches should be 18 ins. apart, and the plants 1 ft. apart. (See illustration facing page 489.)

Where there is no time to prepare trenches, leeks may be grown on the flat.

Manuring

In addition to farmyard manure, poultry manure or a fish fertiliser may be used at 4 ozs. to the square yard, sulphate of potash at 1 oz. to the square yard or wood ashes at 5 ozs. to the square yard, once a month throughout the season.

Liquid manure, or Liquinure, may be watered in between the plants.

Seed Sowing

Sow the seed in gentle heat under glass towards the end of January. A NO-SOIL compost is bought and placed in boxes, and the seed sown thinly on this. They are then stood on the benches of a greenhouse at a temperature of about 60° Fahr. Take care to water and cover the boxes with a sheet of glass and a piece of brown paper until the seedlings have germinated.

When the plants are 1 in. high, they should be pricked out into other boxes, in similar soil, 1½ ins. apart. The boxes should then be watered and placed on the shelf in the greenhouse, near the light, and kept at a temperature of about 55° Fahr. When the plants are 5 ins. high they should be gradually hardened off.

Those who have no greenhouse can sow the seed under cloches or in frames early in March, in drills 9 ins. apart. As soon as the seedlings can be handled they should be transplanted 4 ins. square into soil rich in organic matter. Here they may grow on until they are 8 ins. high, when they can be planted out.

Planting

The plants should be taken out of the soil carefully, so as not to break the roots. If the roots are damaged cut the leaves back so as to equalise things up.

After planting in trenches 1 ft. apart give a good flooding. " On the flat " the rows should be 1 ft. apart and the plants 8 ins. apart. Holes should be made with a dibber 9 ins. deep and the leeks should be dropped into the hole. A little water should be poured into the holes after planting, but the holes should not be filled in.

General Cultivation

Earth up when the plants are half-grown, say, in September. Give a further earthing in October.

Harvesting

Dig as required from December onwards.

Varieties

Three main types :

London Flag or Broad Flag. Thick stems, broad green softish
  leaves, more susceptible to frost than other types.

The Lyon or Prize Taker. The best late leek, slow maturing. Buy
a good strain.

The Musselburgh or Scotch Group. Very hardy, narrower leaves
than any other type. Good strains are : The Emperor,
Monarch, and Giant Musselburgh. The latter is very popular
in Scotland.

LETTUCE

See SALADS, Chapter III, page 540.

MARROWS

The marrow grows well in any odd corner. It is quite suitable
for growing up a wall or fence or for covering up a mound. It
must, of course, be tied in position if necessary.

SOIL

No special cultivation need be done.

MANURING

Plenty of compost should be incorporated when making up the
bed, and a good fish manure at 4 ozs. to the square yard added.

SEED SOWING

Sow the seeds in 3-in. pots in a greenhouse, early in April. The
plants are then ready to put out into open ground towards the
end of May. Those who have no greenhouse may sow the seed
in frames where the plants are to grow 3 to a " station " and then
thin to one per station later. It is inadvisable to sow the seed
much before the first week of May.

PLANTING

Where numbers of marrows are to be grown, the plants should
be 3 ft. apart in the rows with the rows 4 ft. apart. Bush marrows
are preferable under this system. Trailers grown under these
conditions have to be kept pinched back. It is in the odd corner
that they may be allowed to ramble as they please.

GENERAL CULTIVATION

Hoeing should be done regularly and mulchings or rotted leaves
or compost should also be given regularly.

HARVESTING

Marrows should be cut when young and tender and then the

Planting potatoes

Putting potatoes in trays for sprouting

86. & 87. *Earthing up celery*

plants will produce a heavier crop. Regular cutting may treble a crop.

VARIETIES

Bush-shaped Green. An early variety.
Bush-shaped White. Similar to above, but fruits creamy white.
Early Gem. A heavy cropping early, dark green fruits.
Custard Marrow. A flattish saucer-shaped marrow, yellowy white.
Long Green. Dark green marrow—a trailer.
Long White. Large creamy white fruits.
Moore's Cream. Very prolific, small cream-coloured fruits.
Rotherside Orange. Flattened globe-shaped orange-like fruits.

MUSHROOMS

Mushrooms can be grown successfully in all kinds of places—cellars, frames, greenhouses, sheds, or even in the open. Whatever structure is used, a fairly even temperature—never lower than 50° Fahr. or above 70° Fahr. should be maintained. If a greenhouse is employed, some kind of shading will have to be given.

SOIL

This is used for " casing " (see page 514), subsoil being the ideal soil to use.

MANURE

It is usual to use horse manure, though lately it has been found possible to rot down straw with certain activators and obtain similar results. Those who are interested could consult The Horticultural International Advisory Bureau, Arkley, Herts.

The manure or prepared straw must be made. It should be stacked into a neat pile and if it appears rather dry should be watered. In four to six days' time the heap will be turned, the outside to the inside and the top to the bottom. Subsequent turnings are done at intervals of four days. After four turnings the manure should be nut brown in colour, free from any unpleasant odour. The straw when twisted in the two hands should snap easily.

BEDS

These can be either flat, or in single or double ridges. The flat bed is made 8 ins. deep, the manure being firmly trodden down as construction proceeds. The ridge bed is triangular in section, and should be 2 ft. 6 ins. along the base, 2 ft. 6 ins. high and 6 ins. across the top.

SPAWNING

When the beds are made, the temperature is tested with a soil thermometer. It will rise at first to 110°-130° Fahr., and when it has fallen again to 70° Fahr. spawn may be inserted. (See illustration facing page 577.) Use pure culture spawn, and break off pieces about the size of a walnut, inserting these 10 ins. apart and 1 in. deep all over the bed.

CASING

When the white mycelium threads are seen, the beds may be cased from 10 days to 3 weeks after spawning. Apply the subsoil, which should be moist, 1½ ins. deep all over the beds.

GENERAL CULTIVATION

If a temperature of 60° Fahr. can be maintained, mushrooms should appear within 5 to 8 weeks of spawning. Keep the casing soil uniformly moist, but not wet. Avoid draughts and give very little ventilation.

HARVESTING

Pull the mushrooms from the bed, do not cut them, and fill in the hole with a little casing soil. The bed may go on cropping for 2 to 4 months, a square foot of bed yielding about 1 lb. of mushrooms.

ONIONS

It is important for a householder to grow sufficient onions for his own use. The English onion is much more valuable than the Spanish onion.

SOIL

Onions do best on a deeply-cultivated, rich, sandy loam. They will grow on a heavy clay providing this is opened up by the addition of burnt soil, or horticultural peat.

PREPARING THE SOIL

Dig the soil over deeply some time before seed sowing.

MANURING

Farmyard manure should be buried at the rate of 1 good barrow-load to 10 sq. yds. Wood ashes may also be used at ½ lb. per square yard, dried poultry manure at 3 ozs. to the square yard, and fish manure or meat and bone meal at 3-4 ozs. to the square yard.

Firm the surface of the soil before sowing the seed, by treading or rolling. Firming should not be done when the soil is sticky.

SEED SOWING

(1) *Spring*

Sow in March in the south, and April in the north, in rows 1 ft apart and ½ in. deep. Cover the drills by giving a light raking.

GENERAL CULTIVATION

Hoe directly the crop is visible, drawing the soil away from the rows. Thinning should be done as soon as possible so as to leave little groups 3 ins. apart, and later to 6 ins. apart. These thinnings can be used for salads. Eventually, the groups are thinned down to 1 plant, preferably on a cloudy day, and a good bulb is produced. The onion fly lays her eggs near the plants and, to prevent this, apply whizzed naphthalene along the rows (see page 664.)

HARVESTING

The bulbs should ripen naturally in September but, to help them, bend the tops over at the neck. (See illustration facing page 488.) After loosening the soil and pulling them up, the onions are laid on their sides to continue the ripening process. After this they are stored in a cool, airy, dry place. Hang them up in ropes under the shelter of the eaves of a building or in a potting shed or tool shed.

SEED SOWING

(2) *Autumn*

Sow in July or early August. The farther north, the earlier the sowing. For salad onions the rows should be 9 ins. apart, but for onions that are to bulb early the rows should be 12 ins. apart.

Follow onions after a well-manured crop such as early peas, or early potatoes, and then it is only necessary to rake the ground finely and draw out the drills.

Pull regularly. Do not thin salad onions. Thin the varieties that are to bulb in the spring and transplant the thinnings, 12 ins. between the rows and 6-9 ins. between the plants.

(3) *Seed sowing under glass*

For exhibition onions sow in boxes of John Innes seed compost during the first or second week in January. A temperature of about 60° Fahr. is required. As soon as the seedlings are large enough, they should be pricked out 2 ins. apart into further boxes of John Innes potting compost. Grow on slowly, harden off gradually and then set the plants out in the prepared border at 15 ins. between the rows and 9 ins. between the plants. Firm planting is advisable, on a showery day if possible. When the tops have a tendency to fall over after planting a little bamboo stake may be put at the side and the tops tied up to this.

HARVESTING
Use autumn sowings in August, spring sowings during the winter.

VARIETIES

Autumn sowers for bulbing
Giant Rocca. Flattish oval bulb. Mild flavour.
Giant Zittau. Similar to above.
Red Tripoli. Good flavour. Skin tinged with red.
White Tripoli. Excellent flavour but not a good keeper.

Autumn sowers for pulling as spring or salad onions
White Lisbon. A great favourite. Silver-skinned.
White Portugal. Really a Spanish type, but often used as a salad onion.

Spanish Onions
Improved Reading. Juicy flesh, solid. Mild flavour.
James's Keeping. Strong flavour, good keeper.
White Spanish. Good flavour.

Dutch or Flanders Onions
Bedfordshire Champion. Most popular variety for spring sowing. Keeps well, mild.
Selected Ailsa Craig. Large bulbs, tapering in shape. Suitable for exhibition.
The Premier. Pale straw colour. Immense size. Suitable for exhibition.

ONIONS, PICKLING

SEED SOWING
Those who have poor soil and wish to grow onions with very little preparation should grow pickling onions. Broadcast the seed over

the surface of the soil and rake it in lightly. Keep weeded, but not thinned.

HARVESTING
Pickling onions are ready in September.

PARSNIPS

One of the easiest vegetables to grow. It is nice boiled or steamed, or can be par-boiled and then baked in a little fat.

SOIL
Parsnips will grow in almost any soil. If you can't get long, straight roots, then bore holes with an iron rod when sowing, 3 ft. deep and 3 ins. in diameter at the top and 1 ft. apart, and fill these with sifted soil. Sow 3 seeds on the top of each hole, the seedlings being thinned out to 1 later.

PREPARING THE SOIL
Dig the soil deeply in the autumn and leave it rough. It is thus easier to fork down in February or March. Parsnips should be grown on land that has been well manured for a previous crop.

MANURING
Meat and bone meal or a good fish manure may be applied as a top dressing a few days before seed-sowing time at 5-6 ozs. to the square yard.

SEED SOWING
Sow the seed in February or March in the south, and towards the end of March in the north. Sow rather more thickly than for carrots as the seed does not germinate so well. Have the rows 18 ins. apart and 1½ ins. deep. When the seedlings are 1½ ins. high they should be thinned to 8 ins. apart. Regular hoeing should be done.

HARVESTING
The roots may be left in the ground until required. If there is danger of the ground being frozen, thus preventing the roots from being dug up, some of them may be left on the surface of the ground after digging.

Clucas's Intermediate. For shallow soils.
Tender and True. Clear smooth skin. For deeper soils.
The Student. Suitable for the north. For deeper soils.

PEAS

Peas, like beans, have nodules on their roots containing bacteria which extract nitrogen from the air. Therefore, leave pea roots in the ground after the pods have been harvested.

MANURING
Farmyard manure or properly composted vegetable refuse should be dug in when bastard trenching. In addition, meat and bone meal may be added at 3-4 ozs. to the square yard, and wood ashes at 6 ozs. to the square yard.

SEED SOWING
Sow the seed in flat drills, 5-6 ins. wide and 3 ins. deep. (See illustration facing page 505.) Sow 2 ins. apart each way, and for later varieties 3 ins. apart. When the plants are just coming through, protect them by pea boughs or pea guards. Except in the north a first sowing can be made in the autumn, say, November. Draw out the drill on a mild day, in the morning, and sow the seed later in the day.

Further sowings may be made at the beginning of February. Choose dwarf varieties (round-seeded), the rows being 18 ins. apart.

Sowings may also be made under cloches (see pages 581-585).

Sow at regular intervals from early April onwards. (See illustration facing page 505.) Make the next sowing directly the previous row is seen above ground. Sow early-maturing varieties again late in June or early in July and you will get good peas in September.

If the weather is dry, give a good flooding.

Distances between one row and another depend on the varieties sown. A 3-ft. variety needs 18 ins. of room on either side, while a 4-ft. variety should have a 2-ft space.

GENERAL CULTIVATION
Hoe the rows regularly. Mulch as advised for runner beans. Watering is necessary if the weather is dry. To support the plants, bushy twigs may be inserted in the ground near the peas when

they are 3-4 ins. high. Use pea-sticks whenever possible, though dwarf varieties will grow quite well without them. Sticks should be put in at an angle of 45° on either side of the row. The sticks in one row should slope at the opposite angle to the other row.

HARVESTING

Peas should be picked regularly. Don't miss any pods.

VARIETIES

Dwarf, round-seeded

Kelvedon Viscount. Heavy cropper. Popular in north. 1½ ft.

Feltham First. Good type for cloches and open air. 18 ins. high.

Meteor. Hardy dwarf. Only grows 1 ft. high.

Dwarf, wrinkled-seeded

English Wonder. A marrowfat which grows 18 ins. high.

Kelvedon Wonder. One of the best. 18 ins. high. Good for small gardens and allotments.

Little Marvel. Ready 11 weeks after sowing. Large pods, well filled. 2 ft.

Tall earlies

Foremost. Very heavy cropper. Can be sown in February for end May picking. 2½ ft.

Laxton's Superb. Good flavoured pea. 2½ ft.

Springtide. 3 ft. Heavy cropper.

Early maincrops

Monarch. Stands drought well. Excellent flavour. 2½ ft. Marrowfat.

Kelvedon Triumph. Outstanding. Excellent flavour. Good cropper. 1¾ ft.

The Lincoln. 2 ft. high. Very heavy cropper.

Onward. Heavy cropper of excellent flavour. 2½ ft. Marrowfat. One of the best.

Maincrops

Autocrat. Vigorous late variety. Heavy cropper. 3-4 ft.

Chancelot. 3 ft. high. Good exhibition variety. Good flavour.

POTATOES

Potatoes are more cheaply grown on a large scale with tractors and ploughs than in a small garden.

More potatoes are eaten than any other vegetable. They are an excellent cleaning crop.

SOIL

Potatoes may be grown on all soils, though some produce those of an inferior flavour. Heavy soils and peaty soils produce waxy tubers. Damp, low-lying soils should be avoided. The best potatoes are grown on an open sunny situation on deep, well-drained, medium soil.

PREPARING THE SOIL

Ridge the land in the autumn so that air, frost and rain can penetrate and sweeten it. The ridges should run north and south. If this is not possible, ridge the soil in the spring, putting manure and fertilisers into the bottom of the ridges.

MANURING

It is usual to apply farmyard manure or rotted vegetable refuse, well composted, in the rows at planting time. Compost is an excellent substitute for dung. In addition, apply a complete organic manure like a fish fertiliser, at 3-4 ozs. to the yard run.

The tubers should be about the size of a hen's egg and should weigh about 2 ozs. Those who have larger tubers can cut these in such a way that there is an "eye" in each section. Do this just before the tubers are planted.

If potatoes are bought early in the year, they can be placed in shallow trays to sprout, rose end upwards. (See illustration facing page 512.) This ensures a heavier yield.

If possible, use a potato tray 2 ft. 6 ins. long, 1 ft. 6 ins. wide and $3\frac{1}{2}$ ins. deep. In the corners there are small triangular posts standing 2-3 ins. above the sides. The trays may thus be put one on top of the other while the sprouting process is taking place. Store in any light, airy place where there is no frost.

Disbud the tubers as they start to grow, leaving only the two strongest shoots at the rose end, i.e. the end with the largest number of eyes. Sprouted tubers should be put into the furrows carefully, the shoots not being damaged.

PLANTING

Plant earliest potatoes in ridges 18 ins. apart, the tubers being 12 ins. apart in the rows. From this planting, the potatoes should be harvested when quite small. The ridges for ordinary early potatoes should be 1 ft. 9 ins. apart, and the seed 12 ins. apart in the rows. For main crops, the rows should be 2 ft. 6 ins. apart and the tubers 1 ft. 6 ins. apart in the rows. (See illustration facing page 512.)

No seed potatoes should be planted deeper than 4 ins., and 3 ins. will do for the earliest varieties. The rows should run north and south. Soil should be drawn over the rows, to leave a slight ridge, and so mark them.

GENERAL CULTIVATION

Directly the foliage appears, the rows should be hoed. A 2-pronged hoe is a good tool for the purpose. When the tops are half-grown they should be earthed up with a hoe, a 6 in. depth

MAKING A CLAMP ·

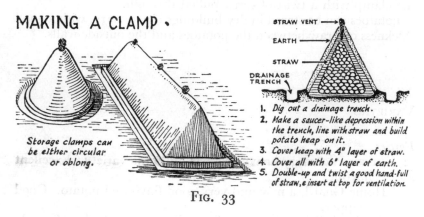

STRAW VENT →

EARTH →

STRAW →

DRAINAGE TRENCH →

1. *Dig out a drainage trench.*
2. *Make a saucer-like depression within the trench, line with straw and build potato heap on it.*
3. *Cover heap with 4″ layer of straw.*
4. *Cover all with 6″ layer of earth.*
5. *Double-up and twist a good hand-full of straw, & insert at top for ventilation.*

Storage clamps can be either circular or oblong.

FIG. 33

of soil being drawn up to the stem, or haulm, on either side. The stems of the plants should then be about 8 ins. high. A further earthing up should be done 3 weeks later, and further ones at fortnightly intervals, as seems necessary.

Keep a look out for potato blight and spray from July onwards with Bordeaux Mixture (see page 645.)

It is possible to obtain potatoes in June, if the tubers are planted under continuous cloches (see pages 581-585.)

LIFTING AND STORING

Early potatoes may be lifted as soon as the tubers are a good size. Do the lifting on a fine day and the potatoes will come out clean and bright. Main crop tubers need not be lifted until the haulm has died down. If diseased tops are present at digging time the spores will drop on to the tubers and infect them. Cut off the tops and put them on the compost heap, and if the heap is properly made, with an accelerator, the spores will thus be killed.

Main crop potatoes will be stored in clamps, hogs, or buries, as they are called. (See Fig. 33.) The ground where the clamp is to stand should be higher than the general level. The potatoes must be fairly dry before clamping, and any diseased tubers should be removed.

Pile the tubers in a ridge-shaped heap about 3½ ft. high and 4 ft. wide. They should then be covered with straw to a depth of about 6 ins. and over the straw 6 ins. of soil should be placed. Make the surface smooth and firm. The soil for the outside of the clamp should be taken from around the clamp and thus a trench can be formed to carry away excess water. Ventilate the top of the clamp with a twist of straw pulled through.

Potatoes can be stored in dry buildings if necessary, with a good thickness of straw between the potatoes and the outside walls.

VARIETIES

Earlies

Arran Pilot, very heavy cropper, immune variety. Excellent flavour.

Home Guard, a new and very good flavoured potato. Good cropper.

Pentland Beauty, a new favourite, cream flesh. Superb quality.

Ulster Chieftain, kidney shaped, soft flesh. Excellent early. Immune.[1]

Ulster Premier, one of the earliest, a red kidney shaped potato.

Ulster Prince, exceptionally heavy cropper, white kidney.

Second Earlies

Pentland Crown, white oval shaped tubers, good cooker.

Ulster Torch, white fleshed, kidney shaped, heavy cropper, good quality. Blight resistant. Later than other Second Earlies.

Dr. Macintosh, kidney shaped, heavy cropper, white fleshed variety, shallow eyes.

[1] This means immune from wart disease only.

Craig's Royal, white skin splashed red, excellent flavour, good quality.

Main Crop

Arran Banner, immune, good flavour. Good cropper, white round tubers, vigorous grower.

Arran Peak, oval shaped tubers, heavy cropper, seems to resist blight.

Ulster Supreme, oval shaped white, excellent keeper, heavy cropper.

Stormont Dawn, heavy yielder, of good quality, oval and round tubers. Stores well.

RHUBARB

Being a permanent crop prepare soil as for seakale (see page 525). Raise plants from seeds sown in March in drills 1 in. deep and 1 ft. apart. Thin seedlings to 10 ins. When a year old, plant out in rows 3 ft. apart and 2 ft. 6 in. between the plants. Propagation is also carried out in February or March by dividing the old crowns into roots bearing only a single bud.

Do not pull until the second year and then only moderately. Water well and mulch with compost. Feed with Liquinure during summer and at end of July dress with fish manure at 4-5 ozs. per square yard. Remove flower spikes immediately they are seen. Never pull after the end of June.

Put roots in a warm dark place for forcing (e.g. under greenhouse staging or in a cellar) from December onwards. Cover with light soil and keep moist. Cover plants outside with straw or leaves, placing a box or cloche over them.

VARIETIES

Dawe's Champion. Very good for outdoors.

Early Albert. Good for forcing.

Hawkes' Champagne. Outstandingly good variety.

Timperley Early. Excellent early variety.

SAVOYS

Savoys are improved by frost, and are well worth growing because of their hardiness.

SOIL

Savoys like firm ground. Prepare the soil as advised for brussels sprouts (see page 499).

MANURING

Apply fish manure or meat and bone meal at 3-4 ozs. to the square yard plus sulphate or muriate of potash at 1 oz. to the square yard.

SEED SOWING

Sow the seed in 3 batches, first at the end of March, the second in mid-April and the last in late April.

Make the drills 9 ins. apart and thin to 3 ins. apart as soon as the seedlings appear. The thinnings can be transplanted if necessary.

PLANTING

Put the plants out into their permanent position at the end of June or early July. With smaller varieties the rows should be 18 ins. apart and the plants 15 ins. in the rows. With a stronger variety 2-ft. square is advised.

HARVESTING

Cut as soon as the hearts are firm and of a good size.

VARIETIES

Small
> Very Early. Small, good flavour.
> Belle Ville. Lovely coloured variety. Hardy, delicious flavour.

Early
> Best of All. Sow March. Firm hearts.
> Pixie Green. Small, suitable for small gardens.

Mid-season
> Christmas Drumhead. Firm hearts. Good flavour.

Late
> Latest of All. Curled leaves. Dark green. Delicious.

Extra Late
> Omega. Slow grower but worth waiting for.

For succession, sow
> Ormskirk Early. For cutting in September and October.
> Ormskirk Medium. For cutting November–February. Hardy.
> Ormskirk Late Green. For cutting January–March. Withstands hard weather.
> Ormskirk Extra Late. For cutting March–April. Very deep colour.

SEAKALE

Seakale is much liked as a forced vegetable.

SOIL

It prefers a heavy well-drained soil, though it will grow in a light loam.

MANURING

Dig in well-rotted manure or compost at the rate of 1 good barrowload per 16 sq. yds. Apply fish manure at 4 ozs. per square yard and work into the top 2 or 3 ins.

PROPAGATION

Seakale may be propagated by seed sowing, root cuttings, or thongs. The last is the usual method. Seeds are sown 1 in. deep in drills 12 ins. apart, and thinned out to 6 ins. apart when large enough. The following February the plants are put out in their permanent positions. Thongs are prepared from the side roots, those of pencil thickness being selected and cut into pieces 6 ins. long, the thickest end being cut level and the thinner end slanting. The thongs are then tied in bundles and put in layers of damp sand till planting time.

PLANTING

Put the " budding " thongs out during the third week in March, in rows 18 ins. apart, with 15 ins. between the plants, placing the top of the thong 1 in. below the surface.

GENERAL CULTIVATION

Hoe regularly throughout the summer and cut off flowering stems. Cut down the foliage by the middle of October.

FORCING

Dig up roots in the winter, cut off the side roots and stand upright in soil or rotted leaves under the greenhouse staging, in frames or in cellars. Moisture, darkness and a temperature of 55-60° Fahr. are required. In the open crowns may be forced by covering with special forcing pots or with boxes and surrounding these with farmyard manure. (See illustration facing page 488.)

VARIETY

Lily White. Pure white, delicate flavour.

SHALLOTS

Shallots are very easy to grow and are not generally attacked by the onion fly.

SOIL
Shallots will grow on almost any soil.

MANURING
Manures may be applied as advised for onions, and, in addition, hoof and horn meal, or a good fish manure, may be worked in at 5-6 ozs. to the square yard.

PLANTING
Planting can be done early in February in the south and a little later in the north. Rows should be 1 ft. apart and the bulbs spaced 4 ins. apart in the rows.

Firm the soil before planting and then push the bulbs in to half their depth. Remove any loose skin. Examine the bed 2 weeks after planting and firm any bulbs that may have become loosened. Planting can be done in odd places such as the tops of celery trenches, along the sides of paths, etc.

GENERAL CULTIVATION
Hoe frequently between the rows, shallowly. Do not bury the bulbs.

HARVESTING
In July when the leaves of the shallots begin to turn yellow they should be lifted and left on the surface of the soil to dry off. Turn them 2 or 3 times each day and when they are thoroughly dry clean them and store in a cool dry place.

VARIETIES
Russian Shallot (sometimes called Dutch or Jersey Shallot). Coppery-red skin, greyish-green leaves. Does not keep very well, but is a heavy cropper.
True Red or Yellow Shallot. Nice firm bulb just right for pickling. Keeps well.

SPINACH

Valuable for its high vitamin and mineral contents.
There are various types which will be dealt with under separate headings.

I. ANNUAL SPINACH (Summer and Winter types)

PREPARING THE SOIL
Spinach will grow almost anywhere, but light soils are best.

Incorporation of plenty of moisture-holding material prevents it going to seed too quickly.

Farmyard manure may be dug in 7-8 ins. down at 1 barrow-load to 12 sq. yds. Also, fork into the top meat and bone, hoof and horn meal or fish manure, or better still, a combination of these, 4-5 ozs. to the square yard.

SEED SOWING

Sow summer spinach at fortnightly intervals from early March onwards to keep up supply. Summer sowings should be made in shady moist positions. Drills 1 in. deep, 1 ft. apart. Thin plants to 6 ins.

Make sowing for winter spinach from early August to early September. In cold, wet soils, a specially raised bed should be made, 5 ft. wide, 3 ins. above surrounding soil level. Have drills 9 ins. apart and thin plants to 6 ins.

GENERAL CULTIVATION

Give summer spinach fortnightly top dressing of Chilean potash nitrate, directly the plants have started into growth. Liable to go to seed quickly if not kept watered.

Winter spinach may need protecting. Put straw, bracken or heather over and between the rows, or use continuous cloches.

HARVESTING

Pick summer spinach regularly and hard, leaving only the youngest inner leaves. Pick winter spinach gently, removing largest leaves only.

VARIETIES

Summer (Round Seeded)
> Giant Lettuce Leaved. Long-standing. Leaves are very large.
> Monstrous Viroflay. Large, upright leaves. Goes to seed quickly.
> The C.O. Has very broad leaves.

Winter (Prickly Seeded)
> Blatchford's New Prickly. Very hardy. Good cropper. For winter and spring use.
> New Giant Leaved. Very large leaves, long-standing. Excellent both for spring and late summer sowings.

II. SPINACH BEET (*Perpetual Spinach*)
Easy to grow and well worthwhile as it can be picked over a long

time. Sown in spring, supplies leaves all summer and, sown in late summer, is picked in spring and early summer when few vegetables are available.

SOIL AND MANURING
As for Beetroot (see page 494).

SEED SOWING
Sow in April and early August. Drills 15 ins. apart, plants thinned gradually to 1 ft. apart.

GENERAL CULTIVATION
Appreciates occasional watering during dry periods.

HARVESTING
Pick leaves regularly, or else the older leaves become coarse and young leaves will not be produced so readily.

III. SEAKALE SPINACH (Silver Beet, Swiss Chard)
An enormous improvement on the last, though similar in habits and requirements. The deep green, puckered leaves are very luscious; stalks and midribs are broad, silvery white and succulent, and may be served separately, cooked like celery.

SOIL, SOWING AND CULTIVATION
As for Spinach Beet.

HARVESTING
Pull leaves regularly, making sure that the entire leaf-stalk is removed, as otherwise formation of new leaves will be hindered.

IV. NEW ZEALAND SPINACH
Not as popular as the ordinary spinach. Half-hardy. Will not go to seed like the other types.

SOIL
Dry, light soils very suitable. Heavier soils will do, if well prepared.

MANURING
As for ordinary spinach.

SEED SOWING
Plants are generally raised under glass, i.e. in greenhouse, frames or under cloches, though sowing in the open about the second

week in May is possible. Under glass, sow in March in boxes of John Innes compost. When large enough to handle, pot plants singly in 3-in. pots and keep in a light position. Harden for planting out end of May.

PLANTING
Plant end of May in rows 3 ft. apart, plants 2 ft. apart in the rows.

GENERAL CULTIVATION
Pick regularly, pinching back plants so as to prevent them from getting entangled with each other. Water generously in dry spells. Cloches placed over the plants in early October will give you a crop into the winter.

SWEDES

Often preferred to winter turnips. Hardier on the whole and of a " different " flavour.

MANURING
As for Turnips.

SEED SOWING
Sow the seed in drills 18 ins. apart. Thin out the plants to 1 ft. apart. Sow in May in the south and in June in the north.

HARVESTING
Leave swedes outside and pull them as required or clamp as for potatoes.

VARIETIES
Bronze Top Swede. Said by epicures to be better flavoured than purple Top Swede.
Purple Top Swede. Well-shaped roots of good colour.

TURNIPS

Can be grown large and used mashed in the winter, or no larger than a tennis ball and be cooked whole.
   Turnips are subject to the club-root disease and so should not be grown after members of the " cabbage " family.

SOIL

Make the soil as near a sandy loam as possible. There must be humus in the land for the plants have a tendency to run to seed in dry weather.

MANURING

Dig in plenty of well-rotted compost and fork damped horticultural peat into the top 2 or 3 ins. at 1 bucketful to the square yard. Add fish manure at the same time at 4 ozs. to the square yard and, finally, apply hydrated lime as a surface dressing at 5 ozs. to the square yard.

SEED SOWING

(a) *In Frames*

Sow about the end of February over a hot bed. Make holes 4 ins. apart and 1 in. deep and drop 3 seeds in each one. Fill in the holes and later thin the seedlings to 1 per station.

(b) *Under Cloches*

Cover the ground in March to warm it. Sow seed about mid-March in drills 1 in. deep and 12 ins. apart. Thin turnips to 6 ins. apart.

(c) *Early Outside*

Sow early April in a warm spot. Rows 8 ins. apart. Thin seedlings down later to 6 ins. apart.

(d) *Main Crop*

Sow seed in May in a shady position if possible. Rows 12 ins. apart. Thin out the plants to 8 ins. apart when they are 1 in. or so high.

(e) *Winter Turnips*

Sow any time from the middle of July to the end of August. Drills 18 ins. apart. Thin first of all to 6 ins. apart then when the roots are fit to use to 1 ft. apart.

(f) *Turnip Tops*

Sow early in September in rows 2 ft. apart. Do no thinning. Allow the plants to grow naturally. Use the leaves and not the roots.

GENERAL CULTIVATION

Control the turnip flea beetle which is the worst pest by dusting with a Gammexane dust. Hoe regularly and in very dry seasons water thoroughly. Put mulchings of lawn mowings along the rows.

HARVESTING

Pull the frame, cloche and spring-sown varieties when the roots are young and fresh, and before they get coarse.

Allow the winter varieties to stand outside and be used as required, though in the north it may be necessary to lift them and clamp them in November.

VARIETIES

(a) and (b)—Frames and Cloches
> Early Long White Frame. Has a blunt nose and a minute tap root.
> Jersey Navet. Pure white with a thin skin.
> Sutton's Gem. The most delicious oval turnip there is.

(c) and (d)—Early Outside and Main
> Early Snowball. Round white turnip, solid and mild.
> Early White Milan. The roots are flat, smooth and white.
> Golden Ball. Yellow fleshed, clean, delicious.

(e) Winter Turnips
> Chirk Castle. Firm white flesh.
> Manchester Market. Similar. Very popular in the north.

(f) Turnip Tops
> Green Globe.

CHAPTER III

Salads

THE modern housewife to-day finds it easy to fill her salad bowl month by month because we really have learned much from the Continent, and so use many more plants for this purpose. The salad may get flavour and aroma from spring onions, or rose petals, cheese or pineapple ; it may be decorated with silvery sardelles or bright blue borage flowers, whilst for the main body of the salad there is a wide choice of plants.

Unfortunately, many people think that anything that can be made tasty with salad cream is good enough and so, having been offered a mixed salad, you may be faced with cold baked beans, cold boiled potatoes, " touched up " perhaps with a blushing slice of beetroot and one apologetic lettuce leaf. It should not be forgotten that a salad ought to be a healthy dish and provide those who eat it with plenty of minerals and vitamins.

ARTICHOKES

The immature heads of the Globe Artichoke make a welcome change from the more usual salads. Boil, remove stem and scales and serve the " cups " cold with a French dressing or mayonnaise. (See Chapter II, Everyday Vegetables, page 484.)

The Jerusalem Artichoke and the Chinese Artichoke are related neither to the Globe Artichoke nor to each other. They can both be utilised in salads.

CELERIAC
(OR TURNIP ROOTED CELERY)

This forms swollen roots the size of a large turnip, but much less even in shape. These roots have a strong celery flavour.

Raise and harden the plants as advised for celery.

PLANTING
Plant late in May or early in June in rich moisture-holding soil, 18 ins. between the rows, plants 15-18 ins. in the rows.

GENERAL CULTIVATION

Water liberally and feed once a fortnight, as soon as the plants are well established, with liquid manure or a complete fertiliser. Remove all side growths as they appear. A fortnight before harvesting, draw up some soil around the base of each plant to bleach the top of the root. Lift in October and store in shed or clamp. The celeriac will usually be fit for use as late as 6 months after lifting.

VARIETIES

Giant Prague. Which grows to great size.
Paris Amélioré. Which is said to be of better quality.

CELERY

Celery is deservedly popular as a salad plant, but should only be grown by those who can give it a good deal of attention. (See Chapter II, Everyday Vegetables, page 506.)

CHICORY

The wild chicory with its lovely, sky-blue flowers is of little value in the garden. But the forced, bleached leaves of the cultivated form make a delicious salad.

SOIL

The soil should be light, but rich in well-decayed organic matter. 2 or 3 ozs. per square yard of a complete organic fertiliser, such as fish manure with potash added should be raked into the surface, before sowing the seed.

SEED SOWING

Sow in early June in the north, in mid-June in the south. The drills are 15 ins. apart and 1 in. deep. Sow thinly and thin out to 12 ins. apart.

The leaves produced during the summer are not eaten, but will furnish the roots with energy to produce fresh shoots when forced in the winter.

FORCING

From the end of September onwards, the roots may be lifted for forcing, a few at a time. Cut off the tops, just above the crown, and place roots, crown upwards, in deep boxes. Cover with 12 ins. of light soil and stand in a dark, warm place. In 2 or 3 weeks' time, the fresh leaves should just begin to show up on the soil surface. The " chicon," as it is called, is then ready to be cut. A second crop may be obtained from the same roots after a further period of 3-4 weeks, but after this cutting the roots will be quite spent and no good for anything but the compost heap.

By bringing in batches of roots in this way, say, every 3 weeks, a supply of the delicious fresh leaves may be kept up from October to May.

Note.—Watering must be done very judiciously at all times. The roots must not get dry, nor must the soil ever be sodden.

TYPES

The Witloof type is the only one extensively grown in this country. The Brunswick and the Magdeburg Chicory used to be grown commercially for their large roots which, dried, ground and roasted, make an unwelcome addition to cheap brands of coffee. The Magdeburg Chicory is also the one most grown in France as a salad plant. It makes loose bunches of narrow leaves.

CORN SALAD

The plants look rather like young forget-me-not clumps. Their smooth leaves are picked for winter salads chiefly, and the plants remain productive for a long time, especially when covered with continuous cloches.

SOIL

Corn salad is not fussy, but appreciates a soil rich in organic matter.

SEED SOWING

Successive sowings made from mid-June to mid-September provide leaves from early autumn to late in spring. Sow on a firm, fine seed-bed in drills 1 in. apart, ¾ in. deep. Thin to 9 ins. apart. The thinnings can be transplanted to other rows.

WATERING

Must be done during dry spells in summer and early autumn.

HARVESTING

Pick leaves singly, or pull up the whole plants and use at once.

The plants may be used when 4-5 leaves have formed, but it pays to wait until nice bushy plants have developed.

TYPES
Two varieties are grown in England :
The Regence, or Italian. Does best under cloches and remains
    productive over a long period.
The Round-leaved. Quick growing and hardy.

CRESS

I. AMERICAN CRESS (Barbarea præcox)
This deserves to be more widely grown, as it is one of the few salad plants available from the open ground in winter. Resembling the ordinary cress in flavour, its appearance is more like that of the watercress. In North America, it grows wild in damp habitats. Position should be shady.

SOIL
Must be moisture holding.

SEED SOWING
Successive sowings may be made from spring to late summer, in drills 9 ins. apart, $\frac{1}{2}$ in. deep. Sow thinly, as this will save thinning out.

WATER
Must be given in dry weather.

HARVESTING
Cut as desired. Never allow the plants to grow tall and lanky.

II. INDIAN CRESS (Tropæolum majus)
This is better known as the "Garden Nasturtium." All its above-ground parts, when young, make good additions to salads. Please note that when grown for salad purposes, the "nasturtium" should be given a rich soil. For culture see page 256.

III. MUSTARD AND CRESS (Sinapis alba and Lepidum sativum)
The popular sandwich "filling," lovely in salads, grown by every child, and yet it needs understanding. For winter supplies mustard and cress is sown indoors, but for spring, summer and autumn use, it can be grown out of doors. Where it is desired

to cut the 2 crops at the same time, the cress should be sown 3 days before the mustard, as the latter is quicker growing. Rape seed can be used instead of mustard and this should be sown at the same time as the cress. It has the advantage of not flagging easily in hot weather.

Soil

Should be friable and firm, moisture holding and well drained. It may be covered with leaf-mould or even sacking before sowing, so that the plants are not gritty when taken up. The soil must be fairly damp at sowing time, so as to make further watering unnecessary.

Seed Sowing

Sow seed closely about their own width apart. Gently press them into the soil surface. It is best to keep the germinating seeds in the dark for at least 5 days after sowing, so as to make them grow tall. The covering—sacks, planks, etc.—must not touch the seed

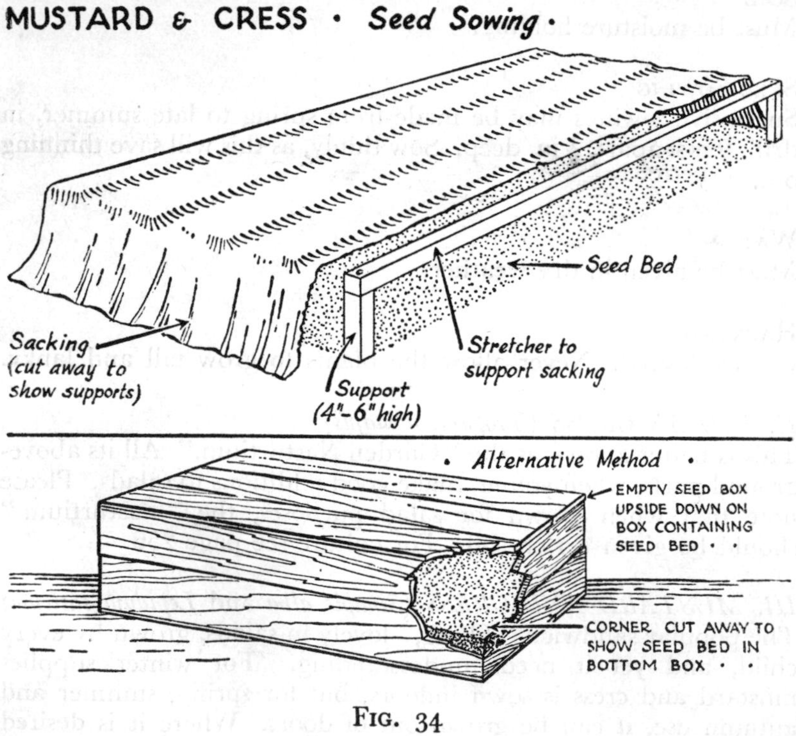

MUSTARD & CRESS · *Seed Sowing* ·

Sacking (cut away to show supports)

Support (4"-6" high)

Stretcher to support sacking

Seed Bed

· *Alternative Method* ·

EMPTY SEED BOX UPSIDE DOWN ON BOX CONTAINING SEED BED · ·

CORNER CUT AWAY TO SHOW SEED BED IN BOTTOM BOX · ·

FIG. 34

of course, but rest on some supporting pegs, 4-6 ins. above the seed bed. If standard size seed-boxes are available, sow in these and cover each box with a second one, turned upside down. (See Fig. 34.)

HARVESTING

Mustard and Cress can be sown, and therefore harvested, all the year round. The crops will be ready 2-3 weeks after sowing, according to temperature conditions. Cut mustard and cress with scissors or razor blade to avoid taking up grit with the plants.

DAMPING OFF

Damping off, a fungus disease, frequently spoils the crop. It can be avoided by sterilising the soil before sowing, using one of the methods described on pages 37-40, and also by avoiding stagnancy of air and water.

IV. WATERCRESS (Nasturtium officinale)

A popular and wholesome salad plant that can be had in summer and winter. Though normally grown in special water-covered beds, it can also be grown in trenches in the ordinary garden, provided a shady and damp spot can be found for it.

PREPARING THE SOIL

A trench should be dug, 2 ft. deep and 2-3 ft. wide. Put a 9-in. layer of well-rotted vegetable refuse in the bottom and soak this with water. Continue giving daily soakings for a fortnight. Then place 4 ins. of good soil over the vegetable refuse and firm it down. The trench is now ready for planting or sowing.

PLANTING

If rooted cuttings are obtained these may be planted 8 ins. square.

SEED SOWING

Seed sowing in the trench can also be carried out, stations of 3 seeds each being placed 8 ins. apart, with a view to thinning later to 1 plant per station. It is best to keep the trench dark during the time of germinating. This may be done by old sacking being laid across the top.

GENERAL CULTIVATION

Weed until plants cover soil surface. Water on all but rainy days, using a can with a fine rose. To obtain bushy plants, pinch the leading shoots when 6 ins. high. Any flowers that form should be removed.

537

HARVESTING

Watercress can be had practically the whole year round, winter supplies being grown in cold frames and summer supplies in several successions in trenches.

CUCUMBER, RIDGE

Only the Ridge Cucumber that is grown out of doors will be discussed here. (For glass-house, frame, and cloche culture see pages 579-582 and 632.)

SOIL

Most soils suit outdoor cucumbers, though heavy cold clays should be lightened with sand, flue dust or similar material. The soil should be warmed by fermenting manure or rotting vegetable refuse, buried about 6 ins. below the surface. If a small mound is made for each plant, the soil will warm up more quickly.

SEED SOWING

This must not be done before the soil has reached a temperature of 60° Fahr. As out of doors this does not usually happen until about the middle of May, most people prefer to raise the plants under glass, sowing them about the middle of April. Use boxes or pots filled with John Innes Potting Compost containing 2 standard doses of fertilisers and chalk (see page 576) and place seed, pointed end down, about $\frac{1}{2}$ in. deep and 3 ins. apart. In 3-in. pots, sow 1 seed in the centre of each pot. Place boxes or pots on top of hot-water pipes or over a hot bed in a frame. When well germinated, remove to lighter position in greenhouse or frame. Water carefully.

PLANTING

This may be done about 1 month after sowing, say mid-May in the south and end of May in the north. Dig holes about 2 ft. square and 1 spade's depth for each plant. Place some strawy manure or other material that will give off heat (see pages 24-25) in the bottom, 6 ins. thick when firmly trodden down. Then place back the soil in the shape of a mound. Have the mounds $2\frac{1}{2}$-3 ft. from each other, and prepare them 2-3 weeks before planting, to give the soil time to warm up.

Strong plants should have the centre nipped out at planting time. In cold weather, the young plants may be protected by 4-sided cloches placed over them or boxes just stood on the windy side.

GENERAL CULTIVATION

Water freely 2-3 times a week. When the plants are bearing, feed once a week with weak liquid manure (see pages 35-37). A mulch of some moisture-holding material such as lawn mowings, damped horticultural peat, given when the plants begin to run, will keep the soil moisture even and prevent the fruits from becoming soiled.

HARVESTING

Cut the fruit several times a week, so as not to let any get over-grown. Remove misshapen fruits regularly. This way a bigger crop will be had. About 40 good fruits per plant may be expected.

VARIETIES

Bedfordshire Prize Ridge. A good cropper.

Burpee Hybrid. A heavy cropper, straight, well formed fruits, smooth skinned.

Perfection Ridge. A similar but better type of Bedfordshire Prize.

DANDELION

The cultivated dandelion is not as well known as its troublesome wild brother The former, when grown, forced and blanched like chicory, makes an excellent salad. It has the advantage of being quite contented on light or chalky soils.

CULTIVATION

As for Chicory (see page 533).

It is possible to bleach single dandelion plants in a flower pot, with another one turned upside down over it, the whole thing then being put in a dark, warm place, as for example, a kitchen cupboard.

ENDIVE

Endive is a salad plant that is far too little grown. When blanched it is ideal for winter use.

SOIL

A rich well-drained soil is required.

SEED SOWING

Successive batches may be sown, from early July to mid-August. Endive is best sown very thinly where it is to remain. This not only saves the labour of transplanting, but prevents an interruption of growth due to the check of transplanting. This is important with crops sown late in summer, with only a short stretch of growing season ahead. Drills should be 1 ft. apart, in the case of the curled endive, and 18 ins. apart in the case of the Batavian. The plants are thinned to the same distance respectively,

GENERAL CULTIVATION
Water freely in dry weather. A mulch of moisture-conserving material is helpful.

BLANCHING
When fully grown, the plants need blanching, as they are very bitter when green. Any of the following methods may be used. They may be left in position and covered, where they grow, either with flower pots that have their drainage hole blocked with a bit of clay or a stone, or with whitewashed continuous cloches over which sacking is laid, care being taken also to cover the ends of the rows. Alternatively the plants may be lifted in succession and packed closely in soil in a cellar, dark outhouse or even a frame keeping the light closed and covered with sacking or mats. When the foliage has turned a yellowy white, it must be used as soon as possible. The best method of blanching is undoubtedly under cloches as you do not have to move the plants.

TYPES
There are 2 main types. The curly Stag Horn and the Green Batavian, which grows leaves more like a lettuce. The latter is becoming particularly popular.

LETTUCE

The gardener should aim at producing lettuces all the year round. This can be done easily if some protection, such as continuous cloches, frame or glasshouse, is available for the winter and early spring crops. Only the out-of-door cultivation of lettuces will be discussed in this chapter. Accounts of the cloche, frame and glasshouse production of lettuces are given in Part VII. Growing Under Glass.

SOIL
There are few soils that will not grow excellent lettuces provided

that the right treatment is given. The lettuce loves a deep loam rich in organic matter, a soil that can be brought to a fine tilth. Very heavy clay soils need feeding with strawy manure, whilst very light sands need to be given " body " by the liberal addition of some bulky, moisture-holding organic manure. Lettuces that are sown in autumn for spring cutting must be given a position in a well-drained soil which should be on the light side.

SEED SOWING

The first sowing for an outdoor crop is usually made under glass in early February (for method see page 635). The seedlings are pricked out as soon as they are fit to handle and will be planted out as soon as weather and soil conditions permit, i.e. probably towards the end of March.

Outdoor sowings are made from March to mid-August. It is very important to make a number of small sowings rather than a few large ones, otherwise you will be swamped with too many lettuces at one time and not enough at another. Lettuce is usually sown in a seed bed where the seed is sown thinly in drills 6-9 ins. apart, the young plants being set out in their permanent positions before they begin to suffer from overcrowding. Late sowings, however, may be made where the lettuce is to grow, as at this time it is unwise to have its growth checked by the transplanting process. In this case, drills should be 1 ft. apart. The seed is sown very thinly, the seedlings being gradually thinned to 10 ins. apart.

PLANTING

Three things must be remembered about lettuce planting :
  (1) It must be done before the plants get large or suffer from being overcrowded. If large, they do not like being disturbed, if crowded they become weak and liable to attack by fungus diseases such as mildew and grey mould.
  (2) The plants must be handled extremely carefully as they are delicate and brittle. Any injury will favour the entrance of fungus diseases. Bruised leaves should be removed.
  (3) Planting must not be done too deeply, for if the growing point is buried, no proper heart will form. Planting is best done with a trowel. Distances depend on variety and soil ; the biggest are given 1 ft. square, while 10 ins. square will be sufficient for the smaller kinds.

VARIETIES

Be careful to choose the right variety for each purpose.

Varieties for early spring sowing, for cutting in spring and early summer

Borough Wonder. A lettuce with solid heart and pale-green pleasant colour. Stands drought well.

Market Favourite. Similar to the above.

Trocadero. Similar but of darker colour, often tinged red at the leaf margins. Heads medium to large of good shape.

Varieties for spring and summer sowing, to be cut in summer and early autumn

All the Year Round. Makes large, firm heads of good colour and flavour. Stands a good deal of drought and heat.

Big Boston. An excellent American variety, growing gigantic, compact, tender, very pale, yellowish-green hearts.

Continuity. Stands drought well. Makes good tender hearts but the leaves tend to be purply or brownish.

Feltham King. Shiny mid-green leaves. Solid hearts, drought resisting. Popular with market growers.

Varieties sown as above, but with crisp curly leaves, and known as Iceberg

New York Giant. Compact, very large, with yellowish-green puckered foliage. Solid hearts.

Webb's Wonderful. Perhaps the best of the group. Large heads of waxy green foliage.

Buttercrunch. Crisp and fresh. Attractive, delicious, slow to go to seed.

Varieties to be sown in late summer outdoors and to be cut in spring

Imperial. A hardy variety producing solid heads of good size.

Winter Crop. Makes immense heads of good, pale green colour, amazingly tender for a winter lettuce.

Most other varieties in this section are either rather coarse or very small.

I. COS LETTUCES

These do not heart as readily as the cabbage type, and they are usually tied round the middle with raffia when they have made about three-quarters of their growth. This causes the centre to bleach and so to become much more tender. (See illustration facing page 544.)

VARIETIES

Mammoth. Sow in spring for summer cutting. Aptly named.

Cordon Bleu. Firm head, tender, crisp, and of fine flavour.

Hicks' Hardy Winter White. Sow in autumn for spring cutting. Rather spreading in habit, so tie up plants when three-quarters grown.

Little Gem. A miniature Cos, usually sown under glass in January. Planted in March and cut in May. Excellent substance and flavour.

Lobjoit's Green Cos. Sow outdoors in autumn or spring for spring or summer cutting. Large, dark green, self-folding.

Osmaston Gem and Winter Density. Belong to the so-called density group, an intermediate type between cabbage and Cos lettuce. Both varieties make hearts of delicious flavour. Winter Density is dark green, Osmaston Gem, yellow.

II. WINTER-HARDY LETTUCES

Some varieties are suitable for late summer sowing and spring cutting, having spent the winter months in the open. These should be sown before the middle of August either in a seed bed or in their permanent position in well-drained soil, as described above. If the sowing has been made in a seed bed, the plants should be set out as soon as possible. If the sowing has been made in the permanent position, the thinnings may be transplanted to further rows. In spring, as soon as the soil begins to warm up, a top dressing of a quick-acting nitrogenous fertiliser, such as nitro-chalk at 1 oz. to the square yard, may be given, to encourage soft growth. The lettuce will be ready to cut end of March to end of April.

HARVESTING

Cut lettuces before there is any sign of bolting. In hot weather it is best to cut them early whilst they are fresh, and keep them in a cool shady place until required. For varieties, see page 542.

III. THE GATHERING LETTUCE

A non-hearting type with crisp, curled leaves. They should never be transplanted.

VARIETIES

Grand Rapids. An American variety, perfectly described by its name. Have rows 18 ins. apart for these.

Green Jade. Has loose, crisp, curled leaves of a bright green colour.

ONIONS, SPRING

SOIL

A light rich loam is preferred. Follow a well-manured crop such as early potatoes.

SEED SOWING

Sow in the first half of August in drills 9 ins. apart. Sowing should be done fairly thinly. No thinning will be necessary as the plants will be pulled in spring as required for salads.

VARIETIES

New Queen. Resistant to mildew.

White Lisbon. A very popular variety, not so resistant to mildew.

RADISHES

A radish, to be any good at all, must be grown quickly. If it is left to " fight for its living " it turns hot and woody. Give radishes all they need for quick and balanced growth.

SOIL

Radishes do not need deep soil.

See that the soil is not lumpy and that it is rich in organic manure.

MANURING

Fork 2 ozs. of fish manure or meat and bone meal per square yard in to the top 3 or 4 ins. when preparing the ground, plus some damped horticultural peat at the same rate.

SEED SOWING

Radish seed should always be sown thinly. Broadcasting is possible but it is better to sow in rows 6 ins. apart, the drills being $\frac{1}{2}$ in. deep. Firm the soil after sowing.

It is possible to make a sowing outside as late as December, in specially sheltered spots. Cover the bed with straw to a depth of 4 ins., but take it off as soon as the seed has germinated.

The next sowing may be early as February in a warm dry border, this being covered with litter as before.

Sowing is possible under cloches, of course, in January and February (see pages 581-584).

Further sowings may be made once a fortnight from the middle of March to the beginning of September. Make the summer sowings in a cool shady place.

Radishes can be grown as an intercrop between rows of other vegetables. They may also be sown in the rows of vegetables like asparagus, parsnips, seakale, and such seeds as take a long time to germinate.

88. *Tying up Cos lettuce to make it heart*

89. *Tomatoes grown out of doors*

90. *Garlic*

91. *Kohl Rabi*

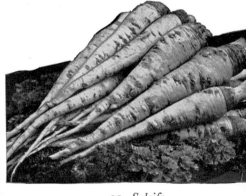

93. *Salsify*

92. *(left) Aubergine*

VARIETIES

Round

> Red Turnip. Crisp, tender, bright red.
> Scarlet Globe. Delicious flavour, large but not coarse.
> Cherry Belle. Scarlet, delicious, crisp with white flesh.

Oval

> French Breakfast. Deep crimson colour, white flesh inside.
> Solid sweet root.
> French Breakfast Early Forcing. Excellent for frames.

Long

> Icicle White. Crisp, excellent quality.

Winter

> Black Spanish, long. Black skin but firm white flesh.
> Black Spanish, round. As above, but round in shape.

TOMATOES

It has now become common knowledge that really good crops of tomatoes can be had from plants grown in the open, especially in the south and the Midlands. (See illustration facing page 544.) In the north, the lower temperatures of the late summer and frequent lack of sunshine make outdoor tomato growing more difficult.

POSITION

A sunny position, sheltered from winds, should be chosen. Tomatoes should, if possible, not be grown near a potato field as they are very liable to infection with potato blight.

SOIL

Tomatoes can be grown successfully in a variety of soils provided they are deeply worked.

PREPARING THE SOIL

Heavy soils should be dug in autumn, a rough surface being left for the frost to act on. Light soils are best dug in spring and will be improved by working in some bulky moisture-holding material, such as well-rotted vegetable refuse. The following mixture applied at planting time will help root formation and healthy, sturdy growth : 2 ozs. each of sulphate of potash, bone meal and either hoof and horn or fish manure to each square yard. On acid soil, or newly dug pasture land, lime should also be applied, e.g. in the form of hydrated lime ¾ lb. per square yard being required.

SEED SOWING

Sowing should be done under glass, end of February or early March. A glasshouse with a temperature of 63-65° Fahr. is suitable, or frames over a hot bed at the same temperature. Sow thinly in boxes of John Innes Seed Compost (see page 576).

RAISING THE PLANTS

As soon as the cotyledons are fully developed, pot the plants singly in 3-in. pots, using the same compost. Where pots are not available boxes can be used. They must be at least 3 in. deep. Keep the plants at a temperature of 60° Fahr. from now on. Water carefully. Ventilate freely as soon as the plants are established in their new quarters. Short-jointed sturdy plants must be aimed at. Gradually harden the plants from mid-May onwards, so that they are ready for planting by the end of May or

METHODS of SUPPORTING TOMATOES

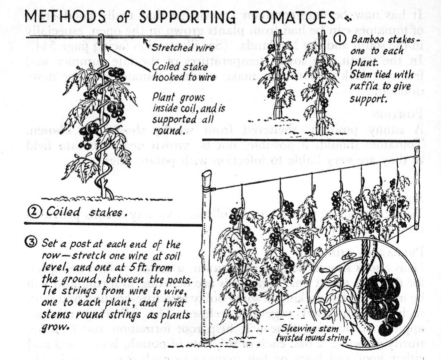

Stretched wire

Coiled stake hooked to wire

Plant grows inside coil, and is supported all round.

① Bamboo stakes— one to each plant. Stem tied with raffia to give support.

② Coiled stakes.

③ Set a post at each end of the row—stretch one wire at soil level, and one at 5ft. from the ground, between the posts. Tie strings from wire to wire, one to each plant, and twist stems round strings as plants grow.

Shewing stem twisted round string.

FIG. 35

beginning of June, according to weather conditions. Do not hurry over the planting, but wait for suitable weather, i.e. a mild period. Excellent plants can be raised under cloches (see pages 581-585).

If glasshouses, frames or continuous cloches are not available, buy plants. But it is no good trying to get them on the cheap by being satisfied with pale, lengthy weaklings. They will only lead to disappointments. Only the best plants will be worth having, that is, short-jointed sturdy plants about 8 ins. high.

PLANTING
Fix supports before planting as the roots would be disturbed by stakes driven down among them. Many methods of support are possible. (See Fig. 35.) Generally a strong stake to each plant is best. Have it 4-5 ft. long and drive it on the side from which the prevailing winds come. Planting distances : allow at least 2 ft. between the rows and 18 ins. from plant to plant in each row. Handle plants carefully. Make holes deep enough to have the ball of roots covered with about ½ in. of new soil. In very light, or very heavy, soils make holes deeper and put some damp horticultural peat or leaf mould in the bottom. This will act as a " sponge " and help root formation. Firm the balls thoroughly and give a good watering unless the soil is really wet.

GENERAL CULTIVATION
Apart from the obvious hoeing and watering, the tomato needs some special attention. Side shoots have to be removed regularly from the axils of the leaves. Care must be taken to see that the plants are adequately fixed to their supports as they grow bigger. Occasional top dressings of a fertiliser with an organic base should be given. The first of these should be rich in potash, whilst the later ones should supply potash plus nitrogen : alternatively, use a proprietary liquid manure like " Liquinure Tomato Special." The bottom leaves should be removed as they turn yellow. Spraying with Bordeaux Mixture, or a good colloidal copper spray such as Bouisol, should be carried out towards the end of July. This will protect the plants from attacks by the potato blight. Give 2 further sprayings at about 3-week intervals and there should then be no trouble. It is very important to stop the plants at the right time. In the south, the first week of August is usually advised for this operation. The end of the main shoot is pinched off at 2 leaves above the last truss. The plant will then give all its energy to ripening its fruit.

The Complete Gardener

VARIETIES
Most varieties have proved successful out of doors but the following are especially good:

Outdoor Girl	Essex Wonder
Hundredfold	Yellow Perfection
Moneymaker	

THE BUSH TOMATO
Some gardeners like the bush-type tomato because it produces a profusion of small sweet fruits. It has the advantage of needing hardly any staking. The plants should be set out four feet apart and the ground should be covered all over with Sedge Peat an inch deep, early in June. This not only acts as a mulch and keeps the moisture in the ground but in addition it prevents the tomatoes from becoming earthy.

VARIETIES

Histon Cropper, produces about 100 fruits per plant, averaging 10 to the lb. Highly resistant to blight.

Amateur Improved, sturdy compact plants, one foot high, usually picked two weeks earlier than any other variety. Often produces 14 lbs. of ripe fruit per plant.

548

CHAPTER IV

Special Crops

SECTION ONE

UNUSUAL VEGETABLES

★

ARTICHOKE, CHINESE

Produces ivory-white tubers which can be used from November to April. Plants only grow 18 ins. high.

PROPAGATION
Done by means of medium-sized tubers produced the previous year.

PLANTING
Carried out in April. Drills 6 ins. deep, rows 18 ins. apart, tubers 9 ins. apart in the rows. An open, sunny situation should be chosen.

SOIL
Well-drained, free-working loam is most suitable. Tubers may rot off in badly-drained land. Heavy clays should be " lightened " and raised beds made to ensure warmth and drainage. Light soils and gravels should be improved by the addition of humus in the form of rotted leaves or peat.

HARVESTING
In well-drained soils the tubers may be left in the ground until required. Lift them from October onwards. Store in soil or sand. When lifting, all the " roots " that have formed should be removed and the tubers kept covered to preserve their whiteness.

ASPARAGUS PEAS

Look more like a vetch than the ordinary pea. Grows 18 ins. high in a bushy form. Pick while young and fresh, say, 1 in. long.

549

Cook pod as picked. Flavour is a cross between asparagus and pea.

SEED SOWING

Sow plants where they are to be grown at same time as ordinary main-crop peas. The rows should be 18 ins. to 2 ft. apart with shallow drills no deeper than ½ in.

GENERAL CULTIVATION

Hoe regularly between the rows, and stick up.

MANURING

See PEAS.

HARVESTING

Pick regularly to prevent seeds forming inside the pods.

AUBERGINE
(*See* EGG PLANT)

BEANS, RUNNER

There are two unusual runner beans, the Blue Coco, which bears blue pods, and the Robin Bean, which bears red-speckled pods. Both should be grown exactly as the Runner Bean (see page 492).

BEANS, SOYA

Sow in drills ½ in. deep with seeds spaced 4 ins. apart. The plants grow 2 ft. high.

The beans may be cooked green or left to ripen, when, after threshing, the beans are used as haricot beans. They are rich in protein.

CAPSICUM

These can be used for flavouring pickles, putting into salads, or for cooking. They are " hot." The fruit may be likened to a long queerly-shaped tomato, red or green.

PROPAGATION

Sow in a lightish compost in March, either in a glasshouse **or** in a heated frame. Place 3 seeds in a 3-in. pot and, after germinating, retain the best one. Plant outside in May. In the north of England grow them in frames or under glass.

PLANTING
Plant out late in May or early June. Rows 18 ins. apart and plants 18 ins. apart in rows.

GENERAL CULTIVATION
Damp overhead to keep down red spider. Hoe regularly.

HARVESTING
Pick regularly. Whole crop gathered before end of September.

CARDOON

This resembles the globe artichoke, has a delicious nutty flavour and the blanched leaf stalks are used as a vegetable or for soups.

PROPAGATION
Sow in March or early in April. Plants do not need a lot of heat, but do well in cold frames. Water sparingly until seedlings have grown. Three seeds may be sown in a pot and thinned out, as suggested for Capsicum.
   Sow in trenches where plants are to grow in April or May.

PLANTING
Trenches made in advance 12 ins. deep, 8 ins. wide, and 4 ft. apart. Dig in manure or organic substitute to a thickness of 6 ins. Plant out 18 ins. apart in the trench.

GENERAL CULTIVATION
Water liberally. Manure from June onwards. Clean away lower yellow leaves. Tie stems loosely together and wrap round with brown paper then earth up in October.

HARVESTING
After blanching lift and use as desired.

VARIETIES
Puvis. Thick leaf-stalk and is solid. Well flavoured.
Spanish Cardoon. Has spineless leaves and easily runs to seed.

Tours. Prickly variety, superior in flavour and length of stem. Hardy.

CELERIAC

Grows like a turnip and tastes like celery. (See Chapter III, Salads, pages 532-533.)

CHOU DE BURGHLEY

A member of the cabbage family, very hardy and does well in the north.

SEED SOWING
Sow in March or early April in a seed bed outside. Rows should be 6 ins. apart. Plants when large enough should be planted in a seed bed 6 ins. square. Transfer to rows 2 ft. apart and plants 18 ins. apart.

GENERAL CULTIVATION
Treat as for cabbage.

HARVESTING
Cut when well hearted ; never allow to get coarse.

COUVE TRONCHUDA

Strong growing, requires plenty of room. Has large midribs which are thick, white and tender.

SEED SOWING
See CHOU DE BURGHLEY.

PLANTING
Transplant into rich well-prepared soil. Plants set out 2 ft. each way.

HARVESTING
Cut off large bottom leaves and detach leaf portion from midrib. Cook each part separately.

COLEWORT

A small, very hardy type of cabbage. For culture see page 509.

EGG PLANT
(AUBERGINE)

A delicious vegetable when stuffed, baked and cut into slices and fried, or flavoured and boiled. Often called Aubergine. (See illustration facing page 545.)

SEED SOWING
Sow in January or February in a warm house with temperature about 60° Fahr., or in March in a frame. Sow 2 or 3 seeds in a 3-in. pot. After a month or six weeks pot into 6-in. pots. It is possible to sow in a frame over a hot bed, or under continuous cloches— say, in April.

PLANTING
Grow in a frame or glasshouse in the north. Plant out on the south border or near a sunny wall in the south. Put plants out in rows 2 ft. square.

GENERAL CULTIVATION
Grow on a single leg at the start, pick out the growing tops to make them branch. Allow only 4-6 fruits to form. Syringe on warm days to keep down the red spider. Hoe regularly and mulch.

VARIETIES
Purple. Throws a large fruit, round and purplish in colour. Fine quality.
Blanche longue de la Chine. Long white aubergine, delicious flavour.
Noire de Pekin. Dark violet fruit, similar to its white cousin above.

GARLIC

Not much grown in this counry but useful in flavourings. (See illustration facing page 545.)

PLANTING
Plant in January or February. Plant " cloves " 2 ins. below surface of soil and as close as 9 ins. apart each way.

HARVESTING
As for shallots. (See page 526.)

GOOD KING HENRY

Known as mercury. Popular in parts of Lincolnshire and known there as Lincolnshire asparagus.

SEED SOWING
Plant in April or May in rows 2 ft. apart, and thin out to 18 ins. apart. Sparse sowing is necessary. Sow seeds in a seed bed and plant out.

GENERAL CULTIVATION
Crops heavily from April to June if grown on well-manured land. Cut shoots in the young stages and tie into bundles. When old the skin toughens quickly and it is necessary to remove this before cooking. Cook like asparagus.

HAMBURG PARSLEY

Grows like a parsnip, while leaves resemble parsley.

SEED SOWING
Prepare soil as for carrots. (See page 503.) Sow in March in drills 18 ins. apart, then thin plants out to half that distance in the rows.

GENERAL CULTIVATION
Hoe regularly. Use whizzed naphthalene along the rows to keep down the carrot fly.

HARVESTING
In season from November till April and may be harvested as early as September. Lift in November and store as for beetroot.

KOHL RABI

Popular on the Continent. Two types—green and purple. Similar flavour to the turnip, but more " nutty." (See illustration facing page 545.)

SEED SOWING
Sow any time from second week in March to the middle of August.
Rows 2 ft. apart, seedlings thinned to 3 ins. apart in early stages
and finally to 6 ins. apart.

GENERAL CULTIVATION
Hoe away from the plants. Treat as turnips.

HARVESTING
Withstands hard frosts. Leave in the ground until required, but
do not grow too large roots. Store in same way as other roots.

ONION, POTATO

Grown similarly to shallots. (See page 526.)

PLANTING
Plant bulbs out in March and lift in August. Plant bulbs 9 ins.
apart in rows 18 ins. apart. Firm bulbs down into the soil, and to
produce large onions artificial manures may be used.

GENERAL CULTIVATION
Earth up to form good clusters. Hoe and mulch if necessary.
Withhold moisture when bulbs begin ripening.

HARVESTING
Fork up in August and leave on surface to ripen, then store in a
cool place.

ONION, TREE

Known as Egyptian onion. Excellent for pickling. Stems thrown
up from the bulbs produce clusters of small bulbs.

PLANTING
Save bulbs formed on stems and in the soil and plant out in
shallow drills early in April. Rows 18 ins. apart, bulbs 6 ins.
apart.

GENERAL CULTIVATION
Keep the soil firm and support plants as onions form.

HARVESTING
Fork up in the autumn and, when dried, remove onions at base
and on the stems.

ONION, WELSH

An herbaceous perennial originating from Siberia. Very hardy
and popular. Neither the red nor white types throw bulbs and
therefore always look like spring onions.

PROPAGATION
To produce supply in spring sow in July or August. Young plants
obtained by the division of older ones, each of which, when put
out, produce thirty or forty onion plants.

OXALIS

A tuberous-rooted plant. As many tubers as possible should be
allowed to form at the base of the stem and these should be the
size of a walnut but longer and more pointed.

PLANTING
Prepare soil as for potatoes. Plant tubers out in May 2 ft. apart
and in rows 3 ft. apart.

GENERAL CULTIVATION
As shoots grow, earth up and continue doing so until September
when tubers should begin to form.

HARVESTING
Dig up early in November and store tubers in sand or dry earth
in a shed. Damp or frost will cause rot.

VARIETIES
Crenata. Has smooth skin and eyes and is rather acid in taste.
Deppi. Roots more tapering, whiter or clearer than Crenata and
less acid. Prefers light soil and should be grown in southern
aspect.

RAMPION

A biennial whose roots are white and fleshy. Used either boiled
or in salads.

SEED SOWING
Grow on a light, moist soil in a shady situation. Sow in May or even June and July. Thin seedlings to 4 ins. apart in drills 12 ins. apart.

GENERAL CULTIVATION
Hoe regularly, keeping soil free from weeds and surface loose.

HARVESTING
Do not dig until required as they over-winter well. The roots may be taken up and stored in sand or dry soil if ground gets frozen.

SALSIFY

Described as the vegetable oyster and is a delicious root crop, having a " nutty " flavour. (See illustration facing page 545.)

SOIL
Prefers a light, deep, moist soil. Heavy soil should be properly prepared, but not enriched with farmyard manure as this causes roots to become fangy and taste earthy.

PREPARING THE SOIL
Bastard trenching, or ridging, should be carried out in the autumn. Apply well-rotted compost well below the top spit. A good fish manure should be used in addition at the rate of 3-4 ozs. to the square yard.

SEED SOWING
Sow in April, the drills being 12 ins. apart and 1 in. deep. Thin out first to 4 ins. and finally to 8 ins. apart.

GENERAL CULTIVATION
Hoe regularly between rows to keep down weeds and to maintain surface soil in a loose crumbly condition.

HARVESTING
Leave in the ground until required or store the roots in sand either outside or in a shed. Possible to use the roots during the second or third week of October. Like beetroot they bleed if they are damaged when lifted.

SCORZONERA

Grown like Salsify. (See page 557.) It is different in appearance, the root being black and the leaves being wider. If left in the ground a second year it grows much larger.

SKIRRET

A rare vegetable, but popular in Japan and China. The roots have a peculiar flavour.

PROPAGATION
Carry out propagation as for Seakale by means of thongs. (See page 525.)
Sow early in April; to help germination keep the seed-bed moist. Thin out to 9 ins. in drills ½ in. deep and 18 ins. apart.

GENERAL CULTIVATION
Plants like deep soil, ample moisture and feeding.

HARVESTING
Lift carefully and spread out on the surface of the ground. Do this in late September or early October. Store as for Salsify. (See page 557.)

SQUASHES AND PUMPKINS

Grow in same way as ridge cucumbers or marrows. (See page 512.) Allow plenty of room.

PROPAGATION
Raise under glass or in frames from seed sown in April or May. Sow in 3-in. pots.
Sow under continuous or lantern cloches, where intended to remain. Keep slugs at bay with bran and Paris green or bran and metaldehyde.

PLANTING OUT
If possible heat soil with old fermenting material such as grass mowings.

HARVESTING
Edible at all stages so harvest directly they are of sufficient size. Hang up for use in winter.

Unusual Vegetables

Gourds can be trained up trellis and fences, are most decorative and crop heavily.

VARIETIES

Squashes

    Acorn Squash. Small variety, good flavour.

    Banana Squash. Has consistency of a banana, delicious flavour. Will keep till winter.

    Golden Scallop Squash. Excellent flavour. Quite round. Good keeper.

    Hubbard Squash. Eat in September or October. Will keep till February. Useful winter variety.

There are no varieties of pumpkins as far as I know.

SUGAR PEAS

Different from the ordinary peas as the pods have no tough interior skin, needing only to be topped and tailed before boiling.

SEED SOWING

Sow in May in rows 4 ft. apart. Often grow 6 ft. high and require staking.

MANURING

See PEAS, page 518.

HARVESTING

Pick regularly. If allowed to set cropping ceases.

SWEET CORN

Becoming very popular.

SOIL

Grows well on any type of soil containing plenty of organic matter.

PREPARING THE SOIL

Dig in organic matter, work half a bucketful of damped horticultural peat into the top 3 ins. with a good fish manure, meat and bone meal, or hoof and horn meal at 3-4 ozs. per square yard.

SEED SOWING

It is better not to transplant. Sow outdoors under cloches the second week of April or in the north at the end of April. If cloches are not available sow during May, or in John Innes compost in 3-in. pots in early April and transplant third week in May. (See illustration facing page 504.)

Draw drills 1½ ins. deep, space seeds 9 ins. apart for Canada Cross and 12 ins. apart for taller varieties. Rows 2 ft. apart.

GENERAL CULTIVATION

Arrange crop in block for better pollination and give full sunshine. Water well and mulch with damp horticultural peat.

HARVESTING

The cobs are ready when, if one of the grains is depressed with the thumb nail, the contents spurt out and have the consistency of clotted cream. Never gather when the contents are still watery and never wait until the grains are hard.

VARIETIES

Canada Cross or John Innes Hybrid. Ready the third week in July.

Courtland Golden Standard. Taller, later, but quite sweet.

Golden Bantam. Very hardy, medium-sized, bright yellow.

UNUSUAL TOMATOES

Those who are fond of tomatoes may like to grow some of the more unusual kinds. These can be grown in accordance with the instructions on pages 545 to 547.

VARIETIES

Pear, small pear-shaped yellow fruits.

Redcurrant, small red tomatoes, in clusters like redcurrants.

Red Cherry, bright red fruits in clusters about the size of cherries.

Yellow Cherry, similar to the above but bearing yellow fruits.

White, produces large white fruits with a yellow tinge.

Oxheart, large golden yellow tomatoes often weighing a pound each.

XIII. *Lilium auratum*

XIV. Cinerarias

HERBS

★

THE VALUE OF HERBS

HERBS are highly aromatic plants, and a little of them goes a long way. But this " little " is of more importance than many people realise. For one thing, herbs are rich in valuable minerals, and for another they give food that extra something which makes all the difference. So if you feel you need a good excuse for wanting a tasty, interesting meal, remember you will benefit much more from food that you have enjoyed eating than from an uninteresting dish.

THE HERB GARDEN

Why not grow your own herbs rather than buying them already dried in packets ? Freshly-picked herbs are much richer in flavour and in vitamin content. Many people are again devoting a special part of their garden to herb growing and there is a great variety of plants that might be included in a herb garden. It is only possible to give notes on a few of the most useful and easily-cultivated kinds.

BALM

Herbaceous perennial with roundish wrinkled leaves and white flowers. Very sweetly scented.

PROPAGATION
Propagate by seed sown or cuttings taken in May, or division of roots in autumn.

PLANTING
Plant 2 ft. apart, preferably in rich, moist soil.

USES
The fresh leaves are used for flavouring soups, salads, claret cups, etc., the dried leaves for an invalid's tea that is supposed to raise

the spirits. (1 pt. of boiling water is poured on $\frac{1}{2}$ oz. of the leaves and allowed to stand for 20 minutes before use.)

BASIL

The Sweet Basil is the most commonly grown and is a half-hardy annual with rather folded leaves of a very strong flavour.

SEED SOWING
Sow seed in heat in March or, if no greenhouse is available, sow in the open late in May.

PLANTING
Planting distances 1 ft. × 8 ins. Basil appreciates rich soil.

HARVESTING
Cut the shoots down to the ground when flowering, and hang up in bunches to dry for winter use. For a supply of fresh leaves throughout the winter, lift and pot a few of the plants and take them into a greenhouse.

USES
The fresh leaves and dried shoots are used for flavouring soups, sausages, stews, salads, etc.

BORAGE

Cousin of the forget-me-not. An herbaceous perennial with very rough-haired stems and leaves, and with bright blue flowers which attract bees.

PROPAGATION
Propagate by seed sown in spring (by root cuttings also in spring), or by division of roots in autumn.

GENERAL CULTIVATION
Cultivation is easy. Any soil suitable. Rows to be 2 ft. apart, plants in the rows 18 ins. apart.

USES
Leaves and flowers as flavouring and brightening of salads and drinks.

Herbs

CARAWAY

Herbaceous biennial of carrot family with delicately feathered leaves and white flowers.

SEED SOWING
Sow in August in light soil. Rows 1 ft. apart. Thin to 6 ins. apart in the rows.

HARVESTING
The plants will flower the following summer and the seed is gathered as soon as ripe.

USES
Seeds as flavouring in cakes and drinks. Leaves may be used in salads. Roots edible, rather like carrot in taste and appearance.

CHERVIL

A hardy herbaceous biennial with finely-cut leaves. There is a curly variety.

SEED SOWING
Sow July–October, i.e. when the seed is quite fresh. May be left to sow itself year after year, but should be thinned, leaving plants 6–9 ins. apart.

GENERAL CULTIVATION
Water freely in hot summers to prevent plants going to seed.

USES
Leaves make pleasant flavouring for soups, stews, sauces, etc.

CHIVES

A hardy herbaceous perennial of the onion family. Small bulbs, delicate onion-like foliage.

PROPAGATION
Sow in May. Divide clumps annually in spring or autumn.

563

GENERAL CULTIVATION

Chives grow best in rich, light soil and make an excellent edging to paths. May be grown in a pot by the kitchen window.

USES

Foliage, finely cut up, used in salads, sauces, soups, sandwiches, etc.

DILL

Another member of the carrot family, an annual of very graceful appearance. Grows to about 3 ft. with delicately fringed leaves and yellow flowers.

SEED SOWING

Sow in April. Rows 9 ins. apart. Thin seedlings to 9 ins. May be left to sow itself year after year. Appreciates rich soil and liberal application of liquid manure.

USES

Fresh leaves are gathered for fish sauces, soups, and salads. The dried plants are used with cucumber pickling.

FENNEL

Herbaceous perennial of somewhat similar appearance to dill, but rather coarser. In England the garden fennel is chiefly grown.

SEED SOWING

Sow in sunny position mid-April to early May. Drills 18 ins. apart. Thin seedlings gradually to 18 ins. apart.

GENERAL CULTIVATION

Plants remain useful for many years if kept from flowering by periodical cuttings down to 1 ft. from the ground.

USES

Chopped leaves in salads and fish sauces, especially salmon and mackerel. The Florence fennel, *Finoccio*, supplies its broad, blanched leaf bases as an excellent vegetable, whilst the sweet fennel, grown in France, has tender young shoots eaten raw in salads. Sweet fennel seeds are also used for flavouring.

HORSE-RADISH

A hardy perennial of the radish family. Has long, dark green, shiny leaves; long, much-branched flesh roots and small white flowers. Tends to spread beyond the space allotted to it.

PROPAGATION
Propagate by " thongs," lengths of root about $\frac{1}{2}$ in. in diameter and 9 ins. long, taken off old plants in winter and laid in ashes or sand till March, when they will have produced a ring of buds at the top end and are planted.

PLANTING
Plant best in specially prepared mounds of rich, light loam. The mounds should be on well-firmed soil, a path or even on concrete. This will prevent the roots from spreading to the rest of the garden. Mounds 2 ft. high, 2 ft. wide. Plants put in 12 ins. asunder, 18 ins. above normal soil level.

GENERAL CULTIVATION
A sunny position and liberal moisture are required.

HARVESTING
Lift in autumn and store over winter, or take up as required.

USES
As a condiment with roast beef and some fish, especially carp. A popular continental Christmas dish is blue carp served with grated horse-radish that has been beaten up with whipped cream.

MARJORAM

Two kinds are grown, the sweet marjoram and the pot marjoram. The latter is more branched and grown as a perennial. It has violet flowers and the whole plant is suffused by a reddish tinge. The sweet marjoram is grown as an annual, has white flowers and makes a compact, bushy plant.

SEED SOWING
Sow in April in rows 1 ft. apart. Thin pot marjoram to 9 ins., sweet marjoram to 6 ins. apart.

Uses

The dried leaves of both are used for flavouring. The sweet marjoram is also incorporated in herb teas.

MINT

Hardy herbaceous perennials with creeping root-stocks. The spear mint is most commonly grown for mint sauce. It is hardy but susceptible to mint rust. The apple mint seems immune against rust and has a pleasant flavour, but is often disliked because of its hairiness.

PROPAGATION

Propagate by " root " division early in March. Plant 12 × 9 ins. in damp position.

FORCING FOR WINTER AND SPRING USE

Lift plant, chop " roots " into about 1-in. long pieces, pack tightly into beds of light, rich soil in a warm greenhouse or frame. Cover with about 1 in. of soil.

DRYING

Cut stems in autumn and hang up in bunches in cool, dry place.

PREVENTING RUST

To prevent rust from settling, move the mint bed each spring to a fresh place. In severe cases give hot-water treatment. Take " roots " up as for replanting, carefully remove all above-ground portions ; wash free of soil and then place in warm water at 110° Fahr. for 20 minutes. The washing alone gives quite a good control too.

PARSLEY

An herbaceous perennial. The most popular herb. Makes good edgings to kitchen garden paths. Likes rich, moist soil.

SEED SOWING

Sow in March for summer, in June for autumn and winter use, or make one sowing in May. Rows 1 in. apart. Thin seedlings early, first to 3 ins., finally to 6 ins. apart. This makes for sturdy plants.

GENERAL CULTIVATION
To prolong season, cover plants with cloches or pot up the best ones and take to cool greenhouse late in September.

VARIETIES
> Champion Moss Curled. Dark green, tightly curled, long-stalked leaves.
> Green Gem Dwarf. Compact habit, not exceeding 5 ins.
> Myatts Garnishing. A long-stalked kind.

SAGE

A shrubby perennial. Several kinds are grown in the herb garden, the green sage being the most popular.

It is best to buy the plants, as the seedlings cannot be relied on. Buy the broad-leaved variety. Have rows 2 ins. apart, plants in the row 1 ft. apart. Once you have made a start, you can increase your stock by cuttings taken with a heel in April or May. They root very readily in sandy soil in frames or in the open.

GENERAL CULTIVATION
Hoe regularly, cut back when attempting to flower. Renew your sage row every 4 years by taking cuttings.

USES
Use as seasoning for duck, sausages and even cheeses. In some districts a gargle for a sore throat is prepared from sage leaves.

SAVORY

Herbs with a strong flavour. The summer savory is an annual, whilst the winter savory is an evergreen perennial and usually propagated by cuttings. But both kinds can be raised from seed.

SEED SOWING
Sow in April in drills 1 ft. apart. Thin seedlings to 6 ins. apart.

HARVESTING
Cut stems when in full flower and hang up in bunches to dry for winter use.

USES
Use as stuffing with veal, turkey, etc., with broad bean dishes and

567

lentil soup. The leaves of both savories are said to give relief from bee stings if rubbed on the affected part.

TARRAGON

A bushy herbaceous perennial that may grow up to 4-5 ft. high. Bears finely-cut leaves on slender shoots.

PROPAGATION
Propagate by division or by cuttings struck in frames or in gentle heat in spring. Plant 2 ft. square in sheltered position.

HARVESTING
Winter supplies may be obtained, as with parsley, by lifting up some plants and taking them to a frame or cool greenhouse.

USES
For flavouring vinegar. Also for salads, sauces, stews, omelettes, etc. The leaves must be used fresh as they lose their aroma when dried.

THYME

An herbaceous perennial with small, agreeably scented leaves Makes an effective edging and may be grown in positions too dry for parsley. The two types chiefly grown are the common thyme and the lemon thyme.

PROPAGATION
Propagate by division of roots in March or April or cuttings taken in early summer. The common thyme can also be grown from seed, but the most usual method for both kinds is root division.

PLANTING
Plant out 2 ft. × 18 ins.

USES
For flavouring soups, stews, etc., and a correct adjunct to jugged hare.

GROWING UNDER GLASS

PART SEVEN

GROWING UNDER GLASS

CHAPTER I

Growing under Glass

PLANNING THE GREENHOUSE

THE greenhouse is becoming more and more popular. Here one can grow all kinds of plants indigenous to other countries, and give them the right climatic conditions. Here one can " force " plants out of season and so increase the food supply when it is most needed. A greenhouse is also invaluable for raising plants of a half-hardy character ; for producing vegetable plants to be planted outside later, and for providing pot plants for home decoration. Greenhouses are used for ferns, cacti and succulents, for orchids or carnations and, in fact, for a very wide range of subjects.

Conditions in the greenhouse can be as near as possible to that in which the plants normally grow outside. It is a great mistake to try and grow too many plants in a house, for they hate crowded conditions. The ideal thing is to grow the species that require much the same treatment and to try and do them well.

TYPES OF GREENHOUSE

There are three main types of greenhouse : (1) the span-roof ; (2) the lean-to, and (3) the three-quarter span. (See illustrations facing page 576.) The span-roof is the most popular for general use. It is independent of other buildings and walls and so the plants obtain the full amount of light possible. The lean-to is most suitable for vines and peaches but, when other plants are grown in it, there is a tendency for them to be drawn towards the light. The best way to use a lean-to is to have the staging built in tiers so that the plants are as near the light as possible. A three-quarter span usually has its long roof facing south, and the back wall provides shelter from the north winds.

SITE

The greenhouse should be situated where it can receive all the light possible, as the question of light in the glasshouse is one of the greatest importance, especially during the winter months. Some shelter should, however, be given from north and east winds. In winter the sun's rays naturally fall more obliquely than in the summer, so that more light is reflected from the glasshouse roof and less will enter the house. The amount of light lost in this way depends to a large extent upon the slope of the roof and the orientation of the house. The ideal seems to be a roof slope of 46°. In the traditional house facing north and south, it has been found that roof slope makes very little difference, but in the east-west house roof slope is of considerable importance. Recent research has shown that there is a considerable gain in winter sunshine in a house facing east and west, and this is particularly important where propagating is to be carried out, say, between December and March. Uneven span houses also seem to make a considerable difference to the amount of light which the plants receive, an uneven span facing south admitting much more light than an even one.

MATERIALS USED

The traditional material for glasshouse building is of course wood, but the present timber shortage has led to the use of other substances, such as concrete, steel and aluminium. These have the advantage of being very durable, the maintenance costs are low as no painting or puttying is required, and in the case of the metal houses the supports can be made very narrow so that there is a minimum of light obstruction.

HEATING

Houses may be heated by oil, by gas, by electricity or by coke or coal. The oil, gas, coke and coal heat water which is circulated through the house in hot-water pipes. In the case of electric heating, which is gaining in favour, especially for the small house, no pipes are needed, there is no stoking to be done and furthermore, the heating can be thermostatically controlled. (See illustration facing page 617.) Firms selling heating systems have technical staffs which can advise on all heating problems.

STAGING

The side staging will probably be 3-4 ft. in height and 3 or 4 ft. wide. (See illustrations facing pages 616 and 617.) The central staging may be tiered, if necessary, so that the plants can be more easily displayed. It is convenient if the surface of the staging is removable. Slates are sometimes used, strips of asbestos, or corrugated iron cut to size. Shingle or ashes may be placed on the staging, but the latter tend to get very damp and sodden and certainly have to be changed every year. Those who are going to grow tomatoes in greenhouses in the soil " on the flat," as it is called, of course, need no staging at all. (See illustration facing page 617.)

TANKS

It is often convenient to sink a tank into the soil, at ground level, where the rain-water from the roof can be collected. In the case of small houses this tank can be outside. A concrete tank lasts longest and it is easiest to keep clean. It should be placed in such a way that it is possible to dip the watering can into it without much effort. It is handy to have water available in the house so that the tank can be refilled from the main.

EQUIPMENT

For one greenhouse a portable potting bench or tray, which can be erected when potting has to be done, will suffice. Those who have a number of greenhouses need a special potting shed for the mixing of composts and actual potting operations. A convenient potting tray is 3 ft. wide, 3 ft. long, with back and sides 1 ft. high.

A small propagating frame, say, 3×3 ft. or 3×4 ft., may be made on the staging at the end nearest the boiler. It can be filled with coconut fibre, or peat into which the pots or pans of cuttings can be plunged. The fibre or peat should be kept moist. Even a box with a sheet of glass placed on the top can be helpful. Electrically-heated frames, with cloche coverage, can now be bought especially for this purpose.

MANAGING THE GREENHOUSE

VENTILATION

Plants must be grown in as natural a condition as possible. It is always better to over-ventilate than under-ventilate. The ventilators are usually opened up early in the morning and are closed down in the afternoon or early evening to help trap the sun-heat and save fuel. Avoid draughts at all costs. Never open the ventilators on the windward side. Never be worried about high temperatures produced by sun-heat, they never do so much harm as overheating by artificial means. The amount of ventilation given depends on weather conditions. Greater heat may be necessary during a damp, dull period to help ensure a buoyant atmosphere, but in the winter this must only be done for short periods or seedy, weak growth will result. The rule, if in doubt, is to give air.

TEMPERATURE

Those who want a cool greenhouse should aim at a temperature of about 50° during the day and 40° at night, but those that go in for plants that need a warmer atmosphere should aim at 55° in the day and 45° at night time. In the autumn and winter, 10° higher in each case than in the spring and summer. (All the foregoing temperatures given in Fahrenheit.)

SHADING

Shading helps to keep down temperatures and to prevent plants drying out quickly. There is never any need to shade unless the sun is very strong, except in the case of certain plants like orchids, ferns, cucumbers, melons and some primulas. Many horticultural sundriesmen sell a special wash for this purpose called Summer Cloud, which, being a pale green, is less conspicuous than the more usual whitewash.

WATERING

Water according to the natural habitat of the plant. If it has a woody stem with tiny leaves, like heaths, little water may be necessary. If the leaves are thick and leathery, watering need not be very frequent. Where plants have large and broad leaves, and are quick growing, water is needed every day. Further, where the plant is growing and is manufacturing food in its leaves, it needs plenty of water, but when it is flowering it needs less water. In the winter, plants are often resting and need hardly any water. Some plants will be drying off and need no water at all.

Remember that a plant that is potted firmly requires less water than a similar plant potted loosely. Flagging may be caused by either under-watering or over-watering.

It is very important never to allow the ball of soil round the roots to become dry, or it shrinks from the pot and it is then impossible to get it to swell to the right size again.

Watering should always be done thoroughly. During summer, normally water in the evening ; in the winter about ten in the morning when the temperature begins to rise. Boxes containing seedlings are best watered by standing in a shallow container filled with water at the right temperature.

DAMPING DOWN

Damping down, or syringing, is important in greenhouses where moist conditions are necessary. It reduces the rate of transpiration of the leaves, helps to keep the atmosphere moist and controls red spider and thrips. The actual damping is done to the paths, staging pipes and walls, with a coarse syringe. (See illustration facing page 577.)

Fine syringing helps to prevent flagging. It is best to syringe the underside of leaves first, then give them a light sprinkling over. Plants in flower, hairy-leaved plants or inactive plants should never be syringed.

CLEANING

Cleanliness is particularly advisable under glass. Pick off and burn dead leaves and flowers. Weed regularly. Pots should be kept clean. Evergreen plants should be syringed to prevent dust collecting. Walls should be whitewashed once a year and inside tanks cleaned out regularly, the insides well scrubbed and painted with a thin Portland cement wash.

The outside of the glass should be cleaned at least once a year and more often if necessary.

During the summer, when plants can be put outside, wash the inside of the house with carbolic soft soap, which should have added to it 6 fluid ounces of formaldehyde and 2 gals. of water.

PAINTING

Paint both the inside and the outside of a timber house every 3 years with genuine white lead paint. Paint should be applied when the surface is free from moisture, so it is important to avoid wet or foggy conditions. Special greenhouse paints are available for use with high-temperature houses. Pipes may be painted with a good vegetable black mixed with boiled linseed oil and turpentine and a little paste drier, which is effective for radiating the heat, or with white lead to reflect as much light as possible.

Remove, wash and replace shingle on the staging once a year.

COMPOSTS AND POTTING

see also page 642

PRINCIPLES AND KINDS OF COMPOSTS

The principles laid down by the John Innes Horticultural Institution, Merton, are that a compost must :

(1) Be in the right physical condition, free from harmful organisms and able to provide an adequate balanced food supply.
(2) Be partially sterilised by heating to a minimum temperature of 180° Fahr. for not more than 30 minutes.
(3) Have fertilisers added in the right proportion, both in the case of seed sowing and potting.

(4) Contain loam, organic material and sand in the right proportions.

(5) Have its ingredients partially sterilised separately, mixed afterwards and phosphates added.

(6) Have strictest hygiene practised in all matters.

For the majority of plants 2 composts should be sufficient. The composts recommended are: (1) John Innes; (2) NO-SOIL (see page 642).

SEED COMPOST

John Innes Seed Compost: 2 parts by bulk, medium loam;
1 part by bulk, good moss peat;
1 part by bulk, coarse sand.

Add to each bushel of this mixture $1\frac{1}{2}$ ozs. superphosphate of lime (16% phosphoric acid) and 1 oz. ground limestone or chalk. (See illustration facing page 577.)

POTTING COMPOST

John Innes Potting Compost : 7 parts by bulk, medium loam ;
3 parts by bulk, good moss peat ;
2 parts by bulk, coarse sand.

Add to each bushel of this mixture $1\frac{1}{2}$ ozs. hoof and horn meal, $\frac{1}{8}$ in. grist (13% nitrogen), $1\frac{1}{2}$ ozs. superphosphate of lime (16% phosphoric acid), $\frac{3}{4}$ oz. sulphate of potash (48% pure potash) and 1 oz. ground limestone or chalk.

Leaf-mould may be used instead of moss peat, and less sand will be required if a light loam is used.

Sift the superphosphate and sulphate of potash through a $\frac{1}{16}$-in. sieve before making up the mixture and adding the fertilisers to the compost. Proportions should be strictly adhered to and weighed carefully.

The potting compost may be used for pricking off the majority of plants.

Though sterilisation has been advised it is not always necessary to treat the sand if it is clean and free from weeds, lime and organic matter. There is no need to sterilise a good horticultural moss peat.

When sterilising soil, riddle so that it is broken down into small pieces. Passed through a $\frac{1}{2}$-in. sieve it will mix well with the fertilisers.

Always measure the temperature of the soil with a thermometer and, after sterilising, remove hot soil immediately to allow excess moisture to evaporate.

Never store a sterilised compost for more than 2 months, but the separate ingredients may be kept after sterilising much longer.

Practise the strictest hygiene. Never allow water tanks to

94. *The modern double glazed greenhouse. Double glazing saves up to 50 per cent of heating costs*

95. *Three-quarter span greenhouse*

96. *Lean-to greenhouse*

97. *Damping down a greenhouse*

98. *John Innes compost heap ready for turning*

99. *Mushroom spawn*

become dirty. The potting bench should be absolutely clean. The house should not be overcrowded. Diseased plants should be removed.

The only special composts necessary are for orchids :

Terrestrial orchids : 1 part fibrous loam ;
1 part orchid peat ;
1 part sphagnum moss ;
1 part cow manure ;
½ part sand, brick dust, charcoal.

Epiphytal orchids : 1 part osmunda fibre ;
1 part sphagnum moss ;
a dash of charcoal.

POT PREPARATION

Always soak new pots before use. Wash old pots to make certain they are clean and porous. Crock well with broken pieces of pot, concave side downwards.

Before starting any potting have all requirements handy. The soil should be moist enough to mould into a ball, but not wet enough to clog when pressed. Rough material, such as the fibres sieved from loam, partially decayed leaves or coarse peat, is needed to put over the crocks to prevent the compost from falling between them and clogging the drainage hole.

Put some compost into the pot and make firm. Then place the plant to be potted in the centre, making sure it will be at the right level when finished. It is at this stage that the alteration of height is determined and the under-soil reduced, or increased accordingly. No amount of extra ramming later will correct it. Add more compost round the plant and firm again, then fill up the pot and level off, leaving a space for watering. For small pots ½ in. is enough, while for large pots 1 in. is needed, and if there is to be a subsequent top dressing when the pot is full of roots, more still is necessary.

When potting on, the old ball of soil must be moist but not water-logged. Remove the old crocks and the top layer of soil with any moss or weeds that may be there ; also take out any worms that may appear. It is important that the new coating of soil should be against the old ball of roots. To ensure this, a flat narrow rammer or old garden label is useful as it will fit down between the pot and roots and compact the soil evenly all through.

HANGING BASKETS

When preparing hanging baskets for planting, there is naturally no need for drainage, the chief problem being to retain moisture. The basket is first lined with sphagnum moss, which, as it starts to green up quite quickly, looks better than ordinary moss. Then a layer of fibrous loam is put in and the remaining space filled in with ordinary potting compost to suit the plant. The layer of fibre must be well firmed as it has to bear a considerable strain. At watering times, for instance, the whole basket is lowered into a tub or tank to soak, and the basket will take up many pounds of water which, when draining away, would find any weak spot in the lining material and allow the compost to run out.

POTTING TERMS

" Potting on " means moving plants from a small pot to a larger one.

" Potting up " or " off " means potting plants, seedlings or cuttings for the first time.

" Re-potting " means the shaking out of the soil from the old ball and potting back into the same size pot.

" Potting back " means the rubbing off of the shoulders of the ball of soil and potting in a smaller pot.

POTTING SUBSTANCES

Horticultural sedge peat is free from acidity, pests, diseases and weed seeds. It holds moisture well.

Sand should be fairly coarse, but should be washed and clean.

Coconut fibre is used for striking cuttings or for growing bulbs in bowls, but to-day it has largely been replaced by peat moss litter.

Mortar rubble opens up soil and adds lime.

Wood ashes contain a small quantity of potash.

Sphagnum is used for lining hanging baskets, sometimes used for orchids.

Polypodium fibre is used for seedling orchids.

Osmunda fibre is used for orchids.

Organic fertilisers are often given as top dressings.

Fish fertilisers are popular because they are organic and are often sold balanced up with potash.

Liquid manures may be given to plants regularly, are best prepared from organic solutions properly balanced and bottled under hygienic conditions.

Liquinure, a proprietary mixture, can be purchased as a balanced feed with a definite formula stated. There are types that are high in potash or high in nitrogen, depending on the plant to be fed. The feeds will, of course, be used in accordance with the instructions on the bottles.

EQUIPMENT FOR POTTING

Brushes can be purchased which fit exactly inside the pots to clean them.

The plants can be supported with wire stakes, green-coloured canes or bamboos. The wire stakes are often fitted with open ring ends.

Rammers are often used to firm soil when potting. A short length of a broom handle is all that is needed, rounded at one end and shaped as a wedge at the other.

Pressers may be round or square, depending on whether they are used for boxes or pots.

Sieves are necessary for sifting soil. A $\frac{1}{4}$-in. meshed sieve is used for soil for smaller pots, a $\frac{1}{2}$-in. meshed sieve for larger pots, and a fine, gauze, wire sieve for sifting sand or fine soil over little seeds in boxes or pans.

Pots may be bought in different sizes from 2 ins. to 18 ins.

FRAMES

There are two types of frames in general use—the span and the half-span or lean-to, the latter being the more commonly used.

Frames should always be situated where they receive the maximum amount of light. The sides may be of wood, or for more permanent structures, of brick or concrete. Average dimensions are : 30 ins. high at the back, 24 ins. at the front, 5 ft. from back to front, and each light 3 ft. wide.

HEATED FRAMES

Frames may be heated by means of hotbeds, by hot-water pipes or by electricity. Such frames are useful for propagation purposes, for early salad crops, and for such crops as melons and cucumbers.

COLD FRAMES

There should be a cold frame in every garden, as there are an infinite number of uses to which it can be put. For instance, raising seedlings and rooting cuttings which require a little protection ; growing early crops of lettuce, radish, turnips and so on ; hardening off tender plants before putting out in the open ; protecting tender plants during the winter, and so on.

DUTCH LIGHTS

This type of frame is becoming increasingly popular. It has the advantage of admitting the maximum amount of light, as there is a single pane of glass and, therefore, no cross bars to cast shade.

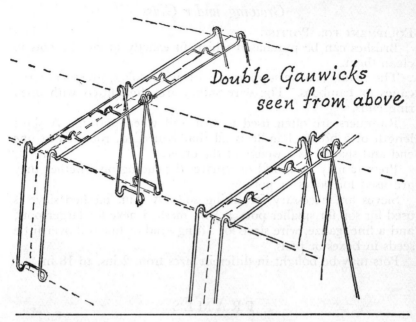

*Double Ganwicks
seen from above*

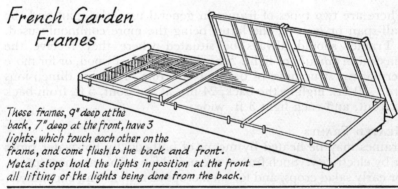

*French Garden
Frames*

*These frames, 9" deep at the
back, 7" deep at the front, have 3
lights, which touch each other on the
frame, and come flush to the back and front.
Metal stops hold the lights in position at the front —
all lifting of the lights being done from the back.*

Fixed Brick Frames

FIG. 36

In addition, the lights are easier to handle than the old-fashioned frame lights. Also, no drip occurs from leaks and cracks in the glass.

As against this, if a light is broken the whole pane must be replaced, and being light in weight, they are more easily lifted and damaged by wind and rain.

Dutch lights are often erected on to temporary frames consisting of wooden boarding, say, three boards 4 ins. wide for the back and two boards 4 ins. for the front. Special "shaped" wooden ends to the frames may be nailed into position.

Dutch lights are much used for lettuces, early carrots, early turnips, early cauliflowers, cucumbers, melons, raising plants for potting out in the open later, for taking root cuttings of perennials like anchusas, delphiniums, etc., and for growing violets and hurrying along various bulbs.

THE USE OF CONTINUOUS CLOCHES

The advantage of continuous cloches may be summarised in the words, " The greenhouse is taken to the plant and not the plant to the greenhouse." The cloches go over the rows of plants, giving

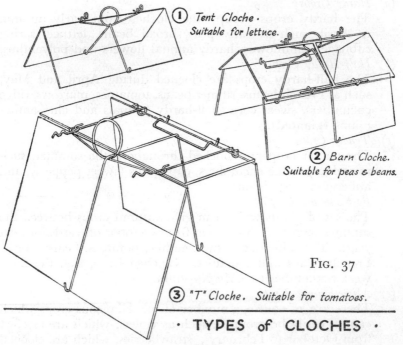

① *Tent Cloche.*
Suitable for lettuce.

② *Barn Cloche.*
Suitable for peas & beans.

Fig. 37

③ *"T" Cloche. Suitable for tomatoes.*

· **TYPES of CLOCHES** ·

all the protection required and yet providing automatic ventilation. They not only protect from frost but from drying winds and, in the winter, from damp. They enable a gardener to take two or more crops off a piece of ground in one year. For this reason, when cultivating land that is to be covered by cloches, twice the quantity of organic matter should be used and very liberal dressings or organic fertilisers should be applied.

In the winter and early spring, the soil should always be covered by cloches for a fortnight before seed sowing. The cloches ensure almost perfect germination and so require thinner sowing than is normally necessary. The ends of the cloche rows should always be sealed with sheets of glass or squares of wood, as this prevents these cloches from being glass funnels down which tremendous draughts of air are blown. The various types of cloches that can be used include tents, barns and Tomato T's. (See Fig. 37.) The barns are the most popular, but the Tomato T's are very useful indeed for the taller crops and, as their name suggests, especially for tomatoes.

The great thing with cloches is to try and ensure that they are used all the year round and this means careful planning. The crops can be divided into groups :

(a) *Hardy Crops*

The hardy crops occupy the cloches from early autumn to April, such as early peas, broad beans, lettuce, spring cabbage, cauliflower, hardy annual flowers and polyanthus.

(b) *Half-Hardy Crops*

The half-hardy crops are cloched during April and May, such as French beans, runner beans, tomatoes, marrows, ridge cucumbers, sweet corn, half-hardy annuals and chrysanthemums (planted).

(c) *Tender Crops*

The tender crops are cloched throughout the summer, such as melons, frame cucumbers, capsicums (sweet peppers), and aubergines (egg plant).

(d) *Post-Summer Crops*

The set of plants which can give autumn crops between the summer ones and those sown from October onwards for next year. These include lettuce, endive, potatoes, "early" peas, French beans and tomatoes. Cloched from, say, the third week September to early November.

(e) *Miscellaneous Crops*

There are, of course, a number of miscellaneous crops which cannot easily be grouped, such as violets, which are cloched from October to February ; strawberries, which are cloched from February to June ; and spring-sown annual flowers, turnips and beetroot, which are usually cloched from early March until early May.

STRIP CROPPING

In order to save time and labour, what is known as strip-cropping is often carried out. (See Figs. 38 and 39.) The garden or allotment is planned in strips so as to use the cloches to their greatest advantage. It is then only necessary to lift the cloches from one

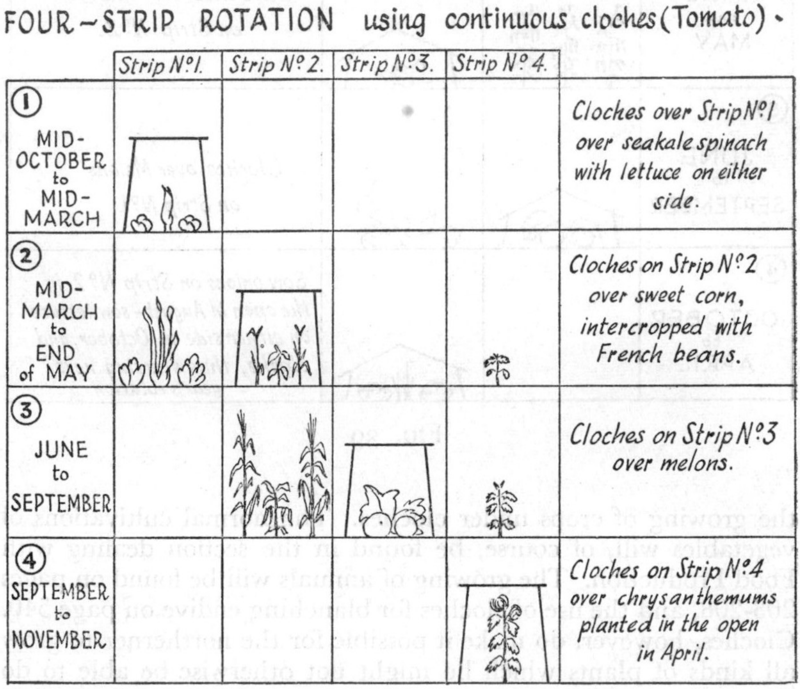

FOUR-STRIP ROTATION using continuous cloches (Tomato).

	Strip Nº 1.	Strip Nº 2.	Strip Nº 3.	Strip Nº 4.	
① MID-OCTOBER to MID-MARCH					Cloches over Strip Nº1 over seakale spinach with lettuce on either side.
② MID-MARCH to END of MAY					Cloches on Strip Nº 2 over sweet corn, intercropped with French beans.
③ JUNE to SEPTEMBER					Cloches on Strip Nº 3 over melons.
④ SEPTEMBER to NOVEMBER					Cloches on Strip Nº 4 over chrysanthemums planted in the open in April.

FIG. 38

row to cover the plants in the row next door. A good working rule is to allow a square yard of ground for every foot run of cloche row, that is to say, an area of 30 sq. yds. to the 30-ft. run of cloches.

The general idea is shown below by means of a 4-strip and 2-strip rotation but, of course, it is just as easy to have a 3-strip rotation.

GROWING THE CROPS

It is impossible, in a book of this size, to go into full details about

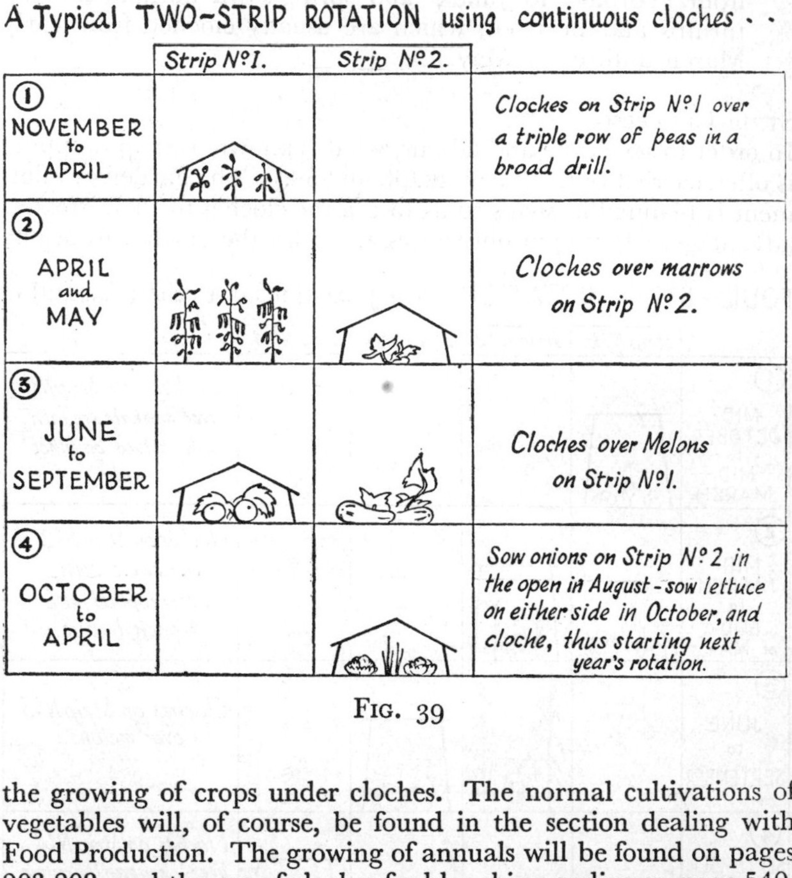

A Typical TWO-STRIP ROTATION using continuous cloches · ·

	Strip Nº 1.	Strip Nº 2.	
① NOVEMBER to APRIL			*Cloches on Strip Nº1 over a triple row of peas in a broad drill.*
② APRIL and MAY			*Cloches over marrows on Strip Nº2.*
③ JUNE to SEPTEMBER			*Cloches over Melons on Strip Nº1.*
④ OCTOBER to APRIL			*Sow onions on Strip Nº2 in the open in August - sow lettuce on either side in October, and cloche, thus starting next year's rotation.*

FIG. 39

the growing of crops under cloches. The normal cultivations of vegetables will, of course, be found in the section dealing with Food Production. The growing of annuals will be found on pages 203-208, and the use of cloches for blanching endive on page 540. Cloches, however, do make it possible for the northerner to grow all kinds of plants which he might not otherwise be able to do because of colder, wetter conditions. The town and city allotment holder in the north uses cloches for spring cabbage and finds, as a result, that he is able to cut good hearts as early as his friends in the south. The southern grower may well delight in the fact that he can grow excellent Cantaloup melons in the open with the aid of continuous cloches (see illustration facing page 609), and frame cucumbers as well.

Taking it by and large, cloches make it possible to harvest crops a fortnight or 3 weeks early. They give wonderful results with strawberries, for instance. They enable a gardener to sow French beans in July and go on picking them from under the cloches until late in October. The market gardener finds he gets enhanced prices for his produce because he is able to deliver it on to the market long before his neighbours. It is possible, for example, to pick runner beans from under cloches in July. Cloches make the autumn sowing of peas and broad beans " a dead cert." Cloches can be used for ripening off onions; for starting off vegetable marrows 3 weeks earlier; for producing very, very early potatoes; for ensuring that lettuces are available all the year round and for making it possible to grow, and fully ripen, tomatoes out of doors.

Continuous cloches also hurry along asparagus in a wonderful way. They make the growing of sweet corn and egg plant well worthwhile, and they can be used for early raspberries and loganberries. When used for giving protection to most annuals, and a large number of perennials, they enable the gardener to cut bloom several weeks earlier than normal.

For the fullest details on the use of continuous cloches see *The A.B.C. of Cloches* by the same author, published by the English Universities Press.

A DAY'S TYPICAL ROUTINE OF A GREEN-HOUSE AND FRAMES IN LATE SPRING

8.0 a.m.   Ventilators of the cool house opened and the temperature recorded.

A start may now be made on disbudding the peach trees. A large number of laterals are seen growing out of the shoots retained in the winter; only 3 of these laterals are retained, the basal growth, the terminal growth and 1, or perhaps 2, growths between. The operation is extended over a period of days so we take only 1 or 2 growths from each shoot to-day.

9.0 a.m.   Ventilators of the warm house opened only slightly, and vine syringed over. Temperature recorded.

11.0 a.m.   Pots tapped and watered. Pots that ring hollow are dry and should be watered to the top of the pot. Plants needing it are syringed after all the watering is done, using a fine spray and soft water. Paths are then damped down in the warm house and the ventilators adjusted again to give more air if necessary.

12.0 a.m.   Pot strawberries are fed with Liquinure and pollinated, each flower which has opened being touched with a rabbit's tail tied to a light stick.

2.0 p.m.   Temperature recorded.
        Seeds sown in frame which had been prepared previously. Annuals for planting out later in the annual border. Runner beans for early crop. Cauliflowers planted out in prepared frame.

3.0 p.m.   Pots are tapped and watered and plants syringed. Warm house damped down and ventilation adjusted.
        Seeds of Cinerarias sown in seed pan.

3.30 p.m. Sweet peas grown in borders tied and disbudded, side shoots being cut out and tendrils removed.
        Tomatoes planted in the border.
        Vines disbudded and laterals tied in.

4.30 p.m. Frames closed where necessary.
        Temperatures recorded and houses closed down.

5.0 p.m.   Cool house fumigated against aphis and left tightly closed. Aphis, which had been observed on strawberry plants, are killed by nicotine.

THE ADVANTAGES OF USING GANWICKS
(For drawing see page 580)

Ganwicks are a cross between a cloche and a frame and combine many of the best points of both. They catch the light right down to ground-level like a cloche, but the tops can be removed for hardening-off like a frame. Also, crops growing in them are completely accessible without having to remove the structure, and, as Ganwicks are specially built to be rapidly dismantled, they make it possible to grow crops in large blocks rather than in rotated strips (strip-cropping). " Block " cropping greatly facilitates mechanical cultivation, and makes any spraying programme, or specialised watering and feeding, easier to carry out.

What is Grown Under Glass

FLOWERING PLANTS UNDER GLASS

★

ALTHOUGH in these days heat is not available for the rare stove plants there are, nevertheless, many beautiful pot plants which may be grown in the cool house often only needing protection during the severe weather. A great many of these subjects will give colour throughout the winter months ; some, such as chrysanthemums and carnations, supply cut flowers for the house ; bulbs which can be forced for early spring display ; annuals both hardy and half-hardy which will also bloom in the spring.

Most of the following plants are quite easy to grow and by a careful choice colour may be had in the glasshouse throughout the year. Propagation details will be found under the heading " Cultivation."

ABELIA Order CAPRIFOLIACEÆ

Evergreen shrub, bearing pinkish flowers in the summer.

CULTIVATION : Propagate by cuttings or layers. Place outdoors in the summer, cold frame from October to January. Re-pot in October. Cut back straggly shoots after flowering.

SPECIES : A. uniflora. 6 ft. high with pinkish-white flowers.

ABUTILON (Flowering Maple) Order MALVACEÆ

Shrubs and semi-climbers, fine foliage and beautifully veined, bell-shaped flowers in spring and early summer.

CULTIVATION : Propagate by cuttings or seed. Re-pot in March or top-dress plants in borders. In February thin shoots and trim into shape.

SPECIES AND A. Darwinii. Orange. Varieties : Boule de Neige,
VARIETIES : white ; Fire Fly, crimson ; Golden Fleece, clear yellow ; Jubilee, pink.

SPECIES AND
CULTIVATION :
A. vexillarium. Flowers red and yellow. Varieties with handsome foliage include *A. Saviizii* and Souvenir de Bonn with silver variegations, and *A. Thompsonii* with leaves mottled yellow and green.

ACACIA (Wattle) Order LEGUMINOSÆ

Trees and shrubs with decorative pinnate leaves and yellow flowers in spring and early summer.

CULTIVATION :
Propagate by heel cuttings of half-ripened shoots or by seeds. Re-pot in summer every 3 or 4 years, water freely in spring and summer. Thin shoots and cut back straggling growths immediately after flowering.

SPECIES :
A. armata. The Kangaroo thorn, 6-10 ft.
A. cordata. 12-18 ft.
A. pulchella. 3-6 ft.

AGAPANTHUS (African Lily) Order LILIACEÆ

Flowering plant with long, narrow, evergreen leaves. Blue or white tubular flowers on a 3-ft. stem in May and June.

CULTIVATION :
Propagate by division in March. Water is given freely during the growing season but sparingly in winter. Dislikes root disturbance.

SPECIES AND
VARIETIES :
A. umbellatus. Bright blue, the variety *albus* is white.

AGAVE (American Aloe, Century Plant, Mexican Soap Plant)
Order AMARYLLIDACEÆ

Ornamental evergreen plants. Flowers are borne on spikes 1-14 ft. high only on old plants.

CULTIVATION :
Propagate by offsets. Re-pot every 5 or 6 years. Water sparingly in winter.

SPECIES AND
VARIETIES :
A. americana, var. *variegata,* with dark green and yellow leaves.

ALOYSIA (Sweet-scented Verbena) Order VERBENACEÆ

Deciduous shrubs with sweetly-scented foliage and small lilac-pink flowers, in August.

CULTIVATION :
Propagate by cuttings. Re-pot in spring when necessary. May be grown as a bush or trained up

CULTIVATION : a pillar. Prune the previous year's growth to 2 or 3
buds in February.
SPECIES : *A. citriodora.* 10-15 ft. high.

ANTIRRHINUM (*see* page 211)

ARALIA (Angelica tree) Order ARALIACEÆ

Ornamental plant with graceful growth and prettily divided
leaves.

CULTIVATION : Propagate by stem cuttings, root cuttings or
grafting. Syringe the plants once a day during
summer.
SPECIES AND *A. Chabrierii.* The False Olive, has long, narrow
VARIETIES : leaves with a dark red midrib.
A. elegantissima. Thread-like dropping leaflets,
petioles mottled with white.
A. Veitchii. Leaves reddish beneath. Variety
gracillima with white midribs.

ASPARAGUS Order LILIACEÆ

Ornamental plants with fern-like foliage.

CULTIVATION : Propagate by seed or division. Re-pot in March,
water and syringe freely during the summer. Feed
established plants weekly.
SPECIES AND *A. plumosus.* Has fern-like shoots 1-10 ft. long and
VARIETIES : makes a good climber. Variety *nanus* makes a
dwarf plant.
A. Sprengeri. Has drooping shoots, 1-4 ft. long,
covered with small leaves and sharp spines. Small
white flowers are followed by bright red berries.

AZALEA Order ERICACEÆ

Three types are commonly grown under glass : (*a*) hybrids and
varieties of the so-called Indian Azaleas ; (*b*) varieties of the
Japanese *Azalea mollis*, a deciduous species ; (*c*) dwarf evergreen
species. They flower from December to May.

CULTIVATION : *Indian Azaleas.* Propagate by seed, cuttings of half-
ripe shoots or grafting.
A. mollis. Propagate by seed, cuttings in August,
grafting or layering.
Soil must be lime free with plenty of peat. Re-pot

The Complete Gardener

CULTIVATION : firmly after flowering every 2 years. Never allow the roots to become dry. Place out of doors in partial shade from July to September. After flowering shorten straggly growths and remove seed pods.

SPECIES AND VARIETIES :

(a) *Indian Azaleas*

    Apollo. A double scarlet.
    Daybreak. A soft pink.
    Niobe. Double ivory white with a yellow tube.
    Theo Finderson. Brick red.
    All flower May–June.

(b) *A. mollis*

    Alphonse Lavallée. Orange.
    Baron Edmund de Rothschild. Red.
    Comte de Gomer. Deep pink.
    Comte de Quincey. Yellow.
    All flower April–May.

(c) *Dwarf Evergreen types*

    A. amœna. Rosy purple. May.
    A. Hinode-giri. Brilliant red.
    A. rosæflora. Double salmon red.

BAMBUSA (Bamboo) Order GRAMINEÆ

Graceful plants with grass-like foliage.

CULTIVATION : Propagate by cuttings or division. Re-pot in March. Water freely in spring and summer.

SPECIES : *B. falcata variegata.* Stems yellowish green. *B. fortunei aurea* (syn. *B. viridi-striata*). Stems purplish green, leaves striped green and yellow.

BEGONIA Order BEGONIACEÆ

Fibrous Rooted Kinds. Winter flowering with masses of small blooms.

CULTIVATION : Propagate by seed or cuttings. Water moderately and syringe daily in summer. Feed with liquid manure. Keep drier and cooler in autumn and winter. Repot in March.

SPECIES : *B. coccinea.* 3-4 ft. Scarlet. *B. manicata.* 2 ft. Pink. *B.* Gloire de Lorraine. 2 ft. Bright pink.

Tuberous Rooted Kinds. Summer flowering. Large double or single flowers in shades of yellow, orange, red and pink.

CULTIVATION : As for fibrous rooted kinds. Can be used outdoors for bedding in the summer.

SPECIES AND   *B. boliviensis.* 2 ft. Single scarlet.
VARIETIES :   Victor Boret. Dwarf orange variety.
Princess Victoria Louise. Pale pink, double.
Evelyn Tavenat. Salmon pink, double.
Ballet Girl. Large white flowers, petals edged with pink.
B. pendula. For hanging baskets. Winter flowering. They are tuberous-rooted and pendulous and include the following charming varieties :
Alice Manning. Lemon yellow.
Edith Manning. Salmon pink.
Golden Shower. Orange.
Irene Manning. Pale pink double.
Lena Manning. Rosy crimson.

BIGNONIA (Trumpet flower) Order BIGNONIACEÆ

Deciduous, strong-growing climber with large flowers in spring, summer and autumn.

CULTIVATION : Propagate by cuttings or layering. Pot firmly in February or March. Water freely in spring and summer. Cut away weak shoots as they appear and shorten the remaining shoots in January.
SPECIES :   *B. jasminoides* (syn. *Tecoma jasminoides*). 10-20 ft., white and red flowers in August.
B. radicans (syn. *Tecoma radicans*). 30-40 ft. Scarlet and orange flowers in August and September.
B. speciosa. 15-20 ft. high. Lavender flowers in spring.

BOUGAINVILLEA Order NYCTAGINACEÆ

Deciduous climber with brightly-coloured bracts in summer and autumn.

CULTIVATION : Propagate by heel cuttings. Pot or top-dress and cut back shoots of the previous year's growth to within 1 in. of their base in February.
SPECIES :   *B. glabra.* 5-8 ft., rose-coloured bracts. Varieties in shades of pink, rose and orange. Flowers throughout the summer.
B. spectabilis. 15 ft. Lilac rose. Summer.

BOUVARDIA Order RUBIACEÆ

Dwarf evergreen shrubs with fragrant flowers from September to March.

591

CULTIVATION : Propagate by stem cuttings, root cuttings or division. Place in a cold frame from June to September then house and feed weekly. Syringe the foliage in summer. Shorten back the previous year's growths to within 1 in. of their base in February.

SPECIES : *B. Humboldtii.* 2-3 ft. White flowers in winter. Hybrids in pink, scarlet and white.

BROWALLIA Order SOLANACEÆ

Very free flowering with blue, violet or white tubular flowers.

CULTIVATION : Sow in spring for summer flowering, or in July for winter flowering. Pinch back 3 or 4 times to encourage bushy growth.

SPECIES : *B. elata.* 18 ins. Flowers blue or white.
B. speciosa major. 2 ft. Bright blue flowers with a white throat.

CALCEOLARIA (Slipperwort) Order SCROPHULARIACEÆ

Plants from 1-3 ft. high with heads of large gaily-coloured flowers marked with blotches and spots.

CULTIVATION : *Herbaceous Species*
Sow seeds in July, pot on young plants as they require it. Plants may be thrown away after flowering.
Shrubby Species.
Propagate by seeds or cuttings. Shade plants from strong sunlight. Pinch back once or twice to produce bushy growth. Re-pot in March and cut back into shape. Feed established plants once a week.

SPECIES : *Herbaceous Species.*
C. gracilis. Pale yellow flowers and varieties. Summer. 1-2 ft.
C. profusa (syn. *C. Clibranii*). Large golden-yellow flowers. Summer, 1-2½ ft.
Shrubby Species.
C. integrifolia (syn. *C. rugosa*). Yellow to red-brown flowers. The parent of the bedding varieties. Summer. 1-3 ft.
C. mexicana. Pale yellow.

CALLISTEMON (Bottle Brush Tree) Order MYRTACEÆ

Evergreen shrubs with leathery leaves and dense spikes of flowers in June.

CULTIVATION : Propagate by cuttings. Re-pot every 2 or 3 years
After flowering cut back lightly.
SPECIES : *C. lanceolatus.* 8-10 ft. Bright crimson flowers.

CAMELLIA Order THEACEÆ or TERNSTRŒMIACEÆ

Large evergreen shrubs, not suitable for small houses ; flowering
in early spring.

CULTIVATION : Propagate by cuttings, layering or grafting. Re-
pot every 3 years in March or April, or top-dress
plants in borders. Plants may be stood out of doors
from June to September. Shorten straggling shoots
in March.
SPECIES : *C. japonica.* The parent of most varieties. Red.
Spring. 15-20 ft.

CAMPANULA Order CAMPANULACEÆ

Although chiefly grown in the open, some species are suited to
pot culture. Flowers are bell-shaped, blue, mauve or white in
June and July.

CULTIVATION : Propagate by seed or basal cuttings of *C. isophylla.*
Water moderately in winter.
SPECIES AND *C. isophylla.* Lilac or lavender-blue flowers suitable
VARIETIES : for hanging baskets. Trailing.
C. pyramidalis. Chimney bell-flower. 4 ft. high.
Blue flowers. Variety *C. p. alba* with white flowers.

CANNA (Indian Shot Plant) Order CANNACEÆ

Broad leaves and brightly-coloured flowers in summer.

CULTIVATION : Propagate by division of roots. Start into growth
in March. Store in winter in a frost-proof shed or
beneath the greenhouse staging.
SPECIES : *C. indica.* Red and yellow flowers. Numerous
varieties. 3 ft.

CARNATION Order CARYOPHYLLACEÆ

The most popular type of carnation for growing in glasshouses
is the Perpetual Flowering, which is especially valuable for its
winter blooms.

If a special greenhouse can be devoted to carnations it should
be one which obtains the maximum of light. The hot flow pipes
from the boiler should be overhead and there should be side, end
and top ventilators.

I. PERPETUAL-FLOWERING CARNATIONS

PROPAGATION

Cuttings are taken from December to February from good healthy plants selecting those of an average size, about 3 ins. long. The cuttings are trimmed with a sharp knife and inserted in clean sharp sand. It is best to place the cuttings in a propagating frame at the warmest end of the house and shade them from the sun.

POTTING

Young cuttings should be removed carefully when rooted and potted up singly in 2-in. pots using John Innes potting compost (see page 576), and then placed where they will get plenty of light and air.

Pot-on as necessary, taking care not to bury the plant any deeper at each successive potting and potting rather firmer each time. Pot finally into 8-in. pots for December or January-rooted cuttings or 5-6-in. pots for March-rooted cuttings.

GROWING-ON

Plants must be supported and galvanised wire supports and rings, which may be bought from any sundriesman, are very good.

Syringe the plants twice a week during the summer. This will freshen the leaves and help to keep down red spider. Plants intended for early winter flowering should be finally potted by the end of June and may then be stood in a frame well protected from rain ; they may then be housed in August.

THE SECOND YEAR

Cut the blooms throughout the winter with long stalks ; this will keep the plants short.

In June the plant will need potting on from a 6-in. to an 8-in. pot and in a week's time may again be stood outside, being housed again early in August.

During the winter keep the house cool and on the dry side with ventilators open on all possible occasions.

STOPPING

The first stopping should be done when there are 8 good pairs of leaves, when the end growth of the plant is pinched out so as to induce it to throw side breaks. The growth stopped will not produce flowers until 5 months later, so that July is late enough in order to get winter blooms. The first stopping may be done in October and the second in June of the following year.

DISBUDDING

Lateral buds should be allowed to develop somewhat before they are removed, much better flowers are produced as a result.

II. MALMAISONS

These are twice the size of the border carnation with a stronger scent and flower only from the end of May to June. Grow them in cool conditions, only closing the ventilators in cases of severe frost.

Propagate them by layering in a cold frame.

III. PERPETUAL MALMAISONS

These flower all the year and have a heavy scent. They should be grown in a cool house with plenty of ventilation. Propagate by heel cuttings. About 2 ft.

VARIETIES : *Perpetual flowering*
Allwood's Primrose. Yellow.
Ditchling. Cherry cerise.
Doris Allwood. Soft salmon rose, shaded French grey.
Joyce Carnation. Very large crimson.
Robert Allwood. Vivid scarlet.
Fancy Varieties
Dairy Maid. White, flaked pink at edge
Pelargonium. White, overlaid crimson maroon.
Tangerine. Flame apricot.
Perpetual Malmaisons
Adriatic. Pure white.
Delicate. Delicate pink, veiled deeper pink.

CELOSIA (Cockscomb) Order AMARANTHACEÆ

Decorative annuals with small flowers in feathery heads in summer.

CULTIVATION : Sow in March. Place pots in full sunlight.
SPECIES : *C. cristata.* 6-9 ins. high. White, golden, orange, crimson and rose-coloured flowers.
C. plumosa. 1-2 ft. high. Various colours may be obtained : yellow, scarlet, crimson, orange scarlet and purple.

CHIONODOXA (Glory of the Snow) (see page 283)

The Complete Gardener

CHRYSANTHEMUM Order COMPOSITÆ

Chrysanthemums for flowering under glass are particularly useful as they may be grown outside in the summer then housed in autumn before the frosts come, thus following after such crops as cucumbers and tomatoes.

PROPAGATION

Cuttings should be removed from the plants when ready, generally in January, selecting shoots that have pushed their way through the soil, 2½ ins. long, sturdy and firm.

Cut the shoots cleanly just below a joint and remove the bottom leaves, then strike the cuttings in compost made up of equal parts of loam and silver sand. Water the cuttings using a fine rose. Then, do not water again until absolutely necessary, but keep the atmosphere of the greenhouse moist.

POTTING

The cuttings should have rooted in 3 weeks and may then be potted singly into 3-in. pots using John Innes potting compost (see page 576). Plants are potted on as necessary until the final potting about the end of May using a 6-10-in. pot according to the variety. The last potting must be quite firm.

STOPPING

This is the pinching out of the growing point in order to encourage the early production of side shoots and to increase the crop. The time of stopping depends upon the variety and, with some varieties, it is not necessary to do any stopping at all, but the first stopping is usually done in April and the second, if needed, in early July.

THE STANDING GROUND

Pots should stand outside during the summer on a foundation of ashes. A 2-in. layer is sufficient and the pots should be stood in rows, or double rows, leaving sufficient pathway to facilitate feeding, weeding and disbudding. Each plant should be staked to a bamboo to which the shoots may be tied and, if 4-ft. posts are erected on the standing ground and a wire stretched between, these bamboos may be tied to the wire to prevent the pots blowing over in the wind. Feeding may start about mid-July and continue once a week until the flowers start to show.

DISBUDDING

Disbudding is the removal of unwanted side shoots and flower buds leaving 1 bud to each shoot. Disbudding should be spread over a period of 4 or 5 days as if all the buds are removed at one time the bud " taken " may go blind. Disbudding is usually started about the middle of August.

HOUSING

Plants may be protected from slight frosts by erecting a framework to be covered with hessian, otherwise they must be housed by the end of September generally. Clean the houses first, then bring the pots in, placing them so that there is room for watering, tying and cutting.

I. ANEMONE-FLOWERED

Chrysanthemums having a raised centre of tubular florets surrounded by a single or double row of tapering ray florets. They grow 2½-3 ft. high and flower from November to January.

VARIETIES :   Bronze Thora. Clear bronze with orange centre.
Caleb Cox. Ray florets are long and deep amber, disc is golden bronze.
Elspeth. Pale, mauve pink.
Snow Queen. White.
Triumph. Mahogany red.

II. CASCADES

This type originated in Japan. They can be trained as cascades or upright in pillar form. Flowers are single, sometimes delicately scented and freely produced from the end of October to the middle of December. These may also be raised from cuttings and grown and trained outside during the summer. The pots are placed on a shelf facing south about 5-6 ft. from the ground as the shoots may grow 4-5 ft. long. One or two leading growths are kept and these are trained *down* the bamboo stake which is secured to the pot from the ground. The plants may be housed at the end of September, the bamboos are removed and the ends of the shoots attached to some support.

VARIETIES :   Hi-No-Hakoma. Red.
Mauveen. Mauve pink.
Niagara. Pure white.
Spider. Pale bronze with narrow petals.
Swallow. Cream.
Yuson. Clear yellow.

III. DECORATIVES

Generally moderate-sized blooms. Most varieties do best if disbudded. Flowering season from October to the end of January. Height 2½-3 ft.

The Complete Gardener

VARIETIES : *Mid-season.*

Alfred Durbin. Reddish terra-cotta.
Astoria. Antique rose, silvery reverse.
Balcombe. Ivory white.
Beacon. Rich red.
Dante. Almost scarlet with rolled petals.
Fiki. Pink.

Late.

Apricot May Wallace. Soft apricot.
Aurora. Orange bronze.
Balcombe Beauty. Pure yellow.
Baldock's Crimson. Bright crimson.
Bronze May Wallace. Deep rosy bronze.
Colham Pink. Rich pink.
Monument. White.

IV. INCURVES

The petals curve inwards to form a globular bloom. The true
incurved forms a much tighter ball than the Japanese. Height
4 ft. Flowers from November to January.

VARIETIES :

Advancement. Bluish white.
Baby Royal. Deep yellow.
Bronze Progress. Bronze.
Frank Trestian. Orange amber.
Mrs. G. Denyer. Soft, bright pink.
Progress. Silvery mauve.

V. JAPANESE

Plants produce very large " mopheads." Flowers may be shaggy,
loosely incurved, reflex and have 2 coloured petals. Height 3-5 ft.
Flowers from November to the end of January.

VARIETIES :

Birmingham. Crimson with gold reverse.
Henry E. Trueman. White.
Majestic. Golden amber.
Mrs. Alg. Davis. Pink.
Mrs. R. C. Pulleng. Ochre yellow.
Red Majestic. Deep rich terra-cotta.
Thos. W. Pockett. Pink with silver reverse.

VI. POMPOMS

A dwarf type which produces small, almost cylindrical blooms.
1½-2½ ft. Flowers September to October.

598

VARIETIES : Ball of Gold. Bright yellow.
Ethel. Bright red.
Hilda Canning. Bronze.
Snowdrop. White.
Thyria. Deep pink.

VII. QUILLED

Sometimes called thread-petalled. The petals are like sharp-pointed tubes and look like those of the cactus dahlia. 2½-3 ft. Flowers November.

VARIETIES : Rayonnante. Pink.
White Rayonnante. White.

VIII. SINGLES

These are more dainty than the blooms of the bigger chrysanthemums and may be grown in spray form or disbudded. 3½-5 ft. Flowers November.

VARIETIES : Bronze Exmouth. Bronze.
Catriona. Rich rose pink, narrow white zone round the yellow eye.
Cygnet. Pure white.
Golden Seal. Deep yellow.
Kirkland's Crimson. Deep crimson.
Mrs. H. Woolman. Bright orange yellow.
Tangerine. Bright chestnut scarlet.

IX. CHARM

A recently introduced type of greenhouse chrysanthemum producing masses of starry scented flowers in a variety of colours. The plants grow only 18 ins. high but may be as much as 2-3 ft. across. They are raised annually from seed which is sown in February under glass, the plants being grown outside during the summer and brought into the greenhouse in October.

CINERARIA Order COMPOSITÆ

Usually grown as an annual. Has heads of daisy-like flowers in shades of pink, red, mauve and blue from December to May.

CULTIVATION : Sow from April to July. Place pots in cold frame from July to October. Need very careful watering.
SPECIES : *C. cruenta* (syn. *Senecio cruentus*). Large flowered, Cactus and *stellata* varieties. 1-2 ft.

CITRUS (Orange) Order RUTACEÆ

Evergreen shrubs with fragrant white flowers in May or July.

CULTIVATION : Propagate by cuttings or seeds. Re-pot when necessary from February to April. Plants may be stood out of doors from June to September.

SPECIES : *C. aurantium japonica.* Kumquat orange.
C. sinensis. Common or Sweet orange.

CLARKIA (see page 217)

CLIANTHUS (Parrot's Bill, Sturt's Desert Pea)
Order LEGUMINOSÆ

Climbers with richly coloured, pea flowers in April and May.

CULTIVATION : Propagate by cuttings or seeds. Pot or plant in March. The plants dislike frequent disturbance. To prune, shorten young shoots to within 2 ins. of their base.

SPECIES : *C. puniceus.* 6 ft. high with crimson flowers.

CLIVIA (Kaffir Lily) Order AMARYLLIDACEÆ

Fleshy-rooted plants with long, narrow, evergreen leaves and showy heads of short tubular flowers in shades of scarlet, orange and yellow in December to July.

CULTIVATION : Propagate by division or seeds. Place pots in the sun as close to the glass as possible. They flower better when slightly pot-bound, but re-pot when necessary in February. Well-established plants should be fed once a week.

SPECIES : *C. nobilis.* Yellow and red. May–July. 1-1½ ft.
C. miniata. Scarlet and yellow. Spring and summer. 1-1½ ft.

COLEUS (Flame Nettle, Nettle Geranium) Order LABIATÆ

Very ornamental plants with bright and variously coloured nettle-shaped leaves.

CULTIVATION : Propagate by cuttings or seed. Pot fairly firmly in February or March. Young plants must be pinched back once to make them bushy.

SPECIES AND
VARIETIES :
C. Blumei. Leaves yellow, red or purple. Flowers dark blue or white. January–April. 2-3 ft. The variety *C. Verschaffelti* is more brilliantly coloured.

What is Grown under Glass

CORONILLA (Crown Vetch, Scorpion Senna) Order LEGUMINOSÆ

Evergreen shrub with numerous fragrant yellow pea-like flowers in spring and summer.

CULTIVATION : Propagate by cuttings or seed. Re-pot in March. Place outside from June to September.

SPECIES AND VARIETIES : *C. glauca.* 8-10 ft. There is a variety *variegata.*

CRINUM (Cape Lily) Order AMARYLLIDACEÆ

Handsome deciduous bulbous plants. The bulbs are large and the flowers are lily-like and borne on 2-3 ft. stems from April to October.

CULTIVATION : Propagate by offsets and seed. Re-pot bulbs in March every 3 or 4 years. Water freely in spring and summer. Store the pots on their sides in the winter.

SPECIES : *C. Macowanii.* Flowers white and purple in autumn. 3 ft.

C. Moorei. Flowers white and red from April to October. 2 ft.

CROCUS (*see* page 284)

CYCLAMEN (Sowbread) Order PRIMULACEÆ

Deciduous perennial-flowering plants. The foliage is often marbled and marked, flowers are white, shades of pink, crimson, cerise or salmon-scarlet in winter.

CULTIVATION : Propagate from seeds. Re-pot in July or August The corm should always be partly above the surface of the soil.

SPECIES : *C. latifolium* (syn. *C. persicum*). 6-9 ins. The parent of numerous varieties.

CYTISUS (Broom) Order LEGUMINOSÆ

Small shrub bearing fragrant, yellow laburnum-like flowers in spring and early summer.

CULTIVATION : Propagate from heel cuttings. Young plants should be stopped 2 or 3 times to produce bushy growth. After flowering cut back shoots to within 2 ins. of their base.

SPECIES : *C. fragrans.* Yellow flowers. 2-3 ft.

DICENTRA (Dutchman's Breeches, Bleeding Heart)
Order FUMARIACEÆ

Perennial which stands gentle forcing. Fern-like foliage and racemes of rosy crimson or white flowers in spring and early summer.

CULTIVATION : Propagate by division of roots in autumn or spring. After flowering the plants should be put out in the open.
SPECIES: *D. spectabilis* (syn. *Dielytra spectabilis*). Rosy carmine. 2 ft.

DIDISCUS (Blue Lace Flower) Order UMBELLIFERÆ

A delightful pot plant with heads of tiny blue flowers in July.

CULTIVATION : Sow in February. Water plants freely as soon as they are well established.
SPECIES : *D. cœruleus* (syn. *Trachymene cœrulea*). 18 ins. high.

EPACRIS (Australian Heath, Tasmanian Heath)
Order EPACRIDACEÆ

Small evergreen shrubs with heath-like flowers from March to June.

CULTIVATION : Propagate from cuttings or seed. Must have a very peaty compost. Directly after flowering cut back shoots of erect kinds to within 1 in. of their base. Pendulous kinds are cut back into shape.
SPECIES : *E. hyacinthiflorus*. 2-3 ft. White or red flowers in March.
Hybrids and varieties in pink, red and white.

ERICA (Heath) Order ERICACEÆ

Shrubby evergreen plants, 1-2½ ft. high, either hard-wooded or soft-wooded types flowering from December to August.

CULTIVATION : Take cuttings of shoots 1 in. long in spring. Must have a very peaty compost free from lime. Re-pot summer-flowering kinds in September, others in March. Place outside from July to October.
SPECIES : *Hard-wooded*
E. cavendishiana. Rich yellow, May to July .
E. ventricosa. Purplish red, June to August.

What is Grown under Glass

SPECIES : *Soft-wooded*
E. gracilis autumnalis. Rosy pink, February to March.
E. gracilis nivalis. White, December to January.
E. hyemalis. Pink, December to March.

ERYTHRINA (Coral Tree) Order LEGUMINOSÆ

Deciduous shrub bearing bunches of scarlet, pea-shaped flowers from June to August.

CULTIVATION : Propagate from heel cuttings. Water freely from April to September. Store pots on their sides during winter. In November cut back shoots close to their base.
SPECIES : *E. Crista-galli.* 6-8 ft. high.

EUCALYPTUS (Australian Gum) Order MYRTACEÆ

Has evergreen leaves covered with a greyish bloom and pleasantly scented.

CULTIVATION : It is best raised from seed each year.
SPECIES : *E. citriodora.* The Citron-scented Gum. 15-20 ft.
E. globulus. The Blue Gum. 15-20 ft.

EUGENIA (Fruiting Myrtle) Order MYRTACEÆ

Evergreen shrub with narrow leaves, white flowers in summer, followed by globular, fragrant fruits.

CULTIVATION : Propagate from cuttings. Re-pot in February or March, and cut back straggling shoots.
SPECIES : *E. myriophylla.* 6 ft. high.

EULALIA (Zebra-striped Rush) Order GRAMINEÆ

Ornamental grasses with narrow leaves.

CULTIVATION : Propagate by division. Water freely in summer, in winter keep the soil just moist.
SPECIES AND VARIETIES : *E. japonica* (syn. *Miscanthus sinensis*). Green leaves with white midrib. 6-10 ft.
E. japonica var. *variegatus.* Leaves striped with yellow or white.
E. japonica var. *zebrinus.* Leaves cross banded with yellow.

EUPHORBIA (Spurge) Order EUPHORBIACEÆ

Flowering shrubs, some with ornamental leaves and bracts, autumn to winter.

CULTIVATION : Propagate from cuttings. Keep plants almost dry from January to May. Cut back shoots of *E. fulgens* to within 1 in. of their base in June.

SPECIES : *E. fulgens*, Scarlet Plume. 2-3 ft. high with scarlet flowers in autumn and winter.
E. splendens, Crown-of-thorns. Red flowers in summer. 4 ft. The stems are spiny and the bracts bright red.

FABIANA (False Heath) Order SOLANACEÆ

Dwarf evergreen shrubs with heath-like foliage and white flowers in spring.

CULTIVATION : Propagate from cuttings. Keep the roots fairly moist all the year round. Cut back shoots lightly after flowering.

SPECIES : *F. imbricata*. 3 ft. White.

FICUS Order MORACEÆ

Evergreen shrubs with decorative foliage.

CULTIVATION : Propagate from cuttings or eyes. Pot or plant from February to April.

SPECIES : *F. pandurata*. Large, fiddle-shaped leaves. 8-10 ft.
F. Parcelli. Green and white leaves. 10-12 ft.
F. radicans. A creeping species.

FITTONIA Order ACANTHACEÆ

Evergreen trailing plants with ornamental foliage.

CULTIVATION : Propagate from cuttings. Water moderately in winter, freely at other times.

SPECIES : *F. argyroneura*. Leaves green, veined with white.
F. gigantea. Leaves green, veined with red.
F. Verschaffeltii. Leaves green, veined with red and glaucous below.

FREESIA Order IRIDACEÆ

Dainty, well-known bulbous plants with fragrant flowers of many colours in winter and early spring.

CULTIVATION : Propagate from offsets or seed. Re-pot each year in August for January flowering, in December for April flowering.

What is Grown under Glass

SPECIES AND VARIETIES :
F. refracta var. *alba.* 1 ft. White and very sweetly scented. Varieties : Amethyst, lavender blue with a white throat ; Buttercup ; rich primrose, yellow shaded with orange ; Jubilee, lilac pink ; *leichtlinii*, creamy white and orange ; Rosa Bonheur, delicate pink with a bronze blotch.

FUCHSIA Order ONAGRACEÆ

Attractive shrubby plants flowering in summer.

CULTIVATION : Propagate from cuttings or seed. Re-pot old plants in February or March. Shade plants from strong sun from March to July and place out of doors from July to October. Pinch young shoots frequently to make bushy plants. Cut back fairly hard in February.

SPECIES : Numerous hybrids and varieties. 2-4 ft. Various colours—red, white, purple.

GARDENIA Order RUBIACEÆ

Evergreen shrubs with fragrant white flowers in spring and summer.

CULTIVATION : Propagate from cuttings. Re-pot or plant in February. Syringe daily in spring and summer except when in bloom. One- or two-year-old plants produce the best flowers.

SPECIES : *G. citriodora.* The Citron-scented Gardenia, 3-5 ft. high, with white fragrant flowers in spring.
G. jasminoides. The Cape Jasmine. Up to 10 ft. Fragrant white flowers in summer.

GLADIOLUS (see page 285)

GLORIOSA (Malabar Glory Lily, Mozambique Lily)
Order LILIACEÆ

Deciduous, tuberous-rooted climbers. Red and yellow lily-like flowers in summer.

CULTIVATION : Propagate from offsets or seed. Pot up the tubers 2 in. deep in February. After flowering water sparingly and then keep dry until potting time.

SPECIES : *G. Rothschildiana.* Ruby red and yellow.
G. superba. 6-10 ft. Orange and red flowers.
G. virescens. 5 ft. high. Yellow and red flowers.

605

GLOXINIA Order **GESNERIACEÆ**

Tuberous-rooted plants with large, velvety, bell-shaped flowers of various colours from June to October.

CULTIVATION : Propagate from cuttings or seeds. Pot up tubers from January to March. The soil should be firm and the tuber not quite buried. Only water the plants when they really need it and dry them off after flowering. A steady heat is needed.

SPECIES : Numerous hybrids and varieties.
Sinningia speciosa. The Gloxinia proper. 6-12 ins. There are numerous varieties.

GODETIA (see page 226)

GREVILLEA (Silk Bark Oak) Order **PROTEACEÆ**

Evergreen shrubs with ornamental foliage, flowering in summer.

CULTIVATION : Propagate from heel cuttings. Re-pot in lime-free soil in March or April. *G. robusta* needs no pruning, other species need cutting back to keep them in good shape.

SPECIES : *G. robusta.* Orange flowers and fern-like leaves. Summer. 10-20 ft.
G. rosmarinifolia. Red flowers in summer. 6-8 ft.

HELIOTROPIUM (Heliotrope, Cherry-pie) Order **BORAGINACEÆ**

Shrubs with fragrant flowers from spring to winter.

CULTIVATION : Propagate from cuttings. Pot or plant from February to May. Cut back old plants closely in February. Pinch back young plants to make bushy growth.

SPECIES : *H. peruvianum* and varieties. 1-6 ft. Blue or white.

HIBISCUS Order **MALVACEÆ**

Evergreen shrubs with large flowers in summer.

CULTIVATION : Propagate from cuttings or by grafting. Re-pot or plant in February or March and cut back into shape.

SPECIES : *H. schizopetalus.* Orange-red flowers. Up to 10 ft. in height.
H. sinensis (syn. *H. rosa-sinensis*). Rose of China, flowers all shades from white to rose red, sometimes double. Up to 30 ft.

What is Grown under Glass

HIPPEASTRUM (Amaryllis, Barbados Lily)
Order AMARYLLIDACEÆ

Showy bulbous plants, long strap-shaped leaves and large funnel-shaped flowers in early spring to early summer in white or shades of pink or red.

CULTIVATION : Propagate by offsets or seed. Re-pot every 3 or 4 years in January. Top-dress each year if not re-potted.

HOYA (Honey-plant, Wax Flower) Order ASCLEPIADACEÆ

Evergreen climber with thick leaves and wheel-shaped flowers in clusters in summer.

CULTIVATION : Propagate from cuttings or by layering. Pot or plant in February or March and cut back into shape.
SPECIES : *H. carnosa.* 10-12 ft. White or pink flowers.

HUMEA (Incense Plant) Order COMPOSITÆ

Biennial, 4-6 ft. high with scented leaves and drooping, feathery sprays of pinkish-brown flowers in June to October.

CULTIVATION : Raise from seeds sown from April to July. Water carefully ; over-watering may cause the plants to die off.
SPECIES : *H. elegans.* Red, pink and crimson.

HYACINTH Order LILIACEÆ

Hardy bulbous plant very suitable for pot work, will flower from December to March. All grow 6-9 ins. high.

CULTIVATION : Plant bulbs between August and September. Keep in the dark until growth is 2 ins. high.
VARIETIES : *Early Dutch Varieties*
    Bismarck. Mid-blue.
    Lady Derby. Light rose pink.
    La Victoire. Deep rosy crimson.
    L'Innocence. White.
    Yellow Hammer. Canary yellow.
    Late-flowering varieties
    City of Haarlem. Deep yellow.
    La Grandesse. White.
    Myosotis. Lavender blue.

VARIETIES : Vesuvius. Brilliant scarlet.
(See also page 286.)

HYDRANGEA Order SAXIFRAGACEÆ

Deciduous shrubby plants with large heads of flowers in spring and summer.

CULTIVATION : Propagate from cuttings. Re-pot in February or March. Give plenty of water in the summer. Pink varieties may be tinted blue by the use of aluminium sulphate, either by adding $\frac{1}{4}$-$\frac{1}{2}$ oz. crystals to the compost when potting, or in water using $\frac{3}{4}$ oz. to 1 gal. Soil must be lime free.

SPECIES AND   *H. hortensis.* Many good varieties include : Europa,
VARIETIES :   deep pink ; La France, bright pink ; Hamburg, red ; Florence Bolt, soft pink.

IMPATIENS (Balsam) Order BALSAMINACEÆ

Plants 18-24 ins. high, with brightly-coloured flowers in summer and autumn.

CULTIVATION : Sow from late March to early May. Plenty of water must be given and the plants may be syringed frequently until the flowers begin to open.

SPECIES :   *I. balsamina.* In shades of pink, red and violet. The improved camellia-flowered strain is best.

IPOMÆA (American Bell-bind, Moon Creeper, Morning Glory) Order CONVOLVULACEÆ

Climbers with convolvulus-like flowers in summer or winter.

CULTIVATION : Propagate from cuttings or seed. Pot or plant from February to April. Cut back straggly growths in February.

SPECIES :   *I. Horsfalliæ.* 10-15 ft. Pink flowers in winter.
I. Learii. 10 ft. Blue flowers in summer.
I. rubro-cærulea. Purplish blue, tube white before opening.

IRIS Order IRIDACEÆ

Dainty little *Iris reticulata* is useful for house decoration in the winter.

CULTIVATION : Plant in 5-in. pots in September and grow on in a cool greenhouse.

100. *A Chinese hibiscus and two good specimens of South African hippeastrum*

101. *Muscat grapes*

102. *Tulips grown under glass*

103. *Cantaloup melons under cloches, half-grown*

104. *Melons netted in a greenhouse*

SPECIES AND   *I. reticulata.* Deep blue.
VARIETIES :   *I. reticulata* var. *cantab.* Pale blue.
               I. reticulata var. *Hercules.* Dark purple.
               (See also page 287.)

JASMINUM (Jasmine, Jessamine) Order OLEACEÆ

Almost evergreen species with white or yellow flowers from summer to winter.

CULTIVATION : Propagate from cuttings in spring. Pot or plant
              and cut back lightly in February.
SPECIES :   *J. grandiflorum.* 10 ft. White flowers in autumn.
              J. revolutum. 9-12 ft. Yellow flowers from June to
              August.

LAPAGERIA Order LILIACEÆ

Evergreens with white or pink flowers in summer.

CULTIVATION : Propagate by layering or from seed. Cut out dead
              or weak shoots in March.
SPECIES AND   *L. rosea.* 15-20 ft. Pink flowers. The variety *alba*
VARIETIES :   has white flowers.

LARKSPUR (*See page* 220)

LILIUM (*See page* 288)

MARGUERITE Order COMPOSITÆ

The white daisy-flowered Marguerite is useful for pots as well as bedding.

CULTIVATION : Propagate from cuttings. Pinch back the plants
              2 or 3 times to make them bushy.
SPECIES :   *Chrysanthemum frutescens.* 3 ft. White or yellow
              flowers in summer.

MIGNONETTE (*See page* 250)

MIMULUS (Monkey Flower) Order SCROPHULARIACEÆ

Perennials with red or yellow tubular flowers in summer.

CULTIVATION : Propagate from cuttings or seed. Pinch back
              plants to make them bushy.
SPECIES :   *M. glutinosus* (syn. *Diplacus glutinosus*). A shrubby

SPECIES :   species 4 ft. high with deep yellow flowers nearly
all the year round.
M. moschatus. 6 ins. high. Pale yellow and brown
flowers.

MYRSIPHYLLUM (Smilax) Order LILIACEÆ

Climbing plant with slender green shoots bearing oval leaves,
small greenish-white flowers and dark purple berries.

CULTIVATION : Propagate from cuttings. Pot or plant in March
and syringe freely during the summer.
SPECIES :   *M. asparagoides.*

NARCISSUS (*See page* 290)

NERINE (Guernsey Lily) Order AMARYLLIDACEÆ

Beautiful bulbous plants. Deciduous with clusters of pink or red
flowers from August to October.

CULTIVATION : Propagate from offsets or from seed sown as soon
as ripe. Re-potting is only necessary every 3 or 4
years. Keep quite dry during the summer and
autumn.
SPECIES :   *N. Bowdenii.* 1½ ft. Pink flowers.
N. curvifolia Fothergillii. 1 ft. Deep scarlet flowers.
N. undulata. 1 ft. Pink flowers.

NERIUM (Oleander) Order APOCYNACEÆ

Evergreen shrubs with fragrant flowers in summer.

CULTIVATION : Propagate from cuttings. Re-pot or plant in
February or March. Water copiously in spring
and summer. Immediately after flowering, shorten
back shoots of previous year's growth to within
3 ins. of their base. Remove young shoots from the
bases of the flower trusses.
SPECIES AND   *N. Oleander.* Rosy flowers. Up to 20 ft.
VARIETIES :   *N. Oleander* var. *album plenum.* Double white.

OLEA (Olive) Order OLEACEÆ

Evergreen shrub with white fragrant flowers in summer.

CULTIVATION : Propagate from cuttings or seed. Re-pot in March
and water freely in summer.
SPECIES :   *O. europæa.* The wild olive. 20-40 ft.

What is Grown under Glass

ORCHIDS Order ORCHIDACEÆ

There are many species of orchids which are not at all difficult to grow, provided that a greenhouse with some heat is available.

TEMPERATURE

A cool house—night temperature not less than 60° Fahr. in summer, and not less than 50° Fahr. in winter, is suitable for Cymbidiums, Odontoglossums and some species of Cypripedium, Cœlogyne, Miltonia and Dendrobium.

An intermediate house—night temperature 65° Fahr. in summer, 60° Fahr. in winter, will suit some kinds of Cattleya, Cœlogyne, Cypripedium, Dendrobium and Miltonia.

A stove house—night temperature 70° Fahr in summer, 65° Fahr. in winter is suitable for Calanthes, and some Cattleyas, Cœlogynes, Cypripediums and Dendrobiums.

FEEDING

No actual feeding should ever be applied in the pots, but diluted liquid manure may be poured on the floor in a warm atmosphere.

VENTILATION

All orchids require plenty of air, but draughts should be avoided.

SHADING

Most orchids dislike bright sunlight, and blinds made of wooden laths may be used in the summer to provide shade. Alternatively, some form of permanent shading may be applied in late March or early April.

WATERING

Rainwater should be used where possible. Plenty of water is required as a rule during the growing season, but very little or none at all at other times. Light syringings may be given early in the day during hot weather, and the house should be damped down three or four times a day during the summer, and once or twice a day in winter.

COMPOSTS

Most orchids will grow in a compost of Osmunda fibre and sphagnum moss, while for some kinds, such as Calanthes and Cypripediums, a proportion of fibrous loam and leaf-mould is added.

POTTING

Potting should always be done as soon as root action starts.

Annual potting is not necessary. The pots must be very well drained, with the crocks placed in an upright position.

CALANTHE

SPECIES : C. *Regnieri* is the only one much grown. It grows 2-3 ft. high and has white or rose-pink flowers in winter.

CATTLEYA

SPECIES : C. *Bowringiana*. 1 ft. Has rosy-purple flowers in October.
C. *labiata*. 1 ft. Mauve-purple and yellow flowers in autumn.
C. *Skinneri*. 10 ins. Rose, purple and white flowers in May.

CŒLOGYNE

SPECIES : C. *cristata*. 6-10 ins. White and yellow flowers from February to April.
C. *speciosa*. 9 ins. Yellow and brown flowers in autumn.

CYMBIDIUM

SPECIES : C. *giganteum*. Yellow, purple and crimson flowers in winter. 2-2½ ft.
C. *Lowianum*. Yellow, cream and maroon flowers in February and March. 2 ft.

CYPRIPEDIUM

STOVE SPECIES : C. *Charlesworthii*. Rose and white flowers in autumn. 1-1½ ft.
C. *Lawrenceanum*. White and purple flowers in April. 1-1½ ft.
GREENHOUSE SPECIES : C. *insigne*. White, purple and brown flowers from December to February. 1 ft.

DENDROBIUM

SPECIES : D. *chrysanthum*. 4-6 ft. Yellow and purple flowers in winter.
D. *densiflorum*. 1½ ft. Yellow and orange flowers in spring.
D. *speciosum*. 1 ft. Creamy yellow and purple flowers in spring.

MILTONIA

SPECIES : *M. vexillaria* is the only species commonly grown. 1½ ft. White, pink, yellow and orange flowers in spring. There are several varieties and hybrids.

ODONTOGLOSSUM

O. Cervantesii. 6 ins. White and brown flowers in spring.
O. crispum. 1-1½ ft. White, rose and crimson flowers in spring.

PALMS Order PALMACEÆ

Decorative foliage plants.

CULTIVATION : Propagate from seeds sown in a temperature of 85° Fahr. The plants may remain in the same pots for several years, provided they are top dressed each spring.

SPECIES : *Chamærops excelsa* and *C. humilis.*
Cocos romanzoffiana (syn. *Arecastrum romanzoffiana*).
Cycas revoluta (the Sage Palm).
Kentia belmoreana (syn. *Howea belmoreana*).
Phoenix Jubæ.

PASSIFLORA (Passion Flower) Order PASSIFLORACEÆ

Vigorous climbers with long spiral tendrils and sometimes edible fruits, flowering in summer.

CULTIVATION : Propagate from cuttings. Re-pot or plant in February or March. Thin weak shoots as they appear.

SPECIES : *P. Belottii.* Flowers pink and blue.
P. cærulea. Flowers white, blue and purple.

PELARGONIUM Order GERANIACEÆ

Several types may be grown in pots, the leaves green or variegated and the flowers of various colours.

I. SHOW PELARGONIUMS
Flower in spring and early summer.

CULTIVATION : Propagate from cuttings in July or August. Pot on rooted cuttings as they require it and pinch once or

CULTIVATION : twice to encourage bushy growth. Water freely from March to June.

VARIETIES : Many varieties in shades of pink, red or white. Regal pelargoniums have semi-double flowers. 2-2½. ft.

II. ZONAL PELARGONIUMS

These may be timed to flower at any season of the year.

CULTIVATION : Propagate from cuttings. Re-pot old plants after flowering and cut back flowering shoots. Water moderately at all times.

VARIETIES : Many varieties in shades of pink, red and white, single or semi-double. 2 ft.

III. IVY-LEAVED PELARGONIUMS

Flowering in summer. Specially suitable for hanging baskets and ornamental vases in the garden.

CULTIVATION : Propagate from cuttings in August and September.

VARIETIES : Single and double varieties in pink, red or white. Trailing.

PETUNIA (*See page* 247)

PHACELIA CAMPANULARIA (*See page* 248)

PIMELEA (Rice Flower) Order **THYMELÆACEÆ**

Dwarf evergreen shrubs with pale pink flowers freely produced in May.

CULTIVATION : Propagate from cuttings or seed. Re-pot firmly as soon as new growth starts in the spring. Cut back into shape immediately after flowering, removing all dead flower heads. Stop young shoots to make bushy growth.

SPECIES : *P. ferruginea.* 2 ft.

PLUMBAGO (Cape Leadwort) Order **PLUMBAGINACEÆ**

Shrubby climber with blue flowers in summer.

CULTIVATION : Propagate from heel cuttings. Pot or plant from February to April. Cut back shoots to within 9 ins. of their base immediately after flowering.

SPECIES : *P. capensis.* 10-15 ft.

POINSETTIA Order EUPHORBIACEÆ

Shrubby plants with insignificant flowers and bracts of bright red or white flowering in autumn and winter.

CULTIVATION : Propagate from cuttings. Re-pot in spring, water and syringe freely while growing, and after flowering keep quite dry. Cut back shoots to 2 or 3 buds in April.

SPECIES : *P. pulcherrima* (syn. *Euphorbia pulcherrima*). 3-6 ft with scarlet bracts.

PRIMULA Order PRIMULACEÆ

Leaves in rosettes and single or double flowers in heads in winter and spring.

CULTIVATION : Propagate from seeds or by division. Keep fairly cool and well ventilated.

SPECIES : *P. Auricula.* Leaves sometimes covered with white farina. Flowers purple, red or yellowish green, sometimes with white, grey or green eye. 6 ins.
P. kewensis. Yellow flowers. 6-12 ins.
P. malacoides. Has small leaves and produces flowers in tiers of pink, rose, lilac and white. 1-1½ ft.
P. obconica. Large flowers in shades of pink, blue and mauve. 9-12 ins.
P. sinensis. Large flowers in shades of pink, red, white and mauve. Frilly petals. 6-9 ins.

PUNICA (Pomegranate) Order PUNICACEÆ

Fairly large deciduous trees with roundish golden-red fruits. Flowers from June to September.

CULTIVATION : Propagate from cuttings or seeds. Pot or plant from October to February. Cut back weak shoots only in early spring.

SPECIES AND *P. granatum.* Red flowers. The variety *flore pleno* is
VARIETIES : double and *Legrellei* has double flowers striped with red and yellow on the outside.

RHODODENDRON Order ERICACEÆ

Greenhouse kinds can be chosen to give bloom for the greater part of the year.

CULTIVATION : Always pot or plant in lime-free soil. Water freely in summer using rain water. Remove seed pods after flowering.

SPECIES : *R. jasminiflorum.* 3 ft. high with white or pink flowers in May. Many hybrids in other colours.

RHYNCOSPERMUM (Chinese Jasmine) Order APOCYNACEÆ

Easily grown evergreen climber with fragrant white flowers in summer.

CULTIVATION : Propagate from cuttings. Pot or plant in April or May and water freely in spring and summer. Thin and cut back into shape after flowering.

SPECIES : *R. jasminoides.* 10-15 ft.

RICHARDIA (Arum or Calla Lily, Lily of the Nile)
Order ARACEÆ

In addition to the white Arum Lily there are species with yellow flowers and variegated leaves.

CULTIVATION : Propagate by division or offsets. Any damaged portion of the tubers must be cut away and the cut ends dusted with lime. Re-pot in August. May be out of doors from June to September. After flowering, pots are dried off and stored on their sides.

SPECIES : *R. africana.* 2 ft. high. White flowers in winter and spring.
R. Elliotiana. Yellow flowers, dark green leaves spotted with white. Summer.
R. Pentlandii. Deep yellow with a brownish-purple blotch at the base of the flower. Summer.

SAINTPAULIA (African Violet) Order GESNERIACEÆ

Perennial with fleshy, hairy leaves and deep violet flowers with yellow stamens from August to March.

CULTIVATION : Propagate from leaf cuttings or seeds. Re-pot from February to May. Need a steady heat.

SPECIES : *S. ionantha.* 4-6 ft. high.

SALPIGLOSSIS (See page 251)

SALVIA Order LABIATÆ

Useful perennials which are easy to grow, flowering in autumn and early winter.

105. *Planting out seedlings on staging*

106. *Lettuces grown in the border*

107. *Tomatoes on staging and in the border.* (*Note the small electrical unit to the right of the door for heating the house*)

108. *Tomatoes on the flat.* *Both rows were planted at the same time, but the right-hand row has had the soil heated electrically*

What is Grown under Glass

CULTIVATION : Propagate from seeds or cuttings. Re-pot in March. Water freely in spring and summer. Young plants should be pinched once or twice to make bushy.

SPECIES : *S. splendens.* Bright scarlet flowers. 2-3 ft.
S. patens. Vivid blue flowers. 2-3 ft.

SAXIFRAGA (Aaron's Beard, Mother of Thousands)
Order SAXIFRAGACEÆ

Has long, trailing shoots terminating in tiny plantlets.

CULTIVATION : The plantlets may be potted up singly in the spring. In the winter the soil should be kept just moist.

SPECIES AND *S. sarmentosa.* Green leaves, the variety *tricolor* is
VARIETIES :   more compact and leaves blotched with cream, white and crimson.

SCHIZANTHUS (*See page* 253)

STATICE (*See page* 254)

STOCKS (*See page* 241)

SELAGINELLA (Creeping Moss, Tree Club Moss)
Order SELAGINELLACEÆ

Green, mossy or fern-like plants.

CULTIVATION : Propagate by division. Re-pot in February or March. Plants should be shaded from strong sunlight and are generally used as edgings.

SPECIES : *S. apoda.* Creeping stems 4 ins. long, covered with small, pale green leaves.
S. kraussiana. Moss-like trailer with bright green leaves.

SOLANUM Order SOLANACEÆ

Climbers and berried shrubs flowering in summer and winter.

CULTIVATION : Propagate from seed and cuttings.

SPECIES : *S. capsicastrum* (Winter Cherry). 18 ins. high. Bright red berries.
S. jasminoides (Jasmine Nightshade). 10 ft. Flowers blue and white.
S. seaforthianum. 10-15 ft. Flowers blue or purple.

617

STRELITZIA (Bird of Paradise Flower, Bird's Tongue Flower)
Order MUSACEÆ

Handsome perennial 3-5 ft. high. The flowers, shaped rather like a bird's head, are borne on stout spikes in spring and early summer.

CULTIVATION : Propagate by division or from suckers. Water sparingly in winter and place in full sun.

SPECIES : *S. augusta.* Up to 18 ft. high. White and purple flowers.
S. Reginæ. 3-4 ft. high. Orange and blue flowers.

STREPTOCARPUS (Cape Primrose) Order GESNERIACEÆ

Large tubular flowers of many shades in summer.

CULTIVATION : Propagate by leaf cuttings or seed. Potting must always be done lightly. Re-pot old plants in March. Water freely from April to October, but keep almost dry in the winter. Shade the pots from bright sunlight.

SPECIES : *S. Wendlandii.* 17 ins. high with violet-blue and white flowers. Hybrids will give a large range of colours.

STREPTOSOLEN Order SOLANACEÆ

Evergreen climber with clusters of bright orange flowers freely produced from April to July.

CULTIVATION : Propagate from cuttings of young shoots. Syringe daily in spring until the flowers appear. Cut shoots back fairly closely after flowering.

SPECIES : *S. Jamesonii.* 4-6 ft. high.

TRACHELIUM (Blue Throat Wort) Order CAMPANULACEÆ

Half-hardy perennial with dense heads of tiny flowers in July and August.

CULTIVATION : Propagate from seed sown in spring or July. Larger plants are obtained from the July sowing. Keep the plants in a cold frame until October then bring them into a cool house.

SPECIES : *T. cœruleum.* Blue flowers. 2 ft.

TULIPS (*See page* 293)

What is Grown under Glass

VALLOTA (Scarborough Lily) Order AMARYLLIDACEÆ

A bulbous plant similar to a small hippeastrum, 2-3 ft. high with scarlet flowers in August and September.

CULTIVATION : Re-potting is only necessary every 3 or 4 years.
SPECIES :   *V. purpurea.*

VERONICA Order SCROPHULARIACEÆ

Shrubby evergreens with flowers of various shades of pink, red, mauve or purple in summer and autumn.

CULTIVATION : Propagate from cuttings. Re-pot in September or March. Water freely in spring and summer. Cut back shoots after flowering.
SPECIES :   *V. Hulkeana.* 4-6 ft. high. Lavender flowers.
V. speciosa. Has a number of varieties with flowers in deep blue, bright crimson and purple. 4-6 ft.

ZEBRINA (Tradescantia) Order COMMELINACEÆ

Plants with ornamental leaves.

CULTIVATION : Propagate from cuttings. Water freely in spring and summer, moderately at other times.
SPECIES :   *Z. discolor* (syn. *Rhœo discolor*). Creeping habit. Leaves dark green above, purple below.
Z. pendula (syn. *Tradescantia zebrina*). Leaves purple beneath and striped with white above.

FRUIT UNDER GLASS

*

FIGS

UNDER glass, figs may be grown as bush trees in pots, or in the border, but they can more often be grown as fan-trained trees against the back wall, or on a wire trellis in the house.

PREPARATION
Take out soil 2 spits deep and place a 6-in. layer of rubble or broken brickbats in the bottom. Ram down to act as drainage and prevent roots coming through into the subsoil.

Then fill in with good soil, adding 2 good handfuls of bone meal, 2 handfuls of wood ashes and 1 handful of ground chalk to each barrowload. Firm down.

A border $3\frac{1}{2}$ ft. wide and $1\frac{1}{2}$ ft. deep is sufficient, as a restricted root run produces short jointed shoots which crop heavily.

STARTING INTO GROWTH
Start trees into growth about January, with a night temperature of 60° Fahr. Raise during fine days to 80° Fahr. with sun-heat. Syringe the house twice daily, morning and afternoon.

STOPPING
When side shoots reach 4 leaves pinch out growing point. Pinch out all sub-laterals at 4 leaves.

Apply plenty of water when baby fruit starts to swell. Feed twice a week with Liquinure when watering.

First crop should ripen in June.

SECOND CROP
This should be produced on young wood stopped when 8 ins. long and be ready to pick in August. Keep a moist atmosphere by syringing and raise the temperature to 90° Fahr. during the day. Bottle up sun-heat by shutting the house early in the afternoon. Keep the greenhouse glass perfectly clean as light is essential. Restrict the root run, never letting them run outside the house. When fruit swells feed with Liquinure (Tomato Special) every 4 days, giving good doses.

Little ventilation is necessary until the fruit starts to colour when air must be given. No syringing or damping down should be done directly ripening starts.

PRUNING

Prune as desired in the winter. Thin shoots where necessary, removing dead wood. Remember the first crop is produced on short-jointed, well-ripened wood of the preceding year's growth.

VARIETIES

Brown Turkey. Popular because it is easy to grow. Very fertile, the fruit has deep red flesh, juicy and sweet.

Brunswick. Bears large fruit, the inside flesh being greenish, the outside skin quite pale green.

Negro Largo. Mid-season variety with very thin skin. Black and shiny. Has brown rather than red flesh and a particularly nice rich flavour.

White Marseilles. Early variety. Fruit is pale green, the flesh inside like opal-tinted china. Considered the richest and sweetest flavoured kind.

GRAPES

Use a stronger wiring system for vine rods than for tomatoes or cucumbers. Low temperatures are normal, except in the case of Muscats, when flowering. Cover openings with small meshed wire netting to prevent entry of birds.

THE BORDER

Vines grow better in inside borders. When preparing the border efficient drainage is essential and the gardener must see that the soil remains fertile for 8 or 9 years. Attract roots of a vine to the surface, never into the subsoil.

PREPARATION OF BORDER

Take out soil to a depth of $2\frac{1}{2}$ ft. then fill bottom with 6 ins. of broken brickbats, etc. Cover with a 2-in. thickness of turf laid grass side downwards, or damped horticultural peat, after which cover with a $\frac{1}{2}$-in. layer of crushed bone. Fill remaining 2 ft. with a good compost.

Vines are normally propagated by cuttings taken from 1-year-old laterals about 4 buds in length. They are struck in sandy soil with a temperature of 65° Fahr. Another method is to cut one bud off a lateral and plant it in the centre of a pot filled with compost in January or February. See that the eye is left exposed and the piece of wood at the base just buried. When the cuttings are well rooted they are usually potted on into 6-in. pots and they finish their first year's growth in these.

Keep the cuttings in the cold house until the beginning of the second year, then cut them back to within 2 buds of their base. When growth starts in the spring give water and keep the night temperature about 65° Fahr. By that time the plants should be in a 12-in. pot.

PLANTING
Plant 2- or 3-year-old canes, if on the cordon system 3 ft. apart. If a rod is allowed to grow naturally it will need 20 ft. to grow. Planting may take place in the autumn or in late March.

GENERAL CULTIVATION
Keep the vine bed moist but not wet. Give ample ventilation during hot weather and early in the morning and last thing at night syringe the vine rod over. In very hot weather it may be necessary to syringe during the day.

At the end of the first year the growth should be about 8 ft. long and should be stopped at the end of August. In December cut the rods back to 6 ft. just above a strong bud. Untie the rod in February and allow it to bend down. When growth has commenced, tie back to the wire. Give the border a good flooding in March. Each eye may send out 2 or 3 growths ; reduce these to 1. Don't allow this lateral to fruit in the second year. When these laterals or side growths are 1 ft. long, stop them and cut back any sub-laterals that develop to 2 joints. Allow the end growth on the rod to grow naturally.

The rod may be allowed to crop in its third year. In the winter, the laterals will be cut back to within 1 bud of their base, the rod bent over as before. When the laterals develop, thin down to 1 per spur and stop them at 2 leaves beyond a bunch. Only allow 8 bunches per rod this year.

In subsequent years, prune back the vine laterals each winter to a plump bud and reduce the leader, or end growth, by about half. When the side growths develop in the spring, thin down to 1 per spur and stop them at 2 joints beyond a bunch of fruit. Any secondary growths which develop should be pinched back beyond the first leaf. The end growth should be stopped when it has grown to the top of the house. Laterals that don't fruit should be stopped at about the same length as those that do.

Fruit under Glass

TEMPERATURE

Normally the temperatures will be between 50 and 60° Fahr. When the vine is in flower it may rise to 70° Fahr., but when the fruit has set it should be lowered to 60° Fahr. until the stoning period has passed. It may then rise to 70° Fahr. again. When the grapes start to colour decrease the temperature to 65° Fahr.

VENTILATION

Ventilate a little in the morning and increase the ventilation as the day advances and close by stages in the afternoon. When the grapes are starting to colour ventilate day and night.

WATERING

Flood the vine border each winter. Give another flooding before flowering and another after thinning. Keep the border well watered until the grapes start to colour and ripen.

FEEDING

Apply well-rotted manure or compost over the borders each winter. Feed with liquid manure after thinning, say, once a fortnight.

SYRINGING

Syringe the leaves regularly with water to keep down red spider. Discontinue when the vines come into flower and again later when the grapes start to ripen. Open the ventilators early to dry off the moisture on the berries before the sun gets on them.

POLLINATION

Tap the rods when the plants are in flower at about midday. Keep the atmosphere charged with moisture at this time and in the case of Muscats close the ventilators for a couple of hours in the middle of the day.

THINNING

Two thinnings are necessary, first when the grapes are the size of a sweet-pea seed, the second when they are the size of marrowfat peas. Cut away at least half the berries removing the inner berries first ; then the smaller berries ; then thin out the side berries. (See Fig. 40.)

WINTER WORK

Cut back the leader, or end growth, by half or a quarter or, when the rod has reached the top of the house, to within, say, $\frac{1}{2}$ in. of

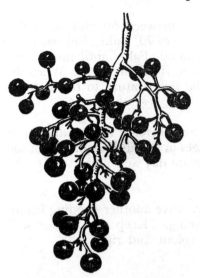

its base. Cut back the side growths to 1 bud ; remove the loose bark, and paint over the rods with a good tar distillate wash. Flood the border, then give a mulching of dung or properly composted vegetable refuse.

VARIETIES

There are a very large number of varieties to chose from, but the following are easy to grow :

Alicante. Free fruiter, excellent keeper, black, late, second quality.

Black Hamburg. Early first quality, black.

FIG. 40 GRAPES CORRECTLY THINNED

Buckland Sweetwater. Early, handsome, white, goes well with Black Hamburg.

Gros Colmar. Large firm berries, black, second quality.

MELONS

Grown like the cucumber and a suitable crop for the low-span roof greenhouse.

PROPAGATION

Sow the first week in January. Clean, crock and fill 3-in. pots with John Innes Seed Compost. Sow 2 seeds per pot $\frac{1}{4}$ in. deep, but retain only the strongest.

Stand pots over the pipes in the house or plunge in hot-bed up to the rim. Cover with glass and a sheet of brown paper in temperature of 75-80° Fahr.

When seedlings appear, remove glass and paper, and stand plant on a shelf near the glass.

POTTING-ON

When plants are 3 or 4 ins. high and well rooted, pot into 5-in. pots, using John Innes Potting Compost.

Syringe regularly with water at the same temperature as the house to keep the atmosphere moist.

Fruit under Glass

MAKING OF BEDS

Make up the beds some days before required so that the soil can warm up. Place a layer of turves grass-side downwards and on the turves a ridge 1 ft. high and 8 ins. wide of a soil mixture as advised for cucumbers (see page 633) this being made moderately firm. Plant firmly 18 ins. apart and stake to keep upright.

Set the ball of soil half-way above soil level, then, as watering proceeds, this will fall away leaving the top of the roots exposed. This prevents collar-rot. If plants are set in the soil in pots with the bottom knocked off, the roots grow into the compost and watering should not be done inside the pot.

TRAINING

Allow plants to run up to the second wire before stopping to allow side shoots to develop. Pinch off those growing below the first wire.

When flowers have set and fruits start to swell, allow 2 melons only per plant. Remove surplus fruit, keeping those of approximately the same size.

To prevent overcrowding restrict growth to 3 or 4 laterals on either side of the stem.

POLLINATION

Transfer pollen from male to female blooms by means of a rabbit's tail when 5 or 6 females are fully expanded. Allow bees to work in a melon house, but never in a cucumber house. Encourage free circulation of air during the middle of the day to dry the foliage and help pollination.

TEMPERATURE AND WATERING

Always use tepid water. Keep collar dry, but soil around the roots moist. Syringe twice daily but avoid draughts. Keep melons drier than cucumbers.

Discontinue watering as flowers open and syringe once only in the afternoon. When fruit changes colour withhold all moisture and give free ventilation.

Keep temperature at 70° Fahr.

MANURING

As roots appear through the compost top-dress with good soil mixed equally with well-decayed farmyard manure. Leave in the house for a day to get warm before applying.

When fruit swells give Liquinure (Tomato Special) at the rate of 2 gals. of feed per 3 plants once a week.

Dried blood may be given twice at intervals of 14 days.

GENERAL REMARKS

As fruit ripens this can be seen by cracking near the stem and smelt by typical melon aroma. Support by nets. (See illustration facing page 609.) Reduce humidity, temperature and water to the roots at this time.

January sowings ensure a good crop from the beginning of May onwards and June sowings from the end of August onwards.

VARIETIES

Blenheim Orange. Scarlet fleshed. Has thick flesh and will do under cooler conditions.

Emerald Gem. Green fleshed. Handsome fruit. Superb in flavour. Of a rich green colour.

Hero of Lockinge. White fleshed. Extremely rich in flavour.

King George. Scarlet fleshed. Good cropper.

Scarlet Hero. Described as a scarlet form of Hero of Lockinge.

PEACHES AND NECTARINES

The nectarine is a smooth-skinned type of peach and can, therefore, be dealt with under the same headings.

Fan-shaped trees with short stems are grown on wires 1 ft. or 18 ins. away from the glass of the house, or against the back wall.

THE BORDER

Dig out soil to a depth of $2\frac{1}{2}$ ft., the hole being 5 ft. long and 3 ft. wide. Place a 6-in. layer of brickbats and coarse rubble in the bottom, covered with turves laid grass side downwards, then fill in with compost : 6 parts good soil ; 1 part of mortar rubble or rough chalk ; $\frac{1}{2}$ part wood ashes or burnt garden refuse ; $\frac{1}{2}$ part bone meal, and $\frac{1}{16}$ part sulphate of potash, or, in place of last, the wood ash content may be doubled.

PLANTING

Plant in October or November, taking care that there is at least 5 ins. between the trunk of the tree and the brickwork. Spread the roots out evenly and shallowly, treading soil firmly round them. Never bury the union of the stock and scion.

FIRST YEAR

Get the trees firmly established. In January, apply damped horticultural peat over the ground to a depth of 4 ins. for 3 ft. around the stem of the tree. Pruning is done at the same time by shortening the shoots to half their length.

MANURING

In February apply dried blood at 2 ozs. per square yard. In November or December, a good fish manure at 3 ozs. per square yard. Liquinure is given after the fruit has stoned. If the ground is not chalky, apply hydrated lime each year after the fruit has been picked at the rate of 4 ozs. per square yard.

WATERING

Apply plenty of water during the spring and summer when dry. A good flooding is necessary in winter too. Syringe branches and leaves after the fruit has set until it begins to ripen. Syringing should continue after harvesting.

TEMPERATURE

When the trees are in flower keep the house at 50° Fahr., after which gradually increase the temperature to 55 or 60° Fahr. at night time. During the daytime the temperature may rise to 75° Fahr.

PRUNING

Both the peach and nectarine flower on the last year's well-ripened growths. The tree should have equal-sized branches radiating evenly from the main stem. Produce the lower branches first and then allow the centre of the fan to be filled in afterwards.

Train the peach on wires fastened 4 ins. away from the wall, spaced 12 or 18 ins. apart, to which the growths should be tied after pruning. Remove older growths in the winter, retaining not over-strong growths spaced 4 ins. apart all over.

Prune in the summer, leaving only 3 or 4 laterals, rubbing out the surplus with the thumb and forefinger when ½ in. long. As well as retaining the leaders, a growth should be left at the base of each length of fruiting wood to take the place of this wood when the fruit has been picked. Dis-shooting should be extended over 10 days.

Trees tending to make too much growth should be root-pruned.

POLLINATION

Pollination can be helped by means of a rabbit's tail attached to a short length of bamboo, although all peaches and nectarines are self-fertile.

MULCHING

After flowering, mulch with damped horticultural peat as suggested under the heading First Year.

THINNING

After the fruits have stoned properly, thin, leaving only 1 per square foot in the case of peaches and 1 per 9 sq. ins. in the case of nectarines. This is usually done in two periods.

GENERAL CULTIVATION

Remove surplus shoots during the summer, but growths required may be kept tied in. Admit air night and day towards the end of summer to ensure proper ripening. Towards October withhold watering.

Place nets in position to catch falling fruit, removing the ripest daily. Syringe the house thoroughly with water after the fruit has been gathered.

VARIETIES

Peaches in order of ripening

Duke of York. Large, rich crimson. Of good flavour and tender flesh.

Peregrine. Large round fruit, brilliant crimson. Very juicy and rich in flavour.

Bellegarde. Fruit large, golden yellow with dark crimson flesh. Excellent flavour.

Sea Eagle. A large fruit, yellow with crimson cheek. Excellent quality.

Nectarines in order of ripening

Cardinal. Round, scarlet. First-class flavour.

Early Rivers. Large, light yellow with rich crimson flesh. Excellent flavour.

Humboldt. Very large, yellow with crimson flush. Very juicy, good flavour.

Pineapple. A deep orange and crimson. Fine flavour, perhaps the best of all.

STRAWBERRIES

PROPAGATION

Obtain runners from healthy vigorous parents of a good strain. Royal Sovereign of the strain Malling 47 are the best.

Set out parents in August or September and so establish before the winter. In late March give a dressing of meat and bone meal at 3 ozs. per square yard, and sulphate of potash at 1 oz. per square yard. Remove blossom trusses as they develop, and runners should begin to appear.

Fruit under Glass

Soak 3-in. pots in water for 2 or 3 hours and, after crocking, fill with John Innes Potting Compost. Firm the soil, but allow space for watering. Then draw a V-shaped drill, 3-4 ins. deep, down one side of each row, in which place a continuous row of pots. Fill in drill so that pots are level when plunged.

As runners develop, peg each into the top of a pot with wire pegs like hairpins. When these are well rooted, sever from parents and, a week later, pot into 5-in. pots using a similar compost. Water pots before potting and, if earthworms are suspected, $\frac{1}{4}$ oz. of corrosive sublimate should be dissolved in 3 gals. of water to kill them, although great care should be taken, as this chemical is deadly poison and corrosive to metal containers.

Pot each plant so that the crown and plant itself points to the edge. Keep in the shade for a week ; after which stand on a good ash base in full sun.

SUMMER WORK
Syringe pots night and morning. Liquinure (Tomato Special) solution may be given twice a week at first and again later, each time the plants are watered, using $\frac{1}{4}$ oz. per $2\frac{1}{2}$-gal. can of water. Arrange pots with crowns pointing south and far enough apart, so that foliage doesn't overlap.

AUTUMN WORK
During the third week of October lay pots on their sides, and a fortnight later place in a cold frame plunged in peat moss. Failing this, stack on their sides in tiers against a wall, ashes being used to keep the pots level, and the crowns pointing outwards.

WINTER WORK
Take plants in early in January to a temperature of 40-45° Fahr. at night and 50° Fahr. during the day. Force slowly until well into flower. After 3 weeks dip plants in a 3% solution of Captan and scrape $\frac{1}{4}$ in. top soil off each pot, replacing same with warm NO-SOIL Compost.

For the first fortnight syringe once a day and afterwards twice.

When the plants flower, raise the temperature to 55° Fahr. at night and 65° Fahr. in the day. Do hand pollination with a rabbit's tail.

Thin fruits as they swell, leaving 10-15 berries per pot. Each fruiting truss should hang over the edge of the pot—the advantage of potting the crown well to the side.

FORCING

When the fruits begin to swell, raise the temperature to 65° Fahr. at night, and 70° Fahr. or over during the day. Continue to syringe the plants twice a day until the berries start to colour, after which syringing should be discontinued.

When the fruits start to colour a little liquid manure may be given. In addition, the pots will need daily watering.

GENERAL REMARKS

Strawberries may be forced by bringing them into heat before Christmas, but really heavy crops can never be expected if this is done.

VARIETIES

Royal Sovereign. Try to get a good strain. This is the best variety for indoor work.

Cambridge Favourite (Shewell-Maudit strain). Strong growing, good flavour.

VEGETABLES UNDER GLASS

*

A GLASSHOUSE may be used for growing large numbers of vegetables, although as a rule in this country the glasshouse is only used for those vegetables that do not grow as perfectly or as succulently out of doors.

BEANS, FRENCH

From the middle of September grow in pots in the greenhouse.

SEED SOWING
Use 10-in pots. Crock and fill with John Innes Potting Compost. Place 8 beans round the edge of the pot, 1½ ins. deep, and, if all grow, reduce to 5. Do not water.

TEMPERATURE
At night from 55-60° Fahr., allowing it to rise a few degrees during the day.

GENERAL CULTIVATION
Syringe twice daily. When pods form water with Liquinure, further feeds given once a week. Support with twiggy sticks. Ventilate well, but do not chill plants with draughts.

VARIETIES
Black Prince and Wonder. Best greenhouse varieties.

BEANS, CLIMBING FRENCH

An alternative to Bush French beans, but grown in the same way.

SEED SOWING
Sow in a narrow border and train vines on wires close to the light. Thin out seedlings to grow 12 ins. apart each way. For earlier sowings, 8 seeds are sown per 3-in. pot, in mid-January in the south, or the beginning of February in the north. The plants thus raised are put out into the borders 12 ins. apart.

PLANTING

As for tomatoes, watering lightly to settle soil round the roots.

GENERAL CULTIVATION

Damp twice a day and give feeds of Liquinure during growing season. Do not over-water. Syringe regularly.

VARIETIES

Guernsey Runner. Best variety.
Princess of Wales.

CAULIFLOWER

Grown in the greenhouse for an early crop.

SEED SOWING

Sow about September 15th on prepared bed out of doors, and cover with continuous cloches or a frame.

POTTING

Pot into 3-in. pots, using a John Innes Potting Compost, when 3 rough leaves develop. Then keep in a cold frame.

PLANTING

Prepare soil as for tomatoes, planting out the third week in January in rows 2 ft. wide, allowing 18 ins. apart.

TEMPERATURE

After this, water the newly planted ball of soil and do not let the temperature fall below 48° Fahr. at night, nor go above 60° Fahr.

GENERAL CULTIVATION

Water once a week and ventilate if warm. Syringe overhead.

VARIETIES

Feltham Forcing. Quick growing. Snow white curd.
Presto. Similar to the above.

CUCUMBER

To grow cucumbers successfully, a good deal of atmospheric moisture is required. The wire supports should run the length of the house, and should be 6 ins. apart. Keep the house always at a temperature of not less than 65° Fahr. at night, even in the

109. *Rose Mildew*

110. *Damping off of seedlings*

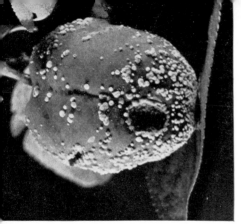

111. Brown rot on plum

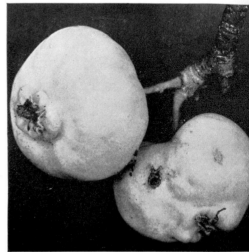

*112. Apples attacked by codling moth
larvae*

*113. Damage done to pear by capsid
bug*

114. Woolly aphis on apple twig

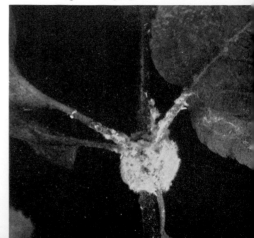

coldest weather. Perfect drainage must be ensured in view of the amount of water that is used, or root troubles will begin.

PROPAGATION

Sowing depends on when planting has to be done. In winter, allow two months from seed sowing to planting time, and in the summer and autumn allow 6 weeks.

Sow the seed in a John Innes Seed Compost (see page 576). Place pots where there is plenty of bottom heat, covering with glass and brown paper, as for tomatoes. Do not let the temperature of the house fall below 70° Fahr. at night time.

POTTING

Plants may be potted up in 10 days or a fortnight into 3-in. pots. Use John Innes Potting Compost (see page 576). Do not pot too firmly. Just consolidate the soil around the seedlings. Insert the plants up to the seed leaf. Give a good watering immediately afterwards with water at the same temperature as the house. Water once a day, when the soil appears dry, but do not allow it to become too wet. Keep up a humid atmosphere all the time.

PREPARING THE GROUND

A normal bed is made up of equal parts stable manure and soil in alternate layers, but soil and straw only may be used. Make the bed up a fortnight before planting, first a layer of straw, then a layer of soil, and so on ; 3 layers of each in all. The bed should be about 2 ft. wide and water it well. It is essential that the bed is made up on well-drained soil, over which has been placed a layer of lime about 2-3 ins. thick.

PLANTING

Allow about 20 ins. between plants, placing them centrally under the panes of glass to avoid drips from the sash bars. The plant is tipped out of the pot with the ball of soil and set into a hole, but not firmed in. Push some light soil round the ball and water in.

VENTILATION

Air should be admitted with caution. Open the ventilators slightly in July on the leeward side, to change air in the house.

TEMPERATURE

A brisk temperature must be maintained at all times. Damping down should be done night and morning, and syringing should be done at midday. The night temperature should be about 70° Fahr. When damping down, as much as a gallon of water is often used per 3 plants.

TRAINING

Train up wires, no side growths or laterals being left below the first wire. Allow the main stem to go to the top of the house, the laterals being stopped when the second leaf has been produced. New sub-laterals are then produced and these are stopped after the second leaf, and so on. Flowers may be produced on the main stem. Cucumbers, however, must not be allowed to develop here. Therefore, remove all flowers from the main stem, and all male flowers from the rest of the plant, otherwise the fruits will be less palatable.

Remove all dead leaves and any young fruits that are distorted or diseased. Leave 2 fruit-bearing joints on every lateral and not more than 3 breaks.

MANURING

Give mulches 3 weeks after planting. First use straw, or strawy stable manure, and then, a week later, give a top dressing of soil all over the bed. Place this in the house at least 12 hours before using. Cucumbers usually come in flushes and the plants should be top dressed after each flush.

Do not over-water. It is usually necessary to soak twice a week. If young fruits tend to damp off, withhold water for a week. Shade the glass in very hot weather.

VARIETIES

Butcher's Disease Resister. Popular variety. Immune from spot disease. Heavy cropper.

Excelsior Telegraph. Long, smooth, good colour. Heavy cropper.

Her Majesty. Perfectly straight fruits of even thickness. Crisp white flesh.

Hurst's Marvel. Handsome, smooth, even fruits. Heavy cropper.

LETTUCE

Lettuces are often grown as a catch crop to follow tomatoes. One planting is usually done in mid-September to mid-October and, as a result, the lettuces are cut in December and January. Another planting can be made in December and January, so as to cut in February and March.

SEED SOWING

Sow the seed about mid-September for mid-October planting, and mid-November for December planting. Fill seed boxes with the John Innes Compost (see page 576) to within $\frac{1}{4}$ in. of the top. Firm evenly and, after watering, sow the seed, spacing it out about $\frac{1}{2}$ in. apart. Sift a little compost over the seeds and press down lightly. Cover the boxes with a sheet of glass and a piece of paper. Germination takes place in 4 days when the glass and paper may be removed. Keep the boxes on the benches in the greenhouse at a temperature of 60° Fahr. In 8 days' time, prick the seedlings out into further seed boxes filled with John Innes Seed Compost, about 1 in. apart. Water and stand the boxes on the bench of the greenhouse at a temperature of about 55° Fahr.

PLANTING

Plant on a well-prepared border where the top $\frac{1}{2}$ in. of soil is raked down as fine as possible. (See illustration facing page 616.) Remove all surface stones. Plant shallowly but firmly 9 ins. apart each way, watering the ground well afterwards. (See illustration facing page 616.) The great thing is to keep the border moist as more lettuces suffer from dryness at the roots than from over-watering. Water so that the lettuces themselves are not made wet. If water is not given regularly then the plants wilt and are attacked by botrytis.[1]

TEMPERATURE

Keep the temperature at 55° Fahr. at night time and at never more than 60° Fahr. in the day. Never attempt to force lettuces.

GENERAL CULTIVATION

Remove decaying leaves with the sharp blade of a knife. Hoe between the plants to keep down weeds.

VARIETIES

Cheshunt Early Giant. A large crisp cabbage lettuce. The best under glass.
Cheshunt 5 B. A very reliable new variety.
Cheshunt Early Ball. Lighter coloured leaves. A little smaller.
Proeftvins Blackpool. Popular especially in the north. Very large.
Note.—Those who like to plant lettuces under glass in the spring should grow Green Frame or May Queen.

[1] Allisan will control Botrytis.

MARROWS

Grow the trailing variety as a catch-crop, training the stems up purlin posts in the houses. Sow singly in 3-in. pots on staging of the house. Plant out in special bed prepared as for marrows in the open. To set fruit, detach male flower and remove petals, then rub stamen over the stigma of fruit-producing flower. Tie to purlin posts for support. Remove side shoots.

Cut fruit when 12 ins. long. Water regularly immediately plants start cropping.

MUSTARD AND CRESS

Sow in boxes placed on staging or directly in beds. Grow and clear in 14 days.

Sterilise the soil for boxes, use John Innes Seed Compost and water well for best results.

After draining sow thickly, but do not cover with soil. Keep boxes in the dark for a few days or cover with brown paper. Sow cress 3 days before mustard. Mustard germinates within 3 days, and should be ready to cut in a week.

RADISHES

SEED SOWING

Sow in beds made up on the staging to be as near the glass as possible. The soil, rich in humus from previous dressings, should be well worked. Sow thinly between mid-October and mid-February and do not cover with more than ½ in. of soil. Water well and ventilate freely as plants grow.

Crop twice between October and March. Do not force. Three essentials are light, air and moisture.

VARIETIES

French Breakfast Early Forcing. Small top. Very early, bright scarlet.

Sparkler 50/50. Half white and half red. Very attractive for salads.

Red Turnip Short Top Forcing. Very few leaves.

TOMATOES

Tomatoes have been grown in varied types of glasshouses. Quite heavy crops can be obtained from plants growing in only 6 ins.

of soil. It is usual to grow them to cover a full season, i.e. the seed is sown in January, the planting is done in late February, or early March, and the picking commences at the end of April and continues till early October. It is possible, on the other hand, to use tomatoes as a catch crop, and to plant them, say, at the end of July, after an early crop of cucumbers and keep them cropping until December ; or to plant them in February, to restrict them to 3 or 4 trusses, and take them out in July. (See illustration facing page 617.)

PROPAGATION

Sow seeds in a John Innes Compost (see page 576). Place this in the greenhouse the week before it is required. Fill seed boxes to within ¾ in. of the top, firm the compost evenly right through, and sift another ¼ in. of compost over the top. Water the soil and, when this has drained away, sow the seed. In the normal seed box this means 6 rows of 9 seeds per row, i.e. they are spaced out at about 1½ ins. apart. Sift the slightest film of compost over the seeds and firm lightly with a firming board. Cover each box with a sheet of glass, and over this place a piece of brown paper ; each morning turn the glass upside down and put the paper back. When the seedlings appear, remove the glass, leaving the paper on for another 2 days. Keep the temperature of the house at this time at 60° Fahr. The atmosphere should be moist and buoyant, so damp down the pathways and soil beneath the staging every day.

POTTING

When 2 leaves have developed, prick the plants out into 3 in. pots, using the John Innes Potting Compost (see page 576). Take care not to pinch the stems of the plants but to hold them by their leaves. Do not pot tightly. Leave about ¼ in. of space at the top of the pot for watering. See that the plant is in the centre of the pot with the seed leaves resting on the soil.

Stand the pots on the staging. Water them well. Keep the temperature of the house at 65° Fahr. Damp down the pathways and pipes. When the plants are established, reduce the temperature to 60° Fahr. Ventilate on all favourable days. Keep the plants on the dry side after this, so as to produce stocky plants. When the plants are 6 ins. high, and have a good root system, plant them out in the border or pot them into large pots or boxes.

PLANTING IN POTS OR BOXES

Fill the boxes, pots or troughs with the John Innes Potting

Compost, put in position a week beforehand to warm. Do not fill the pot or box higher than 4 ins. from the top and thus top dressings may be added later. Make a hole with a trowel, large enough to take the plant with its pot. Stand the pot in the hole for 2 or 3 days before the ball of soil is knocked out, so that the plant in the pot will have become acclimatised to the soil around. Press the ball down firmly so that its top is just below the level of the soil. Disturb the root system as little as possible. Water carefully in the early stages or soft growth may result. Try not to water until the first truss has set and keep the plants going by syringing overhead. It is when the first two trusses have set that the Tomato Liquinure may be given in weekly doses.

Planting in the Border

Dig over the border as early as possible, adding well-rotted dung or composted vegetable refuse at 1 good barrowload to 10 sq. yds. When the same soil has to be used year after year for tomatoes, straw cut into 8-in. lengths is dug into the soil vertically while bastard trenching ; this increased aeration keeps the bacteria working. Always flood the trenches as the digging proceeds to ensure that the subsoil is really wet. Fork into the ground, when preparing it, a complete organic fertiliser like ground hoof and horn or fish manure, at 4 ozs. to the square yard, plus sulphate of potash at 2 ozs. to the square yard. Wood ashes may be given instead of the latter, at ½ lb. per square yard.

Plant 12 ins. apart, with 18 ins. and 30 ins. alternately, to allow space for working, between the rows.

See that the soil is at a temperature of not less than 58° Fahr., or the roots of the plants when put into the soil will die. Make a hole with the trowel, as advised for planting in pots and boxes, and treat the plants similarly. Water the plants for 2 or 3 days after planting, and again a week later. Then do not water until the flowers of the second truss are opening in 6 or 7 weeks' time. After this do not water until the tomatoes really need it, i.e. when the leaves start to look dull and grey, and just before they start to droop. Ventilate as much as possible during the day and keep the air buoyant. Try and not allow the temperature to drop below 60° Fahr.

Top Dressings

Give the plants a top dressing every 14 days after the first truss has set consisting of an organic fertiliser like fish, with a potash content of about 20% and a nitrogen content of 5%. A feeding with Liquinure Tomato Special is an alternative. After the fifth truss has set, it is usual to be a little more liberal, so as to get the plants growing vigorously again. When this happens the normal top dressings may be resumed once more.

In the case of pots and boxes, it is usual to give a top dressing of the John Innes Compost No. 2 to a depth of 2 ins. after the first 3 trusses of fruit have set. Six weeks afterwards another such top dressing is given. A good watering has to be done each time to settle the soil. Remember that pot and box plants require more watering and manuring than those growing in the border.

Training and Tying
One method of training tomatoes is to tie them up to bamboos, a tie being made, as a rule, just below each truss. Another method is to stretch wires tightly along the ground—with others running parallel to them at the top of the house. String, or 4-ply fillis, is then tied from the top wire to the bottom wire and, as each plant grows, it is twisted around its particular length of string or fillis.

Temperature and Ventilation
The minimum night temperature should not fall below 63° Fahr. and should never be above 75° Fahr. A higher temperature in the daytime from sun-heat, of course, does not matter.

Keep the plants cool by overhead syringing in May and June. From June onwards, it is possible to keep the ventilators open, even at night time. To prevent a bad attack of mould or mildew (*Cladosporium*) keep on a little pipe heat so as to cause air movement. Keep the ventilators open at either ends of the house so as to ensure end-on movement of air.

Side Shooting, Stopping and Defoliation
Remove the side shoots regularly by giving them a sharp pull sideways. Pinch out the growing point of a plant (this is known as stopping) when it has reached the top of the house, or 6 weeks before the plants are to be pulled out, whichever occurs the soonest.

Remove the bottom leaves when they turn yellow by cutting them back right to their base. If the foliage is very dense, it is possible to cut off one whole leaf between the second and fourth truss.

Watering, Syringing, Mulching and Shading
Syringing the plants overhead on bright days helps to distribute pollen. Cease syringing when the plants have got to their maximum height. If the borders have been properly flooded in the winter, it should not be necessary to water for 6 weeks after

the first few days after planting. Water in the morning, if possible, and, from June onwards, about once a week, but on very dry soils, twice a week. When the surface of the soil becomes hard, fork it to allow the water to pass through. Insufficient watering can cause uneven ripening of the fruit and the disorder called blossom end rot.

If the surface of the soil is covered with a 6-in. layer of damped horticultural peat or straw, it prevents soil splashing on to the lower fruits—the general cause of buck eye rot.

On the whole, peat is better than straw, and the plants may root into it.

In very hot summers it may be necessary to give the roof of the tomato house a little shading to prevent sun scorch.

VARIETIES

For early work in pots
J. R. 6. Short jointed, sets freely.
Potentate,[1] (Reselected stock) heavy cropper, large fruits.

For winter work in pots
Ailsa Craig, smooth fruits, medium size, good shape.
Dutch Victory, non green-back variety.
Bonne Chose, early fruiting, a Guernsey favourite.

For normal growing in spring and summer
Eurocross A. Heavy cropping, good quality, resistant to Cladosporium. Non green-back, resistant to Cladosporium.
Supercross. Heavy cropping first class hybrid.
Histon Ideal. Heavy cropping, brilliant scarlet, excellent fruit quality.
Moneymaker. Short jointed, fruits solid, round, bright red.
Eurocross B. Heavy cropping, immune to Cladosporium, specially useful in dull seasons.
Ware Cross, first class hybrid, good quality; early. High yield.
Unwin's Prizetaker. Very early, excellent where quality is the first consideration. Stop at the seventh truss.
Be liberal with potash.

Note.—One man's variety is another man's poison! The great thing is to find out the variety that suits your soil and grow it well.

---

[1] This variety will grow well with Cucumbers; so if a house has to be devoted to both crops—this is the one to choose.

115. Raspberry beetle grub

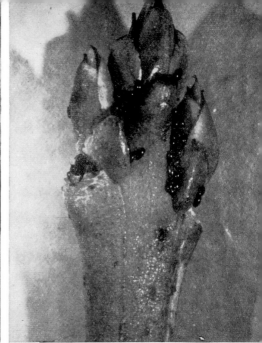

116. Eggs of bean aphis laid on shoot of spindle tree

117. Cherry showing die-back

118. Big bud on blackcurrant

119. Celery fly grubs on back of leaf

120. Turnip plant ravaged by flea beetle

PART EIGHT

FIGHTING THE FOE
GARDEN PESTS AND DISEASES

A special note on NO-SOIL composites
for all pot plants (see page 576)

NO SOIL Seeding Compost

The new Seeding Compost is composed of specially selected and processed Sedge Peat and a specific sand, together with fertilisers, lime and trace elements.

Instructions for use of Seedling Compost

1. Condition Seeding Compost with water at the rate of 8 to 10 pints per bushel or 2½ to 3 gallons per hundredweight of Seedling Compost. Use higher rate if Compost feels dry initially.
2. Mix to distribute and hasten the uniform spread of moisture. It is convenient to moisten up several hours before use and leave in a close heap to facilitate the natural spread of moisture.
3. Fill seed trays evenly and only firm lightly.
4. After sowing and covering, thoroughly moisten Compost by dipping seed trays in shallow water or water from above with a very fine rose.
5. Cover to prevent surface drying out.

NO SOIL Potting Compost

The Seedling Compost is converted into Potting Compost by the addition of the Potting Base supplied. The Potting Base has been specially formulated to give the correct N.P.K. ratios for the Compost. Potting Composts of strengths 1, 2 and 3 may be made up by adding the Potting Base to the Seedling Compost at the following rates per bushel or per cwt. of Seedling Compost.

	Per bushel	Per cwt.
Potting Compost No. 1	11 ozs.	1¾ lb. of Potting Base
Potting Compost No. 2	22 ozs.	3½ lb. of Potting Base
Potting Compost No. 3	33 ozs.	5¼ lb. of Potting Base

NOTE: For small quantities, 1 bushel equals 8 gallons and 3 ozs. Potting Base is approximately 1 level teacup.

Instructions for making-up and use of Potting Compost

1. Add 1¾ lb., 3½ lbs. or 5¼ lbs. of Potting Base per hundredweight of Seedling Compost to make up Potting Composts No. 1, 2 or 3 as required.
2. Mix *very thoroughly* to ensure even spread of Potting Base.
3. Condition with water at the rate of 8 to 10 pints per bushel or 2¼ to 3 gallons per hundredweight.
4. Mix and leave for several hours as suggested under "Seedling Compost."
5. Fill boxes and pots evenly, strike off level and plant with minimum firming. Consolidation will be achieved by subsequent watering.
6. Water in and again in 2 or 3 days in bright weather. In dull weather avoid over-watering in the early stages of plant establishment.
7. Aim to keep the Compost open, particularly in the early stages, by watering gently. Give sufficient water at each application to moisten all the Compost in pot as Compost will absorb more water than a loam Compost.
8. Keep Compost uniformly moist.

Introduction

IT is always a good thing to know why we do a thing, and this applies to gardening quite as much as to other enterprises. Consequently, to understand why we use, say, Karathane for controlling mildew on apples and Derris to rid cabbages of caterpillars, we must know something of the nature of pests and diseases.

Generally speaking, it can be said that a PEST is an INSECT which is feeding upon a plant, while a DISEASE is a minute and primitive PLANT growing upon another plant. The only exception perhaps to this rule is the virus disease which has now been shown to be an " auto-catalytic " protein.

From this simple definition it will be seen that quite different methods must be adopted for the control of these two types of parasite. Pests move about more or less actively over the plant and actually consume the foliage. They have a nervous system which can be paralysed and digestive organs which can often be poisoned. Pests, in fact, *can be killed once they are on the plant.*

On the other hand, the minute plants which constitute diseases usually grow within the plant, and can only be seen when they push outwards to form their myriads of primitive seeds known as " spores."

Plants must be *protected against diseases*—it is too late to do more than check the spread to healthy tissues once the disease is seen.

In the following lists, the various kinds of pests and diseases which harass the gardener are described under the heading of the fruit or vegetable which they normally attack. For example, bean aphis, bean red spider, cabbage flea beetle, cabbage mealy aphis, etc. An exception, however, is made in the case of Flower Pests and Diseases. Here the treatment is reversed and the pests and diseases are described individually, with a list of the main flowers attacked given in each instance.

THE GARDENER'S MEDICINE CHEST

It is a very good thing to have a Garden Medicine Chest containing all the remedies needed to keep plants well and free from diseases and pests.

I have tried to classify them under various headings for ease of reference (*a*) Insecticides, (*b*) Fungicides, (*c*) Baits and (*d*) Fumigants.

INSECTICIDES

Calomel Dust

A 4% dust is used to control onion fly and cabbage root fly. A teaspoonful may be sprinkled round each plant or it may be dusted down the rows. (See illustration facing page 673.)

Derris

A very useful insecticide which can be applied either as a dust (see illustration facing page 672) or as a spray. It will control all kinds of caterpillars and aphids and many other pests including red spider. Can safely be used on plants right up to picking time.

Gammexane—Gamma B.H.C. or Lindane

An effective remedy against flea beetle. For flea beetle dust the rows of seedlings just before they germinate, and again afterwards. For wireworm, work dust into the soil before sowing, or planting at 1 oz. per square yard. (Under suspicion.)

Malathion

A synthetic phosphorous insecticide often wrongly regarded as dangerous. It is in fact non-persistent, relatively non-toxic to humans and birds, and in fact the safest insecticide to use. Controls most pests, including red spider, but is not effective against caterpillars. Has given trouble on some varieties of roses.

Nicotine

An effective remedy for aphids, though very poisonous. Pure nicotine (98%) is used at the rate of $\frac{1}{4}$-$\frac{1}{2}$ fluid ounce to 5 gals. of water, with the addition of a spreader such as Stergene. Alternatively, a nicotine dust may be used.

Pyrethrum

An insecticide of rapid action, very useful against aphides and against most other pests, especially when mixed with Derris.

The Gardener's Medicine Chest

Tar Oil

Used in the winter as a 5% solution on fruit trees. It kills aphis and caterpillar eggs which overwinter on the trees.

Whizzed Naphthalene

Sprinkled along the rows of plants it will keep away carrot and onion flies.

FUNGICIDES

Bordeaux Mixture

Used chiefly against potato blight, but will also control other diseases such as celery blight. It is made by mixing ¾ lb. copper sulphate and 1 lb. of quicklime with 10 gals. of water.

Captan

One of the new synthetic fungicides. Particularly good for apple and pear scab. Also used for storage rots on bulbs and seed dressing against soil-borne funge. Not effective against powdery mildews.

Colloidal Copper

A very fine copper dust which is an effective control for such diseases as black spot of roses, and many of the rusts.

Colloidal Sulphur

Used against mildews and sometimes against apple and pear scab. Does *not* stain the leaves like lime-sulphur.

Dispersible Sulphur

Very effective against powdery mildew of all kinds. A safe form of sulphur for use on sulphur shy varieties of apples where it controls both apple scab and apple mildew.

Karathane

One of the new synthetic fungicides used specifically against powdery mildews.

Lime-Sulphur

Used against scab on fruit trees. Other diseases controlled with this fungicide are gooseberry mildew and raspberry cane spot. It is also used for a pest—big bud mite on blackcurrants.

Mercury

Products based on mercury are used for killing fungus diseases of turf. These products are poisonous and are usually available only through chemists.

Sulphur Dust

A very fine type of sulphur dust should be used for mildews on all types of crops.

645

The Complete Gardener

BAITS AND WORM KILLERS

Metaldehyde

An excellent remedy for slugs when crushed and mixed with moistened bran, damp tea leaves or sawdust, and placed in small heaps 2 ft. apart. 1 oz. of powdered metaldehyde should be mixed with about 3 lbs. of carrier. If domestic animals are likely to be in the garden cover the little heaps with tiles or slates. Sold to-day in pellet form as Slugit.

Mowrah Meal

Used for killing worms on lawns, and also for chafers. It is scattered at the rate of 4-8 ozs. per square yard and well watered in. The worms come to the top and can be swept up.

FUMIGANTS

Calcium Cyanide

A very poisonous white powder used at the rate of $\frac{1}{4}$ oz. per 1,000 cu. ft. in the greenhouse to kill pests. The air must be fairly dry and the temperature up a little. The dust should be sprinkled on the floor working towards the door. The greenhouse should be closed all night and be opened early in the morning before the sun strikes on the plants.

Naphthalene (Grade 16)

Used at 4-6 ozs. per 1,000 cu. ft. in the greenhouse to control red spider and thrips. Also employed as a soil fumigant, dug into vacant ground at the rate of 4 ozs. per square yard.

Nicotine

Vapourised nicotine, using $\frac{1}{4}$ oz. per 1,000 cu. ft. is an excellent control for aphids under glass.

Auto-Shreds

Special treated material which when burnt gives off nicotine smoke which kills insect pests.

Azobenzene

" Smokes " containing this chemical give very good control of red spider under glass.

The gardener will find that the whole subject has been brought up to date in the light of modern research. Control measures are quoted for each pest and disease, but new materials will only be recommended where they are known to mark a definite advance in efficiency of control, safety to the plant and ease of use.

It will be possible to purchase the fungicides and insecticides recommended in this book from any good horticultural chemist or salesman. Very often, however, the specifics are sold under proprietary names.

Garden Pests

FLOWER PESTS

★

A LIMITED range of pests attack flowers in general, so it will be less confusing to describe the pests themselves with a note of the main flowers concerned.

NOTE ON WARM-WATER TREATMENT

The warm-water treatment is recommended at various places in the text for controlling eelworms, mites and bulb fly. The affected plants, or bulbs, washed free of soil, are packed into a wire basket and immersed in a tank of water maintained at 110-112° Fahr. Below 110° Fahr. the pests are not all killed; above 112° Fahr. the plants themselves may succumb.

Time of Treatment
Chrysanthemum stools and strawberry plants, 20 minutes; bulbs, 60 minutes; large bulbs, 90 minutes.

After Treatment
Plunge bulbs or roots into cold water to give rapid cooling. Re-plant in clean or sterilised soil.

APHIDS (Plant Lice)
The commonest of all flower pests. They vary from green to black and reddish. Usually found on young growth, especially in spring. But checked growth, due to dry weather, may allow pests to become established. Leaves crinkled and distorted and growth stunted. Usually, first sign of aphid attack is the activity of ants which feed on the sticky " honeydew " excreted by the aphids.

Control Measures
Spray as soon as insects are seen with Liquid Derris I.T.P. or dust with Derris. Repeat as necessary.

CAPSIDS (The Green Capsid and the Tarnished Plant Bug)

Both common flower pests which are about ¼ in. long, move actively and are seldom seen. They puncture the foliage, and growing points, and distort the flowers. Serious on chrysanthemums, dahlias and delphiniums.

Control Measures
Spray or dust with nicotine or Derris plus pyrethrum as for aphids but, since the bugs drop when disturbed, treat the soil round the plants as well.

CATERPILLARS

Several types cause damage, but the chief types are:

I. ANGLE SHADES MOTH CATERPILLARS
The caterpillars of this shy moth are greenish brown and may be found devouring a wide range of flowering plants. Chrysanthemums, dahlias, gladioli and roses are all attacked.

Control Measures
Spray with liquid Derris and pyrethrum mixed. Repeat as necessary.

II. SWIFT MOTH CATERPILLARS
White soil caterpillars which cause serious root damage to herbaceous plants in general and to many corms, bulbs and rhizomes.

Control Measures
Maintain clean cultivation and work in Flaked Naphthalene, 2-4 ozs. per square yard, where necessary.

III. TORTRIX MOTH CATERPILLARS
These pests draw together several leaves into a sort of tent. Shoots are killed or distorted. Very general.

Control Measures
Habit of rolling leaves protects the pest, but hand-picking, or crushing, is the best control.

Cuckoo Spit

Conspicuous masses of froth on the tips of many plants including lavender, phlox, roses. Small yellow, or greenish, bug sucks the sap and exudes froth as protection.

Control Measures
As for Aphids

Earwigs

Well known to all gardeners. They damage petals of many flowers, and particularly dahlias.

Control Measures
Trap with inverted pots filled with dry grass on supporting canes.

Eelworms

Microscopic, worm-like pests which live within the plant and cause distortion of the stems and foliage, e.g. phlox, leaf yellow and final death, chrysanthemums.

Control Measures
See Warm-Water Treatment, page 647.

Leaf Miners

Tiny grubs which feed within the leaves and produce silvery tunnels. The fly is seldom noticed but lays eggs beneath the leaf. Most common on chrysanthemums.

Control Measures
Spray at weekly intervals with diluted Nicotine Insecticide or spray with Pyrethrum when first seen and again 2 weeks later.

Narcissus Bulb Flies

A fly like a small bee lays eggs at the base of the leaves in May and the grub bores into the fleshy tissue and causes softening, " blindness " and, finally, death of the bulb.

Control Measures
See Warm-Water Treatment, page 647. Spray foliage thoroughly in mid-May, early June and end of June.

RED SPIDERS

Often a serious pest of flowers in hot dry seasons. Particularly bad in 1947. The leaves first show a curious speckling and later turn brown, while the plant is stunted and the flowers small and often distorted.

Control Measures
> The only satisfactory method is thorough spraying—especially beneath the leaves, with liquid derris. Repeat every 14 days until the weather becomes moister.

SLUGS AND SNAILS

Cause all too familiar damage to most garden plants.

Control Measures
> Place small pellets of Metaldehyde known as Slugit around plants. Fork in powdered lime and powdered copper sulphate mixed together in equal parts at 1 oz. per square yard.

SOIL PESTS

Chafer grubs, wireworms, leather jackets, millipedes, cutworms, caterpillars. They attack roots of most plants causing great destruction.

Control Measures
> Control by frequent cultivation. This brings chafers, wireworms etc., to the surface, where they will be eaten by birds and affected by weather.

THRIPS

Tiny insects causing silvering of foliage and "blind" shoots.

Control Measures
> As for APHIDS.

WOODLICE

These greyish creatures live on decaying matter and also attack seedlings and plants with soft stems.

Control Measures
> Derris dusted all round the edges of paths, beds, greenhouse borders and so on, should prevent woodlouse attacks.

FRUIT TREE PESTS

★

APPLE APHIDS (Green Fly)

The aphids attacking apples include the rosy apple aphis, the green apple aphis and the small black apple aphis. However, the effect on the tree is very similar in most cases and the methods of control are the same, so they will be considered as a group.

The colours of the insects vary considerably, but they are all similar to the familiar green fly of the garden. Attack by aphids often results in distortion and curling of the young foliage and shoots. The pest lives through the winter in the form of small, black, shiny eggs which can be easily seen.

Control Measures

> Spray during the fully dormant season with a Tar Distillate Wash at a strength of 1 pt. in $2\frac{1}{2}$ gals. of water. Spray very thoroughly in calm, dry weather, and ensure wetting of all the branches, especially the young growth. Any aphids which escape the winter spraying can be controlled by spraying or dusting with Derris preparations during the growing season.

APPLE BLOSSOM WEEVIL

The insect concerned is a small black beetle, about $\frac{1}{6}$ in. long, with a white V-shaped mark on its back and a long " nose." Eggs are laid in the young blossoms and the developing grub eats away the tissues, which would have otherwise become the fruit, and the petals fail to open. The result is aptly known as a " capped " blossom. If these " capped " blossoms are examined after the normal flowering period, the small yellow chrysalis or the beetle will be found.

Control Measures

> Spray with nicotine emulsion at the "bud-burst" stage.

APPLE CAPSID BUG

A common garden and orchard pest which does considerable damage to both the leaves and fruit. It is a small green insect

651

which can often be seen in early spring moving actively over the leaves. The fruit is punctured and rough, corky patches are produced during growth. Eggs are laid in the bark of young shoots towards mid-summer and the best method of control involves killing these eggs. (See illustration facing page 633.)

Control Measures

The Tar Wash which is applied against aphis has no effect on capsid, and it is necessary to spray with a D.N.C. Wash about the middle of March. Strength to use is 1 pt. in 2 gals. of water, and the best result is obtained when the green tips of the young leaves are just showing in the fruit buds. If this application is omitted, apply a Derris Insecticide at the rate of 1 pt. to 10 gals. of water about a week before the tree is in full bloom.

APPLE CODLIN MOTH

A very common pest of apples which is most frequently the cause of maggoty fruit. The moth which only flies at night, and hence is not seen, lays eggs in the early summer on the young fruit and nearby leaves. The tiny caterpillars, which hatch from the eggs, enter the apple through the eye and sometimes through the side, as with the apple sawfly. The core is gradually eaten away and the apple reduced in value. The fruit often drops before it is ripe, though attacked apples may sometimes remain on the trees until picking time. Since the eggs are laid on the trees over a period of several weeks, it is necessary to use a poison which remains on the fruit for a considerable time. (See illustration facing page 633.)

Control Measures

A suitable material is Lead Arsenate, which is used at the rate of 1 oz. in 2 gals. of water. The application should be made within a week of petal fall, and may be combined with Nicotine Insecticide if trouble has been experienced with apple sawfly in previous seasons. Many of the caterpillars leave the fruit and seek places to hibernate until the following spring. In consequence, bands of sacking tied firmly around the trees just below the main branches will collect many of the caterpillars and the bands may be burnt in the winter.

Garden Pests

APPLE RED SPIDER

This is another widespread pest which attacks all types of fruit trees and it was particularly bad during 1947. Even woodland trees and hedges suffered, and the silvery appearance caused by a heavy attack must be well known to all gardeners. The tree is greatly weakened and the leaves drop prematurely. The insect itself is a tiny spider-like creature, red or brownish in colour, which may be found on the under surface of the leaves, often in very large numbers. The pest over-winters on the trees as bright red, minute eggs which are often clustered around fruit spurs. The whole tree may have a reddish sheen when bare of leaves.

Control Measures

The D.N.C. Wash applied to control capsid will also deal with red spider, but if only spider is present 1 pt. in $2\frac{1}{2}$ gals. of water is sufficient. Any eggs which escape the winter spray and develop into spiders can be controlled by a summer grade of Petroleum Oil, used at 1 pt. in $12\frac{1}{2}$ gals. of water. Derris sprays are also useful.

APPLE SAWFLY

The apple sawfly is an old pest in this country and is one of the insects which cause maggoty fruit. The small, yellowish-red fly lays eggs in the developing fruitlet and the maggot which hatches often eats its way over the surface of the young fruit before tunnelling inwards. The maggot feeds on the fruit which, during June, falls off the tree and the maggot escapes to form a chrysalis in the soil. The best means of distinguishing the maggot of the apply sawfly from that of the codlin moth, which causes similar damage though rather later in the season, is the very unpleasant smell given off by the sawfly " maggot." The codlin moth " maggot " has no odour.

Control Measures

Spray with Nicotine Insecticide at 1 pt. in 10 gals. of water as the blossoms are dropping from the tree. A second spray 1 week later should give complete control. This Nicotine may be added to the Lead Arsenate wash recommended for controlling codlin moth.

APPLE SCALES

Two types of scales can be grouped as one : the mussel scale and the brown soft scale. These are not uncommon on neglected trees and are easily visible on the bark as brown hard shells about $\frac{1}{8}$ in. in length. The outer covering protects the mass of insects which suck the sap from the tree.

Control Measures
> Both types are completely controlled by the usual strength of Tar Wash applied in the dormant season.

APPLE SUCKER

Not a common pest in these days except on neglected trees. Considerable damage may be caused to the developing blossoms, suggesting a spring frost.

Control Measures
> No concern need be felt regarding this pest since it is completely controlled by the usual strength of Tar Wash in the dormant season.

APPLE WINTER MOTH

The general term "winter moth" includes the winter moth proper, the match moth and the mottled umber moth, the caterpillars of which cause considerable damage to leaves and fruit. The male winter moth flies by night between October and January, while the female is wingless and crawls up the stem of the tree to lay her eggs. The eggs are found around the fruit spurs, and in cankers on the bark, and are red in colour but rather longer in shape than the red spider eggs for which they might be mistaken. The damage caused by the caterpillars which develop in the spring may entirely strip the trees of leaves.

Control Measures
> Since the female moth has to traverse the trunk to lay her eggs, she can be trapped by grease bands applied to the trunk during September. The Tar Distillate Wash kills most of the eggs if used at 10%.

APPLE WOOLY APHIS (American Blight)

Common on all kinds of fruit. It can be recognised in spring and summer as conspicuous white woolly patches in cracks in the bark and around young shoots; also prevalent round the unions of newly-grafted trees. (See illustration facing page 633.)

Control Measures

Dab the colonies with neat liquid Derris. The Tar Wash applied against aphis helps considerably. It is useful, however, to add Nicotine Insecticide to a Petroleum Wash to ensure a complete kill. Any colonies which become re-established in the summer are controlled with liquid Derris sprays.

CHERRY BLACK FLY

This pest can cause considerable damage to the young growth on cherry trees.

Control Measures

A satisfactory control is obtained by spraying with the usual strength of Tar Wash in the dormant season.

CHERRY FRUIT MOTH

The caterpillar of this pest destroys the flowers or young fruitlets and may entirely spoil a crop.

Control Measures

A dormant season application of Tar Wash at double strength, i.e. 1 pt. in $1\frac{1}{4}$ gals. of water, will give freedom from this pest.

CHERRY SLUGWORM

See PEAR SLUGWORM

PEAR APHIS (Green Fly)

Similar types of green fly attack pears as apples, but cause, as a rule, much less trouble.

Control Measures

Spray in the dormant season with Tar Wash at 1 pt. in $2\frac{1}{2}$ gals. of water. Use liquid Derris in the spring if this has been omitted.

PEAR MIDGE

The maggot of this pest causes young pear fruitlets to swell very rapidly and then fall from the trees.

Control Measures

This can be largely prevented by clean cultivation and, where serious, by spraying with Nicotine Insecticide at 1 pt. in 10 gals. of water when the trees are in full bloom. The soil should also be sprayed with Tar Oil at normal strength.

PEAR (*also* CHERRY) SLUGWORM

This sawfly is seldom seen, but the slugworm caterpillar is conspicuous on the upper surface of the leaves in June. The caterpillars are at first pale yellow and turn black as they grow. The top surface of the leaf is eaten away producing a skeleton effect. The insects may be found attacking the leaves from June until leaf-fall.

Control Measures

Spray with liquid Derris or Derris mixed with Pyrethrum. Apply as soon as the slugworms are seen.

PLUM APHIS

Several species are concerned, including the leaf-curling aphis and the mealy aphis. Both cause severe distortion and damage to the leaves and young shoots, and spoil the fruit where the attack is heavy.

Control Measures

All types of plum aphis may be readily controlled by spraying with Tar Wash at 1 pt. in $2\frac{1}{2}$ gals. of water in the dormant season, i.e. during December.

PLUM RED SPIDER

The description of this pest and effect on the tree are similar to that for red spider on apple. It is not uncommon in hot dry seasons, such as 1949.

Control Measures

A satisfactory control is obtained by the use of Pyrethrum as the fruit buds are swelling, and Derris washes can be used for summer attacks.

PLUM SAWFLY

The caterpillar of this pest feeds in the fruitlets causing many to drop to the ground while still small.

Control Measures

The trees should be sprayed with a proprietary Derris spray at the full recommended strength when the covering round the fruitlets is just beginning to split. This is usually a week or so after the blossom falls.

SECTION THREE

SOFT FRUIT PESTS

*

A NOTE ON BIRDS

BIRDS are sometimes troublesome in the garden, particularly where soft fruit is grown.

Control Measures

If necessary the bushes may be enclosed in a fruit cage. This is made by fastening wire-netting to stout wooden posts for the sides, as a permanent framework, with fish-netting over the top, which can be removed when the fruit has been picked. The top should not be made of wire netting, as the drips from the galvanised wire may damage the bushes, fruit and the bases of the posts. It is better to have the top removed in late summer, and in fact all the time, except when the fruit is ripening, as the birds do good by " picking up " caterpillars and insects.

Sometimes, birds do damage to gooseberry bushes by pecking the buds, but this trouble can usually be prevented by delaying pruning until late February or early March. Some form of bird-scarer may have to be erected among the crops in districts where birds are especially troublesome.

It has frequently been found that where birds are well provided with water they do not damage the crops. The gardener should, therefore, provide shallow pans of water and see that bird baths are kept filled.

BLACKBERRY BEETLE

See RASPBERRY BEETLE.

BLACKCURRANT GALL MITE (Big Bud)

A well-known and common pest of currants in general, but most conspicuous on blackcurrants where the buds are swollen and distorted, hence the name big bud. On red and white currants the buds are merely killed. This minute insect occurs in great numbers in the swollen buds and prevents normal development. Bad attacks affect the vigour of the plant and reduce the crop. (See illustration facing page 640.)

Control Measures

Spray, when the leaves reach the size of a two-shilling piece, with Lime-sulphur diluted at the rate of 1 pt. in 2½ gals. of water. This strength applies to all varieties except Goliath, Davison's Eight and Triple X; these varieties are sulphur shy, and the strength should be reduced to 1 pt. in 6 gals. of water.

CURRANT APHIDS (Green Fly)

Several types of green fly attack black, red and white currants and cause curling of the leaves with raised red patches, twisting of the new growth and fouling of the fruit with sticky honeydew. The aphids over-winter as eggs which may be found around the buds and stems.

Control Measures

Tar Wash at 1 pt. in 2½ gals. of water during January and February is completely effective. The green fly itself can be killed by liquid Derris at the usual strength, providing spraying is carried out before the insects are protected by the curling of the leaves.

GOOSEBERRY APHIDS

There are 2 common types: (1) the gooseberry aphis, which is dark green or grey and which attacks the leaves and young shoots causing distortion and stunting of the whole bush; and (2) the gooseberry elm aphis which feeds on the roots below ground level and produces masses of woolly material.

Control Measures

The former is cleared by spraying with 5% Nicotine Insecticide in the early summer, while the latter is killed by dipping the washed roots in the same solution.

GOOSEBERRY RED SPIDER

A pest which may be serious to the extent of causing the bushes to become bare of leaves within a few days in early summer. Feeding of large numbers of greyish spiders on under surface of leaves causes sickly appearance and poor fruit.

Control Measures

Spray immediately after flowering with Lime-sulphur, 1 pt. to 6 gals. of water. With sulphur-shy variety Leveller, substitute liquid Derris I.T.P.

GOOSEBERRY SAWFLY

The caterpillars are easily recognised as they are green, marked with black and orange. A bad attack will completely strip the foliage in a few days.

Control Measures

Dust the bushes with Derris powder as soon as the first small caterpillars are seen, or spray with liquid Derris.

LOGANBERRY BEETLE

See RASPBERRY BEETLE.

RASPBERRY BEETLE

A small brownish-yellow beetle which lays eggs in the young fruit soon after flowering. The grub which hatches bores into the fruit and causes the well-known maggots (see illustration, page 640).

Control Measures

Dust with Derris powder thoroughly, 7 days after flowering begins, or spray with liquid Derris, but not while bees are actively pollinating the flowers.

RASPBERRY MOTH

The red grub of this moth feeds on the young developing shoots in April-May, and causes withering and death. The crop may be considerably reduced.

Control Measures

The cocoon of this widespread, and often serious, pest is found in rubbish at the base of the canes. Hence, thorough clearing of all dead material in the autumn reduces the pest. The canes may also be sprayed with Tar Wash during the dormant season at a strength of 1 pt. in 2 gals. of water.

STRAWBERRY APHIDS

At least 4 types of green fly attack strawberries and cause various degrees of leaf curling. Control is important because these aphids carry the virus of such serious diseases as " Yellow Edge." (See VIRUS DISEASES, pages 685-686.)

Control Measures

Spray the plants in April, and again whenever necessary, with 5% Nicotine Wash—1 oz. to 10 gals. of water. Liquid Derris also gives good results.

STRAWBERRY EELWORM

Impossible to diagnose by the gardener, but may be the cause of thickening of the leaf stems, red tints of the leaves and general unthriftiness.

Control Measures
> *See* WARM-WATER TREATMENT, page 647.

STRAWBERRY RED SPIDER

This spider mite causes the leaves to become pale and speckled and may do much damage to the health of the plant. Usually not serious until after the fruit is picked.

Control Measures
> Spray with Lime-sulphur 1 pt. in 6 gals. of water in early May, wetting both sides of the leaves.

STRAWBERRY TARSONEMID MITE

A minute pest which causes young leaves to die before unfolding and older leaves to crinkle and pucker. Runner production is usually very poor and weak.

Control Measures
> *See* WARM-WATER TREATMENT, page 647.

STRAWBERRY WEEVILS

Several weevils cause damage to the fruit or to the developing flower buds and stems. They appear in the spring and have the typically long " noses " of this type of beetle.

Control Measures
> Apply a strong Derris-pyrethrum dust in early May and again in early June.

VEGETABLE PESTS

★

ASPARAGUS BEETLE

Small beetle with black head and red body. The eggs laid from June onwards develop into greyish-yellow grubs which often strip the summer fronds thereby weakening the plant.

Control Measures

The beetles hibernate in rubbish around the plant and this should be cleared in winter and burned. Apply Derris powder as soon as the first grubs are seen. Repeat if necessary.

BEAN APHIS

A black aphis which often completely smothers the heads of broad beans in May. The plant stops growing and the few pods which develop become covered with a black sticky excretion. Also attacks runner beans on occasion. (See illustration facing page 640.)

Control Measures

Spray with liquid Derris or dust with Derris dust. Repeat if necessary. Remove tops of plants as soon as sufficient pods produced. Autumn sown beans suffer least.

BEAN RED SPIDER

Causes runner bean leaves to turn sickly brown in hot dry summers. Spider mites easily visible on under surface of leaves.

Control Measures

Spray thoroughly with summer Petroleum Oil, 1 pt. in $12\frac{1}{2}$ gals. of water, directing the spray beneath the leaves.

BEAN THRIPS

See PEA THRIPS.

BEAN WEEVIL

See PEA WEEVIL.

CABBAGE FLEA BEETLE

Small grey beetles which eat off young seedlings of all cabbage

661

types, turnips and swedes as they come through the soil. Larger seedlings have leaves punctured. (See illustration facing page 641.)

Control Measures

Apply a Derris and Pyrethrum dust along rows as soon as seedlings appear.

CABBAGE GALL WEEVIL

See TURNIP GALL WEEVIL

CABBAGE MEALY APHIS

A greyish-mauve mealy aphis which attacks all members of the cabbage family in great numbers when autumn weather is hot and dry. Leaves are distorted and growth is retarded.

Control Measures

Spray thoroughly with a Pyrethrum Wash or dust with Derris powder. Repeat as necessary.

CABBAGE ROOT FLY

The maggot of this widespread and serious pest attacks the roots and bores into the rootstock. Attacked plants wilt and maggots are easily visible when plants are carefully pulled up.

Control Measures

Pour a little mercuric chloride solution into the holes at planting time. Dip roots before planting in sludge made from 4% Calomel Dust and water.

CABBAGE WHITE CATERPILLARS (and allied types)

The familiar white and yellowish-green butterflies lay their eggs in masses on the leaves and the green and brownish caterpillars feed voraciously. Butterflies of second brood often very common in early autumn.

Control Measures

Dust with Derris and Pyrethrum powder when first small caterpillars seen.

CABBAGE WHITE FLY

Small white flies which weaken plant by sucking sap and disfigure leaves with black frass.

Control Measures

Dust with Derris powder as required.

Garden Pests

CAULIFLOWER PESTS

Cauliflowers are attacked by the same pests as cabbages. Similar control measures apply.

CARROT FLY

Small shiny bottle-green fly which lays eggs in early spring on seedling carrots (also parsley and celery) near ground level. Maggots bore into roots and cause familiar rusty tunnels. Foliage unhealthy and autumn tints develop early.

Control Measures
(1) Deter egg laying by scattering whizzed Naphthalene between rows to mask smell of crop. (2) Spray rows at fortnightly intervals with a Pysect emulsion. (3) Bank soil up to plants after thinning, to hamper egg laying.

CELERY FLY (Leaf Miner)

Eggs laid on under surface of leaves and maggots tunnel within the leaves. Silvery and later brown appearance of leaves easily recognised. (See illustration facing page 641.)

Control Measures
Spray plants with Nicotine when the plants are very young and at planting out time.

LETTUCE APHIS

Leaves distorted and stunted.

Control Measures
Spray with usual strength Malathion, or dust with Derris dust.

LETTUCE ROOT APHIS

A mealy-looking aphis which feeds below ground on the roots. Growth poor and stunted.

Control Measures
Examine late season plants which are growing poorly and, if aphids are found present, water with usual strength of gamma B.H.C. at ½ pt. per plant.

663

MUSHROOM PESTS

For "Fly," Springtails, Woodlice and Mites, use Nicotine smoke.

ONION FLY

Small dark-grey fly lays eggs on young plants near soil level in spring. The pointed, dirty-white grubs eat away the developing bulb and the plant flags and gradually dies.

Control Measures

(1) Deter egg laying by scattering whizzed Naphthalene between rows.

PEA MOTH

Eggs are laid on the young pods and the maggot enters and devours the peas. These familiar maggots are found as the pods mature.

Control Measures

There is at present no really effective control available to amateurs, though infestation may be avoided by adjusting sowing date. Those peas are most affected which flower between early June and mid-August. So those sown either early or very late are most likely to escape.

PEA (and BEAN) WEAVIL

Small grey beetle with typically long nose. The leaves of the young plants are notched and the growing point damaged.

Control Measures

Dust with a Derris-pyrethrum powder as seedlings show through soil and again 14 days later.

PEA (and BEAN) THRIPS

Minute grey or brown insects with double pair of fringed wings which feed beneath the leaves and attack the growing points, causing silvery speckling and distortion. The pods may also assume a silvery appearance.

Control Measures

Reduce by weekly applications of Malathion.

Garden Pests

POTATO COLORADO BEETLE

A pest which was formerly confined to the Continent and America, but local attacks are becoming more frequent in this country. Serious problem in Jersey, Channel Islands. Bright yellow beetles with black stripes running down length of body. Grubs are orange yellow with black spots on side. Beetle about twice the size of a Ladybird.

Control Measures
> Notifiable pest. Send sample in a tin *without* air holes, together with name and address to Ministry of Agriculture, Whitehall Place, London, S.W.1. Do nothing further until advised.

RADISH PESTS

Radishes are members of the cabbage family and are attacked by the same pests. Similar control measures apply.

TURNIP GALL WEEVIL

All the members of the cabbage family are attacked by this weevil, the grub of which produces large galls at ground level or just beneath the soil. Distinguished from club root by presence of small white maggot within galls.

Control Measures
> Dust rows of seedlings, and later base of plants, with a Derris-pyrethrum powder at fortnightly intervals. On cabbages, Calomel treatment for club root and root fly deters gall weevil.

GREENHOUSE PESTS

APHIDS

These pests suck the sap from the leaves and growing points of plants, causing distortion and curling. They reproduce very rapidly.

Control Measures

Spray or fumigate with nicotine smoke.

MEALY BUG

A serious glasshouse pest which sucks sap from the leaves and stems of many greenhouse plants.

Control Measures

Mealy bug is not an easy pest to control because it is covered with a white mealy secretion. Sponge affected leaves with a nicotine solution. Fumigate with calcium cyanide in the winter in the case of vines.

RED SPIDER MITE

Sucks sap from leaves and shoots. It is encouraged by warm, dry conditions.

Control Measures

Fumigate with azobenzene "smokes." Spray with liquid Derris. Syringe the undersides of the leaves regularly to maintain a moist atmosphere.

SCALE INSECTS

These insects are covered by a hard horny scale which protects them and makes control difficult. They pierce the plant tissue and suck the sap from it.

Control measures

Spray with Malathion. Scrape off scales and wash with nicotine solution—$\frac{1}{2}$ oz. nicotine in 10 gals. of water.

THRIPS

Suck sap from leaves and shoots, causing silver-white marks on the foliage.

Control Measures

Spray with nicotine. Fumigate with nicotine smoke.

WHITE FLY

A greenhouse pest which attacks tomatoes, and many other crops and ornamental plants grown under glass.

Control Measures

A small parasitic fly known as *Encarsia formosa* may be introduced into infested houses and forms a good method of control. It lays its eggs on the white flies and so parasitises them. Spray with a nicotine wash.

CHAPTER II

Garden Diseases

FLOWER DISEASES

SUCH a wide range of flowers are grown in the garden and the resistance of different species, and even of varieties, differs so much that to attempt to cover even a portion in detail would be an impossible task in a brief work of this type.

While a host of diseases attack flowering plants, many of these are of more or less casual occurrence, and the important and general diseases are few and are all subject to the same broad methods of control.

Generally speaking, to deal with flower diseases:

(1) Give ample space for development.

(2) Maintain vigorous balanced growth.

(3) Spray or dust early and often when disease prevalent.

Spray both sides of the leaves, *particularly* the under surface.

Disease control specifics have advanced much less than insecticides, but a valuable spray material is available from Murphy's of Wheathampstead, Herts.

Common flower diseases are:

BOTRYTIS (Grey Mould)

Mainly confined to late-blooming flowers when weather is wet and cold. Fluffy dark-grey mould appears and destroys petals, leaves, etc.

Control Measures

Remove infected blooms and dust early with a fine sulphur dust or spray with colloidal sulphur.

DAMPING OFF

A very common disease which attacks seedlings, particularly

under glass and in damp, crowded conditions. The stems of the seedlings shrivel and the little plants topple over and eventually die. (See illustration facing page 632.)

Control Measures
>Water the seed boxes with Cheshunt compound, using ½ oz. of this compound to 1 gal. of water. Treating the seeds with Thiram dust generally helps greatly.

LEAF SPOT

Pale brown spots occur on the leaves and stems causing sometimes " shot hole " effect, sometimes premature leaf drop. Common on most flowers.

Control Measures
>As for RUSTS, or spray with colloidal sulphur plus a few drops of liquid spreader.

MILDEWS

White powdery markings appear on the leaves with distortion and stunting of the plant. Common in cold seasons on most flowers. Encouraged by dryness at the roots. (See illustration facing page 632.)

Control Measures
>Spray with Karathane.

ROOT ROTS

Common on most plants when soil cold and badly drained.

Control Measures
>Improve drainage. Destroy infected plants as shown by general unthriftiness and wilting. Water with usual strength Cheshunt compound in early stages.

RUSTS

Rusty pustules appear beneath the leaves, often in well-marked concentric rings. Pale patches are seen on the upper surface and early shrivelling and leaf drop occurs. Stem may also be attacked.

Plants chiefly attacked
>Antirrhinum, chrysanthemum, carnation, hollyhock, rose, sweet william.

Control Measures
>Spray in anticipation, or as soon as the first signs of the

disease appear, with a colloidal sulphur wash, or with dispersible sulphur.

Note.—Use the colloidal copper or colloidal sulphur at the maker's recommended strength. Remove badly-infected plants. Grow resistant strains where possible, e.g. in the case of antirrhinums.

FRUIT DISEASES

★

APPLE BLOSSOM WILT

A disease which attacks the flower trusses and which causes wilting and death. From a distance, bad attacks resemble fire scorch. Disease may spread back to the spur and branch, causing a bark canker.

Control Measures

> Cut out all cankered spurs as soon as noticed and burn. The Tar Oil wash (see PESTS) and spring Lime-sulphur washes (see APPLE SCAB below) help control this disease. Susceptible varieties : Cox's Orange Pippin, James Grieve, Rival, and especially Lord Derby. Resistant : Bramley's Seedling.

APPLE BROWN ROT

Attacks fruit at all stages and continues to be a source of trouble in store. Young apples become mummified on the trees and constitute a means of re-infection. Stored apples often turn black. (See illustration facing page 633.)

Control Measures

> Remove all mummified fruits and cankered spurs. Control all insect pests and diseases which cause wounds for this disease to get in.

APPLE CANKER

A very destructive disease causing stunting of old trees and, occasionally, death of young trees. First seen as sunken patches of bark surrounding insect punctures or cuts. Gradually spreads to open cankers which may surround branch. The bark usually swells prominently around cankered area. Weak growing varieties, and especially those on " dwarfing " rootstocks, most susceptible. Severe on most dessert varieties, less troublesome on culinary varieties.

Control Measures

> Paint cankers with Medo (see illustration facing page 673) or during winter, cut out all cankers to clean bark and paint over with white lead. Control other pests and diseases which allow the fungus to enter by causing punctures or broken bark, e.g. woolly aphis and scab.

APPLE MILDEW

The leaves become covered with mealy powder and the new shoots distorted and stunted. Often seen on leaves surrounding blossom and young fruit. Usually the fruit fails to develop and the tree is weakened. Bramley's Seedling and Cox's Orange Pippin are both susceptible. Worcester Pearman is fairly resistant.

Control Measures

Remove mildewed leaves and fruit cluster as far as possible. In winter prune away all young growth showing white or grey marking. The Karathane spray keeps mildew in check, but great care must be taken in its use.

APPLE PHYSIOLOGICAL DISEASES

Diseases which are functional and which cannot be traced to fungal attack.

I. BITTER PIT

Brown sunken marks on surface of fruit when ripe or in store, and brown patches scattered about flesh.

Control Measures

Avoid rank growth. Prune lightly. Apply wood ashes at 8 ozs. per square yard.

II. LENTICEL SPOTTING

Surface brown spotting arising from the small " pores," or lenticels, visible on ripe fruit. Usually worst in dry seasons and on sun-side of fruit.

Control Measures

Avoid checks in growth by watering and feeding where necessary.

III. WATER CORE OR GLASSINESS

The flesh around the core appears " glassy " and the trouble gradually spreads outwards to the skin. Attacks some varieties (e.g. Rival) more than others.

Control Measures

Avoid rank growth due to heavy feeding of trees with nitrogenous manures.

There are several more of these diseases, but all are considered to be caused by unbalanced growth.

121. *Spraying cordon apples*

122. *Spraying celery with solo sprayer*

123. *Dusting seedlings with Derris dust*

124. *Painting canker with Medo*

125. *Applying calomel dust round cabbage plants*

Garden Diseases

APPLE SCAB

By far the most general and troublesome disease attacking the apple. Small blister-like swellings are produced on the young wood, the leaves are blotched with black spots and the fruit develops black sunken areas which frequently become hard and crack. Severe attack completely spoils fruit, both in regard to size and appearance. Cox's Orange Pippin is very susceptible, but no really resistant varieties are known.

Balanced growth resists scab, whereas stunted or over-rank growth favours attack.

Control Measures

Captan may be sprayed on to the leaves and branches in all the "stages" mentioned below. It gives excellent results. Prune out and burn all diseased young wood. Spray as follows:

(a) *Green Bud (just as the buds break)*
Spray thoroughly with lime-sulphur according to the instruction on the container. Give the leaves a complete coverage.

(b) *Pink Bud (just before the blossoms open)*
As for "green bud," but add Derris if necessary for caterpillars. (See PESTS.)

(c) *Petal Fall*
Reduce strength of the lime-sulphur to say 1 in 80. Add a nicotine insecticide if sawfly needs controlling. (See PEST.)

(d) 14 *days after Petal Fall*
Repeat as for "Petal Fall."
Usually sprays (a) and (b) are sufficient.

APPLE STORAGE ROTS

A number of rot fungi attack apples in store and constant watch must be kept as spread from diseased to sound fruit is rapid.

Control Measures

Never store damaged fruit. Store in single layers on slatted trays. Spray trees with lime-sulphur in September.

BLACKBERRY BLUE STRIPE WILT

See RASPBERRY BLUE STRIPE WILT.

CHERRY BACTERIAL CANKER

Causes leaves to wither and shoots to die back. Sunken areas appear in the bark, cracking occurs and gum exudes. The whole tree may be killed if the main stem is girdled. Napoleon very susceptible ; Early Rivers fairly resistant.

Control Measures

There is no sure cure, but spraying with Bordeaux mixture at 1¼ lb. in 10 gals. of water in autumn, and ½ lb. in 10 gals. of water after fruit set, is recommended.

CHERRY BACTERIAL DIE-BACK

See PLUM BACTERIAL DIE-BACK. (See illustration facing page 640.)

CHERRY BLOSSOM WILT

Similar affect to that caused on plums and apples.

Control Measures

As for APPLES.

CHERRY WITCHES' BROOMS

A disease which causes a cluster of shoots to grow out into a broom-like structure.

Control Measures

Remove all abnormal growths in winter and spray with Bordeaux mixture, ½ lb. in 10 gals. of water, as leaves unfurl in spring.

CURRANT LEAF SPOT

Small brown spots appear on the leaves in early summer and the entire leaf may turn brown and fall off. Bushes seriously weakened.

Control Measures

Rake up and burn all fallen leaves in autumn and spray at fruit set stage as for Rust.

CURRANT REVERSION

A virus disease which causes the bushes to become unfruitful.

Leaves become smaller, dark green and altered in shape. Examine a typical leaf half-way down a young shoot. If there are less than 5 side veins running from the centre vein to the top leaf lobe, the bush is reverted.

Control Measures
> Pull out and burn diseased bushes and control big bud mite (see PESTS), since these pests spread the virus.

CURRANT RUST

Small yellow lumps appear beneath the leaves in summer and brownish marks appear on the upper surface. Later in the season, usually after picking, the leaves turn dark brown or nearly black. The bushes gradually become weakened.

Control Measures
> Spray with full strength Bordeaux mixture as soon as fruit is set, directing spray beneath the leaves. Spray with Thiram after picking and again twice at 10 day intervals.

GOOSEBERRY AMERICAN MILDEW

The most serious disease attacking this fruit. Disease first seen as white powdery patches on the young leaves and developing shoots. The disease spreads to the fruit which becomes covered with a white web and fails to develop. As the season passes, black spots can be seen on the white mildewed surfaces, and these are the spores which carry the disease over the winter.

Control Measures
> Avoid overcrowding of the bushes and maintain clean cultivation and well-balanced growth by high potash fertilisers. As soon as disease is seen, dust bushes with sulphur or spray with Karathane.

GOOSEBERRY CLUSTER CUP RUST

Orange blotches appear on the leaves, fruit and shoots. Wart-like effect produced on fruit.

Control Measures
> Spray Bordeaux mixture with full strength, about 14 days before the flowers open.

GOOSEBERRY EUROPEAN MILDEW

Rather similar to American Mildew but mildew mainly confined to top surface of the leaves and rarely attacks the berries.

Control Measures

Avoid overcrowding the bushes and dust with sulphur as necessary.

LOGANBERRY BLUE STRIPE WILT

See RASPBERRY BLUE STRIPE WILT.

PEACH LEAF CHLOROSIS

Paleness of leaves due to deficiency of soil iron, or inability of the plant to take up iron.

Diagnosis

Spray 1 small branch bearing pale leaves with a solution of sulphate of iron, 1 oz. in 1 gal. of water, with the addition of a few drops of liquid wetter. Marked greening of these leaves within a few days proves iron deficiency.

Control Measures

Spray whole tree with iron solution as above. Avoid liming soil and feed several times during season with 1 oz. per square yard of sulphate of ammonia. Maintain adequate water supply.

PEACH LEAF CURL

Leaves develop prominent raised red blotches and become twisted and swollen. Leaf drop occurs early and health of tree impaired.

Control Measures

Remove affected leaves early in the season. Spray with colloidal copper towards end of February, when buds are just swelling.

PEAR CANKER

The appearance is exactly similar to the lesions caused on apples and the disease is identical.

Control Measures

As described for apples. The variety Fertility is very susceptible to canker.

PEAR SCAB

A slightly different fungus from that attacking the apple, but appearances and effects on leaves, shoots and fruits are identical.

Most varieties other than Conference are very susceptible and spraying should be carried out.

Control Measures

As for apple scab; use lime-sulphur. A prepared form is most convenient and should be made up by mixing with a little water to a "cream" and diluting with clean water. Keep the suspension well stirred during use. The stages for application are: (1) Green Bud; (2) White Bud; (3) Petal Fall; and if possible (4) 14 days later.

PLUM BACTERIAL DIE-BACK

General name for a group of more or less obscure bacterial and fungal diseases which cause branches to die back to main trunk, and may even kill the tree. Victoria rather susceptible.

Control Measures

Prune away all dead wood to live tissue and paint cuts which are over $\frac{1}{4}$ in. across.

PLUM BLOSSOM WILT

May cause complete loss of crop when the weather is wet at blossoming time. The same fungus causes withering of the tips of new growth, spur canker and brown rot of the fruit.

Control Measures

Remove all withered shoots, cankered spurs and mummified fruit. Spray with normal strength Captan or Bordeaux mixture at White Bud stage.

PLUM BRANCH DIE-BACK

Similar effect on Bacterial Die-back, but frequently small gelatinous bodies can be seen on dead wood when the weather is moist.

Control Measures

Prune away all dead wood.

PLUM FRUIT GUMMING

The fruit exudes blobs of transparent gum. No disease concerned, and caused probably by poor growing conditions.

Control Measures

Maintain steady growing conditions by correct manuring and watering where necessary.

PLUM SILVER LEAF

A very serious disease, especially on Victorias. Infected branches bear silvery leaves and the wood is stained brown. Death gradually occurs, sometimes after several seasons. Usually the whole tree dies if infected branches are not dealt with properly.

Control Measures
> Cut out branches bearing silvered leaves in autumn after first appearance of trouble and *burn* the branches. Paint the cuts with White Lead at once. This is a " scheduled disease " and branches which have not been cut as soon as noticed and have reached the wilting stage must, by law, be removed before July 15th, as after this time bracket-like purple growths appear on the bark and the spores given off are highly infectious to neighbouring trees.

PLUM SOOTY BLOTCH

A disease which causes sooty patches on the fruit, especially in wet seasons. It is most obvious on pale skinned varieties such as Victorias.

Control Measures
> Spray with lime sulphur ½ pt. to 6 gals. of water, 14 days after blossoming.

RASPBERRY BLUE STRIPE WILT

Blueish stripe appears on canes, starting usually at the base. Leaves on the affected side develop yellow blotches between veins. The leaves curl inwards exposing the white under surface. Mainly confined to raspberries.

Control Measures
> Improve cultivation, apply balanced manures and remove badly affected canes.

RASPBERRY CANE BLIGHT

The leaves wilt and wither and the canes become brittle at ground level and often break off. Lloyd George is particularly susceptible.

Control Measures
> Remove all diseased canes right at the base and burn at once. Maintain balanced growth.

Garden Diseases

RASPBERRY CANE SPOT (Anthracnose)

Small purple circular spots appear at the base of the new canes in early summer. The spots later turn into sunken cankers. Heavy attacks may kill the canes, especially at the tips. Lloyd George susceptible ; Pyne's Royal resistant.

Control Measures

Apply full strength Bordeaux mixture when leaf buds commence to " move," and half-strength Bordeaux mixture when flower buds show white tips.

STRAWBERRY LEAF SPOT

Leaves become covered with reddish spots causing early death.

Control Measures

Burn off the leaves and straw after picking. Destroy stock if disease very prevalent.

STRAWBERRY MILDEW

Black blotches appear on leaves which later curl up. Royal Sovereign fairly resistant.

Control Measures

Apply a fine dust up to time of picking and burn off leaves and straw after picking. Strawberries grown with a deep mulch of sedge peat or powdery compost seldom if ever get mildew.

STRAWBERRY VIRUS DISEASES

The Strawberry is subject to a number of virus diseases which cause yellowing of the leaf edges, crinkling of the leaves, distortion of the plant and gradual degeneration.

Control Measures

None. Burn all unthrifty plants and apply nicotine preparations to healthy plants to control aphids which spread Virus diseases. (See PESTS.)

VIRUS DISEASES

Very widespread and serious group caused, not by pests or fungus diseases, but by physiological disorders.

Examples

Mosaic (see page 686), Spotted Wilt (see page 686), Crinkle, Yellow Edge (see above).

Control Measures

None known. Burn all infected plants.

679

VEGETABLE DISEASES

★

ASPARAGUS ROOT ROT

A coppery coloured "web" appears on the rootstock and main roots causing death of the plant.

Control Measures

Dig out infected section of the bed and replace with fresh soil to depth of 12 ins. or fork in 4% Calomel dust at rate of 4 ozs. per square yard.

ASPARAGUS RUST

Brown rusty blisters appear on the stems during summer, and the leaflets turn brown. The plant is weakened.

Control Measures

Spray with full strength Bordeaux mixture as soon as rust is seen. Remove fronds before leaflets fall to the ground and burn at once.

BEAN DISEASES—DWARF AND RUNNER

I. BEAN ANTHRACNOSE

Plants covered with small black spots often surrounded by red patches. Particularly bad in wet cold seasons when whole plant may fail. Infected seed is spotted or blotched and should not be sown.

Control Measures

Spray as soon as disease is seen with half-strength Bordeaux mixture (i.e. ½ lb. in 10 gals. water).

II. BEAN HALO BLIGHT

Dark angular spots surrounded by a lighter " halo " appear on all parts of the plant. Infected portions wilt and die.

Control Measures

Sow only reliable seed. Remove and burn all infected plants as soon as seen. Avoid overcrowding.

III. BROAD BEAN CHOCOLATE SPOT

All parts of the plant are dotted with irregular chocolate-coloured spots or streaks, especially in wet seasons.

Garden Diseases

Control Measures

Encouraged by excessive growth. Apply ample potash and lime before sowing. Avoid overcrowding.

BEET LEAF SPOT

Disease causing spotting, and later, perforation, of the leaves. Crop is reduced.

Control Measures

Burn all fallen leaves and spray with full-strength Bordeaux mixture as soon as first spots appear. Soak seeds as for " black leg." (See below.)

BEETROOT DAMPING OFF (Black Leg)

Seedlings damp off and roots of somewhat older plants turn black and fail to develop.

Control Measures

This disease is usually seed carried and reliable firms treat their beet seed. Added precaution is to soak seed for 10 minutes in formaldehyde solution, 1 tablespoonful to 1 pt. of water. Dress the seed with thiram dust before sowing.

CABBAGE CLUB ROOT (Finger and Toe, Anbury)

The most serious disease which attacks members of the cabbage family including turnips, wallflowers, stocks, etc. Roots become swollen, distorted and often clubbed to prodigious size. Plant fails to develop and may die.

Control Measures

Lime soil thoroughly each year. Follow routine outlined for control of cabbage root fly (see PESTS), i.e. use 4% calomel dust in seed bed and dip plants before spacing out in sludge of 4% calomel dust and water. Raise healthy plants by watering seed beds with a solution of 1 oz. mercuric chloride to 12 gals. of water. Repeat 14 days later. A similar solution should be poured into the holes at planting out time.

CABBAGE DOWNY MILDEW

Mainly disease of seedlings which causes yellowing of the leaves and distortion. White downy patches appear beneath the leaves.

Control Measures

Spray with colloidal sulphur in water.

CELERY LEAF SPOT

Most serious and widespread disease of celery. Discoloured areas occur on foliage and black spores appear on these areas. Whole leaf rapidly destroyed.

Control Measures
Disease is seed borne, and all reliable seed is treated with formaldehyde. Spray with full strength Bordeaux mixture as soon as disease appears and repeat 4 times at 14-day intervals. Spray both sides of leaves.

CELERY SOFT ROT

Disease causing soft rotting of the heart of mature plants, usually from December onwards.

Control Measures
Lift as soon as mature and store in insect-free moist sand or sterilised soil.

LEEK RUST

Common throughout the country, especially in the north. Rusty pustules appear, usually in rows, on the leaves.

Control Measures
Remove diseased leaves as soon as seen. Spray with full-strength Bordeaux mixture at first sign of disease. Stimulate rapid growth by feeding with sulphate of ammonia.

LEEK WHITE ROT

See ONION WHITE ROT.

LEEK WHITE TIP

Tips of leaves turn white and droop. Water-soaked areas appear on the stems and decay sets in.

Control Measures
Spray with Bordeaux mixture making several applications from autumn until spring. Cut off infected tips and burn.

LETTUCE DOWNY MILDEW

Leaves become mildewed and yellow and finally die off.

Control Measures
Disease usually due to checked growth in cold moist weather.

Maintain rapid growth by feeding with sulphate of ammonia and dust with sulphur.

LETTUCE GREY MOULD (Botrytis)

Another cold damp weather disease. The plants become covered with a grey mould and wilt away. Serious mainly on seedlings.

Control Measures

Maintain rapid growth—water the soil well and dust several times with Folosan.

LETTUCE RING SPOT

Often serious in cold wet weather. Leaves become spotted and perforated and rusty marks occur on ribs of leaves.

Control Measures

Maintain vigorous growth with nitrogenous manures, and give adequate potash. Dust with sulphur.

MARROW MILDEW

White powdery growth on leaves which restricts growth. Very common when plant checked in growth.

Control Measures

Dust with a fine sulphur at frequent intervals or spray with colloidal sulphur.

MINT RUST

Rusty pustules and yellow patches appear on the foliage. Leaves drop early in the season.

Control Measures

Spray with full-strength Bordeaux mixture as soon as disease first seen. Remove and burn all growth in the autumn.

ONION DOWNY MILDEW

Serious disease, especially in wet seasons. Leaves become yellow, wilt, and whole plant may rot and die. May attack shallots, but seldom leeks.

Control Measures

Maintain rapid but balanced growth and avoid waterlogged soil. Spray with colloidal sulphur.

ONION SMUT

Very serious disease, the appearance of which must be notified to the local N.A.A.S. (National Agricultural Advisory Service) authorities. Black streaks appear on the leaves and black powdery masses of spores later appear.

Control Measures

Burn all plants infected. Avoid growing onions on the particular piece of ground for upwards of 5 years.

ONION WHITE ROT

Foliage becomes yellow and wilted and the fungus spreads as a white mass round the base of the bulb. Very contagious and a whole bed may be dried up and dead by August.

Control Measures

Work in 4% Calomel dust at rate of 2 ozs. per square yard of bed before sowing or planting.

PEA MILDEW

A late summer disease which covers stems, leaves and pods with white powder.

Control Measures

Dust with sulphur, making several applications. Water well.

POTATO BLIGHT

The leaves develop black blotches and a whole patch may become leafless in a few days. Usually first seen in warm moist weather in July–August. The sickly smell of " blight " is very characteristic. Spores fall to the soil and may affect tubers near the surface.

Control Measures

Spray with full-strength Bordeaux mixture commencing in late June and repeat 3 times at 14-day intervals. Remove and burn blighted haulms to prevent spread to tubers.

POTATO SCAB

Brown rough or corky areas appear on tubers. Usually caused by excessive liming of soil.

Control Measures

Dig in plenty of fresh green vegetable refuse. Use lawn mowings along trenches at one handful per tuber.

POTATO WART DISEASE

Huge unsightly black warts appear on tubers. As soon as found notify local N.A.A.S. (National Agricultural Advisory Service) official. Henceforth grow immune varieties.

SHALLOT WHITE ROT
See ONION WHITE ROT.

SPINACH DOWNY MILDEW

Common disease which causes leaves to yellow on the top side and a greyish mould to appear on the under surface. May be serious in cold wet weather.

Control Measures
Dust frequently with sulphur.

TOMATO BLIGHT

The same as Potato Blight. Leaves blackened, fruit develops dark sunken areas and later rots.

Control Measures
As for POTATO BLIGHT.

TOMATO BLOSSOM END ROT

Dark green, hard, sunken patches occur at blossom end of fruit. Tissue beneath the skin is black.

Control Measures
This is a physiological disease and indicates unsuitable growing conditions. Ensure good drainage, ample moisture and generally balanced growth.

TOMATO ROOT AND COLLAR ROTS

Common at all stages from seed box to mature plant. Similar fungi cause " damping off." Roots turn brown and rot, or stem develops a cankered area near the soil and the plant collapses.

Control Measures :
Remove and burn all infected plants. Water at all stages with Cheshunt compound, 1 oz. in 2 galls. of water. Harmless, apply frequently.

VIRUS DISEASES

Viruses are extremely minute bodies, and it is not yet known whether they consist of living or non-living matter. It has been

The Complete Gardener

suggested that they are of a protein nature. Plants affected by virus diseases seldom recover.

Most virus diseases are very infectious, and can be transmitted from plant to plant by insects, chiefly aphids and thrips; on the knives or hands of workers; on seeds; on plant refuse left lying about, and so on.

Control Measures

There are no known cures for virus diseases, and affected plants should be pulled up and burned as soon as they are seen. Other measures which may be taken are:
(1) Elimination of the sources of infection.
(2) Controlling the insects which spread the viruses.
(3) Breeding resistant varieties.

TOMATO VIRUS DISEASES

I. SPOTTED WILT

The young leaves develop pale ring spots, and later a bronzing appears, the upper leaves curl downwards and the plant may be killed.

Control Measures

Any young plants showing symptoms of the disease should be rejected. Pull up and burn immediately any diseased plants seen in the houses. Keep down thrips, which carry the disease, by spraying with nicotine.

II. MOSAIC

The leaves are mottled, with dark green raised patches, and the young leaves are distorted.

Control Measures

Only save seed from healthy plants. Burn affected plants and sterilise the soil.

N.B.—Damping off of seedlings and pre-emergence rots in all vegetables can be prevented by treating the seeds with thiram dust before sowing. This is especially useful in the case of peas and beans.

PART NINE

ORDERS FOR THE MONTH

Orders for the Month

IT is very useful, at least I find it so, to have someone to remind you just how important it is to do the jobs in the garden exactly when they ought to be done. A gardener finds it most difficult to " catch up." He has to think ahead, and very often 12 months ahead.

It is hoped, therefore, that these " Orders for the Month " will prove useful. They are purposely put in as orders rather than as suggestions so that the terse terminology may (1) save time and space, and (2) serve to indicate the urgency of the work.

In order to help those who are only keen on one particular branch of gardening the orders are issued under separate headings. A vegetable gardener, therefore, will only have need to consult the vegetable section, the fruit grower the fruit section, and so on.

It is impossible to include every single little operation that might have to be done in any one month. Therefore, only the more important jobs have been included. It is equally impossible to give details as to how the work has to be done, but having read an order and realised its application, all that is necessary is to look up the details in the appropriate section in the book, using the index at the back for guidance if necessary.

SPECIAL NOTE TO NORTHERN GARDENERS
Northern gardeners who handle and read this book must, of course, realise that they will probably be a fortnight or 3 weeks later than their confrères in the south. It is, however, impossible to make hard and fast rules. I have known spring cabbage turn in for use 3 weeks earlier in Cheshire and in Flintshire than in Kent. There is at least one garden in Cumberland that is early, and far more sheltered and warm than many gardens in Warwickshire, and it is often a case of east versus west, rather than north versus south. The west on the whole will be wetter and the east drier. The orders refer to an average garden and not, of course, to a lovely warm valley in Cornwall or a garden in a bleak position on the Yorkshire moors.

JANUARY

Make out your seed order immediately and post it.

THE GARDEN BEAUTIFUL

Do any path-making necessary.

Fight slugs in rock garden with Metaldehyde.

Renew protection over tender bulbs with dry organic matter.

Plant deciduous shrubs or rose trees.

Protect tender shrubs.

Roll lawns if necessary, providing soil is not too wet.

Top-dress alpine plants with correct compost or stone chippings.

Tread along rows of cuttings after a frost.

Fork through shrubberies—never damage roots of rhododendrons.

Top-dress rhododendrons and pieris with horticultural peat or coarse leaf-mould.

Top-dress lily of the valley with well-rotted compost. Make new beds if necessary.

Prune winter jasmine when it goes out of flower.

Plant imported lilies in perfectly-drained soil. Keep heavy rains off by using continuous cloches.

Keep rabbits out at all costs.

Attend to lawns, eradicating weeds.

Plant hardy perennials. See that they are firm.

Tread around perennials planted in November or December.

Protect alpines with hairy foliage with sheets of glass held above them on wire clips.

Go over labels and renew them.

Trim grass verges.

Layer some hardy shrubs if the weather proves open.

Prepare sites for chrysanthemums and dahlias if necessary.

Protect auriculas during severe weather.

Pick blooms of *Iris stylosa*, and winter aconites.

Pick Christmas roses, jasmine, laurustinus, winter sweet, and witch hazels.

FRUIT GROWING

Do what planting is necessary. Continue work already begun.

Continue spraying fruit trees with recognised winter wash.

Fork shallowly through strawberry beds.

Fork shallowly between rows of raspberries, adding ample decayed manure or compost.

Feed trees and bushes where necessary.

Put black cotton in among branches of gooseberry bushes to prevent birds damaging buds.

Cut autumn fruiting raspberries down to ground level at end of month.

Take cuttings of bush fruits. Burn diseased wood.
Carry out any root pruning necessary.
Protect fruit trees from severe frosts.
Prune outdoor vines and tie in.
Shorten tall canes of raspberries to 5 ft.
Stake and tie in properly all newly-planted trees.
Prune newly-planted blackcurrants down to ground level.
Prepare and clean ground for new planting to be done. This matter is urgent.

VEGETABLE GROWING

Protect rows of celery with continuous cloches or straw.
Sow seed of exhibition onions in boxes under glass.
Force rhubarb, seakale and chicory.
Sow broad beans in warm border if weather and district suitable.
Sow round-seeded peas in warm border if weather and district suitable.
Plant shallots, tilth permitting.
Hoe lightly between cauliflowers in frames.
Lift parsnips and prepare ground for succeeding crop.
Lift Jerusalem artichokes and store in sand in shed.
Plant lettuce in frames.
Get all the bastard trenching done possible.
Sow parsnips towards the end of month, tilth permitting.
Prepare trenches for peas and beans, towards the end of the month for later sowings.
Sow lettuce seed in boxes in the greenhouse for planting out later.
Sow radishes on a warm border.
Under continuous cloches sow broad beans, peas, carrots, cauliflowers, lettuce, leeks, onions, radish and spinach.

THE GREENHOUSE

(a) *Floral*

Start introducing bulbs for forcing.
Propagate chrysanthemums.
Top-dress backward chrysanthemum plants with John Innes Compost No. 2.
Cut back and remove chrysanthemums in pots when plants have finished flowering.
Sow seed of tuberous-rooted begonias in boxes.
Re-pot ferns if pot-bound.
Pot up pelargoniums.
Remove spent blooms and dead foliage from all plants.
Feed freesias with Liquinure twice weekly.

The Complete Gardener

Sow seeds of gloxinias, streptocarpus, grevillea, and
   eucalyptus.
Sow seed of asparagus species and *Solanum Capsicastrum.*
Divide maidenhair ferns.
Take cuttings of perpetual-flowering carnations.
Sow annual hollyhocks and antirrhinums.
Propagate coleus, heliotrope and marguerites towards the
   end of the month.
Sow seeds of such shrubs as genista, erica, pieris, cistus and
   helianthemum.
Sow sweet peas in pots towards the end of the month.
Sow ageratum and East Lothian stocks.
Pot on herbaceous calceolarias.

(*b*) *Food*
   Flood fig tree borders.
   Sow melon seeds in 3-in. pots.
   Syringe early peach trees to start them into growth.
   Start forcing strawberries in pots.
   Cease syringing vines when well on the move. Flood the
      border.
   Top-dress borders of late vines.
   Sow peas for indoor crop. Variety Harbinger.
   Sow cucumber seeds for early crop.
   Sow onion seeds in boxes for large bulbs.
   Sow early Brussels sprouts in boxes.
   Sow seed of cauliflower for summer crops, in boxes.
   Sow French beans for growing under glass.
   Sow mustard and cress in boxes.
   Force mint on staging of greenhouse.
   Force seakale and chicory under staging of house in dark.
   Sow tomato seed for early crops.

FEBRUARY

February is considered a wet month. It is often a treacherous
month, because although spring is in the air, winter may come
again.

THE GARDEN BEAUTIFUL
   Make all structural alterations, improvements and additions in
      the garden, rock gardens, water gardens, etc.
   Lay turf for new lawns.

Orders for the Month

Make first mowing of lawns when weather is suitable, afterwards top dressing with a nitrogenous fertiliser.

Roll lawns and paths regularly each week.

Plant hardy perennials in prepared ground in the herbaceous border.

Lift and divide some of the hardier perennials and replant.

Plant roses.

Prune climbing roses.

Plant hardy shrubs.

Prune hardy shrubs.

Fork over shrubberies, working in compost if necessary.

Plant remaining spring-flowering bulbs.

Plant out bulbs, after forcing, in the wild garden.

Protect early-flowering irises.

Lift Primulinus Gladioli corms, sort and replant in fresh soil.

Sow sweet peas.

Renew plants and labels in rock garden and see that protection against rain and fog is sufficient.

Lightly fork borders and between spring bedding.

Re-firm bedding and all newly-planted stock after frost.

Dress vacant flower borders with Naphthalene to destroy soil pests.

Use Arsenical weed killer on gravel paths and drives.

Complete all trenching in the flower garden.

Fruit Growing

Complete all winter spraying operations.

Plant wall trees if weather is favourable.

Mulch newly-planted trees with light material.

Prune and tie in apricot trees growing on walls.

Thin out spurs on old pear and plum trees if necessary.

Top-dress peaches and nectarines and spray with Burgundy Mixture.

Prune and tie in morello cherries.

Fork fruit tree borders after pruning and training.

Protect wall fruits with netting against frost.

Cut down newly-planted raspberry canes (summer fruiting) to 6 ins.

Commence pruning of gooseberries not done in autumn.

Vegetable Growing

Sow parsnip seed if possible and not done before.

Sow broad beans if possible and not done before.

Sow early round peas for succession.

Plant shallots if possible.

Plant horse radish thongs.

Use recently cleared celery trenches for making sites for peas.

Divide chives and replant.

Hoe between spring cabbage towards end of month and apply nitro-chalk.

Treat winter spinach similarly.

Prepare onion bed.

Thin out autumn-sown onions and transplant.

Fork surface of established asparagus beds and apply good dressing of manure.

Prepare new asparagus beds.

Sow early carrots in cold frame or hot-bed.

Plant first early potatoes in warm border.

Prepare seed bed for brassicas.

Sow cauliflower seed for early crop towards end of month.

Sow spinach seed in warm border.

Sow turnips.

Complete all ground operations by the end of the month.

The Greenhouse

(a) *Floral*

Bring in more bulbs for forcing.

Stake daffodils and hyacinths.

Bring in stools of *Salvia patens* and dahlias for production of cuttings.

Pot up rooted cuttings of chrysanthemums for bush plants.

Take further cuttings of border chrysanthemums.

Take further cuttings of perpetual-flowering carnations.

Take cuttings of abutilons and salvias.

Take further cuttings of pelargoniums and pot up those already rooted.

Sow in a cool house seeds of delphinium hybrids, cytisus, genista and lupins.

Sow seeds of border and perpetual carnations, china asters, scabious.

Sow freesias for August flowering.

Sow in moderate heat seeds of *Asparagus Sprengeri*, and *Grevillea robusta*.

Pot up rooted cuttings of *Crassula coccinea*.

Divide and re-pot old plants of *Francoa ramosa*.

Re-pot established plants of *Hydrangea*.

Cut over plants of *Salvia splendens* to obtain cuttings.

Bring in shrubs for flowering indoors. *Azalea mollis*, lilacs, etc.

Top-dress borders with fresh soil after removing a little of
the surface soil.

Feed plants of mignonette, cineraria and primula with liquid
manure twice weekly.

Look out for aphis and fumigate on its first appearance.

Increase the ventilation through the month, but avoid cold
draughts.

(b) Food

Disbud early fig tree growing in pots.

Plant out melon seedlings in prepared beds and make further
sowings of melons for main crop.

Pollinate peach trees.

Syringe strawberry plants daily and bring in further plants
for succession.

Rub off weak shoots on early vines and tie down one lateral.

Transfer early sowings of lettuce to the cold frame and make
further sowings in boxes for transplanting.

Sow mustard and cress and radishes.

Plant a few chicory roots and keep dark.

Plant out cucumber plants.

Pot tomato seedlings into 3-in. pots and re-pot autumn-sown
plants to 10-in. pots.

Sow tomatoes for planting in frames or open ground.

Plant more asparagus for forcing.

Sow dwarf beans at 3-week intervals and syringe growing
plants daily.

Sow early shorthorn carrots.

Plant potatoes in frames.

Sow early forcing turnips in frames.

Sow vegetable marrows in heat for cropping in frames.

MARCH

Planting and transplanting not done in the autumn should be
done now. Remember to stake as you plant.

THE GARDEN BEAUTIFUL

Prepare surface soil in borders for sowing seeds.

Commence tying up perennial plants and protect from slugs.

Plant out carnations which have been wintered in frames.

Complete the pruning of climbing roses and commence the
pruning of bush roses.

Fork over rose beds and work in manure if not already done.

Complete the pruning of hardy shrubs.

Top-dress azaleas and rhododendrons with horticultural peat, leaf-mould and loam.

Sow anemones in drills.

Plant hardy gladioli.

Plant hardy lilies.

Sow stocks out of doors in a warm bed.

Sow seeds of hardy annuals out of doors.

Sow sweet peas in prepared trenches if not already done. Plant out seedlings sown under glass.

Thin out autumn-sown annuals.

Remove protecting material from the rock garden and clean.

Top-dress with a mixture of sandy loam, leaf-mould and manure.

Plant out Sweet Williams and Canterbury bells to flower.

FRUIT GROWING

Complete all fruit planting.

Complete pruning of gooseberries.

Prune and train in fig trees.

Spray peaches and nectarines with Colloidal Sulphur against mildew.

Spray blackcurrant bushes with Lime-sulphur against big bud mite.

Fork soil around fruit bushes and mulch with half-decayed manure.

VEGETABLE GROWING

Plant Jerusalem artichokes.

Plant out broad beans sown in heat and make further sowing for succession.

Make further sowings of shorthorn carrots in sheltered borders.

Sow maincrop leeks.

Plant shallots if not already done.

Make further sowings of peas for succession.

Sow turnips in warm border if not already done.

Plant early potatoes.

Sow, where they are to mature, radish, spinach, beet, kohl rabi, globe beet and lettuce.

Make sowings in the seed bed of broccoli, cabbage, savoy cabbage and cauliflower.

Continue to plant out cabbages.

Make new beds and plant seakale sets.

Force seakale outside.

Orders for the Month

(a) *Floral*

Pot up cuttings of perpetual flowering carnations into thumb pots.

Pot on *Schizanthus wisetonensis* and *Clarkia elegans* into flowering pots.

Pot up autumn-sown cyclamens in 3-in. pots.

Divide and re-pot *Primula kewensis*.

Shift sweet peas into their flowering pots.

Take further cuttings of zonal geraniums for winter flowering.

Make sowings of *Kochia trichophylla* in gentle heat.

Sow in gentle heat *Primula malacoides*, *P. obconica* and *P. sinensis*.

Divide cannas and start into growth in moderate heat.

Bring crinums into light to start growth.

Start tuberous-rooted begonias.

Prune *Plumbago capensis* and start into growth.

Start *Gloriosa spp.*

Take cuttings of *Trachelium cœruleum*, *Veronica Hulkeana* and *Campanula isophylla*.

Sow the following seeds : ten-week stocks, nemesia, salpiglossis, *Phlox Drummondii*, nicotiana, petunia, mimulus, tagetes, *Meconopsis spp.*, celosia, sweet alyssum and gerbera hybrids.

(b) *Food*

Spray fig trees to prevent red spider.

Disbud early peach trees and thin out fruit.

Thin fruit on strawberry plants and feed 3 times a week.

Start the late vinery and water the borders.

Thin early grapes while the berries are small, thin bunches to one per shoot.

Sow seeds of celery, celeriac, angelica and vegetable marrow.

Sow cucumber seeds for use in cold houses.

Syringe cucumber plants freely.

Plant lettuce in frames.

Plant out maincrop tomatoes.

Pot on vegetable marrow plants into 5-in. pots.

APRIL

Weeds will be troublesome now so keep the hoe working. Insect pests are also getting numerous—keep a watch for them and have remedies ready.

The Complete Gardener

The Garden Beautiful

Apply lawn sand to lawns.

Clip ivy growing on house and walls.

Continue staking in herbaceous borders and commence hoeing.

Plant out border carnations and chrysanthemums, gladioli, violet runners from frames and unstarted dahlias.

Complete pruning of bush roses.

Plant out bedding plants, pansies, antirrhinums, calceolarias, pentstemons.

Divide and re-plant kniphofia and *Gentiana ornata*.

Plant out perennials raised in heat.

Commence propagation of perennial plants.

Cut off all dead flower heads.

Fruit Growing

Complete pruning of fruit trees on walls.

Destroy woolly aphis by application of neat liquid derris.

Disbud apricots, peaches and nectarines in good weather.

Spray top fruit with Lime-sulphur at green bud stage.

Spray against gooseberry sawfly.

Spray against scab.

De-flower strawberries for runner production.

Clean up fruiting strawberry beds, fork and mulch with well-rotted manure.

Plant hardy vines from pots and disbud established outdoor vines.

Graft fruit trees.

Vegetable Growing

Sow in the open ground seeds of the following crops : peas, French beans, beet, carrots, turnips, onions, spinach, brassicas, kohl rabi, lettuce, endive, corn salad, cardoon, chicory, globe artichoke, salsify and scorzonera.

Plant out asparagus.

Put in support for early sown peas.

Plant out cauliflowers.

Earth up early potatoes.

Pinch out tops of broad beans.

Prepare celery trenches.

Plant maincrop potatoes.

The Greenhouse

(a) *Floral*

Sow seeds of zinnias, *Lobelia tenuior* and cinerarias.

698

Take cuttings of delphiniums hybrids, leptospermums, *Mimulus variegatus*, *Plumbago capensis*, *Ceratostigma spp.*, *Deutzia gracilis*, abutilons and some greenhouse rhodo-dendrons.

Pot up *Humea elegans*.

Pot up tuberous-rooted begonias.

Re-pot ivy-leaved geraniums, abutilons, and *Clivia miniata*.

Re-pot azaleas which have flowered.

Take seeds of good cinerarias and primulas.

(*b*) *Food*

Syringe fig trees twice daily and increase temperature.

Pollinate melon blooms.

Thin peach fruits as necessary and syringe to check red spider.

Plant young vines early in the month.

Make up hot-beds for unheated melon frames.

Sow the following seeds : runner beans, gourds, vegetable marrows, and cucumbers.

Feed cropping cucumbers frequently with liquid manure.

Plant marrows on hot-beds.

MAY

Be careful not to put out tender plants early in the month—there is danger of frost during the night.

THE GARDEN BEAUTIFUL

Continue to mow lawns at regular intervals.

Plant out dahlias and stake immediately.

Attend to training of wall shrubs.

Sow seeds of wallflowers, auriculas, polyanthus and biennials.

Plant out half-hardy annuals and tender bedding plants.

Divide polyanthus and plant out in shady border.

Lift tulips and heel in to ripen.

Continue to stake border plants.

Cut down early-flowered herbaceous plants and mulch.

FRUIT GROWING

Bark-ring over-vigorous apple and pear trees.

Remove all shoots below the graft on newly-grafted trees.

Complete disbudding of peaches and nectarines leaving only shoots for extension and replacements.

Thin stone fruits on walls.

Disbud Morello cherries.

Plant out forced strawberries.
Protect strawberry beds from birds and straw to keep fruit clean.
Lay-in strawberry runners from de-flowered plants.
Thin gooseberries for cooking.

Vegetable Growing

Make sowings of runner beans, swedes, New Zealand spinach, ridge cucumbers, beetroot and curled endive.
Make weekly sowings of lettuce.
Sow marrows under cloches.
Plant out vegetable marrows, brassicas and leeks.
Plant out main batch of celery, celeriac, cardoons and globe artichokes.
Plant out tomatoes in a sheltered position.
Thin out carrots and other crops.
Earth up potatoes.
Top-dress onions.
Feed asparagus beds with liquid manure.
Take cuttings of sage with a heel.

The Greenhouse

(a) *Floral*

Transfer young plants of perpetual-flowering carnations to the cold frame.
Stake and tie carnations, pelargoniums and calceolarias.
Harden off bedding plants.
Stand chrysanthemums on ashes out of doors, and stake.
Pot up zonal pelargoniums and move to standing ground.
Sow seed of herbaceous calceolaria and pansies in gentle heat.
Sow seed of cinerarias, balsams and cockscombs in unheated houses.
Take cuttings of *Hydrangea hortensis*, cape heaths and hardy tree heaths.
Prick off primula seedlings into boxes and place in a frame.
Start on the final potting of chrysanthemums.
Cut back and re-pot *Acacia spp.*
Plant out *Richardia africana* in trenches.
Bring flowered amaryllis into warmth to make growth.
Pot up any rooted cuttings taken last month.
Damp the paths on sunny mornings.
Shade cyclamens from bright sun.

(b) *Food*

Stop syringing fig trees.
Water fig-tree borders with liquid manure.

See that melon fruits are supported.
Syringe and damp down late peach houses twice a day.
Thin grapes and stop sub-laterals.
Put out cucumber plants in hot-bed frames.
Top-dress tomatoes with compost and manure.
Pollinate flowers of vegetable marrows and pinch out the
  shoots regularly.
Make sowing of sweet corn early in the month.

JUNE

Routine work will occupy much time. Shading will be necessary
when the sun becomes hot.

THE GARDEN BEAUTIFUL
  Finish planting out summer bedding.
  Prune hardy shrubs as they finish flowering.
  Fork over shrubberies after pruning.
  Take cuttings of rock plants and insert in a shady border.
  Cut lupins, delphiniums and anchusas down to the ground and
    mulch.
  Disbud border carnations.
  Divide pyrethrums.
  Lift narcissi to dry off.
  Plant wallflowers in the nursery border.
  Complete the staking of herbaceous plants.
  Pinch out the tops of annuals such as clarkias to get bushy plants.
  Propagate perennials from root cuttings.
  Clip box edgings.
  Apply weed killer to paths and drives.

FRUIT GROWING
  Look out for insect attack and spray against scab.
  Thin out top fruit as necessary.
  Keep peach borders well watered.
  Mulch raspberry beds with rotted manure.
  Thin fruits on strawberry plants.
  Thin dessert gooseberries severely.

VEGETABLE GROWING
  Feed onions to the end of the month and dust or spray against
    mildew.
  Stop cutting asparagus and give a heavy dressing of manure.

Plant out tomatoes on a sunny border early in the month.
Plant out sweet corn early in the month.
Continue to plant out winter greens.
Lift early potatoes for seed.
Make a last sowing of peas.
Sow French beans for succession.
Make a further sowing of endive and parsley.
Thin out carrots and dust with spent soot.
Make a late sowing of carrots.
Stake runner beans.
Look out for attacks of cabbage root fly.

THE GREENHOUSE

(*a*) *Floral*

Stake and tie all chrysanthemums.
Prick out cinerarias into boxes and place in cold frames.
Sow streptocarpus, *Primula sinenis* and herbaceous calceolarias.
Raise alpines from seeds as they ripen.
Take cuttings of most alpines in a sand frame.
Take cuttings of *Salvia coccinea*, kalmia, *Coronilla spp.*
Layer *Hoya carnosa.*
Stake and tie lilies.
Bring stove plants into the cool greenhouse.
Syringe daily carnations, cyclamen, azaleas and chrysanthemums.
Dry off nerines and freesias.
Damp down morning and afternoon.
Ventilate freely.

(*b*) *Food*

Soak peach borders with plenty of water after fruit is gathered.
Thin late grapes.
Shade cucumbers and melons from bright sun.
Syringe and damp down cucumber houses frequently.
Feed tomatoes in pots and borders.
Sow tomato seeds for winter cropping.

JULY

Irrigation will be needed if the month is dry, but pay attention to staking in case of sudden storms.

Orders for the Month

THE GARDEN BEAUTIFUL

Bud roses or propagate by cuttings.

Layer shrubs such as rhododendrons, lilacs and heaths

Feed choice shrubs with liquid manure.

Continue the pruning of hardy shrubs.

Divide and re-plant bearded irises. Lift, clean and store May-flowering tulips.

Plant hardy cyclamen, colchicums, erythroniums, etc.

Feed border chrysanthemums and dahlias.

Feed florist's flowers and exhibition plants.

Feed plunged pot plants.

Remove runners from violets intended for forcing.

Lift Canterbury bells and sweet williams.

Continue to propagate alpines.

Take pink cuttings.

Layer border carnations.

Prick out seedling polyanthus and auriculas.

Prick out seedling perennial plants and biennials.

Sow hollyhocks, East Lothian stocks, antirrhinums and wall-flowers.

Make sowing of *Cynoglossum amabile.*

Clip formal hedges.

Continue routine work of hoeing and weeding beds and paths.

FRUIT GROWING

Bud fruit trees.

Commence summer pruning of apple and pear trees.

Thin dessert plums, train in all shoots required and stop the others.

Thin early dessert apples.

Water cordon apples and pears.

Thin out all dessert pears.

Water peach and nectarine borders and mulch.

Cut out old loganberry canes as fruit is picked and tie up the young shoots.

Hoe through raspberry beds and remove superfluous canes.

Layer strawberries for pot work.

Clear old strawberry beds.

Start planting new strawberry runners.

Feed late strawberries with liquid manure and water well.

Pinch lateral growths on outdoor vines.

VEGETABLE GROWING

Lift early potatoes.

Give maincrop potatoes final earthing up and spray against potato blight.

Keep new asparagus beds weeded and watered.

Spray runner beans in dry weather.

Prepare ground for autumn-sown onions.

Bend over tops of winter onions as soon as tops begin to die down.

Lift shallots as tops die down.

Continue to plant winter greens.

Cultivate and earth up Jerusalem artichokes.

Remove side shoots and basal growths from tomatoes and feed with liquid manure.

Sow turnips and lettuce for winter use, Batavian and broad-leaved endive, and spring cabbage.

THE GREENHOUSE

(a) Floral

Remove forced shrubs to standing ground to ripen.

Sow cinerarias and freesias to flower in the spring.

Sow hardy primulas and *P. malacoides*.

Cut back the flowered stems of second-year perpetual carnations.

Pot on cyclamens to final pots.

Pot on new stock of perpetual carnations.

Pot on *Salvia splendens* to flowering pots and keep close.

Take cuttings of such plants as bay laurel, roses, leptospermums, helianthemums, philadelphus and lithospermum.

Continue to propagate pelargoniums, *Hydrangea hortensis*, and abutilons.

Propagate *Gypsophila paniculata* and *Calceolaria violacea*.

Prick off herbaceous calceolarias.

Pot up seedlings of *Humea elegans*.

(b) Food

Thin the second crop of figs.

Stand finished pot fruit trees in the open, and feed with liquid manure.

Syringe late peach trees twice a day and ventilate freely.

Top-dress cucumbers.

Pot June-sown tomatoes into 3-in. pots.

Top-dress main crop tomatoes.

Syringe cucumbers in frames and feed freely.

Sow parsley in frames.

Orders for the Month

AUGUST

Prepare your sheds and stores now—this is the beginning of the harvest.

The Garden Beautiful

Disbud early chrysanthemums.
Prepare ground for planting of new evergreens, roses and shrubs.
Complete pruning of hedges.
Prune rambler roses and take further cuttings.
Plant out seedling delphiniums into the flower border.
Divide and transplant *Hippeastrum pratense* and *Amaryllis Bella-donna*.
Prepare beds for planting bulbs.
Plant out Brompton stocks to give early bloom.
Take half-ripe cuttings of veronicas, olearias, escallonias, cistus, cytisus, and *Buddleia Davidii*.
Dig over vacant ground early.
Make preparations for winter bedding.

Fruit Growing

Prepare ground for planting new fruit stocks.
Give top fruit a final thinning.
Pinch out lateral growth on peaches and nectarines.
Prune early peach varieties when fruit is picked.
Cut out old canes from raspberries and tie in new canes.
Prune blackcurrants after fruiting if necessary.
Complete the planting of strawberry runners.
Clean established strawberry beds after fruiting and lightly fork.
Keep fruiting strawberry plants free of runners.
Layer late-fruiting strawberries for spring planting.

Vegetable Growing

Sow spring cabbage if not already done.
Sow winter spinach and hardy lettuce for spring.
Sow Brussels sprouts, cauliflowers and autumn-sown onions.
Sow turnips for winter use.
Lift potatoes as ready, first removing blighted tops.
Lift spring-sown beet and early carrots.
Commence to earth up celery.
Transplant spring cabbage.

The Greenhouse

(a) Floral

Apply liquid manure to chrysanthemums when showing bud.

Pot up calceolarias into 3-in. pots.

Pot up cinerarias into 4-in. pots.

Sow *Cyclamen persicum*, keep close and shaded.

Pot up 2-year cyclamen from frames.

Lift richardias from open ground and pot up.

Re-pot nerines and lachenalias.

Pot up freesia bulbs.

Pot on *Primula sinensis* and *P. malacoides* into flowering pots.

Bring in pelargoniums from standing ground to cold frame and take cuttings as they become available.

Take cuttings of coleus, begonia, heliotrope and verbena.

Propagate evergreens by cuttings in cold frames.

Take internodal cuttings of fuchsias.

Propagate succulents early in the month.

Dry off gloxinias in frames.

Sow seeds of annuals for late spring.

Prepare frames for violets.

(*b*) *Food*

Sow seeds of lettuce and endive to prick off into cold frames.

Prepare manure or compost for mushroom beds.

Pot on June-sown tomatoes into 5-in. pots.

Feed maincrop tomatoes frequently.

Overhaul paintwork of houses and frames and the boiler system.

SEPTEMBER

The days will now be drawing in—get as much planting done as possible.

THE GARDEN BEAUTIFUL

Prepare sites for new lawns and sow seed.

Plant out alpines and herbaceous plants.

Start planting bulbs, except tulips.

Plant out rooted pinks and border carnation layers.

Layer evergreens.

Take cuttings of cherry laurel and privet.

Clear annual borders as flowers finish and start sowing hardy annuals for next summer.

Stop feeding flowering plants.

Prune back wall climbers and tie in long shoots.

Propagate by means of cuttings, shrubs, herbaceous perennials and bedding plants.

Take further basal cuttings of pansies and violas.
Plant out polyanthuses.

FRUIT GROWING

Prepare fruit room ready for storing.
Start grease-banding fruit trees.
Prepare ground for planting new trees.
Trench ground for new raspberry beds and manure heavily.
Cut out fruiting canes of loganberries and tie young canes into
   position.
Destroy wasps' nests.

VEGETABLE GROWING

Dry onions in open sheds or warm houses if weather is wet.
Give late sown dwarf beans protection against early frosts.
Earth up celery again.
Plant out endive.
Lift and store potatoes, beet and carrots.
Gather and dry supplies of herbs.

THE GREENHOUSE

(*a*) *Floral*

Pot up bulbs for forcing
Pot first batch of *Lilium longiflorum* in cold frame.
Lift and pot up *Solanum Capsicastrum* and bouvardias.
Bring in rooted pelargoniums from frames to greenhouse.
Pot up rhododendrons for forcing under glass.
Sow clarkia and schizanthus and place in cold frame.
Sow sweet peas to bloom under glass.
Disbud chrysanthemums.
Re-pot pelargoniums when starting fresh growth.
Plant violets in prepared frame.
Sow snapdragons for bedding, and conservatory.
Prune plumbago and other specimen plants as they finish
   flowering.
Collect seed of tuberous-rooted begonias.

(*b*) *Food*

Discontinue syringing melons.
Ventilate peach houses freely night and day.
Prune off sub-lateral growth on early vines.
Pot up seedling cauliflowers and place in cold frame.
Pot on tomatoes into 10-in. pots for winter cropping.
Make up mushroom beds in warm dark sheds.

OCTOBER

Reduce watering and see that the glasshouses are ready for the winter months.

THE GARDEN BEAUTIFUL

Lay new lawns and repair old ones.
Complete the planting of herbaceous perennials.
Lift border chrysanthemums when finished.
Lift gladiolus corms.
Divide and re-plant pæonies.
Plant lily of the valley.
Cut down dahlias and lift the roots to store.
Plant out spring bedding.
Plant new roses.
Layer deciduous shrubs such as cydonia, syringa, clematis, hamamelis and *Daphne spp.*
Take root cuttings of *Anemone japonica, Papaver orientale, Romneya Coulteri*, morisia, statice, yuccas, etc.
Sow magnolia seed.
Top-dress the rock garden with fine soil and protect tender plants against too much rain.
Make a start on structural alterations in the garden.

FRUIT GROWING

Pick apples and pears and store.
Start winter pruning of apples and pears when growth has ceased.
Plant fruit trees, and stake securely.
Renovate exhausted fruit borders.
Prune and train Morello cherries.
Prune peaches and nectarines.
Prune red and white currants.
Take cuttings of bush fruits.
Plant raspberries in prepared ground.
Lift rhubarb for forcing and leave exposed to frost.

VEGETABLE GROWING

Start trenching or bastard trenching.
Finish lifting potatoes.
Earth up celery for the last time.
Protect cauliflowers sown in August.
Protect broccoli by heeling over.
Remove all foliage from asparagus.

Protect plants of vegetable marrows with cloches or frames.
Protect crowns of globe artichokes with ashes.
Gather fruits of outdoor tomatoes and ripen in a warm glasshouse.
Harvest and store cardoons, celeriac and salsify.
Start blanching endive.

THE GREENHOUSE

(*a*) *Floral*

> Stand cannas, liliums, crinums and fuchsias on their sides under the staging.
> Plant gladioli for flowering under glass and place in a cold frame.
> Continue to disbud chrysanthemums.
> Bring all chrysanthemums indoors and feed with liquid manure twice a week.
> Move *Primula sinensis* and *Cyclamen persicum* from cold frame to glasshouse.
> Pot up *Dicentra spectabilis* and place in a cold frame.
> Take cuttings of Lorraine begonias.
> Disbud perpetual-flowering carnations.
> Pinch clarkias, schizanthuses and sweet peas when 4-in. tall.
> Shake out tuberous-rooted begonias and store.
> Pot on cinerarias into flowering pots.

(*b*) *Food*

> Prune all pot fruit trees, re-pot and plunge in sheltered position out of doors.
> Prune early peach trees.
> Renovate peach borders.
> Cut out the sub-lateral growth on late vines.
> Move pot strawberries into frames.
> Make a sowing of lettuce.
> Plant lettuce and endive in frames.
> Set potato tubers for forcing.
> Start retarded seakale crowns in heat.
> Damp the mushroom house daily.
> Sow seeds for early tomato crop.

NOVEMBER

Get as much digging and trenching done as possible all through the garden.

THE GARDEN BEAUTIFUL
Continue structural alterations and renovations.
Plant biennials for winter bedding.
Protect less hardy perennials with ashes.
Protect christmas roses from cold and wet.
Plant tulips.
Put in plants in the wild garden and water garden.
Plant shrubs and trees, hardy climbers and roses.
Apply naphthalene to vacant land.
Continue to dig over vacant land.

FRUIT GROWING
Continue the pruning of fruit trees.
Dig between fruit trees and bushes as pruning is finished.
Root prune over-vigorous trees.
Plant gooseberry bushes and raspberry canes.

VEGETABLE GROWING
Lift chicory for forcing.
Sow longpod broad beans in a sheltered border.
Sow round-seeded peas.
Plant colewort.
Plant horseradish thongs.
Store ripe marrows and a few parsnips.

THE GREENHOUSE

(a) *Floral*
Start forcing bulbs.
Take cuttings of Japanese and in-curved chrysanthemums.
Pot on calceolarias into 5-in. pots.
Take cuttings of perpetual-flowering carnations.
Bring in Indian azaleas.
Start clivias.
Sow seed of most alpines.
Collect and stack turf for next season's requirements.
Collect and stack leaves to form leaf-mould.

(b) *Food*
Clean fig houses and top-dress borders.
Prune late peach trees.
Plant young peach trees.
Prune mid-season vines.
Lift asparagus to force on hot-beds.
Lift seakale for forcing.
Bring in rhubarb crowns for forcing.

DECEMBER

Weather will be very uncertain so take the opportunity to get pots cleaned, labels repainted, sheds tidy and everything clean, stacked and ready to hand.

THE GARDEN BEAUTIFUL
Plant shrubs and trees when weather permits.
Fork through shrubberies if mulched system is not followed.
Insert more shrub cuttings.
Plant new hedges.
Tread round newly-planted stock to re-firm after frost.
Protect the not-quite hardy plants from frost.
Remove snow collected on specimen plants or the branches may break.
Renovate lawns when possible.

FRUIT GROWING
Start winter spraying.
Continue winter pruning.
Dig between raspberry rows incorporating manure.
Protect fruit trees from rabbits.

VEGETABLE GROWING
Continue trenching, bastard trenching and ridging as weather permits.
Remove decaying leaves from brassicas.
Protect broccoli from frost.
Examine stored vegetables and remove any which are diseased.
Start forcing seakale on the bed.

THE GREENHOUSE

(a) *Floral*
Take cuttings of chrysanthemums.
Cut down chrysanthemums as they go out of bloom.
Take cuttings of carnations.
Pot on autumn-sown sweet peas.
Pinch schizanthuses to make bushy growth and support with temporary stakes.
Feed cinerarias with liquid manure weekly.
Start forcing hydrangeas.
Top-dress or re-pot cypripediums.

(b) *Food*

Start pot figs in temperature of 50° Fahr.

Clean late peach houses.

Start the early vinery.

Prune late vines.

Sow melons for early crop.

Sow early peas and dwarf beans for cropping under glass.

Blanch endive.

Pot up seakale for early forcing.

Sow carrots in frames.

Commence forcing chicory.

Bring in rhubarb crowns for forcing.

Sow tomatoes for summer crop.

INDEX

INDEX

Topics such as Manuring, Planting, Pruning, etc., are treated under each plant or group of plants, and therefore only the general references are entered in the Index.

715

Index

Index

Index

Index

Index

Index

Index

729

Index